Test Bank

to accompany

Carson • Butcher • Mineka

ABNORMAL PSYCHOLOGY AND MODERN LIFE
Tenth Edition

Prepared by

Gerald I. Metalsky
Lawrence University

and

Rebecca Laird

HarperCollins*CollegePublishers*

ISBN: 0-673-55594-1

1 2 3 4 5 6 - XXX - 01 00 99 98 97 96

PREFACE

About the Test Bank

The questions in this **Test Bank** are based on the textbook **ABNORMAL PSYCHOLOGY AND MODERN LIFE, Tenth Edition**, by Robert C. Carson, James N. Butcher, and Susan Mineka.

The **Test Bank** was designed for use by instructors at both small and large institutions of learning, where class size may vary from a handful of students taking a tutorial or small seminar to hundreds of students taking a large lecture class. Toward this aim and new to the tenth edition of the **Test Bank** are twenty short-answer questions for each chapter. In addition, we have increased the number of essay questions from the prior edition to fifteen per chapter. Insofar as one of the authors of the **Test Bank** (GM) has taught undergraduate-level Abnormal Psychology at both a small liberal arts college -- where short-answer questions often are emphasized -- and at a large university -- where multiple-choice questions often are emphasized -- it is our hope that instructors from all types of institutions of learning will find the **Test Bank** useful.

Each chapter of the **Test Bank** includes 110 multiple-choice questions as well as 20 short-answer questions and 15 essay questions. In any given chapter, the multiple-choice questions include up to 5 questions from the **Study Guide** by Don Fowles, providing instructors with the option of including such questions on quizzes or exams so as to reinforce the serious student who uses the **Study Guide** to learn the material.

We have divided questions into three categories -- factual, conceptual, and applied -- in order to provide instructors with flexibility when preparing their exams or quizzes. Any mixture of factual, conceptual, and applied questions can be selected when preparing an exam or quiz. In addition, the **TestMaster and QuizMaster User's Guide** provides instructions for editing questions from the **Test Bank** should an instructor wish to make any changes, such as incorporating lecture material into a given question.

Acknowledgments

We are extremely grateful to members of the HarperCollins organization who were always available throughout the process of preparing the **Test Bank**, particularly Evie Owens, Diane Wansing, and Catherine Woods. Diane Wansing's enthusiasm was contagious and we are extremely grateful for her day-to-day commitment to the project.

We also wish to thank Bob Carson, Jim Butcher, and Sue Mineka for their valuable input on prior versions of the **Test Bank**. Sue Mineka was a source of neverending support and inspiration for which we are deeply grateful.

We thank Florence Laird-Lohman and Jerry Blackburn for helping our family to stay in stride while we worked on this project. Our five-year-old son, Alex Laird Metalsky, was extraordinarily patient with us during the preparation of the **Test Bank**. We are extremely grateful for having such a wonderful son.

Gerald I. Metalsky and Rebecca S. Laird

Contents

CHAPTER 1 Abnormal Behavior in Our Times

Multiple-Choice

Choose the one alternative that best completes the statement or answers the question.

Pages: 5
Topic: Abnormal Behavior In Our Times
Skill: Factual   Other1:
1. Abnormal psychology
   A) is the attempt to understand problematic human behavior through the analysis of as many case studies as possible.
   B) is primarily concerned with finding the biological underpinnings of psychological phenomena.
   C) is a discipline which contains multiple conceptualizations of problematic behavior.
   D) focuses primarily on developing treatments for mental disorders.
   Answer: C

Pages: 5
Topic: Abnormal Behavior In Our Times
Skill: Conceptual   Other1:
2. Which of the following is NOT an important consideration in discriminating among the many existing conceptualizations of abnormal behavior?
   A) the practical utility of the conceptualization
   B) the scientific adequacy of the conceptualization
   C) the extent to which it takes into account the enormous complexity of human behavior
   D) the length of time that it has dominated research in the field
   Answer: D

Pages: 5-6
Topic: Popular Views of Abnormal Behavior
Skill: Conceptual   Other1:
3. The beliefs held by most people about abnormal behavior
   A) are surprisingly accurate compared to what scientists actually do know about abnormal behavior.
   B) tend to be oversimplified and biased because they are based on the most aberrant and unusual mental disorders.
   C) have become quite sophisticated and accurate due to extensive coverage of this topic in literature and in the media.
   D) have become quite sophisticated but inaccurate due to extensive coverage of this topic in literature and the media.
   Answer: B

Pages: 6
Topic: Popular Views of Abnormal Behavior
Skill: Applied   Other1:
4. The abnormal behavior of others is a popular and recurring theme on television and radio talk shows. Which of the following statements is true?
   A) These shows provide a very useful function because they tend to provide a rather accurate depiction of abnormal behavior.
   B) These shows do a disservice by downplaying the dangerousness of people with mental problems.
   C) The "armchair" diagnoses provided by the mental health professionals on such shows are usually accurate and helpful.
   D) These shows give misinformation about the causes and treatment of abnormal behavior.
   Answer: D

Pages: 7
Topic: Popular Views of Abnormal Behavior
Skill: Factual   Other1:
5. Which of the following statements is true?
   A) Most former mental patients are no more dangerous or volatile than "normal" people.
   B) Actually, most people will develop manifestations of mental illness at some point in their lives.
   C) Normal and abnormal behavior are fundamentally different in kind, even though they may appear to be similar.
   D) Most behaviors exhibited by people diagnosed with a mental disorder are quite distinct from "normal" individuals.
   Answer: A

Pages: 7
Topic: Popular Views of Abnormal Behavior
Skill: Applied   Other1:
6. Candace is a former mental patient. We might expect that her behavior is
   A) noticeably odd but not dangerous or volatile.
   B) bizarre and unusual, but not dangerous.
   C) probably indistinguishable from that of any "normal" person.
   D) secretive and withdrawn.
   Answer: C

Pages: 7
Topic: Popular Views of Abnormal Behavior
Skill: Applied   Other1:
7. Mary has developed a mental illness. Her chances of recovering completely are
    A) not very good.
    B) poor, especially if her behavior is extremely bizarre.
    C) fair.
    D) very good.
    Answer: D

Pages: 7
Topic: Popular Views of Abnormal Behavior
Skill: Applied   Other1:
8. The Neighborhood Preservation Society is protesting the establishment of a group home for
    former mental patients in its subdivision. Which of the following reasons they've cited
    for this protest is valid?
    A) Former mental patients pose a threat to the safety of the other neighborhood residents.

    B) Once hospitalized, individuals rarely recover sufficiently to become fully productive
       members of society again.
    C) Their bizarre and often unpredictable behavior makes such individuals poor candidates
       as "good neighbors."
    D) none of the above
    Answer: D

Pages: 8
Topic: What Do We Mean by Abnormal Behavior: Dilemmas of Definition
Skill: Conceptual   Other1:
9. What role do values play in attempting to define abnormal behavior?
    A) Attempts to define abnormal behavior are invalid without first developing an explicit,
       rational system of ethics.
    B) Defining abnormal behavior should be a neutral, value-free enterprise.
    C) Most abnormal behaviors actually are highly desirable in our society.
    D) Valuational statements are always implicit in scientific attempts to define abnormal
       behavior.
    Answer: D

Pages: 8
Topic: What Do We Mean by Abnormal Behavior: Dilemmas of Definition
Skill: Factual   Other1:
10. The standard working definition for mental disorder and its subclasses is contained in the
    A) American Psychological Association's bylaws.
    B) American Psychiatric Association's bylaws.
    C) World Health Organization's bylaws.
    D) Diagnostic and Statistical Manual of Mental Disorders.
    Answer: D

Pages: 8-9
Topic: What Do We Mean by Abnormal Behavior: Dilemmas of Definition
Skill: Factual   Other1:
11. Which of the following characteristics is NOT associated with the DSM-IV definition of
    mental disorder?
    A) A mental disorder is associated with present distress or disability.
    B) A mental disorder may be an expectable and culturally sanctioned response to a
       particular event.
    C) A mental disorder is a clinically significant behavioral or psychological syndrome or
       pattern.
    D) Conflicts between the individual and society need not be regarded as a mental disorder.
    Answer: B

Pages: 8-9
Topic: What Do We Mean by Abnormal Behavior: Dilemmas of Definition
Skill: Conceptual   Other1:
12. According to the DSM-IV's definition of mental disorder, impairment in one or more areas
    of functioning (disability)
    A) must be present in order to make a diagnosis.
    B) may be present but is not a necessary condition for making a diagnosis.
    C) is one of the less important features of a mental disorder.
    D) must be present for at least six months to be considered a true disability.
    Answer: B

Pages: 8-9
Topic: What Do We Mean by Abnormal Behavior: Dilemmas of Definition
Skill: Applied   Other1:

13. In some of the parts of the world, an individual who hears voices talking to him or her (auditory hallucinations) is viewed as having a special gift and insight into the unknown. According to the DSM-IV, this person
    A) should not be considered as having a mental disorder because he or she is exhibiting a culturally sanctioned behavior.
    B) should be given a diagnosis of a mental disorder because auditory hallucinations are known to be a hallmark feature of mental illness.
    C) should not be considered as having a mental disorder because in this case the auditory hallucinations are not associated with any distress, disability, or increased risk of death, pain, or loss of freedom.
    D) A and C
    Answer: D

Pages: 9
Topic: What Do We Mean by Abnormal Behavior: Dilemmas of Definition
Skill: Factual   Other1:

14. A syndrome is
    A) a symptom.
    B) a group of symptoms that tend to co-occur.
    C) another name for clinical depression.
    D) a category in DSM-IV.
    Answer: B

Pages: 9
Topic: What Do We Mean by Abnormal Behavior: Dilemmas of Definition
Skill: Applied   Other1:

15. A racing heart, clammy skin, and nervousness are all indications of anxiety. Together they comprise a
    A) syndrome.
    B) cluster analysis.
    C) prototype.
    D) schema.
    Answer: A

16. The Solarists are a cult whose members believe that they control the movements of the sun with special hand gestures. What would the DSM-IV say about this group?
A) The group suffers from Shared Delusion Psychosis.
B) Because a group of persons share a belief, however strange, the group must be considered emotionally healthy.
C) While some of this group's individual members may meet criteria for a DSM-IV diagnosis, the DSM-IV does not diagnose groups.
D) none of the above
Answer: C

17. Historically, the two major approaches to defining abnormality or mental disorder differ in the importance that each assigns to _____ in determining whether or not a given behavior is abnormal.
A) science
B) history
C) culture
D) value judgments
Answer: C

18. Alex believes that behavior can be considered abnormal only if society labels it as abnormal. This position is known as
A) valuational relativism.
B) clinical culturalism.
C) social absolutism.
D) cultural relativism.
Answer: D

19. Ava advocates a cultural relativism view of abnormal behavior. She would suggest that
A) most societies around the world should be defined as "sick."
B) social acceptance makes behavior normal.
C) abnormal behavior is consistent across cultures.
D) a psychotherapist should urge his or her clients to rebel against society.
Answer: B

Pages: 9
Topic: What Do We Mean by Abnormal Behavior: Dilemmas of Definition
Skill: Applied   Other1:
20. People in some rural parts of the world accept the practice of infanticide to get rid of
    girl babies. According to the DSM definition of mental disorder, which of the following
    statements is true?
    A) The individuals who practice infanticide are not mentally disordered.
    B) Only those individuals who have had sufficient education to "know better" are mentally
       disordered.
    C) Causing the death of another is always indicative of a DSM-IV mental disorder.
    D) The society in which infanticide is practiced is sick, not the individuals themselves.
    Answer: A

Pages: 10
Topic: Abnormal Behavior: Mental Disorder as Maladaptive Behavior
Skill: Factual   Other1:
21. The authors define abnormal behavior as
    A) behavior that is persistent and contrary to the continued well-being of an individual
       or his or her community.
    B) any behavior that is not accepted by society.
    C) limited not only to individuals but may occur in couples and groups as well.
    D) A and C
    Answer: D

Pages: 10
Topic: Abnormal Behavior: Mental Disorder as Maladaptive Behavior
Skill: Applied   Other1:
22. Adolph Eichmann was a high-ranking Nazi official who actively participated in Hitler's
    "final solution"--to rid the world of people with Jewish ancestry. According to the
    authors' definition of abnormal behavior,
    A) Eichmann did not have a mental disorder because his behavior was culturally sanctioned.
    B) Eichmann did have a mental disorder because he ordered the death of millions, which
       clearly indicates that his behavior was maladaptive.
    C) Eichmann did not have a mental disorder because he was proud of his "accomplishments."
    D) Eichmann did have a mental disorder because his behavior clearly was unusual.
    Answer: B

Pages: 10
Topic: Abnormal Behavior: Mental Disorder as Maladaptive Behavior
Skill: Conceptual   Other1:
23. According to the authors, treatment for abnormal behavior includes
    A) helping individuals adjust to their personal situations.
    B) helping alleviate the social conditions that are associated with abnormal behavior.
    C) promoting conformity to social roles.
    D) A and B
    Answer: D

Pages: 10
Topic: Abnormal Behavior: Mental Disorder as Maladaptive Behavior
Skill: Factual   Other1:
24. The field that most closely corresponds to clinical psychology is
    A) psychiatry.
    B) religious counseling.
    C) social work.
    D) psychiatric nursing.
    Answer: A

Pages: 11
Topic: Abnormal Behavior: Mental Disorder as Maladaptive Behavior
Skill: Factual   Other1:
25. Most research on abnormal behavior is conducted by
    A) psychiatrists.
    B) social workers.
    C) counselors.
    D) psychologists.
    Answer: D

Pages: 11
Topic: Classifying Abnormal Behavior
Skill: Conceptual   Other1:
26. Defining the clinical picture of any abnormal behavior is critical to
    A) developing a classification system.
    B) investigating the causes of the disorder.
    C) developing and evaluating the effectiveness of treatments.
    D) all of the above
    Answer: D

Pages: 11
Topic: Classifying Abnormal Behavior
Skill: Conceptual   Other1:
27. In medicine, an illness typically is diagnosed on the basis of its cause. In abnormal psychology and psychiatry, a given mental illness typically is diagnosed on the basis of
   A) its responsiveness to a given type of treatment.
   B) its cause.
   C) its severity.
   D) its clinical picture.
   Answer: D

Pages: 11
Topic: Classifying Abnormal Behavior
Skill: Conceptual   Other1:
28. We know we have a good classification system in abnormal psychology when
   A) the system has remained unchanged for a long period of time.
   B) medical insurance companies concur with the system.
   C) the reliability and validity of the system are adequate for classifying individuals.
   D) none of the above
   Answer: C

Pages: 11
Topic: Classifying Abnormal Behavior
Skill: Conceptual   Other1:
29. Accurate diagnostic classification systems allow for all of the following EXCEPT
   A) meeting the needs of medical insurance companies.
   B) assigning each individual to one and only one diagnostic category.
   C) enhanced communication among professionals.
   D) enabling adequate statistical counts of the incidence of the various disorders.
   Answer: B

Pages: 11
Topic: Classifying Abnormal Behavior
Skill: Factual   Other1:
30. The degree to which a test or measuring device produces the same result each time it is used to measure the same thing is called _____.
   A) validity
   B) converging operations
   C) reliability
   D) testability
   Answer: C

Pages: 12
Topic: Classifying Abnormal Behavior
Skill: Factual   Other1:
31. In the context of classification, reliability is
    A) the usefulness of a classification system.
    B) an index of the extent to which independent observers can agree that a given individual's behavior fits into a particular category.
    C) the extent to which a diagnostic category accurately conveys the characteristics of membership in that category.
    D) the extent to which a classification system stands the test of time.
    Answer: B

Pages: 12
Topic: Classifying Abnormal Behavior
Skill: Factual   Other1:
32. A classification system which "carves nature at its joints" may be said to possess substantial
    A) simplicity.
    B) diversity.
    C) validity.
    D) convergence.
    Answer: C

Pages: 11-12
Topic: Classifying Abnormal Behavior
Skill: Applied   Other1:
33. A group of psychologists at a community mental health center interview a patient. All of the psychologists agree that the patient is depressed. In fact, the patient is not depressed but has been taking a medication that gives the appearance of depression. The psychologists are
    A) reliable, but not valid.
    B) valid, but not reliable.
    C) neither reliable nor valid.
    D) both reliable and valid.
    Answer: A

Pages: 12
Topic: Classifying Abnormal Behavior
Skill: Conceptual   Other1:

34. In the context of classification, validity means
    A) that people with different diagnoses share the same underlying cause of their disorders.
    B) that people with different diagnoses will respond to the same treatment.
    C) that people with the same diagnoses will share clinically meaningful similarities to one another.
    D) that people with the same diagnosis will respond equally to a given treatment.
    Answer: C

Pages: 12
Topic: Classifying Abnormal Behavior
Skill: Factual   Other1:

35. Which of these statements about classification systems is TRUE?
    A) The validity of a classification system normally presupposes diagnostic reliability.
    B) Diagnostic reliability presupposes the validity of a diagnostic class.
    C) Diagnostic reliability alone is sufficient for valid classification.
    D) Reliability and validity are culturally relative concepts.
    Answer: A

Pages: 12
Topic: Classifying Abnormal Behavior: DSM Classification/Mental Disorders
Skill: Applied   Other1:

36. Gail visited a psychologist because she was experiencing interpersonal difficulties and temper outbursts. The psychologist administered a battery of psychological tests. In diagnosing Gail, the psychologist will use Gail's subjective description of her problems as _____, and the test results as _____.
    A) signs; symptoms
    B) symptoms; signs
    C) signs; criteria
    D) symptoms; criteria
    Answer: B

Pages: 12
Topic: Classifying Abnormal Behavior: DSM Classification/Mental Disorders
Skill: Factual   Other1:

37. The DSM-IV diagnostic criteria assigns diagnoses on the basis of
    A) psychological testing.
    B) response to treatment.
    C) causal factors.
    D) symptoms and signs.
    Answer: D

Pages: 13
Topic: Classifying Abnormal Behavior: DSM Classification/Mental Disorders
Skill: Factual   Other1:
38. The greatest innovation in the DSM-III and later editions of the DSM has been
    A) the attempt to define all disorders according to an integrated theoretical framework.
    B) the elimination of "wastebasket" or residual categories.
    C) the use of more reliable operational criteria for defining different disorders.
    D) enhancing the role of subjective observation by expert clinicians in diagnosis.
    Answer: C

Pages: 13
Topic: Classifying Abnormal Behavior: DSM Classification/Mental Disorders
Skill: Conceptual   Other1:
39. A drawback associated with the use of "wastebasket" or residual diagnostic categories is
    A) the sacrifice in reliability that results.
    B) the sacrifice in validity that results.
    C) the sacrifice in both reliability and validity that results.
    D) the need for later rediagnosis.
    Answer: B

Pages: 13
Topic: Classifying Abnormal Behavior: DSM Classification/Mental Disorders
Skill: Conceptual   Other1:
40. The use of very precise criteria to enhance the reliability of the DSM-IV has led to very
    narrowly defined categories, thereby inflating the occurrence of comorbidity. This means
    that
    A) by enhancing reliability, validity also has been enhanced.
    B) by enhancing reliability, validity may have suffered.
    C) enhancing reliability inevitably leads to greater validity.
    D) none of the above
    Answer: B

Pages: 13
Topic: Classifying Abnormal Behavior: DSM Classification/Mental Disorders
Skill: Conceptual   Other1:
41. Which of the following is a drawback associated with enhancing the reliability of a
    diagnostic classification system?
    A) the resulting failure to detect the co-occurrence of two or more disorders in the same
       individuals
    B) the decreasing lack of actual "clinical reliability" that the classification system
       will have
    C) the unintended sacrifice in validity that can result
    D) none of the above
    Answer: C

42. "Comorbidity" is
   A) the occurrence of the same disorder in two or more persons simultaneously, as in members of the same cult.
   B) the occurrence of the same disorder in two or more genetically related individuals.
   C) the presence of an Axis III disorder.
   D) when two or more supposedly separate disorders occur together in the same person.
   Answer: D

43. In some studies, statistical analyses have revealed a significant correlation between major depression and bulimia. This is an example of
   A) a residual or "wastebasket" category.
   B) covalidity.
   C) comorbidity.
   D) a prototype.
   Answer: C

44. Axis I of the DSM-IV is used to describe
   A) any long-standing personality problems that meet diagnostic criteria for one or more personality disorders.
   B) any general medical conditions that may be relevant to understanding and treating an individual.
   C) psychosocial and environmental problems.
   D) the particular clinical syndromes or conditions that may be a focus of clinical attention.
   Answer: D

Pages: 13
Topic: Classifying Abnormal Behavior: DSM Classification/Mental Disorders
Skill: Applied   Other1:
45. Frederick avoids most social situations because he is extremely fearful of rejection. A therapist diagnosed Frederick with Avoidant Personality Disorder. On which Axis of DSM-IV would this information be contained?
    A) Axis I
    B) Axis II
    C) Axis IV
    D) Axis V
    Answer: B

Pages: 14
Topic: Classifying Abnormal Behavior: DSM Classification/Mental Disorders
Skill: Applied   Other1:
46. Marla is a diabetic psychiatric patient who was admitted to the hospital following a suicide attempt. She is despondent over the debilitating progress of her disease. Her DSM-IV diagnosis might look like which of the following:
    A) Axis I: Diabetes; Axis II: Major depressive disorder
    B) Axis I: Major depressive disorder; Axis III: None
    C) Axis I: Major depressive disorder; Axis III: Diabetes
    D) Axis II: Major depressive disorder; Axis III: Diabetes
    Answer: C

Pages: 14
Topic: Classifying Abnormal Behavior: DSM Classification/Mental Disorders
Skill: Factual   Other1:
47. Axis IV assesses
    A) various categories of impinging life problems.
    B) global functioning.
    C) childhood developmental disorders.
    D) medical conditions.
    Answer: A

Pages: 14
Topic: Classifying Abnormal Behavior: DSM Classification/Mental Disorders
Skill: Factual   Other1:
48. Which DSM-IV Axis uses a checklist for assessing various categories of psychosocial and environmental problems?
    A) Axis II
    B) Axis III
    C) Axis IV
    D) Axis V
    Answer: C

Pages: 14
Topic: Classifying Abnormal Behavior: DSM Classification/Mental Disorders
Skill: Factual   Other1:
49. The Global Assessment of Functioning (GAF) Scale is used to
    A) evaluate physical functioning.
    B) assess an individual's life problems.
    C) evaluate longstanding childhood developmental disorders.
    D) evaluate an individual's overall psychological, social, and occupational functioning.
    Answer: D

Pages: 14
Topic: Classifying Abnormal Behavior: DSM Classification/Mental Disorders
Skill: Factual   Other1:
50. Which axes are considered optional for diagnosis?
    A) III and IV
    B) IV and V
    C) III and IV
    D) All are necessary.
    Answer: B

Pages: 14
Topic: Classifying Abnormal Behavior: DSM Classification/Mental Disorders
Skill: Factual   Other1:
51. Which of the following would NOT be found as a category of mental disorder in the DSM-IV?
    A) Alzheimer's disease
    B) alcohol abuse
    C) grief following the death of a spouse
    D) mental retardation
    Answer: C

Pages: 16
Topic: Classifying Abnormal Behavior: DSM Classification/Mental Disorders
Skill: Applied   Other1:
52. Greg has suffered from ongoing feelings of depression and low self-esteem for years. His disorder is
    A) acute.
    B) chronic.
    C) episodic.
    D) recurrent.
    Answer: B

Pages: 16
Topic: Classifying Abnormal Behavior: DSM Classification/Mental Disorders
Skill: Applied   Other1:

53. Connie was admitted to the hospital exhibiting manic psychotic symptoms. This is her fourth admission for the same disorder. In between hospitalizations she is symptom-free. Her disorder is
    A) chronic and recurrent.
    B) episodic and recurrent.
    C) chronic and nonrecurrent.
    D) episodic and nonrecurrent.
    Answer: B

Pages: 16
Topic: Classifying Abnormal Behavior: The Problem of Labeling
Skill: Conceptual   Other1:

54. One of the problems with using psychiatric diagnoses is that
    A) individuals who are diagnosed are very resistant to adopt that label.
    B) such labels are often assumed to be an accurate and complete description of the individual.
    C) such diagnoses usually do not convey the seriousness and intensity of the disorder.
    D) such diagnoses are designed to describe the person rather than the person's behavioral pattern.
    Answer: B

Pages: 16
Topic: Classifying Abnormal Behavior: The Problem of Labeling
Skill: Applied   Other1:

55. Angela has been diagnosed as mentally ill, a label that is known to the people in her community. They are likely to
    A) maintain a greater social distance from her.
    B) consider her harmless.
    C) perceive her as experiencing "problems in living" rather than a mental illness.
    D) see her as a normal person.
    Answer: A

Topic: Classifying Abnormal Behavior: The Problem of Labeling
Skill: Conceptual   Other1:

56. Many contemporary mental health professionals prefer to refer to the people they treat as "clients" rather than as "patients" because
    A) most of these professionals do not have MD's.
    B) the connotations of the "client" label differ in implying more self-responsibility for one's own treatment and recovery in therapy.
    C) the DSM-IV does not regard individuals in treatment as medically sick.
    D) psychological treatments are not covered by medical health insurance.
    Answer: B

Pages: 17
Topic: The Extent of Abnormal Behavior
Skill: Factual   Other1:

57. Mental health epidemiology is
    A) the study of epidemics in mental disorders among the general population.
    B) the study of organic brain diseases among different ethnic populations of a defined geographic region.
    C) the study of the distribution of mental disorders in a given population.
    D) a sociological study of psychological disorders.
    Answer: C

Pages: 17
Topic: The Extent of Abnormal Behavior
Skill: Factual   Other1:

58. _____ rates are often reported in terms of the lifetime risk of contracting a particular disorder.
    A) Prevalence
    B) Point prevalence
    C) Point incidence
    D) Incidence
    Answer: D

Pages: 17
Topic: The Extent of Abnormal Behavior
Skill: Factual   Other1:

59. The proportion of active cases in a given population or during a particular point in time is the
    A) prevalence rate.
    B) incidence rate.
    C) lifetime incidence rate.
    D) occurrence rate.
    Answer: A

Topic: The Extent of Abnormal Behavior
Skill: Applied   Other1:
60. Individuals who were born in the winter months have a greater chance of having become schizophrenic at some point in their lives than were individuals who were born in the summer months. An epidemiologist would say that the _____ rate for winter-born schizophrenics is higher than that for summer-born schizophrenics.
A) point prevalence
B) capitance
C) lifetime prevalence
D) comorbidity
Answer: C

Topic: The Extent of Abnormal Behavior
Skill: Factual   Other1:
61. The NIMH epidemiological studies found that about _____ of the population suffer from mental or substance abuse disorders in any given month.
A) one percent
B) five percent
C) fifteen percent
D) fifty percent
Answer: C

Topic: The Extent of Abnormal Behavior
Skill: Factual   Other1:
62. In terms of one-year prevalence, the NIMH and Kessler et al. studies found that about _____ of individuals are likely to experience a mental disorder or substance abuse.
A) one percent
B) ten percent
C) thirty percent
D) seventy-five percent
Answer: C

Topic: The Extent of Abnormal Behavior
Skill: Factual   Other1:
63. The NIMH epidemiological study found that
A) rates of almost all disorders are similar for men and women.
B) phobia and depression are among the most frequently occurring disorders.
C) lifetime prevalence rates for various disorders are consistent in different parts of the country.
D) mental disorders and substance abuse are uncommon in some parts of the country.
Answer: B

Pages: 18
Topic: The Extent of Abnormal Behavior
Skill: Factual   Other1:
64. The NIMH epidemiological study found that _____ are more common among women whereas _____ are more common among men.
   A) mood and substance abuse disorders; anxiety and somatization disorders
   B) mood disorders and antisocial personality disorders; anxiety and substance abuse disorders
   C) mood and anxiety disorders; substance abuse and antisocial personality disorders
   D) mood and somatization disorders; anxiety and somatization disorders
   Answer: C

Pages: 18
Topic: The Extent of Abnormal Behavior
Skill: Factual   Other1:
65. The trend toward deinstitutionalization in recent years means that
   A) inpatient hospitalization in public institutions has declined markedly.
   B) people with psychological problems more often receive outpatient treatment than inpatient treatment.
   C) many people who need professional help do not receive any help at all.
   D) all of the above
   Answer: D

Pages: 19
Topic: Research in Abnormal Psychology: Observation of Behavior
Skill: Factual   Other1:
66. Self-observation as a source of information is limited in which of the following ways?
   A) It lacks intersubjective reliability.
   B) It includes information about automatic and unconscious processes, which are not valid sources of knowledge.
   C) It does not provide information about the mental activity that occurs outside of awareness.
   D) A and C
   Answer: D

Pages: 19
Topic: Research in Abnormal Psychology: Observation of Behavior
Skill: Factual   Other1:
67. _____ are more or less plausible ideas used to explain something (e.g., a behavior) and can be tested using research methods.
   A) Observations
   B) Hypotheses
   C) Variables
   D) Correlations
   Answer: B

Pages: 19-20
Topic: Research in Abnormal Psychology: Observation of Behavior
Skill: Conceptual   Other1:

68. Several competing hypotheses usually exist to explain a given pattern of abnormal behavior. One result of this is that
    A) the prevalence of the disorder may be artificially inflated.
    B) psychological diagnoses are rendered less reliable.
    C) a variety of therapeutic approaches may exist for treating the same disorder.
    D) psychopathology is less scientific than a discipline like physics or chemistry.
    Answer: C

Pages: 20
Topic: Research in Abnormal Psychology: Sampling and Generalization
Skill: Applied   Other1:

69. Sidney developed a theory of the causes of anxiety by studying one of his clients in therapy. Which of the following limitations is Sidney likely to face?
    A) His observations may have more to do with Sidney's own characteristics and observational biases than with his client.
    B) There may be different causes of anxiety in other individuals though they share similar symptoms.
    C) Sidney may be basing his theory on characteristics of the client that are unrelated to the origin of the anxiety.
    D) all of the above
    Answer: D

Pages: 20
Topic: Research in Abnormal Psychology: Sampling and Generalization
Skill: Applied   Other1:

70. A psychologist is studying a group of individuals suffering from depression. Although these individuals all suffered a loss in childhood, they differ in many other ways. The psychologist would assume that the loss in childhood
    A) is the cause of the depression.
    B) is not the cause of the depression.
    C) may be related to the depression if the loss does not occur as often among persons who are not depressed.
    D) is unrelated to the depression.
    Answer: C

Pages: 20-21
Topic: Research in Abnormal Psychology: Sampling and Generalization
Skill: Conceptual   Other1:
71. An important FIRST step in studying a particular disorder is
    A) selecting the appropriate subjects for study.
    B) determining the criteria for identifying people who have the disorder.
    C) deciding upon the appropriate statistical analyses to use on the data to be collected.
    D) selecting the best case study for analysis.
    Answer: B

Pages: 21
Topic: Research in Abnormal Psychology: Sampling and Generalization
Skill: Conceptual   Other1:
72. To ensure validity using a sampling approach, it is important that
    A) criteria be broad enough to create a large enough sample.
    B) the sample be obtained primarily from individuals who have never been treated for a psychiatric disorder.
    C) an epidemiological approach using correlational analysis be employed.
    D) every person in the larger group of study has an equal chance of being included in the sample.
    Answer: D

Pages: 21
Topic: Research in Abnormal Psychology: Sampling and Generalization
Skill: Applied   Other1:
73. A current debate in the field of abnormal psychology centers around whether it is appropriate to apply findings from studies of depressed college students to clinical populations of depressives. This is an example of an issue concerning
    A) reliability.
    B) the adequacy of the DSM-IV classification system.
    C) an inappropriate control group.
    D) sampling and generalization.
    Answer: D

Pages: 21
Topic: Research in Abnormal Psychology: Sampling and Generalization
Skill: Conceptual   Other1:
74. To determine whether certain characteristics are true of people in general, and not just of people with mental disorders, it is important to use
    A) an experimental design.
    B) a representative sample of individuals with the disorder.
    C) a control group.
    D) a criterion group.
    Answer: C

Pages: 21
Topic: Research in Abnormal Psychology: Sampling and Generalization
Skill: Applied   Other1:
75. Jane wished to test the hypothesis that schizophrenia is more prevalent in lower socioeconomic classes. She evaluated 25 schizophrenics for socioeconomic background and found that 20 percent of them did indeed live in poverty. What can she conclude?
A) Poor socioeconomic conditions cause schizophrenia.
B) Schizophrenics drift downward into the lower classes because of their disorder.
C) Depression is not caused by poor socioeconomic conditions.
D) Nothing
Answer: D

Pages: 21
Topic: Research in Abnormal Psychology: Sampling and Generalization
Skill: Applied   Other1:
76. A good control group for a sample of snake phobics is one which
A) is equated to the snake phobics on socioeconomic level.
B) is comparable to the snake phobics in all characteristics except for the presence of a snake phobia.
C) does not differ from the snake phobics in chance factors.
D) is drawn from the snake phobic sample.
Answer: B

Pages: 21
Topic: Research in Abnormal Psychology: Correlation and Causation
Skill: Conceptual   Other1: In Student Study Guide
77. Which of the following may be safely inferred when a sizable positive correlation is found between variables x and y?
A) People high on x will usually be high on y.
B) People low on x will usually be high on y.
C) x causes y.
D) y causes x.
Answer: A

Pages: 21
Topic: Research in Abnormal Psychology: Correlation and Causation
Skill: Applied   Other1:
78. A psychologist found that individuals who abuse alcohol were more likely to have
experienced physical abuse by a parent in childhood than were individuals in a control
group who do not abuse alcohol. The psychologist can conclude that
A) childhood abuse causes later alcohol abuse.
B) childhood abuse and alcohol abuse are both caused by some other factor.
C) individuals who do not experience physical abuse in childhood will not become alcohol
   abusers.
D) none of the above
Answer: D

Pages: 21
Topic: Research in Abnormal Psychology: Correlation and Causation
Skill: Conceptual   Other1:
79. Individuals who have alcohol problems tend to come from families with other individuals
who have alcohol problems. This would suggest that
A) genetic factors cause an individual to have alcohol problems.
B) environmental factors cause an individual to have alcohol problems.
C) both genetic and environmental factors cause an individual to have problems.
D) No causation can be determined from this statement.
Answer: D

Pages: 21
Topic: Research in Abnormal Psychology: Correlation and Causation
Skill: Conceptual   Other1:
80. One way to improve our ability to disentangle correlated variables is
A) by manipulating the variables after all data has been collected.
B) by using statistical techniques like path analysis.
C) by not conducting correlational studies and relying on the experimental method instead.
D) none of the above
Answer: B

Pages: 22
Topic: Research in Abnormal Psychology: Correlation and Causation
Skill: Factual   Other1:
81. An epidemiologist would most likely use a(n) _____ approach in studying variations in the
incidence of a mental disorder.
A) correlational
B) experimental
C) prospective
D) retrospective
Answer: A

Pages: 22
Topic: Research in Abnormal Psychology: Experimental Strategies
Skill: Factual   Other1:
82. The most reliable scientific findings result when psychologists use the _____ method.
    A) correlational
    B) experimental
    C) retrospective
    D) case study
    Answer: B

Pages: 23
Topic: Research in Abnormal Psychology: Experimental Strategies
Skill: Factual   Other1:
83. A psychologist wishes to test the hypothesis that the experience of chronic physical pain can cause clinical depression, but the Ethics Committee of his university won't allow him to conduct a study in which he inflicts pain on the subjects. What kind of research design might best allow the psychologist to test this hypothesis while circumventing the committee's objection?
    A) experimental
    B) prospective
    C) analogue
    D) longitudinal
    Answer: C

Pages: 23
Topic: Research in Abnormal Psychology: Experimental Strategies
Skill: Conceptual   Other1:
84. Inducing temporary depression by having normal subjects concentrate on negative thoughts is an example of
    A) an analogue study.
    B) a path analysis.
    C) a case study.
    D) a correlational study.
    Answer: A

Pages: 23
Topic: Research in Abnormal Psychology: Experimental Strategies
Skill: Applied   Other1:

85. In a study, Carol presented false feedback to students about the result of an exam they'd taken. In a random fashion, some were told they got an "A," and others were told that they failed. The students were then asked to rate their self-esteem on a questionnaire in order for Carol to see what impact the feedback had on their subsequent feelings about themselves. This is an example of a(n) _____ study.
A) correlational
B) analogue
C) laboratory
D) prospective
Answer: B

Pages: 23
Topic: Research in Abnormal Psychology: Experimental Strategies
Skill: Conceptual   Other1:

86. The major scientific problem with analogue studies is
A) the difficulty of disentangling intercorrelated factors.
B) the difficulty of manipulating variables in a laboratory.
C) the inability to draw causal inferences from such studies.
D) establishing a convincing connection between the experimentally contrived behavior and the naturally occurring phenomenon.
Answer: D

Pages: 23
Topic: Research in Abnormal Psychology: Experimental Strategies
Skill: Conceptual   Other1:

87. Seligman's early learned helplessness research with dogs is a good example of
A) the correlational method adapted to laboratory research.
B) the difficulty in generalizing from laboratory models to the real world.
C) the disappointing results typically obtained with the experimental use of electric shock.
D) a successful animal model of depression.
Answer: B

Pages: 23
Topic: Research in Abnormal Psychology: Experimental Strategies
Skill: Applied   Other1:
88. In one study, infant monkeys were isolated from their mothers and were given either wire or cloth "substitute mothers." The infant monkeys became withdrawn and behaved in a manner that, in humans, suggests depression. What condition would need to be satisfied in order for this kind of generalization to the human population to be valid?
    A) Science must establish the major commonalities between the monkeys' behavior and depression as it occurs in humans.
    B) The monkeys must meet the same DSM-IV criteria for depression as humans.
    C) The same study must be done with human infants in order to compare results in the two populations.
    D) Any generalization of this type would be invalid.
    Answer: A

Pages: 23
Topic: Research in Abnormal Psychology: Experimental Strategies
Skill: Factual   Other1:
89. The most powerful research method that can be used in the evaluation of the efficacy of various treatment approaches is the _____ method.
    A) case study
    B) experimental
    C) correlational
    D) retrospective
    Answer: B

Pages: 24
Topic: Research in Abnormal Psychology: Experimental Strategies
Skill: Factual   Other1:
90. A psychologist using a waiting list control group or a comparative outcome strategy would be testing a hypothesis about
    A) treatment outcomes.
    B) learned helplessness in humans.
    C) different possible causes of a mental disorder.
    D) factors that might be correlated with a particular mental disorder.
    Answer: A

Pages: 24
Topic: Research in Abnormal Psychology: Experimental Strategies
Skill: Applied   Other1:
91. Dr. Brown's experimental and control groups differ significantly in educational level.
    What might she do to "correct" her results for this difference?
    A) There is nothing she can do about it.
    B) She may be able to use retrospective controls to adjust for the difference.
    C) She may be able to use statistical techniques to adjust for the difference.
    D) She can safely ignore the difference in educational level.
    Answer: C

Pages: 24
Topic: Research in Abnormal Psychology: Clinical Case Studies
Skill: Conceptual   Other1:
92. One of the biggest limitations with the case study approach is
    A) the need to rely too heavily on psychological testing in gathering data.
    B) too little emphasis on biological factors that may be involved in causing the abnormal
       behavior.
    C) the difficulty in finding multiple observers to use with only one subject.
    D) in attempting to generalize to other cases.
    Answer: D

Pages: 24
Topic: Research/Abnormal Psychology: Retrospective/Prospective Strategies
Skill: Applied   Other1: In Student Study Guide
93. A psychologist identifies fifty children who have schizophrenic mothers. At adolescence,
    the researcher compares those who break down with those who don't. This is an example of
    a _____ study.
    A) clinical case
    B) comparative outcome
    C) prospective
    D) retrospective
    Answer: C

Pages: 24
Topic: Research/Abnormal Psychology: Retrospective/Prospective Strategies
Skill: Applied   Other1:
94. When confronted with the occurrence of abnormal behavior in an acquaintance, ordinary
    people often try to figure out why the behavior occurred by contemplating events in that
    individual's past. This is an example of the _____ method.
    A) prospective
    B) retrospective
    C) introspective
    D) correlational
    Answer: B

Pages: 24
Topic: Research/Abnormal Psychology: Retrospective/Prospective Strategies
Skill: Conceptual   Other1:
95. "Be careful what you look for--you just may find it." This warning might best apply to
researchers using _____ strategies.
A) experimental
B) prospective
C) analogue
D) retrospective
Answer: D

Pages: 25
Topic: Research/Abnormal Psychology: Retrospective/Prospective Strategies
Skill: Factual   Other1:
96. In most prospective studies,
A) the backgrounds of individuals with a disorder are studied to determine causative
factors.
B) an unselected sample of a general population of adults is used.
C) analogue research is used because of the ethical problems with other experimental
research.
D) children sharing a risk factor known to be associated with high rates of a disorder are
studied over time.
Answer: D

Pages: 24
Topic: Research/Abnormal Psychology: Retrospective/Prospective Strategies
Skill: Applied   Other1:
97. Loren is assessing a large group of college students believed to be at risk for developing
schizophrenia. He is following these college students through subsequent years to
determine which of them do, in fact, become schizophrenic. This is an example of a(n)
_____ research design.
A) prospective
B) retrospective
C) experimental
D) postdictive
Answer: A

Topic: Unresolved Issues on Classification
Skill: Conceptual   Other1:

98. A major advantage that prospective studies have over retrospective studies is that
    A) in retrospective studies, subjects' memories of past events may be colored by present mental disorders.
    B) in retrospective studies, it is more difficult to disentangle effects of present mental disorders from effects of past events.
    C) prospective studies allow an experimenter to control all relevant variables while manipulating only one at a time.
    D) A and B
    Answer: D

Pages: 26
Topic: Unresolved Issues on Classification
Skill: Conceptual   Other1:

99. One of the biggest difficulties in improving our diagnostic classification system remains
    A) the problem of enhancing interdiagnostic reliability.
    B) clarifying the nature of the diseases described in the DSM medical model.
    C) the problem of enhancing reliability without sacrificing validity.
    D) reducing the focus on the treatment of disorders at the expense of attention to the causes of the disorders.
    Answer: C

Pages: 26
Topic: Unresolved Issues on Classification
Skill: Factual   Other1:

100. The DSM-IV is based on a _____ model.
    A) prototype
    B) medical
    C) dimensional
    D) cluster
    Answer: B

Pages: 26
Topic: Unresolved Issues on Classification
Skill: Conceptual   Other1:

101. DSM-IV assumes that
    A) mental disorders consist of discrete, discontinuous categories with clearcut boundaries.
    B) human behavior is ultimately too complex to be captured in a medical model.
    C) Axis I and II disorders should be diagnosed using a dimensional approach.
    D) normal and abnormal behavior differ only in degree, not in kind.
    Answer: A

Pages: 27
Topic: Unresolved Issues on Classification
Skill: Conceptual   Other1:
102. DSM-IV assumes that the current use of _____ to diagnose mental disorders will give way to the use of _____ when future research makes this possible.
    A) symptoms; signs
    B) symptoms; causes
    C) treatment approach; causes
    D) causes; biological factors
    Answer: B

Pages: 27
Topic: Unresolved Issues on Classification
Skill: Conceptual   Other1:
103. Objections to the current diagnostic system include all of the following EXCEPT
    A) the DSM-IV focuses excessively on the causes of various disorders and not sufficiently on treatment.
    B) the DSM-IV is based on a medical model that fails to convey the complexity of human behavior.
    C) the use of a categorical system of classification is an oversimplification of reality.
    D) the reliance on symptoms in the classification system is rudimentary.
    Answer: A

Pages: 27
Topic: Unresolved Issues on Classification
Skill: Factual   Other1:
104. Three basic approaches to classifying abnormal behavior are the _____ methods.
    A) categorical, prospective, and retrospective
    B) categorical, medical, and dimensional
    C) categorical, dimensional, and prospective
    D) categorical, dimensional, and prototypal
    Answer: D

Pages: 27
Topic: Unresolved Issues on Classification
Skill: Applied   Other1:
105. Dr. Gray rates his clients according to varying degrees of extraversion, negative affectivity, and agreeableness. He is using a _____ classification approach.
    A) DSM-IV
    B) prototypal
    C) categorical
    D) dimensional
    Answer: D

Pages: 27
Topic: Unresolved Issues on Classification
Skill: Factual   Other1:
106. Some people have suggested amending Axis II and even Axis I to abandon the categorical approach to classification in favor of the _____ approach.
    A) dimensional
    B) medical
    C) prospectival
    D) cluster
    Answer: A

Pages: 27
Topic: Unresolved Issues on Classification
Skill: Factual   Other1:
107. Which of the following uses a dimensional scale?
    A) Axis I
    B) Axis II
    C) Axis IV
    D) Axis V
    Answer: D

Pages: 27
Topic: Unresolved Issues on Classification
Skill: Factual   Other1:
108. A conceptualized entity depicting an idealized combination of characteristics that occur with some regularity in a less perfect way in the real world is a
    A) dimension.
    B) category.
    C) core concept.
    D) prototype.
    Answer: D

Pages: 27
Topic: Unresolved Issues on Classification
Skill: Conceptual   Other1:
109. One advantage of a prototypal classification model is that
    A) it would allow diagnosis on the basis of causal factors rather than symptoms.
    B) it allows people to be sharply divided into normal and abnormal categories.
    C) an individual's abnormal behavior may be seen as an instance of more than one prototype of mental disorder, thereby making "comorbidity" more understandable.
    D) none of the above
    Answer: C

Pages: 27
Topic: Unresolved Issues on Classification
Skill: Conceptual   Other1:
110. Which of the following classification systems are most similar?
      A) the categorical and dimensional systems
      B) the symptom and prototypical systems
      C) the categorical and prototypical systems
      D) the dimensional and prototypical systems
      Answer: D

Short Answer

Write the word or phrase that best completes each statement or answers the question.

Pages: 5-10
Topic: Abnormal Behavior: Mental Disorder as Maladaptive Behavior
Skill: Factual   Other1:
1. Identify two approaches to defining abnormal behavior.
    Answer: Popular views tend to regard abnormal behavior (incorrectly) as bizarre,
             dangerous, and very different from "normal" behavior. Cultural relativists view
             abnormal as meaningful only with reference to a given culture, as deviating from
             social norms. DSM-IV adopts the medical model in viewing mental disorder as a
             syndrome reflecting individual dysfunction. The authors' working definition
             focuses on the maladaptive nature of abnormal behavior.

Pages: 8
Topic: What Do We Mean by Abnormal Behavior: Dilemmas of Definition
Skill: Conceptual   Other1:
2. What do issues of value judgment have to do with defining abnormal behavior?
    Answer: Gorenstein noted that they are "hopelessly intertwined" because most of the
             behavior that we regard as abnormal we also regard as undesirable.
             Statistically deviant behaviors like heroism that are not seen as undesirable
             are not considered "abnormal" at all, in the sense of being problematic
             conditions, dysfunctions, or diseases that can, or even ought to be, treated for
             the social good. Any definition of abnormal behavior contains implicit within
             it an assertion of values.

Pages: 9
Topic: Abnormal Behavior: Mental Disorder as Maladaptive Behavior
Skill: Factual   Other1:
3. _____ is the view that any behavior should be considered normal if it is sanctioned by the
    culture in which it occurs.
    Answer: Cultural relativism

Pages: 10
Topic: Abnormal Behavior: Mental Disorder as Maladaptive Behavior
Skill: Factual   Other1:
4. According to the authors, abnormal behavior is _____.
    Answer: maladaptive

Pages: 11-12
Topic: Classifying Abnormal Behavior
Skill: Conceptual   Other1:
5. Identify and define two characteristics that a useful diagnostic classification system
    must have.
    Answer: Reliability is an index of the extent to which observers can agree that a given
             individual's behavior fits into a particular diagnostic category. Validity is
             the extent to which a diagnostic category accurately conveys clinically
             important information basic to that particular category.

Pages: 11-12
Topic: Classifying Abnormal Behavior
Skill: Conceptual   Other1:
6. What is reliability and why is it important to a diagnostic classification system?
    Answer: In classification, reliability is the extent to which different observers agree
             that a given individual's behavior fits a particular diagnostic category.
             Without reliability it would not be possible to determine whether or not a
             particular disorder were present or absent. Typically, the validity of a
             classification system presupposes its reliability.

Pages: 12
Topic: Classifying Abnormal Behavior
Skill: Conceptual   Other1:
7. What is validity and why is it important to a diagnostic classification system?
    Answer: Validity is the extent to which a measuring instrument actually measures what it
             claims to measure. In classification, validity refers to the extent to which a
             category will accurately convey something clinically important or basic about an
             individual's behavior. Without validity a classification system would be
             irrelevant and useless.

Pages: 12-13
Topic: Classifying Abnormal Behavior: DSM Classification/Mental Disorders
Skill: Conceptual   Other1:
8. Evaluate the DSM-IV in terms of its reliability and validity.
   Answer: The DSM-IV has explicit operational criteria for assigning diagnoses on the
   basis of specific symptoms and signs. Thus, the interdiagnostic reliability for
   many categories is high. However, the DSM-IV may have enhanced reliability at
   the expense of validity. In reality, people's disorders often do not fall
   neatly into distinct DSM-IV categories. Many cases fall into broad residual
   ("wastebasket") categories that don't convey much about the actual nature of the
   varied disorders lumped together in them. A too fine-grained taxonomic approach
   may also artificially inflate comorbidity.

Pages: 13-16
Topic: Classifying Abnormal Behavior: DSM Classification/Mental Disorders
Skill: Factual   Other1:
9. How does the DSM-IV evaluate individuals to determine a diagnosis?
   Answer: The DSM-IV contains explicit operational criteria for determining whether an
   individual's behavior (based on signs and symptoms) fits a diagnostic category
   on Axes I and II. These first two axes assess a person's psychological
   condition, with the focal syndrome or condition contained on Axis I, and
   longer-standing personality problems on Axis II. Axis III contains information
   about general medical conditions potentially related to the case. Axis IV uses
   a checklist to assess relevant psychosocial stressors. Axis V uses a 100-point
   scale to assess a person's level of functioning.

Pages: 16
Topic: Classifying Abnormal Behavior: The Problem of Labeling
Skill: Conceptual   Other1:
10. What are two of the problems associated with carrying a label of mental illness?
    Answer: One danger is that a diagnostic label may influence an individual to accept a
    redefined identity and act out the expectations of that role. Bearing a label
    of mental illness may be devastating to a person's morale and self-esteem. Some
    research suggests that individuals who have been mental patients tend to be
    rejected by others, who regard them as dangerous.

Pages: 17
Topic: The Extent of Abnormal Behavior
Skill: Factual   Other1:
11. The two major statistics used in epidemiological studies are _____ and _____ rates.
    Answer: incidence; prevalence

12. Identify three of the findings obtained by large-scale epidemiological studies like those conducted by the NIMH.

    Answer: The one-month prevalence rate of mental or substance abuse disorder is about 16 percent, and the one-year prevalence rate about 30 percent. There are differences in lifetime prevalence rates for various disorders in different sites studied. Anxiety and depressive disorders were most prevalent overall. Men had more substance abuse and antisocial personality disorders, while women had more mood and anxiety disorders.

13. The technique by which a researcher selects a limited number of individuals for study from a larger population is called _____.

    Answer: sampling

14. What is the difference between correlational studies and those using the experimental method?

    Answer: Correlational studies test hypotheses about whether two or more variables co-occur on a regular basis. It is not possible to draw a conclusion about whether any sort of causal relationship exists between two correlated variables. In order to test a causal hypothesis, the experimental method must be used. Here researchers control all variables but the one of interest, which they manipulate in order to see whether changes in that variable are associated with changes in a second variable. If so, the effect may be assumed to be caused by what was manipulated.

15. Dr. Smythe wished to study the causes of juvenile delinquency in teenagers. He found that an overwhelming number of them came from single-parent households compared to a control group of nondelinquent teenagers. What can he conclude from this?

    Answer: He can not draw any firm causal inferences about the relationship between single-parent homes and juvenile delinquency. Some other factor or complex pattern of factors could be causally linked to BOTH delinquency and broken homes.

Pages: 23
Topic: Research in Abnormal Psychology: Experimental Strategies
Skill: Applied   Other1:
16. Dr. Lansford wishes to test the hypothesis that lack of social stimulation in the early months of infancy causes long-term impairment in social relationships. However, to run a study in which infants are systematically deprived in this way would be clearly unethical. How might she test her hypothesis?
   Answer: She might test this hypothesis in an analogue study, in which she would simulate the social deprivation conditions with animals. She also might conduct a longitudinal study, in which she examines deprived and non-deprived children over time.

Pages: 23
Topic: Research in Abnormal Psychology: Experimental Strategies
Skill: Applied   Other1:
17. The type of research design that would be optimal to use in testing the efficacy of various treatment approaches for a particular mental disorder is the _____ method.
   Answer: experimental

Pages: 24
Topic: Research/Abnormal Psychology: Retrospective/Prospective Strategies
Skill: Conceptual   Other1:
18. What are retrospective studies? What are their limitations?
   Answer: Retrospective research involves gathering data about mentally disordered subjects by reconstructing past events in their lives and using other historical data that might be available. However, individuals' memories of past events may be biased by their present disorders. Relevant historical information may be unavailable. Further, investigators using the retrospective method may be especially likely to find what they expect to find.

Pages: 24-25
Topic: Research/Abnormal Psychology: Retrospective/Prospective Strategies
Skill: Conceptual   Other1:
19. What are prospective studies? What are some of the advantages associated with this strategy?
   Answer: Prospective studies follow a group of individuals through time who are hypothesized to be at high risk for developing a particular mental disorder (for example, through genetic liability). Investigators attempt to predict which of the individuals, or which of two or more groups, will become disordered. Prospective studies circumvent the problems that retrospective studies have in gathering information about events prior to becoming disordered, and allow greater confidence in the causal hypotheses that can be generated from findings.

Pages: 27-28
Topic: Unresolved Issues on Classification
Skill: Factual   Other1:

20. Briefly describe the three types of classification systems discussed in the text.

    Answer: A categorical model assumes that categories are discrete and discontinuous, each with a unique core and definable boundary. A dimensional model assumes that behavior can be conceptualized in terms of various dimensions of behavior (such as mood, extraversion) which vary in strength or intensity. Everyone's behavior can be described as a configuration of dimensional traits using the same set of dimensions for all. Prototypal models assume some overlap between categories. Specific instances may belong to two or more categories and may have only a subset of characteristics of any category.

Essay

Write your answer in the space provided or on a separate sheet of paper.

Pages: 5-11
Topic: What Do We Mean by Abnormal Behavior: Dilemmas of Definition
Skill: Conceptual   Other1:

1. Discuss some of the difficulties involved in attempting to define abnormal behavior.

    Answer: There are many widespread misconceptions among the general public about mental disorders and individuals who are mentally ill. "Abnormal" presupposes some norm from which behavior deviates, but there is no definition of "normal" about which people can all agree. Issues of value come into play, as does sociocultural context. Decisions must be made as to whether to apply the label to couples or groups as well as individuals.

Pages: 5-6
Topic: Popular Views of Abnormal Behavior
Skill: Factual   Other1:

2. Many people gain their understanding of abnormal behavior from the popular media, such as radio, television, and newspapers. What problems does this create?

    Answer: The popular media typically simplifies abnormal behavior. The media often appear to give answers when they barely succeed in posing the correct questions. The descriptions of individuals provided in the media are likely to be extreme cases that give a distorted picture and minimize the less spectacular maladjustments that are far more common.

Pages: 9-10
Topic: What Do We Mean by Abnormal Behavior: Dilemmas of Definition
Skill: Conceptual   Other1:

3. What are the two broad historical perspectives that have attempted to define abnormality in behavior?

    Answer: Cultural relativism defines abnormal entirely in terms of the culture in which it occurs--behavior is abnormal only if the culture defines it as such. A less extreme view regards abnormal behavior as maladaptive behavior. This perspective considers behavior to be abnormal if it results in harm to an individual or to the society in which the individual lives. Thus, it is a less culturally variable stance.

Pages: 10
Topic: Abnormal Behavior: Mental Disorder as Maladaptive Behavior
Skill: Factual   Other1:

4. The authors offer a working definition of abnormal behavior as maladaptive behavior. What do they mean by this?

    Answer: Behavior is abnormal if it is persistent and poses potential harm to an individual and/or the society in which the individual functions. This definition takes a moderate position on the issue of cultural relativism without denying the significance of cultural context. The definition may be applied to individuals, couples, and groups, without any implication about the mental health of individual group members. Therapy is viewed from this perspective in terms of both helping people adjust to their personal situations and helping to change social conditions that may influence the behavior.

Pages: 11-12
Topic: Classifying Abnormal Behavior
Skill: Conceptual   Other1:

5. Why is a classification system so important in the field of psychopathology?

    Answer: It is necessary for clear professional communication in research as well as in clinical settings. Clear, consistent diagnostic criteria are necessary for selecting appropriate research subjects and for gathering statistics on the incidence of various disorders. It is also necessary to have standardized, reliable diagnoses available to clinicians in order for them to be able to treat individuals, as well as to satisfy medical insurance companies.

Pages: 11-12
Topic: Classifying Abnormal Behavior
Skill: Conceptual   Other1:

6. What characteristics must a classification system have in order to be useful in the field of psychopathology?
    Answer: The two most important characteristics are reliability and validity. Reliability in this case is an index of the extent to which independent observers can agree that a particular individual's behavior fits into a particular diagnostic category. Validity, which typically presupposes interdiagnostic reliability, refers to the extent to which a particular diagnostic category actually refers to the behaviors it purports to refer to. A reliable diagnosis that lacks validity will not be clinically meaningful.

Pages: 13
Topic: Classifying Abnormal Behavior: DSM Classification/Mental Disorders
Skill: Conceptual   Other1:

7. Enhancing interdiagnostic agreement by using extremely precise diagnostic criteria has important limitations. What are they?
    Answer: By using such precise criteria to improve reliability, some argue the DSM-IV has sacrificed the validity of some of its diagnostic categories. Thus, the usefulness and relevance of the DSM-IV has been hampered. In addition, these highly precise criteria artificially inflate the occurrence of comorbidity. Further, too many residual or "wastebasket" diagnostic categories have resulted. Such categories are too broad to give us a hint as to the real nature of the different disorders that are all lumped together.

Pages: 13-16
Topic: Classifying Abnormal Behavior: DSM Classification/Mental Disorders
Skill: Applied   Other1:

8. How would you go about evaluating an individual based on the axes of DSM-IV?
    Answer: Appropriate and reliable clinical assessment techniques would be used to assess the individual's presenting symptoms and signs. The individual is evaluated along five dimensions or Axes according to the DSM's explicit operational criteria. Axis I is used to diagnose the clinical syndrome or condition that is a focus of treatment. Axis II contains personality disorders. Axis III contains medical information that may be relevant. Axis IV is diagnosed using a checklist to evaluate psychosocial stressors. Axis V is assessed with the GAF rating scale evaluating level of functioning.

Pages: 12-13
Topic: Classifying Abnormal Behavior: DSM Classification/Mental Disorders
Skill: Conceptual   Other1:

9. Every diagnostic system has its problems and the DSM-IV is no exception. What are the limitations of this diagnostic system?
    Answer: The categories in the DSM describe rather than explain. Only individual behavior is covered, excluding familial and societal problems. There are questions about validity, as well as whether a medical model is an appropriate one for mental disorders. Similarly, a categorical classification model may be inadequate.

Pages: 17-18
Topic: The Extent of Abnormal Behavior
Skill: Applied   Other1:

10. Assume that you are reading a newspaper story concerning a major epidemiological study of abnormal behavior. The story provides incidence and prevalence data. First, what are these? Second, what might be some of the data presented in the story regarding the prevalence of psychiatric disorders in this country?
    Answer: Incidence is the rate of occurrence of a given disorder in a given population. Prevalence refers to the number of active cases that can be identified at a given point in time. The most common disorders are phobias, depression, and alcohol/substance abuse. Rates vary according to location and gender.

Pages: 20-21
Topic: Research in Abnormal Psychology: Sampling and Generalization
Skill: Applied   Other1:

11. Assume that you work for the National Institute of Mental Health. You are about to participate in a major epidemiological study to determine the prevalence of psychiatric disorders in society. Discuss how the issues of sampling and generalization will affect your study.
    Answer: A representative sample of the population to be described is very important. To ensure the validity of generalizations from the sample to the population, each person in the larger population from which the sample is drawn must have an equal chance of being selected for study.

Pages: 21-22
Topic: Research in Abnormal Psychology: Correlation and Causation
Skill: Applied   Other1:
12. Assume that a study finds that parents of children with schizophrenia give their children confusing communications. Thus, there is a correlation between childhood schizophrenia and disordered parental communications. Discuss the issues of causality between these variables.

    Answer: Correlation does not imply causation. Some factor associated with the childhood of schizophrenics may result in more disordered communication, or vice versa. Both could be caused by some other variable, or both could be involved in a more complex pattern of variables influencing both in similar ways.

Pages: 22-24
Topic: Research in Abnormal Psychology: Experimental Strategies
Skill: Conceptual   Other1:
13. The experimental method is the most powerful research method. What are the advantages and disadvantages of this method with regard to studying abnormal behavior?

    Answer: It allows for an understanding of causation. Unfortunately, practical and ethical considerations limit the use of this method in the study of many problems in abnormal psychology. Analogue studies are often used to overcome these problems, but they may have limited applicability to naturally occurring disorders. The experiemental method is especialy useful in evaluating treatment approaches.

Pages: 24
Topic: Research in Abnormal Psychology: Clinical Case Studies
Skill: Factual   Other1:
14. What is the case study method? What are its advantages and disadvantages?

    Answer: A case study is an indepth investigation of one individual. Case studies provide highly detailed and rich information about an individual's life and development, which may be very useful in generating further hypotheses about psychopathology. However, there is a risk that the case study will be biased by the assumptions of the author. Also, they are often difficult to generalize to other individuals.

Pages: 26-28
Topic: Unresolved Issues on Classification
Skill: Conceptual   Other1:

15. There is much controversy over the DSM-IV. What are some of the major criticisms?
    Describe alternative approaches to classification.

    Answer: The four major objections to DSM-IV are: 1) DSM-IV is based on a medical model
             and inadequately conveys the complexity of human behavior; 2) the categorical
             system is an oversimplification of reality; 3) the reliance on symptoms in the
             classification system is rudimentary; and 4) enhancing interdiagnostic
             reliability in the DSM-IV has sometimes resulted in a sacrifice in validity.
             The dimensional and prototypal approaches are alternatives.

CHAPTER 2   Historical Views of Abnormal Behavior

Multiple-Choice

Choose the one alternative that best completes the statement or answers the question.

Pages: 31
Topic: Historical Views of Abnormal Behavior
Skill: Factual   Other1:
1. In a broad sense, the evolution of popular views of psychopathology has progressed from
   A) beliefs based on scientific awareness to religiously based views.
   B) a focus on supernatural causes to natural causes.
   C) beliefs based on religious views to beliefs based on superstition.
   D) beliefs based on medical causes to beliefs based on natural causes.
   Answer: B

Pages: 31
Topic: Historical Views of Abnormal Behavior
Skill: Conceptual   Other1:
2. Which of the following statements is true?
   A) The Greeks thought so little of the human body that they did not consider human anatomy important.
   B) Psychological beliefs typically have dominated physiological explanations until the last fifty years.
   C) Religious views were important, but have not played much of a role in the past 1000 years.
   D) Currently there is a renewed emphasis on biological approaches to the point of sometimes undervaluing psychological approaches.
   Answer: D

Pages: 32
Topic: Abnormal Behavior in Ancient Times: Demonology, Gods and Magic
Skill: Factual   Other1:
3. The early writings of Chinese, Egyptians, Hebrews and Greeks show that in ancient times abnormal behavior often was attributed to
   A) black bile.
   B) magnetic forces inside the body.
   C) demons and gods who had taken possession of a person.
   D) brain dysfunction.
   Answer: C

Pages: 32
Topic: Abnormal Behavior in Ancient Times: Demonology, Gods and Magic
Skill: Factual   Other1:
4. In ancient societies, if a person's abnormal conduct consisted of speech that appeared to
    have a religious or mystical significance, then the person was
    A) assumed to have willingly entered into a pact with the devil.
    B) thought to be a witch.
    C) thought to be possessed by a good spirit or god.
    D) assumed to have something physically wrong with the heart.
    Answer: C

Pages: 32
Topic: Abnormal Behavior in Ancient Times: Demonology, Gods and Magic
Skill: Factual   Other1:
5. In ancient cultures, flogging or starving were sometimes used as part of exorcism rituals
    to
    A) see if God would step in to save the individual from death.
    B) make the body of a possessed person so unpleasant that the evil spirit would be driven
       out.
    C) make the possessed individual suffer for his or her sins.
    D) try to exact a confession from the individual.
    Answer: B

Pages: 32
Topic: Abnormal Behavior in Ancient Times: Demonology, Gods and Magic
Skill: Factual   Other1:
6. Demonic possession was primarily treated by
    A) trephining.
    B) realligning magnetic forces in the body.
    C) an early form of hypnosis.
    D) exorcism.
    Answer: D

Pages: 32
Topic: Abnormal Behavior in Ancient Times: Demonology, Gods and Magic
Skill: Factual   Other1:
7. In ancient cultures, more humane treatment of people exhibiting abnormal behavior began
    when
    A) the treatment was taken over by priests.
    B) there was a shift from a belief in supernatural forces to physiological forces.
    C) the culture recognized that abnormal behavior was out of the person's control.
    D) it came to be believed that the person did not willingly enter into a pact with the
       devil.
    Answer: A

Pages: 32
Topic: Abnormal Behavior in Ancient Times: Demonology, Gods and Magic
Skill: Factual   Other1:
8. Dream interpretation was first used by
    A) Sigmund Freud.
    B) Mesmer.
    C) ancient priests of Asclepius.
    D) Hippocrates.
    Answer: C

Pages: 33
Topic: Abnormal Behavior/Ancient Times: Early Philosophical/Medical Concepts
Skill: Factual   Other1:
9. Hippocrates hypothesized that abnormal behavior is primarily caused by
    A) demonic possession.
    B) brain pathology.
    C) absence of dream activity.
    D) environmental factors.
    Answer: B

Pages: 33
Topic: Abnormal Behavior/Ancient Times: Early Philosophical/Medical Concepts
Skill: Factual   Other1:
10. The three categories of mental disorders developed by Hippocrates included all but which
    of the following?
    A) schizophrenia
    B) mania
    C) melancholia
    D) phrentis (brain fever)
    Answer: A

Pages: 33
Topic: Abnormal Behavior/Ancient Times: Early Philosophical/Medical Concepts
Skill: Factual   Other1:
11. In his theory of the etiology of mental disorders, Hippocrates emphasized the importance
    of
    A) liver dysfunction.
    B) humors such as black bile.
    C) demonic possession.
    D) hysteria.
    Answer: B

Topic: Abnormal Behavior/Ancient Times: Early Philosophical/Medical Concepts
Skill: Factual   *Other1:*

12. Hippocrates offered _____ as a cure for hysteria.
    A) bleeding
    B) phlegm reduction
    C) marriage
    D) celibacy
    Answer: C

Topic: Abnormal Behavior/Ancient Times: Early Philosophical/Medical Concepts
Skill: Factual   *Other1:*

13. Which of the following was true regarding Hippocrates?
    A) He divided all mental disorders into neurosis and psychosis.
    B) He relied heavily on clinical observation.
    C) He believed that dreams were an indication of the gods' displeasure.
    D) He utilized the experimental method in evaluating his treatments.
    Answer: B

Topic: Abnormal Behavior/Ancient Times: Early Philosophical/Medical Concepts
Skill: Factual   *Other1:*

14. Xerxes is feeling depressed. He sought help from Hippocrates. Hippocrates would probably have
    A) prescribed the roots of certain plants and unusual elixirs.
    B) utilized a talking cure.
    C) prescribed exercise, tranquility, and celibacy.
    D) performed an exorcism.
    Answer: C

Topic: Abnormal Behavior/Ancient Times: Early Philosophical/Medical Concepts
Skill: Factual   *Other1:*

15. Blood, black bile, yellow bile, and phlegm are
    A) the names of demons thought to inhabit the brain.
    B) causes of physical disorders that mimic mental disorders.
    C) physical causes of the four primary personality traits described by Plato.
    D) the four bodily humors of Hippocratic theory.
    Answer: D

Pages: 34
Topic: Abnormal Behavior/Ancient Times: Early Philosophical/Medical Concepts
Skill: Factual   Other1:
16. Plato's belief, which was similar to the present-day insanity defense, was that individuals
    A) should not be held responsible for their actions if they suffer from neuroses.
    B) who are incapable of comprehending their trials should be released immediately.
    C) must be judged insane based on their actions at the time of the trial and not at the time their acts were committed.
    D) afflicted with insanity should not be held responsible for their actions nor punished in the same way as normal people.
    Answer: D

Pages: 34
Topic: Abnormal Behavior/Ancient Times: Early Philosophical/Medical Concepts
Skill: Conceptual   Other1:
17. Plato anticipated Freud's notion of
    A) free association.
    B) hypnotic treatment.
    C) dreams as substitute satisfactions.
    D) the pleasure principle.
    Answer: C

Pages: 34
Topic: Abnormal Behavior/Ancient Times: Early Philosophical/Medical Concepts
Skill: Factual   Other1:
18. Aristotle, an early student of Plato, wrote extensively about
    A) the psychological causes of mental disorders.
    B) mental disorders and the contents of consciousness.
    C) mental disorders and the contents of the unconscious mind.
    D) the principle of opposite by opposite.
    Answer: B

Pages: 34
Topic: Abnormal Behavior/Ancient Times: Early Philosophical/Medical Concepts
Skill: Conceptual   Other1:
19. Aristotle anticipated Freud's notion of
    A) hypnosis.
    B) a talking cure.
    C) the pleasure/pain principle.
    D) unconscious thought.
    Answer: C

Pages: 34
Topic: Abnormal Behavior/Ancient Times: Early Philosophical/Medical Concepts
Skill: Conceptual   Other1:
20. Aristotle and Hippocrates were similar in that both believed that
    A) many mental disorders could not be treated.
    B) hysteria was more common in men than in women.
    C) psychological factors like frustration and conflict caused some mental disorders.
    D) bodily humors were a direct cause of mental disorders.
    Answer: D

Pages: 34
Topic: Abnormal Behavior/Ancient Times: Early Philosophical/Medical Concepts
Skill: Factual   Other1:
21. In ancient Egypt, temples of Saturn were used as _____ in treating disturbed individuals.
    A) prisons
    B) sanatoriums
    C) sleeping facilities
    D) schools
    Answer: B

Pages: 34
Topic: Abnormal Behavior/Ancient Times: Early Philosophical/Medical Concepts
Skill: Factual   Other1:
22. Galen is an important historical figure because he
    A) contributed to knowledge about the nervous system.
    B) maintained a scientific approach.
    C) divided the causes of psychological disorders into physical and mental categories.
    D) all of the above
    Answer: D

Pages: 35
Topic: Abnormal Behavior/Ancient Times: Early Philosophical/Medical Concepts
Skill: Factual   Other1: In Student Study Guide
23. The "Dark Ages" in the history of abnormal psychology began with the
    A) "Black Death" of the fifteenth century A.D.
    B) death of Galen in 200 A.D.
    C) fall of Rome in the fifth century A.D.
    D) Roman monarchs around 100 A.D.
    Answer: B

Pages: 35
Topic: Abnormal Behavior in Ancient Times: Views During the Middle Ages
Skill: Conceptual   Other1:
24. During the Middle Ages, the most enlightened treatment of mental disorders was found in
    A) Europe.
    B) China.
    C) Islamic countries.
    D) England.
    Answer: C

Pages: 35
Topic: Abnormal Behavior in Ancient Times: Views During the Middle Ages
Skill: Factual   Other1:
25. The outstanding figure of Islamic medicine was
    A) Damascus.
    B) Paracelcus.
    C) Avicenna.
    D) Polvan.
    Answer: C

Pages: 36
Topic: Abnormal Behavior in Ancient Times: Views During the Middle Ages
Skill: Conceptual   Other1:
26. Ritual and superstition were most commonly used to explain abnormal behavior by
    A) Hippocrates.
    B) Galen.
    C) Islamic cultures in the Middle Ages.
    D) Western Europeans in the Middle Ages.
    Answer: D

Pages: 36
Topic: Abnormal Behavior in Ancient Times: Views During the Middle Ages
Skill: Conceptual   Other1:
27. Ancient Chinese treatment of mental disorders was similar to that in ancient Europe in that both cultures
    A) viewed social conditions as primary causes of abnormal behavior.
    B) devalued the role of physicians.
    C) emphasized supernatural forces.
    D) believed that the disorders were caused by physiological causes.
    Answer: D

Pages: 36
Topic: Abnormal Behavior in Ancient Times: Views During the Middle Ages
Skill: Factual   Other1:
28. During the Middle Ages in Europe,
    A) mental disorders were almost nonexistent.
    B) demonology grew in popularity but also coexisted with naturalistic views.
    C) demonology triumphed as the only recognized theory of insanity.
    D) physicians almost always viewed insanity as being caused by sin.
    Answer: B

Pages: 37
Topic: Abnormal Behavior in Ancient Times: Views During the Middle Ages
Skill: Factual   Other1:
29. During the Middle Ages, the phenomenon known as _____ developed.
    A) mass madness
    B) Saint Vitus's dance
    C) dancing manias
    D) all of the above
    Answer: D

Pages: 37
Topic: Abnormal Behavior in Ancient Times: Views During the Middle Ages
Skill: Factual   Other1:
30. In tarantism, or St. Vitus's dance, individuals
    A) believed they were possessed by demons.
    B) believed they had been bitten by a demon.
    C) danced as a cure for the orgiastic rituals in which they had engaged.
    D) believed that they had turned into werewolves.
    Answer: C

Pages: 37
Topic: Abnormal Behavior in Ancient Times: Views During the Middle Ages
Skill: Conceptual   Other1:
31. The condition in which people believed themselves to be werewolves was an example of
    A) schizophrenic delusions.
    B) psychosis.
    C) mass hysteria.
    D) demon possession.
    Answer: C

Pages: 37
Topic: Abnormal Behavior in Ancient Times: Views During the Middle Ages
Skill: Factual   Other1:
32. The disorder in which an individual believes that he or she is a werewolf is called
    A) tarantism.
    B) vampirism.
    C) lycanthropy.
    D) St. Vitus's delusion.
    Answer: C

Pages: 37
Topic: Abnormal Behavior in Ancient Times: Views During the Middle Ages
Skill: Factual   Other1:
33. The peak of the incidence of mass hysteria was associated with
    A) the invasion of Attaturk.
    B) cataclysmic events including famine and the Black Death plague.
    C) unexplained invasions of tarantulas in southern Europe.
    D) a dramatic increase in the wolf population of Europe.
    Answer: B

Pages: 38
Topic: Abnormal Behavior in Ancient Times: Views During the Middle Ages
Skill: Factual   Other1:
34. Contemporary incidents of group hysteria usually mimics
    A) mania.
    B) substance abuse, such as alcoholism.
    C) a physical disorder.
    D) schizophrenia.
    Answer: C

Pages: 38
Topic: Abnormal Behavior in Ancient Times: Views During the Middle Ages
Skill: Factual   Other1:
35. After hearing about some individuals who were poisoned by cyanide-laced Tylenol capsules,
    a sudden wave of illness gripped a large crowd of people who drank soda at a football
    game. This is an example of
    A) tarantism.
    B) mass hysteria.
    C) infectious delusion.
    D) psychosomatic delusion disorder.
    Answer: B

Pages: 38
Topic: Abnormal Behavior in Ancient Times: Views During the Middle Ages
Skill: Factual   Other1:
36. During the Middle Ages, the mentally disturbed of Europe were treated primarily by
    A) demonologists.
    B) shamans.
    C) physicians.
    D) clergy.
    Answer: D

Pages: 38
Topic: Abnormal Behavior in Ancient Times: Views During the Middle Ages
Skill: Factual   Other1:
37. A common treatment for mental illness during the Middle Ages in Europe was
    A) exorcism.
    B) fresh air and supportive surroundings.
    C) banishment.
    D) Benedictine liqueur.
    Answer: A

Pages: 38
Topic: Abnormal Behavior/Ancient Times: Witchcraft/Mental Illness
Skill: Factual   Other1:
38. In today's society there has been another resurgence of
    A) mass hysteria.
    B) mass delusion.
    C) lycanthropy.
    D) superstitious belief in the supernatural and exorcism.
    Answer: D

Pages: 39
Topic: Abnormal Behavior/Ancient Times: Witchcraft/Mental Illness
Skill: Factual   Other1:
39. Martin Luther advocated the belief in two types of
    A) mental disorder.
    B) demonic possession.
    C) witchcraft.
    D) hysteria.
    Answer: B

Pages: 39
Topic: Abnormal Behavior/Ancient Times: Witchcraft/Mental Illness
Skill: Conceptual   Other1:
40. The distinction between corporal and spiritual possession may account for recent thought that witches in the Middle Ages were
   A) usually but not always mentally ill.
   B) not usually mentally ill.
   C) never mentally ill.
   D) no more likely to be viewed as being mentally ill than were other people.
   Answer: B

Pages: 40
Topic: The Growth Toward Humanitarian Approaches
Skill: Factual   Other1:
41. The emergence of humanism brought about changes in all of the following EXCEPT
   A) a resurgence of belief in supernatural causes of behavior.
   B) scientific questioning.
   C) more humane treatment.
   D) fewer superstitious beliefs about demonic possession.
   Answer: A

Pages: 40
Topic: Humanitarian Approaches: Scientific Questioning in Europe
Skill: Factual   Other1:
42. During the early Renaissance, Paracelsus advocated the idea that
   A) witches are corporally but not spiritually possessed.
   B) exorcism is a treatment for mental illness.
   C) dancing mania is a form of group demonic possession.
   D) the instinctual and spiritual natures of human beings are in conflict.
   Answer: D

Pages: 39
Topic: Humanitarian Approaches: Scientific Questioning in Europe
Skill: Factual   Other1:
43. A strong advocate of the belief that madness was a form of demonic possession was
   A) Teresa of Avila.
   B) Reginald Scot.
   C) Paracelsus.
   D) Martin Luther.
   Answer: D

Pages: 40
Topic: Humanitarian Approaches: Scientific Questioning in Europe
Skill: Factual   Other1:

44. The suggestion that a mind can be sick just like a body can be sick was first suggested by
    A) Paracelsus.
    B) Teresa of Avila.
    C) Martin Luther.
    D) Galen.
    Answer: B

Pages: 40-41
Topic: Humanitarian Approaches: Scientific Questioning in Europe
Skill: Factual   Other1:

45. Johann Weyer (Joannus Wierus) and Reginald Scot suggested that the behaviors attributed to witchcraft and demonology were due to
    A) sickness.
    B) uncontrollable unconscious impulses.
    C) possession by the devil that came of the individual's free will.
    D) possession by the devil that was contrary to the individual's choice.
    Answer: A

Pages: 41
Topic: Humanitarian Approaches: Scientific Questioning in Europe
Skill: Factual   Other1: In Student Study Guide

46. Which of the following did NOT argue that those showing abnormal behavior should be seen as mentally ill and treated with humane care?
    A) Paracelsus
    B) Teresa of Avila
    C) King James I of England
    D) Johann Weyer (Johannus Wierus)
    Answer: C

Pages: 41
Topic: Humanitarian Approaches: Establishment of Early Asylums and Shrines
Skill: Factual   Other1:

47. Early asylums of the sixteenth century were characterized by
    A) the humane conditions in which people were kept.
    B) the fact that they were exclusively devoted to the care of women.
    C) being squalid places in which troublesome individuals who couldn't care for themselves were kept.
    D) the clean conditions in which people lived.
    Answer: C

Pages: 41
Topic: Humanitarian Approaches: Establishment of Early Asylums and Shrines
Skill: Factual   Other1:
48. One of the first asylums, St. Mary of Bethlehem (Bedlam), was well known for its
    A) use of new and innovative therapies, such as "talk therapies."
    B) deplorable and degrading conditions.
    C) emphasis on serenity and tranquility.
    D) use of physiological therapies, such as bloodletting.
    Answer: B

Pages: 41
Topic: Humanitarian Approaches: Establishment of Early Asylums and Shrines
Skill: Factual   Other1:
49. Shackling a patient to a wall with little food or heat would be most typical of
    A) hospitals run by Philippe Pinel.
    B) the sanatoriums of Alexandria, Egypt.
    C) the early asylums in Europe.
    D) treatment advocated by Hippocrates.
    Answer: C

Pages: 42
Topic: Humanitarian Approaches: Establishment of Early Asylums and Shrines
Skill: Factual   Other1:
50. Early asylums in the United States
    A) were much more humane than those in Europe.
    B) used gentle physical treatments.
    C) were as inhumane as those in Europe.
    D) allowed family members to room with their mentally ill relatives while they were being
       treated.
    Answer: C

Pages: 42
Topic: Humanitarian Approaches: Establishment of Early Asylums and Shrines
Skill: Factual   Other1:
51. Early asylums in the United States based treatment on the belief that
    A) patients had to be intimidated into choosing rationality over insanity.
    B) kind, caring concern was central to successful treatment.
    C) talking therapy was the best treatment for mental disorders.
    D) patients were guilty of sinning and must be induced to experience a religious revival.
    Answer: A

Pages: 42
Topic: Humanitarian Approaches: Establishment of Early Asylums and Shrines
Skill: Applied   Other1:
52. Beth was a mental patient at the Public Hospital in Virginia in the late 1700's. She was severely depressed. Her treatment was likely to include
    A) classical music.
    B) animal magnetism.
    C) a form of group therapy.
    D) bleeding and blistering.
    Answer: D

Pages: 42
Topic: Humanitarian Approaches: Establishment of Early Asylums and Shrines
Skill: Factual   Other1:
53. The treatment offered mental patients in the colony of Geel
    A) stood out for its squalor and torture of patients.
    B) was the first to include hypnosis.
    C) emphasized kindness and generosity.
    D) involved icy water baths and shock treatments.
    Answer: C

Pages: 42
Topic: Humanitarian Approaches: Establishment of Early Asylums and Shrines
Skill: Factual   Other1:
54. The shrine at Geel in Belgium
    A) still exists today as a hospital surrounded by a residential community for mentally ill individuals living with foster families.
    B) was an imaginary setting in medieval lore.
    C) was destroyed by religious fanatics hunting witches.
    D) became a squalid asylum, although it initially provided humane treatment for the mentally ill.
    Answer: A

Pages: 42
Topic: The Growth Toward Humanitarian Approaches: Humanitarian Reform
Skill: Factual   Other1:
55. Philippe Pinel was a major figure in the history of treating mental disorders because he
    A) developed more humane straight jackets.
    B) was the first to use hypnosis.
    C) unchained mental patients and revolutionized care of the mentally ill.
    D) was the first to develop a medication to treat mental disorders.
    Answer: C

Pages: 43
Topic: The Growth Toward Humanitarian Approaches: Humanitarian Reform
Skill: Factual   Other1:
56. When Philippe Pinel first began to unchain the mentally ill from their hospital walls,
    A) they mobbed and almost killed him.
    B) they were instantly cured.
    C) they responded with joy and by being orderly and peaceful.
    D) his experiment failed and had to be tried several times before the right conditions
       could be found.
    Answer: C

Pages: 44
Topic: The Growth Toward Humanitarian Approaches: Humanitarian Reform
Skill: Factual   Other1:
57. A contemporary of Pinel's in England who started a Quaker religious retreat for the
    mentally ill was
    A) John Wesley.
    B) Benjamin Alvarez.
    C) William Tuke.
    D) John Pussin.
    Answer: C

Pages: 44
Topic: The Growth Toward Humanitarian Approaches: Humanitarian Reform
Skill: Factual   Other1:
58. Benjamin Rush was
    A) an Englishman who fought the humane revolution in treatment of mental illness.
    B) the founder of American psychiatry.
    C) the founder of an English Quaker religious retreat for the mentally ill.
    D) the founder of the first mental hospital in the United States.
    Answer: B

Pages: 44
Topic: The Growth Toward Humanitarian Approaches: Humanitarian Reform
Skill: Factual   Other1:
59. Benjamin Rush
    A) believed in chaining patients to walls for extended periods of time.
    B) believed that most disorders resulted from genetic causes.
    C) argued against the reforms of Pinel and Tuke.
    D) advocated more humane treatment, although he continued to use bloodletting and
       purgatives.
    Answer: D

Pages: 44
Topic: The Growth Toward Humanitarian Approaches: Humanitarian Reform
Skill: Factual   Other1:
60. Moral management advocated that
    A) mental disorders were the result of inherited deficiencies.
    B) mentally disturbed individuals should be treated as humans, not as animals, because of fear of divine retribution.
    C) social, individual, and occupational therapy were necessary forms of treatment.
    D) mentally disordered individuals suffered because they had sinned.
    Answer: C

Pages: 44
Topic: The Growth Toward Humanitarian Approaches: Humanitarian Reform
Skill: Factual   Other1:
61. The theory of moral management viewed mental disturbance as resulting from
    A) excessive guilt for past wrongdoing.
    B) lack of a proper moral upbringing.
    C) social isolation.
    D) severe psychological and social stresses.
    Answer: D

Pages: 44
Topic: The Growth Toward Humanitarian Approaches: Humanitarian Reform
Skill: Factual   Other1:
62. Moral management therapy
    A) was very effective in treating the mentally ill.
    B) was not very effective in treating the mentally ill.
    C) was a humane approach but not very effective.
    D) used powerful tranquilizing drugs.
    Answer: A

Pages: 47
Topic: The Growth Toward Humanitarian Approaches: Humanitarian Reform
Skill: Factual   Other1:
63. Neurasthenia referred to
    A) a brain injury.
    B) an early form of lobotomy.
    C) the Victorian belief that certain conditions like depression were caused by a person using up his or her nerve force or bodily energies.
    D) a temporary type of paralysis caused by bloodletting.
    Answer: C

Pages: 48
Topic: The Growth Toward Humanitarian Approaches: Humanitarian Reform
Skill: Factual   Other1:
64. Victorian views influenced nineteenth-century medicine in that
    A) emotional problems were believed to result from immorality.
    B) only women and not men were considered to have emotional problems.
    C) women were regarded as especially susceptible to emotional illness because of uterine dysfunction.
    D) most physicians believed that sexual repression caused emotional problems.
    Answer: C

Pages: 45
Topic: The Growth Toward Humanitarian Approaches: Humanitarian Reform
Skill: Factual   Other1:
65. The reasons for the demise of moral management include all BUT which of the following?
    A) advances in biomedical science
    B) empirical demonstrations that it was ineffective as a mode of therapy
    C) ethnic and racial predjudice against the rising immigrant population
    D) the rise of the mental hygiene movement
    Answer: B

Pages: 46
Topic: The Growth Toward Humanitarian Approaches: Humanitarian Reform
Skill: Conceptual   Other1:
66. Advances in biomedical science in the nineteenth century resulted in a belief in biology as the explanation for mental disorders. This led to
    A) the idea that psychological and social treatments were largely irrelevant.
    B) the development of clinical psychology as the leading treatment.
    C) the idea that children should be tested early to determine who would be susceptible to mental disorders.
    D) the addition of many biological treatments to psychological and social treatments.
    Answer: A

Pages: 46
Topic: The Growth Toward Humanitarian Approaches: Humanitarian Reform
Skill: Factual   Other1:
67. Dorothea Dix
    A) urged that religious conversion was a primary means of treatment for the mentally disturbed.
    B) was a major impediment to the mental hygiene movement in this country.
    C) was a leading force in the emphasis on finding biological cures for mental disorders.
    D) is credited with establishing numerous humane mental hospitals in many countries.
    Answer: D

Pages: 49
Topic: The Foundations of Twentieth-Century Views
Skill: Conceptual   Other1:
68. At the start of the twentieth century in America, public attitudes toward the mentally ill
A) had become enlightened and humane.
B) associated mental disorder with "tainted genes" and divine retribution.
C) had become a conviction that the mentally ill were incurable and should be executed or jailed for the rest of their lives.
D) were characterized by fear, horror, and ignorance.
Answer: D

Pages: 49
Topic: The Foundations of Twentieth-Century Views
Skill: Factual   Other1:
69. Clifford Beers did much to revolutionize public attitudes toward the mentally ill by
A) publishing an account of his own bout with mental illness and his treatment.
B) leading mentally ill patients in revolts against their alienists.
C) advocating the use of physical restraints like straitjackets to quiet excited patients.
D) leading a Congressional investigation of the treatment of mentally ill in hospitals of the day.
Answer: A

Pages: 50
Topic: Scientific Research: The Roots of the Biological Viewpoint
Skill: Factual   Other1:
70. A major biomedical breakthrough in psychopathology was
A) the discovery of the cause and later a cure for general paresis (syphilitic insanity).
B) the discovery of penicillin as a cure for syphilis.
C) the development of electroshock therapy for general paresis (syphilitic insanity).
D) the discovery that brain injuries could be associated with mental disorders.
Answer: A

Pages: 50
Topic: Scientific Research: The Roots of the Biological Viewpoint
Skill: Conceptual   Other1:
71. The discovery of the cause of general paresis and a successful treatment of this disorder were important in that
A) it marked the origin of the manufacture of antipsychotic drugs.
B) it allowed scientists to understand the general nature of Alzheimer's disease.
C) this was the first time in history that a physical cause and a successful treatment of a mental disorder were discovered.
D) it marked the realization that lead was a toxin involved in several brain disorders.
Answer: C

Pages: 50
Topic: Scientific Research: Brain Pathology as a Causal Agent
Skill: Conceptual   Other1:
72. Major early breakthroughs in biological psychiatry
    A) discovered the bacterial cause of schizophrenia.
    B) demonstrated the link between sexual conflict and mental disorders that was proposed by
       Freud.
    C) demonstrated that uterine dysfunction was indeed a cause of several emotional disorders
       in women.
    D) enabled people to predict the course of certain disorders, but not to understand why
       some individuals developed them and some didn't.
    Answer: D

Pages: 51
Topic: Scientific Research: Brain Pathology as a Causal Agent
Skill: Factual   Other1:
73. The forerunner of our present-day classification system for mental disorders is
    A) Emil Kraepelin.
    B) Wilhelm Greisinger.
    C) William James.
    D) Wilhelm Wundt.
    Answer: A

Pages: 52
Topic: Scientific Research: The Beginnings of a Classification System
Skill: Conceptual   Other1:
74. Kraepelin viewed mental disorders as distinct patterns of symptoms with a predetermined
    and predictable course and outcome. This provided a basis for
    A) a system of classification for mental disorders.
    B) the medical model of mental disorders.
    C) research into the specific causes of specific mental disorders.
    D) all of the above
    Answer: D

Pages: 51
Topic: Scientific Research: Advances Achieved/Early Biological Views
Skill: Factual   Other1:
75. Early research into the specific causes of different types of mental disorders focused on
    A) bacterial infections.
    B) gross brain pathology.
    C) psychosocial causes of neurological malfunction.
    D) sexual dysfunction.
    Answer: B

Pages: 52
Topic: Scientific Research: Advances Achieved/Early Biological Views
Skill: Conceptual   Other1:
76. The medical model perspective
    A) was confined to biological psychiatry.
    B) fell into disrepute when advances were made in identifying psychosocial causes of
       mental disorders.
    C) invaded psychosocial theory as the view that abnormal behavior is a symptom of some
       underlying illness.
    D) was dismissed by Freudian psychoanalytic theory.
    Answer: C

Pages: 52
Topic: Scientific Research: Psych Understand/Mental Disorders: Psychodynamic
Skill: Factual   Other1:
77. One of the earliest attempts to understand the psychological causes of mental disorder was
    the work of
    A) Alois Alzheimer.
    B) Wilhelm Griesinger.
    C) Clifford Beers.
    D) Sigmund Freud.
    Answer: D

Pages: 53
Topic: Scientific Research: Psych Understand/Mental Disorders: Psychodynamic
Skill: Factual   Other1:
78. Psychoanalysis has its roots in
    A) the study of the cause of general paresis.
    B) the study of hypnosis and hysteria.
    C) attempts to treat mental retardation.
    D) the mental hygiene movement.
    Answer: B

Pages: 53
Topic: Scientific Research: Psych Understand/Mental Disorders: Psychodynamic
Skill: Applied   Other1:
79. Elizabeth is experiencing a paralysis of the left hand. Her treatment includes sitting in
    a dark room while a man in a lilac robe applies iron rods to her body. She is being
    treated by
    A) a young Sigmund Freud.
    B) an ancient shaman.
    C) Jean Charcot.
    D) Franz Mesmer.
    Answer: D

Pages: 53
Topic: Scientific Research: Psych Understand/Mental Disorders: Psychodynamic
Skill: Conceptual   Other1:
80. Mesmerism includes many of the phenomena later associated with
    A) hypnosis.
    B) electromagnetic theory.
    C) free association.
    D) operant conditioning.
    Answer: A

Pages: 54
Topic: Scientific Research: Psych Understand/Mental Disorders: Psychodynamic
Skill: Conceptual   Other1:
81. The Nancy School believed that
    A) hysteria is caused by degenerative brain changes.
    B) hysteria is a form of self-hypnosis.
    C) hysteria is caused by an imbalance of magnetic forces in the body.
    D) mental disorders have biological causes.
    Answer: B

Pages: 54
Topic: Scientific Research: Psych Understand/Mental Disorders: Psychodynamic
Skill: Applied   Other1:
82. Anna Q. is experiencing a loss of feeling in her right leg. She visits Jean Charcot in
    Paris for treatment early in his career as head of the Salpetriere Hospital. What is he
    likely to diagnose her with?
    A) hysterical self-hypnosis
    B) a mental disorder with a psychological cause
    C) a degenerative brain disorder
    D) an unresolved Electra complex
    Answer: C

Pages: 54
Topic: Scientific Research: Psych Understand/Mental Disorders: Psychodynamic
Skill: Conceptual   Other1:
83. The Nancy School proposed a theory of hysteria that was important in the history of
    psychopathology because
    A) it identified the area of the brain implicated in hysterical symptoms.
    B) it represented the first widespread recognition of a psychologically caused mental
       disorder.
    C) it identified degenerative brain pathology as a cause of hysteria.
    D) none of the above
    Answer: B

Pages: 54
Topic: Scientific Research: Psych Understand/Mental Disorders: Psychodynamic
Skill: Factual   Other1:
84. The Nancy School-Charcot debate was finally resolved when
    A) Charcot acknowledged that the cause of hysteria and other mental disorders was psychological rather than physical in nature.
    B) Charcot acknowledged the biological basis of hysteria.
    C) Freud proved Charcot wrong.
    D) the Nancy School disbanded due to lack of evidence for their theory.
    Answer: A

Pages: 55
Topic: Scientific Research: Psych Understand/Mental Disorders: Psychodynamic
Skill: Factual   Other1:
85. Influences on Freud's early work included all of the following EXCEPT
    A) Charcot.
    B) Ivan Pavlov.
    C) the Nancy School.
    D) Josef Breuer.
    Answer: B

Pages: 55
Topic: Scientific Research: Psych Understand/Mental Disorders: Psychodynamic
Skill: Factual   Other1:
86. Josef Breuer treated hysterical patients by
    A) hypnosis.
    B) encouraging them to talk about their problems.
    C) counterconditioning.
    D) A and B
    Answer: D

Pages: 55
Topic: Scientific Research: Psych Understand/Mental Disorders: Psychodynamic
Skill: Applied   Other1:
87. Josephine was a patient of Josef Breuer. He employed a method called _____ to enable her to discharge emotion and experience emotional release after talking about her problems under hypnosis.
    A) self-induced trance
    B) dream analysis
    C) transference
    D) catharsis
    Answer: D

Pages: 55
Topic: Scientific Research: Psych Understand/Mental Disorders: Psychodynamic
Skill: Factual   Other1:
88. Breuer and Freud jointly published a milestone paper announcing
    A) the neurological foundation of hysteria.
    B) that hysteria is a false phenomenon involving patients who feign symptoms in order to gain attention.
    C) that unconscious processes can determine behavior and result in mental disorders.
    D) that hypnosis does not work with mentally ill people.
    Answer: C

Pages: 55
Topic: Scientific Research: Psych Understand/Mental Disorders: Psychodynamic
Skill: Conceptual   Other1:
89. After discovering that he could dispense with hypnosis, Freud employed two main methods for exploring unconscious thought processes,
    A) ego and superego analysis.
    B) mesmerism and free association.
    C) free association and dream analysis.
    D) dream analysis and id catharsis.
    Answer: C

Pages: 55
Topic: Scientific Research: Advances in Psychological Research
Skill: Factual   Other1:
90. Wilhelm Wundt
    A) established the first experimental psychology laboratory.
    B) was the first to use hypnosis in clinical practice.
    C) established the first clinic for juvenile delinquents.
    D) was the first to propose the existence of sociocultural causal factors in mental disorders.
    Answer: A

Pages: 56
Topic: Scientific Research: Advances in Psychological Research
Skill: Factual   Other1:
91. The first American psychological clinic was established at the University of Pennsylvania in 1896. The clinic focused on problems of mentally deficient children both in terms of research and therapy. The clinic was established by
    A) William James.
    B) J. McKeen Cattell.
    C) Lightner Witmer.
    D) Wilhelm Wundt.
    Answer: C

Pages: 56
Topic: Scientific Research: Advances in Psychological Research
Skill: Factual   Other1:
92. William Healy
    A) established the first experimental psychology laboratory.
    B) proposed the first environmental, or sociocultural, causal factor for abnormal behavior.
    C) founded the first abnormal psychology journal.
    D) established the first American psychology clinic.
    Answer: B

Pages: 56
Topic: Scientific Research: Advances in Psychological Research
Skill: Factual   Other1:
93. The study of subjective experience through free association and dream analysis was criticized by
    A) followers of Breuer.
    B) the Nancy School.
    C) William Healy.
    D) behavioral psychologists.
    Answer: D

Pages: 56
Topic: Scientific Research: Advances in Psychological Research
Skill: Conceptual   Other1:
94. According to the behavioral perspective, all of the following are viewed as legitimate areas of scientific inquiry EXCEPT
    A) external stimuli evoking behavioral responses.
    B) directly observable behavior.
    C) subjective reports of sensations.
    D) conditions that reinforce behaviors.
    Answer: C

Pages: 56
Topic: Scientific Research: Advances in Psychological Research
Skill: Conceptual   Other1:
95. The role of _____ is a central theme of the behavioral perspective.
    A) learning
    B) operant conditioning
    C) classical conditioning
    D) observational conditioning
    Answer: A

Pages: 57
Topic: Scientific Research: Advances in Psychological Research
Skill: Factual   Other1:
96. Pavlov's discovery of the conditioned reflex was seminal in inspiring the development of
_____ theory.
A) psychodynamic
B) biomedical
C) behavioral
D) experimental
Answer: C

Pages: 57
Topic: Scientific Research: Advances in Psychological Research
Skill: Factual   Other1:
97. The first American to use the principles of classical conditioning in psychology was
A) Pavlov.
B) Thorndike.
C) Skinner.
D) Watson.
Answer: D

Pages: 57
Topic: Scientific Research: Advances in Psychological Research
Skill: Conceptual   Other1:
98. "Give me any healthy child and I can train it to be any kind of adult I wish." This was
the boastful claim of
A) Sigmund Freud.
B) B. F. Skinner.
C) John B. Watson.
D) Ivan Pavlov.
Answer: C

Pages: 56-57
Topic: Scientific Research: Advances in Psychological Research
Skill: Conceptual   Other1:
99. Although differing in many respects in their perspectives on abnormal behavior, William
Healy and John B. Watson both proposed the importance of which of the following in the
etiology of abnormal behavior?
A) unconscious processes
B) sexual conflict
C) gross brain pathology
D) the role of the social environment
Answer: D

Pages: 57
Topic: Scientific Research: Advances in Psychological Research
Skill: Factual   Other1:
100. Thorndike and Skinner are associated with the discovery and understanding of
    A) classical conditioning.
    B) operant conditioning.
    C) psychodynamic theory.
    D) biological psychiatry.
    Answer: B

Pages: 57
Topic: Scientific Research: Advances in Psychological Research
Skill: Conceptual   Other1:
101. Over time, behavior has consequences which, in turn, influence future behavior. This is the principle behind
    A) classical conditioning.
    B) observational conditioning.
    C) operant conditioning.
    D) Pavlovian conditioning.
    Answer: C

Pages: 57
Topic: The Foundations of Twentieth-Century Views
Skill: Factual   Other1:
102. Operant conditioning is also known as
    A) Pavlovian conditioning.
    B) vicarious conditioning.
    C) instrumental conditioning.
    D) classical conditioning.
    Answer: C

Pages: 57
Topic: Scientific Research: Advances in Psychological Research
Skill: Conceptual   Other1: In Student Study Guide
103. Classical and instrumental conditioning differ primarily with respect to
    A) the types of reinforcers involved.
    B) an emphasis on animal versus human subjects.
    C) the number of trials to reach criterion performance.
    D) whether the outcome (reinforcer) is dependent on the animal's behavior.
    Answer: D

Pages: 58
Topic: Unresolved Issues on Interpreting Historical Events
Skill: Conceptual   Other1:
104. Accurately interpreting historical events is
A) straightforward compared to interpreting abnormal behavior.
B) often difficult and open to reinterpretation.
C) not usually very difficult.
D) not very important.
Answer: B

Pages: 58
Topic: Unresolved Issues on Interpreting Historical Events
Skill: Conceptual   Other1:
105. One of the major problems in identifying historical trends in abnormal behavior is that
A) historical analysis allows for prospective but not retrospective analysis.
B) there has been little attempt throughout history to identify the causes of abnormal behavior.
C) abnormal behavior did not receive much written attention until the early twentieth century.
D) we cannot rely on direct observation.
Answer: D

Pages: 58
Topic: Unresolved Issues on Interpreting Historical Events
Skill: Conceptual   Other1:
106. One of the problems with historical analysis of abnormal behavior is that
A) the fewer the sources available, the more likely an existing bias may go undetected.
B) only high political figures have generally done the writing of historical texts.
C) writings have typically ignored the role of religious influences in the lives of individuals.
D) prospective analysis is the major method used.
Answer: A

Pages: 58-60
Topic: Unresolved Issues on Interpreting Historical Events
Skill: Conceptual   Other1:
107. Which of the following is true with regard to bias in the historical analysis of abnormal behavior?
A) There are so few writings that we really can get almost no idea of how abnormal behavior has been viewed.
B) Retrospective analysis is limited and so we must rely on prospective analysis.
C) Bias occurs in both the views of the writer and the reader.
D) The fewer the sources surveyed, the less likely any existing bias will be detected.
Answer: C

Pages: 60
Topic: Unresolved Issues on Interpreting Historical Events
Skill: Conceptual   Other1:
108. The text used the example of the concept of "possession" to illustrate
    A) the changing history of the meaning of the phrase "nervous breakdown."
    B) that concepts may have very different meanings now than they did in prior historical eras.
    C) that some concepts remain constant in their meaning throughout history.
    D) a superstitious belief that ended with the close of the Middle Ages.
    Answer: B

Pages: 60
Topic: Unresolved Issues on Interpreting Historical Events
Skill: Factual   Other1:
109. The field of study that involves applying psychological theory to the interpretation of historical events and figures is called
    A) psychohistory.
    B) historical reinterpretation.
    C) historical psychoanalysis.
    D) psychoanalytic reconstruction.
    Answer: A

Pages: 60
Topic: Unresolved Issues on Interpreting Historical Events
Skill: Conceptual   Other1:
110. The use of psychological autopsy
    A) has become a valuable tool in determining past events with great accuracy.
    B) involves dissecting the brains of individuals who were mentally ill in order to establish possible physical causal factors associated with their illness.
    C) should be done with great caution since even recent events are open to bias and a variety of conflicting interpretations.
    D) is the method by which psychotherapists attempt to reconstruct the life events leading up to the onset of a mental disorder in a particular patient.
    Answer: C

Short Answer

Write the word or phrase that best completes each statement or answers the question.

Pages: 32
Topic: Abnormal Behavior in Ancient Times: Demonology, Gods and Magic
Skill: Factual   Other1:
1. What was the most common explanation for abnormal behavior among many ancient peoples including the Chinese, Egyptians, Hebrews, and Greeks?
    Answer: The most common explanation was possession by a demon or a god.

Pages: 33
Topic: Abnormal Behavior/Ancient Times: Early Philosophical/Medical Concepts
Skill: Factual   Other1:
2. What type of causes did Hippocrates attribute mental disorders to?
    Answer: He believed in natural causes for mental disorders involving imbalance in the bodily humors. He also acknowledged the role of heredity and predisposition, as well as head injury.

Pages: 34
Topic: Abnormal Behavior/Ancient Times: Early Philosophical/Medical Concepts
Skill: Factual   Other1:
3. Who first discussed the idea of insanity as a "legal defense"?
    Answer: Plato, who argued that mentally disturbed persons who committed criminal acts were in some "obvious" sense not responsible for their acts and should not receive punishment in the same way as a normal person.

Pages: 35
Topic: Abnormal Behavior in Ancient Times: Views During the Middle Ages
Skill: Conceptual   Other1:
4. Where was the most humane and scientifically enlightened treatment of the mentally ill found during the Middle Ages?
    Answer: It was found in the Islamic countries, where humane mental hospitals were established. Avicenna was a notable thinker in the field, writing of various mental disorders and offering unique but humane treatments.

Pages: 37
Topic: Abnormal Behavior in Ancient Times: Views During the Middle Ages
Skill: Factual   Other1:
5. What are tarantism and lycanthropy?
    Answer: These are two types of mass hysteria disorders that spread through Europe in the later Middle Ages. Tarantism was a dancing mania believed to be caused by a tarantula bite. Lycanthropy occurred in isolated areas and involved a person thinking he or she had been possessed by a wolf.

Pages: 38
Topic: Abnormal Behavior in Ancient Times: Views During the Middle Ages
Skill: Conceptual   Other1:
6. What was the major treatment for mental disorders in the Middle Ages in Europe?
    Answer: Most often mentally ill individuals were thought to be possessed by demons, and
            exorcism was used in an attempt to restore normalcy.

Pages: 40
Topic: Abnormal Behavior in Ancient Times: Views During the Middle Ages
Skill: Factual   Other1:
7. The first person to suggest that a mind could be "as if sick" was _____.
    Answer: Teresa of Avila

Pages: 41
Topic: Humanitarian Approaches: Establishment of Early Asylums and Shrines
Skill: Factual   Other1:
8. What sort of treatment and conditions characterized the earliest asylums?
    Answer: They were dirty and squalid, modeled on penal institutions and were used to
            confine people who were considered troublesome. They lived in filth and
            darkness, chained to walls with little food. They were sometimes exhibited to
            the public for a fee.

Pages: 42-43
Topic: The Growth Toward Humanitarian Approaches: Humanitarian Reform
Skill: Applied   Other1:
9. Simone was a patient at a hospital in Paris run by Philippe Pinel. What would her
    treatment have been like?
    Answer: Pinel took the chains off of mental patients, who had been kept in conditions of
            filth and abuse. They were given sunny rooms and allowed to exercise outside,
            and generally treated humanely. The experiment resulted in peace and orderly
            behavior.

Pages: 44
Topic: The Growth Toward Humanitarian Approaches: Humanitarian Reform
Skill: Conceptual   Other1:
10. What was moral management?
    Answer: This was the belief that mentally ill people would benefit from moral and
            spiritual development and the rehabilitation of their character. Treatment
            included individual, social, and occupational therapy and was highly effective.

Pages: 46
Topic: The Growth Toward Humanitarian Approaches: Humanitarian Reform
Skill: Factual   Other1:

11. _____ was the founder of the mental hygiene movement.
    Answer: Dorothea Dix

Pages: 45-46
Topic: The Growth Toward Humanitarian Approaches: Humanitarian Reform
Skill: Conceptual   Other1:

12. What was the mental hygiene movement?
    Answer: This movement, led by Dorothea Dix, focused almost exclusively on improving the
            physical well-being of hospitalized mental patients, and did not provide any
            substantive treatment for the mental problems of these patients. This movement
            became widespread in mental hospitals in the nineteenth century and resulted in
            improvements in the conditions of mental hospitals.

Pages: 49-50
Topic: Twentieth-Century Views: Changing Attitudes Toward Mental Health
Skill: Conceptual   Other1:

13. What was Clifford Beers's major contribution to the growth of humane treatment of mental
    patients?
    Answer: A Yale graduate, he wrote a book describing his own mental breakdown and
            subsequent cruel treatments in three institutions of the day. He campaigned
            actively to make people aware of the deplorable conditions in hospitals and
            attracted the interest and support of eminent figures in psychology and
            psychiatry.

Pages: 50
Topic: Scientific Research: The Roots of the Biological Viewpoint
Skill: Conceptual   Other1:

14. The first and perhaps most important biomedical breakthrough in the history of abnormal
    psychology may be the discovery of the physical cause and treatment of _____.
    Answer: general paresis (syphilitic insanity)

Pages: 50
Topic: Scientific Research: The Roots of the Biological Viewpoint
Skill: Conceptual   Other1:

15. What was the importance of the discovery of the cause of general paresis?
    Answer: This was the first time a physical cause of a mental disorder was found. This
            led to a widespread attempt to link many mental disorders with an organic cause,
            typically involving gross brain pathology. It also contributed to the
            widespread influence of the medical model of mental illness.

Pages: 51
Topic: Scientific Research: The Beginnings of a Classification System
Skill: Factual   Other1:

16. The classification system that was the forerunner of today's classification system for mental disorders was developed by _____.
    Answer: Emil Kraepelin

Pages: 54
Topic: Scientific Research: Psych Understand/Mental Disorders: Psychodynamic
Skill: Conceptual   Other1:

17. Mesmer's work treating hysterical phenomena led to the Nancy School's later interest in the relationship between hysteria and _____.
    Answer: hypnosis

Pages: 54
Topic: Scientific Research: Psych Understand/Mental Disorders: Psychodynamic
Skill: Conceptual   Other1:

18. The acceptance of the Nancy School's theory of the origin of hysteria marked the first time that a _____ cause of a mental disorder was widely recognized.
    Answer: psychological

Pages: 55
Topic: Scientific Research: Psych Understand/Mental Disorders: Psychodynamic
Skill: Applied   Other1:

19. Imagine that you are an early patient of Freud's. Briefly describe what your treatment would include.
    Answer: The treatment might use hypnosis and involve talking freely without reservation about problems. Freud later dropped hypnosis and used the techniques of free association and dream analysis, which he believed provided information about the unconscious conflicts and processes underlying mental problems.

Pages: 56
Topic: Scientific Research: Advances in Psychological Research
Skill: Conceptual   Other1:

20. Briefly describe the central belief of the behavioral perspective regarding scientific inquiry into psychopathology.
    Answer: Behavioral psychologists believed that the only valid area of scientific inquiry is directly observable behavior, the external stimuli that elicit behavioral responses, and the external conditions that reinforce behaviors.

Essay

Write your answer in the space provided or on a separate sheet of paper.

Pages: 32-50
Topic: Abnormal Behavior in Ancient Times: Demonology, Gods and Magic
Skill: Factual   Other1:

1. Abnormal behavior often has been attributed to the influence of supernatural forces. Describe how these forces were used to explain abnormal behavior during various time periods, and the treatments that resulted.
   Answer: Early writings of Egyptian, Chinese, Hebrews, and Greeks show they attributed such behavior to possession by a demon or god. This was treated by exorcism. In the Middle Ages, the clergy were largely responsible for treatment because possession was considered causal. In fifteenth and sixteenth century Europe, witchcraft became another related explanation for which torture, burning, and other such methods were used. Recent historical analyses, however, suggest that the mentally ill may not have been taken to be witches, as was often once thought.

Pages: 32-34
Topic: Abnormal Behavior/Ancient Times: Early Philosophical/Medical Concepts
Skill: Factual   Other1:

2. In ancient Greece, explanations and treatments of abnormal behavior changed significantly. Discuss the role played by Hippocrates in questioning previously held beliefs about demonology and mental illness.
   Answer: Ancient Greeks began to question demonology as a cause of mental disorder. Hippocrates proposed that they had natural causes and required treatment like other diseases. He also acknowledged the causal role of heredity and brain injury and used dream analysis.

Pages: 35-38
Topic: Abnormal Behavior in Ancient Times: Views During the Middle Ages
Skill: Conceptual   Other1:

3. How did conceptualizations of abnormal behavior and treatments for the mentally ill differ in Islamic countries and in Europe during the Middle Ages?
   Answer: Islamic countries were enlightened and scientific, continuing Greek thought. Humane mental hospitals were established. Avicenna wrote a medical work describing many mental disorders and offering unusual but humane treatments. In Europe, demonological possession, "sin," and older naturalistic causal theories coexisted. Clergy initially treated mentally ill with kindness, later with increasingly harsh exorcism.

Pages: 37
Topic: Abnormal Behavior in Ancient Times: Views During the Middle Ages
Skill: Conceptual   Other1:

4. Mass disorders were prevalent in the Middle Ages. What are some examples of these disorders? What were seen as causes of the disorders at the time? How do we view them now?

   Answer: Dancing manias spread throughout Europe, thought then to be symptoms caused by tarantula bites and cured by dancing. In isolated areas lycanthropy outbreaks occurred, in which individuals thought they were possessed by wolves and imitated their behavior. One such person was "treated" by having his limbs amputated. Factors now thought to be involved in these cases are famine, plague, oppression, pestilence, and the enormous fears that were generated.

Pages: 36-37
Topic: Abnormal Behavior in Ancient Times: Views During the Middle Ages
Skill: Applied   Other1:

5. Assume that you were severely depressed in the Middle Ages. What kinds of treatment would you have been likely to receive had you lived in Europe?

   Answer: This disorder would have been seen as a form of possession. It may have been treated with old potions derived from Galen and gentle religious techniques earlier in the medieval era. Later, exorcisms came to be used, with an emphasis on ever-escalating insults to Satan to get him to leave a body. Later witchcraft may have been used as an explanation for the disorder, involving the belief that an individual made a pact with the devil which gave them special powers. Some mentally ill people may have been mistaken for witches, for which they were punished or killed.

Pages: 39-42
Topic: Humanitarian Approaches: Scientific Questioning in Europe
Skill: Conceptual   Other1:

6. In the early Renaissance, scientific questioning began to influence explanations and treatments for mentally disturbed individuals. How did the explanations used during this time period differ from previous explanations? Who were the major individuals during this era, and what were their roles?

   Answer: Scientific questioning was a response to the demonology and witchcraft explanations of the Middle Ages. This rational humanism attributed disturbed behavior to more natural causes. Teresa of Avila first suggested that a mind can be "as if sick." Weyer argued that disturbed individuals were really sick in mind or body. Paracelsus said dancing manias were a disease. Reginald Scot denied the existence of demons.

Pages: 41-42
Topic: Humanitarian Approaches: Establishment of Early Asylums and Shrines
Skill: Conceptual   Other1:

7. When were the first asylums established, what events led to their development, and what were the conditions like in many of them?

    Answer: Starting in the sixteenth century, asylums were established, when demonological explanations no longer dominated thinking about abnormal behavior. They were originally used as a way of confining people who were considered troublesome. Most resembled penal institutions. Patients were chained to walls and treated like animals, exhibited to the public for money, kept in the cold and dark. Early American asylums used aggressive and painful treatments to intimidate patients into "choosing" rationality over insanity. The Geel shrine was a notable exception.

Pages: 42-48
Topic: The Growth Toward Humanitarian Approaches: Humanitarian Reform
Skill: Conceptual   Other1:

8. In the late eighteenth century, a movement developed to reform asylums. What were the major issues in this reform? Who were the major individuals and what roles did they play? What were moral management and mental hygiene?

    Answer: Deplorable conditions in asylums led individuals like Pinel and Tuke to establish places where patients were treated humanely. Their successes inspired Rush in America and also gave rise to widespread use of moral management, a treatment emphasizing moral development that used individual, social, and occupational therapy and was highly effective. The mental hygiene movement focused on patients' physical well-being but essentially ignored treatment of their mental problems.

Pages: 47-48
Topic: The Growth Toward Humanitarian Approaches: Humanitarian Reform
Skill: Conceptual   Other1:

9. How did Victorian ideas about morality influence doctors' attempts to understand and treat mental disorders in the nineteenth century?

    Answer: Rudimentary medical treatments were used in conjunction with moral management therapy by early alienists. They believed that Victorian morality was beneficial to mental health. Certain excesses, like sex, for example, led to the depletion of a person's store of nerve force or bodily energy. This would result in neurasthenia, a disorder of "shattered nerves." Sex, work, and excessive study were seen as energy-depleting activities for men, whereas women were viewed as weaker in nerve force due to frequent uterine disturbances. Women were not expected to experience sexual pleasure.

Pages: 50-51
Topic: Scientific Research: The Roots of the Biological Viewpoint
Skill: Conceptual   Other1:

10. What was the import of the discovery of a cause and a treatment for general paresis?

    Answer: This breakthrough was the first time a physical cause of a mental disorder was demonstrated, and the first effective physical treatment for this disorder was developed. The medical community hoped that an organic cause would be found for every mental disorder, and focused their efforts on attempting to find the brain pathology causing various disorders. Some successes followed, such as Alzheimer's discoveries, and Kraepelin's classification system aided this research. The medical model of mental disorders is still used today.

Pages: 51-52
Topic: Scientific Research: The Beginnings of a Classification System
Skill: Conceptual   Other1:

11. Discuss the origins of our modern day classification system for mental disorders.

    Answer: In the nineteenth century, Emil Kraepelin emphasized the importance of brain pathology in mental disorders. He believed that each mental disorder was characterized by its own distinct pattern of symptoms, predetermined course, and predictable outcome. He proceeded to develop a classification system based on his observational descriptions of various mental disorders in terms of their symptoms, course, and prognoses. This model of classification was a forerunner of our current classification system.

Pages: 52
Topic: Scientific Research: Brain Pathology as a Causal Agent
Skill: Conceptual   Other1:

12. What is the medical model of mental disorders? How has it influenced biological and psychosocial theories of abnormal behavior?

    Answer: This model regards abnormal behavior as symptoms of an underlying illness, analogous to a fever as a symptom of an underlying infection. In early biological research in psychopathology, scientists looked exclusively for physical causes of psychological problems, assuming that most would be associated with gross brain pathology. The medical model extended to psychosocial theories like Freud's by assuming that psychological symptoms are caused by underlying biological pathology.

Pages: 53-55
Topic: Scientific Research: Psych Understand/Mental Disorders: Psychodynamic
Skill: Conceptual   Other1:
13. Describe the main historical events that led to early psychoanalytic thought.
     Answer: In the 1700's, Mesmer treated many hysteria-like disorders by a process that
                   included phenomena resembling hypnosis. The Nancy School became interested in
                   the relationship between hypnosis and hysteria, proposing that both were due to
                   suggestion. Charcot became interested which leant credence to this idea, and
                   later came to agree with the Nancy School. Freud studied with Charcot and
                   worked with Breuer, who treated hysterics by having them talk about their
                   problems under hypnosis and achieve catharsis. This led them to suggest
                   unconscious influence on behavioral manifestations of hysteria.

Pages: 56-57
Topic: Scientific Research: Advances in Psychological Research
Skill: Conceptual   Other1:
14. Describe the major historical events that led to the behavioral perspective.
     Answer: It arose out of Pavlov's experimental studies of learning in which he
                   demonstrated the phenomenon of classical conditioning. Watson was searching for
                   a scientific method for studying psychological phenomenon, and reasoned that
                   this entails studying overt, directly observable behavior, along with the
                   stimuli evoking behavioral responses and the conditions reinforcing the
                   behaviors. He did not accept subjective mental processes or unconscious
                   processes as valid scientific areas of inquiry. Later Thorndike and Skinner
                   developed operant conditioning principles.

Pages: 58-60
Topic: Unresolved Issues on Interpreting Historical Events
Skill: Conceptual   Other1:
15. What are some of the difficulties one must face when interpreting historical events?
     Answer: Historical interpretation always involves retrospective analysis rather than
                   direct observation. Sources may be limited or unavailable, may require
                   inference and extrapolation, are biased, may be viewed out of context and thus
                   may have a different meaning to us than they did in the past, or the meaning may
                   simply be unclear. We have our own biases, too, that we bring to the
                   interpretive process--some of which we may not be aware of.

CHAPTER 3 Causal Factors and Viewpoints in Abnormal Psychology

Multiple-Choice

Choose the one alternative that best completes the statement or answers the question.

Pages: 63
Topic: What Causes Abnormal Behavior?
Skill: Conceptual   Other1:
1. A knowledge of the causes of abnormal behavior might enable us to do all but which of the following?
   A) classify mental disorders according to their causes rather than their symptoms
   B) prevent the conditions that lead to mental disorders
   C) prevent or reverse the conditions that serve to maintain mental disorders
   D) use symptom clusters to better classify mental disorders
   Answer: D

Pages: 64
Topic: Abnormal Behavior: Necessary/Sufficient/Contributory Causes
Skill: Applied   Other1:
2. An individual develops general paresis as a result of being infected by syphilitic spirochetes. These spirochetes, which eventually invade the central nervous system if left untreated, must be present in order for the person to develop general paresis. Thus, syphilitic spirochetes are a(n) _____ cause of general paresis.
   A) reinforcing
   B) contributory
   C) necessary
   D) etiological
   Answer: C

Pages: 64
Topic: Abnormal Behavior: Necessary/Sufficient/Contributory Causes
Skill: Factual   Other1:
3. One prominent theory of the origin of depression hypothesizes that, if one becomes hopeless about his or her future, then he or she will become depressed. Thus, in this theory, hopelessness may be said to be a _____ cause of depression.
   A) contributory
   B) sufficient
   C) necessary
   D) distal
   Answer: B

Pages: 64
Topic: Abnormal Behavior: Necessary/Sufficient/Contributory Causes
Skill: Factual   Other1:

4. A cause that increases the probability of the occurrence of a disorder, but is neither
   necessary nor sufficient for the disorder to develop, is
   A) contributory and distal.
   B) contributory and proximal.
   C) contributory, whether distal or proximal.
   D) contributory, and neither distal nor proximal.
   Answer: C

Pages: 64
Topic: Abnormal Behavior: Necessary/Sufficient/Contributory Causes
Skill: Conceptual   Other1:

5. Suppose that the presence of a particular gene is a necessary cause for the occurrence of
   schizophrenia. Which of the following statements is true?
   A) The gene is also a sufficient cause for the occurrence of schizophrenia.
   B) Schizophrenia can occur in the absence of that gene.
   C) Most people with schizophrenia will have that gene.
   D) A person with that gene may or may not become schizophrenic.
   Answer: D

Pages: 64
Topic: Abnormal Behavior: Necessary/Sufficient/Contributory Causes
Skill: Factual   Other1:

6. Distal causes differ from proximal causes in that
   A) distal causes are of much greater severity than are proximal causes.
   B) distal causes tend to be biological or genetic in nature, whereas proximal causes are
      usually social stressors.
   C) proximal causes occur closer in time to the onset of symptoms of a disorder than distal
      causes.
   D) proximal causes are merely contributory, whereas distal causes are necessary or
      sufficient.
   Answer: C

Pages: 64
Topic: Abnormal Behavior: Necessary/Sufficient/Contributory Causes
Skill: Applied   Other1:

7. Steve is extremely fearful of rejection by his peers. When others try to act friendly toward him, he suspects ulterior motives and responds with aggressive outbursts. As a result, the other children have gradually come to ignore Steve, which has led to an even greater sense of rejection. Steve's aggressive behavior is a _____ cause of his fear of rejection.
   A) secondary
   B) multiple
   C) primary
   D) reinforcing
   Answer: D

Pages: 65
Topic: Abnormal Behavior: Feedback/Circularity in Abnormal Behavior
Skill: Conceptual   Other1:

8. The behavioral sciences rarely follow a simple linear cause-and-effect model because
   A) there is usually more than one causal factor involved in any particular condition.
   B) they lack the more sophisticated measurement methods of the "hard" sciences.
   C) they draw on diverse theoretical perspectives to explain the etiology of psychopathological disorders.
   D) complex groups of causal factors often operate through feedback and circularity.
   Answer: D

Pages: 65
Topic: Abnormal Behavior: Feedback/Circularity in Abnormal Behavior
Skill: Applied   Other1:

9. A couple is in counseling. She states that she drinks because he rejects her. He states that he rejects her because she drinks. It appears that
   A) the drinking is probably the actual predisposing cause for the problems in this marriage.
   B) the rejection is probably the actual predisposing cause for the problems in this marriage.
   C) the drinking and rejection influence and maintain each other.
   D) the drinking and rejection are caused by another third variable unknown to the couple.
   Answer: C

Pages: 65
Topic: What Causes Abnormal Behavior: Diathesis-Stress Models
Skill: Factual   Other1:
10. A diathesis is
    A) a distal, sufficient cause of a mental disorder.
    B) a stressor which interacts with another contributory cause to produce a disorder.
    C) a distal predisposition toward developing a disorder.
    D) always a biological or genetic vulnerability to developing a disorder.
    Answer: C

Pages: 66
Topic:
Skill: Factual   Other1:
11. In the context of diathesis-stress models, _____ factors make it less likely that a person
    will experience the adverse consequences of a stressor, thereby promoting successful
    adaptation despite challenging or threatening circumstances, which is known as _____.
    A) proximal; adaptation
    B) protective; resilience
    C) reciprocal; adaptation
    D) circulatory; resistance
    Answer: B

Pages: 66
Topic: What Causes Abnormal Behavior: Diathesis-Stress Models
Skill: Applied   Other1:
12. Peter was forced to move frequently when he was growing up because his father was in the
    military. He found it somewhat stressful to have to make new friends all the time, though
    he usually was able to do so. The "steeling" or "inoculation" effect would predict that
    A) Peter may find it easier than many people to deal with new and unfamiliar social
       situations as an adult.
    B) Peter may be unable to establish truly intimate bonds with others later in life.
    C) Peter may be especially vulnerable to the possibility of rejection in new social
       situations.
    D) Peter may be unable to develop the resistance needed to adapt to new and unfamiliar
       social situations later in life.
    Answer: A

Pages: 65-66
Topic: What Causes Abnormal Behavior: Diathesis-Stress Models
Skill: Conceptual   Other1:
13. Suppose that low self-esteem is a diathesis for developing depression later in life. This means that
    A) people who currently are depressed will have low self-esteem.
    B) people who currently have low self-esteem will be depressed.
    C) people who currently have low self-esteem will be at increased risk for developing depression later in life.
    D) both A and C
    Answer: C

Pages: 67
Topic: Models or Viewpoints For Understanding Abnormal Behavior
Skill: Factual   Other1:
14. Many research-oriented clinical psychologists have criticized Freud's theory of abnormal behavior and have moved toward behavioral and cognitive-behavioral viewpoints. This is an example of a
    A) revisionist paradigm.
    B) meta-shift.
    C) paradigm shift.
    D) Copernican revolution.
    Answer: C

Pages: 68
Topic: Biological Viewpoints
Skill: Conceptual   Other1:
15. What is the major difference between the medical and the biopsychological models of mental disorders?
    A) The medical model focuses on more distal causes of mental disorders.
    B) The biopsychological model focuses on biological and genetic causes but also allows for other kinds of causal factors.
    C) The medical model focuses on biological and genetic causes but also allows for other kinds of causal factors.
    D) The medical model assumes that all mental disorders are ultimately caused by neurological diseases.
    Answer: B

Pages: 69
Topic: Biological Causal Factors: Neurotransmitter and Hormonal Imbalances
Skill: Factual   Other1:
16. The transmission of impulses from one nerve cell in the brain to the next occurs when
    A) special neuronal enzymes relay the "message" between the cells.
    B) chemical neurotransmitters are released into the gap between the cells.
    C) hormonal messengers in the body make their way to the brain to carry the "message"
       between the cells.
    D) the re-uptake process between the cells is completed.
    Answer: B

Pages: 69
Topic: Biological Causal Factors: Neurotransmitter and Hormonal Imbalances
Skill: Factual   Other1: In Student Study Guide
17. After being released into the synaptic cleft, the neurotransmitter substance may be
    reabsorbed into the presynaptic axon button, a process called _____.
    A) re-uptake
    B) deactivation
    C) recapture
    D) active transport
    Answer: A

Pages: 69
Topic: Biological Causal Factors: Neurotransmitter and Hormonal Imbalances
Skill: Factual   Other1:
18. Biochemical imbalances in the brain can occur in which of the following ways?
    A) There may be an excess production of a neurotransmitter.
    B) There may be a deficiency in the reabsorption of a neurotransmitter into the
       presynaptic neuron.
    C) The postsynaptic neuronal receptors may be abnormally sensitive or insensitive to the
       neurotransmitter.
    D) all of the above
    Answer: D

Pages: 69
Topic: Biological Causal Factors: Neurotransmitter and Hormonal Imbalances
Skill: Factual   Other1:
19. Disturbances in the endocrine system directly influence the body's
    A) genes.
    B) chromosomes.
    C) nutrition.
    D) hormones.
    Answer: D

Pages: 71
Topic: Biological Causal Factors: Genetic Defects
Skill: Factual   Other1:
20. In general, heredity determines
    A) the specifics of human behavior.
    B) the range within which characteristic behavior can be modified by other factors.
    C) physiological characteristics, but rarely psychological behavior.
    D) all of the above
    Answer: B

Pages: 71
Topic: Biological Causal Factors: Genetic Defects
Skill: Conceptual   Other1:
21. A child born with a genetic endowment to be introverted
    A) is unlikely to ever become truly extraverted.
    B) is likely to be more or less introverted depending on childhood experiences growing up.
    C) developed this genetic endowment at conception.
    D) all of the above
    Answer: D

Pages: 71
Topic: Biological Causal Factors: Genetic Defects
Skill: Conceptual   Other1:
22. Which of the following statements is FALSE?
    A) Some genetic vulnerability factors may not become manifest until later in life.
    B) Genetic factors alone do not fully account for all mental disorders.
    C) Heredity is an important source of individual differences as well as similarities
       between members of the same species.
    D) There is not enough evidence as of yet to know whether heredity plays an important
       causal role in the occurrence of mental disorders.
    Answer: D

Pages: 71
Topic: Biological Causal Factors: Genetic Defects
Skill: Factual   Other1:
23. Normal human cells have
    A) twenty-two autosomal chromosome pairs and one pair of sex chromosomes.
    B) twenty-one trisomy chromosome pairs, one autosomal pair and one pair of sex
       chromosomes.
    C) twenty-one autosomal chromosome pairs and two trisomy chromosome pairs.
    D) twenty-three autosomal chromosome pairs.
    Answer: A

Pages: 71
Topic: Biological Causal Factors: Genetic Defects
Skill: Factual   Other1:
24. In a normal male the sex chromosomes are
    A) XX.
    B) XY.
    C) XXY.
    D) YY.
    Answer: B

Pages: 71
Topic: Biological Causal Factors: Genetic Defects
Skill: Factual   Other1:
25. In abnormal psychology, genetic influences
    A) tend to express themselves in a linear, straightforward manner.
    B) affect behavior only indirectly.
    C) affect behavior directly.
    D) operate through simple known laws of inheritance.
    Answer: B

Pages: 72
Topic: Biological Causal Factors: Genetic Defects
Skill: Applied   Other1:
26. Ian is predisposed to being very aggressive with his peers in school, who respond by
    rejecting him. Later in life Ian began to associate with other aggressive youth and to
    participate in a variety of delinquent behaviors. This is an example of
    A) phenotypic vulnerability to aggression.
    B) a phenotypic diathesis.
    C) polygenic expression.
    D) the way the genotype may shape the phenotype.
    Answer: D

Pages: 72
Topic: Biological Causal Factors: Genetic Defects
Skill: Factual   Other1:
27. Most of the genetic influences in abnormal behavior involve
    A) a dominant gene.
    B) a recessive gene.
    C) a polygenic effect.
    D) a defect associated with the sex chromosomes.
    Answer: C

Pages: 72-73
Topic: Biological Causal Factors: Genetic Defects
Skill: Factual   Other1:

28. Which of the following is NOT a common method for studying genetic influences?
A) the study of specific gene defects
B) twin studies
C) adoption studies
D) family history (pedigree) studies
Answer: A

Pages: 72
Topic: Biological Causal Factors: Genetic Defects
Skill: Factual   Other1: In Student Study Guide

29. In genetic studies the subject, or carrier, of the trait or disorder in question who serves as the starting point is known as the
A) proband.
B) zygote.
C) risk person.
D) initiation point.
Answer: A

Pages: 72
Topic: Biological Causal Factors: Genetic Defects
Skill: Conceptual   Other1:

30. Which of the following would be most likely to serve as a control group in a twin study of abnormal behavior?
A) dizygotic twins
B) monozygotic twins
C) normal twins
D) same-sex siblings
Answer: A

Pages: 72
Topic: Biological Causal Factors: Genetic Defects
Skill: Conceptual   Other1:

31. If genetic factors play an important causal role in the occurrence of a particular mental disorder, we would expect
A) the concordance rate for the disorder in identical twins to be significantly higher than in fraternal twins.
B) the concordance rate for the disorder in identical twins to be 100 percent.
C) the concordance rate for the disorder in fraternal twins to be significantly higher than in identical twins.
D) the concordance rate for the disorder to differ little between identical and fraternal twins.
Answer: A

Pages: 74
Topic: Biological Causal Factors: Genetic Defects
Skill: Conceptual.   Other1:
32. Which of the following statements about the heredity of mental disorders is true?
    A) Disorders that run in families are genetic, and those that don't run in families are not genetic.
    B) Stronger genetic influence means environmental influence must not be very important.
    C) Even strongly genetically determined traits can be substantially influenced by environmental conditions.
    D) Genetic effects decrease with age.
    Answer: C

Pages: 73
Topic: Biological Causal Factors: Constitutional Liabilities
Skill: Factual   Other1:
33. A detrimental characteristic that is either innate or is acquired very early on in life, often prenatally, is called a(n)
    A) functional genetic equivalent.
    B) genetic liability.
    C) constitutional liability.
    D) embryological abnormality.
    Answer: C

Pages: 74
Topic: Biological Causal Factors: Constitutional Liabilities
Skill: Factual   Other1:
34. The most common birth difficulty associated with later mental disorders is
    A) low birth weight.
    B) infant drug addiction.
    C) premature delivery.
    D) fever at birth.
    Answer: A

Pages: 75
Topic: Biological Causal Factors: Constitutional Liabilities
Skill: Conceptual   Other1:
35. Which of the following statements about individual differences in infant characteristics is true?
    A) Newborns do not show differences in temperament until they are about a year old.
    B) Differences in reactivity and arousal among newborns are genetic in origin, while differences in temperament among older infants are due primarily to environmental factors.
    C) The dimensions of temperament identified in infants correspond to the central dimensions found in adult personality.
    D) Temperament in infancy and childhood probably has little to do with later forms of psychopathology.
    Answer: C

Pages: 76
Topic: Biological Causal Factors: Brain Dysfunction
Skill: Conceptual   Other1:
36. Although gross brain pathology is rare among children with abnormal behavior, more subtle deficiencies in brain function may
    A) linger but diminish during adolescence.
    B) enhance vulnerability to more serious disorders later in life.
    C) lead to more serious brain pathology later in life.
    D) lead to a gradual and steady destruction of brain tissue throughout adult life.
    Answer: B

Pages: 76-77
Topic: Biological Causal Factors: Physical Deprivation or Disruption
Skill: Factual   Other1:
37. Severe malnutrition in infancy is most closely associated with
    A) irreversible brain damage.
    B) irreversible stunting of physical growth.
    C) psychological difficulties and lower than expected IQ.
    D) A and C
    Answer: A

Pages: 77-78
Topic: Biological Causal Factors: Physical Deprivation or Disruption
Skill: Factual   Other1:
38. With regard to environmental stimulation during infancy, it appears likely that
    A) too little stimulation is significantly worse than too much stimulation.
    B) too much stimulation is significantly worse than too little stimulation.
    C) each individual has an optimal level of stimulation that may vary over time.
    D) stimulation is overrated as a contributory cause of mental disturbances.
    Answer: C

Pages: 78
Topic: Biological Causal Factors: The Impact of the Biological Viewpoint
Skill: Conceptual   Other1:
39. Some biological psychiatrists argue that if a biological factor can be causally related to
    a mental disorder, then that mental disorder can be regarded strictly as an illness that
    has exclusively biological causes. Which of the following statements provides a
    counter-argument to this biological viewpoint?
    A) All behavior, normal and abnormal, has a biological substrate.
    B) Differences between people in normal as well as in abnormal behaviors are associated
       with biological differences.
    C) All psychological causes, once they have an effect on a person, are mediated by
       biological processes.
    D) all of the above
    Answer: D

Pages: 79
Topic: Psychosocial Viewpoints: The Psychodynamic Perspectives
Skill: Factual   Other1:
40. Sigmund Freud theorized that mental disorders result from unresolved
    A) defense mechanisms.
    B) primary processes.
    C) id anxieties.
    D) intrapsychic conflicts.
    Answer: D

Pages: 79
Topic: Psychosocial Viewpoints: The Psychodynamic Perspectives
Skill: Factual   Other1:
41. According to Freud, the id operates through _____ whereas the ego operates through _____.
    A) the reality principle; secondary process thinking
    B) the pleasure principle; primary process thinking
    C) secondary process thinking; primary process thinking
    D) the pleasure principle; the reality principle
    Answer: D

Pages: 79
Topic: Psychosocial Viewpoints: The Psychodynamic Perspectives
Skill: Factual   Other1:
42. Ego-defense mechanisms are
    A) rational strategies used by the ego to defend against anxiety.
    B) irrational protective measures used by the ego to defend against anxiety.
    C) strategies used by the superego to defend the ego against real external dangers.
    D) defenses against forbidden Oedipal wishes.
    Answer: B

Pages: 81
Topic: Psychosocial Viewpoints: The Psychodynamic Perspectives
Skill: Conceptual   Other1:
43. Freud's theory of psychological development suggests that
    A) the individual passes from id to ego to superego as he or she matures.
    B) the individual passes through psychosexual stages which each have distinct patterns of pleasure-seeking activity.
    C) a child must negotiate and resolve a series of Oedipal or Electra complexes.
    D) repression is the final and most mature stage of development.
    Answer: B

Pages: 82
Topic: Psychosocial Viewpoints: The Psychodynamic Perspectives
Skill: Conceptual   Other1:
44. Contemporary psychodynamic theories differ from Freud's in
    A) their focus on primary processes and abnormal symptoms.
    B) their emphasis on superego functioning.
    C) their focus on internalized representations of significant people in a child's life.
    D) their emphasis on more basic manifestations of libidinal energy.
    Answer: C

Pages: 82
Topic: Psychosocial Viewpoints: The Psychodynamic Perspectives
Skill: Conceptual   Other1:
45. Object-relations theory emphasizes which of the following?
    A) the impact of early relationships on a person's later interactions
    B) inner conflicts associated with the conflicting properties of internalized objects
    C) the successful completion of early developmental phases like separation-individuation
    D) all of the above
    Answer: D

Pages: 83
Topic: Psychosocial Viewpoints: The Psychodynamic Perspectives
Skill: Conceptual   Other1:
46. One of the central limitations of Freudian theory is
    A) the lack of scientific evidence for many fundamental psychoanalytic explanations.
    B) its failure to describe the impact of early childhood experiences on later psychological functioning.
    C) its failure to include any extensive account of the role of unconscious processes in mental life.
    D) its failure to take into consideration the role of parent-child relationships.
    Answer: A

Pages: 83
Topic: Psychosocial Viewpoints: The Behavioral Perspective
Skill: Conceptual   Other1:
47. Behaviorists argue that abnormal behavior results from
    A) improper reinforcement schedules.
    B) inadequate response generalization.
    C) lack of differential reinforcement.
    D) learning maladaptive responses to environmental stimuli.
    Answer: D

Pages: 83
Topic: Psychosocial Viewpoints: The Behavioral Perspective
Skill: Conceptual   Other1:
48. The behaviorist perspective views psychoanalysis as not providing acceptable scientific
    data because
    A) the study of subjective experience through dream analysis and free association is not
       open to verification by other investigators.
    B) hypnosis can not be studied in an empirically objective manner.
    C) abnormal behavior develops through abnormal experiences which can not be studied using
       the scientific method.
    D) the idea that children have sexual urges is difficult, if not impossible, to test
       empirically.
    Answer: A

Pages: 84
Topic: Psychosocial Viewpoints: The Behavioral Perspective
Skill: Factual   Other1:
49. Establishing a specific response to a previously neutral stimulus which has been paired
    with an unconditioned stimulus is known as
    A) classical conditioning.
    B) operant conditioning.
    C) instrumental conditioning.
    D) avoidance conditioning.
    Answer: A

Pages: 84
Topic: Psychosocial Viewpoints: The Behavioral Perspective
Skill: Factual   Other1:
50. Which of the following is NOT important in establishing a classically conditioned
    response?
    A) the repeated pairing of CS and US
    B) an optimum rate of reinforcement of the CS by the US
    C) The CS must provide nonredundant information about the occurrence of a US.
    D) The CS must be a reliable predictor of the occurrence of the US.
    Answer: B

Pages: 84
Topic: Psychosocial Viewpoints: The Behavioral Perspective
Skill: Applied   Other1:
51. Debbi was bitten by a dog when she was a child. As an adult, she has an enormous fear of dogs. Debbi can be said to have a(n)
A) conditioned emotional response.
B) automatically conditioned response.
C) generalized response.
D) unconditioned response.
Answer: A

Pages: 84
Topic: Psychosocial Viewpoints: The Behavioral Perspective
Skill: Applied   Other1:
52. Julie and her behavioral therapist have worked together to eliminate Julie's fear of spiders. Which of the following statements about Julie's prognosis is FALSE?
A) The fear may reemerge when Julie encounters a spider on an upcoming camping trip.
B) The fear may reemerge spontaneously years after successful treatment.
C) Julie's fear of spiders has been extinguished.
D) Julie has effectively unlearned her fear and shouldn't be troubled by it anymore.
Answer: D

Pages: 84
Topic: Psychosocial Viewpoints: The Behavioral Perspective
Skill: Factual   Other1:
53. A learned response-outcome expectancy is associated with
A) operant conditioning.
B) classical conditioning.
C) stimulus generalization.
D) discriminative learning.
Answer: A

Pages: 84
Topic: Psychosocial Viewpoints: The Behavioral Perspective
Skill: Factual   Other1:
54. A type of learning that involves the acquisition of behaviors necessary to achieve a desired goal is called
A) positive conditioning.
B) operant conditioning.
C) differential reinforcement.
D) classical conditioning.
Answer: B

Topic: Psychosocial Viewpoints: The Behavioral Perspective
Skill: Factual   Other1:

55. Which of the following is NOT associated with operant conditioning?
    A) extinction
    B) discrimination
    C) unconditioned stimulus
    D) conditioned avoidance response
    Answer: C

Pages: 84
Topic: Psychosocial Viewpoints: The Behavioral Perspective
Skill: Applied   Other1:

56. John is afraid of snakes and keeps away from a variety of situations in which he may encounter a snake. John has developed a(n)
    A) generalization gradient.
    B) avoidant personality.
    C) conditioned avoidance response.
    D) adaptive way of managing his fear.
    Answer: C

Pages: 85
Topic: Psychosocial Viewpoints: The Behavioral Perspective
Skill: Applied   Other1:

57. Laurie has learned that if she acts coy and flirtatious with others, she is likely to get her way. However, she has also learned that this behavior works only with men and not with other women. This is an example of
    A) differential reinforcement leading to discriminant responses.
    B) a conditioned avoidance response.
    C) a classically conditioned response.
    D) cognitive restructuring.
    Answer: A

Pages: 85
Topic: Psychosocial Viewpoints: The Behavioral Perspective
Skill: Conceptual   Other1:

58. Which of the following statements is NOT a plausible behavioral reinterpretation of psychoanalytic principles?
    A) Anxiety is a conditioned fear response.
    B) Neurosis is a failure to condition.
    C) The principle of positive and negative reinforcement corresponds to the pleasure principle of the id.
    D) Repression is conditioned thought-stoppage reinforced by anxiety-reduction.
    Answer: B

Topic: Psychosocial Viewpoints: The Behavioral Perspective
Skill: Applied   Other1:

59. Bill is afraid of flying and has been postponing an important business trip. A behavior therapist recommends a treatment whereby Bill progressively imagines more frightening situations associated with flying while he is in a state of deep relaxation. This technique is called
A) aversive conditioning.
B) positive reinforcement.
C) shaping and modeling.
D) systematic desensitization.
Answer: D

Pages: 86
Topic: Psychosocial Viewpoints: The Behavioral Perspective
Skill: Applied   Other1:

60. Beth often complains to her husband that she is depressed and unable to perform everyday tasks. Her husband responds with sympathy and helps her accomplish the things she must do each day. A behavior therapist recommending a program of reinforcement withdrawal would suggest
A) punishing her for depressive behavior.
B) modeling competent, nondepressive behavior.
C) ignoring depressive behavior and providing positive reinforcement for nondepressive behavior.
D) desensitizing her to her depressive behaviors.
Answer: C

Pages: 87
Topic: Psychosocial Viewpoints: The Cognitive-Behavioral Perspective
Skill: Conceptual   Other1:

61. From the cognitive-behavioral perspective, an important limitation with the behavioral perspective is the fact that
A) behaviorists went too far in attacking the psychoanalytic perspective.
B) behaviorists failed to attend to the importance of mental processes.
C) behaviorists held an overly stringent view of what constitutes scientific inquiry.
D) behaviorists overemphasized the importance of subjective experience.
Answer: B

Pages: 87
Topic: Psychosocial Viewpoints: The Cognitive-Behavioral Perspective
Skill: Factual   Other1:
62. Cognitive-behavioral psychologists believe that abnormal behavior
    A) consists of learned maladaptive response patterns.
    B) results from distorted thinking and information processing.
    C) results from neurotic thought processes.
    D) results from impaired patterns of interpersonal relationships.
    Answer: B

Pages: 88
Topic: Psychosocial Viewpoints: The Cognitive-Behavioral Perspective
Skill: Factual   Other1:
63. "Internal reinforcement" refers to
    A) the positive "self-talk" used in self-actualization therapy.
    B) positive causal attributions.
    C) the way people learn to regulate their behavior by internal symbolic processes.
    D) the lessening of anxiety associated with performing an instrumental avoidance response.
    Answer: C

Pages: 87-89
Topic: Psychosocial Viewpoints: The Cognitive-Behavioral Perspective
Skill: Factual   Other1:
64. Which of the following statements is NOT associated with the cognitive-behavioral
    perspective?
    A) Individuals interpret the world according to a system of personal constructs.
    B) Different forms of psychopathology are associated with differences in attributional
       style.
    C) Human beings are the sum of their choices.
    D) Adverse early learning experiences may lead to the development of maladaptive schemas
       associated with various forms of psychopathology.
    Answer: C

Pages: 87
Topic: Psychosocial Viewpoints: The Cognitive-Behavioral Perspective
Skill: Conceptual   Other1:
65. Although the psychoanalytic and cognitive-behavioral perspectives differ in many ways, one
    similarity is the emphasis placed by both perspectives on people's
    A) subjective experiences.
    B) internal conflicts.
    C) need for gratification.
    D) all of the above.
    Answer: A

Pages: 89
Topic: Psychosocial Viewpoints: The Cognitive-Behavioral Perspective
Skill: Factual   Other1:

66. Schemas are defined as
    A) cognitive representations of knowledge that guide information processing.
    B) the mental images that clients use during systematic desensitization.
    C) maladaptive ideas about oneself and others.
    D) internal, stable, global causes ascribed to negative events.
    Answer: A

Pages: 88-89
Topic: Psychosocial Viewpoints: The Cognitive-Behavioral Perspective
Skill: Conceptual   Other1:

67. From a cognitive-behavioral perspective, attributional style and schemas are similar in that both
    A) focus on maladaptive internal images that produce abnormal behavior.
    B) focus on the manner in which people provide causal explanations for events in their lives.
    C) help to explain adaptive and maladaptive emotions and behavior.
    D) emphasize the importance of interpersonal relationships as precursors to adaptive and maladaptive ways of viewing the world.
    Answer: C

Pages: 88
Topic: Psychosocial Viewpoints: The Cognitive-Behavioral Perspective
Skill: Applied   Other1:

68. Susan does poorly on a midterm exam and attributes the poor grade to some enduring flaw in herself ("I'm stupid"). She typically interprets negative events in her life in such a fashion. Susan may be said to have a
    A) negative construct.
    B) negative internal reinforcement schedule.
    C) schematic neurosis.
    D) depressive attributional style.
    Answer: D

Topic: Psychosocial Viewpoints: The Humanistic Perspective
Skill: Conceptual   Other1:

69. Which of the following is NOT a principle of humanistic psychology?
    A) A fundamental striving of the individual is toward self-actualization.
    B) Each individual is ultimately responsible for choosing the value and meaning that his or her life will have.
    C) Psychopathology is the blocking of an individual's natural tendency toward mental health and personal growth.
    D) Therapy is a way of moving individuals from maladjustment to adjustment.
    Answer: D

Pages: 89
Topic: Psychosocial Viewpoints: The Humanistic Perspective
Skill: Conceptual   Other1:

70. Compared with other perspectives, the humanist perspective
    A) places less emphasis on the self as an important part of the personality.
    B) suggests that people who shape their personal destiny are active participants in life.
    C) suggests that people are likely to have personal problems even under the most favorable circumstances.
    D) suggests that people tend to be influenced more by irrational forces, resulting in greater emphasis on emotions.
    Answer: B

Pages: 93
Topic: Psychosocial Viewpoints: The Interpersonal Perspective
Skill: Applied   Other1:

71. According to Freud, six-month-old Jason is in the oral stage of development. In contrast to Freud's notion of oral gratification, interpersonal theorists would focus on what aspect of Jason's development?
    A) development of trust or mistrust in others
    B) development of personal constructs
    C) development of self-actualization
    D) development of a foundation of inner needs
    Answer: A

Topic: Psychosocial Viewpoints: The Interpersonal Perspective
Skill: Factual   Other1: In Student Study Guide
72. Harry Stack Sullivan noted that we sometimes screen out of consciousness some especially frightening aspect of our self-experience and perceive it as _____.
A) "bad-me"
B) "good-me"
C) "not-me"
D) "vulnerable-me"
Answer: A

Pages: 94
Topic: Psychosocial Viewpoints: The Interpersonal Perspective
Skill: Applied   Other1:
73. Cecilia is having difficulty with her husband. She feels much stress and anxiety in this relationship. A psychologist working from the approach of Harry Stack Sullivan would probably focus on
A) the love that she has experienced in previous romantic relationships.
B) discrepancies between the "ideal other" and "real other."
C) the lack of growth and fulfillment of her potential that she is experiencing.
D) the personifications (mental prototypes) she has of "husband" that influence the relationship.
Answer: D

Pages: 94
Topic: Psychosocial Viewpoints: The Interpersonal Perspective
Skill: Factual   Other1:
74. Recent influences on interpersonal thought include which of the following?
A) viewing interpersonal relationships in terms of social roles
B) interpersonal behavioral accomodation
C) social exchange theory
D) all of the above
Answer: D

Pages: 95
Topic: Psychosocial Viewpoints: Summary
Skill: Conceptual   Other1:
75. With regard to the various theoretical perspectives for understanding psychopathology, it appears that
    A) the cognitive-behavioral and psychodynamic viewpoints, but not the humanistic and interpersonal viewpoints, are supported by empirical research.
    B) the interpersonal and behavioral viewpoints are most useful in explaining psychopathology.
    C) each viewpoint limits the types of evidence that may be examined and the way it will be interpreted.
    D) the behavioral and cognitive-behavioral viewpoints are the most thorough in their search for the truth.
    Answer: C

Pages: 96
Topic: Psychosocial Causal Factors: Schemas and Self-schemas
Skill: Factual   Other1:
76. New perceptions and experiences tend to be worked into our existing schemas, even if the new information must be distorted to fit them. This process is called
    A) accomodation.
    B) assimilation.
    C) appropriation.
    D) adumbration.
    Answer: B

Pages: 96
Topic: Psychosocial Causal Factors: Schemas and Self-schemas
Skill: Conceptual   Other1:
77. An important goal of virtually all therapeutic approaches is _____, changing an individual's existing cognitive frameworks to incorporate discrepant and often threatening information.
    A) accomodation
    B) assimilation
    C) catharsis
    D) reality testing.
    Answer: A

Pages: 97
Topic: Psychosocial Causal Factors: Schemas and Self-schemas
Skill: Factual   Other1:
78. One source of vulnerability to later psychological problems is the failure to learn appropriate ways of processing experience. Mischel identified five ways in which children differ from one another in this regard. Which of the following is NOT one of these?
    A) They differ in the way they process new information.
    B) They develop different expectations based on their own unique experiences.
    C) They learn different ways of regulating their impulses and behavior.
    D) Some fail to develop schemas.
    Answer: D

Pages: 97
Topic: Psychosocial Causal Factors: Schemas and Self-schemas
Skill: Factual   Other1:
79. Which of the following factors is NOT included in Barlow's and Mineka's models of clinical anxiety?
    A) experience with unpredictable negative outcomes
    B) desire to observe frightening events during childhood
    C) a biological vulnerability
    D) exposure to uncontrollable negative events
    Answer: B

Pages: 98
Topic: Psychosocial Causal Factors: Early Deprivation or Trauma
Skill: Applied   Other1:
80. A cognitive psychologist might offer which of the following as an interpretation of the effects of parental deprivation on an individual?
    A) The child will be unable to develop a sense of basic trust.
    B) The child will remain fixated at the oral stage.
    C) The child will be unable to actualize itself to its fullest potential.
    D) The child will acquire dysfunctional schemas and self-schemas.
    Answer: D

Pages: 98
Topic: Psychosocial Causal Factors: Early Deprivation or Trauma
Skill: Factual   Other1:
81. Which of the following is NOT a protective factor against later psychopathology for children institutionalized during early childhood?
    A) later positive social relationships
    B) moving from the institution into a harmonious, rather than a discordant, family environment
    C) having little desire for nurturance
    D) experiencing later athletic or academic success
    Answer: C

Pages: 99
Topic: Psychosocial Causal Factors: Early Deprivation or Trauma
Skill: Factual   Other1:

82. One serious outcome of early parental deprivation and rejection is "failure to thrive" (FTT) syndrome. Which of the following statements about FTT is NOT true?
    A) This disorder is fairly common in low-income families.
    B) FTT is associated with low birth weight.
    C) The FTT infant is likely to be stunted in growth but emotionally recovered in later childhood.
    D) The FTT infant may be severely depressed.
    Answer: C

Pages: 99
Topic: Psychosocial Causal Factors: Early Deprivation or Trauma
Skill: Applied   Other1:

83. Marla was physically abused by her mother in childhood. Compared to other children, Marla is more likely to
    A) exhibit signs of autism.
    B) be impulsive and overly aggressive.
    C) be extremely passive and withdrawn.
    D) exhibit psychotic symptoms.
    Answer: B

Pages: 96
Topic: Psychosocial Causal Factors: Early Deprivation or Trauma
Skill: Applied   Other1:

84. Sally was abused as an infant and toddler by both her father and mother. As a result, she has developed a schema that others can not be trusted. According to the processes of assimilation and accomodation,
    A) she will be likely to view new encounters in a manner consistent with her mistrustful schema, and may be unable to experience relationships that would disconfirm her schema.
    B) she will view all of her relationships in a mistrustful way until someone shows her that he or she can be trusted.
    C) she will learn to be overly accomodating in her behavior toward others in order to ensure that she is well-treated.
    D) she will overcompensate and become a "caretaker" later in life.
    Answer: A

Pages: 99
Topic: Psychosocial Causal Factors: Early Deprivation or Trauma
Skill: Factual   Other1:
85. Kaufman and Zigler estimated that as many as 30 percent of the children who have been physically abused by a parent will go on to abuse their own children. Which of these factors might protect against this tragic scenario?
    A) the child's physical attractiveness
    B) a good relationship with some other adult during childhood
    C) higher IQ
    D) all of the above
    Answer: D

Pages: 100
Topic: Psychosocial Causal Factors: Early Deprivation or Trauma
Skill: Factual   Other1:
86. Psychic traumas are likely to be most damaging during
    A) infancy or early childhood.
    B) adolescence.
    C) early adulthood.
    D) old age.
    Answer: A

Pages: 100
Topic: Psychosocial Causal Factors: Early Deprivation or Trauma
Skill: Conceptual   Other1:
87. Psychic traumas are especially likely to leave lasting psychological wounds because
    A) they fail to generalize to other situations, thus never diluting in intensity.
    B) they may reactivate memories of stressors that never really happened.
    C) they are established in situations that evoke strong emotions which make them highly resistant to extinction.
    D) they involve separation from the parent.
    Answer: C

Pages: 100
Topic: Psychosocial Causal Factors: Early Deprivation or Trauma
Skill: Factual   Other1:
88. Bowlby found that in a normal response to prolonged separation from the parents, a child will
    A) exhibit few signs of distress during separation.
    B) show significant despair during the separation and temporary detachment from the parents upon reunion.
    C) exhibit excessive aggressiveness and impulsivity for some time following reunion with the parents.
    D) turn quickly to another adult as a parent substitute.
    Answer: B

Pages: 100
Topic: Psychosocial Causal Factors: Early Deprivation or Trauma
Skill: Applied   Other1:

89. Brad experienced the death of his father when he was four years old. The long-term consequences of this traumatic event are
    A) highly dependent upon the support he receives from his mother or other significant people.
    B) likely to be vulnerability to severe depression in adolescence with high risk for suicidality.
    C) likely to generalize to other situations resulting in an extreme fear of abandonment.
    D) unlikely to be serious, since the event happened when Brad was very young.
    Answer: A

Pages: 101
Topic: Psychosocial Causal Factors: Inadequate Parenting
Skill: Applied   Other1:

90. Dana's mother suffers from serious depressive episodes. Dana is likely to
    A) be at risk for a wide range of developmental difficulties and later psychopathology.
    B) become depressed herself because of shared genetic factors.
    C) have difficulties in adolescence with alcohol and substance abuse.
    D) develop a dissociative disorder.
    Answer: A

Pages: 102
Topic: Psychosocial Causal Factors: Inadequate Parenting
Skill: Factual   Other1:

91. The text describes four different parenting styles that are each associated with a different developmental outcome for children. Which of the following is NOT one of these styles?
    A) authoritarian
    B) indulgent
    C) authoritative
    D) abusive
    Answer: D

Pages: 102
Topic: Psychosocial Causal Factors: Inadequate Parenting
Skill: Factual   Other1:
92. The four parenting styles described in the text differ along two dimensions, warmth and control. The style associated with the most positive developmental outcome is _____ in warmth and _____ in control.
    A) high; low
    B) low; high
    C) high; moderately high
    D) low; moderately high
    Answer: C

Pages: 102
Topic: Psychosocial Causal Factors: Inadequate Parenting
Skill: Factual   Other1:
93. Children from authoritarian families
    A) tend to have problems with cognitive and social skills.
    B) tend to have demanding and exploitive relationships.
    C) may show increased aggressive behavior if their parents also use severe discipline.
    D) A and C
    Answer: A

Pages: 102
Topic: Psychosocial Causal Factors: Inadequate Parenting
Skill: Factual   Other1:
94. Severe discipline in the form of physical punishment by authoritarian parents is associated with
    A) childhood depression.
    B) social withdrawal.
    C) increased aggressiveness in the child.
    D) spoiled and selfish behavior.
    Answer: C

Pages: 103
Topic: Psychosocial Causal Factors: Inadequate Parenting
Skill: Factual   Other1:
95. Children whose parents show a permissive-indulgent style tend to develop self-schemas that include
    A) demanding and "entitlement" features.
    B) flexibility in coping with stress.
    C) permissiveness in the context of later romantic relationships.
    D) a lack of trust in the world.
    Answer: A

Pages: 103
Topic: Psychosocial Causal Factors: Inadequate Parenting
Skill: Factual   Other1:

96. Children growing up in a high risk environment, such as an urban inner city, do best when
    A) parents are warmer and more indulgent.
    B) parents are more restrictive and less democratic.
    C) parents exhibit a strict, authoritarian style utilizing physical punishment to maintain control.
    D) parents adopt a neglecting-uninvolved style.
    Answer: B

Pages: 104
Topic: Psychosocial Causal Factors: Pathogenic Family Structures
Skill: Conceptual   Other1:

97. Which of these statements is true about children from divorced families?
    A) They will show enhanced adjustment if the custodial parent remarries soon after the divorce.
    B) They are at high risk for a wide variety of serious difficulties, especially if the divorce happens later in life (e.g., while in college).
    C) Infants and very young children are at greatest risk for adverse consequences from a divorce.
    D) They are often better off than children in intact but high-conflict families.
    Answer: D

Pages: 105
Topic: Psychosocial Causal Factors: Maladaptive Peer Relationships
Skill: Factual   Other1:

98. A major factor associated with a child's rejection by peers is
    A) overly aggressive behavior.
    B) shyness.
    C) socioeconomic background.
    D) a lack of empathy.
    Answer: A

Topic: Psychosocial Causal Factors: Maladaptive Peer Relationships
Skill: Applied   Other1:

99. A psychotherapist working with a child who has been rejected by peers might best focus on
   A) uncovering and exploring earlier psychic traumas that might be related to current interpersonal difficulties.
   B) treating the parents for conflicts they may be having that are reflected in the child's difficulty.
   C) teaching the child social skills like how to join ongoing group activities and how to moderate aggressive behavior.
   D) helping the child not to worry about it too much, since his position in the peer group is likely to change by itself with time.
   Answer: C

Pages: 106
Topic: Sociocultural Viewpoint: Sociocultural Factors/Cross-Cultural Studies
Skill: Conceptual   Other1:

100. Research indicates that
   A) abnormality is a culturally defined concept.
   B) while many psychological disturbances are universal, cultural factors serve as causal factors and modifying influences.
   C) there are few differences between cultures in the forms that various disorders take.
   D) children in other cultures tend to be better adjusted than American children.
   Answer: B

Pages: 109
Topic: Sociocultural Viewpoint: Sociocultural Factors/Cross-Cultural Studies
Skill: Factual   Other1:

101. Cross-cultural studies conducted by Weisz and colleagues examine the prevalence of undercontrolled and overcontrolled behavior problems in children and adolescents from Thailand and the United States. The findings of these studies indicated that
   A) Thai children and adolescents had a greater prevalence of undercontrolled problems than did American children and adolescents, consistent with their cultural backgrounds.
   B) Thai children and adolescents had a greater prevalence of overcontrolled problems than did American children and adolescents, consistent with their cultural backgrounds.
   C) Thai children and adolescents had a similar rate of overcontrolled problems compared to American children and adolescents, consistent with their cultural backgrounds.
   D) A and C
   Answer: B

Pages: 111
Topic: Sociocultural Causal Factors: The Sociocultural Environment
Skill: Conceptual   Other1:
102. In terms of the sociocultural environment, it is likely that
    A) groups do not differ nearly as much as was previously believed.
    B) the likelihood that inborn potentialities will be actualized has remained constant over
       time.
    C) groups living in the same general geographical area typically have very similar values
       and behavior.
    D) the more uniform and thorough the education of the younger members of a particular
       cultural group, the more alike they will become.
    Answer: D

Pages: 111
Topic: Sociocultural Causal Factors: The Sociocultural Environment
Skill: Conceptual   Other1:
103. Of the following, the individual who is most likely to be vulnerable to maladaptive
    behavior is the
    A) female who is low in masculinity.
    B) male who is low in masculinity.
    C) female who is high in masculinity.
    D) A and B
    Answer: D

Pages: 111
Topic: Sociocultural Causal Factors: The Sociocultural Environment
Skill: Factual   Other1:
104. Low masculinity in women may be associated with
    A) reduced chance of divorce.
    B) female attractiveness.
    C) low self-esteem and/or learned helplessness.
    D) high socioeconomic status.
    Answer: C

Pages: 111
Topic: Sociocultural Causal Factors: Pathogenic Societal Influences
Skill: Factual   Other1:
105. Compared with individuals in the middle and upper classes, lower-class individuals
    encounter
    A) more stressors, but these stressors are no more severe.
    B) fewer stressors, but these stressors are more severe.
    C) more stressors, and these stressors are more severe.
    D) fewer stressors, and these stressors are no more severe.
    Answer: C

Pages: 113
Topic: Sociocultural Causal Factors: Pathogenic Societal Influences
Skill: Factual   Other1:

106. Which of the following statements is true?
    A) Women who work in the home tend to be less depressed and anxious than women who work outside the home.
    B) Traditional masculine roles put men at greater risk for psychopathology than women.
    C) Many more women seek psychological treatment than do men.
    D) The traditional female role seems to have an inoculating effect against psychopathology in women.
    Answer: C

Pages: 113
Topic: Sociocultural Causal Factors: Pathogenic Societal Influences
Skill: Factual   Other1:

107. During periods of extensive unemployment, we might expect which of the following?
    A) an increase in psychological problems, especially among individuals in the middle class
    B) an increase in physical health problems due to lack of health insurance, but no substantial increase in psychological problems
    C) permanent mental health problems among affected individuals
    D) a rise in physical and psychological health problems, especially among lower socioeconomic groups.
    Answer: D

Pages: 114
Topic: Issues on Theoretical Viewpoints/Causation of Abnormal Behavior
Skill: Factual   Other1:

108. Psychologists who accept working ideas from several existing viewpoints have adopted a(n) _____ perspective.
    A) psychointegrative
    B) eclectic
    C) elliptic
    D) synthesized
    Answer: B

Pages: 114
Topic: Issues on Theoretical Viewpoints/Causation of Abnormal Behavior
Skill: Conceptual   Other1: In Student Study Guide

109. According to the authors, the problematic proliferation of diverse viewpoints about psychopathology can best be solved by
    A) adhering to a single point of view for consistency's sake.
    B) becoming an eclectic.
    C) developing a unified point of view.
    D) divorcing oneself from all major perspectives.
    Answer: C

Pages: 114-115
Topic: Issues on Theoretical Viewpoints/Causation of Abnormal Behavior
Skill: Conceptual   Other1:
110. Which of these statements is NOT associated with the biopsychosocial model?
    A) Most disorders are a product of the interaction of many types of causal factors.
    B) For a given person, the particular combination of causal factors may be relatively unique.
    C) A scientific understanding of the causes of abnormal behavior will enable us to predict abnormal behavior in individuals.
    D) A large number of "unexplained" influences may make it impossible for scientists to ever be able to predict abnormal behaviors in individuals with exact certainty.
    Answer: C

Short Answer

Write the word or phrase that best completes each statement or answers the question.

Pages: 64
Topic: Abnormal Behavior: Necessary/Sufficient/Contributory Causes
Skill: Factual   Other1:
 1. Define necessary, sufficient, and contributory causes.
    Answer: A necessary cause is a condition that MUST exist in order for a disorder to occur. A sufficient cause is a condition that guarantees the occurrence of a disorder. A contributory cause is a condition that increases the probability that a disorder will develop but is itself neither necessary nor sufficient.

Pages: 65-67
Topic: What Causes Abnormal Behavior: Diathesis-Stress Models
Skill: Factual   Other1:
 2. Briefly describe the diathesis-stress model of abnormal behavior.
    Answer: The diathesis-stress model views a mental disorder as the result of stress operating on an individual with a diathesis for developing that disorder. A diathesis is a predisposition or pre-existing vulnerability to develop that disorder, and can derive from biological, psychosocial, or sociocultural factors.

Pages: 68-76
Topic: Biological Causal Factors
Skill: Factual   Other1:

3. Identify and briefly describe three categories of biological factors that are relevant to the development of mental disorders.

Answer: Biochemical imbalances in the brain--Disruption of neurotransmitter substances in the brain, which may lead to a disruption in the transmission of neural impulses.

Genetic defects--Research shows that heredity is an important predisposing causal factor in several mental disorders.

Constitutional liabilities--These are detrimental characteristics that are either hereditary or acquired very early.

Brain dysfunction--Gross pathology and subtle deficiencies in brain function.

Physical Deprivation or Disruption--Lack of fulfillment of basic physical needs such as food, sleep, or stimulation.

Pages: 72-73
Topic: Biological Causal Factors: Genetic Defects
Skill: Conceptual   Other1:

4. Identify three research methods for studying genetic influences in abnormal behavior. Suppose that genetic endowment is a causal factor involved in the development of schizophrenia. What would each of the three research methods show when used to investigate schizophrenia?

Answer: Family history (pedigree) studies, twin studies, and adoption studies. In the pedigree study, we'd expect to find a higher rate of schizophrenia in the relatives of schizophrenic probands compared to the relatives of control probands. In the twin studies, we'd expect the concordance rate for schizophrenia to be higher in monozygotic than in dizygotic twins. In adoption studies, if we identify schizophrenic probands in adulthood who had been adopted at a young age, we'd expect to find a higher rate of schizophrenia in their biological parents than in their adoptive parents.

Pages: 75
Topic: Biological Causal Factors: Constitutional Liabilities
Skill: Factual   Other1:

5. Research has identified five dimensions of temperament that appear as early as two months of age. Two of these dimensions are _____ and _____.

Answer: In the child, these dimensions are fearfulness, irritability and frustration, positive affect, activity level, and attentional persistence. In the adult these dimensions correspond to neuroticism or negative emotionality, extraversion or positive emotionality, and constraint or control (conscientiousness and agreeableness).

Pages: 79-81
Topic: Psychosocial Viewpoints: The Psychodynamic Perspectives
Skill: Factual   Other1:

6. Briefly describe Freud's theory of anxiety and conflict, including the three types of anxiety.

    Answer: Behavior results from the interaction of three subsystems that constitute human personality (id, ego, and superego). Intrapsychic conflict results when these three make incompatible demands on an individual. Neurotic anxiety results when the id's unconscious impulses threaten to break through ego controls. Moral anxiety results when an individual commits or contemplates an action that conflicts with the superego. Reality anxiety arises from actual external dangers.

Pages: 82
Topic: Psychosocial Viewpoints: The Psychodynamic Perspectives
Skill: Conceptual   Other1:

7. Briefly describe one of the main differences between object-relations theory and traditional psychoanalytic thought.

    Answer: Psychoanalytic theory focuses on psychosexual development and on relations among the three subsystems of personality (id, ego and superego). Object-relations theory focuses on the child's early relationships with significant others who the child has introjected into his or her own personality. Freud emphasized intrapsychic conflicts resulting from contradictory demands of id, ego, and superego; object-relations theorists emphasize the conflicting properties that internalized, split-off object representations may have.

Pages: 83
Topic: Integration of Viewpoints
Skill: Conceptual   Other1:

8. Briefly describe one of the central criticisms of psychoanalytic theory made by behaviorists.

    Answer: Behaviorists claim that the psychoanalytic study of subjective experience does not provide acceptable scientific data because such data are not open to direct observation and independent verification by other investigators.

Pages: 84
Topic: Psychosocial Viewpoints: The Behavioral Perspective
Skill: Factual　　　　　*Other1:*
9. Describe three factors that may influence the establishment and strength of a classically
    or operantly conditioned response.
    Answer:　In classical conditioning, the CS and US must be paired repeatedly, and the CS
    　　　　　must be a reliable predictor of the US. In addition, the CS must provide
    　　　　　nonredundant information about the occurrence of the US. In operant
    　　　　　conditioning, the initial reinforcement rate must usually be high in order to
    　　　　　establish a conditioned response. Afterward, an intermittent rate of
    　　　　　reinforcement may produce an especially persistent response. A conditioned
    　　　　　avoidance response is especially difficult to extinguish.

Pages: 85-86
Topic: Psychosocial Viewpoints: The Behavioral Perspective
Skill: Factual　　　　　*Other1:*
10. Identify and briefly describe three therapeutic techniques derived from the behavioral
    perspective.
    Answer:　Positive reinforcement--rewarding desired behavior. Use of aversive
    　　　　　stimuli--punishing undesirable behavior. Withdrawal of reinforcement--to
    　　　　　extinguish undesirable behavior. Systematic desensitization--repeatedly pairing
    　　　　　feared stimuli with positive stimuli to inhibit or reduce fear and avoidance
    　　　　　behavior. Shaping--reinforcing successive approximations of a desired behavior.
    　　　　　Cognitive restructuring--using reinforcement to modify covert behavior
    　　　　　(cognitions).

Pages: 88
Topic: Psychosocial Viewpoints: The Cognitive-Behavioral Perspective
Skill: Conceptual　　　　　*Other1:*
11. _____ are the causes that individuals assign to events in order to explain them.
    Answer:　Attributions

Pages: 89
Topic: Psychosocial Viewpoints: The Cognitive-Behavioral Perspective
Skill: Conceptual　　　　　*Other1:*
12. What are "schemas" and what role do they play in abnormal behavior?
    Answer:　Schemas are underlying representations of knowledge that guide current
    　　　　　information-processing. Schemas may lead to distortions in perception,
    　　　　　attention, memory, and other cognitive processes, thereby resulting in
    　　　　　maladaptive emotions and behaviors. Some cognitive psychopathologists associate
    　　　　　different kinds of psychopathology with different kinds of maladaptive schemas.

Pages: 89
Topic: Psychosocial Viewpoints: The Humanistic Perspective
Skill: Factual   Other1:
13. The perspective that focuses on freeing people from disabling attitudes with the goal of attaining personal growth is the _____ perspective.
Answer: humanistic

Pages: 79-94
Topic: Integration of Viewpoints
Skill: Conceptual   Other1:
14. Briefly describe one of the similarities between the views of Harry Stack Sullivan, Sigmund Freud, and Aaron Beck.
Answer: All three describe abnormal behavior in terms of the incongruity that may result between an individual's perceptions of the world, and the world as it really is. Further, all three allow for the possibility that some of our perceptions are based on factors out of our immediate consciousness (the "not-me" for Sullivan; the unconscious for Freud; implicit schematic assumptions for Beck).

Pages: 95
Topic: Psychosocial Viewpoints: Summary
Skill: Conceptual   Other1:
15. How does adopting one theoretical perspective on psychopathology limit us?
Answer: It limits us in the type of evidence we consider, in how we perceive maladaptive behavior, and in how we interpret data.

Pages: 98-99
Topic: Psychosocial Causal Factors: Early Deprivation or Trauma
Skill: Factual   Other1:
16. Name two protective factors that influence later outcome in a child who has experienced early parental deprivation.
Answer: An improvement in the care-giving environment; good experiences at school (social, academic, athletic); institutionalization later rather than earlier in childhood in a child who has already had good attachment experiences; going from an institution into a harmonious family environment.

Pages: 102
Topic: Psychosocial Causal Factors: Inadequate Parenting
Skill: Factual   Other1:
17. The _____ style of parenting is high in warmth, careful to set limits concerning acceptable behavior, but also allows considerable freedom within those limits.
Answer: authoritative

Pages: 105-106
Topic: Psychosocial Causal Factors: Maladaptive Peer Relationships
Skill: Factual   Other1:
18. What are the major features associated with children who are rejected by their peers?
    Answer: Rejected children are typically overly aggressive, excessively demanding, and
              too ready to take offense.

Pages: 112
Topic: Sociocultural Causal Factors: Pathogenic Societal Influences
Skill: Factual   Other1:
19. The sociocultural perspective suggests that certain social roles may prescribe deviant
    behaviors, or may produce maladaptive reactions. One example of a psychological disorder
    that is associated with a difficult social role is _____.
    Answer: depression or anxiety in women

Pages: 114
Topic: Issues on Theoretical Viewpoints/Causation of Abnormal Behavior
Skill: Factual   Other1:
20. Briefly describe the biopsychosocial model of abnormal behavior.
    Answer: This theoretical perspective highlights the importance of the interaction of
             biological, psychosocial, and sociocultural factors in the development of
             psychopathology.

Essay

Write your answer in the space provided or on a separate sheet of paper.

Pages: 65-67
Topic: What Causes Abnormal Behavior?
Skill: Applied   Other1:
1. What is a diathesis-stress model of psychopathology? Give an example of a disorder
   conceptualized from this perspective, including a description of the proposed diathesis
   and stressor giving rise to the disorder.
   Answer: This model conceptualizes many mental disorders as resulting from stressors
            interacting with pre-existing vulnerability factors that are associated with a
            given disorder. The vulnerability may be biological, psychosocial, or
            sociocultural in nature, and is a more distal necessary or contributory cause.
            By itself, however, it is not sufficient to cause the disorder; more proximal
            contributory or necessary causes impinge upon an individual at risk, resulting
            in the development of a disorder. Example: depressogenic attributional style
            (diathesis), and failure on an exam (stressor).

Pages: 69-73
Topic: Biological Causal Factors: Genetic Defects
Skill: Applied   Other1:

2. Design a study to test the following hypothesis: genetic endowment is a causal factor in the etiology of clinical depression. Describe the methodology you would use, the control group(s), and what you would expect to find if the hypothesis is true.

    Answer: Using a family history (pedigree) design, clinical depressives would serve as probands with nondepressives as controls. There should be a higher rate of depression among relatives of depressed probands than among relatives of controls. In a twin study, the concordance rate for depression in monozygotic twins should be higher than in dizygotic twins. In an adoption study, the rate of depression in biological relatives of adult depressives who had been adopted as children should be higher than the rate of depression in the adoptive relatives.

Pages: 79-82
Topic: Psychosocial Viewpoints: The Psychodynamic Perspectives
Skill: Conceptual   Other1:

3. Charlotte suffers from intense anxiety. How would Freud explain this anxiety? In your answer, describe the different parts of the personality from a Freudian perspective, and how these parts of personality interact to produce anxiety.

    Answer: Freud suggests that behavior results from interaction of three subsystems in personality: id, ego, and superego. Each should be described. Inner (intrapsychic) conflicts arise when these three make incompatible demands on the individual. Freud suggests three types of anxiety: reality, neurotic, and moral anxiety. Reality anxiety arises from external threats, neurotic anxiety from the threat of the id's unconscious impulses breaking through ego controls, and moral anxiety from action in conflict with the superego. The ego handles anxiety either rationally or with ego-defense mechanisms.

Pages: 84
Topic: Psychosocial Viewpoints: The Behavioral Perspective
Skill: Conceptual   Other1:

4. The behavioral viewpoint suggests that classical and operant conditioning are the major principles involved in abnormal behavior. What are these principles, and how are they involved in abnormal behavior? Give an example.

    Answer: In classical conditioning, a previously neutral stimulus (CS) is presented repeatedly preceding an unconditioned stimulus until the CS acquires the capacity to elicit the desired response. In operant conditioning, the individual learns to achieve a desired goal via reinforcement (the delivery of a reward or escape from an aversive stimulus). Behaviorists view both adaptive and maladaptive behavior as patterns learned according to these principles, and apply techniques derived from learning theory to change maladaptive behavior. Give example (e.g., snake phobia after snakebite).

Pages: 87-89
Topic: Psychosocial Viewpoints: The Cognitive-Behavioral Perspective
Skill: Conceptual   Other1:
5. What are the basic ideas behind the cognitive-behavioral approach? Compare this approach with the psychodynamic and behavioral viewpoints.
    Answer: The cognitive approach focuses on how basic information processing and higher-order cognitive processes can become distorted, resulting in the development and maintenance of maladaptive emotions and behaviors. Different patterns of distorted information processing can be associated with different forms of psychopathology. Like psychodynamic theory, mental products and processes are considered valid areas of scientific inquiry and therapeutic treatment. Like the behavioral approach, therapy focuses on present thoughts and behaviors rather than on underlying intrapsychic conflicts.

Pages: 89-92
Topic: Psychosocial Viewpoints: The Humanistic Perspective
Skill: Factual   Other1:
6. Discuss the assumptions of the humanistic and existential perspectives.
    Answer: Freedom for self-definition and self-direction is a primary human experience and, thus, people are fundamentally responsible for creating a meaningful and constructive life. Abnormal behavior is related to disturbances in the process of personal growth, in the quest for meaning and value, and in self-actualization. Humanistic therapy is directed at removing the blocks to growth and self-actualization. These blocks may include the exaggerated use of self-defense mechanisms, unfavorable social conditions, inauthenticity, and excessive stress.

Pages: 92-95
Topic: Psychosocial Viewpoints: The Interpersonal Perspective
Skill: Factual   Other1:
7. Describe the fundamental principles of the interpersonal perspective on psychopathology and interpersonal therapy for mental disorders.
    Answer: The interpersonal perspective suggests that much psychopathology is rooted in difficulties individuals have in their past and present interpersonal relationships. Psychopathology in turn has a negative impact on present and future relationships. Therapy focuses on analyzing past and present relationships to alleviate problem-causing factors and enhance satisfaction in relationships. This focus includes verbal and nonverbal communication, social roles, accomodation and attribution processes, social skills training, and social exchange. May include discussion of Erikson, Sullivan, and others.

Pages: 83-95
Topic: Psychosocial Viewpoints: The Psychodynamic Perspectives
Skill: Conceptual   Other1:

8. Describe the criticisms leveled at the psychoanalytic perspective by adherents to the behavioral and interpersonal perspectives. In addition, from your own perspective, evaluate the merits of these criticisms.

     Answer: Behaviorists argue that psychoanalytic theory does not meet the criteria of a true scientific theory because its data and theoretical assertions are not empirically observable and independently verifiable. Interpersonal psychologists disagree with the psychoanalytic emphasis on early development through gratification of sexual impulses, as well as with the emphasis placed on intrapsychic conflicts as sources of maladaptive behavior. The student should evaluate these criticisms.

Pages: 106-110
Topic: Sociocultural Viewpoint
Skill: Conceptual   Other1:

9. Within our diagnostic system, we tend to overlook the sociocultural viewpoint. What is this viewpoint? What evidence supports or refutes it?

     Answer: The sociocultural viewpoint suggests that social, cultural, and economic conditions affect the rates and expression of psychopathology. Evidence supporting this view comes from the fact that psychopathology is found more often in the lower socioeconomic class and that cross-cultural studies show that individuals with the same disorders may express them differently. Evidence refuting this explanation comes from the fact that certain disorders tend to be found universally.

Pages: 67-95
Topic: Models or Viewpoints For Understanding Abnormal Behavior
Skill: Conceptual   Other1:

10. Provide an example of a paradigm shift that has occurred in the field of psychopathology. In doing so, also describe the essential characteristics of a paradigm shift.

     Answer: Until fairly recently, clinical psychology was dominated by the psychoanalytic paradigm. This paradigm defined the nature of psychopathology and set the parameters for investigations into the etiology of mental disorders, as well as the type of treatments available. Gradually criticisms of psychoanalytic theory and alternative explanations for the nature, origins, and treatment of abnormal behavior were offered by behaviorists, cognitive-behaviorists, and biopsychologists. These new insights constitute paradigm shifts, fundamental reorganizations of how people think about the entire field.

Pages: 67-95
Topic: Integration of Viewpoints
Skill: Conceptual   Other1:

11. The text discussed a variety of theoretical perspectives on abnormal behavior including biological, psychodynamic, behavioral, humanistic, and interpersonal. Using clinical depression as an example, describe how three of these different theoretical perspectives would define depression, the kinds of causal factors they would focus on in exploring the etiology of depression, and the kind of treatment each would prescribe for an individual suffering from clinical depression.

    Answer: Biological: a defect in physiological structure or function caused by biochemical, hormonal, genetic, or other physical factors. Treatment would be directed at correcting biological malfunction. Psychodynamic: depression is a manifestation of unconscious intrapsychic conflict and inadequate psychosexual development. Make conflicts conscious to handle rationally. Behavioral: maladaptive learned pattern of behavior is the focus of treatment. Humanistic: focus on growth and self-actualization. Interpersonal: analyze past and present relationships for dysfunction, seen as causal.

Pages: 102-103
Topic: Psychosocial Causal Factors: Inadequate Parenting
Skill: Factual   Other1:

12. Describe the four different types of parenting styles described in the text. In addition, discuss the developmental outcome associated with each type of parenting style.

    Answer: Authoritarian style: low in warmth and high in control. The children tend to be conflicted and irritable, overly aggressive if severe punishment is used, with a negative outcome in adolescence, especially for boys. Permissive-indulgent style: parents are high in warmth but low in control. Children are aggressive, impulsive, spoiled, exploitive. Neglecting-uninvolved style: parents are low in warmth and control. Disrupted attachment, low self-esteem, poor peer relations, conduct problems. Authoritative: high in warmth, set clear but moderate limits. Most positive social and general outcome.

Pages: 98-100
Topic: Psychosocial Causal Factors: Early Deprivation or Trauma
Skill: Factual   Other1:

13. Discuss the effects often seen among children and adults who have experienced deprivation, neglect, and abuse in infancy and childhood.

    Answer: Institutionalization is associated with poor attachment, retarded speech and language development, apathy, and poor personality development. Rejection and deprivation are associated with "failure to thrive" syndrome. Abuse may lead to aggressive, impulsive behavior; social, emotional and linguistic impairment; bizarre and disrupted attachment to mother; and poor organization of self. Childhood abuse predicts violence in adolescence and adulthood (especially in men); and in women, self-injurious and suicidal behavior, depression, and anxiety.

Pages: 114-115
Topic: Issues on Theoretical Viewpoints/Causation of Abnormal Behavior
Skill: Applied   Other1:
14. Describe the biopsychosocial model of psychopathology. Give an example of how it would characterize a particular disorder like alcoholism.
    Answer: This is an attempt at integrating diverse theoretical viewpoints into a unified model which acknowledges the interaction of biological, psychosocial, and sociocultural causal factors in the etiology and treatment of mental disorders. This model emphasizes that many causal factors may be involved in a disorder, and a given combination of causal factors may be unique to a given individual or a subset of individuals who share the disorder. Alcoholism may result from a genetic vulnerability and early deprivation experiences with alcoholic parents interacting with later stressors.

Pages: 68-95
Topic: Integration of Viewpoints
Skill: Conceptual   Other1:
15. The various perspectives regarding abnormal behavior have all had an important impact on the field. Describe a major contribution of four of the seven major viewpoints.
    Answer: Biological: biochemical factors, genetic transmission, drug therapies. Psychodynamic: emphasis on importance of some early experiences, notion of the unconscious. Behavioral and Cognitive: therapeutic techniques, attention to scientific rigor in testing theory and efficacy of therapies. Humanistic: emphasis on human potential and growth. Interpersonal: emphasis on the important role relationships play in psychopathology. Sociocultural: focus on role of economic and cultural influences in development and expression of disorders.

CHAPTER 4 Stress and Adjustment Disorders

Multiple-Choice

Choose the one alternative that best completes the statement or answers the question.

Pages: 119
Topic: Stress and Adjustment Disorders
Skill: Factual   Other1:
1. The impact that a stressful event will have on an individual depends on
    A) the severity of the stressor.
    B) whether or not it is a psychosocial event.
    C) the individual's preexisting vulnerabilities.
    D) A and C
    Answer: D

Pages: 119
Topic: Stress and Adjustment Disorders
Skill: Factual   Other1:
2. According to a diathesis-stress model of mental disorder, stressors interact with _____
    to cause the occurrence of a disorder.
    A) precipitating factors
    B) predisposing factors
    C) preexisting factors
    D) intrapsychic conflictual factors
    Answer: B

Pages: 119
Topic: Stress and Stressors
Skill: Factual   Other1:
3. When conditions of overwhelming stress occur, a previously stable person will usually
    A) not be affected by the stress in any way.
    B) show a temporary reaction to the stress.
    C) experience a sudden, rather than a gradual, breakdown in adaptive functioning.
    D) not even recognize the stressor.
    Answer: B

Pages: 120
Topic: Stress and Stressors
Skill: Factual   Other1:
4. What relationship do stress and coping have with one another?
   A) They are interrelated and interdependent.
   B) They are independent.
   C) They are mutually exclusive.
   D) Coping results from stress.
   Answer: A

Pages: 120
Topic: Stress and Stressors
Skill: Factual   Other1:
5. Which of the following is true concerning stress?
   A) Both distress and eustress tax an individual's coping skills, although eustress is usually more damaging.
   B) Both distress and eustress tax an individual's coping skills, although distress is usually more damaging.
   C) Both distress and eustress are equally damaging.
   D) Neither distress nor eustress are potentially damaging to an individual.
   Answer: B

Pages: 120
Topic: Stress and Stressors: Categories of Stressors
Skill: Factual   Other1:
6. The three basic categories of stressors described in the text are
   A) frustrations, obstacles, and distress.
   B) frustrations, obstacles, and demands.
   C) frustrations, conflicts, and pressures.
   D) conflicts, pressures, and obstacles.
   Answer: C

Pages: 120
Topic: Stress and Stressors: Categories of Stressors
Skill: Applied   Other1:
7. Eartha is frustrated because she is not able to achieve her goals. If she is like most people, frustration can be particularly difficult for her to cope with because
   A) people become frustrated primarily when they set low goals instead of high goals.
   B) the fact that she became frustrated shows that she has few coping skills.
   C) frustration typically leads to depression.
   D) frustration often leads to self-devaluation.
   Answer: D

Pages: 120
Topic: Stress and Stressors: Categories of Stressors
Skill: Applied   Other1:
8. Rivkah wants to pursue a career in medicine, but lives far from the nearest medical school. If she moves to a larger (and more expensive) university town, however, she would have to adopt a much lower standard-of-living for herself and her children. Rivkah faces a(n) _____ conflict.
    A) approach-avoidance
    B) double-approach
    C) external
    D) double-avoidance
    Answer: A

Pages: 121
Topic: Stress and Stressors: Categories of Stressors
Skill: Applied   Other1:
9. Joe has been accepted into a graduate program at two different schools. He wants to attend both of them but, of course, can select only one. Joe faces a(n) _____ conflict.
    A) double-approach
    B) double-external
    C) double-avoidance
    D) approach-avoidance
    Answer: A

Pages: 121
Topic: Stress and Stressors: Categories of Stressors
Skill: Applied   Other1:
10. John has a strong desire to get into graduate school. Soon he will take the Graduate Record Exam (GRE). John is probably experiencing a considerable amount of
    A) strain.
    B) frustration.
    C) conflict.
    D) pressure.
    Answer: D

Pages: 121
Topic: Stress and Stressors: Categories of Stressors
Skill: Factual   Other1:
11. In a study on stress and coping, individuals were assessed for maladaptive behavior and anxiety on the seventeen days preceding and following a career-determining exam. Which of the following statements is true?
    A) Individuals with maladaptive coping strategies were actually less anxious overall than individuals who used more adaptive coping strategies.
    B) Individuals using maladaptive coping strategies showed greater anxiety and maladaptive behavior under high stress, but actually performed better on the exam than those with adaptive coping strategies.
    C) Both groups were similar in both anxiety level and test performance.
    D) Individuals using maladaptive coping strategies experienced more anxiety but were similar in test performance compared to individuals with adaptive coping strategies.
    Answer: D

Pages: 121
Topic: Stress and Stressors: Categories of Stressors
Skill: Factual   Other1:
12. Which of the following statements is true?
    A) Some occupations have such high levels of stress that they put individuals at risk for heart disease.
    B) While some occupations are extremely stressful, they appear to have little impact on physical health.
    C) As of yet there is no clear association between type of occupation and coronary heart disease.
    D) There is apparently less coronary heart disease today than in earlier centuries.
    Answer: A

Pages: 122-123
Topic: Stress and Stressors: Factors Predisposing a Person to Stress
Skill: Conceptual   Other1:
13. The extent to which a stressor disrupts functioning is determined by
    A) chance factors.
    B) the characteristics of the stressor.
    C) the resources of the person experiencing the stress.
    D) B and C
    Answer: D

Pages: 122
Topic: Stress and Stressors: Factors Predisposing a Person to Stress
Skill: Factual   Other1:
14. Which of the following is true about stressors?
    A) Stressors that involve important aspects of an individual's life tend to be highly
       stressful for most people.
    B) The less time a stressor operates, the more severe its effects.
    C) Temporary fatigue actually imposes more intense stress than does prolonged exhaustion.
    D) Stressors typically are discrete and do not have a cumulative effect.
    Answer: A

Pages: 123
Topic: Stress and Stressors: Factors Predisposing a Person to Stress
Skill: Factual   Other1:
15. A situation is most likely to be experienced as stressful if
    A) the resources for dealing with the situation are inadequate, regardless of the
       individual's perception.
    B) the individual has low self-esteem but has the ability to cope with the situation.
    C) the person perceives the situation to be threatening, regardless of whether it really
       is.
    D) the person perceives the situation to be threatening, but only if it actually is.
    Answer: C

Pages: 123
Topic: Stress and Stressors: Factors Predisposing a Person to Stress
Skill: Applied   Other1:
16. Tom is facing major surgery. To help him cope with the stress, his doctors should
    A) give him realistic information about it and as much control over the circumstances as
       possible.
    B) tell him only the most optimistic aspects of the surgery and outcome to avoid a
       negative self-fulfilling prophecy.
    C) spare him from having to make any decisions about his treatment.
    D) tell him as little as possible.
    Answer: A

Pages: 123
Topic: Stress and Stressors: Factors Predisposing a Person to Stress
Skill: Factual   Other1:
17. To deal more effectively with a stressful event, it is important to
    A) give up any sense of control over the situation and simply not worry about it.
    B) try to ignore the upcoming event as much as possible.
    C) know how long the stressor will last, even if this is a long time.
    D) have optimistic expectations of the event even if these expectations are unrealistic.
    Answer: C

Pages: 124
Topic: Stress and Stressors: Factors Predisposing a Person to Stress
Skill: Factual   Other1:
18. Follow-up assessments of Chernobyl employees after the nuclear reactor accident found
    A) short-term increases in symptoms of stress, but a return to normal after 20 months.
    B) significant increases in physical stress symptoms but no increase in psychological problems.
    C) a significant increase in both physical and psychosocial problems.
    D) no differences in the stress symptom profiles between Chernobyl survivors and employees of other Russian nuclear plants.
    Answer: C

Pages: 123
Topic: Stress and Stressors: Factors Predisposing a Person to Stress
Skill: Factual   Other1:
19. Stress tolerance refers to
    A) the network of family and social supports available to an individual faced with stressors.
    B) a person's ability to withstand stress without becoming seriously impaired.
    C) the ability to not be affected at all by stressors, not even the most traumatic.
    D) none of the above
    Answer: B

Pages: 123
Topic: Stress and Stressors: Factors Predisposing a Person to Stress
Skill: Factual   Other1:
20. Which of the following statements is FALSE?
    A) Positive social and family relationships can have a moderating effect on stress, illness, and early death.
    B) Different people are vulnerable to different stressors.
    C) Problems faced by other family members usually have little impact on an individual's own stress level.
    D) People vary greatly in biological and psychological vulnerability to stressors.
    Answer: C

Pages: 123
Topic: Stress and Stressors: Factors Predisposing a Person to Stress
Skill: Factual   Other1:
21. In a recent study conducted in mainland China, people reported that the most common stressor they experienced in daily life was
    A) the death of a spouse.
    B) the birth of a daughter rather than a son.
    C) difficulty in interpersonal relationships.
    D) divorce.
    Answer: C

Pages: 123
Topic: Stress and Stressors: Factors Predisposing a Person to Stress
Skill: Applied   Other1:
22. Bill's wife died a few months ago. Bill is more likely to experience psychological problems if
    A) he thinks a lot about the positive experiences they shared together.
    B) he lacks external supports.
    C) he continues to put the same amount of effort into his job.
    D) he seeks out social support from family members.
    Answer: B

Pages: 123
Topic: Stress and Stressors: Factors Predisposing a Person to Stress
Skill: Applied   Other1:
23. Both Emily and Elmer have had their spouses die in the past year. This is likely to be hardest on
    A) Emily.
    B) Elmer.
    C) both, as there is no difference between men and women.
    D) whoever was married the longest.
    Answer: B

Pages: 124
Topic: Stress and Stressors: Factors Predisposing a Person to Stress
Skill: Factual   Other1:
24. One of the reasons that crises are often especially stressful is
    A) their long duration.
    B) some people do not have social support systems.
    C) the coping techniques that people usually use are not likely to work.
    D) people tend to expect the worst, which becomes a self-fulfilling prophecy.
    Answer: C

Pages: 125
Topic: Stress and Stressors: Factors Predisposing a Person to Stress
Skill: Factual   Other1:
25. Crisis intervention has become an important tool in treatment because
    A) there is much sound research about the impact of life changes indicating that crisis intervention is helpful.
    B) the outcome of a crisis has a great impact on a person's subsequent adjustment.
    C) the rate of suicide in individuals experiencing crisis is extraordinarily high.
    D) individuals do not know how to use their usual coping strategies when confronted with crisis situations.
    Answer: B

Pages: 125
Topic: Stress and Stressors: Factors Predisposing a Person to Stress
Skill: Conceptual   Other1:
26. Research examining the relationship between life stressors and possible physical and mental disorder has
   A) showed conclusively that life stressors result in increased physical, but not mental, disorders.
   B) showed conclusively that life stressors result in increased mental, but not physical, disorders.
   C) showed conclusively that life stressors result in increased mental and physical disorders.
   D) been criticized because of numerous methodological problems.
   Answer: D

Pages: 125
Topic: Stress and Stressors: Factors Predisposing a Person to Stress
Skill: Factual   Other1:
27. A recent improvement in assessing significant life events involves using a semi-structured interview instead of the questionnaires previously used in life stress studies. How is this an improvement over the older method?
   A) The ratings obtained by the interviews are more reliable.
   B) The interview assesses the meaning that the event has to the individual.
   C) Life event rating variables are placed in a clearly defined and specific context.
   D) all of the above
   Answer: D

Pages: 126
Topic: Coping Strategies
Skill: Factual   Other1:
28. Recent research has found which of the following to be true concerning the relationship between cognitions and stressful events?
   A) Stressful events often cause cognitions to become distorted.
   B) People who have disordered cognitions actually have experienced fewer and less severe life stressors than others, which is one reason their cognitions are, in fact, distorted.
   C) People may actually produce stressful life events by virtue of the kinds of cognitions that they have.
   D) People who are depressed or anxious tend to perceive fewer external situations as stressful because of self-preoccupation.
   Answer: C

Pages: 126-127
Topic: Coping Strategies: General Principles of Coping With Stress
Skill: Conceptual   Other1:
29. What is the relationship between the three interactional levels of defense against stress?
    A) Biological defenses are fundamental to the defenses of the other two levels, but the reverse is not true.
    B) Vulnerability in an individual's sociocultural defenses is less important than in an individual's psychological or biological defenses.
    C) Coping failure on any one of these levels may seriously increase an individual's vulnerability on the other levels.
    D) Biological and psychological defenses impact on one another, but sociocultural defenses operate relatively independently.
    Answer: C

Pages: 127
Topic: Coping Strategies: General Principles of Coping With Stress
Skill: Factual   Other1: In Student Study Guide
30. When we are faced with a stressor, we need to do two things. One thing is meet the requirements of the stressor, and the other is to
    A) protect the self from damage and disorganization.
    B) change the way we think about the problem.
    C) protect the self from defense-oriented response.
    D) make sure that we do not face a stressor again.
    Answer: A

Pages: 127
Topic: Coping Strategies: General Principles of Coping With Stress
Skill: Factual   Other1:
31. A major difference between task-oriented and defense-oriented coping strategies is
    A) how much prior experience a person has had in dealing with a particular stressor.
    B) how competent or inadequate a person feels about handling a particular stressor.
    C) that men tend to use task-oriented strategies while women tend to use defense-oriented strategies.
    D) that task-oriented strategies are directed toward external situations whereas defense-oriented strategies are directed internally.
    Answer: B

Pages: 127
Topic: Coping Strategies: General Principles of Coping With Stress
Skill: Conceptual   Other1:
32. A task-oriented response helps a person to _____ , whereas a defense-oriented response helps a person to _____ .
    A) meet the requirements of stressors; protect the self from psychological damage
    B) retreat from a problem; approach a problem
    C) attack a problem and never retreat from it; retreat from the problem
    D) protect the id; protect the ego
    Answer: A

Pages: 127
Topic: Coping Strategies: General Principles of Coping With Stress
Skill: Factual   Other1:
33. Crying, repetitive talking, and mourning are examples of
    A) defense-oriented responses.
    B) ego-defense mechanisms.
    C) pathological reactions to stress.
    D) typical posttraumatic stress symptoms.
    Answer: A

Pages: 127
Topic: Coping Strategies: General Principles of Coping With Stress
Skill: Conceptual   Other1:
34. Denial and repression are
    A) defense-oriented strategies used to protect the self from internal or external stressors.
    B) examples of maladaptive behaviors.
    C) task-oriented strategies by which an individual changes his or her internal cognitive situation.
    D) all of the above
    Answer: A

Pages: 128
Topic: Coping Strategies: Decompensation Under Excessive Stress
Skill: Factual   Other1:
35. A serious breakdown in adaptive functioning is called
    A) an alarm reaction.
    B) resistance.
    C) decompensation.
    D) a defense-oriented response.
    Answer: C

36. Adam was a fourth-year medical student who had been struggling for years to keep up with his school work. After a particularly grueling exam, he began to experience feelings of unreality and to hear voices telling him to jump out of the window. This is an example of
    A) a defense-oriented response.
    B) denial.
    C) regression.
    D) decompensation.
    Answer: D

37. The perception of an internal or external threat may be associated with
    A) increased rigidity of cognitive processes, with a resulting inability to see available alternatives.
    B) perceptual overload as the perceptual field expands to include more sensory information than an individual can process.
    C) a rallying of immunological defenses with a resulting heightened ability to ward off invaders.
    D) increased cognitive flexibility.
    Answer: A

38. Selye suggested that experiments examining stress on animals have shown that
    A) defense mechanisms are not helpful in limiting the effects of stress.
    B) after even a very stressful experience, rest can be completely restorative.
    C) each exposure to stress takes its toll and has its impact.
    D) prolonged stress leads to pathological insensitivity to stressors rather than to pathological overresponsiveness.
    Answer: C

Topic: Coping Strategies: Decompensation Under Excessive Stress
Skill: Factual   Other1:
39. It appears that an organism's coping resources are limited. One consequence of this is that
    A) prolonged psychological stress can lead to biological impairment, and vice versa.
    B) an organism requires regular rest periods in order to fully restore its adaptive resources.
    C) prolonged stress results in pathological underresponsiveness rather than in overresponsiveness.
    D) an organism must select the defense mechanisms that are the most effective in repairing emotional damage to the organism.
    Answer: A

Pages: 128
Topic: Coping Strategies: Decompensation Under Excessive Stress
Skill: Factual   Other1:
40. Five years after the nuclear accident at Three Mile Island, residents
    A) had finally recovered from the effects of stress.
    B) had recovered physiologically although they continued to have psychological problems.
    C) showed both physiological and psychological symptoms of high stress.
    D) continued to experience ever greater increases in their stressful responses.
    Answer: C

Pages: 128
Topic: Coping Strategies: Decompensation Under Excessive Stress
Skill: Factual   Other1:
41. According to Selye's general adaptation syndrome, when first confronted by a stressor the body will
    A) be at a resting state of biological adaptation.
    B) call up maintenance mechanisms to ward off damage.
    C) respond with an alarm reaction by activating the autonomic nervous system.
    D) ignore it unless it persists.
    Answer: C

Pages: 128
Topic: Coping Strategies: Decompensation Under Excessive Stress
Skill: Factual   Other1:
42. According to Selye's general adaptation syndrome, biological adaptation is at its maximum level of resources used during the _____ stage.
    A) alarm reaction
    B) resistance
    C) exhaustion
    D) decompensation
    Answer: B

Pages: 128
Topic: Coping Strategies: Decompensation Under Excessive Stress
Skill: Factual   Other1:
43. According to Selye's general adaptation syndrome, the final stage of the body's reaction to sustained stress involves
   A) complete psychological decompensation.
   B) depletion of adaptive resources.
   C) recovery to normal levels of functioning.
   D) organic damage such as heart disease or cancer.
   Answer: B

Pages: 129
Topic: Coping Strategies: Decompensation Under Excessive Stress
Skill: Factual   Other1:
44. Once a severe stressor has ceased, according to Selye's general adaptation syndrome, maintenance mechanisms begin to repair damage and reorganize normal functioning. Which of the following statements is true?
   A) With enough time, an organism usually returns to its previous level of functioning.
   B) An individual is more apt to recover completely from physiological damage than from psychological damage.
   C) A permanent lowering of the prior level of integration and functioning may occur.
   D) An individual is more likely to recover from psychological damage than from physiological damage.
   Answer: C

Pages: 129
Topic: Coping Strategies: Decompensation Under Excessive Stress
Skill: Conceptual   Other1:
45. Biological and psychological decompensation
   A) differ in that psychological decompensation follows a much more variable course than biological decompensation.
   B) differ in that biological decompensation usually involves much more severe and long lasting impairment.
   C) are similar in the course that each tends to follow.
   D) are similar in that both end with an alarm reaction by the autonomic nervous system.
   Answer: C

Pages: 130
Topic: Coping Strategies: Decompensation Under Excessive Stress
Skill: Factual   Other1:
46. According to Selye's general adaptation syndrome, which of the following might we expect
    to see in an individual as the stage of exhaustion begins?
    A) the use of new and untried ego-defense mechanisms
    B) a shift from task-oriented to defense-oriented coping strategies
    C) the appearance of symptoms of maladjustment
    D) delusions and/or hallucinations
    Answer: D

Pages: 130
Topic: Coping Strategies: Decompensation Under Excessive Stress
Skill: Factual   Other1:
47. Recent studies have found that severe stress
    A) has little apparent causal effect on organic diseases like cancer and heart disease.
    B) can influence brain structure and function, especially in young children.
    C) is often offset by the release of endogenous opiates.
    D) may actually result in a temporary boost in immune system functioning.
    Answer: B

Pages: 130-131
Topic: Coping Strategies: Decompensation Under Excessive Stress
Skill: Factual   Other1:
48. Sustained exposure to stress results in
    A) the release of norepinephrine from noradrenergic brain systems.
    B) elevated cortisol levels.
    C) a reduction in an organism's immunity to disease.
    D) all of the above
    Answer: D

Pages: 131
Topic: Adjustment Disorder: Reactions to Common Life Stressors
Skill: Conceptual   Other1:
49. Stress resulting from situations or events that are out of our control may
    A) increase immune system functioning by activating the fight or flight response.
    B) increase immune system functioning by activating task-oriented responses.
    C) decrease immune system functioning by increasing the release of endorphins.
    D) decrease immune system functioning, although the mechanisms by which this comes about
       are not clear.
    Answer: D

Pages: 131
Topic: Adjustment Disorder: Reactions to Common Life Stressors
Skill: Factual   Other1:

50. What role do stressors play in the DSM-IV?
    A) They are included in diagnostic formulations.
    B) They are included on Axis III as a medically-related condition.
    C) They are not included in diagnostic formulations.
    D) They are considered for only a few Axis I disorders.
    Answer: A

Pages: 131
Topic: Adjustment Disorder: Reactions to Common Life Stressors
Skill: Applied   Other1:

51. Bill lost his job last month and has been unable to function as usual. He would be
    diagnosed as having a(n)
    A) anxiety disorder.
    B) acute stress disorder.
    C) posttraumatic stress disorder.
    D) adjustment disorder.
    Answer: D

Pages: 131
Topic: Adjustment Disorder: Reactions to Common Life Stressors
Skill: Factual   Other1:

52. The mildest and least stigmatizing disorder in the DSM-IV is probably
    A) posttraumatic stress disorder.
    B) adjustment disorder.
    C) generalized anxiety disorder.
    D) acute stress disorder.
    Answer: B

Pages: 131
Topic: Adjustment Disorder: Reactions to Common Life Stressors
Skill: Factual   Other1:

53. What determines whether a person has an adjustment disorder?
    A) if the person's reaction to a stressor is excessive
    B) if the person is unable to function as usual following exposure to the stressor
    C) if the person's reaction to a stressor is maladaptive
    D) all of the above
    Answer: D

Pages: 131
Topic: Adjustment Disorder: Reactions to Common Life Stressors
Skill: Factual   Other1:
54. Axis IV in DSM-IV is especially useful for which three Axis I disorders?
    A) adjustment disorder, acute stress disorder, and posttraumatic stress disorder
    B) adjustment disorder, anxiety disorder, and posttraumatic stress disorder
    C) adjustment disorder, acute stress disorder, and depression
    D) adjustment disorder, depression, and schizophrenia
    Answer: A

Pages: 131
Topic: Adjustment Disorder: Reactions to Common Life Stressors
Skill: Applied   Other1:
55. Darrell has been diagnosed with an adjustment disorder. This would suggest that
    A) the disorder is likely to become a permanent condition.
    B) Darrell's maladjustment will lessen once the stressor has subsided.
    C) Darrell's condition is likely to be resistant to psychotherapy.
    D) the disorder may go into remission, but is likely to reappear a few years later.
    Answer: B

Pages: 131
Topic: Adjustment Disorder: Reactions to Common Life Stressors
Skill: Factual   Other1:
56. What does DSM-IV say about the duration of an adjustment disorder?
    A) It has no particular duration.
    B) If it persists longer than six months, the diagnosis should be changed to some other
       mental disorder.
    C) It lasts a maximum of four weeks.
    D) If it lasts longer than one year, the diagnosis was wrong and a different diagnosis
       should be given.
    Answer: B

Pages: 132
Topic: Adjustment Disorder: Stress From Unemployment
Skill: Conceptual   Other1:
57. Which of the following statements is NOT true?
    A) While potentially debilitating in the short run, unemployment is not associated with
       serious long-term psychological consequences.
    B) Unemployment rates among young black men are over 50 percent.
    C) Employee-based intervention programs have been successful in promoting more effective
       coping strategies for unemployed individuals.
    D) The lower socioeconomic segment of society contributes disproportionately high numbers
       to both unemployment figures and mental hospitals.
    Answer: A

Pages: 133
Topic: Adjustment Disorder: Stress From Bereavement
Skill: Factual   Other1:
58. A normal grieving process lasts no longer than about
    A) four months.
    B) one year.
    C) three years.
    D) There is no particular length of time that a normal grieving period should last.
    Answer: B

Pages: 133
Topic: Adjustment Disorder: Stress From Bereavement
Skill: Factual   Other1:
59. Which of the following situations is NOT typically associated with a complicated or prolonged bereavement?
    A) an untimely or unexpected death
    B) when an individual strongly disliked or resented the deceased
    C) when an individual has had prior emotional problems
    D) the expected death of a spouse after many years of marital happiness
    Answer: D

Pages: 134
Topic: Adjustment Disorder: Stress From Divorce or Separation
Skill: Factual   Other1:
60. Divorce and separation
    A) are rarely associated with psychological problems.
    B) are only stressful for people who have preexisting psychological problems.
    C) are markedly overrepresented among people with psychological problems.
    D) are often associated with posttraumatic stress disorder.
    Answer: C

Pages: 135
Topic: Acute Stress/Posttraumatic Stress Disorder: Severe Life Stressors
Skill: Factual   Other1:
61. Acute and posttraumatic stress disorders differ in
    A) the duration of illness.
    B) the severity of the stressor preceding onset of the disorder.
    C) the presence of depression and social withdrawal.
    D) all of the above
    Answer: A

Pages: 131
Topic: Acute Stress/Posttraumatic Stress Disorder: Severe Life Stressors
Skill: Applied   Other1:
62. Harry's mother was killed in an automobile accident when he was a child. When his wife left him as an adult, he refused to leave the house for weeks at a time. Harry might be diagnosed with
    A) acute stress disorder.
    B) posttraumatic stress disorder.
    C) adjustment disorder.
    D) delayed stress disorder.
    Answer: C

Pages: 134
Topic: Acute Stress/Posttraumatic Stress Disorder: Severe Life Stressors
Skill: Factual   Other1:
63. To be diagnosed as having posttraumatic stress disorder, the individual must
    A) be afraid of the situation that originally caused the problem, even if the person does not avoid this situation.
    B) have repressed the situation that originally brought on the anxiety.
    C) have experienced a stressor that is unusually severe and psychologically traumatic.
    D) suffer a depersonalization experience in addition to the anxiety.
    Answer: C

Pages: 135
Topic: Acute Stress/Posttraumatic Stress Disorder: Severe Life Stressors
Skill: Factual   Other1:
64. All of the following are symptoms of posttraumatic stress disorder EXCEPT
    A) increased physiological arousal.
    B) increased sexual arousal.
    C) persistent avoidance of stimuli associated with the trauma.
    D) impaired concentration and memory.
    Answer: B

Pages: 135
Topic: Acute Stress/Posttraumatic Stress Disorder: Severe Life Stressors
Skill: Factual   Other1:
65. Acute stress disorder and posttraumatic stress disorder are categorized under which section of the DSM-IV?
    A) stress disorders
    B) depressive (mood) disorders
    C) anxiety disorders
    D) adjustment disorders
    Answer: C

Pages: 135
Topic: Acute Stress/Posttraumatic Stress Disorder: Severe Life Stressors
Skill: Factual   Other1:
66. If symptoms last for six weeks following a life-threatening traumatic event, the diagnosis is
    A) acute stress disorder.
    B) adjustment disorder.
    C) posttraumatic stress disorder.
    D) disaster syndrome, short duration.
    Answer: C

Pages: 135
Topic: Acute Stress/Posttraumatic Stress Disorder: Severe Life Stressors
Skill: Conceptual   Other1:
67. The most difficult disorder to diagnose accurately may be
    A) acute posttraumatic stress disorder.
    B) acute stress disorder.
    C) disaster syndrome.
    D) delayed posttraumatic stress disorder.
    Answer: D

Pages: 135-136
Topic: Acute Stress/Posttraumatic Stress Disorder: Catastrophic Events
Skill: Factual   Other1:
68. Shock, suggestibility, and recovery are three stages of _____
    A) the general adaptation syndrome.
    B) posttraumatic adjustment disorder syndrome.
    C) the disaster syndrome.
    D) the normal grieving process.
    Answer: C

Pages: 135
Topic: Acute Stress/Posttraumatic Stress Disorder: Catastrophic Events
Skill: Applied   Other1:
69. Darby has just experienced a tornado that severely damaged his home. If he is typical of most individuals with "disaster syndrome," then he will
    A) proceed through a suggestible stage, followed by a shock stage and then recovery stage.
    B) be free of anxiety and apprehension once he reaches the recovery stage.
    C) want to repetitively tell about this tornado most often in the suggestible stage.
    D) be most willing to take directions from rescue workers once he is in the suggestible stage.
    Answer: D

Pages: 136
Topic: Acute Stress/Posttraumatic Stress Disorder: Catastrophic Events
Skill: Factual   Other1:
70. Studies found that the most devastating psychological effects of Hurricane Hugo were associated with
A) the elderly.
B) young children.
C) those who experienced the most severe exposure to the hurricane.
D) B and C
Answer: D

Pages: 136
Topic: Acute Stress/Posttraumatic Stress Disorder: Catastrophic Events
Skill: Applied   Other1:
71. Anne was in a serious car accident which killed the driver of the automobile she was in. During the following weeks, Anne told the story of the accident over and over to anyone who would listen. What might a therapist say about this?
A) Anne is showing a pathological obsession with the details of the accident.
B) This is a natural and fairly typical part of Anne's recovery process.
C) Anne has posttraumatic stress disorder.
D) Anne is still in the initial shock stage.
Answer: B

Pages: 138
Topic: Acute Stress/Posttraumatic Stress Disorder: Catastrophic Events
Skill: Applied   Other1:
72. Dena was just involved in a very traumatic incident. To minimize the likelihood of her developing posttraumatic stress disorder, she should
A) receive supportive counseling immediately after the incident.
B) act as if the incident didn't occur.
C) resume her normal activities immediately.
D) avoid dwelling on and retelling the incident.
Answer: A

Pages: 137
Topic: Acute Stress/Posttraumatic Stress Disorder: Catastrophic Events
Skill: Conceptual   Other1:
73. Recurrent nightmares and the need to tell the same story about a disaster again and again appear to be
A) symptoms of pathological adjustment.
B) symptoms of acute adjustment disorder.
C) mechanisms for reducing anxiety.
D) pathological ways of coping with guilt feelings.
Answer: C

Pages: 137
Topic: Acute Stress/Posttraumatic Stress Disorder: Catastrophic Events
Skill: Factual   Other1:
74. Serious car accidents are relatively common, as are subsequent personal damage law suits. Research on traumatic reactions to car accidents indicates that personal damage law suits
    A) help people recover more quickly.
    B) prolong the recovery process.
    C) have no effect on posttraumatic symptoms.
    D) none of the above
    Answer: B

Pages: 138
Topic: Acute Stress/Posttraumatic Stress Disorder: Catastrophic Events
Skill: Factual   Other1: In Student Study Guide
75. Resnick et al. found high rates of traumatic events among women, suggesting that they are especially vulnerable to victimization. Which of the following was NOT found in their survey?
    A) One-fourth were abandoned by husbands with no support for their children.
    B) Sixty-nine percent experienced at least one type of traumatic event.
    C) One-third reported a crime such as physical or sexual assault.
    D) Over fifty percent experienced multiple incidents.
    Answer: A

Pages: 138
Topic: Acute Stress Disorder: Causal Factors in Posttraumatic Stress
Skill: Conceptual   Other1:
76. A key causal factor in all cases of posttraumatic stress appears to be
    A) low self-esteem.
    B) conditioned fear.
    C) the severity of the stressor.
    D) the number of prior traumas experienced.
    Answer: B

Pages: 138
Topic: Acute Stress Disorder: Causal Factors in Posttraumatic Stress
Skill: Conceptual   Other1:
77. Prompt psychotherapy following a traumatic event is crucial because
    A) it prevents conditioned fear from establishing itself and becoming resistant to change.
    B) it distracts the victim.
    C) the victim is in a suggestible state for only a short while following a trauma before becoming too agitated for effective treatment.
    D) none of the above
    Answer: A

Pages: 138
Topic: Acute Stress/Posttraumatic Stress Disorder: The Trauma of Rape
Skill: Factual   Other1:
78. In an "acquaintance" rape, a person is more likely to feel _____ than in the case of "stranger" rape.
    A) reluctance to seek help
    B) guilt
    C) betrayed
    D) all of the above
    Answer: D

Pages: 139
Topic: Acute Stress/Posttraumatic Stress Disorder: The Trauma of Rape
Skill: Applied   Other1:
79. Marie was raped two weeks ago. Which of the following statements is probably NOT true?
    A) She is experiencing difficulty in her social relationships.
    B) She is unable to resume normal sexual activity.
    C) She is unable to concentrate.
    D) Her anxiety is markedly diminished from the time immediately following the rape.
    Answer: D

Pages: 139
Topic: Acute Stress/Posttraumatic Stress Disorder: The Trauma of Rape
Skill: Factual   Other1:
80. Which of the following is NOT associated with poor long-term adjustment to rape?
    A) attitude and behavior of husband or boyfriend
    B) exhibiting a controlled emotional style immediately following the rape rather than venting feelings
    C) excessive self-blame
    D) prior level of psychological functioning
    Answer: B

Pages: 140
Topic: Acute Stress/Posttraumatic Stress Disorder: The Trauma of Rape
Skill: Conceptual   Other1:
81. A recent study found that causal attributions play an important role in the recovery of rape victims because
    A) women do not tend to blame themselves for the occurrence of rape.
    B) the attributions determined the severity of posttraumatic stress disorder.
    C) the attributions determined whether they felt in control of their future circumstances.
    D) they prevent an unhealthy denial from taking place.
    Answer: C

Pages: 141
Topic: Acute Stress Disorder/Posttraumatic Disorder: Trauma/Military Combat
Skill: Factual   Other1:
82. The prevalence of posttraumatic stress disorder is highest in individuals who served in which war?
   A) World War II
   B) Korean War
   C) Vietnam War
   D) There is no difference.
   Answer: C

Pages: 141-142
Topic: Acute Stress Disorder/Posttraumatic Disorder: Trauma/Military Combat
Skill: Factual   Other1:
83. A study of identical twins who served in the military during the Vietnam War found that
   A) if one twin suffered from posttraumatic stress disorder, the other also was likely to.
   B) whether or not a twin had posttraumatic stress disorder depended on whether or not he had served in southeast Asia.
   C) the twins had a significantly low rate of posttraumatic stress disorder, perhaps because of the special social support each twin was able to give one another.
   D) twins who did not serve in southeast Asia nevertheless showed symptoms of posttraumatic stress disorder if their co-twin also showed these symptoms.
   Answer: B

Pages: 142
Topic: Acute Stress Disorder/Posttraumatic Disorder: Trauma/Military Combat
Skill: Factual   Other1:
84. Which of the following statements is NOT true?
   A) The prevalence of posttraumatic stress symptoms increases with an increase in the degree of combat exposure.
   B) The symptoms of combat-related stress follow a very consistent and predictable pattern from one person to the next.
   C) Different degrees of stress symptoms are associated with different types of war trauma.
   D) Two of the most common emotional symptoms of combat stress are anger and overwhelming anxiety.
   Answer: B

Pages: 143
Topic: Acute Stress Disorder/Posttraumatic Disorder: Trauma/Military Combat
Skill: Factual   Other1: In Student Study Guide
85. Which of the following biological causes of combat stress do we know the most about?
    A) constitutional differences in sensitivity
    B) differences in temperament
    C) differences in vigor
    D) the conditions of battle that tax a soldier's stamina
    Answer: D

Pages: 144
Topic: Acute Stress Disorder/Posttraumatic Disorder: Trauma/Military Combat
Skill: Factual   Other1:
86. Individuals who are most likely to have difficulties coping with combat stress are
    A) sociopaths.
    B) those who are already accustomed to dealing with anxiety on a day-to-day basis.
    C) those who are psychologically immature.
    D) those who are psychologically well-adjusted prior to combat.
    Answer: C

Pages: 144
Topic: Acute Stress Disorder/Posttraumatic Disorder: Trauma/Military Combat
Skill: Factual   Other1:
87. Which of the following soldiers would be most likely to break down in combat? The soldier
    A) whose parents fostered self-reliance and flexibility.
    B) who sees his leaders as strong parental figures.
    C) who has had the war goals explained realistically.
    D) who believes strongly in himself and does not have much of a sense of group
       identification.
    Answer: D

Pages: 145
Topic: Acute Stress Disorder/Posttraumatic Disorder: Trauma/Military Combat
Skill: Factual   Other1:
88. Five years after serving as combat veterans
    A) many men were still reporting frequent nightmares, anger, and fears.
    B) very few of the men showed any posttraumatic stress symptoms.
    C) most of the men experienced delayed posttraumatic stress disorder.
    D) the suicide rate was still very high in this group.
    Answer: A

Pages: 145
Topic: Acute Stress Disorder/Posttraumatic Disorder: Trauma/Military Combat
Skill: Factual   Other1:

89. The increased incidence of delayed posttraumatic stress disorder
    A) is due in part to its popularity.
    B) indicates that individuals may be faking their symptoms.
    C) is related specifically to having engaged in long periods of continual combat.
    D) suggests that the delayed syndrome is worse than the acute syndrome.
    Answer: A

Pages: 145
Topic: Acute Stress/Posttraumatic Stress Disorder: Prisoner of War
Skill: Factual   Other1:

90. The immediate residual damage to Nazi concentration camp survivors was
    A) surprisingly slight given the trauma of their ordeal.
    B) extensive, both physically and psychologically.
    C) much more severe psychologically than physically.
    D) much more severe physically than psychologically.
    Answer: B

Pages: 146
Topic: Acute Stress/Posttraumatic Stress Disorder: Prisoner of War
Skill: Factual   Other1:

91. Which of the following statements is true?
    A) About half of a large group of prisoners of war reported posttraumatic stress symptoms
       in the year following release from captivity.
    B) Posstraumatic stress symptoms peak in intensity within the first year, and then
       typically disappear.
    C) Length of imprisonment has little to do with the likelihood of developing psychiatric
       problems.
    D) Reentry to society is difficult for concentration camp survivors, but not for former
       prisoners of war.
    Answer: A

92. Following World War II and the Korean War, symptoms of depression in men who had been prisoners of war
    A) were extensive soon after returning home but dissipated once problems of malnourishment were addressed.
    B) were prominent even forty years after imprisonment.
    C) were extensive soon after returning home but dissipated soon after soldiers were reunited with their families.
    D) were common only among those who had low self-esteem prior to entering the military.
    Answer: B

93. Performance on cognitive memory tasks was significantly worse in individuals who experienced
    A) the longest imprisonment.
    B) severe trauma-induced weight loss.
    C) harsh treatment and isolation during imprisonment.
    D) the greatest number of posttraumatic stress symptoms.
    Answer: B

94. Which of these statements is true?
    A) Concentration camp survivors tend to be so deeply scarred that even their children suffer the effects.
    B) Concentration camp survivors tend to recover psychologically, but not physically, in the years following their ordeal.
    C) Most concentration camp survivors still suffer from posttraumatic stress disorder.
    D) Community samples of concentration camp survivors show them to be remarkably resilient and functioning well over time.
    Answer: D

Pages: 148
Topic: Acute Stress/Posttraumatic Stress Disorder: Being Held Hostage
Skill: Conceptual   Other1:
95. Mr. A, who was kidnapped and assaulted by a gang of youths, began to recover from posttraumatic stress disorder during two years of therapy when he
   A) was able to work through self-blame and accept his feelings of rage toward his abductors.
   B) stopped retelling the incident to his wife and children.
   C) was able to confront groups of tough teenagers without anxiety.
   D) was able to see the gang convicted for their act in a court of law.
   Answer: A

Pages: 149
Topic: Acute Stress/Posttraumatic Stress Disorder: Being Held Hostage
Skill: Factual   Other1:
96. A recent study of fifty-five torture victims who had been Turkish political prisoners found
   A) that few were able to function in society after their ordeal.
   B) that those who had experienced some cognitive control over the circumstances of torture were less affected psychologically in the long run.
   C) that they were extremely psychologically disturbed but fully recovered physically.
   D) that they were physically debilitated but exhibited few symptoms of posttraumatic stress.
   Answer: B

Pages: 148
Topic: Acute Stress/Posttraumatic Stress Disorder: The Trauma of Relocation
Skill: Factual   Other1:
97. In the case of Pham, the Vietnamese immigrant who killed himself and his sons,
   A) he had a past history of mental disorder in Vietnam before he ever came to the United States.
   B) he is typical of refugees from southeast Asia who are usually unable to adjust to Western culture.
   C) his problems did not stem from stressors associated with relocation.
   D) he was unable to adapt to the circumstances of life in a new culture.
   Answer: D

Topic: Acute Stress/Posttraumatic Stress Disorder: The Trauma of Relocation
Skill: Factual   Other1:

98. A ten-year longitudinal study of Hmong refugees found all BUT which of the following?
    A) Over half of the refugees were off welfare and were now employed.
    B) Many still had not learned English.
    C) Psychological adjustment had improved, although some refugees still experienced anxiety, hostility, and paranoia.
    D) There was an excess of family violence among the refugees.
    Answer: D

Pages: 150
Topic: Treatment/Prevention/Stress Disorders: Treatment After Severe Trauma
Skill: Factual   Other1:

99. A study of the effectiveness of brief therapy immediately following a traumatic event found
    A) that a large number of people showed improvement in posttraumatic stress symptoms following the therapy.
    B) that few people who have experienced traumatic events benefit from treatment that is very brief in duration.
    C) that most people needed long-term treatment before showing much improvement in symptoms.
    D) it was inferior to proper rest, with or without sedatives, in producing any improvement in symptoms.
    Answer: A

Pages: 150
Topic: Treatment/Prevention/Stress Disorders: Treatment After Severe Trauma
Skill: Factual   Other1:

100. Which of the following does NOT appear to be helpful in recovering from a trauma?
    A) reliving the trauma in fantasies
    B) a prior stable and integrated personality
    C) therapy immediately following the trauma
    D) resuming normal activities immediately in order to avoid thinking about the trauma
    Answer: D

Pages: 150-151
Topic: Treatment/Prevention/Stress Disorders: Treatment After Severe Trauma
Skill: Factual   Other1:

101. Disaster-area workers
    A) often develop psychological symptoms, such as depression and anxiety.
    B) typically find short-term therapy beneficial.
    C) need to vent pent-up or unmanageable emotions.
    D) all of the above
    Answer: D

Pages: 152
Topic: Treatment/Prevention of Stress Disorders: Stress Prevention/Reduction
Skill: Factual   Other1:
102. Which of the following is NOT associated with a more successful emotional adjustment following surgery?
A) accurate information about procedures and pain
B) low levels of fear prior to surgery
C) moderate levels of fear before surgery
D) inoculating self-statements
Answer: B

Pages: 152
Topic: Treatment/Prevention of Stress Disorders: Stress Prevention/Reduction
Skill: Applied   Other1:
103. Jim is in training to be a paramedic. How might stress-inoculation techniques be used in his training program?
A) to help those he rescues
B) to enable him to practice coping with stressful situations ahead of time
C) to help him to endure physical pain
D) to immunize him against the viruses he is likely to encounter in his future work
Answer: B

Pages: 152
Topic: Treatment/Prevention/Stress Disorders: Posttraumatic Stress Symptoms
Skill: Factual   Other1:
104. A recent treatment outcome study found that
A) medication is superior to psychotherapy in treating posttraumatic stress disorder.
B) psychotherapy is superior to medication in treating posttraumatic stress disorder.
C) psychotherapy and medication together are more effective than medication alone.
D) medication is only effective when given early or very soon after a traumatic event.
Answer: C

Pages: 153
Topic: Treatment/Prevention/Stress Disorders: Posttraumatic Stress Symptoms
Skill: Conceptual   Other1:
105. Crisis intervention is
A) similar to stress inoculation in that both techniques can be used to help a person cope with an anticipated traumatic event.
B) long-term therapy designed to help individuals suffering from posttraumatic stress disorder.
C) a technique whereby individuals practice self-statements to cope with traumatic events they have experienced.
D) the exposure to stimuli that have come to be associated with a traumatic event.
Answer: A

Pages: 153
Topic: Treatment/Prevention of Stress Disorders: Direct Therapeutic Exposure
Skill: Factual   Other1:
106. Direct therapeutic exposure is
    A) too direct and extreme a therapeutic approach to use safely with victims of posttraumatic stress disorder.
    B) potentially useful along with other behavioral methods in treating posttraumatic stress symptoms.
    C) the therapeutic process by which an individual relaxes and repeats calming self-statements while imagining pleasant scenes.
    D) effective only when combined with medication.
    Answer: B

Pages: 153
Topic: Unresolved Issues on the Politics of Posttraumatic Stress Disorder
Skill: Conceptual   Other1:
107. The text presented the case of an employee of an air cargo company who was fired. Later he was arrested on charges of property destruction and assault. His case was an example of how
    A) stress from being fired can bring back other stress-related experiences, such as combat.
    B) combat predisposes an individual to be less resistant to stress throughout his or her lifetime.
    C) posttraumatic stress is completely unpredictable in most individuals.
    D) the diagnosis of posttraumatic stress disorder is used as a legal strategy to justify criminal acts.
    Answer: D

Pages: 154
Topic: Unresolved Issues on the Politics of Posttraumatic Stress Disorder
Skill: Factual   Other1:
108. The posttraumatic stress syndrome is less often being used in _____ cases, and more often used in _____ cases.
    A) civil; criminal
    B) civil; insanity
    C) criminal; civil
    D) personal damage; murder
    Answer: C

Pages: 154
Topic: Unresolved Issues on the Politics of Posttraumatic Stress Disorder
Skill: Factual   Other1:
109. The text presented a description of the litigation following a Delta Airline crash. This case illustrates that
    A) survivors often have problems before a trauma occurs.
    B) proving the existence of posttraumatic stress disorder is very difficult.
    C) survivors' problems were symptoms of posttraumatic stress that could be alleviated within one year by therapy.
    D) it is relatively easy to establish a causal link between stressors and symptoms.
    Answer: B

Pages: 153-154
Topic: Unresolved Issues on the Politics of Posttraumatic Stress Disorder
Skill: Applied   Other1:
110. To successfully use the posttraumatic stress defense in a trial,
    A) there must be sufficient evidence that the stressor was causally related to the behavior in question.
    B) the individual must be in a job in which stress is clearly expected.
    C) it must be established that the individual suffers from the diagnostic criteria defined in DSM-IV.
    D) the individual must show other indications of legal insanity in addition to posttraumatic stress symptoms.
    Answer: A

Short Answer

Write the word or phrase that best completes each statement or answers the question.

Pages: 120
Topic: Stress and Stressors: Categories of Stressors
Skill: Factual   Other1:
1. The three categories of stressors discussed in the text are _____, _____, and _____.
   Answer: frustrations; conflicts; pressures.

Pages: 122
Topic: Stress and Stressors: Factors Predisposing a Person to Stress
Skill: Factual   Other1:

2. Many factors determine the impact that a stressor will have on an individual. Briefly describe five of these factors.
    Answer: These factors include the importance of the stressful event to the person; the duration of the stressor; the cumulative effect of stressors in a person's life; chronicity of the stressor; the controllability of the stressor; whether two or more stressors are operating simultaneously; the closer a person gets in time to having to deal with a stressful event; the more closely a person is involved in a traumatic event.

Pages: 123
Topic: Stress and Stressors: Factors Predisposing a Person to Stress
Skill: Applied   Other1:

3. Describe two ways to improve an individual's ability to cope with a serious anticipated stressor.
    Answer: Giving the individual a sense of adequacy and control will improve his or her stress tolerance. Adequacy is achieved by gaining realistic and accurate knowledge about the nature of the stressor, its duration, and its likely aftermath. An individual also might receive specialized training in which he or she is given repeated exposure to controlled stressors until coping patterns become automatic. Control can be achieved by allowing an individual to choose the stressful situation voluntarily or by having control over some of the circumstances surrounding the stressor.

Pages: 125
Topic: Stress and Stressors: Factors Predisposing a Person to Stress
Skill: Conceptual   Other1:

4. What is crisis intervention and why is it important?
    Answer: The outcome of a crisis has a profound effect on a person's subsequent adjustment. If a person has not coped well with the crisis, his or her ability to cope with similar stressors in the future may be seriously impaired. An individual may develop an expectation of failure. Thus crisis intervention, which is therapy designed to help individuals during times of acute and severe stress, is extremely important in helping a person develop new coping strategies to adjust to new demands.

Pages: 127
Topic: Coping Strategies: General Principles of Coping With Stress
Skill: Factual   Other1:

5. The text describes two basic categories of coping strategies that individuals use. _____ responses are used when a person feels adequate to cope with a stressor. When feelings of adequacy are threatened, _____ responses tend to occur.

    Answer: task-oriented; defense-oriented. In task-oriented responses, behavior is directed primarily toward satisfying the requirements of the stressor in order to resolve the situation. When feelings of adequacy are threatened, a defense-oriented response tends to occur in which behavior is directed primarily at protecting the self from hurt and disorganization. This type of response includes ego-defense mechanisms like denial, and damage-repair mechanisms like crying.

Pages: 128
Topic: Coping Strategies: Decompensation Under Excessive Stress
Skill: Factual   Other1:

6. _____ is a serious lowering of adaptive functioning in the face of a severe or sustained stressor that leads to psychological disintegration.

    Answer: Decompensation

Pages: 128-130
Topic: Coping Strategies: Decompensation Under Excessive Stress
Skill: Factual   Other1:

7. Briefly describe Selye's general adaptation syndrome.

    Answer: In this biological model, the body typically goes through three major phases in its reaction to sustained and excessive stress. In the alarm reaction, the autonomic nervous system signals the body's defensive forces. During the stage of resistance, biological adaptation is at a maximum level in the use of bodily resources. During the exhaustion stage, these resources are depleted and the body loses its power to resist. This can lead to illness and death.

Pages: 129-130
Topic: Coping Strategies: Decompensation Under Excessive Stress
Skill: Factual   Other1:

8. Briefly describe the characteristics of psychological decompensation.

    Answer: Its course is usually gradual and resembles biological decompensation. Coping resources are mobilized during the alarm and mobilization stage. Task-oriented and defense-oriented mechanisms are used. Symptoms of maladjustment may appear if resources are inadequate. During resistance, task-oriented strategies may resolve the situation. The use of ego-defense mechanisms may intensify and rigidify. During exhaustion, adaptive resources are depleted; psychological disintegration, delusions, and hallucinations may occur.

Topic: Adjustment Disorder: Reactions to Common Life Stressors
Skill: Factual   Other1:

9. Individuals whose response to a common stressor is excessive, or who are unable to funtion as usual following the experience of a common stressor, would qualify for a diagnosis of

    ____.

    Answer: adjustment disorder

Pages: 133
Topic: Adjustment Disorder: Stress From Bereavement
Skill: Factual   Other1:

10. Briefly describe the normal grieving process.

    Answer: Initially an individual typically reacts with disbelief. Then feelings of sadness, despair, and grief emerge. An individual may feel angry at the deceased. He or she may feel quite overwhelmed by these feelings. Emotional upset will continue, but the normal grieving process lasts about a year.

Pages: 135
Topic: Acute Stress/Posttraumatic Stress Disorder: Severe Life Stressors
Skill: Factual   Other1:

11. Briefly define posttraumatic stress disorder and list four of the symptoms associated with it.

    Answer: Posttraumatic stress disorder describes a syndrome of stress symptoms lasting at least one month following exposure to an unusually severe stressor. Symptoms include persistently reexperiencing the traumatic event in thoughts or nightmares; persistently avoiding stimuli associated with the stressor; increased physiological arousal; impaired concentration and memory; depression and social withdrawal.

Pages: 135
Topic: Acute Stress/Posttraumatic Stress Disorder: Severe Life Stressors
Skill: Applied   Other1:

12. Three weeks ago David lost his house in a flood. Since this occurred, he has complained of an inability to sleep or eat. He sits in a dark hotel room unwilling to meet with friends or go to work. What would David's diagnosis be and why?

    Answer: He meets criteria for acute stress disorder on Axis I in the DSM-IV by virtue of the nature and severity of the stressor, and his excessive reaction to it, as well as the fact that his symptoms began within four weeks of the event, and have lasted more than two days and less than four weeks.

Pages: 135-136
Topic: Acute Stress/Posttraumatic Stress Disorder: Catastrophic Events
Skill: Applied   Other1:

13. Kari was in an office building that exploded because of a faulty gas line. Describe the typical series of responses and behaviors that she is likely to experience following the explosion.

    Answer: The disaster syndrome describes this typical progression of responses in such victims. Immediately after the explosion, in the shock stage, she probably will be stunned, dazed, and apathetic. In the suggestible stage that follows, she is likely to be very passive and suggestible, amenable to help and suggestions from rescue workers. In the recovery stage, Kari probably is tense, anxious, and fearful. She may need to describe the event repeatedly, gradually regaining her equilibrium.

Pages: 138
Topic: Acute Stress Disorder: Causal Factors in Posttraumatic Stress
Skill: Factual   Other1:

14. Briefly identify three causal factors associated with the occurrence of posttraumatic stress symptoms.

    Answer: These include preexisting problems in psychological functioning and adjustment; emotional insecurity; interpersonal skill deficits; the social context of recovery; and probably a person's biological makeup. Some research suggests that the level of stress moderates the effect of preexisting personality factors.

Pages: 138-140
Topic: Acute Stress/Posttraumatic Stress Disorder: The Trauma of Rape
Skill: Factual   Other1:

15. Identify three factors that influence a victim's response to rape.

    Answer: These factors include prior level of psychological functioning; age and life circumstances; whether the rapist was a stranger or an acquaintance; attitude and behavior of spouse or romantic partner.

Pages: 139
Topic: Acute Stress/Posttraumatic Stress Disorder: The Trauma of Rape
Skill: Factual   Other1:

16. The four phases that have been found to describe the emotional and psychological processes of a rape victim are ____, ____, ____, and ____.

    Answer: anticipatory; impact; posttraumatic recoil; reconstitution. First is the anticipatory phase when a victim is being set up. The rape occurs during the impact phase. The posttraumatic recoil stage begins immediately after the rape and continues until the reconstitution phase, when a victim begins to make plans for leaving an emergency room or crisis center. Reconstitution continues until the experience has been assimilated and shared, and the victim's self-concept restored.

Topic: *Acute Stress Disorder/Posttraumatic Disorder: Trauma/Military Combat*
Skill: *Conceptual*   Other1:

17. Identify three factors that are associated with a poor adjustment to combat or to the later development of posttraumatic stress disorder after having served in the military.
    Answer: These factors include prior level of psychological functioning; degree of intensity of combat exposure; the type of war trauma exposed to (abusive violence, handling corpses); possibly constitutional factors; personal immaturity; self-reliant background; acceptance of realistic war goals; identification with combat unit and esprit de corps; respect for leadership; returning to an accepting social environment.

Pages: 145
Topic: *Acute Stress Disorder/Posttraumatic Disorder: Trauma/Military Combat*
Skill: *Factual*   Other1:

18. What have studies found about the long-term effects of posttraumatic stress in veterans?
    Answer: Many veterans report posttraumatic symptoms more than five years after discharge, including recurrent nightmares, depression, anger, and interpersonal difficulties. Combat veterans report certain symptoms twice as often as noncombat veterans. Posttraumatic stress disorder symptoms diminish somewhat with age, and symptoms are similar across wars.

Pages: 150-153
Topic: *Treatment/Prevention/Stress Disorders: Posttraumatic Stress Symptoms*
Skill: *Applied*   Other1:

19. Briefly describe two treatment and/or prevention strategies for treating stress-related symptoms.
    Answer: Studies show that individuals who are facing a major stressful event benefit from receiving realistic and accurate advance information about the stressor. Stress-inoculation training is another preventive strategy whereby people are prepared to tolerate an anticipated stressor by learning adaptive self-statements and practicing them under situations of controlled stressors. Crisis intervention is a brief problem-focused therapeutic approach. Exposure therapy can be very successful with PTSD. Medication can be helpful but more successful when it is combined with psychotherapy.

Topic: Unresolved Issues on the Politics of Posttraumatic Stress Disorder
Skill: Conceptual   Other1:

20. What is the major difficulty confronting individuals who attempt to use posttraumatic stress disorder as a legal defense?

    Answer: The major difficulty is in demonstrating that the stressful event is clearly causally connected to the posttraumatic stress symptoms. It is difficult to make this determination when an individual has had psychological difficulties or experienced other stressful situations prior to the stressor that is the focus of litigation.

Essay

Write your answer in the space provided or on a separate sheet of paper.

Pages: 120-121
Topic: Stress and Stressors: Categories of Stressors
Skill: Conceptual   Other1:

1. The text describes three different categories of stressors. Describe and give examples for each. How do these different categories relate to the concepts of distress and eustress?

    Answer: Frustrations occur when one's strivings are thwarted. Conflicts result from the simultaneous occurrence of two or more incompatible needs or motives. Conflicts include variations of approach and avoidance conflicts. Pressures to achieve specific goals or to behave in certain ways force a person to speed up or intensify effort. Examples of each should be given. Stress can be broken down into eustress (positive stress) and distress (negative stress). Stress in each of the three categories can be positive or negative.

Pages: 122
Topic: Stress and Stressors: Factors Predisposing a Person to Stress
Skill: Applied   Other1:

2. Dennis is about to enter a highly stressful position as an air-traffic controller. Describe the factors that will predispose Dennis to respond to the stressors in an adaptive or maladaptive way.

    Answer: The impact of a stressor depends on its importance, duration, cumulative effect, multiplicity, imminence, and controllability. His perception of the threat and his tolerance for stress are important. External resources and social supports can exacerbate or mitigate his stress.

Pages: 123-124
Topic: Stress and Stressors: Factors Predisposing a Person to Stress
Skill: Conceptual   Other1:

3. Discuss the relationship between stress and external social supports.

    Answer: There is much research evidence that family and social support can moderate the psychological effects of stress on an individual, as well as reducing illness and even death. For example, widowers who attended church or temple became less depressed than those who did not. Men may have a harder time coping with the death of a spouse than women because of fewer social resources. Cultural and religious rituals provide comfort for people going through certain kinds of stresses. Interpersonal difficulties can be a significant source of stress as well.

Pages: 128-131
Topic: Coping Strategies: Decompensation Under Excessive Stress
Skill: Conceptual   Other1:

4. Some individuals are able to handle a significant amount of stress. However, under sustained or severe stress, individuals may decompensate. What is decompensation? What happens biologically and psychologically to individuals who decompensate?

    Answer: Decompensation involves a lowering of adaptive efficiency. The individual may be biologically less able to fight off infections; psychologically, may have a narrowed perceptual field and cognitive rigidity. Decompensation also results in a lowering of resistance to other stressors, and wear on the organism. Selye's general adaptation syndrome is useful in describing decompensation, with its stages of alarm, resistance, and exhaustion.

Pages: 131
Topic: Acute Stress/Posttraumatic Stress Disorder: Severe Life Stressors
Skill: Applied   Other1:

5. Alexa came to your clinic complaining of symptoms associated with stress. Using the DSM-IV as a guide, what information would you collect in order to make a diagnosis?

    Answer: Her symptoms must be evaluated according to the explicit criteria in DSM-IV and will probably be associated with one of these Axis I disorders: adjustment disorder, acute stress disorder, or PTSD. The nature and severity of the stressor she experienced can be evaluated with the checklist on Axis IV. If the stressor is unusually severe, her diagnosis is probably acute stress disorder or PTSD; if her symptoms reflect a maladaptive response to an ordinary stressor, adjustment disorder. Time frames during which the three disorders occur also differ and must be assessed.

Topic: Adjustment Disorder: Stress From Divorce or Separation
Skill: Applied   Other1:

6. Donna, the mother of two young children, was divorced two months ago. She has become very depressed and anxious and has withdrawn significantly. She did not have any psychological problems before the divorce. What would be her diagnosis? What information is necessary to make this diagnosis? What are the issues Donna is likely to have to face having been recently divorced?

    Answer: She would be diagnosed with adjustment disorder, which requires that an individual be unable to function as usual or have an excessive reaction to an identifiable stressor. Symptoms must start not more than three months following the stressor and are expected to last less than six months, or another diagnosis should be given. Donna is likely to have to work through issues involving acknowledging failure in the relationship, explaining the divorce to people, losing friendships and financial security, and having problems associated with child custody and visitation.

Pages: 134-135
Topic: Acute Stress/Posttraumatic Stress Disorder: Severe Life Stressors
Skill: Applied   Other1:

7. Davina has been diagnosed with posttraumatic stress disorder as the result of having been raped. What symptoms are necessary for this diagnosis? What other conditions are necessary for this diagnosis to be applied?

    Answer: The individual must persistently reexperience the trauma in nightmares or intrusive thoughts and must avoid stimuli associated with it. Other symptoms may include hyperarousal, depression, social withdrawal, anxiety, impaired concentration, and memory. The symptoms must last for at least one month and may be considered acute or delayed depending on their onset in relation to the stressor. The stressor must be unusually severe for a posttraumatic stress disorder diagnosis to be made (e.g., life-threatening).

Pages: 135-137
Topic: Acute Stress/Posttraumatic Stress Disorder: Catastrophic Events
Skill: Factual   Other1:

8. Describe the disaster syndrome.

    Answer: During the initial shock phase, individuals are stunned and dazed. They may wander around not knowing what happened and appear apathetic. During the second phase, suggestibility, they are extremely passive and dependent. During the final recovery stage, victims may be tense, hypersensitive, and show generalized anxiety. They may need to tell the story of the event over and over. Intense grief or depression may occur. Feelings of personal responsibility and inadequacy may arouse strong guilt feelings.

Pages: 139-140
Topic: Acute Stress/Posttraumatic Stress Disorder: The Trauma of Rape
Skill: Applied   Other1:
9. Andrea is a rape victim. Describe the phases that Andrea is likely to go through in
    dealing with this traumatic event. What are the long-term effects of this event?
    Answer: She is likely to go through four phases. The anticipatory phase involves the
              use of defense mechanisms like denial. The impact phase involves intense fear
              for her life. The posttraumatic recoil phase begins immediately after the rape
              and may involve an expressed or controlled style. The reconstitution phase may
              involve self-protective activity, frightening nightmares, and phobias. On a
              long-term basis, she will feel the rape continues to have an impact on her. If
              she has had prior psychological problems, she may have significant adjustment
              problems after the rape.

Pages: 140-145
Topic: Acute Stress Disorder/Posttraumatic Disorder: Trauma/Military Combat
Skill: Factual   Other1:
10. Combat is an intense, traumatic experience. Describe the psychosocial and sociocultural
    factors that play important roles in determining an individual's adjustment to combat.
    Answer: Psychosocial factors include reduction in personal freedom, frustrations,
              separations, stresses from combat, and the individual's personality make-up.
              Sociocultural factors include clarity and acceptability of war goals, group
              identification, esprit de corps, quality of leadership, and returning to an
              accepting social environment.

Pages: 145
Topic: Acute Stress Disorder/Posttraumatic Disorder: Trauma/Military Combat
Skill: Applied   Other1:
11. Jeff was involved in some of the heaviest infantry combat in the Persian Gulf War.
    Compared to other soldiers, for what long-term effects is he at greater risk? What are
    some of the factors that will influence whether he later has a disorder?
    Answer: He is at greater risk for posttraumatic stress, with guilt feelings over
              casualties if he was personally responsible. He is more likely to have
              depression and difficulties in close interpersonal relationships. These
              symptoms may continue for years. Factors that make such problems less likely
              include whether he was treated immediately upon exhibiting symptoms, whether he
              has social support, and his pre-military coping resources.

Pages: 145-147
Topic: Acute Stress/Posttraumatic Stress Disorder: Prisoner of War
Skill: Factual   Other1:

12. What effects are typical in individuals who are imprisoned as prisoners of war or in a concentration camp?

    Answer: Individuals are often physically debilitated, with a very high death rate during imprisonment and in the years following release. Residual damage is severe, extensive, and includes physical ailments, generally low stress tolerance, anxiety, depression, nightmares, irritability, impotence and, in individuals sustaining extreme trauma-induced weight loss, impaired cognitive performance. Duration of imprisonment, harshness of treatment, and isolation are factors predisposing people to later problems, though studies of community samples of camp survivors show that many function remarkably well.

Pages: 150-153
Topic: Treatment/Prevention/Stress Disorders: Posttraumatic Stress Symptoms
Skill: Applied   Other1:

13. As a psychologist, you've just received word that an airplane has crashed in your town and you are in charge of handling psychological resources for survivors. Describe the sort of treatment program you would establish.

    Answer: Studies show that individuals given supportive treatment immediately following a trauma experience a reduction in PTSD symptoms, so counseling survivors should begin right away. Individuals probably will need to tell their story over and over and vent their feelings to a supportive listener. They will benefit from receiving accurate and realistic information about the event, as well as about what they might expect to experience in the way of symptoms and recovery in the future. Medications may be helpful together with brief psychotherapy. Long-term treatment might include exposure therapy.

Pages: 152
Topic: Treatment/Prevention of Stress Disorders: Stress Prevention/Reduction
Skill: Applied   Other1:

14. Assume that you have been hired to work with patients who undergo potentially dangerous brain surgery. What are some of the things that you can do to help these patients minimize post-operation problems?

    Answer: Patients will benefit from receiving accurate and realistic information about the procedures, risks, pain, and recovery. They would also benefit if they could be given some control over the procedure or its circumstances, such as regulating their own pain medication. Stress inoculation training may be helpful, in which patients are taught adaptive self-statements to use in coping with their fear and discomfort.

Pages: 153-154
Topic: Unresolved Issues on the Politics of Posttraumatic Stress Disorder
Skill: Conceptual   Other1:

15. Discuss the use of posttraumatic stress disorder as a legal defense.

    Answer: The defense is being used less often in criminal cases, but more often in civil
             cases such as those involving compensation and personal injury. Establishing
             legal justification for this defense usually involves expert witnesses on both
             sides. The major difficulty in using it is establishing a clear causal
             connection between the past stressor and the behavior in question, as evidenced
             by the Delta Airline suit.

CHAPTER 5   Panic, Anxiety, and Their Disorders

Multiple-Choice

Choose the one alternative that best completes the statement or answers the question.

Pages: 157
Topic: Panic, Anxiety, and Their Disorders
Skill: Factual   Other1:
1. According to the psychodynamic view, which of the following statements is NOT true of neurotic behavior?
A) Neurotic behavior always reflects intrapsychic conflict.
B) Neurotics are out of touch with reality.
C) Neurotic behavior can involve extreme avoidance behavior.
D) A neurotic's social relationships and work performance are likely to be impaired.
Answer: B

Pages: 157
Topic: Panic, Anxiety, and Their Disorders
Skill: Factual   Other1:
2. To Freud, anxiety was a sign of
A) neurological malfunction.
B) hormonal malfunction.
C) breakdown of the id.
D) intrapsychic conflict between id and ego or superego.
Answer: D

Pages: 158
Topic: Panic, Anxiety, and Their Disorders
Skill: Factual   Other1:
3. Editions of the DSM since 1980 categorize what used to be called neuroses into different categories based on
A) their symptom picture.
B) the type of neurotic-like behavior.
C) the cause of each disorder.
D) the types of defense mechanisms characteristic of each disorder.
Answer: A

Pages: 158
Topic: Panic, Anxiety, and Their Disorders
Skill: Conceptual   Other1:
4. Freud's views on anxiety and neurosis have been criticized for all BUT which of the
    following?
    A) He regarded anxiety as the cause of many disorders which did not include symptoms of
       anxiety.
    B) His concept of anxiety could not always be observed and measured.
    C) He believed that the presence of anxiety was masked in some cases because it was
       defended against.
    D) He believed that symptoms of anxiety create serious psychological problems for some
       people.
    Answer: D

Pages: 158
Topic: Panic, Anxiety, and Their Disorders
Skill: Conceptual   Other1:
5. The DSM diagnostic criteria for anxiety disorders are very clearly defined. This allows
    for
    A) enhanced reliability of diagnosis.
    B) the study of more homogeneous groups of people sharing a common diagnosis.
    C) an increased ability to investigate potential causal factors involved in the etiology
       of anxiety disorders as well as effective treatments.
    D) all of the above
    Answer: D

Pages: 158
Topic: The Fear and Anxiety Response Patterns
Skill: Factual   Other1:
6. Historically the most common way of distinguishing between fear and anxiety was
    A) whether there was an obvious source of real danger.
    B) by their different symptoms.
    C) by the severity of the symptoms.
    D) B and C
    Answer: A

Pages: 158
Topic: The Fear and Anxiety Response Patterns
Skill: Applied   Other1:
7. Stanley ran out of the house when he saw a mouse. This is an example of the _____ component of a fear response.
   A) physiological
   B) cognitive
   C) subjective
   D) behavioral
   Answer: D

Pages: 158
Topic: The Fear and Anxiety Response Patterns
Skill: Applied   Other1:
8. Home alone one night, Alicia suddenly heard someone trying to break into her apartment. Based on contemporary research and theory, such as Barlow's, Alicia is likely to experience
   A) a diffuse blend of emotions and cognitions.
   B) anxiety.
   C) an irrational fear.
   D) fear or panic.
   Answer: D

Pages: 159
Topic: The Fear and Anxiety Response Patterns
Skill: Conceptual   Other1:
9. Fear and anxiety are similar in that
   A) both can be adaptive responses.
   B) both involve the activation of the "fight or flight" response of the sympathetic nervous system.
   C) both contain physiological and behavioral components, although only anxiety contains a significant cognitive/subjective dimension.
   D) both contain certain physiological and cognitive/subjective components, although only anxiety contains a significant behavioral component.
   Answer: A

Pages: 159
Topic: The Fear and Anxiety Response Patterns
Skill: Conceptual   Other1:
10. Fear and anxiety differ in that
   A) anxiety consists of a more diffuse blend of emotions and cognitions than fear.
   B) only fear is adaptive.
   C) only anxiety involves a strong urge to flee the immediate situation.
   D) only fear is a conditionable response.
   Answer: A

Pages: 159
Topic: The Fear and Anxiety Response Patterns
Skill: Factual   Other1:
11. According to Barlow, anxiety
    A) involves activation of the fight or flight response.
    B) involves preparation for the fight or flight response if it becomes necessary.
    C) involves the intense urge to flee a threatening situation immediately.
    D) reflects a state of chronic underarousal.
    Answer: B

Pages: 159
Topic: The Fear and Anxiety Response Patterns
Skill: Conceptual   Other1:
12. When anxiety becomes chronic and severe, it is
    A) a fear response.
    B) maladaptive.
    C) often adaptive in helping an individual plan for potential threats.
    D) no longer possible to extinguish.
    Answer: B

Pages: 159
Topic: The Fear and Anxiety Response Patterns
Skill: Factual   Other1:
13. Which of the following statements is true?
    A) Unlike fear, anxiety is a highly conditionable response pattern.
    B) Unlike anxiety, fear is a highly conditionable response pattern.
    C) Thoughts and bodily sensations each can acquire the capacity to elicit a conditioned
       response in humans.
    D) Anxiety is an irrational conditioned response, whereas fear is a rational conditioned
       response.
    Answer: C

Pages: 159
Topic: Anxiety Disorders
Skill: Factual   Other1:
14. An anxiety disorder
    A) includes an unrealistic and irrational fear of disabling intensity.
    B) includes an unrealistic but rational fear of diabling intensity.
    C) includes a realistic but irrational fear of disabling intensity.
    D) includes a realistic and rational fear of disabling intensity.
    Answer: A

Pages: 159
Topic: Anxiety Disorders
Skill: Factual   Other1:
15. Which of the following is NOT an example of a DSM-IV anxiety disorder?
    A) social phobia
    B) posttraumatic stress disorder
    C) anxiety-induced stress disorder
    D) obsessive-compulsive disorder
    Answer: C

Pages: 160
Topic: Anxiety Disorders
Skill: Factual   Other1:
16. According to an NIMH epidemiological study, anxiety disorders are
    A) relatively uncommon.
    B) relatively common in women but not in men.
    C) relatively common in men but not in women.
    D) relatively common in both men and women.
    Answer: D

Pages: 160
Topic: Anxiety Disorders
Skill: Factual   Other1: In Student Study Guide
17. In the New Haven-Baltimore-St. Louis Epidemiological Catchment Area (ECA) program
    sponsored by the National Institute of Mental Health, _____ were the most common
    psychiatric disorders reported for women and the second-most common for men.
    A) obsessive-compulsive disorders
    B) generalized anxiety disorders
    C) panic disorders
    D) phobias
    Answer: D

Pages: 160
Topic: Anxiety Disorders
Skill: Factual   Other1:
18. Comorbidity data indicate that 25-50 percent of all individuals who receive an anxiety
    disorder diagnosis also will receive a diagnosis of _____ at some point in their lives.
    A) a mood disorder like depression
    B) schizophrenia
    C) adjustment disorder
    D) sexual dysfunction
    Answer: A

Pages: 160
Topic: Anxiety Disorders: Phobic Disorders
Skill: Applied   Other1:
19. Mel would go to great lengths to avoid having to take an elevator, which terrifies him.
    If this is his only feared situation, he might be diagnosed with
    A) social phobia.
    B) specific phobia.
    C) agoraphobia.
    D) panic disorder.
    Answer: B

Pages: 160-161
Topic: Anxiety Disorders: Phobic Disorders
Skill: Applied   Other1:
20. Maurine is afraid of elephants. However, she lives in Chicago and has only seen elephants
    at the circus. Her anxiety level remains low if she keeps her distance from elephants.
    What would the DSM-IV say about her?
    A) She has a specific phobia to elephants.
    B) She does not have a specific phobia.
    C) She has a specific phobia, avoidable type.
    D) She has animal phobia.
    Answer: B

Pages: 160
Topic: Anxiety Disorders: Phobic Disorders
Skill: Factual   Other1:
21. A cardinal characteristic of phobias is
    A) spontaneous panic attacks.
    B) an exaggerated fear of something everyone fears to a lesser extent.
    C) avoidance of the feared object or situation.
    D) a unique physiological response pattern involving fainting.
    Answer: C

Pages: 161
Topic: Anxiety Disorders: Phobic Disorders
Skill: Factual   Other1:
22. Blood-injury phobia is a unique specific phobia because
    A) it involves an increase in blood pressure and heart rate.
    B) it is the most common phobia in women.
    C) its physiological response pattern differs from other phobias in that a rise in blood
       pressure and heart rate are followed by a drop in both.
    D) it is the most common phobia in men.
    Answer: C

Pages: 161
Topic: Anxiety Disorders: Phobic Disorders
Skill: Factual   Other1:
23. Which of the following statements is NOT true of blood-injury phobia?
    A) It has a stronger familial component than other phobias.
    B) It often involves nausea, dizziness, and fainting.
    C) It is associated with a physiological response pattern that is common to all specific phobias.
    D) It is more common in women than in men.
    Answer: C

Pages: 162
Topic: Anxiety Disorders: Phobic Disorders
Skill: Factual   Other1:
24. Specific phobias
    A) are common, especially in women.
    B) differ from one another in typical age of onset.
    C) differ in relative prevalence by gender.
    D) all of the above
    Answer: D

Pages: 162
Topic: Anxiety Disorders: Phobic Disorders
Skill: Factual   Other1:
25. Lifetime prevalence rates for specific phobias indicate that
    A) men are more likely than women to suffer from specific phobias.
    B) women and men are equally likely to suffer from specific phobias.
    C) women are more likely than men to suffer from specific phobias, although the relative sex ratios vary considerably according to the type of specific phobia.
    D) none of the above
    Answer: C

Pages: 162
Topic: Anxiety Disorders: Phobic Disorders
Skill: Applied   Other1:
26. Milly claims that she first began experiencing claustrophobia as an adult. Which of these statements is true?
    A) Milly's phobic disorder probably began in childhood, even though she doesn't remember earlier difficulties with it.
    B) Her claustrophobic symptoms are likely to be masking some other disorder.
    C) Her claustrophobia is likely to be a precursor to panic disorder with agoraphobia.
    D) Milly's case is typical because claustrophobia, like agoraphobia, often begins in adolescence or early adulthood.
    Answer: D

Pages: 162
Topic: Anxiety Disorders: Phobic Disorders
Skill: Conceptual   Other1:
27. Each time a feared situation is avoided,
    A) phobic behavior is reinforced by the anxiety reduction that results.
    B) conditioned fear responses may weaken.
    C) the likelihood of a panic attack occurring in the future increases.
    D) an individual becomes increasingly agoraphobic.
    Answer: A

Pages: 162
Topic: Anxiety Disorders: Phobic Disorders
Skill: Factual   Other1:
28. Anxiety reduction from avoidance behavior and secondary gains have a(n) _____ effect on phobic behavior.
    A) reinforcing
    B) diminishing
    C) adaptive
    D) unpredictable
    Answer: A

Pages: 163
Topic: Anxiety Disorders: Phobic Disorders
Skill: Factual   Other1:
29. According to Freud, Little Hans's horse phobia was caused by
    A) an early trauma involving witnessing his pet pony being castrated.
    B) an early trauma involving witnessing an accident with a horse.
    C) anxiety from a repressed Oedipal conflict which was displaced onto horses.
    D) generalization from his original fear of dogs.
    Answer: C

Pages: 163
Topic: Anxiety Disorders: Phobic Disorders
Skill: Factual   Other1:
30. According to learning theory, Little Hans's horse phobia is best explained by
    A) traumatic classical conditioning.
    B) operant conditioning principles.
    C) vicarious conditioning.
    D) all of the above
    Answer: A

Pages: 163
Topic: Anxiety Disorders: Phobic Disorders
Skill: Applied   Other1:

31. Kenneth's mother is intensely afraid of spiders. On many occasions he watched her running out of the house to get a neighbor for help when she found a spider in the house. Eventually Kenneth developed a phobia for spiders as well. This is an example of
    A) traumatic classical conditioning.
    B) observational conditioning.
    C) operant conditioning.
    D) counter-immunization.
    Answer: B

Pages: 163
Topic: Anxiety Disorders: Phobic Disorders
Skill: Factual   Other1:

32. In their examination of fear acquisition using rhesus monkey subjects, Mineka, Cook, and colleagues demonstrated that
    A) initially fearless monkeys can rapidly develop a phobic-like fear of snakes through observing other monkeys behaving fearfully with snakes.
    B) initially fearless monkeys can rapidly develop a phobic-like fear of snakes through traumatic classical conditioning.
    C) initially fearless monkeys can rapidly develop a phobic-like fear of snakes through vicarious conditioning.
    D) A and C
    Answer: D

Pages: 163
Topic: Anxiety Disorders: Phobic Disorders
Skill: Factual   Other1:

33. Which of the following statements about Mineka, Cook, and colleagues' animal studies is NOT true?
    A) Laboratory-reared monkeys with no previous exposure to snakes developed a phobic-like fear of snakes after simply observing a wild-reared monkey behaving fearfully with snakes.
    B) Observationally conditioned fear responses were acquired quickly but did not last more than a day or two.
    C) Observationally acquired fear responses were undiminished after three months.
    D) Observationally acquired fear responses could be acquired by watching videotapes of fearful monkeys.
    Answer: B

Pages: 163
Topic: Anxiety Disorders: Phobic Disorders
Skill: Factual   Other1:
34. The traditional learning model of phobia acquisition
    A) failed to recognize the importance of traumatic conditioning in the origin of phobias.
    B) presented a theory of immunization to account for individual differences in experiential variables.
    C) failed to account for individual differences in the development and maintenance of phobias.
    D) regarded all phobias as instances of stimulus generalization from internal anxiety conflicts.
    Answer: C

Pages: 164
Topic: Anxiety Disorders: Phobic Disorders
Skill: Conceptual   Other1: In Student Study Guide
35. The concept that explains why phobias often are not learned even though we observe models responding fearfully is
    A) counter-conditioning.
    B) stimulus pre-exposure.
    C) immunization.
    D) reciprocal inhibition.
    Answer: B

Pages: 164
Topic: Anxiety Disorders: Phobic Disorders
Skill: Applied   Other1:
36. Mari grew up with a pet golden retriever. When she was ten, a neighbor's new dog bit her. Which of the following statements is likely to be true?
    A) Mari's traumatic experience with the neighbor's dog will probably result in fear that will generalize to other dogs, including her own.
    B) Mari is likely to become dog phobic, although she won't develop a fear of her own dog.
    C) Mari will develop a temporary fear of dogs that will disappear in a few days.
    D) Mari's extensive positive experience with her own dog prior to being bit probably immunized her against acquiring a traumatic conditioned fear response to dogs.
    Answer: D

Pages: 164
Topic: Anxiety Disorders: Phobic Disorders
Skill: Factual   Other1:

37. Experiencing a trauma that is uncontrollable is
    A) more likely to result in a strong conditioned fear response than if an individual has some control over this event.
    B) an example of lack of preparedness.
    C) less likely to result in a strong conditioned fear response than if an individual has some control over the event.
    D) not likely to result in a strong conditioned fear response.
    Answer: A

Pages: 164
Topic: Anxiety Disorders: Phobic Disorders
Skill: Conceptual   Other1:

38. Two individuals undergoing the same traumatic experience may end up with very different responses to it. Which of the following might account for this difference?
    A) differences in prior experience with the same stimulus
    B) differences in preparedness
    C) differences in learning ability
    D) differences in intelligence
    Answer: A

Pages: 164
Topic: Anxiety Disorders: Phobic Disorders
Skill: Factual   Other1:

39. A person who acquires a mild conditioned fear might develop a full-blown phobia if a later traumatic experience occurred, even if that later experience had nothing to do with the original conditioning stimulus. This is an example of
    A) immunization.
    B) vicarious conditioning.
    C) a cognitive variable.
    D) the inflation effect.
    Answer: D

40. One way in which phobic individuals differ from nonphobics is in
    A) phobics' tendency to screen out dangerous stimuli as a way of attempting to defend against threatening cues.
    B) phobics' tendency to underestimate the probability of the occurrence of fearful events following aversive stimuli.
    C) phobics' tendency to be constantly on the alert for phobic stimuli.
    D) phobics' biological preparedness level.
    Answer: C

41. All of the following are variables that may account for individual differences in the development of phobias EXCEPT for
    A) immunization experiences.
    B) temperament.
    C) the controllability vs. uncontrollability of the traumatic stimulus.
    D) All of the above do help account for individual differences in the development of phobias.
    Answer: D

42. Personality variables
    A) appear to be irrelevant in the acquisition of phobias.
    B) may affect the speed and strength of conditioned fear responses.
    C) are important in the acquisition of phobias because Kagan and colleagues found elevated rates of phobias in uninhibited children.
    D) determine whether an individual will most readily condition to objects associated with prepared fears or to other kinds of objects.
    Answer: B

43. Prepared fears are
    A) fears that are especially easily acquired and/or especially resistant to extinction.
    B) inborn and innate.
    C) arbitrary groups of objects that have become associated with fear responses.
    D) fears indigenous to subhuman species involving specific classes of objects.
    Answer: A

Pages: 165
Topic: Anxiety Disorders: Phobic Disorders
Skill: Factual   Other1:

44. In human laboratory studies, Öhman and colleagues found that fear is conditioned more readily to some stimuli than to others. This research provides evidence for the theory of
A) observational conditioning.
B) temperamental differences in conditionability.
C) subliminally acquired phobias.
D) biological preparedness.
Answer: D

Pages: 165
Topic: Anxiety Disorders: Phobic Disorders
Skill: Factual   Other1:

45. Öhman and colleagues found that responses conditioned to fear-relevant stimuli
A) were more resistant to extinction than responses conditioned to fear-irrelevant stimuli.
B) were stronger only when stimuli were presented subliminally.
C) were easier to extinguish than responses conditioned to fear-irrelevant stimuli.
D) were as strong when toy snakes were used as stimuli as when real snakes were used.
Answer: A

Pages: 165
Topic: Anxiety Disorders: Phobic Disorders
Skill: Factual   Other1:

46. After human subjects had acquired a conditioned fear response in Öhman's studies, subliminal presentation of stimuli to these same subjects
A) elicited conditioned fear responses when stimuli were fear-irrelevant but not when they were fear-relevant.
B) elicited conditioned fear responses only when stimuli were fear-relevant.
C) failed to elicit conditioned fear responses.
D) elicited conditioned fear responses for all stimuli whether or not they were fear-relevant or fear-irrelevant.
Answer: B

Pages: 165
Topic: Anxiety Disorders: Phobic Disorders
Skill: Conceptual   Other1:
47. Phobics may not be able to control their irrational fears because their fear may arise from cognitive structures that are not under conscious control. Evidence for this assertion is provided by
A) Mineka's animal studies.
B) the effects of subliminal presentation of fear-relevant stimuli.
C) the difficulty in extinguishing conditioned fear responses to fear-relevant stimuli.
D) the existence of immunization and inflation effects.
Answer: B

Pages: 165
Topic: Anxiety Disorders: Phobic Disorders
Skill: Factual   Other1:
48. In one of their studies with rhesus monkeys, Mineka, Cook, and colleagues showed fearless monkeys videotapes of other monkeys behaving fearfully to stimuli such as toy snakes and flowers. What did these investigators find?
A) The monkeys readily acquired conditioned fear responses to both the toy snakes and to the flowers.
B) The monkeys readily acquired conditioned fear responses to the toy snakes but not to the flowers, consistent with preparedness theory.
C) The monkeys developed a conditioned fear response only to those stimuli they had prior experience with, a finding unanticipated by preparedness theory.
D) The monkeys acquired conditioned fear responses only when they observed fearful monkeys directly, not from videotapes, consistent with Öhman's revision of preparedness theory.
Answer: B

Pages: 165-166
Topic: Anxiety Disorders: Phobic Disorders
Skill: Factual   Other1:
49. One important piece of information obtained by Mineka and Cook's animal research, which could not be demonstrated in Öhman's human studies, was that
A) snakes appear to be a powerful fear-conditioning stimulus.
B) only monkeys with prior exposure to the fear-relevant stimuli acquired a conditioned fear response to these stimuli.
C) prepared conditioned fear responses can be acquired even when subjects have no preexisting negative association to fear-relevant stimuli.
D) conditioned fear responses to fear-relevant stimuli do not extinguish readily.
Answer: C

Pages: 165-166
Topic: Anxiety Disorders: Phobic Disorders
Skill: Conceptual   Other1:
50. Taken together, the research by Öhman and by Mineka, Cook, and colleagues on conditioned fear responses to fear-relevant stimuli converge to support the idea that
    A) fears and phobias tend to occur to a relatively arbitrary group of objects or situations that may have been associated with trauma.
    B) our evolutionary history has affected which stimuli we are most likely to come to fear.
    C) fears and phobias tend to occur to dangerous objects or situations, such as snakes and guns.
    D) phobia acquisition is more likely to occur through observational conditioning than through traumatic classical conditioning.
    Answer: B

Pages: 166
Topic: Anxiety Disorders: Phobic Disorders
Skill: Factual   Other1:
51. Fear of negative evaluation by others is a hallmark of
    A) social phobia.
    B) panic disorder.
    C) generalized anxiety disorder.
    D) obsessive-compulsive disorder.
    Answer: A

Pages: 166
Topic: Anxiety Disorders: Phobic Disorders
Skill: Factual   Other1:
52. Intense fear of public speaking is the most common
    A) generalized social phobia.
    B) specific social phobia.
    C) obsession.
    D) anxiety disorder.
    Answer: B

Pages: 166
Topic: Anxiety Disorders: Phobic Disorders
Skill: Applied   Other1:
53. John fears being rejected by others and the humiliation that would bring. As a result he tends to avoid social situations whenever possible. He would probably have a diagnosis of
    A) avoidant phobia.
    B) specific phobia.
    C) specific social phobia.
    D) generalized social phobia.
    Answer: D

Pages: 166
Topic: Anxiety Disorders: Phobic Disorders
Skill: Factual   Other1:

54. Social phobias and specific phobias differ in that
    A) social phobias are uncommon.
    B) social phobias usually begin during childhood.
    C) social phobias occur about equally often in women and men.
    D) none of the above
    Answer: C

Pages: 166
Topic: Anxiety Disorders: Phobic Disorders
Skill: Applied   Other1:

55. Joann is unable to avoid attending an office party, though she suffers from social phobia and fears this situation immensely. What is likely to happen?
    A) She may resort to alcohol use, such as drinking before the party, in order to cope with her anxiety.
    B) She is likely to feel uneasy at first but her initial anxiety should subside once she starts interacting with others.
    C) She is likely to come down with a psychosomatic illness that conveniently prevents her from attending the party.
    D) She may experience a panic attack shortly before the party, but will be able to function normally once she gets there.
    Answer: A

Pages: 166
Topic: Anxiety Disorders: Phobic Disorders
Skill: Applied   Other1:

56. Sharon has a diagnosis of social phobia. It wouldn't be unusual to find that at some point she also obtained a diagnosis of
    A) depression.
    B) panic disorder.
    C) generalized anxiety disorder.
    D) any of the above
    Answer: D

Pages: 167
Topic: Anxiety Disorders: Phobic Disorders
Skill: Factual   Other1:
57. Öhman and colleagues have suggested an evolutionary origin for specific and social
     phobias. Which of the following do they cite as evidence for their theory?
     A) Social phobias involve panic and fight or flight responses as if an individual were
        threatened by a predator.
     B) Specific phobias often involve fears of potential predators and other threats to
        safety, accompanied by a strong urge to flee. By contrast, social phobia often
        involves fear of social stimuli signalling dominance and aggression, accompanied by
        submissive behaviors but rarely by attempts to actually flee the feared situation.
     C) Social phobia is accompanied by a strong urge to flee the feared situation, whereas
        specific phobia is not associated with an urge to flee the feared stimulus situation.
     D) Specific phobias often are associated with direct traumatic conditioning, but social
        phobias are usually associated with vicarious conditioning.
     Answer: B

Pages: 167
Topic: Anxiety Disorders: Phobic Disorders
Skill: Factual   Other1:
58. Many social phobias originate from
     A) operant conditioning experiences.
     B) direct classical conditioning experiences.
     C) vicarious conditioning exprinces.
     D) B and C
     Answer: D

Pages: 167
Topic: Anxiety Disorders: Phobic Disorders
Skill: Factual   Other1:
59. Öhman's conditioning studies using social stimuli found all BUT which of the following?
     A) Subjects develop stronger conditioned responses when mild electric shocks are paired
        with slides of angry faces rather than with neutral or happy faces.
     B) Following conditioning, extremely brief presentations of angry or contemptuous faces
        elicited the conditioned response.
     C) Conditioning was most likely to occur when the angry face was directed at the subject.
     D) The only individuals who acquired the conditioned response to angry faces were those
        who had been shocked randomly prior to stimulus exposure.
     Answer: D

Pages: 168
Topic: Anxiety Disorders: Phobic Disorders
Skill: Conceptual   Other1:
60. Individuals exposed to the same types of traumatic social experiences differ as to whether they will develop a social phobia. What might account for these differences?
    A) individual differences in intellectual level
    B) being from a lower socioeconomic background is associated with being less confident socially
    C) preexisting differences in individuals' temperament and experience
    D) early childhood experiences with a pleasant but dominant opposite-sexed parent, leading to unresolved Oedipal wishes
    Answer: C

Pages: 168
Topic: Anxiety Disorders: Phobic Disorders
Skill: Factual   Other1:
61. Genetic studies of social phobia show that
    A) there is no genetic component to social phobia.
    B) the monozygotic twin concordance rate for social phobia is nearly 100 percent.
    C) there is probably a rather modest genetic contribution to social phobia, although the contribution of genetic and environmental factors needs to be disentangled.
    D) the first degree relatives of social phobics are not likely to be socially phobic themselves.
    Answer: C

Pages: 168
Topic: Anxiety Disorders: Phobic Disorders
Skill: Applied   Other1:
62. Bill has a diagnosis of generalized social phobia. Which of the following statements probably applies to him?
    A) He is afraid of public speaking but otherwise has no fears about handling social situations.
    B) He selectively screens out information that people around him are judging him negatively unless forced to acknowledge that this is true.
    C) His high degree of self-consciousness in public situations makes it more likely that he will behave inappropriately.
    D) none of the above
    Answer: C

Pages: 168
Topic: Anxiety Disorders: Phobic Disorders
Skill: Conceptual   Other1:

63. Hypervigilance, expectations of rejection, and self-preoccupation are examples of
    A) symptoms of specific phobia.
    B) cognitive factors that may be involved in the origin and maintenance of social phobias.
    C) preparedness schemas in humans and animals.
    D) nonpathological social behaviors.
    Answer: B

Pages: 169
Topic: Anxiety Disorders: Panic Disorder and Agoraphobia
Skill: Factual   Other1: In Student Study Guide

64. The two features of panic attacks that distinguish them from other types of anxiety are their characteristic _____ and their _____.
    A) focal stimulus; intensity
    B) brevity; mildness
    C) focal stimulus; constancy
    D) brevity; intensity
    Answer: D

Pages: 168-169
Topic: Anxiety Disorders: Panic Disorder and Agoraphobia
Skill: Factual   Other1:

65. According to the DSM-IV, which of the following criteria is NOT characteristic of panic disorder?
    A) Panic disorder must be preceded by agoraphobia.
    B) A person must have recurrent and mostly unexpected panic attacks.
    C) Panic attacks involve the abrupt onset of symptoms that usually reach a peak intensity within ten minutes.
    D) A person must be concerned about having another attack for at least one month.
    Answer: A

Pages: 169
Topic: Anxiety Disorders: Panic Disorder and Agoraphobia
Skill: Conceptual   Other1:

66. Panic disorder can be difficult to diagnose because
    A) its symptoms are sometimes mistaken for various medical conditions.
    B) it is such a rare disorder.
    C) panic attacks are difficult to assess.
    D) people with panic attacks are afraid to leave the house and therefore rarely seek treatment.
    Answer: A

Pages: 169
Topic: Anxiety Disorders: Panic Disorder and Agoraphobia
Skill: Factual   Other1:
67. Barlow regards panic attacks as
    A) involving the activation of the fight or flight response to a "true alarm."
    B) a masked form of anxiety.
    C) involving the activation of the fight or flight response to a "false alarm."
    D) identical in characteristics to a phobic fear response.
    Answer: C

Pages: 169
Topic: Anxiety Disorders: Panic Disorder and Agoraphobia
Skill: Conceptual   Other1:
68. Agoraphobics usually suffer from a variety of fears. What is currently thought to be the
    underlying theme of these different fears?
    A) fear of one or more forms of travel
    B) fear of leaving one's house
    C) fear of being in a crowded place
    D) fear of being in places from which escape would be impossible or embarassing
    Answer: D

Pages: 169
Topic: Anxiety Disorders: Panic Disorder and Agoraphobia
Skill: Factual   Other1:
69. Which of the following statements is true of the relationship between agoraphobia and
    panic disorder?
    A) Panic disorder always occurs in conjunction with agoraphobia.
    B) Agoraphobia usually occurs without panic disorder.
    C) Agoraphobia usually occurs with panic disorder, although it can occasionally also occur
       in the absence of panic attacks.
    D) Agoraphobia usually precedes panic disorder.
    Answer: C

Pages: 169
Topic: Anxiety Disorders: Panic Disorder and Agoraphobia
Skill: Factual   Other1:
70. Panic disorder and agoraphobia
    A) both usually involve the repeated occurrence of panic attacks.
    B) may be genetically linked.
    C) both are common in women but relatively rare in men.
    D) both A and B
    Answer: D

Pages: 169
Topic: Anxiety Disorders: Panic Disorder and Agoraphobia
Skill: Factual   Other1:

71. Some people who have a history of repeated panic attacks become fearful of situations where they might experience a panic attack, and become reluctant to leave home. This would qualify for a diagnosis of
A) generalized panic disorder.
B) panic disorder with agoraphobia.
C) panic disorder without agoraphobia.
D) none of the above
Answer: B

Pages: 170
Topic: Anxiety Disorders: Panic Disorder and Agoraphobia
Skill: Factual   Other1:

72. The text presented the case of Anne Watson, who had panic disorder with agoraphobia. Her case was typical of individuals with this disorder in that
A) her panic attacks began in childhood.
B) her agoraphobia preceded the onset of panic attacks.
C) her panic attacks eventually subsided on their own.
D) her panic attacks began in adulthood after experiencing a highly stressful event.
Answer: D

Pages: 172
Topic: Anxiety Disorders: Panic Disorder and Agoraphobia
Skill: Conceptual   Other1: In Student Study Guide

73. The common mechanism underlying the effects of all the various panic provocation agents is that they
A) mimic the physiological cues that normally precede a panic attack.
B) stimulate the locus coeruleus.
C) interfere with processes that inhibit anxiety.
D) increase activity in the anxious apprehension system.
Answer: A

Pages: 172
Topic: Anxiety Disorders: Panic Disorder and Agoraphobia
Skill: Conceptual   Other1:
74. What is problematic about drawing causal inferences about the particular neurobiological system involved in the origin of panic attacks on the basis of biological challenge studies?
    A) The studies are few in number and need to be replicated.
    B) There are a large number of pharmacological panic provocation agents that are associated with different and even mutually exclusive neurobiological processes.
    C) The challenge agents produce panic attacks in people who do not have panic disorder, as well as in patients with panic disorder.
    D) none of the above
    Answer: B

Pages: 173
Topic: Anxiety Disorders: Panic Disorder and Agoraphobia
Skill: Factual   Other1:
75. One theory about the neurobiology of panic disorder proposed by Gorman and colleagues suggests that panic, anticipatory anxiety, and phobic avoidance are three components of panic disorder with agoraphobia which differ in
    A) intensity.
    B) the extent to which each is genetically determined.
    C) the area of the brain in which each of the components originates.
    D) the kindling threshold.
    Answer: C

Pages: 173
Topic: Anxiety Disorders: Panic Disorder and Agoraphobia
Skill: Factual   Other1:
76. Genetic studies of panic disorder suggest that
    A) the heritability for panic disorder is very strong while the environment appears to play a very small role in determining who develops the disorder.
    B) the heritability for panic disorder is very strong and the environment also appears to play a very important role in determining who develops the disorder.
    C) the heritability for panic disorder is modest and the environment appears to play a very important role in determining who develops the disorder.
    D) the heritability for panic disorder is virtually nonexistent and the environment appears to account almost fully for determining who develops the disorder.
    Answer: C

Pages: 173
Topic: Anxiety Disorders: Panic Disorder and Agoraphobia
Skill: Factual   Other1:
77. The "fear of fear" hypothesis about panic disorder holds
   A) that panic attacks are most likely to develop in people who already are in a state of
      generalized fear or anxiety.
   B) that agoraphobics come to fear panic attacks because they are so terrifying and because
      they begin to interpret mild internal signs of anxiety as a signal that a panic attack
      might occur; they react with anxiety to their anxiety.
   C) that automatic thoughts often trigger panic.
   D) that the seat of brain activity underlying all panic and anxiety responses is the
      limbic system.
   Answer: B

Pages: 173
Topic: Anxiety Disorders: Panic Disorder and Agoraphobia
Skill: Factual   Other1:
78. Conditioning to one's own internal bodily sensations is called
   A) kindling.
   B) automatic thinking.
   C) interoceptive conditioning.
   D) exteroceptive conditioning.
   Answer: C

Pages: 174
Topic: Anxiety Disorders: Panic Disorder and Agoraphobia
Skill: Factual   Other1:
79. According to the cognitive model of panic, individuals panic because
   A) they have catastrophizing automatic thoughts about the meaning of their bodily
      sensations.
   B) they become interoceptively conditioned to their internal bodily sensations.
   C) they've developed a learned panic response to a variety of external stimuli.
   D) of random firing of neurons in the locus coeruleus.
   Answer: A

Pages: 175
Topic: Anxiety Disorders: Panic Disorder and Agoraphobia
Skill: Conceptual   Other1:
80. A variety of biological challenge studies have been conducted in which subjects' interpretations about their internal bodily sensations were manipulated. These studies found that such manipulations altered the probability of occurrence and the intensity of panic attacks in those subjects who had a diagnosis of panic disorder. These studies provide supportive evidence for which model of panic?
A) biochemical
B) interoceptive
C) proprioceptive
D) cognitive
Answer: D

Pages: 174
Topic: Anxiety Disorders: Panic Disorder and Agoraphobia
Skill: Conceptual   Other1:
81. One drawback of the cognitive model of panic is that
A) it doesn't explain why only a subgroup of individuals who have a panic attack will go on to develop panic disorder.
B) it doesn't specify what factors cause an individual to develop a tendency to catastrophize about bodily sensations.
C) it doesn't explain why simple cognitive manipulations can block panic.
D) it is difficult to test empirically.
Answer: B

Pages: 175
Topic: Anxiety Disorders: Panic Disorder and Agoraphobia
Skill: Conceptual   Other1:
82. The cognitive model predicts that a misinterpretation of internal bodily sensations leads to a panic attack in individuals who have a diagnosis of panic disorder. What might this suggest about the results of biological challenge studies?
A) No generalizations can be drawn about panic attacks occurring outside of laboratory conditions because the panic attacks in the laboratory are caused by artificial means.
B) The misinterpretation of hyperarousal does not cause panic attacks in these studies.
C) There is no relationship between panic provocation agents and the occurrence of panic attacks.
D) Sensitivity to panic provocation agents is probably a consequence, not a cause, of having panic disorder.
Answer: D

Pages: 175
Topic: Anxiety Disorders: Panic Disorder and Agoraphobia
Skill: Applied   Other1:
83. Florence has been diagnosed with panic disorder. In a biological challenge study, she was told that she could control the amount of carbon dioxide she inhaled by turning a dial, although she never opted to turn the dial. Based on the results of the study by Sanderson, Rapee, and Barlow, which of the following statements would be most likely to be true?
   A) Florence's level of physiological arousal was much lower than subjects who did not have the perceived control over the amount of gas they inhaled.
   B) Florence was more likely to experience a panic attack because of anxiety associated with the additional responsibility of controlling the amount of gas.
   C) Being told that she controlled the gas had no impact on whether she was likely to have a panic attack.
   D) none of the above
   Answer: A

Pages: 175
Topic: Anxiety Disorders: Panic Disorder and Agoraphobia
Skill: Factual   Other1:
84. Recently it has been suggested that differing levels of preexisting "anxiety sensitivity" may account for
   A) individual differences in readiness to acquire classically conditioned fear responses in specific phobias.
   B) individual differences in extinction rates of conditioned fear responses.
   C) individual differences in who develops catastrophic misinterpretations of bodily sensations and, thus, panic disorder.
   D) differences in individuals who develop specific phobias and those who develop social phobias.
   Answer: C

Pages: 173-176
Topic: Anxiety Disorders: Panic Disorder and Agoraphobia
Skill: Factual   Other1:
85. According to your text, which of the following is NOT a cognitive vulnerability factor that has been proposed for panic disorder?
   A) biases in processing threatening information
   B) perceptions of controllability
   C) sensitivity to biologically prepared stimuli
   D) anxiety sensitivity
   Answer: C

Pages: 176
Topic: Anxiety Disorders: Generalized Anxiety Disorder
Skill: Factual   Other1:
86. One difference between generalized anxiety disorder and all of the other anxiety disorders is that
    A) the central emotion in generalized anxiety disorder is anxiety, whereas the central emotion is fear in the other anxiety disorders.
    B) only individuals with generalized anxiety disorder have hyperresponsive autonomic nervous systems.
    C) individuals with generalized anxiety disorder are often also depressed, but this is less often so for individuals with other anxiety disorders.
    D) people with generalized anxiety disorder lack the effective anxiety-avoidance mechanisms usually seen with the other anxiety disorders.
    Answer: D

Pages: 176
Topic: Anxiety Disorders: Generalized Anxiety Disorder
Skill: Factual   Other1:
87. Barlow refers to generalized anxiety disorder as the "basic" anxiety disorder because
    A) anxious apprehension is the essence of generalized anxiety disorder, but is only one feature of the other anxiety disorders.
    B) it precedes the onset of other anxiety disorders in an individual.
    C) other anxiety disorders appear to be variants of generalized anxiety disorder.
    D) all the other anxiety disorders are genetically linked to generalized anxiety disorder.
    Answer: A

Pages: 177
Topic: Anxiety Disorders: Generalized Anxiety Disorder
Skill: Factual   Other1:
88. Among the most common symptoms of generalized anxiety disorder are all BUT which of the following?
    A) feeling keyed up or on edge
    B) autonomic hyperactivity
    C) difficulty concentrating or mind going blank
    D) muscle tension
    Answer: B

Pages: 178
Topic: Anxiety Disorders: Generalized Anxiety Disorder
Skill: Factual   Other1:
89. Generalized anxiety disorder
   A) often co-occurs with other Axis I disorders, especially mood disorders and other
      anxiety disorders.
   B) almost always begins in adulthood.
   C) is rarely associated with alcohol or substance abuse.
   D) is relatively rare compared to the other anxiety disorders, especially in women.
   Answer: A

Pages: 179
Topic: Anxiety Disorders: Generalized Anxiety Disorder
Skill: Factual   Other1:
90. According to the psychoanalytic view, the difference between specific phobias and
    generalized anxiety is that
   A) people with generalized anxiety have not repressed their anxiety and displaced it onto
      an external object, as have people with specific phobias.
   B) generalized anxiety results from an excessively harsh repression of superego impulses,
      whereas specific phobias involve an inability to repress anxiety.
   C) specific phobias result from intrapsychic conflicts but generalized anxiety does not.
   D) generalized anxiety involves fear of a real danger, whereas specific phobias involve
      fear of an imaginary threat.
   Answer: A

Pages: 179
Topic: Anxiety Disorders: Generalized Anxiety Disorder
Skill: Factual   Other1:
91. Generalized anxiety is currently regarded as consisting largely of worry about a variety
    of negative things that may happen. This differs from the earlier behavioral formulation
    of generalized anxiety as
   A) a group of many individual specific fears conditioned to internal stimulus cues.
   B) fear of many external and internal stimulus situations.
   C) a response to uncontrollable aversive events.
   D) a deficit in the ability to inhibit a conditioned fear response.
   Answer: B

Pages: 179
Topic: Anxiety Disorders: Generalized Anxiety Disorder
Skill: Conceptual   Other1:
92. A major area of research into the etiology of generalized anxiety disorder has been the importance of prior experience with uncontrollable and unpredictable aversive events. In support of this research, Mineka and colleagues found that
    A) frequent early experiences with control and mastery had no effect on monkeys' later behavior in fear-eliciting situations.
    B) frequent early experiences with control and mastery seemed to immunize monkeys to some extent against the harmful effects of later exposure to fear-eliciting situations.
    C) monkeys reared with no control over their reinforcers could later have been diagnosed with DSM-IV generalized anxiety disorder.
    D) monkeys who developed symptoms of generalized anxiety disorder first showed conditioned fear responses to innocuous stimuli.
    Answer: B

Pages: 180
Topic: Anxiety Disorders: Generalized Anxiety Disorder
Skill: Applied   Other1:
93. "It's always best to assume the worst." "I must be prepared for danger at all times." These statements are examples of
    A) maladaptive schemas.
    B) safety signals.
    C) threat cues.
    D) anti-affirmations.
    Answer: A

Pages: 181
Topic: Anxiety Disorders: Generalized Anxiety Disorder
Skill: Factual   Other1:
94. Which of the following statements is NOT true concerning information-processing biases in individuals with generalized anxiety disorder?
    A) These individuals have an automatic, unconscious bias toward selectively attending to threatening cues when presented with both threat and nonthreat cues.
    B) These individuals are likely to interpret ambiguous information in a threatening way.
    C) These individuals are especially likely to remember and ruminate about the threat cues that they've experienced.
    D) These individuals do not have an especially good memory for threatening cues that they've experienced.
    Answer: C

Pages: 181
Topic: Anxiety Disorders: Generalized Anxiety Disorder
Skill: Factual   Other1:

95. The area of the brain and neurotransmitter system most strongly implicated in panic disorder and in generalized anxiety disorder, respectively, are
    A) the frontal cortex and serotonin; the locus coeruleus and norepinephrine.
    B) the limbic system and serotonin; the hypothalamus and norepinephrine.
    C) the locus coeruleus and norepinephrine; the limbic system and GABA (gamma aminobutyric acid).
    D) the medulla oblongata and GABA; the frontal cortex and norepinephrine.
    Answer: C

Pages: 181
Topic: Anxiety Disorders: Generalized Anxiety Disorder
Skill: Conceptual   Other1:

96. Neurobiological factors involved in panic disorder and generalized anxiety disorder provide evidence for the hypothesis that
    A) fear and anxiety are fundamentally distinct.
    B) both disorders are caused by an excess of the GABA neurotransmitter.
    C) the two disorders are genetically identical.
    D) panic may be an acute version of generalized anxiety disorder.
    Answer: A

Pages: 182
Topic: Anxiety Disorders: Obsessive-Compulsive Disorder
Skill: Factual   Other1:

97. Most people with obsessive-compulsive disorder
    A) experience obsessions, but compulsions are relatively rare.
    B) experience compulsions, but obsessions are relatively rare.
    C) experience both obsessions and compulsions.
    D) develop compulsions in childhood, and obsessions in adolescence or adulthood.
    Answer: C

Pages: 182
Topic: Anxiety Disorders: Obsessive-Compulsive Disorder
Skill: Factual   Other1:

98. Which of the following is true of obsessive-compulsive disorder?
    A) This disorder is fairly evenly distributed between men and women.
    B) This disorder tends to have a chronic course, although the severity of symptoms usually waxes and wanes.
    C) Obsessive thoughts often involve themes of contamination, aggression, or sexual impulses.
    D) all of the above
    Answer: D

Pages: 183
Topic: Anxiety Disorders: Obsessive-Compulsive Disorder
Skill: Conceptual   Other1:
99. Obsessive-compulsive disorder tends to be a homogeneous disorder. One example of this is that
    A) symptoms tend to wax and wane over time.
    B) some people are "cleaners" and some people are "checkers."
    C) there are numerous different types of obsessions.
    D) nearly all individuals with this diagnosis fear that something terrible will happen to themselves or others, for which they will be responsible.
    Answer: D

Pages: 183
Topic: Anxiety Disorders: Obsessive-Compulsive Disorder
Skill: Factual   Other1:
100. Compulsive behaviors are reinforced by
    A) external rewards for performing behaviors that are positively valued in society.
    B) the reduction of anxiety following performance of the compulsive act.
    C) the covert obsessions that follow these compulsive acts.
    D) increases in anxiety.
    Answer: B

Pages: 183
Topic: Anxiety Disorders: Obsessive-Compulsive Disorder
Skill: Factual   Other1:
101. One very important feature of obsessive-compulsive disorder is
    A) that it is usually preceded by a viral infection.
    B) the tendency to judge risks to safety unrealistically.
    C) that it does not tend to co-occur with other anxiety disorders.
    D) that obsessions involving aggressive impulses often result in violent acts.
    Answer: B

Pages: 186
Topic: Anxiety Disorders: Obsessive-Compulsive Disorder
Skill: Conceptual   Other1:
102. Mowrer's two-process theory of avoidance learning provides a theoretical rationale for an effective treatment for obsessive-compulsive disorder. What is this treatment?
    A) response activation therapy
    B) exposure prevention therapy
    C) response provocation therapy
    D) exposure therapy with response prevention
    Answer: D

Pages: 188
Topic: Anxiety Disorders: Obsessive-Compulsive Disorder
Skill: Factual   Other1:

103. As discussed in your text, much evidence now suggests a number of biological causal factors in obsessive-compulsive disorder including all of the following EXCEPT
    A) a moderate genetic contribution.
    B) abnormalities in the functioning of the basal ganglia.
    C) abnormalities in serotonin systems.
    D) All of the above have been implicated as possible biological causal factors.
    Answer: D

Pages: 189
Topic: Anxiety Disorders: Sociocultural Causal Factors
Skill: Conceptual   Other1:

104. Anxiety disorders
    A) exist only in technologically advanced cultures.
    B) probably exist in all societies, but take different forms in different cultures.
    C) are especially prevalent in Japan, where strong pressures exist to compete and succeed.
    D) involve different causal factors in different cultures.
    Answer: B

Pages: 191
Topic: Treatments and Outcomes: Pharmacological Therapies
Skill: Factual   Other1:

105. One of the greatest disadvantages of pharmacological treatment for anxiety disorders is that
    A) all of the drugs used are very addictive.
    B) the drugs are effective in fewer than ten percent of the individuals treated with them.
    C) relapse rates following discontinuation of medication range from moderate to very high unless medication is combined with psychotherapy.
    D) all of the drugs used have serious side-effects.
    Answer: C

Pages: 192
Topic: Treatments and Outcomes: Psychological Therapies
Skill: Factual   Other1:

106. Treatment outcome studies have found
    A) that psychodynamic therapy is highly effective for treating generalized anxiety disorder.
    B) that psychodynamic therapy is not very effective for treating panic disorder, agoraphobia, and obsessive-compulsive disorder.
    C) that behavior therapy is not very successful in treating anxiety disorders without some psychodynamic treatment being used as well.
    D) that cognitive therapy is better than behavioral therapy for all anxiety disorders.
    Answer: B

Pages: 192
Topic: Treatments and Outcomes: Psychological Therapies
Skill: Applied   Other1:
107. In therapy for her anxiety, Joanna was asked to imagine a series of fearful situations while in a state of deep relaxation. This treatment is called
A) interoceptive exposure.
B) cognitive retraining.
C) graded exposure.
D) systematic desensitization.
Answer: D

Pages: 193
Topic: Treatments and Outcomes: Psychological Therapies
Skill: Factual   Other1:
108. _____ treatments are a central core of most behavioral treatments for many anxiety disorders.
A) Desensitization
B) Muscle relaxation
C) Exposure-based
D) Avoidance retraining
Answer: C

Pages: 193
Topic: Treatments and Outcomes: Psychological Therapies
Skill: Factual   Other1:
109. Adding a cognitive therapy component to behavioral treatments
A) adds little in the way of effectiveness to existing exposure treatments for anxiety disorders.
B) enhances effectiveness for treating some, but not all, anxiety disorders.
C) adds substantially to treatment efficacy for any disorder.
D) tends to dilute the efficacy of the behavioral treatments.
Answer: B

Pages: 196
Topic: Unresolved Issues on the Anxiety Disorders
Skill: Factual   Other1:
110. Of all the approaches taken to understanding the anxiety disorders, it is an unfortunate state of affairs that the LEAST progress has been made by the
A) sociocultural approach.
B) biological approach.
C) biopsychosocial approach.
D) cognitive approach.
Answer: C

Short Answer

Write the word or phrase that best completes each statement or answers the question.

Pages: 157
Topic: Anxiety Disorders
Skill: Factual   Other1:
1. The exaggerated use of avoidance behaviors or defense mechanisms was historically known as
_____.
Answer: neurosis

Pages: 157
Topic: Anxiety Disorders
Skill: Factual   Other1:
2. How did Freud define neurosis?
Answer: Freud viewed neurotic behavior as caused by intrapsychic conflict between id demands and the prohibitions of ego or superego. Anxiety was a sign of this inner conflict, although it was not always obvious and its existence was, in many cases, inferred.

Pages: 158-159
Topic: The Fear and Anxiety Response Patterns
Skill: Factual   Other1:
3. Briefly define fear and anxiety as contemporary researchers view them.
Answer: Fear or panic is a basic emotion involving the activation of the sympathetic nervous system's fight or flight response. Anxiety, according to Barlow, is a more complex and diffuse blend of emotions and cognitions which involves preparation for possible future danger and, should it occur, the subsequent activation of the fight or flight response.

Pages: 160
Topic: Anxiety Disorders
Skill: Factual   Other1:
4. Briefly describe three findings of epidemiological studies pertaining to anxiety disorders.
Answer: They are relatively common, more prevalent in women than in men. It is also common for there to be two or more diagnoses of an anxiety disorder in the same person. Between 25 and 50 percent of all individuals diagnosed with an anxiety disorder will also, at some point, receive a diagnosis of an affective disorder.

Pages: 160
Topic: Anxiety Disorders: Phobic Disorders
Skill: Factual   Other1:

5. What is a phobia? What are the three main categories of phobias in DSM-IV?
    Answer: A phobia is a persistent and disproportionate fear of a specific object or
             situation that in reality presents little or no actual danger. The three
             categories of phobias in DSM-IV are specific phobia, social phobia, and
             agoraphobia.

Pages: 162-165
Topic: Anxiety Disorders: Phobic Disorders
Skill: Conceptual   Other1:

6. What does learning theory tell us about the origins and maintenance of specific phobias?
    Answer: Specific phobias appear to involve fear responses that are classically
             conditioned through either direct experience with a traumatic event, or by
             observing someone interacting fearfully with an object. The phobic avoidance
             response results in anxiety reduction, which provides a powerful reinforcement
             each time the feared stimulus is avoided. Phobic responses are especially
             resistant to extinction.

Pages: 163-166
Topic: Anxiety Disorders: Phobic Disorders
Skill: Conceptual   Other1:

7. Briefly describe the results of animal studies conducted by Mineka, Cook, and colleagues
    as they pertain to specific phobias.
    Answer: These investigators demonstrated the acquisition of a conditioned fear response
             to snakes in rhesus monkeys by means of observational conditioning. Monkeys
             readily acquired conditioned fear responses to fear-relevant stimuli such as
             snakes, but not to fear-irrelevant stimuli such as flowers, even when they had
             no prior experience with the fear-relevant stimuli.

Pages: 165
Topic: Anxiety Disorders: Phobic Disorders
Skill: Factual   Other1:

8. What is biological preparedness?
    Answer: Some researchers have suggested that primates and humans have a
             biologically-based preparedness to rapidly associate certain objects or
             situations with aversive events. Thus, conditioned fear responses to these
             fear-relevant objects or situations are more readily acquired and more resistant
             to extinction. These prepared fears may have an evolutionary basis.

Pages: 166-168
Topic: Anxiety Disorders: Phobic Disorders
Skill: Factual   Other1:
9. Briefly identify and describe two cognitive variables that may play a role in the origin or maintenance of social phobias.
  Answer: Perceptions of uncontrollability may lead to submissive and fearful behavior. Social phobics tend to believe that others control events in their lives. They may have "danger schemas," latent expectations that others will reject them. They may have distortions in information processing, such as hypervigilance and overattention to possible social threats. They may be so preoccupied with negative self-evaluative thoughts that they actually do behave in a socially unskillful manner. This may, in turn, lead others to reject them, thereby confirming the phobics' original expectations.

Pages: 169-172
Topic: Anxiety Disorders: Panic Disorder and Agoraphobia
Skill: Conceptual   Other1:
10. What is the relationship between panic disorder and agoraphobia?
  Answer: Agoraphobia usually begins in an individual who already has experienced panic attacks, when he or she begins to fear and avoid the situations in which future panic attacks might occur. Cases of agoraphobia without panic disorder are very rare clinically, though less rare in epidemiological studies. The two disorders may be genetically linked.

Pages: 172
Topic: Anxiety Disorders: Panic Disorder and Agoraphobia
Skill: Factual   Other1:
11. What are biological challenge procedures?
  Answer: In these investigations of panic disorder, panic provocation agents (such as sodium lactate or carbon dioxide) are administered to individuals with and without diagnoses of panic disorder. The agents produce stress on certain neurobiological systems, which then produce intense physical symptoms. These agents are associated with a higher rate of subsequent panic attacks in people with panic disorder.

Pages: 174
Topic: Treatments and Outcomes: Psychological Therapies
Skill: Factual   Other1:
12. Briefly describe the cognitive model of panic.
  Answer: Individuals with panic disorder are hypersensitive to their own bodily sensations and tend to automatically interpret these sensations as indicating that something catastrophic will happen to them (such as a racing heart means a heart attack). These automatic thoughts trigger further increases in autonomic functioning, more catastrophic interpretations, and hence a downward spiral into a full-blown panic attack.

Pages: 176
Topic: Anxiety Disorders: Generalized Anxiety Disorder
Skill: Applied   Other1:

13. For as long as he can remember, Steve has been a "worrier." He feels tense and restless, irritable, and easily fatigued. He has difficulty concentrating and sleeping. What DSM-IV diagnosis does Steve probably qualify for? What other DSM diagnoses would he be most likely to exhibit?

    Answer: The most likely diagnosis is generalized anxiety disorder. He would therefore be at risk for a diagnosis of another anxiety disorder, a depressive disorder, and alcohol or substance abuse/dependence. The most common additional disorders are panic disorder with agoraphobia, social phobia, and specific phobia.

Pages: 181
Topic: Anxiety Disorders: Generalized Anxiety Disorder
Skill: Factual   Other1:

14. Generalized anxiety disorder is believed to be associated with a dysfunction in the neurotransmitter system _____ in the region of the brain known as the _____.

    Answer: GABA (gamma aminobutyric acid); limbic system

Pages: 187
Topic: Anxiety Disorders: Obsessive-Compulsive Disorder
Skill: Factual   Other1:

15. Briefly describe the most effective behavioral treatment for obsessive-compulsive disorder.

    Answer: Treatment involves exposure therapy with response prevention. Exposure may be in imagination (in vitro) or in real life (in vivo). Response prevention involves preventing the individual from performing the compulsive act associated with anxiety reduction.

Pages: 189-190
Topic: Anxiety Disorders: Sociocultural Causal Factors
Skill: Conceptual   Other1:

16. In Japan, taijin kyofusho (TKS) is a disorder involving fear of social situations. Briefly describe the similarities between TKS and the anxiety disorder that it is most similar to.

    Answer: TKS is rooted in Japanese concerns about the social presentation of self. Other-centered group conformity is emphasized in Japanese culture, putting the individual on stage at all times. This transforms ordinary social awkwardness into a more serious social and moral failing (Kirmayer, 1991). TKS, therefore, is most similar to social phobia, although some of the symptoms differ. For example, TKS includes a phobia about eye contact.

Pages: 190-191
Topic: Treatments and Outcomes: Pharmacological Therapies
Skill: Factual   Other1:

17. In treating anxiety disorders, medical practitioners rather than mental health professionals often use, and misuse, drugs from the benzodiazepine category for tension relief and for relaxation. An example of a benzodiazepine that often is prescribed is _____.

Answer: Valium, Xanax, and any of the other benzodiazepines

Pages: 193
Topic: Treatments and Outcomes: Psychological Therapies
Skill: Factual   Other1:

18. A very promising new variant of exposure therapy being used in the treatment of panic disorder targets the fear that patients have of their internal sensations. This new variant of exposure therapy is known as _____.
Answer: interoceptive exposure

Pages: 193
Topic: Treatments and Outcomes: Psychological Therapies
Skill: Factual   Other1:

19. Professional therapists appear to be increasing their willingness to learn and employ a combination of varied approaches that may be used in treatment of clients with an anxiety disorder. This more integrative approach to treatment is called _____.
Answer: multimodal therapy

Pages: 196
Topic: Unresolved Issues on the Anxiety Disorders
Skill: Conceptual   Other1:

20. What are the impediments to progress in developing a coherent biopsychosocial model of anxiety disorders?
Answer: Some impediments arise from difficulties that professionals have in understanding the research of colleagues in different areas than theirs. Some fields are advancing and changing so quickly that it is hard to keep up with the research literature. Some lack of progress is also due to biases in the thinking of professionals who champion their own point-of-view as superior to those who differ from them.

Essay

Write your answer in the space provided or on a separate sheet of paper.

Pages: 157
Topic: Anxiety Disorders
Skill: Conceptual   Other1:

1. What is the history of the term "neurosis?" How was it used by Freud? How is it viewed by the DSM today?
   Answer: "Neurosis" was first used in the 1700's to mean disordered sensations of the nervous system. Freud viewed neurosis as a psychological disorder resulting from intrapsychic conflict between id demands and prohibitions of ego or superego. Anxiety, whether conscious or unconscious, arose from this conflict and caused neurotic behaviors. Historically, anxiety disorders were considered examples of neurotic behavior involving the exaggerated use of defense mechanisms and avoidance behaviors. In DSM-IV, "neurosis" is not used, and anxiety is the prominent symptom of anxiety disorders.

Pages: 159
Topic: Anxiety Disorders
Skill: Conceptual   Other1:

2. Identify and briefly describe each of the main categories of anxiety disorders.
   Answer: Generalized anxiety disorder is marked by chronic worry about two or more life circumstances whereas phobia disorders are characterized by fear and worry about a specific stimulus. With panic disorder there are recurrent panic attacks, anticipatory anxiety, and phobic avoidance. Obsessive-compulsive disorder is marked by obsessions or compulsions or both. Posttraumatic stress disorder involves a severe emotional reaction to a catastrophic event beyond the realm of ordinary human experience.

Pages: 163-166
Topic: Anxiety Disorders: Phobic Disorders
Skill: Conceptual   Other1:

3. How have analogue studies with animals contributed to our knowledge of anxiety disorders?
   Answer: A series of studies by Mineka, Cook, and colleagues demonstrated the acquisition of phobic-like fear behavior in rhesus monkeys through observational conditioning. Additional studies in which monkeys observed other monkeys interacting nonfearfully with fear-relevant stimuli were associated with an immunization effect. Further studies provided or withheld early experiences with mastery and control to monkeys, and found an inoculation effect in the Mastery group. Other animal studies provided evidence of biological preparedness that may be similar to that involved in human specific phobias.

Pages: 165-168
Topic: Anxiety Disorders: Phobic Disorders
Skill: Conceptual   Other1:

4. What is biological preparedness? Describe studies that are relevant to this concept and discuss preparedness in relation to two of the anxiety disorders.

   Answer: Preparedness, developed in the course of evolution, is the biologically-based tendency to associate certain types of potentially threatening objects and situations with aversive events. Fears to these stimuli are more easily conditioned and very resistant to extinction. Preparedness is especially relevant to specific and social phobias and obsessive-compulsive disorder. Ö hman and Mineka conducted studies which provided evidence for the role of preparedness in the acquisition of phobias. Conditioned fears to hypothesized prepared stimuli were more readily acquired and resistant to extinction.

Pages: 161-189
Topic: Anxiety Disorders
Skill: Conceptual   Other1:

5. Discuss the evidence for a hereditary basis of the anxiety disorders.

   Answer: The genetic evidence for anxiety disorders is based on family history (pedigree) studies which show a higher incidence of these disorders among first-degree relatives of the proband than in members of the general population. The higher prevalence is particularly true of agoraphobia, OCD, and blood-injury phobia. The risk of developing anxiety disorder increases with the number of afflicted parents and with the degree of genetic similarity to the affected person.

Pages: 165-189
Topic: Anxiety Disorders
Skill: Conceptual   Other1:

6. Describe biological hypotheses about causal factors and biological treatments for anxiety disorders.

   Answer: Generalized anxiety disorder involves underactivity of the neurotransmitter GABA in the limbic system. Panic disorder is characterized by norepinephrine dysfunction in the locus coeruleus. OCD involves a dysfunction in serotonin metabolism, and abnormalities in the basal ganglia and possibly the striatum. For generalized anxiety disorder, benzodiazepines and tricyclic antidepressants are most effective. Panic disorders require the use of antidepressants or high potency benzodiazepines, and OCD is treated with medications that influence serotonin metabolism.

Pages: 163-188
Topic: Anxiety Disorders
Skill: Conceptual   Other1:

7. Describe the various psychological explanations for anxiety disorders and the corresponding psychotherapies.

    Answer: Psychodynamic theories hold that anxiety disorders stem from intrapsychic conflicts that induce anxiety, requiring the construction of ego-defenses. Behavioral explanations focus on the role of maladaptive learning. Exposure therapies with response prevention are the backbone of behavioral therapies. Cognitive therapy is designed to identify and change the faulty thinking that causes anxiety.

Pages: 168-176
Topic: Anxiety Disorders: Panic Disorder and Agoraphobia
Skill: Applied   Other1:

8. Elvira suffers from unexpected panic attacks that are not triggered by her being the focus of others' attention. She experiences these attacks about once a week. She has now become afraid of situations where escape is difficult. What is her diagnosis? Explain the other components of the diagnosis that are not provided in the above description. What are the causes of her disorder and how might she be treated?

    Answer: Elvira has panic disorder with agoraphobia. Such individuals have a lengthy list of symptoms. These panic attacks are not provoked by the immediate situation but are often observed to follow earlier periods of stress. Agoraphobia is a frequent complication and may share a genetic linkage. Antidepressants may be helpful along with behavioral and cognitive interventions.

Pages: 176-182
Topic: Anxiety Disorders: Generalized Anxiety Disorder
Skill: Applied   Other1:

9. What is generalized anxiety disorder? What are the symptoms of this disorder? How does it differ from other anxiety disorders?

    Answer: It is characterized by chronic unrealistic or excessive worry. Symptoms involve motor tension, vigilance and scanning, restlessness, and difficulty concentrating. It differs from other anxiety disorders primarily in the "free-floating" source of distress and the lack of adequate means of avoiding anxiety-eliciting situations.

Pages: 182-189
Topic: Anxiety Disorders: Obsessive-Compulsive Disorder
Skill: Applied   Other1:

10. Egan feels a need to wash his hands as much as fifteen times an hour. This seems to reduce his anxiety temporarily. What would be his diagnosis? What are the characteristics of this disorder? How would Egan view his disorder?

Answer: His diagnosis is obsessive-compulsive disorder, which involves a persistent preoccupation with obsessions and/or feeling compelled to engage in some behavior that is highly ritualistic. These thoughts and behaviors usually appear irrational to the individual and interfere considerably with everyday life.

Pages: 163-188
Topic: Treatments and Outcomes: Psychological Therapies
Skill: Conceptual   Other1:

11. Select two of the anxiety disorders and discuss what role cognitive variables might play in the origin and maintenance of these disorders.

Answer: In panic disorder, individuals may be hypersensitive to bodily sensations, with attacks that involve misinterpreting internal sensations as having catastrophic and uncontrollable consequences. They may also have high levels of preexisting "anxiety sensitivity." GAD may be associated with a history of experiencing unpredictable, uncontrollable events, lack of safety signals, and maladaptive schemas. Maintenance involves biased information-processing for anxiety-related stimuli, overestimating probabilities of threat, and underestimating one's control over important aspects of the environment.

Pages: 163-175
Topic: Anxiety Disorders
Skill: Conceptual   Other1:

12. Discuss the role of individual differences in the origin of anxiety disorders.

Answer: Early behavioral theories failed to explain why some individuals exposed to a traumatic event acquired conditioned fear responses and others did not. Most anxiety disorders show modest heritability (more in OCD). Abnormalities in neurological structure and function and temperamental differences also may play a role. Preparedness accounts for why some stimuli are more associated with conditioned fear. Mineka's studies point to the importance of prior experience in controlling versus not controlling important aspects of one's environment.

Pages: 182-188
Topic: Treatments and Outcomes: Psychological Therapies
Skill: Applied   Other1:

13. Jaye came to your clinic complaining that she feels an urgent need to wash her hands for five minutes every time she touches a doorknob or a piece of furniture. What is her probable diagnosis? Describe in detail a behavioral treatment program based on what you know about research on treatment efficacy for this disorder.

    Answer: The treatment of choice for her obsessive-compulsive disorder is exposure therapy with response prevention. Patient and therapist develop a hierarchy of aversive stimuli rated 1-100 according to their potential to evoke the compulsive behavior. The patient then exposes herself to the situations in guided fantasy and in vivo, progressing up the hierarchy as her discomfort level in each situation drops. She will be exposed to the situations without being allowed to perform the compulsive act. Adjuncts may include treatment with serotonergic reuptake inhibitors.

Pages: 192-195
Topic: Treatments and Outcomes: Psychological Therapies
Skill: Conceptual   Other1:

14. Discuss cognitive treatments for anxiety disorders.

    Answer: They are valuable when added to behavioral therapy for panic disorder, social phobia and generalized anxiety disorder, but not for specific phobia and OCD. Cognitive therapy involves identifying and modifying maladaptive cognitions. One highly successful model of treatment is a three-phase program for panic disorder. Phase I involves teaching patients the cognitive model of panic disorder. They are taught to systematically examine the evidence supporting the validity of their fears and to decatastrophize. Phase II teaches arousal-reduction techniques. Phase III uses exposure therapy.

Pages: 195-196
Topic: Unresolved Issues on the Anxiety Disorders
Skill: Conceptual   Other1:

15. Discuss the current state of theory and research in developing a coherent biopsychosocial model of anxiety disorders.

    Answer: With enhanced reliability of anxiety disorder diagnoses in the DSM, much progress in identifying possible biological causal factors has occurred, as well as in identifying possible cognitive and behavioral causal factors. However, little communication between researchers in biology and psychology occurs because of differences in understanding one another's research, as well as biases that one approach is superior to the other. There is also much less interest in sociocultural factors. Thus, minimal progress has been made in developing a coherent biopsychosocial model of anxiety disorders.

CHAPTER 6   Mood Disorders and Suicide

Multiple-Choice

Choose the one alternative that best completes the statement or answers the question.

Pages: 201
Topic: Mood Disorders and Suicide
Skill: Factual   Other1:
1. Which of the following is used as a means of differentiating among the various mood disorders?
    A) severity
    B) symptoms
    C) duration
    D) all of the above
    Answer: D

Pages: 201
Topic: Mood Disorders and Suicide
Skill: Factual   Other1:
2. Which of the following is true of unipolar major depression?
    A) It is the most prevalent mood disorder.
    B) It is equally common in men and women.
    C) It occurs five times as often in elderly people as in middle-aged adults.
    D) It does not begin until adolescence.
    Answer: A

Pages: 202
Topic: Unipolar Mood Disorders: Normal Depression
Skill: Applied   Other1:
3. Kathleen is suffering from a normal depression. Which of the following is most likely?
    A) She probably has experienced recent stress.
    B) Her depression is most easily treated with antidepressant medication.
    C) Her depression will probably become a major depressive episode.
    D) She probably has a biological predisposition for developing a major depressive episode.
    Answer: A

Pages: 202
Topic: Unipolar Mood Disorders: Normal Depression
Skill: Applied   Other1:
4. Ervin was widowed six months ago. He is depressed and withdrawn, and spends a lot of time fantasizing about and yearning for his wife. Which of these statements is true?
   A) He is in what Bowlby described as phase one of the normal grieving process.
   B) He will probably spend another year or two grieving before moving into the final rebuilding phase.
   C) He is in what Bowlby described as phase two of the normal grieving process.
   D) He is probably also experiencing mood-congruent delusions or hallucinations.
   Answer: C

Pages: 203
Topic: Unipolar Mood Disorders: Normal Depression
Skill: Factual   Other1:
5. Recent evidence suggests that depression occuring in the postpartum period is most often
   A) a brief episode of major depression.
   B) a period of depressive feelings that are within the normal range of mood variation.
   C) a precursor to a major depressive episode.
   D) a hormone disorder.
   Answer: B

Pages: 205-206
Topic: Unipolar Mood Disorders: Mild to Moderate Mood Disorders
Skill: Applied   Other1:
6. The text presented the case study of a 28-year-old junior executive who experienced dysthymia. She was typical of individuals with this disorder in that she
   A) responded well to antianxiety medication.
   B) experienced alternating periods of hypothymia and mild depression.
   C) had no outward signs of her depression.
   D) had experienced moderate depression for over two years.
   Answer: D

Pages: 205
Topic: Unipolar Mood Disorders: Mild to Moderate Mood Disorders
Skill: Factual   Other1:
7. Dysthymia differs from adjustment disorder with depressed mood in
   A) behavioral manifestations.
   B) duration; adjustment disorder does not exceed six months in duration.
   C) an identifiable psychosocial stressor within three months of onset of depressed symptoms, which is required for adjustment disorder but not for dysthymia.
   D) B and C
   Answer: D

Pages: 205
Topic: Unipolar Mood Disorders: Mild to Moderate Mood Disorders
Skill: Applied   Other1:

8. One week ago, Lillian got a permanent at her beauty salon. The beautician left the solution on too long and much of Lillian's hair fell out. Since that time, Lillian has spent her days crying, refusing to go to work or even to leave the house. How would you diagnose Lillian?
    A) dysthymia
    B) posttraumatic stress syndrome
    C) adjustment disorder with depressed mood
    D) no diagnosis is appropriate; Lillian's reaction is normal under the circumstances.
    Answer: C

Pages: 229
Topic: Unipolar Mood Disorders: Mild to Moderate Mood Disorders
Skill: Factual   Other1:

9. The currently prominent tripartite model of anxiety and depression developed by Watson and colleagues suggests that anxiety and depression
    A) differ in that anxiety is characterized by anxious hyperarousal, while depression is characterized by low positive affectivity.
    B) differ in that anxiety is characterized by anxious hyperarousal, while depression is characterized by high negative affect.
    C) differ in that anxiety involves low positive affect, while depression involves high negative affect.
    D) differ in that depression involves negative affect while anxiety involves both low positive affect and high negative affect.
    Answer: A

Pages: 229
Topic: Unipolar Mood Disorders: Mild to Moderate Mood Disorders
Skill: Factual   Other1:

10. Alloy, Mineka, and colleagues have expanded the hopelessness model of depression in order to explain the features of comorbidity between depression and anxiety. All of the following statements are true of their model EXCEPT
    A) When an individual becomes convinced of the certainty of uncontrollability of future events, and also becomes certain that bad outcomes will occur, hopelessness and depression set in.
    B) Anxiety disorders are characterized by a sense of helplessness.
    C) Helplessness and a diagnosis of an anxiety disorder often occur sequentially before the onset of hopelessness and depression.
    D) Phobias are the most likely anxiety disorders to be associated with depression, and panic and obsessive-compulsive disorders the least likely, because phobias are associated with hopelessness.
    Answer: D

Pages: 206
Topic: Unipolar Mood Disorders: Major Depressive Disorder
Skill: Factual   Other1:
11. Major depression differs from dysthymia in that
    A) intermittent normal moods may last a few days or weeks in major depression, but not in dysthymia.
    B) a person must have experienced a manic or hypomanic episode to receive a diagnosis of major depression.
    C) more symptoms must be present and symptoms must occur every day for at least two weeks in order to diagnose major depression.
    D) cognitive and motivational symptoms occur only in major depressive disorder.
    Answer: C

Pages: 207
Topic: Unipolar Mood Disorders: Major Depressive Disorder
Skill: Factual   Other1:
12. Kerry suffers from depression. He is experiencing delusions that his brain is deteriorating and that he is aging quickly. These delusions
    A) are uncommon in depression and suggest a diagnosis of schizophrenia.
    B) are typical of depressive delusions because they are mood-congruent.
    C) suggest that he is suffering from a bipolar rather than a unipolar disorder.
    D) are most likely to persist after the depression remits.
    Answer: B

Pages: 207
Topic: Unipolar Mood Disorders: Major Depressive Disorder
Skill: Factual   Other1:
13. Depression that is worse in the morning and is accompanied by an inability to experience pleasure, significant weight loss, and early morning awakening is known as the _____ type of major depression.
    A) seasonal
    B) melancholic
    C) dysthymic
    D) premenstrual
    Answer: B

Pages: 207
Topic: Unipolar Mood Disorders: Major Depressive Disorder
Skill: Factual   Other1:
14. Major depression of the melancholic type was traditionally thought to be linked to
    A) mood-incongruent delusions.
    B) double depression.
    C) endogenous causes.
    D) prior stressful events.
    Answer: C

Pages: 207
Topic: Unipolar Mood Disorders: Major Depressive Disorder
Skill: Factual   Other1:
15. Double depression
   A) is very uncommon.
   B) involves a diagnosis of major depression in a person with dysthymia.
   C) is another name for recurrent depressive episodes.
   D) is a major depressive episode that lasts longer than the usual six months.
   Answer: B

Pages: 208
Topic: Unipolar Mood Disorders: Major Depressive Disorder
Skill: Applied   Other1:
16. Ruth was diagnosed with a major depressive episode and began treatment with an
   antidepressant medication. She discontinued the medication after a month when she began
   feeling better, but quickly experienced a return of her depressive symptoms. This is
   likely to be an example of a
   A) recurrence of her major depressive episode.
   B) relapse.
   C) major depression of the melancholic type.
   D) depressive episode in the context of bipolar disorder.
   Answer: B

Pages: 208
Topic: Unipolar Mood Disorders: Major Depressive Disorder
Skill: Factual   Other1:
17. Left untreated, a major depressive episode will last, on average, about
   A) one month.
   B) six months.
   C) two years.
   D) It's impossible to predict.
   Answer: B

Pages: 208
Topic: Unipolar Mood Disorders: Major Depressive Disorder
Skill: Factual   Other1:
18. Which of the following is true of recurrent episodes of depression?
   A) Recurrent episodes occur almost exclusively in women, whereas men tend to experience
      only a single episode.
   B) Depressive episodes are more likely to recur in elderly patients than in young people.
   C) Once an individual experiences one major depressive episode, he or she is no more
      likely to experience another episode than someone who's never had a depression.
   D) Recurrent episodes may leave scars that increase a person's risk for future episodes,
      especially for younger persons.
   Answer: D

Pages: 208
Topic: Unipolar Mood Disorders: Major Depressive Disorder
Skill: Factual   Other1:
19. Abdul has made an appointment with a psychologist because he gets depressed in the winter and improves in the summer. This type of mood disorder is called
A) winter mood disorder.
B) winter depression.
C) periodic affective disorder.
D) seasonal affective disorder.
Answer: D

Pages: 209
Topic: Bipolar Disorders
Skill: Factual   Other1:
20. Bipolar disorders are marked by periods of mania or _____ and depression.
A) hypermania
B) hypomania
C) hypersomnia
D) hypersomnolence
Answer: B

Pages: 209
Topic: Bipolar Disorders: Cyclothymia
Skill: Factual   Other1: In Student Study Guide
21. A disorder that involves mood swings between subclinical levels of depression and mania is
A) bipolar disorder.
B) manic depression.
C) dysthymic disorder.
D) cyclothymic disorder.
Answer: D

Pages: 209
Topic: Bipolar Disorders: Cyclothymia
Skill: Conceptual   Other1:
22. Evidence that cyclothymia is a milder form of bipolar disorder was obtained by
A) studies in which it was noted that depressive symptoms are very mild in both these disorders.
B) studies in which a relationship was found between a cyclothymic temperament and an excess of depressive and manic or hypomanic episodes during prospective follow-up.
C) studies in which a hypomanic personality inventory was able to identify individuals who had experienced both hypomanic episodes and depression.
D) both B and C
Answer: D

Pages: 210
Topic: Bipolar Disorders: Bipolar Disorder
Skill: Applied   Other1:
23. Lee has Bipolar I disorder. This means that she has
    A) a much deeper depression than someone with unipolar major depression.
    B) had recurrent dysthymic episodes.
    C) had at least one manic episode.
    D) had a prior diagnosis of cyclothymia.
    Answer: C

Pages: 210
Topic: Bipolar Disorders: Bipolar Disorder
Skill: Factual   Other1:
24. Bipolar I and Bipolar II disorders are
    A) probably distinct disorders.
    B) different in that people with Bipolar II disorder experience hypomanic rather than
       manic episodes.
    C) similar in that people with either disorder experience depressive episodes.
    D) all of the above
    Answer: D

Pages: 211
Topic: Bipolar Disorders: Bipolar Disorder
Skill: Factual   Other1:
25. The text presented the case study of a 46-year-old woman who was in a hospital during a
    manic episode. She was typical of individuals who experience bipolar disorder because she
    A) had inflated self-esteem and made erotic overtures.
    B) had much anxiety, especially in interpersonal situations.
    C) was lethargic.
    D) had delusions that others were persecuting her.
    Answer: A

Pages: 211
Topic: Bipolar Disorders: Bipolar Disorder
Skill: Conceptual   Other1:
26. Unipolar and bipolar disorders have all of the following in common EXCEPT
    A) Both are typically recurrent disorders.
    B) Either may exhibit a seasonal pattern.
    C) The majority of individuals with either diagnosis have periods of intermittent normal
       functioning.
    D) They share a common genetic loading.
    Answer: D

Pages: 211
Topic: Bipolar Disorders: Bipolar Disorder
Skill: Conceptual   Other1:
27. The bipolar individual who is most likely to be misdiagnosed by DSM-IV is the one who
    A) experiences numerous manic episodes, but no depressive episodes.
    B) is hyperverbal and delusional during a manic episode.
    C) has anxiety along with depression.
    D) has an initial depressive episode with no previous episodes of mania or hypomania.
    Answer: D

Pages: 211-212
Topic: Bipolar Disorders: Bipolar Disorder
Skill: Factual   Other1:
28. Over 90 percent of individuals with bipolar disorder
    A) experience a single manic episode but many recurrent depressive episodes.
    B) experience recurrent manic and/or depressive episodes.
    C) show a full recovery after lithium treatment.
    D) exhibit rapid cycling.
    Answer: B

Pages: 212
Topic: Bipolar Disorders: Bipolar Disorder
Skill: Factual   Other1:
29. Rapid cycling refers to
    A) four or more episodes of mania or depression every year.
    B) episodes of depression and remission alternating at least once every two months.
    C) the mood changes associated with cyclothymia.
    D) all of the above
    Answer: A

Pages: 212
Topic: Bipolar Disorders: Schizoaffective Disorder
Skill: Applied   Other1:
30. Logan has been diagnosed with schizoaffective disorder. This means that Logan
    A) has manic and depressive symptoms simultaneously.
    B) has two or more major symptoms of schizophrenia in addition to a major mood disorder.
    C) has a good prognosis compared to individuals with unipolar depression.
    D) experiences symptoms only in the winter.
    Answer: B

Pages: 212
Topic: Bipolar Disorders: Schizoaffective Disorder
Skill: Conceptual   Other1:
31. Schizoaffective disorder
    A) is a psychotic type of mood disorder.
    B) is a subtype of schizophrenia.
    C) is a distinctive diagnostic entity, separate from mood disorders and schizophrenia.
    D) is controversial in that it is not yet clear which of the above might be true.
    Answer: D

Pages: 213-214
Topic: Causal Factors in Unipolar Disorders: Biological Factors
Skill: Factual   Other1:
32. Which of the following statements is true about hereditary factors in unipolar depression?
    A) Adoption studies have provided substantial evidence that unipolar depressions result
       from a very high genetic loading.
    B) Heritability estimates from twin studies range from 33 percent to 45 percent depending
       on the diagnostic criteria used to select unipolar depressives.
    C) Hereditary factors are much more important in unipolar than in bipolar disorder.
    D) Adoption studies indicate that environmental factors, and not genetic factors, are
       causally implicated in unipolar depression.
    Answer: B

Pages: 214
Topic: Causal Factors in Unipolar Disorders: Biological Factors
Skill: Factual   Other1:
33. Researchers in the 1960's noted that tricyclic antidepressants increased the availability
    of serotonin and norepinephrine in the brain. This led to
    A) the monoamine hypothesis.
    B) the neurotransmitter depletion hypothesis.
    C) the dexamethasone suppression test (DST).
    D) the hemispheric imbalance hypothesis.
    Answer: A

Pages: 215
Topic: Causal Factors in Unipolar Disorders: Biological Factors
Skill: Conceptual   Other1:
34. Which of the following is true of biochemical theories of the etiology of unipolar depression?
    A) They are probably correct in suggesting that the depletion of serotonin and norepinephrine is a key causal factor in unipolar depression.
    B) They are probably correct in suggesting that the excess of serotonin and norepinephrine is a key causal factor in unipolar depression.
    C) They are probably not sufficient to account for the etiology of unipolar depression without taking into account other kinds of biochemical systems.
    D) none of the above
    Answer: C

Pages: 214-215
Topic: Causal Factors in Unipolar Disorders: Biological Factors
Skill: Factual   Other1:
35. All of the following have been associated with unipolar depression EXCEPT
    A) high levels of cortisol.
    B) low levels of thyroid hormone.
    C) hemispheric asymmetry in brain activity.
    D) excessive levels of dopamine.
    Answer: D

Pages: 215
Topic: Causal Factors in Unipolar Disorders: Biological Factors
Skill: Factual   Other1:
36. Lower activity in the left prefrontal cortex (relative to the right prefrontal cortex)
    A) is associated with bipolar disorder.
    B) is present during manic episodes.
    C) may be a risk marker for depression.
    D) is associated with the presence of psychotic delusions.
    Answer: C

Pages: 216
Topic: Causal Factors in Unipolar Disorders: Biological Factors
Skill: Conceptual   Other1:
37. According to recent research, many of the clinical symptoms of depression may result from disruptions in the
    A) circadian rhythms of various bodily cycles.
    B) manufacture of serotonin.
    C) regulation of body temperature.
    D) quantity of artificial light available to people.
    Answer: A

Pages: 216
Topic: Causal Factors in Unipolar Disorders: Biological Factors
Skill: Factual   Other1:
38. One current theory of the etiology of unipolar depression suggests a failure of regulation of different, interrelated biological systems. These systems include those that regulate all but which of the following?
    A) neurotransmitters
    B) hormone production
    C) the sleep-waking cycle
    D) mood biorhythms
    Answer: D

Pages: 216
Topic: Causal Factors in Unipolar Disorders: Biological Factors
Skill: Factual   Other1:
39. Research on the treatment of seasonal affective disorder indicates that
    A) controlled exposure to light, even artificial light, is effective.
    B) controlled exposure to light is effective but the light must be real, not artificial.
    C) controlled exposure to light, whether real or artificial, is ineffective.
    D) studies on the treatment of seasonal affective disorder are so rare that no conclusion can be drawn.
    Answer: A

Pages: 217
Topic: Causal Factors in Unipolar Disorders: Biological Factors
Skill: Factual   Other1:
40. Which part of the brain regulates many of the biological functions that are disturbed in depression?
    A) the limbic system
    B) the temporal lobe
    C) the inner cortex
    D) the medulla oblongata
    Answer: A

Pages: 218-219
Topic: Causal Factors in Unipolar Disorder: Psychosocial Factors
Skill: Factual   Other1:
41. Sophisticated studies of stressful life events and depression (that do not rely on self-report) have found that
A) stressful events are no more frequent for depressives than for nondepressives.
B) depressives experience more events involving loss, physical injury, and social disruption than nondepressives.
C) depressives experience more threatening and dangerous events than nondepressives.
D) negative events are associated with endogenous depression, but not other types of depression.
Answer: B

Pages: 219
Topic: Causal Factors in Unipolar Disorder: Psychosocial Factors
Skill: Conceptual   Other1:
42. A recent review of the literature on the occurrence of stressful events and depression cited in your text concluded that
A) chronic stressors and minor events are associated with the onset of major depression.
B) chronic stressors and minor events are associated with an increase in depressive symptoms but probably not major depression.
C) depressive symptoms are associated with minor events, whereas major depression is associated with chronic strain.
D) major life stressors cause endogenous depressions but not other types of depression.
Answer: B

Pages: 219
Topic: Causal Factors in Unipolar Disorder: Psychosocial Factors
Skill: Factual   Other1:
43. In a classic study by Brown and Harris, which of the following factors seemed to protect women against becoming depressed following the experience of a severely stressful event?
A) being involved in an intimate relationship
B) having at least four children at home to take care of
C) not having to work outside the home
D) all of the above
Answer: A

Pages: 221
Topic: Causal Factors in Unipolar Disorder: Psychosocial Factors
Skill: Factual   Other1:
44. Lucy suffers from major depression. One of the factors that may make her vulnerable to depression is
    A) an increased suppression of cortisol.
    B) a strong religious commitment.
    C) the death of a parent before the age of eleven.
    D) living too near to her relatives.
    Answer: C

Pages: 214-220
Topic: Causal Factors in Unipolar Disorder: Psychosocial Factors
Skill: Factual   Other1:
45. Results from studies of potential diatheses for unipolar depression find that
    A) a genetic diathesis appears to operate in over 90% of the cases of depression.
    B) only about one-third to one-half of the variance is accounted for by genetic variables.
    C) environmental factors are almost exclusively responsible for the origin of depression.
    D) genetic factors are involved in bipolar, but not in unipolar, disorder.
    Answer: B

Pages: 220-221
Topic: Causal Factors in Unipolar Disorder: Psychosocial Factors
Skill: Factual   Other1:
46. Among the personality variables that have been suggested as potential diatheses for depression are
    A) a temperamental sensitivity to negative stimuli.
    B) hypersensitivity to interpersonal loss and rejection.
    C) a pessimistic attributional style.
    D) all of the above
    Answer: D

Pages: 220
Topic: Causal Factors in Unipolar Disorder: Psychosocial Factors
Skill: Applied   Other1:
47. Sarah measured high on a scale of neuroticism. This may mean that
    A) she is at risk for depression and anxiety disorders.
    B) she is nonsociotropic.
    C) she is high in positive affectivity.
    D) she is selectively insensitive to negative stimuli.
    Answer: A

Pages: 220
Topic: Causal Factors in Unipolar Disorder: Psychosocial Factors
Skill: Applied   Other1:
48. Marc is very concerned about how others think of him and is extremely sensitive to criticism and rejection. He is most likely to be
    A) low in sociotropy.
    B) low in emotional resilience.
    C) high in autonomy.
    D) high in sociotropy.
    Answer: D

Pages: 220
Topic: Causal Factors in Unipolar Disorder: Psychosocial Factors
Skill: Applied   Other1:
49. Erin is extremely preoccupied with academic success and being "first" in all of her extracurricular activities. She is most likely to be
    A) high in sociotropy.
    B) low in sociotropy.
    C) high in autonomy.
    D) low in autonomy.
    Answer: C

Pages: 220
Topic: Causal Factors in Unipolar Disorder: Psychosocial Factors
Skill: Conceptual   Other1:
50. An individual who is high in sociotropy is most likely to become depressed following
    A) an achievement failure.
    B) a negative interpersonal event.
    C) a situation involving threat or danger.
    D) a symbolic loss.
    Answer: B

Pages: 220-221
Topic: Causal Factors in Unipolar Disorder: Psychosocial Factors
Skill: Factual   Other1:
51. According to Beck, psychosocial stressors may activate _____, and thereby lead to the onset of a depression.
    A) pessimistic attributional styles
    B) dysfunctional beliefs
    C) repressed memories of childhood traumas
    D) hormonal dysregulation
    Answer: B

Topic: Causal Factors in Unipolar Disorder: Psychosocial Factors
Skill: Factual   Other1:

52. Dysfunctional schemas and pessimistic attributional styles are examples of
    A) psychosocial stressors.
    B) sociocultural variables.
    C) cognitive diatheses.
    D) biopsychosocial diatheses.
    Answer: C

Pages: 221
Topic: Causal Factors in Unipolar Disorder: Psychosocial Factors
Skill: Factual   Other1:

53. Early parental loss
    A) has little to do with adult depression, although it is associated with depression in children.
    B) appears to be a risk factor for adult depression, especially if the loss is followed by poor parental care.
    C) is a risk factor for later depression only if the loss is due to the death of the parent.
    D) is a risk factor only for psychotic depression.
    Answer: B

Pages: 222
Topic: Causal Factors in Unipolar Disorder: Psychosocial Factors
Skill: Conceptual   Other1:

54. There is probably a genetic basis for neuroticism. Neuroticism is highly correlated with negative attributional style. Thus, heredity may operate as a _____ diathesis and attributional style as a more _____ diathesis for depression.
    A) necessary; sufficient
    B) vulnerability; stressor-like
    C) fundamental; superficial
    D) distal; proximal
    Answer: D

Pages: 222
Topic: Causal Factors in Unipolar Disorder: Psychosocial Factors
Skill: Conceptual   Other1:

55. Jordan has recurrent episodes of depression. Freud would say that
    A) his self-accusations are unconsciously directed at a lost love object (real or symbolic).
    B) his depressions reflect a regression back to the oral stage of development.
    C) his needs for nurturance probably were not fulfilled during the first year of life.
    D) all of the above
    Answer: D

Pages: 222
Topic: Causal Factors in Unipolar Disorder: Psychosocial Factors
Skill: Factual   Other1:
56. More recent psychodynamic theorists have emphasized the importance of _____ as a vulnerability factor to depression.
    A) "anger turned inward"
    B) oral fixation
    C) insecure early attachment to the parental figures
    D) anal fixation
    Answer: C

Pages: 223
Topic: Causal Factors in Unipolar Disorder: Psychosocial Factors
Skill: Factual   Other1:
57. Lewinsohn's behavioral model of depression suggests that
    A) depression is reinforced by the anxiety reduction associated with depressive social withdrawal.
    B) depression develops through traumatic conditioning.
    C) depression is caused by a lack of positive reinforcement that is contingent on one's responses.
    D) depression is a conditioned state associated with early trauma in a person who has an introverted temperament.
    Answer: C

Pages: 223
Topic: Causal Factors in Unipolar Disorder: Psychosocial Factors
Skill: Conceptual   Other1:
58. A major difficulty with behavioral models of depression is that
    A) they are hard to operationalize in research.
    B) research hasn't demonstrated the direction of causality between depressive symptoms and response-contingent reinforcements.
    C) there has been little research associated with these models.
    D) they emphasize lack of positive reinforcement but ignore punishment.
    Answer: B

Pages: 223
Topic: Causal Factors in Unipolar Disorder: Psychosocial Factors
Skill: Factual   Other1:
59. Beck's cognitive theory of depression posits _____ as a diathesis for depression.
    A) depressogenic schemas
    B) negative introjects
    C) inadequate reinforcements
    D) dysfunctional behaviors
    Answer: A

Pages: 223
Topic: Causal Factors in Unipolar Disorder: Psychosocial Factors
Skill: Factual   Other1:
60. According to Beck's diathesis-stress model of depression, stressors activate dysfunctional beliefs, resulting in
    A) internal, stable, global attributions.
    B) negative automatic thoughts.
    C) the development of a depressogenic schema.
    D) regression to an earlier stage of development.
    Answer: B

Pages: 223
Topic: Causal Factors in Unipolar Disorder: Psychosocial Factors
Skill: Factual   Other1:
61. In Beck's model of depression, the negative cognitive triad
    A) refers to the three dimensions of attributions (internality, globality, and stability).
    B) involves negative thoughts about self, world, and future.
    C) refers to the three major cognitive distortions (overgeneralization, selective abstraction, and all-or-none reasoning).
    D) all of the above
    Answer: B

Pages: 224
Topic: Causal Factors in Unipolar Disorder: Psychosocial Factors
Skill: Applied   Other1:
62. "If I don't get the highest grade in the class on this exam, then I'm a total failure as a person." According to Beck, this is an example of
    A) selective abstraction.
    B) the negative cognitive triad.
    C) underrationalization.
    D) overgeneralization.
    Answer: D

Pages: 224-225
Topic: Causal Factors in Unipolar Disorder: Psychosocial Factors
Skill: Conceptual   Other1:
63. According to Teasdale's concept of the "vicious cycle" of depression, _____ may maintain and exacerbate a depression.
    A) unstable attributions
    B) learned hopelessness
    C) positive reinforcements
    D) cognitive biases
    Answer: D

Pages: 225
Topic: Causal Factors in Unipolar Disorder: Psychosocial Factors
Skill: Conceptual   Other1:
64. Which of the following statements is true regarding research on Beck's cognitive theory of depression?
    A) The research tends to support descriptive aspects of the theory, but more research is needed to evaluate causal aspects of the theory.
    B) The research has not found much evidence for Beck's theory.
    C) The research has provided substantial support for both descriptive and causal hypotheses in Beck's theory.
    D) As yet there has not been enough research testing his theory to draw any conclusions about either the descriptive or the causal aspects of the theory.
    Answer: A

Pages: 225
Topic: Causal Factors in Unipolar Disorder: Psychosocial Factors
Skill: Factual   Other1:
65. In laboratory experiments in the late 1960's, Seligman and colleagues found major learning deficits in dogs who had earlier experienced
    A) separation from their mothers.
    B) isolation from peers.
    C) uncontrollable shocks.
    D) malnutrition.
    Answer: C

Pages: 225
Topic: Causal Factors in Unipolar Disorder: Psychosocial Factors
Skill: Factual   Other1:
66. In Seligman's studies, after dogs were exposed to uncontrollable shocks, they
    A) became hyperaggressive.
    B) exhibited behaviors that are similar to those of an individual experiencing a panic attack.
    C) learned how to control shocks in a new situation much more quickly than other dogs.
    D) failed to try to learn to control shocks when they were put into a new situation.
    Answer: D

Topic: Causal Factors in Unipolar Disorder: Psychosocial Factors
Skill: Factual   Other1:
67. When an organism learns that it has no control over aversive events, it will become passive and depressed. This is a central hypothesis of the
    A) hopelessness theory of depression.
    B) attribution theory of depression.
    C) learned helplessness theory of depression.
    D) cognitive theory of depression.
    Answer: C

Pages: 225
Topic: Causal Factors in Unipolar Disorder: Psychosocial Factors
Skill: Factual   Other1:
68. According to Seligman and his colleagues, learned helplessness will produce three kinds of deficits. Which of the following is NOT one of them?
    A) hopelessness
    B) motivational
    C) cognitive
    D) emotional
    Answer: A

Pages: 226
Topic: Causal Factors in Unipolar Disorder: Psychosocial Factors
Skill: Factual   Other1:
69. In the reformulated helplessness theory of depression, Abramson and colleagues proposed that the experience of an uncontrollable negative event contributes to developing depressed symptoms depending on _____.
    A) the type of social support system a person has.
    B) the severity of the uncontrollable negative events.
    C) whether the uncontrollable event is achievement-oriented or interpersonally-oriented.
    D) the kinds of causal attributions a person makes for experiencing the uncontrollable negative event.
    Answer: D

Pages: 226
Topic: Causal Factors in Unipolar Disorder: Psychosocial Factors
Skill: Factual   Other1:
70. The attributional style of depressed individuals is characterized by a tendency to make _____ attributions for negative events.
    A) internal, unstable, specific
    B) internal, unstable, global
    C) internal, stable, global
    D) external, unstable, specific
    Answer: C

Pages: 226
Topic: Causal Factors in Unipolar Disorder: Psychosocial Factors
Skill: Factual   Other1:
71. In a revision of the reformulated helplessness theory of depression, Abramson, Metalsky, and colleagues proposed that a _____ expectancy is a proximal necessary cause of one subtype of depression.
A) helplessness
B) hopelessness
C) controllability
D) predictability
Answer: B

Pages: 226
Topic: Causal Factors in Unipolar Disorder: Psychosocial Factors
Skill: Factual   Other1:
72. In a prospective study testing the hopelessness theory of depression, Metalsky and colleagues found that
A) learned helplessness interacted with a negative stressor to produce depression.
B) a pessimistic attributional style led to depression, which in turn produced symptoms of hopelessness.
C) hopelessness is a symptom and not a cause of depression.
D) a pessimistic attributional style and low self-esteem, when combined with a negative stressor, culminated in hopelessness-mediated depressed symptoms.
Answer: D

Pages: 228-230
Topic: Causal Factors in Unipolar Disorder: Psychosocial Factors
Skill: Factual   Other1:
73. Which of the following appears to be an interpersonal causal factor in the origin of depression?
A) poor social skills
B) restricted social support networks
C) marital distress
D) all of the above
Answer: D

Pages: 228
Topic: Causal Factors in Unipolar Disorder: Psychosocial Factors
Skill: Factual   Other1:
74. When a nondepressed student lives with a depressed roommate, which of the following often results?
    A) frequent verbal fights which may even become physical
    B) increased depression and hostility in the roommate who was not originally depressed
    C) a decrease in depression in the depressed roommate
    D) increased caretaking by the nondepressed roommate, but only after the nondepressed roommate becomes depressed
    Answer: B

Pages: 230
Topic: Causal Factors in Unipolar Disorder: Psychosocial Factors
Skill: Factual   Other1:
75. Research investigating the association between marital distress and depression has found that
    A) marital distress is related to depression in women, but not in men.
    B) marital distress is probably both a causal factor and a result of depression.
    C) marital distress is often a result of depression in one of the spouses, but does not appear to be a causal factor.
    D) marital distress usually stops when depression remits.
    Answer: B

Pages: 230
Topic: Causal Factors in Unipolar Disorder: Psychosocial Factors
Skill: Factual   Other1:
76. Parental depression
    A) is a risk factor for depression in children.
    B) is probably both a genetic and a psychosocial vulnerability factor for the children of a depressed parent.
    C) is associated with adaptive failure and a variety of psychiatric diagnoses in children.
    D) all of the above
    Answer: D

Pages: 231
Topic: Causal Factors in Bipolar Disorders: Biological Factors
Skill: Factual   Other1:

77. In 1922 Kraepelin estimated that about 80 percent of his manic-depressive patients had a "hereditary taint." More recent data from family history (pedigree), twin, and adoption studies suggests that
    A) actually, that is true of unipolar disorder and not bipolar disorder.
    B) there is no significant genetic liability for bipolar disorder.
    C) he was right; about 80 percent of the variance in liability for bipolar disorder is genetic.
    D) there is about the same genetic liability for bipolar disorder as for any other mood disorder.
    Answer: C

Pages: 231
Topic: Causal Factors in Bipolar Disorders: Biological Factors
Skill: Conceptual   Other1:

78. Elevated rates of unipolar disorder have been found in genetic studies of bipolars. Why might this be true?
    A) Much evidence suggests that unipolar disorder is a milder form of bipolar disorder.
    B) Genes for bipolar disorder may also predispose to unipolar disorder.
    C) Bipolar disorder "breeds true."
    D) none of the above
    Answer: B

Pages: 231-232
Topic: Causal Factors in Bipolar Disorders: Biological Factors
Skill: Conceptual   Other1:

79. The gene mapping study of bipolar disorder in an Amish community is an example of
    A) the first time scientists were successful in identifying the exact gene responsible for a mental disorder.
    B) a study flawed because of using outdated, unreliable diagnostic criteria.
    C) premature acceptance of scientific findings without evaluating contradictory evidence.
    D) a successful genetic linkage study.
    Answer: C

Pages: 232
Topic: Causal Factors in Bipolar Disorders: Biological Factors
Skill: Factual   Other1:
80. Abnormalities with which of the following neurotransmitters has NOT been implicated in
bipolar disorder?
A) serotonin
B) dopamine
C) lithium
D) norepinephrine
Answer: C

Pages: 232
Topic: Causal Factors in Bipolar Disorders: Biological Factors
Skill: Factual   Other1:
81. The drug of choice in treating bipolar disorder is
A) sodium.
B) lithium.
C) thyroid hormone.
D) Prozac.
Answer: B

Pages: 233-234
Topic: Causal Factors in Bipolar Disorders: Psychosocial Factors
Skill: Factual   Other1:
82. A sophisticated prospective study of the role of stressful life events in bipolar disorder
found that
A) low levels of stress protected an individual against manic episodes.
B) low levels of stress protected an individual against depressive episodes.
C) high levels of stress were not associated with the occurrence of manic or depressive
    episodes.
D) high levels of stress were associated with the occurrence of manic, hypomanic, and
    depressive episodes.
Answer: D

Pages: 234
Topic: Causal Factors in Bipolar Disorders: Psychosocial Factors
Skill: Factual   Other1:
83. Mania and depression may reflect defensive strategies for coping with severe stress. This
is a theory associated with the _____ approach.
A) interpersonal
B) cognitive-behavioral
C) psychodynamic
D) humanistic
Answer: C

Pages: 235
Topic: Mood Disorders: Sociocultural Factors for Unipolar/Bipolar Disorders
Skill: Factual   Other1:
84. The prevalence of mood disorders is
    A) very high in cultures like Japan and China.
    B) stable across different cultures.
    C) relatively low and decreasing in Western cultures.
    D) variable among different societies.
    Answer: D

Pages: 236
Topic: Treatments/Outcomes: Pharmacotherapy and Electroconvulsive Therapy
Skill: Applied   Other1:
85. Nina has a diagnosis of adjustment disorder with depressed mood following the death of her boyfriend. The most appropriate treatment for her would probably be
    A) antidepressants.
    B) psychotherapy.
    C) antianxiety medication.
    D) lithium.
    Answer: B

Pages: 236
Topic: Treatments/Outcomes: Pharmacotherapy and Electroconvulsive Therapy
Skill: Factual   Other1:
86. Today the drug of choice for moderate to severe depression is usually
    A) a tricyclic like imipramine.
    B) a selective serotonin reuptake inhibitor like Prozac.
    C) electroconvulsive therapy.
    D) lithium therapy.
    Answer: B

Pages: 237
Topic: Treatments/Outcomes: Pharmacotherapy and Electroconvulsive Therapy
Skill: Factual   Other1:
87. Electroconvulsive therapy may be preferable to pharmacological treatment in all BUT which of the following cases?
    A) an individual who is an immediate and serious suicide risk
    B) an elderly person who can't tolerate antidepressant drugs
    C) in conjunction with lithium for a cyclothymic
    D) in a bipolar patient who has not been able to tolerate lithium
    Answer: C

Pages: 237
Topic: Treatments/Outcomes: Pharmacotherapy and Electroconvulsive Therapy
Skill: Factual   Other1:

88. Lithium
   A) is free of side effects when used over extended periods of time.
   B) is useful for treating manic episodes, but not bipolar depressive episodes.
   C) is the only current treatment for bipolar disorder.
   D) has sometimes been associated with kidney damage when used long-term.
   Answer: D

Pages: 239
Topic: Treatments and Outcomes: Psychotherapy
Skill: Factual   Other1:

89. A recent multisite study sponsored by the National Institute of Mental Health found that
   A) interpersonal and cognitive therapy are as effective as antidepressant medication for milder cases of major depression.
   B) antidepressant medication is much more effective than either interpersonal or cognitive therapy even for milder cases of depression.
   C) cognitive therapy is superior to interpersonal therapy in preventing recurrent episodes of depression.
   D) interpersonal therapy is less effective than antidepressant medication and cognitive therapy.
   Answer: A

Pages: 239
Topic: Treatments and Outcomes: Psychotherapy
Skill: Factual   Other1:

90. One factor that is especially likely to produce depression relapse is
   A) family members ignoring the depressed behavior expressed by the depressed individual.
   B) excessive attention from family members.
   C) family members discussing the depressed individual's negative thoughts and feelings with him or her.
   D) behavior by a spouse that can be interpreted as criticism.
   Answer: D

Pages: 240
Topic: Suicide
Skill: Factual   Other1:

91. Most individuals who commit suicide do so
   A) soon after the onset of a major depressive episode.
   B) during the deepest phase of an episode of depression.
   C) during the recovery phase of a depressive episode.
   D) several months or even years after they have recovered from a depressive episode.
   Answer: C

Pages: 240
Topic: Suicide
Skill: Applied   Other1:
92. Melissa is severely depressed and wants to commit suicide. If she is typical of most individuals who commit suicide,
    A) she is determined to kill herself and will choose a lethal means such as a gun to ensure that she is successful.
    B) she is ambivalent about committing suicide.
    C) she will change her mind at the last minute and reexamine her problems in a more objective fashion.
    D) she will give no outward signs of her distress.
    Answer: B

Pages: 241
Topic: Suicide: The Clinical Picture and the Causal Pattern
Skill: Factual   Other1:
93. The majority of individuals who ATTEMPT suicide are _____ and the majority of those who COMPLETE suicide are _____.
    A) women and people under age 35; men and people over age 65
    B) men and people over age 65; women and people under age 35
    C) adolescents; the elderly
    D) the elderly; adolescents
    Answer: A

Pages: 241
Topic: Suicide: The Clinical Picture and the Causal Pattern
Skill: Factual   Other1:
94. The highest rate of COMPLETED suicides is in the
    A) elderly (65 and over).
    B) adolescent population.
    C) college-aged population.
    D) population of middle-aged women.
    Answer: A

Pages: 241
Topic: Suicide: The Clinical Picture and the Causal Pattern
Skill: Factual   Other1:
95. In contrast to men, women
    A) complete suicide more often.
    B) complete suicide more often, although men attempt suicide more often than women.
    C) attempt suicide more often, although men complete suicide more often.
    D) attempt and commit suicide more often.
    Answer: C

Pages: 241
Topic: Suicide: The Clinical Picture and the Causal Pattern
Skill: Factual   Other1:
96. In contrast to women, men who commit suicide
    A) tend to ingest drugs or a combination of drugs and alcohol.
    B) tend to use a more lethal method, particularly gunshot.
    C) tend to leave a suicide note.
    D) do not give any warning or show obvious signs that they are in severe distress.
    Answer: B

Pages: 241
Topic: Suicide: The Clinical Picture and the Causal Pattern
Skill: Factual   Other1:
97. A recent trend is an alarming increase in completed suicides among
    A) children and adolescents.
    B) the elderly.
    C) the middle-aged.
    D) white-collar male executives.
    Answer: A

Pages: 242
Topic: Suicide: The Clinical Picture and the Causal Pattern
Skill: Factual   Other1:
98. Risk factors for suicide in adolescents include all of the following EXCEPT
    A) drug abuse.
    B) depression.
    C) exposure to other people who have attempted or committed suicide.
    D) all of the above
    Answer: D

Pages: 243
Topic: Suicide: The Clinical Picture and the Causal Pattern
Skill: Factual   Other1:
99. College students who attempt suicide tend to be
    A) doing poorly in school.
    B) superior students who expect a great deal of themselves in terms of academic
       achievement, although their grades are not usually regarded as significant
       precipitating factors.
    C) apparently happy and well-adjusted, showing no warning signs of possible suicide.
    D) none of the above
    Answer: B

Pages: 243
Topic: Suicide: The Clinical Picture and the Causal Pattern
Skill: Factual   Other1:
100. The major precipitating factor for most suicidal college students is
    A) the failure to establish, or the loss of, a close interpersonal relationship.
    B) academic failure.
    C) physical injury or debilitating illness.
    D) difficulty with separation from parents.
    Answer: A

Pages: 244
Topic: Suicide: The Clinical Picture and the Causal Pattern
Skill: Factual   Other1:
101. Suicide often is associated with a variety of different kinds of negative events. These different kinds of negative events have a common theme underlying them, which is
    A) financial loss.
    B) loss of social status.
    C) hopelessness about the future or loss of a sense of meaning to life.
    D) a traumatic event causing serious damage to the individual or to the individual's property.
    Answer: C

Pages: 244
Topic: Suicide: The Clinical Picture and the Causal Pattern
Skill: Conceptual   Other1:
102. There is great variability in suicide rates from one country to another. An important determinant of suicide rates is
    A) the particular racial make-up of the population of a given society.
    B) the extent to which obedience to parents is emphasized in a given society.
    C) whether the right to suicide is endorsed by law.
    D) the predominant attitude of the society toward death.
    Answer: D

Pages: 244
Topic: Suicide: The Clinical Picture and the Causal Pattern
Skill: Factual   Other1:
103. In the nineteenth century, Emile Durkheim analyzed records of suicides in different countries. The conclusion he came to, which still holds true in contemporary studies, is that the greatest deterrent to committing suicide in times of personal stress is
    A) financial security.
    B) a higher education.
    C) a sense of involvement and identity with other people.
    D) socioeconomic class.
    Answer: C

Pages: 245
Topic: Suicide: Suicidal Ambivalence
Skill: Factual   Other1:
104. Individuals differ in the degree of intent associated with suicidal behavior. According
to one recent analysis, individuals in the "to be" category of intent
A) comprise a very small percentage of the suicidal population.
B) do not really wish to die, but instead want to communicate a dramatic message to others
about their distress.
C) are usually male.
D) are intent on dying and usually use lethal methods of suicide.
Answer: B

Pages: 245
Topic: Suicide: Suicidal Ambivalence
Skill: Factual   Other1:
105. Suicidal individuals in the "to be or not to be" group
A) are ambivalent about committing suicide.
B) usually lead stormy, stress-filled lives and make repeated suicide attempts.
C) are intent on dying.
D) A and B
Answer: D

Pages: 245
Topic: Suicide: Suicidal Ambivalence
Skill: Applied   Other1:
106. Arnie has just attempted suicide, but was found in time and has made a physical recovery.
He is likely to
A) feel a marked reduction in emotional turmoil for at least a short period.
B) feel extremely distressed that his suicide attempt was unsuccessful, and immediately
attempt suicide again.
C) recover from his previous depression and remain stabilized for many years.
D) direct his despair at others in the form of anger, and may commit a violent act.
Answer: A

Pages: 246
Topic: Suicide: Suicidal Ambivalence
Skill: Factual   Other1:
107. Most people who commit suicide
A) never give any warning that they are contemplating suicide.
B) communicate their intent to a mental health professional, but not to friends or family
members.
C) communicate their intent to friends or family members, either directly or indirectly.
D) do so impulsively, with no time to give any warning.
Answer: C

Topic: Suicide: Suicide Prevention
Skill: Factual   Other1:
108. The prevention of suicide is extremely difficult because most people who are contemplating suicide
   A) are members of the "not to be" group who are intent on dying.
   B) give prior warning of their intentions, but do not actively seek help from either family members, friends, or mental health professionals.
   C) seek help from mental health professionals, but do not convey their intentions to family members or friends.
   D) do so on the spur of the moment when no one is around to stop them from acting.
   Answer: B

Pages: 247
Topic: Suicide: Suicide Prevention
Skill: Factual   Other1:
109. As part of crisis intervention, workers at suicide prevention centers may help avert an actual suicide attempt by
   A) fostering a dependent relationship and giving highly directive suggestions about courses of action to take.
   B) maintaining contact for as long as possible, such as weekly contacts for six months to a year.
   C) attempting to get at underlying causes of the problem rather than dealing directly with the immediate problem.
   D) none of the above
   Answer: A

Pages: 250
Topic: Unresolved Issues on Mood Disorders and Suicide
Skill: Conceptual   Other1:
110. In cases of patients who are suffering from mental illness and who have thoughts of committing suicide, the most prudent and ethical course for a psychologist to take is
   A) to honor the patient's "right to suicide."
   B) to help such patients make a final decision about killing themselves.
   C) to actively intervene in an attempt to alleviate the suicidality.
   D) to hospitalize such patients immediately, even if the thoughts of suicide are relatively mild.
   Answer: C

Short Answer

Write the word or phrase that best completes each statement or answers the question.

Pages: 202-203
Topic: Unipolar Mood Disorders: Normal Depression
Skill: Factual   Other1:
1. Give an example of a "normal" depression.
   Answer: Grief associated with a significant loss, the majority of cases of post-partum depression, depression associated with a recent, obviously painful stressor. Normal depressions are fairly common in college students.

Pages: 204
Topic: Unipolar Mood Disorders: Mild to Moderate Mood Disorders
Skill: Factual   Other1:
2. What is dysthymia?
   Answer: It is an Axis I mood disorder wherein a person displays a persistently depressed mood, more days than not, for at least two years. Normal moods may occur for only a few days or weeks at a time. Two of six additional symptoms must be present: appetite disturbance, sleep disturbance, low energy level, low self-esteem, hopelessness, problems concentrating or making decisions.

Pages: 205
Topic: Unipolar Mood Disorders: Mild to Moderate Mood Disorders
Skill: Factual   Other1:
3. Briefly describe the difference between adjustment disorder with depressed mood and major depression.
   Answer: The depression associated with an adjustment disorder occurs as a response to an identifiable stressor, within three months of that stressor, and the depression is more severe than the stressor would warrant, or is associated with impaired social or occupational functioning. Adjustment disorder depression is milder in severity than a major depression and must remit by six months.

Pages: 229
Topic: Unipolar Mood Disorders: Major Depressive Disorder
Skill: Conceptual   Other1:
4. Briefly describe one current theory that attempts to account for the comorbidity of anxiety and depression.
   Answer: Watson and colleagues suggest that the depression/anxiety overlap is accounted for by the broader dimension of negative affect. Depression is associated with low positive affect and anxiety with anxious hyperarousal. Beck suggests that depression and anxiety differ in cognitive content. Alloy, Mineka, and colleagues propose that anxiety is characterized by feeling uncertain helplessness. As certainty about helplessness develops, but uncertainty about bad outcomes remains, mixed anxiety/depression is likely. As uncertainty in both areas increases, hopelessness and depression result.

Pages: 206-207
Topic: Unipolar Mood Disorders: Major Depressive Disorder
Skill: Factual   Other1:
5. Identify five of the symptoms of major depression.
   Answer: Symptoms include markedly depressed mood or marked loss of interest in pleasurable activities most of every day for at least two weeks together with four or more of the following: fatigue or energy loss, insomnia or hypersomnia, appetite disturbance, psychomotor agitation or retardation, diminished ability to think or concentrate, self-denunciation such as feelings of worthlessness or disproportionate guilt, and recurrent thoughts of death or suicidal ideation.

Pages: 207
Topic: Unipolar Mood Disorders: Major Depressive Disorder
Skill: Factual   Other1:
6. According to DSM-IV, what are three of the symptoms of major depression of the melancholic type that differentiate this subtype from nonmelancholic depression?
   Answer: In addition to meeting criteria for major depression, an individual must experience loss of interest or pleasure in almost all activities, or not react to usually pleasurable stimuli or desired events. The individual must also experience three or more of the following: early morning awakening, depression worse in the morning, marked psychomotor agitation or retardation, significant loss of appetite and weight, inappropriate or excessive guilt, or a depressive mood qualitatively unlike that characteristic of a nonmelancholic depression.

Pages: 210
Topic: Bipolar Disorders: Bipolar Disorder
Skill: Applied   Other1:

7. Bob is in a manic episode. Identify five symptoms that he might be experiencing.

   Answer: He may be experiencing excessive excitement, elation or euphoria, inflated self-esteem or grandiosity. He may feel restless, have a decreased need for sleep and experience racing thoughts or a "flight of ideas." He may engage in reckless and impulsive activity that has a potential for harmful consequences, such as overspending, promiscuous sex, alcohol or substance abuse.

Pages: 209
Topic: Bipolar Disorders: Cyclothymia
Skill: Factual   Other1:

8. Cyclical mood changes that include mild depression and hypomania are characteristic of

   _____.

   Answer: cyclothymia

Pages: 210
Topic: Bipolar Disorders: Bipolar Disorder
Skill: Conceptual   Other1:

9. What is the most important clinical feature distinguishing unipolar from bipolar disorder?

   Answer: Bipolar disorder includes at least one episode of mania or hypomania, whereas there have been no manic or hypomanic episodes for a diagnosis of unipolar disorder.

Pages: 212
Topic: Bipolar Disorders: Schizoaffective Disorder
Skill: Applied   Other1:

10. Sally has symptoms of mania, although she experienced mood-incongruent hallucinations and delusions for several weeks in the absence of any prominent mood symptoms. According to the DSM-IV, her diagnosis is probably _____.

    Answer: schizoaffective disorder

Pages: 214
Topic: Causal Factors in Unipolar Disorders: Biological Factors
Skill: Factual   Other1:

11. What is the monoamine hypothesis?

    Answer: This theory, prominent in the 1960's and 1970's, viewed depression (and mania) as being caused by deficits (or excesses) in neurotransmitter substances of the monoamine class, norepinephrine and serotonin.

Pages: 216
Topic: Causal Factors in Unipolar Disorders: Biological Factors
Skill: Conceptual   Other1:
12. Briefly describe one causal theory of depression and mania that involves the dysregulation of bodily rhythms.
    Answer: One theory proposes that the primary disturbance in these disorders is in the regulation of the circadian system. Alterations in neurotransmitter substances may occur as a consequence of these disturbed circadian rhythms. Another more comprehensive theory suggests that there is a homeostatic regulation system for neurotransmitters as well as for other systems. Disruption in neurotransmitter systems cause irregularities in circadian rhythms and in the endocrine system, which in turn leads to depression or mania.

Pages: 220-222
Topic: Causal Factors in Mood Disorders
Skill: Factual   Other1:
13. Briefly identify three diatheses that have been proposed for unipolar or bipolar disorder.
    Answer: Biological factors include biochemical dysfunction, genetic loading, dysregulation of neurotransmitter and neuroendocrine systems and circadian rhythms, and abnormalities in brain activity and glucose metabolism. Cognitive diatheses include dysfunctional beliefs and pessimistic attributional style. Personality factors include neuroticism, sociotropy, and autonomy. Other diatheses include early parental loss, inadequate parenting, and interpersonal skill deficits.

Pages: 223-228
Topic: Causal Factors in Unipolar Disorder: Psychosocial Factors
Skill: Factual   Other1:
14. Briefly describe one of the major current cognitive theories of depression.
    Answer: Beck's theory proposes depressogenic schemas or dysfunctional beliefs as the underlying diathesis for depression. These beliefs are activated by stressors, causing negative automatic thoughts about self, world and future and a variety of cognitive distortions. The hopelessness theory proposes pessimistic attributional style as a distal diathesis of depression which interacts with stressors to result in hopelessness, the proximal necessary cause of hopelessness depression, the subtype proposed in the theory.

Pages: 231
Topic: Causal Factors in Bipolar Disorders: Biological Factors
Skill: Conceptual   Other1:
15. The strongest evidence for a substantial genetic component to a mood disorder is for _____ disorder.
    Answer: bipolar

Pages: 231-232
Topic: Causal Factors in Bipolar Disorders: Biological Factors
Skill: Conceptual   Other1:

16. What can we learn about science and discovery when considering the work done on bipolar disorder in Amish families?
    Answer: We see the danger in the premature acceptance of preliminary scientific findings, while failing to examine contradictory evidence and to withhold judgment until independent confirmation of results has been obtained.

Pages: 236-237
Topic: Treatments/Outcomes: Pharmacotherapy and Electroconvulsive Therapy
Skill: Factual   Other1:

17. The treatment of choice for bipolar depression is _____, while for unipolar depression it may be either _____ or _____.
    Answer: lithium; psychotherapy, antidepressants.

Pages: 238-239
Topic: Treatments and Outcomes: Psychotherapy
Skill: Conceptual   Other1:

18. Briefly describe cognitive therapy for depression.
    Answer: Clients learn to become aware of their negative automatic thoughts, how to systematically evaluate their thoughts and beliefs to identify biases and correct distortions of logic and information processing. It is a scientific approach in that clients learn to act like scientists, treating their beliefs like hypotheses and empirically testing them for accuracy.

Pages: 240-245
Topic: Suicide
Skill: Factual   Other1:

19. Briefly list three risk factors for suicide.
    Answer: These risk factors include being under age thirty-five or being elderly, being separated or divorced, having a mood disorder, schizophrenia or alcoholism, living alone, belonging to certain ethnic groups, being in certain professions, and recent experience of severe loss.

Pages: 241
Topic: Suicide
Skill: Factual   Other1:

20. Fill in the blanks to indicate which is true of men and which is true of women: More _____ become clinically depressed than _____; of these, more _____ attempt suicide, but more _____ commit suicide.
    Answer: women; men; women; men

Essay

Write your answer in the space provided or on a separate sheet of paper.

Pages: 202-203
Topic: Unipolar Mood Disorders: Normal Depression
Skill: Conceptual   Other1:

1. Is there such a thing as a "normal" depression? If so, what might bring one on? In addition, what kinds of behavior might be expected?

    Answer: Normal depressions usually result from recent stressful events like the death of a loved one or some other significant loss like retirement, leaving home for college, childbirth, or even a success. During normal grieving, numb disbelief interrupted by outbursts of intense upset often occur early on. This is typically followed by sadness and yearning, disinterest in the outside world, and later disorganization and despair, until a person begins to reengage with the world. Normal depression in college students was found to be associated with dependency, self-criticism, and feeling inadequate.

Pages: 204-205
Topic: Unipolar Mood Disorders: Mild to Moderate Mood Disorders
Skill: Factual   Other1:

2. Dysthymia and cyclothymia are two of the mood disorders in DSM-IV. What is the symptomatology of each?

    Answer: Dysthymia involves a persistently depressed mood more days than not for two years or more, plus two or more of these symptoms: appetite or sleep disturbance, low self-esteem, hopelessness, difficulty concentrating. Cyclothymia involves the occurrence of frequent episodes of hypomania and depression during at least a two-year span. Symptoms of the depressed phase are similar to dysthymia and do not qualify for major depression. Symptoms of the hypomanic phase are essentially the opposite of the symptoms of dysthymia. Evidence suggests that cyclothymia is a milder variant of bipolar disorder.

Pages: 205-207
Topic: Unipolar Mood Disorders: Major Depressive Disorder
Skill: Applied   Other1:

3. Pretend that you are a therapist interviewing a man who complains of feeling depressed for the past month. How would you evaluate him for a DSM-IV diagnosis of a mood disorder? How would you distinguish between major depression and bipolar disorder?

Answer: DSM-IV major depression requires depressed mood or loss of interest in pleasurable activities most of every day for at least two weeks, plus four or more of these symptoms: loss of energy, sleep problems, appetite disturbance, psychomotor agitation or retardation, diminished ability to think, self-denunciation, recurrent thoughts of death or suicide. If he's ever had an episode of mania or hypomania, he would require a diagnosis of bipolar disorder. Cyclothymia would involve many hypomanic and depressive episodes for two years without meeting criteria for full mania or major depression.

Pages: 207
Topic: Unipolar Mood Disorders: Major Depressive Disorder
Skill: Applied   Other1:

4. Leon has been diagnosed with a major depression, melancholic type. Describe the symptoms that he is likely to have. What treatment would you prescribe?

Answer: Leon will display loss of interest or pleasure in most activities. He will also experience three or more of the following: early morning awakening, depression worse in the morning, marked psychomotor agitation or retardation, significant loss of appetite and weight, inappropriate or excessive guilt, or qualitatively distinct depressed mood. He is more likely to respond to electroconvulsive treatment or antidepressant medication than to psychotherapy. Melancholic depression has been linked theoretically to endogenous causation.

Pages: 210
Topic: Bipolar Disorders: Bipolar Disorder
Skill: Applied   Other1:

5. Lenore has been diagnosed as suffering from bipolar disorder. What are her symptoms? How would she be treated?

Answer: She has experienced at least one manic episode or one clearcut hypomanic episode. She also may have experienced one or more major depressive episodes. If she has not yet experienced a depressive episode, it's assumed that she eventually will. When manic she probably is euphoric, grandiose, extremely restless, talkative with a flight of ideas, needs little sleep, behaves impulsively and recklessly. Lithium therapy is quite successful in regulating moods. Electroconvulsive therapy is also quite useful with manic episodes.

Pages: 213-214
Topic: Causal Factors in Unipolar Disorders: Biological Factors
Skill: Factual   Other1:

6. What is the evidence for a genetic basis for unipolar depression?

    Answer: Research evidence supports some genetic liability in unipolar depression,
              although it is not as strong as for bipolar disorder. A review of family
              (pedigree) studies indicated that about 15 percent of first degree relatives of
              unipolar depressives had the same diagnosis. Monozygotic co-twins of unipolars
              are twice as likely to develop major depression as dizygotic co-twins, in a
              review of twin studies. Heritability estimates for unipolar depression range
              from 33-50 percent. There are no good adoption studies focusing solely on
              unipolar disorder.

Pages: 214-215
Topic: Causal Factors in Unipolar Disorders: Biological Factors
Skill: Conceptual   Other1:

7. Discuss theories and research about biochemical factors that may be involved in unipolar
   depression.

    Answer: Biochemical theories stem from observations that antidepressants modify levels
              of norepinephrine and serotonin in brain synapses, and alter the number and
              sensitivity of certain neuronal receptors. Modifications of neurotransmitter
              levels involve both short-term increases and longer-term decreases in their
              availability, so there are undoubtedly factors other than biochemistry at work.
              Some propose that neurotransmitter disturbances result from dysregulation in the
              circadian system. Others propose that the primary disturbance is in a
              homeostatic regulatory system for neurotransmitters.

Pages: 222
Topic: Causal Factors in Unipolar Disorder: Psychosocial Factors
Skill: Conceptual   Other1:

8. Discuss the psychodynamic view of depression. What evidence exists in support of this
   view?

    Answer: Freud viewed depression (melancholia) as similar to mourning. In depression
              there is a real, symbolic, or imagined loss. Depression involves lowered
              self-esteem and greater self-criticality because unconscious negative feelings
              toward the lost love object are directed toward the self. Freud viewed the early
              loss of mother or early lack of nurturance as a vulnerability factor for later
              depression. Much research supports the importance of a child's secure
              attachment to a parent for later resistance to depression. Research does not
              support Freud's theory of depression as anger turned inward.

Pages: 222-223
Topic: Causal Factors in Unipolar Disorder: Psychosocial Factors
Skill: Conceptual   Other1:

9. How do behaviorists view the causes of depression? What does the research indicate about the merits of this view?

    Answer: One prominent theory views depression as resulting when a person's behavior no longer brings accustomed reinforcement, or when negative reinforcements increase. This leads to a reduction in effort, which in turn leads to even less gratification. A person's sensitivity to reinforcers may change as they become depressed, and people may differ in the number of activities they find reinforcing. Research does not provide evidence to confirm the direction of causality hypothesized by behaviorists, although much research shows that depressives do obtain fewer reinforcements in life.

Pages: 229
Topic: Causal Factors in Unipolar Disorder: Psychosocial Factors
Skill: Conceptual   Other1:

10. Diagnoses of anxiety and depression often co-occur. Discuss this overlap in terms of current theories about it and the research associated with these theories.

    Answer: Genetic studies demonstrate some shared liability. One model shows that overlap in various measures of the two are due to a broad dimension of negative affect (found in both depression and anxiety), while measures of the two differ in positive affect (low in depression) and anxious hyperarousal (high in anxiety). Another theory proposes that expectations of helplessness and uncertainty about being able to control important outcomes are associated with anxiety. As helplessness increases but uncertainty remains, mixed anxiety/depression develops. As hopelessness sets in, depression results.

Pages: 223-225
Topic: Causal Factors in Unipolar Disorder: Psychosocial Factors
Skill: Conceptual   Other1:

11. Describe Beck's theory of the origin of depression. Discuss findings from research that has tested his model.

    Answer: Beck proposed that dysfunctional beliefs or depressogenic schemas can develop during childhood and serve as a vulnerability factor for later depression. When stressors activate these beliefs, negative automatic thoughts arise about self, world, and future (the negative cognitive triad). Cognitive biases in information processing maintain the automatic thoughts and reinforce the dysfunctional beliefs. Negative thoughts cause emotional and motivational symptoms. Much research supports descriptive features of Beck's theory, but causal aspects of his theory haven't yet been adequately tested.

Pages: 225-228
Topic: Causal Factors in Unipolar Disorder: Psychosocial Factors
Skill: Conceptual   Other1:

12. Describe the learned helplessness model of depression. Also discuss later modifications of this theory, including the reformulated helplessness and hopelessness theories of depression. Discuss related research findings.

   Answer: The learned helplessness model arose from studies where dogs who experienced uncontrollable shocks developed a learning deficit involving passivity and depression-like symptoms. The reformulated helplessness theory added pessimistic attributional style (internal, stable, global attributions for negative events) as a diathesis for depression. In the hopelessness theory these attributions result in hopelessness, which leads to the subtype of depression proposed in the theory. Research provides much evidence for descriptive features and some for causal hypotheses.

Pages: 231-232
Topic: Causal Factors in Bipolar Disorders: Biological Factors
Skill: Conceptual   Other1:

13. What is the evidence for a genetic liability for bipolar disorder?

   Answer: A review of family (pedigree) studies shows 19 percent of bipolars' first-degree relatives have unipolar or bipolar disorder. Concordance rates for monozygotic and dizygotic twin pairs are 69 percent and 19 percent. One adoption study has been done, and found that 31 percent versus 2 percent of the biological versus adoptive parents of a bipolar also had either bipolar or unipolar disorder. Estimates are that genes may account for about 80 percent of the variance in liability for bipolar disorder.

Pages: 236-240
Topic: Treatments and Outcomes
Skill: Conceptual   Other1:

14. Describe the various treatments that exist for mood disorders. Discuss studies pertaining to treatment efficacy for the various treatment modalities.

   Answer: Pharmacological treatments for unipolar depression include tricyclics (especially for moderate and severe depression) and selective serotonin reuptake inhibitors (commonly prescribed for milder depressions). Drugs are often effective but tricyclics may have unpleasant side-effects and only prevent relapse if taken continuously. Electroconvulsive therapy is effective for severe depression and mania. Lithium therapy is very effective for bipolar disorder, although it can have serious side-effects. Cognitive and interpersonal therapies are as effective as drug therapy for unipolar depression.

Pages: 240-246
Topic: Suicide
Skill: Conceptual   *Other1:*

15. Who are the individuals most likely to attempt and commit suicide? What are some of the psychosocial and sociocultural factors associated with suicide?

Answer: Women are more likely to attempt and men to commit suicide. The rate for women, children, and adolescents is increasing. Other high-risk groups include the elderly, people with mood disorders, schizophrenics, alcoholics, individuals living alone, separated and divorced people, the unemployed, certain ethnic groups and certain professionals. Most attempts are associated with interpersonal discord or other severe stress, involving loss of meaning to life or hopelessness. Preventive cultural factors include religious taboos against suicide and a sense of involvement and identity with others.

CHAPTER 7   Somatoform and Dissociative Disorders

Multiple-Choice

Choose the one alternative that best completes the statement or answers the question.

Pages: 253
Topic: Somatoform and Dissociative Disorders
Skill: Factual   Other1:
1. Conditions involving physical complaints or disabilities occurring in the absence of any physical pathology that could account for them are
   A) hypochondriacal disorders.
   B) anxiety disorders.
   C) dissociative disorders.
   D) somatoform disorders.
   Answer: D

Pages: 253
Topic: Somatoform and Dissociative Disorders
Skill: Factual   Other1:
2. Conditions involving a disruption in the sense of a coherent and stable personal identity are
   A) dissociative disorders.
   B) somatoform disorders.
   C) identity disorders.
   D) neuroses.
   Answer: A

Pages: 253
Topic: Somatoform and Dissociative Disorders
Skill: Conceptual   Other1:
3. According to Freud, somatoform and dissociative disorders were caused by
   A) neurological dysfunction.
   B) intrapsychic conflict.
   C) hysterical neurosis.
   D) self-hypnosis.
   Answer: B

Pages: 253-254
Topic: Somatoform and Dissociative Disorders
Skill: Conceptual   Other1:
4. Historically, a number of psychologists have suggested a connection between
   A) trauma, dissociative patterns, and somatoform symptoms.
   B) dissociative disorders and liver dysfunction.
   C) hypnosis as a cause of dissociative disorders.
   D) agoraphobia and somatization disorder.
   Answer: A

Pages: 253-254
Topic: Somatoform and Dissociative Disorders
Skill: Conceptual   Other1:
5. Hisorically, psychologists have suggested that _____ characterize(s) the underlying
   pathology in somatoform and dissociative disorders, although this hasn't been thoroughly
   investigated by contemporary researchers.
   A) neurotic displacement
   B) superego dysfunction
   C) dissociative tendencies
   D) sexual impulses
   Answer: C

Pages: 254
Topic: Somatoform Disorders
Skill: Factual   Other1:
6. The most important difference between somatoform and factitious disorders is that
   A) factitious disorders involve feigned symptoms, whereas somatoform disorders involve
      sincere complaints of physical malady.
   B) factitious disorders involve exaggerations of actual physical illnesses.
   C) somatoform disorders involve symptoms that are feigned in order to gain some specific
      objective.
   D) factitious disorders involve causing physical symptoms in someone else in order to gain
      some personal gratification.
   Answer: A

Pages: 254
Topic: Somatoform Disorders
Skill: Factual   Other1:
7. Individuals with somatoform disorders
   A) feign their illnesses in order to obtain some special treatment.
   B) generally have an organic basis for their illness.
   C) believe that their symptoms are real and serious.
   D) usually have little concern over their state of health.
   Answer: C

Pages: 254
Topic: Somatoform Disorders
Skill: Factual   Other1:
8. The physical symptoms seen in somatoform disorder are believed to be
   A) under voluntary control.
   B) not under voluntary control.
   C) fabricated for the purpose of assuming a sick role.
   D) under voluntary control initially, yet after years of experiencing the problem, the symptoms become involuntary.
   Answer: B

Pages: 254
Topic: Somatoform Disorders
Skill: Other1:
9. All of the following are somatoform disorders EXCEPT
   A) hypochondriasis.
   B) somatization disorder.
   C) conversion disorder.
   D) fugue disorder.
   Answer: D

Pages: 254
Topic: Somatoform Disorders: Somatization Disorder
Skill: Applied   Other1:
10. Marla, twenty-five years old, has been admitted to the hospital for tests on three occasions when she complained of nausea, vomiting, and diarrhea. Doctors have not been able to find anything organically wrong with her. She would be diagnosed as having
    A) body dysmorphic disorder.
    B) factitious disorder.
    C) somatization disorder.
    D) conversion disorder.
    Answer: C

Pages: 255
Topic: Somatoform Disorders: Hypochondriasis
Skill: Factual   Other1:
11. In contrast to somatization disorder, an individual with hypochondriasis is more likely to
    A) complain of having a specific and serious disease, such as cancer.
    B) have an early onset of the disorder.
    C) stay away from doctors.
    D) all of the above
    Answer: A

Pages: 255
Topic: Somatoform Disorders: Hypochondriasis
Skill: Applied   Other1:
12. Evan is terrified because he is convinced that he has colon cancer. He has consulted with several physicians about it, but he can not clearly describe any particular symptoms that he is experiencing and no evidence of any illness has been found. His diagnosis is probably
A) somatization disorder.
B) hypochondriasis.
C) pain disorder.
D) conversion disorder.
Answer: B

Pages: 255
Topic: Somatoform Disorders: Hypochondriasis
Skill: Factual   Other1:
13. Hypochondriasis and somatization disorder differ in that
A) hypochondriasis does not seem to focus on any specific set of symptoms.
B) hypochondriasis involves feigning symptoms, while somatization disorder does not.
C) individuals with hypochondriasis usually suffer from panic attacks associated with their extreme fear of the disease they believe they have.
D) individuals with somatization disorder are morbidly preoccupied with their excretory and digestive functions.
Answer: A

Pages: 256
Topic: Somatoform Disorders: Hypochondriasis
Skill: Applied   Other1:
14. Ford has been diagnosed with hypochondriasis. He is likely to
A) be reassured when he is not found to have any organic disorder.
B) provide a very precise description of his symptoms.
C) have little interest in health matters.
D) have a need to communicate to others the extent of his suffering.
Answer: D

Pages: 256
Topic: Somatoform Disorders: Hypochondriasis
Skill: Factual   Other1:
15. Hypochondriacal individuals
A) are concerned primarily with dysfunctions of their hands, feet, and limbs.
B) show losses or distortions of sensory functioning, such as sight or hearing.
C) typically have delusions similar to those found in psychotic disorders.
D) often use a wide range of self-medications.
Answer: D

Pages: 257
Topic: Somatoform Disorders: Hypochondriasis
Skill: Factual   Other1:

16. Compared with medical patient controls, hypochondriacs
    A) have a history of astonishing health.
    B) more often report psychological trauma and abuse in childhood.
    C) tend to be elderly.
    D) tend to have been healthier in childhood.
    Answer: B

Pages: 257
Topic: Somatoform Disorders: Hypochondriasis
Skill: Conceptual   Other1:

17. Hypochondriasis can be viewed as
    A) an organic brain disorder.
    B) malingering.
    C) a kind of needy interpersonal communication.
    D) a rare disorder compared to other somatoform disorders.
    Answer: C

Pages: 257
Topic: Somatoform Disorders: Hypochondriasis
Skill: Conceptual   Other1:

18. The hypochondriacal adult is most likely saying,
    A) "If only I could get over this pain in one area of my body, I would be fine."
    B) "I am faking these physical problems so that I can get something from other people."
    C) "I deserve more of your attention and concern."
    D) "I am afraid of the world."
    Answer: C

Pages: 255-256
Topic: Somatoform Disorders: Hypochondriasis
Skill: Factual   Other1:

19. Which of the following statements about hypochondriasis is NOT true?
    A) It is frequently associated with other Axis I diagnoses.
    B) Hypochondriacs were often sick in childhood, requiring absences from school more often than the average child.
    C) Hypochondriacs typically report a shifting and incoherent set of symptoms and complaints.
    D) Hypochondriacs deliberately feign illnesses to gain attention.
    Answer: D

Pages: 257
Topic: Somatoform Disorders: Pain Disorder
Skill: Factual   Other1:
20. Which disorder is marked by complaints of pain in the absence of medical pathology that would explain the magnitude of the pain observed?
    A) body dysmorphic pain disorder
    B) dyspareunia
    C) psychosomatic pain disorder
    D) pain disorder
    Answer: D

Pages: 257
Topic: Somatoform Disorders: Pain Disorder
Skill: Applied   Other1:
21. Hans suffered a broken leg with some minor residual damage to his knee. Fourteen years later, he says that he is still unable to work because of severe pain in his leg. Hans probably suffers from
    A) somatization disorder.
    B) hypochondriasis.
    C) conversion disorder.
    D) pain disorder.
    Answer: D

Pages: 257
Topic: Somatoform Disorders: Pain Disorder
Skill: Applied   Other1:
22. Farley has had severe pain for the last nine months. He had some very minor surgery twelve months ago, but his pain appears unrelated and is greatly in excess of what would be expected from this surgery. He suffers from
    A) conversion disorder.
    B) panic disorder.
    C) somatization disorder.
    D) pain disorder.
    Answer: D

Pages: 257
Topic: Somatoform Disorders: Pain Disorder
Skill: Factual   Other1:
23. Pain disorder
    A) is more commonly diagnosed among women.
    B) is usually alleviated once a physician tells a patient that there is no organic basis
       for the complaint.
    C) involves a multitude of vague physical complaints about numerous areas of the body.
    D) is highly resistant to psychological treatment but amenable to physiological treatment.
    Answer: A

Pages: 257
Topic: Somatoform Disorders: Pain Disorder
Skill: Factual   Other1:
24. The pain experienced by individuals with pain disorder
    A) rarely leads to a disabling lifestyle.
    B) is feigned to gain attention.
    C) usually disappears after placebo medication is administered.
    D) may fluctuate in perceived intensity according to the amount of stress the individual
       is experiencing.
    Answer: D

Pages: 257
Topic: Somatoform Disorders: Pain Disorder
Skill: Conceptual   Other1:
25. In many cases, pain disorder patients
    A) are easily diagnosed by physicians, who appropriately refer them for psychological
       treatment.
    B) wind up being disabled either through addiction to pain medication or through surgery
       they have been able to obtain.
    C) deal with their pain through distraction and other adaptive coping mechanisms and don't
       allow the disorder to get the better of them.
    D) none of the above
    Answer: B

Pages: 258
Topic: Somatoform Disorders: Conversion Disorder
Skill: Factual   Other1:
26. The pattern of pseudoneurological symptoms of physical malfunction or loss of control
    without any underlying organic pathology is
    A) somatization disorder.
    B) conversion disorder.
    C) hypochondriasis.
    D) pseudoneurological disorder.
    Answer: B

Pages: 258
Topic: Somatoform Disorders: Conversion Disorder
Skill: Factual   Other1:
27. Freud's concept of conversion hysteria is referred to today as
    A) hypochondriasis.
    B) somatization disorder.
    C) conversion disorder.
    D) dissociative identity disorder.
    Answer: C

Pages: 258
Topic: Somatoform Disorders: Conversion Disorder
Skill: Factual   Other1:
28. Freud believed that hysterical symptoms resulted from
    A) a displacement of frustrated ego demands.
    B) a frustrated desire to have children.
    C) uterine dysfunction.
    D) repressed sexual energy.
    Answer: D

Pages: 258
Topic: Somatoform Disorders: Conversion Disorder
Skill: Applied   Other1:
29. Felicia has a conversion disorder. According to contemporary thought, her disorder is due
    to
    A) excessive information about the physical functioning of the body.
    B) excessive monitoring of bodily functions, almost to the point of becoming a compulsion.
    C) physical symptoms enabling a person to escape or avoid stressful situations without
        having to take responsibility for doing so.
    D) an expression of repressed sexual energy.
    Answer: C

Pages: 258
Topic: Somatoform Disorders: Conversion Disorder
Skill: Factual   Other1:
30. _____ refer(s) to external circumstances that tend to reinforce the maintenance of a
    disability or mental illness.
    A) Primary gain
    B) Secondary gain
    C) Tertiary gain
    D) none of the above
    Answer: B

Pages: 259
Topic: Somatoform Disorders: Conversion Disorder
Skill: Factual   Other1:
31. Compared with their incidence in the last century, conversion disorders appear to be
    A) increasing as the stress of everyday life increases.
    B) maintaining a consistent incidence rate.
    C) reported more often as more individuals with this disorder seek treatment.
    D) decreasing because of growing sophistication about medical and psychological disorders.
    Answer: D

Pages: 259
Topic: Somatoform Disorders: Conversion Disorder
Skill: Conceptual   Other1:
32. An individual suffering from conversion disorder today is more likely to have symptoms
    A) that simulate a more sophisticated disease.
    B) that are extremely dramatic, like being suddenly struck blind.
    C) that are feigned.
    D) that are unrelated to stress.
    Answer: A

Pages: 259-260
Topic: Somatoform Disorders: Conversion Disorder
Skill: Conceptual   Other1:
33. The text presented the case of a twenty-nine year old physician who had a conversion
    disorder. He is typical of individuals with such a disorder because
    A) his difficulty in speaking allowed him to escape from unwanted responsibility.
    B) he began to experience some depersonalization as his stress increased.
    C) he began to believe that he suffered from many diseases as he learned more about
       medical disorders.
    D) his numerous, vague physiological complaints were found to have no organic basis.
    Answer: A

Pages: 260
Topic: Somatoform Disorders: Conversion Disorder
Skill: Conceptual   Other1:
34. The diagnostic distinction between conversion disorder and pain disorder in the DSM-IV is
    A) based on whether or not there is an underlying physical disease that fully accounts for
       symptoms.
    B) the presence of depersonalization symptoms.
    C) somewhat unclear and needs refining in future research.
    D) dependent upon the age of the individual and the duration of symptoms.
    Answer: C

Pages: 260
Topic: Somatoform Disorders: Conversion Disorder
Skill: Factual   Other1:
35. In a study of hysterical visual symptoms among airmen in World War II, it was found that
    A) the optic nerves of the airmen had been damaged, creating an actual organic cause for
       what was thought to be a psychological problem.
    B) the symptoms each airman reported were closely related to his performance duties.
    C) day fliers were more subject to night blindness once their flights for the day had been
       completed.
    D) most airmen who suffered from conversion disorder also experienced panic disorder.
    Answer: B

Pages: 261
Topic: Somatoform Disorders: Conversion Disorder
Skill: Factual   Other1:

36. In a study of conversion reactions among student aviators, which of the following was NOT considered by the researchers to be one of the etiological factors implicated in the conversion reactions?
    A) the age of the aviators
    B) the unacceptability of quitting the training program
    C) previous use of somatic complaints to avoid responsibility
    D) parental models who had significant physical illnesses similar to those reported by the aviators
    Answer: A

Pages: 261
Topic: Somatoform Disorders: Conversion Disorder
Skill: Factual   Other1:

37. In a study of student aviators with conversion reactions, it was found that
    A) the students had few physical symptoms prior to enlistment.
    B) in previous athletic training, physical illness had been an acceptable means of avoiding difficult situations.
    C) in the past, the students had a significant incidence of voluntarily quitting projects before they were completed.
    D) what appeared to be conversion reactions were actually incidences of malingering.
    Answer: B

Pages: 260
Topic: Somatoform Disorders: Conversion Disorder
Skill: Conceptual   Other1:

38. A hysterically blind person resembles an individual who has been hypnotically induced to be unable to "see" an object in that
    A) both are actually blind.
    B) neither is likely to endanger himself or herself by bumping into anything.
    C) both conditions will probably result in hysteria.
    D) both are feigning blindness.
    Answer: B

Pages: 260
Topic: Somatoform Disorders: Conversion Disorder
Skill: Factual   Other1:
39. A hysterically deaf person
  A) is similar to an actual deaf person in that auditory stimuli do not register in the brain.
  B) can hear but feigns having the problem.
  C) screens the auditory sensory input from consciousness to the point that the stimuli do not register in the brain.
  D) has auditory stimuli register in the brain but screens this information from consciousness.
  Answer: D

Pages: 260
Topic: Somatoform Disorders: Conversion Disorder
Skill: Applied   Other1:
40. Renee's left arm is paralyzed and anesthetic. Yet, extensive testing has indicated perfectly normal neurological and circulatory function. Renee is probably suffering from
  A) conversion disorder.
  B) hypochondriasis.
  C) multiple sclerosis.
  D) somatoform pain disorder.
  Answer: A

Pages: 260
Topic: Somatoform Disorders: Conversion Disorder
Skill: Applied   Other1:
41. Kelly is a piano student with conversion disorder. Her hand is paralyzed so that she can not perform. Which of the following is probably true of her?
  A) Her paralysis will spread to her arms and legs.
  B) She will develop hysterical deafness.
  C) Her paralysis developed in response to a severe shock.
  D) She can use the hand for other functions like writing.
  Answer: D

Pages: 262
Topic: Somatoform Disorders: Conversion Disorder
Skill: Factual   Other1:

42. In conversion disorder, individuals
    A) are usually extremely upset and concerned about their symptoms and long-range prognosis.
    B) usually display symptoms that do not mimic any organic disease.
    C) may exhibit symptoms of an actual disease (e.g., malaria) to the extent that they run a high temperature.
    D) do not simulate a disease very well.
    Answer: C

Pages: 262
Topic: Somatoform Disorders: Conversion Disorder
Skill: Applied   Other1:

43. Susan recently developed hysterical blindness. She is likely to
    A) frantically try to find out what is wrong.
    B) act in a matter-of-fact way, with little of the anxiety that would be expected from a person who has a loss of sight.
    C) fluctuate between being frantic and acting in a matter-of-fact way.
    D) act in a matter-of-fact way, although some people with hysterical blindness exhibit a level of concern "appropriate" to the disability they display.
    Answer: D

Pages: 262
Topic: Somatoform Disorders: Conversion Disorder
Skill: Factual   Other1:

44. Distinguishing features between conversion disorders and actual organic disturbances include
    A) removal, shifting, or reinduction of symptoms through hypnotic suggestion.
    B) the selective nature of the dysfunction, such as "paralyzed" muscles being used for some activities but not others.
    C) "la belle indiffé rence."
    D) all of the above
    Answer: D

Pages: 262
Topic: Somatoform Disorders: Conversion Disorder
Skill: Factual   Other1:
45. Unlike individuals suffering from conversion disorder, people who are feigning symptoms
    A) tend to want to discuss their symptoms in excruciating detail.
    B) tend to be evasive and defensive.
    C) enjoy visiting physicians for examinations to see if they can outsmart the professionals.
    D) exhibit "la belle indifference," a strange unconcern about their symptoms.
    Answer: B

Pages: 262
Topic: Somatoform Disorders: Conversion Disorder
Skill: Conceptual   Other1:
46. An individual usually develops conversion disorder
    A) after experiencing a fleeting wish, quickly suppressed, to get sick in order to escape a stressful situation.
    B) without any apparent precipitating stressor.
    C) after experiencing a genuine serious illness that has been successfully treated.
    D) none of the above
    Answer: A

Pages: 262
Topic: Somatoform Disorders: Conversion Disorder
Skill: Conceptual   Other1: In Student Study Guide
47. All of the following are part of a chain of events in the development of a conversion disorder except
    A) a conscious plan to use illness as an escape.
    B) a desire to escape from an unpleasant situation.
    C) a fleeting wish to be sick in order to avoid the situation.
    D) the appearance of the symptoms of some physical ailment.
    Answer: A

Pages: 262-263
Topic: Somatoform Disorders: Conversion Disorder
Skill: Factual   Other1:
48. Conversion symptoms often develop in association with all BUT which of the following?
    A) an opportunity for financial recompensation for injury
    B) as symbols of a major conflict in one's life
    C) feelings of guilt and the desire to punish oneself
    D) several experiences of panic attacks
    Answer: D

Pages: 263
Topic: Dissociative Disorders
Skill: Factual   *Other1:*
49. Contemporary cognitive psychologists have embraced the general notion of _____ that psychodynamic psychologists had long ago adopted.
    A) sexual repression
    B) conversion
    C) unconscious mental activity
    D) depersonalization
    Answer: C

Pages: 263
Topic: Dissociative Disorders
Skill: Factual   *Other1:*
50. The human mind has the ability to conduct complex mental activity in channels that are independent of conscious awareness. This is called
    A) depersonalization.
    B) dissociation.
    C) conversion.
    D) disintegration.
    Answer: B

Pages: 264
Topic: Dissociative Disorders
Skill: Factual   *Other1:*
51. Dissociative disorders are similar to somatoform disorders in that
    A) both involve the development of symptoms of physical illnesses.
    B) both have a clearcut organic causal basis.
    C) both appear mainly to be ways of avoiding anxiety and managing potentially overwhelming stress.
    D) both involve amnesia states.
    Answer: C

Pages: 264
Topic: Dissociative Disorders
Skill: Conceptual   *Other1:*
52. An individual who avoids anxiety by "slipping out of" his or her personal identity suffers from
    A) a dissociative disorder.
    B) somatization disorder.
    C) conversion disorder.
    D) body dysmorphic disorder.
    Answer: A

Pages: 264
Topic: Dissociative Disorders
Skill: Conceptual   Other1:
53. Ross conceives of _____ as a continuum underlying a variety of states and disorders, such as conversion disorder and what used to be referred to as multiple personality disorder.
A) somatization
B) depersonalization
C) disintegration
D) dissociation
Answer: D

Pages: 265
Topic: Dissociative Disorders: Dissociative Amnesia and Fugue
Skill: Factual   Other1:
54. In contrast to amnesia due to brain pathology, psychogenic amnesia is more likely to involve
A) information that is permanently lost.
B) information that is not registered and does not enter memory store.
C) a failure to recall information that is still there beneath the level of consciousness.
D) the person forgetting his or her entire life history.
Answer: C

Pages: 265
Topic: Dissociative Disorders: Dissociative Amnesia and Fugue
Skill: Factual   Other1:
55. An individual with dissociative amnesia will, under hypnosis,
A) still be unable to recall forgotten information.
B) dissociate further into a decompensated state.
C) recall material that was forgotten.
D) relive early traumas uncontrollably.
Answer: C

Pages: 265
Topic: Dissociative Disorders: Dissociative Amnesia and Fugue
Skill: Factual   Other1:
56. Localized psychogenic amnesia
A) is extremely rare compared to other forms of psychogenic amnesia.
B) involves a person remembering nothing that happened during a specific period of time.
C) involves amnesia accompanied by an actual flight away from home.
D) involves the forgetting of a person's entire life history.
Answer: B

Pages: 266
Topic: Dissociative Disorders: Dissociative Amnesia and Fugue
Skill: Applied   Other1:
57. Judy suffers from psychogenic amnesia. She probably
    A) remembers only events from the past, not how to do such things as arithmetic.
    B) can perform only simple, basic work regardless of the complex work that she was able to
       do previously.
    C) is able to recognize close friends and relatives but not acquaintances.
    D) seems quite normal other than for her amnesia.
    Answer: D

Pages: 265
Topic:
Skill: Other1:
58. Jan became amnesic, wandered away from home and assumed a completely new identity as a
    shoe salesman. He suffers from
    A) depersonalization.
    B) dissociative identity disorder.
    C) malingering identity disorder.
    D) a fugue state.
    Answer: D

Pages: 266
Topic: Dissociative Disorders: Dissociative Amnesia and Fugue
Skill: Factual   Other1:
59. People who have dissociative amnesia tend to
    A) have a long history of panic attacks and depressive episodes.
    B) be highly suggestible.
    C) forget everything except for childhood memories.
    D) behave in bizarre and unusual ways.
    Answer: B

Pages: 266
Topic: Dissociative Disorders: Dissociative Amnesia and Fugue
Skill: Conceptual   Other1:
60. The text presented the case of Burt Tate, a 42-year-old short order cook, who suffered
    from a dissociative fugue reaction. He was typical of such individuals because
    A) his symptoms appeared in the context of extreme stress.
    B) he displayed unusual and bizarre behavior in addition to his memory problems.
    C) he appeared to be a very mature, altruistic, and capable person before the disorder
       appeared.
    D) he remembered a lot about threatening experiences in his life but could not remember
       much about day to day experiences.
    Answer: A

Pages: 266
Topic: Dissociative Disorders: Dissociative Identity Disorder
Skill: Conceptual   Other1:
61. Dissociative identity disorder is still usually known as _____ by ordinary people.
    A) amnesia
    B) multiple personality disorder
    C) hysteria
    D) an "identity crisis"
    Answer: B

Pages: 266
Topic: Dissociative Disorders: Dissociative Identity Disorder
Skill: Factual   Other1:
62. An individual with dissociative identity disorder
    A) is usually male.
    B) has a host personality that controls the other alter personalities.
    C) has two or more complete and distinct systems of personality.
    D) has two or more personalities that are very similar to one another.
    Answer: C

Pages: 266
Topic: Dissociative Disorders: Dissociative Identity Disorder
Skill: Factual   Other1:
63. In dissociative identity disorder, alter personalities
    A) are unaware of the existence of the host and are unaware of each other.
    B) tend to be unstable and not very distinct from one another.
    C) are always of the same gender as the host.
    D) usually display behaviors that are inhibited in the host personality.
    Answer: D

Pages: 267
Topic: Dissociative Disorders: Dissociative Identity Disorder
Skill: Conceptual   Other1:
64. The text presented the case of Mary Kendall, who suffered from dissociative identity
    disorder. She is typical of individuals with this disorder in that
    A) she was sexually abused as a child.
    B) she had been unable to function in society for many years before receiving her
       diagnosis.
    C) a course of psychotherapy succeeded in eliminating all personalities except that of the
       host.
    D) she suffered from chronic pain.
    Answer: A

Pages: 266-267
Topic: Dissociative Disorders: Dissociative Identity Disorder
Skill: Factual   Other1:
65. Alter personalities
    A) may express rejected parts of the self.
    B) may be nonhuman in form.
    C) often take certain roles like persecutor and protector.
    D) all of the above
    Answer: D

Pages: 267
Topic: Dissociative Disorders: Dissociative Identity Disorder
Skill: Factual   Other1:
66. In dissociative identity disorder,
    A) the host usually knows about alter personalities, but the alters usually are not aware of each other.
    B) the host personality usually controls the actions of the alter personalities.
    C) alter personalities usually know about each other and about the host, but the host is usually unaware of the alter personalities.
    D) no single personality usually knows about all of the others.
    Answer: C

Pages: 268
Topic: Dissociative Disorders: Dissociative Identity Disorder
Skill: Conceptual   Other1:
67. One reason for the gender discrepancy in the incidence of dissociative identity disorder may be that
    A) there is a hormonal dysregulation that usually accompanies this disorder, making it more common in women.
    B) girls are much more likely to be sexually abused than boys.
    C) women are more susceptible to stress than men.
    D) women are more likely to feign this disorder.
    Answer: B

Pages: 268
Topic: Dissociative Disorders: Dissociative Identity Disorder
Skill: Factual   Other1:
68. The diagnosis of dissociative identity disorder
    A) is viewed with skepticism by most clinicians.
    B) has been declining over the past century.
    C) cannot be faked.
    D) has been increasing dramatically in recent years.
    Answer: D

Pages: 269
Topic: Dissociative Disorders: Depersonalization Disorder
Skill: Factual   Other1:
69. The disorder involving the experience of sudden loss of the sense of self is
    A) derealization disorder.
    B) psychogenic amnesia.
    C) disidentity disorder.
    D) depersonalization disorder.
    Answer: D

Pages: 269
Topic: Dissociative Disorders: Dissociative Identity Disorder
Skill: Factual   Other1:
70. Depersonalization disorder occurs mostly in
    A) women.
    B) adolescents and young adults.
    C) children.
    D) the elderly.
    Answer: B

Pages: 269
Topic: Dissociative Disorders: Depersonalization Disorder
Skill: Factual   Other1:
71. Derealization experiences frequently accompany
    A) dissociative identity disorder.
    B) conversion disorder.
    C) somatoform disorders.
    D) depersonalization disorder.
    Answer: D

Pages: 269
Topic: Dissociative Disorders: Depersonalization Disorder
Skill: Applied   Other1:
72. Dody complains of experiences in which she feels like she is floating above her body and
    sometimes she feels that she floats to visit relatives in distant places. What is her
    diagnosis?
    A) derealization disorder.
    B) depersonalization disorder.
    C) conversion disorder.
    D) dissociative identity disorder.
    Answer: B

Pages: 269
Topic: Dissociative Disorders: Depersonalization Disorder
Skill: Conceptual   Other1:
73. The text presented the case of Charlotte D., who was referred to a mental health service because of depersonalization experiences. She was typical of individuals with this disorder because she
A) had her first incident of depersonalization after an acute stress.
B) was elderly.
C) also suffered from a dissociative identity disorder.
D) had suffered sexual abuse as a child.
Answer: A

Pages: 269
Topic: Dissociative Disorders: Depersonalization Disorder
Skill: Factual   Other1:
74. Individuals who experience depersonalized states
A) have considerable difficulty functioning between episodes.
B) are very rare.
C) are usually able to function normally between episodes.
D) are almost always male.
Answer: C

Pages: 269
Topic: Dissociative Disorders: Depersonalization Disorder
Skill: Conceptual   Other1:
75. A diagnostic problem that may arise with depersonalization disorder is that
A) individuals usually are too ashamed to admit to having these experiences.
B) depersonalization experiences sometimes signal the onset of decompensation and psychotic states.
C) this disorder mimics somatoform disorders.
D) these experiences are rare.
Answer: B

Pages: 269-270
Topic: Factors in Somatoform/Dissociative Disorders: Biological Factors
Skill: Factual   Other1:
76. According to psychodynamic views, somatoform and dissociative disorders are similar to anxiety disorders in the central causal role that _____ plays.
A) derealization
B) projection
C) depression
D) anxiety
Answer: D

Pages: 270
Topic: Factors in Somatoform/Dissociative Disorders: Biological Factors
Skill: Factual   *Other1:*
77. Research on the origins of somatoform and dissociative disorders is
    A) clear that these disorders have a biological origin.
    B) generally sparse and not very advanced.
    C) converging on dysregulation in neurotransmitter systems as the primary cause of these disorders.
    D) clear that there is a substantial genetic contribution to these disorders.
    Answer: B

Pages: 270
Topic: Factors in Somatoform/Dissociative Disorders: Biological Factors
Skill: Factual   *Other1:*
78. Genetic studies of somatoform and dissociative disorders
    A) find that there is a strong genetic contribution to both disorders.
    B) find that there is no genetic contribution to either disorder.
    C) are inconclusive.
    D) find a genetic contribution for dissociative disorders but not for somatoform disorders.
    Answer: C

Pages: 270
Topic: Factors in Somatoform/Dissociative Disorders: Biological Factors
Skill: Factual   *Other1:*
79. Some researchers hypothesize that somatoform disorders involving nervous system and musculoskeletal symptoms reflect a dysfunction in the right cerebral hemisphere because
    A) that is the area of the brain responsible for fantasy and imagination.
    B) that is the area of the brain responsible for physical pain.
    C) it is the dominant side of the brain in most people.
    D) these symptoms show a pronounced tendency to be located on the left side of the body.
    Answer: D

Pages: 270
Topic: Factors in Somatoform/Dissociative Disorders: Biological Factors
Skill: Factual   *Other1:*
80. Research investigating evoked potential responses in the brains of individuals with dissociative disorder found that
    A) their evoked potentials are unusually spiked.
    B) they show deficits in responses to sensory stimuli that are associated with the origin of their symptoms.
    C) the biological substrate, if any, of these disorders has not been revealed.
    D) their evoked potentials are unusually flat.
    Answer: C

81. The strongest evidence implicates _____ as a risk factor for dissociative disorders.
    A) death of a parent during childhood
    B) traumatic childhood abuse
    C) low self-esteem developed during childhood
    D) parental use of strict discipline with excessive punishment
    Answer: B

82. Current research strongly suggests that dissociative identity disorder resembles
    A) generalized anxiety disorder.
    B) panic disorder without agoraphobia.
    C) conversion disorder.
    D) posttraumatic stress disorder.
    Answer: D

83. Kathleen was sexually assaulted by her father throughout her childhood. During these
    traumatic episodes she found herself thinking, "This isn't happening to me; it's happening
    to someone else." Kathleen was probably
    A) coping with this intolerable situation by developing somatization symptoms.
    B) experiencing derealization.
    C) attempting to cope with an intolerable situation by dissociating.
    D) decompensating.
    Answer: C

84. In studies of childhood abuse suffered by individuals with dissociative identity disorder,
    reports of sexual abuse often are accompanied by reports of _____.
    A) early loss of a parent
    B) physical abuse
    C) psychosis in the mother
    D) poverty
    Answer: B

Pages: 270-271
Topic: Factors in Somatoform/Dissociative Disorders: Psychosocial Factors
Skill: Factual   Other1:
85. The research evidence is probably strongest for a connection between childhood sexual abuse and
    A) anxiety disorder.
    B) somatoform disorder.
    C) dissociative identity disorder.
    D) depersonalization disorder.
    Answer: C

Pages: 271
Topic: Factors in Somatoform/Dissociative Disorders: Psychosocial Factors
Skill: Conceptual   Other1:
86. Concerning the recall of possible childhood abuse, memory may be viewed as
    A) infallible; it is virtually impossible to have false memories of sexual abuse.
    B) interpretive reconstructions of past events.
    C) fabrications.
    D) accurate; some distortions may occur but these typically pertain to minor incidents.
    Answer: B

Pages: 271
Topic: Factors in Somatoform/Dissociative Disorders: Psychosocial Factors
Skill: Conceptual   Other1:
87. In cases of recalling childhood sexual abuse,
    A) adults who recover repressed memories of the abuse are actually mistaken.
    B) adults may be influenced by untrained psychotherapists to construct repressed memories of abuse when no abuse occurred.
    C) one should assume that the person recalling repressed memories is mistaken, unless proven otherwise.
    D) one should assume that the person recalling repressed memories is accurate, unless proven otherwise.
    Answer: B

Pages: 273
Topic: Factors in Somatoform/Dissociative Disorders: Psychosocial Factors
Skill: Conceptual   Other1:
88. Some contemporary books provide a list of symptoms that they claim are indicators of past sexual abuse. These typically include depression, anxiety, and low self-esteem. Which of the following statements is true?
    A) These symptoms are so common in clinical populations that the list is worthless as a diagnostic tool, and potentially very dangerous.
    B) This list is inaccurate and instead should include symptoms like panic attacks and periods of time unaccounted for.
    C) People who have repressed memories of past abuse do not experience these particular symptoms.
    D) none of the above
    Answer: A

Pages: 273
Topic: Factors in Somatoform/Dissociative Disorders: Psychosocial Factors
Skill: Factual   Other1:
89. There is no established clinical justification for the practice of
    A) hypnosis.
    B) prevailing upon a client to confront and condemn the alleged perpetrator of childhood sexual abuse.
    C) narcotherapy.
    D) behavioral interventions in treating pain disorder.
    Answer: B

Pages: 273
Topic: Factors in Somatoform/Dissociative Disorders: Psychosocial Factors
Skill: Factual   Other1:
90. According to a recent review of the false memory issue by Loftus,
    A) there is no such thing as a false memory.
    B) recall of repressed childhood traumas is false.
    C) it is very difficult to create a false memory.
    D) it is not difficult to create a false memory.
    Answer: D

Pages: 273
Topic: Factors in Somatoform/Dissociative Disorders: Psychosocial Factors
Skill: Factual   Other1:
91. Memories for events that have actually never taken place are
    A) pseudomemories.
    B) hypnotic memories.
    C) implicit memories.
    D) false autobiographical memories.
    Answer: A

Pages: 273
Topic: Factors in Somatoform/Dissociative Disorders: Psychosocial Factors
Skill: Factual   Other1:
92. Hypnosis may encourage
    A) repression of memories of abuse.
    B) rich elaborations of pseudomemories.
    C) the development of dissociative episodes.
    D) decompensation.
    Answer: B

Pages: 271
Topic: Factors in Somatoform/Dissociative Disorders: Psychosocial Factors
Skill: Factual   Other1:
93. Dissociative identity disorder
    A) never occurs in the absence of childhood trauma.
    B) never occurs without a history of childhood sexual abuse.
    C) only occurs when there is a family history of dissociative disorders.
    D) may occur in the absence of childhood trauma.
    Answer: D

Pages: 271
Topic: Factors in Somatoform/Dissociative Disorders: Psychosocial Factors
Skill: Factual   Other1:
94. Factors that may be associated with the development of dissociative tendencies are
    A) a high capacity for personal absorption.
    B) ease of hypnotizability.
    C) a high capacity for fantasy.
    D) all of the above
    Answer: D

Pages: 271
Topic: Factors in Somatoform/Dissociative Disorders: Psychosocial Factors
Skill: Factual   Other1:
95. One valid indicator of the propensity to dissociate is
    A) low birth weight.
    B) a high score on the Dissociative Experience Scale.
    C) resistance to hypnosis.
    D) a history of chronic physical illness.
    Answer: B

Pages: 271-274
Topic: Factors in Somatoform/Dissociative Disorders: Psychosocial Factors
Skill: Factual   Other1:

96. The personality patterns and psychiatric disorders associated with somatoform disorders include all BUT which of the following?
    A) hysterical (histrionic) personality disorder
    B) alexithymia
    C) neuroticism
    D) depression
    Answer: A

Pages: 274
Topic: Factors in Somatoform/Dissociative Disorders: Sociocultural Factors
Skill: Factual   Other1:

97. In non-Western cultures where the expression of emotional distress is considered unacceptable,
    A) dissociative identity disorder is commonplace.
    B) somatizing patterns are more common.
    C) somatizing patterns are less common.
    D) dissociative disorders are practically nonexistent.
    Answer: B

Pages: 274
Topic: Factors in Somatoform/Dissociative Disorders: Sociocultural Factors
Skill: Conceptual   Other1:

98. Cultural tolerance plays a role in the incidence of
    A) dissociative disorders.
    B) somatoform disorders.
    C) A and B
    D) none of the above
    Answer: C

Pages: 274
Topic: Treatment and Outcomes
Skill: Factual   Other1:

99. Medical interventions to treat somatoform disorders
    A) are highly effective.
    B) are rarely effective in giving sustained relief from primary symptoms.
    C) should be confined to antianxiety medication.
    D) improves the prognosis for full recovery.
    Answer: B

Pages: 274
Topic: Treatment and Outcomes
Skill: Factual   *Other1:*
100. The prognosis for full recovery from most somatoform disorders is
    A) very good.
    B) poor.
    C) very good with the help of medication.
    D) unclear; not enough data is available to know.
    Answer: B

Pages: 274
Topic: Treatment and Outcomes
Skill: Factual   *Other1:*
101. Research suggests that _____ is promising for treating conversion and pain disorders.
    A) psychodynamic therapy
    B) pharmacotherapy
    C) cognitive-behavioral therapy
    D) interpersonal therapy
    Answer: C

Pages: 274
Topic: Treatment and Outcomes
Skill: Factual   *Other1:*
102. Kluft recently has proposed a three-stage consensus model for treating
    A) depersonalization disorder.
    B) dissociative identity disorder.
    C) somatization disorder.
    D) conversion disorder.
    Answer: B

Pages: 274
Topic: Treatment and Outcomes
Skill: Factual   *Other1:*
103. In the early stage of treatment of dissociative identity disorder, according to Kluft's consensus model,
    A) ground rules and trust are established.
    B) the client is encouraged to relive early traumas.
    C) the client is "introduced" to alter personalities.
    D) behavioral interventions are instituted.
    Answer: A

Pages: 274-275
Topic: Treatment and Outcomes
Skill: Conceptual   Other1:

104. The goal of Kluft's consensus model of therapy for dissociative identity disorder is
    A) amnesia for early traumas.
    B) cathartic reliving of traumas.
    C) integration of the separate personality systems.
    D) confronting the abuser.
    Answer: C

Pages: 274-275
Topic: Treatment and Outcomes
Skill: Factual   Other1:

105. The second stage of Kluft's consensus model of therapy for dissociative identity disorder involves
    A) explaining the nature of the problem to the patient.
    B) working through traumas and resolution of dissociative defenses.
    C) repair and compensation for years of poor adjustment.
    D) grieving for losses.
    Answer: B

Pages: 275
Topic: Treatment and Outcomes
Skill: Conceptual   Other1:

106. One difficulty in treating individuals with dissociative identity disorder is
    A) their inability to remember the contents of past therapy sessions.
    B) their tendency to disappear for months at a time in fugue states.
    C) their tendency to switch between personalities as a defensive maneuver.
    D) their tendency to drop out of therapy early in treatment.
    Answer: C

Pages: 275
Topic: Treatment and Outcomes
Skill: Factual   Other1:

107. During the postintegration stage of therapy in Kluft's consensus model,
    A) an individual often experiences grief and profound loneliness.
    B) there is a marked danger of decompensation into a psychotic state.
    C) medication has proven useful.
    D) hypnosis is employed.
    Answer: A

Pages: 275
Topic: Treatment and Outcomes
Skill: Conceptual   Other1:
108. The use of hypnosis in treating dissociative states
    A) is very effective.
    B) is not very effective.
    C) has not been systematically tested for its effectiveness.
    D) is no longer done.
    Answer: C

Pages: 275
Topic: Unresolved Issues at the Somatoform/Dissociative Interface
Skill: Factual   Other1:
109. The DSM-III and DSM-IV created the two diagnostic categories of somatoform and
    dissociative disorders on the basis of
    A) research into the biological causes of these disorders.
    B) genetic studies.
    C) historical concepts of hysterical diseases.
    D) the presence or absence of somatic manifestations.
    Answer: D

Pages: 275
Topic: Unresolved Issues at the Somatoform/Dissociative Interface
Skill: Factual   Other1:
110. Kihlstrom and others have argued that future classification systems might best classify
    _____ as a dissociative disorder.
    A) pain disorder
    B) somatization disorder
    C) conversion disorder
    D) hypochondriasis
    Answer: C

Short Answer

Write the word or phrase that best completes each statement or answers the question.

Pages: 254
Topic: Somatoform and Dissociative Disorders
Skill: Factual   Other1:
1. Briefly state the defining characteristics of somatoform disorders.
    Answer: They are conditions involving physical complaints or disabilities for which
            there is no satisfactory organic basis. These somatic symptoms are involuntary.

Pages: 263-264
Topic: Somatoform and Dissociative Disorders
Skill: Factual   Other1:
2. Briefly state the defining characteristic of dissociative disorders.
   Answer: These are conditions involving a disruption in the sense of a coherent and stable personal identity.

Pages: 253
Topic: Somatoform and Dissociative Disorders
Skill: Conceptual   Other1:
3. How did Freud view somatoform and dissociative disorders?
   Answer: He considered them to be neuroses, manifestations of unconscious intrapsychic conflict involving the repression of forbidden sexual and aggressive impulses which were converted to symbolic psychological and somatic symptoms.

Pages: 254
Topic: Somatoform Disorders: Somatization Disorder
Skill: Factual   Other1:
4. Briefly characterize somatization disorder.
   Answer: This is characterized by multiple complaints of physical ailments over a long period of time, with onset before the age of thirty. These physical symptoms can not be adequately explained by organic causes and result in either medical treatment or significant life impairment.

Pages: 255
Topic: Somatoform Disorders: Hypochondriasis
Skill: Conceptual   Other1:
5. Individuals who are preoccupied with their bodily functions and complain of a shifting, incoherent pattern of physical ailments which have no apparent organic basis probably suffer from _____.
   Answer: hypochondriasis

Pages: 257
Topic: Somatoform Disorders: Pain Disorder
Skill: Factual   Other1:
6. Briefly describe somatoform pain disorder.
   Answer: This disorder involves complaints of pain that cause significant life disruption in the absence of organic causes that would provide an adequate explanation for the pain even if some medical condition is present.

Pages: 258
Topic: Somatoform Disorders: Conversion Disorder
Skill: Applied   Other1:

7. Lonnie lost his ability to control his leg movements when he tries to run, although he is able to walk without difficulty. Tests have found no medical basis for his complaint. What is his probable diagnosis and why?

    Answer: He probably has conversion disorder because the loss of function has no apparent organic basis and involves a pseudoneurological problem that is selective in functional loss.

Pages: 262-263
Topic: Somatoform Disorders: Conversion Disorder
Skill: Conceptual   Other1:

8. What factors tend to be associated with the onset of conversion disorder?

    Answer: An individual typically experiences an intolerable stressor, has the fleeting thought that it would be desirable to be sick in order to escape dealing with the stressor, but immediately suppresses this thought as unacceptable. Conversion symptoms then develop and provide an escape from the unwanted situation, although the individual sees no connection between the situation and the symptoms. Guilt, self-punishment, and the opportunity for financial compensation following injury are also associated with the origin of conversion disorder.

Pages: 263-264
Topic: Dissociative Disorders
Skill: Conceptual   Other1:

9. Briefly describe how the unconscious is viewed by contemporary cognitive psychologists.

    Answer: It is now widely recognized that unconscious mental activity does indeed exist. Many complex mental activities can and do occur outside of conscious awareness involving such areas as perception and memory. When this multi-channel capacity loses some of its integrative quality, however, clinical conditions may result. Dissociative phenomena are an example of this.

Pages: 265
Topic: Dissociative Disorders: Dissociative Amnesia and Fugue
Skill: Factual   Other1:

10. The disorder in which an individual escapes an intolerable situation by forgetting personal identifying information and leaving his or her life behind is called _____.

    Answer: a fugue state

Pages: 266
Topic: Dissociative Disorders: Dissociative Identity Disorder
Skill: Factual   Other1:

11. Briefly describe the defining characteristics associated with dissociative identity disorder.
    Answer: This disorder is characterized by the simultaneous existence of two or more personalities. Each personality has well-developed and distinct emotional and thought processes. There is usually a "host" personality which is unaware of the alter personalities, who tend to display characteristics that are inhibited in the host.

Pages: 268
Topic: Dissociative Disorders: Dissociative Identity Disorder
Skill: Factual   Other1:

12. The incidence of _____ disorder has been decreasing in recent years whereas the incidence of _____ disorder has been increasing.
    Answer: conversion; dissociative identity

Pages: 269
Topic: Dissociative Disorders: Depersonalization Disorder
Skill: Factual   Other1:

13. What are depersonalization and derealization experiences?
    Answer: Depersonalization is the feeling that one has lost one's sense of self, such as by becoming another person or by a dramatic and grotesque physical change. This may often be experienced as floating out of the body and looking down at oneself, or even as visiting far away places. Derealization is the experience that the external world appears distorted, unstable, and intangible.

Pages: 270
Topic: Factors in Somatoform/Dissociative Disorders: Biological Factors
Skill: Conceptual   Other1:

14. What is the genetic basis for somatoform and dissociative disorders?
    Answer: There is little research in this area. Limited evidence suggests a modest genetic contribution to somatoform disorders. No evidence exists at present of a genetic contribution to dissociation, although it is too soon to draw firm conclusions about heredity for either disorder at the present time.

Pages: 270-271
Topic: Factors in Somatoform/Dissociative Disorders: Psychosocial Factors
Skill: Conceptual   Other1:

15. Available evidence suggests that _____ is a major risk factor for development of dissociative identity disorder.
    Answer: childhood sexual and/or physical abuse

Pages: 271-274
Topic: Factors in Somatoform/Dissociative Disorders: Psychosocial Factors
Skill: Factual   Other1:
16. Alexithymia and neuroticism are personality patterns associated with ____.
    Answer: somatoform disorders

Pages: 274
Topic: Factors in Somatoform/Dissociative Disorders: Sociocultural Factors
Skill: Conceptual   Other1:
17. Briefly describe the influence that sociocultural factors may have on somatoform and dissociative disorders.
    Answer: Cultural acceptance of emotional distress influences the prevalence of somatoform disorders. It is less acceptable in certain non-Western cultures to express emotional distress directly. In such cultures, somatizing patterns are more common than in Western cultures. Similarly, social acceptance and tolerance of dissociative phenomena seem to influence the prevalence of these patterns.

Pages: 274-275
Topic: Treatment and Outcomes
Skill: Conceptual   Other1:
18. What does research tell us about effective treatments for conversion and pain disorders?
    Answer: Controlled clinical studies indicate that both behavioral and cognitive-behavioral therapies are very promising. The prognosis for full recovery from these two disorders is good.

Pages: 274-275
Topic: Treatment and Outcomes
Skill: Factual   Other1:
19. Briefly describe Kluft's three-stage consensus model for treating dissociative identity disorder.
    Answer: The first stage, stabilization, involves setting ground rules, establishing trust, explaining the nature of the disorder to the patient, and halting further maladaptive reactions to current stressors. The second stage, working through trauma and resolution of dissociative defenses, has integration as its goal. The third stage, postintegration therapy, involves repair, compensation, and grieving.

Pages: 275-276
Topic: Unresolved Issues at the Somatoform/Dissociative Interface
Skill: Conceptual   Other1:

20. Briefly identify and describe one of the unresolved issues surrounding somatoform and dissociative disorders that was addressed in the text.

Answer: One issue involves whether conversion disorder isn't actually a dissociative disorder. Another issue concerns whether somatoform pain disorder is essentially identical to sensory forms of conversion disorder. Body dysmorphic disorder may not belong to the somatoform group. The distinction between somatization disorder and hypochondriasis is fuzzy. Dissociation may be a broader dimension underlying somatoform and dissociative disorders.

Essay

Write your answer in the space provided or on a separate sheet of paper.

Pages: 253
Topic: Somatoform and Dissociative Disorders
Skill: Factual   Other1:

1. Describe the history of the way in which somatoform and dissociative disorders have been conceptualized.

Answer: In the 19th century, Janet proposed that conversion disorder, which he called hysteria, was associated with the dissociated expression of traumatic memories. Freud added the notion of intrapsychic conflict and anxiety converted into somatic symptoms that were symbolically associated with features of the underlying conflict. Currently some psychologists regard dissociation as a broad dimension underlying dissociative and some somatoform disorders. However, the DSM-IV regards these as two distinct classes of disorders differing in the presence or absence of central somatic symptoms.

Pages: 254-258
Topic: Somatoform Disorders
Skill: Factual   Other1:

2. Describe three types of somatoform disorders other than conversion disorder. How are these three different disorders distinguished from one another?

Answer: Somatization disorder is characterized by multiple complaints of physical ailments over a long period, beginning before age thirty, with no apparent or adequate organic cause. Hypochondriasis is similar but may begin after age thirty and typically involves shifting, vague symptoms and morbid preoccupation with bodily functions. Pain disorder involves severe or lasting pain symptoms with no physical cause, or a medical condition inadequate to explain the pain.

Pages: 255-257
Topic: Somatoform Disorders: Hypochondriasis
Skill: Conceptual   Other1:
3. What is hypochondriasis? Describe the typical hypochondriacal individual. What are the risk factors for developing this disorder?

Answer: This somatoform disorder involves somatic complaints with no apparent physical basis. The age of onset may be after thirty. The individual tends to report a diffuse, vague pattern of symptoms that shifts and fluctuates over time. They often are abnormally preoccupied with their bodily processes, major consumers of over-the-counter medications, and avid followers of popular medical articles. Many hypochondriacs experienced childhood abuse and trauma, much childhood sickness and school absence, and have other Axis I diagnoses. This disorder may be seen as a kind of needful communication.

Pages: 258-263
Topic: Somatoform Disorders: Conversion Disorder
Skill: Applied   Other1:
4. Edward was a pilot in the Persian Gulf War. On the eve of his first bombing mission, he began to experience night blindness. There appeared to be no organic reason for this problem, and his eyesight would return to normal during the day. What is the probable diagnosis? How is his case typical or different from most such individuals? How would his disorder be distinguished from an organic disorder?

Answer: He probably has conversion disorder. He's typical in that his problem occured when faced with extreme stress, and his loss of function was selective, providing an escape from a specific stressor. Unlike organic disorders, Edward's disorder probably included la belle indifference, and under hypnosis symptoms could be removed, shifted, and reinduced.

Pages: 262-263
Topic: Somatoform Disorders: Conversion Disorder
Skill: Conceptual   Other1:
5. How does a conversion disorder typically develop? What are the risk factors associated with its onset?

Answer: Typically an individual faces an intolerable stressor, has the fleeting thought that being sick would provide an escape, but that thought is unacceptable and is promptly suppressed. The individual then develops conversion symptoms, but doesn't associate them with the stressor. Symptoms may be associated with secondary gain or may be symbolic of a major conflict situation. They may involve self-punishment for intense guilt, and may also arise when an opportunity for injury compensation occurs.

Pages: 263-264
Topic: Dissociative Disorders
Skill: Factual   Other1:

6. Identify and briefly describe the dissociative disorders.

    Answer: These disorders involve avoiding potentially overwhelming stress by escaping
          from one's personal identity or memory. Dissociative amnesia involves forgetting
          important personal information and, in fugue states, leaving home and sometimes
          assuming a new identity. Depersonalization involves sudden feelings that one
          has lost one's sense of self, often felt as an out-of-body experience, and may
          be accompanied by derealization experiences. Dissociative identity disorder
          involves two or more distinct, relatively stable personalities coexisting in one
          individual.

Pages: 265
Topic: Dissociative Disorders: Dissociative Amnesia and Fugue
Skill: Applied   Other1:

7. After a series of severe arguments with her husband, Fionnula claims to have problems
    recalling certain events. If this is not an organic disorder, then what is it likely to
    be? How is it differentiated from a fugue state? When do these disorders typically occur
    and what are some of the personality characteristics associated with them?

    Answer: This is psychogenic amnesia. She has limited recall, whereas in a fugue state
          she would leave and possibly adopt a new identity. This disorder usually occurs
          after great stress, and is fairly common after a traumatic experience.
          Individuals who become amnesic are typically highly suggestible and have past
          experiences of wanting to just forget it all and flee, but they are too
          inhibited to do so.

Pages: 266-268
Topic: Dissociative Disorders: Dissociative Identity Disorder
Skill: Conceptual   Other1:

8. Dissociative identity disorder receives a lot of media attention. Describe this disorder.
    How common is it? What is an example of a typical case?

    Answer: Two or more personalities coexist, each with distinct emotional and thought
          processes. Usually a "host" personality exists unaware of the alter
          personalities, who may themselves know about some of the others. Alters often
          express behaviors inhibited in the host and assume distinct roles like
          protector. Often one alter knows about all of the other personalities. The
          incidence of reported cases is increasing, which may be artifactual or may be
          associated with increasing child sexual abuse, a major risk factor. It's more
          common in females with a history of sexual and/or physical abuse.

Pages: 268
Topic: Dissociative Disorders: Dissociative Identity Disorder
Skill: Conceptual   Other1:

9. What is the evidence for and against the suggestion that dissociative identity disorder is a form of malingering?

   Answer: Evidence against this suggestion includes the fact that some clinicians, by virtue of unwise use of hypnosis, are themselves responsible for eliciting this disorder in highly suggestible patients. Concerns about malingering also arise due to the frequency with which defendants and their attorneys use the diagnosis in an attempt to escape punishment for crimes. However, these criticisms fail to fully account for all of the observations reported, such as the elaborate pretreatment personal histories of patients with dissociative identity disorder.

Pages: 270
Topic: Factors in Somatoform/Dissociative Disorders: Biological Factors
Skill: Factual   Other1:

10. Discuss the research evidence for the involvement of biological causal factors in somatoform disorders.

    Answer: There has not been a lot of research in this area. Family history (pedigree) studies provide limited evidence of a possible genetic contribution to somatoform disorders. However, these studies can not separate the possible effects of environmental and genetic causal factors. One interesting piece of evidence comes from studies that have found a remarkably strong tendency of nervous system and musculoskeletal symptoms to appear on the left side of the body, which suggests right cerebral hemisphere involvement.

Pages: 270-274
Topic: Factors in Somatoform/Dissociative Disorders: Psychosocial Factors
Skill: Conceptual   Other1:

11. Discuss the role of traumatic childhood abuse as an etiological factor in dissociative disorders.

    Answer: It has been strongly implicated in dissociative identity disorder (DID), which resembles posttraumatic stress disorder and seems to be a kind of posttraumatic dissociative disorder. About 80 percent of the cases of DID investigated in two studies reported childhood sexual abuse and many also reported various types of physical abuse. Dissociation may develop as a means of coping during victimization.

Pages: 272-273
Topic: Factors in Somatoform/Dissociative Disorders: Psychosocial Factors
Skill: Conceptual   Other1:

12. Discuss the issue of recovering repressed memories of childhood abuse. What problems have been created by overzealous clinicians and how can these problems be averted?

    Answer: This is a currently heated issue because of the preponderance of cases being "discovered" and the difficulty verifying these memories. Some psychotherapists appear to be "planting" the idea of past abuse in clients, who recover memories that are false. Research demonstrates the reconstructive nature of memory and tendency under hypnosis for increasing elaboration on pseudomemories. Loftus's work is notable in showing the ease with which false memories can be created. Clinicians should be familiar with the research on false memories and take every precaution possible to minimize this risk.

Pages: 274-275
Topic: Treatment and Outcomes
Skill: Conceptual   Other1:

13. What treatments have been used for somatoform disorders and how effective have they been?

    Answer: Most professionals advise caution in prescribing medication for somatoform disorders. Antianxiety and antidepressant drugs may help for awhile, but the long-term prognosis for full recovery from somatoform disorders is not very good. A supportive relationship with a health professional may be the best available approach at present. Many patients with these disorders will refuse psychological treatment because they are convinced of the physical reality of their symptoms. However, clinical studies show that pain disorder is very amenable to behavioral and cognitive-behavioral therapies.

Pages: 274-275
Topic: Treatment and Outcomes
Skill: Conceptual   Other1:

14. Describe Kluft's three-stage consensus model for treating dissociative identity disorder (DID).

    Answer: The goal of this model is integration of personalities in the context of enhanced general functioning. Stage one, stabilization, involves establishing ground rules, trust, understanding of the problem, and halting further maladaptive reactions to current stressors. Stage two involves working through and reconnecting to memories of past traumas, dealing with defensive propensities to "switch," and reestablishing connections between separate identities. Stage three involves grieving, repair and compensation. Research is needed to evaluate the effectiveness of this and other treatments for DID.

Pages: 275-276
Topic: Unresolved Issues at the Somatoform/Dissociative Interface
Skill: Conceptual   Other1:

15. DSM-IV considers somatoform and dissociative disorders to be categorically distinct, but not all current researchers agree with this distinction. Discuss the basis for the distinction and why some investigators take issue with it.

Answer: DSM-IV divides these two categories on the basis of the presence or absence of somatic symptoms. However, as Kihlstrom notes, one might best regard conversion disorder symptoms as cognitive in nature, and the central feature of this disorder to be the dissociation of mental contents and processes from conscious awareness, affecting memory and identity. Some suggest that a dissociative tendency is a dimension underlying both DSM-IV classes.

CHAPTER 8   Psychological Factors and Physical Illness

Multiple-Choice

Choose the one alternative that best completes the statement or answers the question.

Pages: 279
Topic: Psychological Factors and Physical Illness
Skill: Factual   Other1:
1. The interdisciplinary approach to the treatment of physical disorders thought to have psychological factors as a major aspect of their causal patterns is known as
    A) psychoneurological medicine.
    B) pathophysiological medicine.
    C) psychosocial medicine.
    D) behavioral medicine.
    Answer: D

Pages: 279
Topic: Psychological Factors and Physical Illness
Skill: Conceptual   Other1:
2. Behavioral medicine emphasizes
    A) replacing traditional medical methods with psychological methods in the treatment of physical illness.
    B) the role of psychological factors in the occurrence, maintenance, and prevention of physical illness.
    C) integrating psychology and sociology in an effort to replace surgery for physical illness.
    D) utilizing imagery to treat disabling illnesses such as cancer.
    Answer: B

Pages: 279-280
Topic: Psychological Factors and Physical Illness
Skill: Factual   Other1:
3. Psychogenic illnesses are
    A) physical illnesses with psychological consequences.
    B) diseases that are psychologically induced or maintained.
    C) psychological disorders caused by concurrent medical diseases.
    D) illnesses that involve individuals feigning symptoms, usually to gain attention.
    Answer: B

Pages: 280
Topic: Psychological Factors and Physical Illness
Skill: Factual   Other1:
4. The subspecialty within behavioral medicine that deals specifically with diagnosis, treatment, and prevention of the psychological components of physical illness is
A) health psychology.
B) medical psychology.
C) integrative medicopsychology.
D) environmental psychology.
Answer: A

Pages: 280
Topic: Psychological Factors and Physical Illness
Skill: Conceptual   Other1:
5. The behavioral medicine approach suggests that
A) it is often more important to know what kind of patient has the disease than what kind of disease the patient has.
B) the traditional medical approach has been found to be hopelessly inadequate for treating most diseases.
C) the context in which disease occurs usually plays a small but important role in the progression of the disease.
D) physicians should be replaced by psychologists in treating many physical illnesses.
Answer: A

Pages: 280
Topic: Psychological Factors and Physical Illness
Skill: Factual   Other1:
6. Unlike previous editions of the DSM, the DSM-IV includes
A) psychosomatic disorders on Axis II.
B) a category called Psychological Factors Affecting Medical Condition on Axis I.
C) an Axis III for medical conditions.
D) organic mental disorders on Axis V.
Answer: B

Pages: 281
Topic: Psychological/Health/Disease: Health/Attitudes/Coping Resources
Skill: Factual   Other1:
7. A major factor buffering against disease is
A) a pessimistic outlook.
B) an optimistic outlook.
C) ignorance, in the tradition of "ignorance is bliss."
D) a belief that one should assign complete responsibility for one's health care to one's physician.
Answer: B

Pages: 281
Topic: Psychological/Health/Disease: Health/Attitudes/Coping Resources
Skill: Factual   Other1:
8. The two types of optimism delineated in the text are
   A) helplessness and hopelessness.
   B) sense of efficacy and lack of hopelessness.
   C) sense of efficacy and defensive denial.
   D) defensive denial and coping.
   Answer: C

Pages: 281
Topic: Psychological/Health/Disease: Health/Attitudes/Coping Resources
Skill: Factual   Other1:
9. The defensive type of optimism
   A) constitutes a significantly enhanced risk for health problems.
   B) reflects an unwillingness or inability to acknowledge symptoms.
   C) is unhelpful in the health context.
   D) all of the above
   Answer: D

Pages: 281
Topic: Psychological/Health/Disease: Health/Attitudes/Coping Resources
Skill: Factual   Other1:
10. In a study of baseball hall-of-famers, an attitude of _____ predicted poor health outcomes.
    A) helplessness
    B) optimism
    C) efficacy
    D) apathy
    Answer: A

Pages: 282
Topic: Psychological/Health/Disease: Health/Attitudes/Coping Resources
Skill: Conceptual   Other1:
11. How do life changes affect health?
    A) Positive changes always have a beneficial effect on health, while negative changes have a detrimental effect.
    B) Positive changes can have a detrimental effect on a person's health if the amount of adjustment required by the change taxes a person's coping resources.
    C) Neither positive nor negative life changes have a very significant effect on health.
    D) Negative life changes only impact on an individual's health status if he or she is a Type A personality.
    Answer: B

Pages: 282
Topic: Psychological/Health/Disease: Health/Attitudes/Coping Resources
Skill: Conceptual   Other1:
12. Any type of chronic negative affect or emotion appears to
    A) enhance the risk of disease.
    B) lower the risk of disease.
    C) enhance the risk of disease, but only in individuals who have chronically low
       self-esteem.
    D) enhance the risk of disease, but only in individuals who have high self-esteem.
    Answer: A

Pages: 282
Topic: Psychological/Health/Disease: Health/Attitudes/Coping Resources
Skill: Factual   Other1:
13. Ordinary frustrations of everyday life provoking extreme emotional reactions is
    characteristic of
    A) the Type B personality.
    B) the defensive pessimist.
    C) the Type A personality.
    D) the Disease-prone personality.
    Answer: C

Pages: 282
Topic: Psychological/Health/Disease: Health/Attitudes/Coping Resources
Skill: Applied   Other1:
14. A person predisposed to allergies who experiences severe emotional stress may experience
    the onset or increase of allergic symptoms. This is in keeping with
    A) the biogenic model of illness.
    B) the stress theory of illness.
    C) the placebo effect.
    D) the diathesis-stress model of illness.
    Answer: D

Pages: 282
Topic: Psychological/Health/Disease: Health/Attitudes/Coping Resources
Skill: Conceptual   Other1:
15. Which of the following is true?
    A) Negative emotions make an individual susceptible to disease, but positive emotions do not have much of an effect.
    B) Positive emotions seem to produce a certain immunity to disease, but negative emotions do not have much of an effect.
    C) Negative emotions make an individual susceptible to disease and positive emotions seem to produce a certain immunity.
    D) Neither negative emotions nor positive emotions affect the course of disease nearly as much as was previously thought.
    Answer: C

Pages: 282
Topic: Psychological/Health/Disease: Health/Attitudes/Coping Resources
Skill: Factual   Other1:
16. The person who believes that treatment is going to be effective has a much better chance of showing improvement than the patient who is neutral or pessimistic. This is known as the
    A) Hawthorne effect.
    B) placebo effect.
    C) Premack effect.
    D) double-blind effect.
    Answer: B

Pages: 282
Topic: Psychological/Health/Disease: Health/Attitudes/Coping Resources
Skill: Applied   Other1: In Student Study Guide
17. A patient who shows improvement after a trusted physician gives him or her an injection of sterile water is demonstrating
    A) the Hawthorne effect.
    B) the placebo effect.
    C) demand characteristics.
    D) faith healing.
    Answer: B

Pages: 283
Topic: Psychological Factors/Health/Disease: Autonomic Excess/Tissue Damage
Skill: Factual   Other1:

18. Arousal of the autonomic nervous system is associated with
    A) hormonal depletions.
    B) the fight or flight syndrome.
    C) delayed physiological responses to stress.
    D) the resistance stage of the general adaptation syndrome.
    Answer: B

Pages: 283
Topic: Psychological Factors/Health/Disease: Autonomic Excess/Tissue Damage
Skill: Factual   Other1:

19. Many have suggested that the unduly repetitive or long-continued activation of the autonomic nervous system may result in
    A) depression.
    B) disease, such as high blood pressure.
    C) a decrease in the magnitude of the body's alarm reaction.
    D) inhibition of the musculoskeletal system.
    Answer: B

Pages: 283
Topic: Psychological Factors/Health/Disease: Autonomic Excess/Tissue Damage
Skill: Factual   Other1:

20. The alarm stage of Selye's general adaptation syndrome is dominated by
    A) increased arousal of the autonomic nervous sytem.
    B) the inhibited secretion of neurotransmitters.
    C) the inhibition of excessive defenses.
    D) voluntary physiological processes.
    Answer: A

Pages: 283
Topic: Psychological Factors/Health/Disease: Autonomic Excess/Tissue Damage
Skill: Conceptual   Other1:

21. Some have suggested that chronic internal sources of threat may
    A) counteract the effects of chronic external stress.
    B) be unimportant in their effects on health relative to the effects of chronic external stress.
    C) lead to the flattening out of the alarm reaction to external threats.
    D) put an individual's health at serious risk.
    Answer: D

Pages: 283
Topic: Psychological/Health/Disease: Psychosocial Factors/Immune System
Skill: Factual   Other1:
22. During Selye's resistance stage of the general adaptation syndrome,
    A) the autonomic nervous system triggers a fight or flight reaction.
    B) the individual becomes aware of the existence of a threat.
    C) an organism's protective resources are mobilized.
    D) none of the above.
    Answer: C

Pages: 283
Topic: Psychological/Health/Disease: Psychosocial Factors/Immune System
Skill: Factual   Other1:
23. The immune system is a major component underlying an organism's _____ stage of the general adaptation syndrome.
    A) resistance
    B) revolt
    C) alarm
    D) autonomic
    Answer: A

Pages: 284-285
Topic: Psychological/Health/Disease: Psychosocial Factors/Immune System
Skill: Factual   Other1:
24. The primary components of the immune system include all of the following EXCEPT
    A) white blood cells.
    B) B-cells.
    C) T-cells.
    D) antigens.
    Answer: D

Pages: 284
Topic: Psychological/Health/Disease: Psychosocial Factors/Immune System
Skill: Factual   Other1:
25. A foreign substance in the body is called a(n)
    A) leukocyte.
    B) antigen.
    C) B-cell.
    D) macrophage.
    Answer: B

Pages: 284
Topic: Psychological/Health/Disease: Psychosocial Factors/Immune System
Skill: Factual   Other1:
26. Humoral immune functioning is primarily associated with _____, while cellular immune functioning is primarily associated with _____.
   A) blood cells; antigens
   B) B-cells; blood cells
   C) T-cells; lymph nodes.
   D) B-cells; T-cells
   Answer: D

Pages: 284
Topic: Psychological/Health/Disease: Psychosocial Factors/Immune System
Skill: Factual   Other1: In Student Study Guide
27. B-cells produce antibodies which are involved chiefly with protection against the more common varieties of
   A) bacterial infection.
   B) cancerous growth.
   C) cellular dysfunction.
   D) viral infection.
   Answer: A

Pages: 284
Topic: Psychological/Health/Disease: Psychosocial Factors/Immune System
Skill: Conceptual   Other1:
28. The front line of immune defense is contained in
   A) the white blood cells.
   B) the bone marrow.
   C) the antigens circulating in the blood.
   D) the thalamus.
   Answer: A

Pages: 285
Topic: Psychological/Health/Disease: Psychosocial Factors/Immune System
Skill: Factual   Other1:
29. A study of the effects of psychosocial factors on immune functioning in HIV-infected men showed that
   A) behavioral interventions had psychological benefits, but no apparent effect on immunocompetence due to the virulent nature of the virus.
   B) antigens are completely resistant to the effects of psychological interventions.
   C) depressed mood had no effect on immunocompetence.
   D) behavioral interventions had positive psychological and immunocompetence effects.
   Answer: D

Pages: 285
Topic: Psychological/Health/Disease: Psychosocial Factors/Immune System
Skill: Conceptual   Other1:
30. Psychosocial stressors can impact on the immune system
    A) only when the immune system already is in a weakened state.
    B) once the organism has been depleted of white blood cells.
    C) only when powerful stressors seem capable of significantly reducing immunocompetence.
    D) to the point of enhancing vulnerability to virtually any antigen.
    Answer: D

Pages: 285
Topic: Psychological/Health/Disease: Psychosocial Factors/Immune System
Skill: Factual   Other1:
31. In an important recent study, induced negative self-evaluations were found to
    A) be causally linked to subsequent diminished levels of natural killer cell cytotoxicity.
    B) have a significant correlation with suppression of immune function.
    C) have little impact on immune function unless accompanied by several severe life
       stressors.
    D) provide a paradoxical buffer against the onset of later physical illness.
    Answer: A

Pages: 285
Topic: Psychological/Health/Disease: Psychosocial Factors/Immune System
Skill: Factual   Other1:
32. In an important recent study, each of the following psychosocial factors was found to be
    causally associated with contracting a cold virus EXCEPT
    A) lack of exercise.
    B) stressful life events.
    C) self-perceived stress.
    D) negative emotion.
    Answer: A

Pages: 285
Topic: Psychological/Health/Disease: Psychosocial Factors/Immune System
Skill: Conceptual   Other1:
33. Two recent reviews of studies investigating the relationship between psychosocial factors
    and immune functioning found that
    A) psychosocial factors are relatively unimportant as predictors of illness.
    B) depressed individuals make much less use of health care in health maintenance
       organizations than nondepressed individuals.
    C) depressed affect is reliably associated with suppressed immune functioning.
    D) depressed affect is associated with suppressed immune functioning only if accompanied
       by severely low self-esteem.
    Answer: C

Pages: 286
Topic: Psychological/Health/Disease: Psychosocial Factors/Immune System
Skill: Factual   Other1:
34. The field that explores psychological influences on the nervous system's control of immune responsiveness is called
    A) behavioral medicine.
    B) health psychology.
    C) psychoneuroimmunology.
    D) neuropsychological medicine.
    Answer: C

Pages: 286
Topic: Psychological/Health/Disease: Psychosocial Factors/Immune System
Skill: Factual   Other1:
35. Psychoneuroimmunology is concerned with
    A) the mediating role that the central nervous system presumably plays in presiding over the relationship between negative psychological states and diminished immune functioning.
    B) medical causes of immune system dysfunction.
    C) investigating whether there are any links between psychological factors and physical illness.
    D) the impact of physical illness on immune functioning.
    Answer: A

Pages: 286
Topic: Psychological/Health/Disease: Psychosocial Factors/Immune System
Skill: Factual   Other1:
36. All of the following have been implicated in affecting immune function EXCEPT
    A) a variety of neurochemicals including endorphins.
    B) adrenocortical hormones (steroids).
    C) spinal fluid.
    D) testosterone.
    Answer: C

Pages: 286
Topic: Psychological/Health/Disease: Psychosocial Factors/Immune System
Skill: Conceptual   Other1:
37. There is evidence that immunosuppression
    A) can be affected by mental states.
    B) can be classically conditioned, possibly even to mental stimuli.
    C) can affect mental states.
    D) all of the above
    Answer: D

Pages: 286
Topic: Psychological/Health/Disease: Psychosocial Factors/Immune System
Skill: Factual   Other1:

38. During the exhaustion stage of Selye's general adaptation system,
    A) the resources of the immune system may be depleted.
    B) the resources of the immune system are mobilized.
    C) the immune system reserves are replenished.
    D) the autonomous nervous system triggers an alarm reaction.
    Answer: A

Pages: 287
Topic: Psychological/Health/Disease: Psychosocial Factors/Immune System
Skill: Conceptual   Other1:

39. With regard to the relationship between stressors and the immune system, it appears that the
    A) immune system can be operantly but not classically conditioned.
    B) white blood cells are not affected by external stressors.
    C) adequacy of the immune response to a particular antigen diminishes proportionately with the quantity and intensity of other stressors.
    D) the resources of the immune system are almost infinitely replenishable.
    Answer: C

Pages: 288
Topic: General Psychological Factors in Health and Disease: Life Style
Skill: Conceptual   Other1:

40. Life-style patterns
    A) are rarely associated with physical illness.
    B) can be very difficult to change.
    C) may not always be as strongly associated with physical illness as some have suggested.
    D) B and C
    Answer: D

Pages: 288
Topic: Psychosocial Factors in Specific Disease Processes
Skill: Factual   Other1:

41. Stressful life circumstances tend to
    A) be associated with diseases in specific organ systems.
    B) cause disruption of autonomous nervous system functioning.
    C) cause neurological disease.
    D) be diffuse and nonspecific in terms of the organ systems affected.
    Answer: D

Pages: 288
Topic: Psychosocial Factors in Specific Disease Processes
Skill: Factual   Other1:
42. All of the following are factors affecting specific organ systems or diseases EXCEPT
    A) congenital predispositions.
    B) destructive life-style patterns.
    C) personality factors.
    D) interpersonal functioning.
    Answer: B

Pages: 288
Topic: Psychosocial Factors/Disease Processes: Heart Disease/Type A Behavior
Skill: Applied   Other1:
43. Erich is experiencing a blockage of the arteries that supply blood to the heart muscle.
    He suffers from
    A) angina pectoris.
    B) angioplasty.
    C) coronary heart disease.
    D) Type A personality.
    Answer: C

Pages: 288
Topic: Psychosocial Factors/Disease Processes: Heart Disease/Type A Behavior
Skill: Applied   Other1:
44. Elmo suffers from angina pectoris and myocardial infarction. These are both clinical
    manifestations of
    A) thrombosis.
    B) stroke.
    C) coronary heart disease.
    D) "silent" heart disease.
    Answer: C

Pages: 289
Topic: Psychosocial Factors/Disease Processes: Heart Disease/Type A Behavior
Skill: Factual   Other1:
45. The number-one killer in the United States today is
    A) cancer.
    B) coronary heart disease.
    C) violence.
    D) alcohol-related automobile accidents.
    Answer: B

Pages: 290
Topic: Psychosocial Factors/Disease Processes: Heart Disease/Type A Behavior
Skill: Factual   Other1:
46. Atherosclerosis is
A) sudden, chaotic, and uncoordinated contractions of the heart's ventricles.
B) a blood clot in one of the arteries leading to the heart.
C) blockage and reduction in elasticity of the coronary vessels feeding the heart.
D) a blood clot in the brain, which may be associated with stroke.
Answer: C

Pages: 289
Topic: Psychosocial Factors/Disease Processes: Heart Disease/Type A Behavior
Skill: Factual   Other1:
47. More than half of the risk for coronary heart disease is
A) biological in nature.
B) not clearly understood.
C) due to environmental stressors.
D) due to life-changing stressors.
Answer: B

Pages: 289
Topic: Psychosocial Factors/Disease Processes: Heart Disease/Type A Behavior
Skill: Applied   Other1:
48. Geoffrey is extremely impatient when he has to wait in line or in traffic. He often feels enormous rage but tries to control it. Geoffrey suffers from
A) Type A/B behavior pattern.
B) hostility personality disorder.
C) Type B behavior pattern.
D) Type A behavior pattern.
Answer: D

Pages: 289
Topic: Psychosocial Factors/Disease Processes: Heart Disease/Type A Behavior
Skill: Factual   Other1: In Student Study Guide
49. According to Friedman and Rosenman, all of the following indications are involved in the type A behavior pattern EXCEPT
A) excessive competitive drive with poorly defined goals.
B) hostility.
C) impatience or time urgency.
D) decelerated speech and motor activity.
Answer: D

Pages: 289
Topic: Psychosocial Factors/Disease Processes: Heart Disease/Type A Behavior
Skill: Factual   Other1:

50. Various measures of the Type A behavior pattern construct
    A) are not as strongly intercorrelated as one would expect.
    B) are highly intercorrelated and all point to a single dimension underlying coronary
       risks.
    C) measure the same component of Type A behavior.
    D) have not been significantly associated with coronary artery deterioration.
    Answer: A

Pages: 289
Topic: Psychosocial Factors/Disease Processes: Heart Disease/Type A Behavior
Skill: Factual   Other1:

51. Among the differing components of Type A behavior, the one most clearly associated with
    coronary artery deterioration is
    A) impatience.
    B) hyperaggressivity/hostility.
    C) violence proneness.
    D) verbal expression of anger.
    Answer: B

Pages: 291
Topic: Psychosocial Factors/Disease Processes: Heart Disease/Type A Behavior
Skill: Conceptual   Other1:

52. Overall, the research evidence indicates that the general cluster of behaviors associated
    with the Type A pattern
    A) do not tend to predict coronary heart disease.
    B) predict coronary heart disease independent of other risk factors.
    C) predict coronary heart disease only in association with several other independent
       factors.
    D) predict coronary heart disease for women but not for men.
    Answer: B

Pages: 291
Topic: Psychosocial Factors/Disease Processes: Heart Disease/Type A Behavior
Skill: Factual   Other1:

53. Two important prospective studies of the relationship between the Type A behavior pattern
    and coronary heart disease found that
    A) Type A behavior predicts coronary heart disease independently of other risk factors.
    B) Type A predicts certain kinds of cancer but does not predict coronary heart disease.
    C) the relationship was true only for cigarette smokers.
    D) the relationship was true only for men who were overweight and did not exercise.
    Answer: A

Pages: 292
Topic: Psychosocial Factors/Disease Processes: Anorexic/Bulimic Syndromes
Skill: Factual   Other1:

54. All of the following characteristics are often associated with anorexia EXCEPT
    A) overactivity.
    B) being female.
    C) onset in adolescence or young adulthood.
    D) periods of obesity alternating with periods of starvation.
    Answer: D

Pages: 293
Topic: Psychosocial Factors/Disease Processes: Anorexic/Bulimic Syndromes
Skill: Applied   Other1:

55. Ginger suffers from anorexia. With regard to her family, she probably
    A) describes her mother as overbearing and intrusive.
    B) describes her father as nurturing and supportive.
    C) suffered repeated familial traumas early in childhood.
    D) feels excessively close to her mother and hostile toward her father.
    Answer: A

Pages: 293
Topic: Psychosocial Factors/Disease Processes: Anorexic/Bulimic Syndromes
Skill: Factual   Other1:

56. Analyses of the communications between family members of anorexics reveal that
    A) they are characterized by overt hostility and frequent arguments.
    B) the parents often give "double messages" of nurturant affection and simultaneous disregard.
    C) the parents tend to be openly hostile toward one another, but not toward the children.
    D) parents tend to be indifferent to the children.
    Answer: B

Pages: 293
Topic: Psychosocial Factors/Disease Processes: Anorexic/Bulimic Syndromes
Skill: Applied   Other1:

57. Jorma began dieting in anticipation of her first day of high school. By the time school began, she had dropped from 120 pounds to less than 80 pounds by restricting her eating severely and exercising for several hours every day. She is typical of an anorexic girl because
    A) her anorexia began with normal dieting.
    B) her disorder began in adolescence.
    C) her anorexic disorder began with a major life change requiring new coping skills.
    D) all of the above
    Answer: D

Pages: 293-294
Topic: Psychosocial Factors/Disease Processes: Anorexic/Bulimic Syndromes
Skill: Applied   Other1:

58. The text presented the case of Mary S., a 16-year-old who suffered from anorexia. Mary was typical of individuals with this disorder because she
    A) had shown excessive weight gain in the three months prior to the development of the anorexia.
    B) suffered a weight loss of about 10 percent.
    C) recognized that she had a serious problem early on but couldn't control her behavior.
    D) maintained high activity levels even as she became dizzy and weak.
    Answer: D

Pages: 295
Topic: Psychosocial Factors/Disease Processes: Anorexic/Bulimic Syndromes
Skill: Applied   Other1:

59. The text presented the case of Nicole, a bulimic college student. She is typical of such individuals because she
    A) had suffered few health problems.
    B) had few thoughts of food except when she was eating.
    C) experienced shame, guilt, and self-deprecation.
    D) did not realize that her eating habits were abnormal.
    Answer: C

Pages: 294
Topic: Psychosocial Factors/Disease Processes: Anorexic/Bulimic Syndromes
Skill: Factual   Other1:

60. Purging and nonpurging are subtypes of the _____ diagnostic category in DSM-IV.
    A) anorexia
    B) bulimia nervosa
    C) obesity
    D) overeating
    Answer: B

Pages: 294
Topic: Psychosocial Factors/Disease Processes: Anorexic/Bulimic Syndromes
Skill: Factual   Other1:

61. In a study using figure drawings as stimuli, it was found that
    A) men were dissatisfied with their own current figures.
    B) women judged their current figures as too thin.
    C) men believed women liked thinner female figures more than they actually did.
    D) women believed men liked thinner female figures more than they actually did.
    Answer: D

Pages: 294
Topic: Psychosocial Factors/Disease Processes: Anorexic/Bulimic Syndromes
Skill: Factual   Other1:
62. In recent years in the United States,
    A) more and more males have become anorexic.
    B) anorexia has increased while bulimia has decreased.
    C) anorexia and bulimia both have become much more common.
    D) bulimia has increased while anorexia has decreased.
    Answer: C

Pages: 294-296
Topic: Psychosocial Factors/Disease Processes: Anorexic/Bulimic Syndromes
Skill: Factual   Other1:
63. Individuals with bulimia and anorexia
    A) often have suffered from early sexual abuse.
    B) share traits of perfectionism and dysfunctional thought processes.
    C) tend to be from poorer socioeconomic backgrounds.
    D) have experienced sustained parental neglect.
    Answer: B

Pages: 296
Topic: Psychosocial Factors/Disease Processes: Anorexic/Bulimic Syndromes
Skill: Factual   Other1:
64. Power struggles between patients and their parents concerning personal autonomy and identity are
    A) common for individuals with anorexia, but not those with bulimia.
    B) common for individuals with bulimia, but not those with anorexia.
    C) common for individuals with anorexia or bulimia.
    D) not common for individuals with either anorexia or bulimia.
    Answer: C

Pages: 296
Topic: Psychosocial Factors/Disease Processes: Anorexic/Bulimic Syndromes
Skill: Factual   Other1:
65. Compared to individuals with bulimia, those with anorexia are
    A) likely to have had more extensive sexual experience.
    B) assumed to be at a relatively less advanced stage of identity development.
    C) more likely to use diuretics and laxatives.
    D) more likely to have achieved a measure of independence from their families.
    Answer: B

Pages: 296
Topic: Psychosocial Factors/Disease Processes: Anorexic/Bulimic Syndromes
Skill: Factual   Other1:
66. Chronic anorexia and bulimia are associated with
   A) serious psychological consequences in many areas of life, but minimal physical damage.
   B) the tendency for individuals to gain increasing control over their disorder as
      biological systems shut down.
   C) serious physical problems and eventual loss of control over the behavior.
   D) brain degeneration.
   Answer: C

Pages: 296
Topic: Psychosocial Factors/Disease Processes: Anorexic/Bulimic Syndromes
Skill: Conceptual   Other1:
67. Prior to the 1960's, thinking about the relationship between psychosocial factors and
    disease
   A) was unknown.
   B) involved the suggestion that a given emotional conflict was necessary and sufficient in
      causing the instance of a particular disease.
   C) was confined to behavioral explanations for the origin of physical disease.
   D) contained elements of the supernatural.
   Answer: B

Pages: 297
Topic: Psychosocial Factors in Disease Processes: Essential Hypertension
Skill: Factual   Other1:
68. All of the following are examples of an empirically established relationship between a
    specific emotional state and a particular physical illness EXCEPT
   A) coronary heart disease and some components of the Type A behavior pattern.
   B) leukemia and hostility.
   C) recurrent headaches and emotional tension.
   D) essential hypertension and emotional stress.
   Answer: B

Pages: 297
Topic: Psychosocial Factors in Disease Processes: Essential Hypertension
Skill: Factual   Other1:
69. Constricted blood vessels, accelerated heart rate, restricted blood flow to visceral
    organs: these symptoms jointly reflect
   A) atherosclerosis.
   B) hypertension.
   C) myocardial infarction.
   D) migraine headache.
   Answer: B

Pages: 297
Topic: Psychosocial Factors in Disease Processes: Essential Hypertension
Skill: Factual   Other1:
70. In contrast to hypertension, essential hypertension
    A) is a chronic condition.
    B) is notable for its many overt warning symptoms.
    C) has no known physical cause.
    D) is relatively rare.
    Answer: C

Pages: 297
Topic: Psychosocial Factors in Disease Processes: Essential Hypertension
Skill: Factual   Other1:
71. Hypertension
    A) is higher among white-collar males.
    B) is higher among blacks.
    C) is higher among women.
    D) is lower among blacks.
    Answer: B

Pages: 297-298
Topic: Psychosocial Factors in Disease Processes: Essential Hypertension
Skill: Conceptual   Other1:
72. Current evidence for the psychoanalytic hypothesis that essential hypertension is caused
    by suppressed rage
    A) shows that this hypothesis is completely false.
    B) indicates that it may be correct insofar as individuals who develop high blood pressure
       tend to have strong yet suppressed urges to engage in socially disapproved behavior.
    C) shows that anorexia, and not essential hypertension, is caused by suppressed rage.
    D) shows that emotional conflicts are not involved in causing essential hypertension.
    Answer: B

Pages: 299
Topic: Psychosocial Factors in Disease Processes: Recurrent Headaches
Skill: Factual   Other1:
73. Most cases of recurrent headaches seem to be related to
    A) nonspecific organic causes.
    B) alterations in the brain's electrical activity.
    C) a disorder of histamine metabolism.
    D) emotional tension.
    Answer: D

Pages: 299
Topic: Psychosocial Factors in Disease Processes: Recurrent Headaches
Skill: Conceptual   Other1:
74. Some evidence suggests that
   A) tension headache sufferers are unusually reactive to stress and pain.
   B) migraine headache sufferers are especially abnormal in their psychological profiles.
   C) migraine headaches may result from internal conflicts over power and dependency.
   D) cluster headache sufferers have psychological rather than physical causes.
   Answer: A

Pages: 300
Topic: Psychogenic Physical Disease: Additional Etiologic Considerations
Skill: Factual   Other1:
75. When considering psychogenic illnesses, the problem of specificity involves
   A) investigating the specific organic cause of a particular disease.
   B) investigating the particular psychological cause of a particular disease.
   C) understanding the impact that specific diseases have on psychological functioning.
   D) investigating why, under stress, one person develops anorexia and another person
      develops some other disease.
   Answer: D

Pages: 301
Topic: Psychogenic Physical Disease: Biological Factors
Skill: Conceptual   Other1:
76. A study of identical twins discordant for coronary heart disease found numerous
   psychological differences between the twins. This suggests that
   A) genetic factors are not important in heart disease.
   B) genetic factors are the most important factors in heart disease.
   C) genetic factors may be necessary but not sufficient for heart disease.
   D) psychosocial factors are not important for heart disease.
   Answer: C

Pages: 301
Topic: Psychogenic Physical Disease: Biological Factors
Skill: Conceptual   Other1:
77. Individual differences in autonomic reactivity
   A) are present in infancy but tend to disappear by adulthood.
   B) are present in infancy and persist into adulthood and may be associated with individual
      differences in susceptibility to disease.
   C) have not been empirically associated with individual differences in temperament.
   D) cause thyroid dysfunction, which is associated with recurrent headaches.
   Answer: B

Pages: 301
Topic: Psychogenic Physical Disease: Biological Factors
Skill: Applied   Other1:
78. A person who has inherited a "weak stomach"
    A) will always develop stomach problems.
    B) has genetic liability as a sufficient cause of any stomach disorders that develop.
    C) will not tend to develop problems with other organ systems when faced with stress.
    D) may be especially prone to react with stomach complaints under stress.
    Answer: D

Pages: 301
Topic: Psychogenic Physical Disease: Biological Factors
Skill: Conceptual   Other1:
79. The corticovisceral control mechanisms
    A) are thought to regulate homeostatic equilibrium in the body.
    B) trigger Type A behaviors.
    C) are controlled by the autonomic nervous system.
    D) have often been associated with migraine headaches.
    Answer: A

Pages: 301
Topic: Psychogenic Physical Disease: Biological Factors
Skill: Conceptual   Other1:
80. At present, the most influential contemporary theories about biological factors involved
    in psychogenic diseases include all of the following EXCEPT
    A) specific emotional conflicts cause specific physical diseases.
    B) the vulnerability of specific organ systems to stress.
    C) dysregulation of the homeostatic control systems of the brain.
    D) differences in an individual's characteristic autonomic activity.
    Answer: A

Pages: 301-302
Topic: Psychogenic Physical Disease: Psychosocial Factors
Skill: Conceptual   Other1:
81. Which of the following statements is true about our knowledge of the relationship between
    personality factors and disease?
    A) Personality variables have been shown to be relatively unimportant in the occurrence of
       disease.
    B) Specific personality factors have been conclusively linked to particular diseases.
    C) Only the personality factor hostility has been conclusively linked to various
       illnesses.
    D) Particular personality factors have been significantly although only weakly correlated
       with the occurrence of certain illnesses.
    Answer: D

Pages: 302
Topic: Psychogenic Physical Disease: Psychosocial Factors
Skill: Factual   Other1:
82. Experimental subjects who are deliberately frustrated, experiencing increases in heart rate and blood pressure,
    A) will always show a very slow return to normal bodily functioning.
    B) show rapid return to normal body function if they are allowed to fantsize about aggressive responses.
    C) show quicker recovery of bodily processes only if they are given an opportunity to physically or verbally express their aggressive feelings.
    D) show a rapid return to normal bodily functioning.
    Answer: C

Pages: 302-303
Topic: Psychogenic Physical Disease: Psychosocial Factors
Skill: Factual   Other1:
83. Following the death of a spouse, survivor mortality is influenced by
    A) the gender of the survivor.
    B) the suddenness of the death.
    C) the age and ethnicity of the survivor.
    D) all of the above
    Answer: D

Pages: 303
Topic: Psychogenic Physical Disease: Psychosocial Factors
Skill: Applied   Other1:
84. Gigi is a young asthmatic girl who is overdependent and insecure. These personality traits
    A) are risk factors for asthma.
    B) may predispose her to asthma or may result from having the disease.
    C) are genetically determined necessary causes of the onset of asthma.
    D) result from her mother's neglectful behavior toward her.
    Answer: B

Pages: 304
Topic: Psychogenic Physical Disease: Psychosocial Factors
Skill: Conceptual   Other1:
85. In a study of asthma subjects, some individuals developed asthma after breathing in a substance that they only thought contained allergens. This shows that
    A) suggestion alone can contribute to asthma.
    B) subjects can feign asthma.
    C) subjects had developed asthma in childhood as a result of suggestion.
    D) conditioning has little to do with autonomic nervous activity.
    Answer: A

Pages: 304
Topic: Psychogenic Physical Disease: Psychosocial Factors
Skill: Applied   Other1:
86. Nelly has chronic back pain which involves secondary gains. This means that
    A) she benefits indirectly by continuing to stay ill.
    B) the pain is due to a neurological deficit.
    C) the pain was caused by the suggestion of others.
    D) she does not have anything physically wrong with her.
    Answer: A

Pages: 304
Topic: Psychogenic Physical Disease: Psychosocial Factors
Skill: Conceptual   Other1:
87. Physical disorders may be _____ in the same way as other behavior patterns.
    A) acquired but not maintained
    B) maintained but not acquired
    C) acquired and/or maintained
    D) neither acquired nor maintained
    Answer: C

Pages: 305
Topic: Psychogenic Physical Disease: Sociocultural Factors
Skill: Conceptual   Other1:
88. Eating disorders may be especially influenced by
    A) the rise of industrialization in the nineteenth century.
    B) environmental toxins.
    C) sociocultural factors.
    D) Type A behavior patterns.
    Answer: C

Pages: 305
Topic: Treatments and Outcomes
Skill: Conceptual   Other1:
89. Removing a particular environmental stressor that has been causally implicated in the development of an illness
    A) is sufficient to cause recovery from the illness.
    B) has no impact on recovery from the illness.
    C) may be insufficient for recovery if irreversible organic changes have occurred.
    D) none of the above
    Answer: C

Pages: 305
Topic: Treatments and Outcomes
Skill: Conceptual   Other1:
90. Developing an effective treatment program requires a thorough assessment of
    A) the nature and severity of the organic pathology.
    B) psychosocial and biological factors that may play a role in the onset or maintenance of the disease.
    C) sociocultural factors that may play a role in the illness.
    D) all of the above
    Answer: D

Pages: 305-306
Topic: Treatments and Outcomes: Biological Measures
Skill: Factual   Other1:
91. Biological treatments of milder psychogenic diseases often involve the use of _____ to allow an individual to reduce emotional tension.
    A) tranquilizers
    B) acupuncture
    C) biological challenge
    D) biofeedback
    Answer: A

Pages: 306
Topic: Treatments and Outcomes: Psychosocial Measures
Skill: Conceptual   Other1:
92. The most effective psychological treatment for psychogenic disease appears to be
    A) cognitive-behavioral therapy.
    B) psychoanalytic therapy.
    C) biofeedback.
    D) behavior modification.
    Answer: A

Pages: 306
Topic: Treatments and Outcomes: Psychosocial Measures
Skill: Factual   Other1:
93. Biofeedback
    A) is not used anymore because it has proven ineffective.
    B) is very effective.
    C) has not proven very effective, although the verdict is still out on its effectiveness using newer and more sophisticated equipment.
    D) is very effective for bulimia and anorexia but not for other psychogenic illnesses.
    Answer: C

Pages: 306
Topic: Treatments and Outcomes: Psychosocial Measures
Skill: Conceptual   Other1:
94. Behavior-modification techniques are based on the assumption that
    A) internal conflicts are associated with physical illnesses.
    B) extinction and differential reinforcement may be effective ways of modifying autonomic responses.
    C) dysfunctional cognitions cause maladaptive behaviors that are associated with physical illness.
    D) psychological states can be conditioned even if physical responses can not be.
    Answer: B

Pages: 306
Topic: Treatments and Outcomes: Psychosocial Measures
Skill: Applied   Other1:
95. The text presented the case of June C., a seventeen year-old girl who had been sneezing every few seconds for five months. She was treated with behavior modification. This case showed how
    A) physiological treatments are usually necessary to maintain the effectiveness of behavior modification.
    B) responses can be unlearned.
    C) such responses can be initially altered but rarely maintained.
    D) ineffective such therapy is.
    Answer: B

Pages: 307
Topic: Treatments and Outcomes: Psychosocial Measures
Skill: Factual   Other1:
96. Behavioral relaxation techniques are
    A) effective for simple tension headaches.
    B) not very effective for treating psychogenic illnesses.
    C) extremely effective for treating almost all psychogenic illnesses.
    D) only effective in conjunction with medication and surgery.
    Answer: A

Pages: 307
Topic: Treatments and Outcomes: Psychosocial Measures
Skill: Factual   Other1:
97. Behavioral interventions may be most useful in
    A) curing essential hypertension.
    B) eliminating migraines.
    C) treating depression.
    D) altering harmful life-style habits and patterns.
    Answer: D

Pages: 307
Topic: Treatments and Outcomes: Psychosocial Measures
Skill: Factual   Other1:
98. Bulimia nervosa has responded especially well to
    A) behavioral modification.
    B) antianxiety medication.
    C) cognitive-behavioral therapy.
    D) psychodynamic therapy.
    Answer: C

Pages: 307
Topic: Treatments and Outcomes: Psychosocial Measures
Skill: Factual   Other1:
99. Cognitive-behavior therapy has proven effective in treating
    A) Type A behavior.
    B) bulimia nervosa.
    C) stress reduction.
    D) all of the above
    Answer: D

Pages: 308
Topic: Treatments and Outcomes: Combined Treatment Measures
Skill: Conceptual   Other1:
100. Psychogenic diseases usually require
    A) psychosocial treatment but little medical intervention.
    B) medical treatment but little psychosocial intervention.
    C) both medical and psychosocial intervention.
    D) behavioral and psychodynamic treatment.
    Answer: C

Pages: 308
Topic: Treatments and Outcomes: Combined Treatment Measures
Skill: Factual   Other1:
101. The treatment for anorexia nervosa
    A) primarily requires hospitalization and medical interventions.
    B) primarily requires psychological interventions.
    C) can be treated successfully with family therapy alone.
    D) requires both medical interventions and psychological treatment.
    Answer: D

Pages: 308
Topic: Treatments and Outcomes: Combined Treatment Measures
Skill: Factual   Other1:
102. Weight gain in hospitalized anorexics
    A) typically occurs regardless of the type of psychological treatment employed.
    B) is only possible in conjunction with cognitive-behavioral techniques.
    C) is only possible with family therapy.
    D) is likely to be long-term.
    Answer: A

Pages: 308
Topic: Treatments and Outcomes: Combined Treatment Measures
Skill: Applied   Other1:
103. Gilda is in a hospital program for anorexia. This program promotes daily weight gain by making Gilda stay in isolation. Gilda is likely to
    A) show no change in her behavior.
    B) actually lose weight.
    C) gain weight but then lose weight as soon as she leaves the hospital.
    D) gain weight and maintain more normalized eating patterns once she leaves the hospital.
    Answer: C

Pages: 308
Topic: Treatments and Outcomes: Combined Treatment Measures
Skill: Factual   Other1:
104. An influential treatment program at the Mayo Clinic treats anorexics by combining medical and psychological therapies, and includes _____ as a crucial component of treatment.
    A) psychoanalytic techniques
    B) family therapy
    C) confrontational therapy
    D) aerobic exercise
    Answer: B

Pages: 308
Topic: Treatments and Outcomes: Sociocultural Measures
Skill: Factual   Other1:
105. Treatments that are targeted at prevention of illness among certain subgroups are
    A) behavioral measures.
    B) sociocultural measures.
    C) cognitive measures.
    D) ethnic treatments.
    Answer: B

Pages: 308
Topic: Treatments and Outcomes: Sociocultural Measures
Skill: Conceptual   Other1:
106. Sociocultural treatment measures are most likely to be aimed at
    A) altering life-style behaviors.
    B) helping individuals understand the childhood experiences responsible for their
       behaviors.
    C) developing large-scale vaccination programs.
    D) individuals who have been diagnosed with serious disorders.
    Answer: A

Pages: 308-309
Topic: Treatments and Outcomes: Sociocultural Measures
Skill: Factual   Other1:
107. The results of the North Karelia Project, a prevention program which was designed to
    reduce atherosclerosis,
    A) proved to be successful for white-collar workers and upper-class individuals, but not
       for blue-collar workers.
    B) was not successful in preventing risk of coronary heart disease.
    C) was successful in reducing risk of coronary heart disease in women but not in men.
    D) was successful in reducing risk of coronary heart disease in men and women.
    Answer: D

Pages: 309
Topic: Unresolved Issues on Containing the AIDS Epidemic
Skill: Conceptual   Other1:
108. One of the greatest problems remaining that pertains to the interface between psychology
    and physical illness is
    A) how to get people to modify the life-style choices that put them at risk for diseases
       like AIDS.
    B) how to get women to comply with the same preventive measures as men already do.
    C) to demonstrate that psychosocial factors may be causally implicated in some physical
       illnesses.
    D) to demonstrate empirically that it may be possible to reduce susceptibility to certain
       diseases by changing life-style patterns.
    Answer: A

Pages: 309-310
Topic: Unresolved Issues on Containing the AIDS Epidemic
Skill: Factual   Other1:
109. The failure to use measures for preventing HIV infection is greatest among
    A) gay males in large urban cities who identify with the gay subculture.
    B) minority gays.
    C) gay men who do not identify themselves as homosexuals.
    D) B and C
    Answer: D

Pages: 309
Topic: Unresolved Issues on Containing the AIDS Epidemic
Skill: Factual   Other1:
110. Risk factors for engaging in unsafe sex include all BUT which of the following?
    A) alcohol consumption
    B) youth
    C) being a gay male in the urban gay subculture
    D) being a heterosexual college student
    Answer: C

Short Answer

Write the word or phrase that best completes each statement or answers the question.

Pages: 280
Topic: Psychological Factors and Physical Illness
Skill: Applied   Other1:
1. How would DSM-IV code a person with chronic back pain and complaints of anxiety and tension that you suspect are associated with the person's medical condition?
    Answer: Axis III would contain the back-related medical condition. Axis I provides a category for Psychological Factors Affecting Medical Condition, which may include psychological symptoms such as anxiety and tension.

Pages: 281
Topic: Psychological/Health/Disease: Health/Attitudes/Coping Resources
Skill: Conceptual   Other1:
2. What are the two types of optimism described in the text, and how are they related to health?
    Answer: They are sense of efficacy and defensive denial. Sense of efficacy involves a belief in one's ability to cope with adversity. Its absence, helplessness, has been associated with poor health outcomes. Defensive denial produces a significantly enhanced risk for health problems.

Pages: 282
Topic: Psychological/Health/Disease: Health/Attitudes/Coping Resources
Skill: Factual   Other1:

3. The belief that a particular treatment will work can actually help a person show improvement from the treatment. This is called a _____.
   Answer: placebo effect

Pages: 286-287
Topic: Psychological Factors/Health/Disease: Autonomic Excess/Tissue Damage
Skill: Conceptual   Other1:

4. According to Selye's general adaptation syndrome, the alarm stage and resistance respectively involve the _____ system and the _____ system.
   Answer: autonomic nervous; immune

Pages: 285-287
Topic: Psychological/Health/Disease: Psychosocial Factors/Immune System
Skill: Factual   Other1:

5. Identify two psychosocial factors that have been empirically associated with immunosuppression.
   Answer: These factors include depression and dysphoria, induced negative self-evaluation, anxiety, general negative emotion, self-perceived stress, stressful life changes requiring substantial adaptation, sleep deprivation, marathon running, death of a spouse, space flight, normal diurnal mood variation, and maladaptive conditioning.

Pages: 289-292
Topic: Psychosocial Factors/Disease Processes: Heart Disease/Type A Behavior
Skill: Conceptual   Other1:

6. Describe the Type A behavior pattern.
   Answer: This includes excessive competition in the absence of well-defined goals, impatience or time urgency, and hostility manifested in accelerated speech and motor activity. Components of Type A that have been identified include hyperaggressivity/hostility and negative affect that has been suppressed.

Pages: 293-296
Topic: Psychosocial Factors/Disease Processes: Anorexic/Bulimic Syndromes
Skill: Conceptual   Other1:

7. Briefly characterize the families of anorexic and bulimic girls.
   Answer: They tend to describe their mothers as intrusive and overbearing, their fathers as emotionally absent. They seem to be engaged in struggles with parents for power, autonomy, and identity. Parents often give them "double messages" involving nurturant affection together with disregard for their attempts at self-expression.

Pages: 294-296
Topic: Psychosocial Factors/Disease Processes: Anorexic/Bulimic Syndromes
Skill: Conceptual   Other1:

8. Some people suggest that bulimia nervosa and anorexia nervosa are not distinct disorders, as they are categorized in DSM-IV. Briefly state three ways in which bulimics and anorexics are similar.

    Answer: They share many of the same symptoms as well as the goal of maintaining a suboptimal body weight. They have some personality characteristics in common such as perfectionism, overachievement, and dysfunctional thought processes. Both are associated with socioeconomically advantaged backgrounds. Individuals may move between the two disorders. Both may have similar family problems, including power and autonomy/separation struggles.

Pages: 297
Topic: Psychosocial Factors in Disease Processes: Essential Hypertension
Skill: Applied   Other1:

9. John is a black male living in the inner city. Joe is a white male executive living in the suburbs. Which of these two men is at greater risk for essential hypertension and why?

    Answer: John is. Essential hypertension is about twice as high in blacks as whites. This may be associated with poorer diet and the chronic stresses specifically associated with inner-city life.

Pages: 297-298
Topic: Psychosocial Factors in Disease Processes: Essential Hypertension
Skill: Conceptual   Other1:

10. Identify two of the psychosocial factors that have been associated with essential hypertension.

    Answer: These factors include suppressed rage, suppressed need for power, poor life-style habits, chronic emotional stress, Type A behavior, and the inhibition or suppression of strong urges to perform socially unacceptable acts.

Pages: 299-300
Topic: Psychosocial Factors in Disease Processes: Recurrent Headaches
Skill: Conceptual   Other1:

11. What are two of the psychosocial factors associated with tension headaches?

    Answer: These include individuals who are overreactive to stress and pain, show general increases in psychopathology on psychological tests, and a need to feel in control.

Pages: 300-301
Topic: Psychogenic Physical Disease: Biological Factors
Skill: Conceptual   Other1:
12. A major study of coronary heart disease in identical twins found that the twins who were suffering from heart disease had many more problems at home, were more work-oriented, and generally more dissatisfied with life than were there discordant co-twins. What conclusion can you draw from this study?
    Answer: This study provides rather compelling evidence for the possibility of a psychosocial contribution to coronary heart disease. A genetic liability may or may not be necessary, but it is not sufficient.

Pages: 300-301
Topic: Psychogenic Physical Disease: Biological Factors
Skill: Factual   Other1:
13. Identify three biological factors associated with individual differences in susceptibility to psychogenic disease.
    Answer: These factors include genetic liability, differences in autonomic reactivity, vulnerability in specific organ systems, differences in the regulation of the autonomic nervous system by corticovisceral control mechanisms, and dysregulation of hormonal function associated with excessive hypothalamic activation.

Pages: 301
Topic: Psychogenic Physical Disease: Biological Factors
Skill: Factual   Other1:
14. The systems thought to maintain homeostatic equilibrium in the body are called the _____.
    Answer: corticovisceral control mechanisms

Pages: 302-303
Topic: Psychogenic Physical Disease: Psychosocial Factors
Skill: Conceptual   Other1:
15. What role do interpersonal relationships play in psychogenic disease?
    Answer: Physical illness is associated with marital problems, divorce, death of a spouse, loneliness, and absence of positive social support.

Pages: 303-304
Topic: Psychogenic Physical Disease: Psychosocial Factors
Skill: Conceptual   Other1:
16. What role may operant conditioning play in psychogenic illness?
    Answer: It may be involved in either the origin of illness or in its maintenance. The autonomic nervous system can be operantly conditioned. Some physical disorders may arise through the accidental reinforcement of symptom and behavioral patterns. Receiving extra attention and secondary gain are examples of these reinforcements.

Pages: 306-307
Topic: Treatments and Outcomes: Psychosocial Measures
Skill: Factual   Other1:
17. Briefly give an example of a behavioral technique that has been used successfully for a specific psychogenic disease.
    Answer: Relaxation techniques are effective for simple tension headaches. Biofeedback may be useful as a relaxation procedure. Behavioral programs have had some success with altering Type A behavior patterns and self-injurious life-style patterns like cigarette smoking. Counter-conditioning therapy was successful in treating an involuntary response (intractable sneezing).

Pages: 307
Topic: Treatments and Outcomes: Psychosocial Measures
Skill: Factual   Other1:
18. The most effective therapeutic technique for bulimia nervosa is _____ .
    Answer: cognitive-behavioral therapy

Pages: 308
Topic: Treatments and Outcomes: Psychosocial Measures
Skill: Conceptual   Other1:
19. Family therapy has proven a crucial part of the treatment for _____ .
    Answer: anorexia

Pages: 308
Topic: Treatments and Outcomes: Psychosocial Measures
Skill: Factual   Other1:
20. What is a sociocultural treatment measure?
    Answer: It is typically aimed at prevention of disorders among certain selected high-risk groups. It aims to alter the individuals' life-style habits or patterns to reduce their risk for a particular disease.

Essay

Write your answer in the space provided or on a separate sheet of paper.

Pages: 279-280
Topic: *Psychological Factors and Physical Illness*
Skill: *Conceptual*   Other1:

1. Behavioral medicine is a rapidly growing field. What is it? What are some of the problem areas examined from this perspective?
   Answer: Behavioral medicine is an interdisciplinary approach to the treatment of physical disorders thought to have psychological factors as a major aspect of their causal patterns. Problem areas include etiology, host resistance, disease mechanism, patient decision-making, early intervention and prevention. Subdisciplines include health psychology and psychoneuroimmunology.

Pages: 280
Topic: *Psychological Factors and Physical Illness*
Skill: *Applied*   Other1:

2. Barbara comes to you complaining of anxiety and recurrent headaches. You suspect that psychological factors are contributing to her medical condition. How would you use the DSM-IV Axes to evaluate her and code her diagnoses?
   Answer: Her medical condition would be coded on Axis III. If she qualifies for an anxiety disorder diagnosis, that diagnosis would be coded on Axis I. Any psychological factors suspected as contributing to initiating and/or exacerbating her medical illness would also be coded on Axis I under the category Psychological Factors Affecting Medical Condition. These factors must fall into one or more of six subcategories that include mental disorder, psychological symptoms, personality traits or coping style, maladaptive health behaviors, stress-related physiological response, or other/unspecified.

Pages: 285-287
Topic: *Psychological/Health/Disease: Psychosocial Factors/Immune System*
Skill: *Conceptual*   Other1:

3. The immune system has long been thought to be unresponsive to psychosocial factors. What evidence is there that this may not be the case? What are some of the potential psychosocial factors that have been identified in more recent research?
   Answer: Behavioral interventions like aerobic exercise have had positive immunocompetence effects on even as virulent a virus as AIDS. Depressed mood also impacts on immune function in HIV-infected men and in many other studies. Psychosocial and mental states may depress immune function to the point of enhancing vulnerability to almost any antigen. These stressors seem to operate through a variety of pathways. Other factors from recent studies include negative self-evaluations, stressful life events, perceived stress, dysphoric mood, sleep deprivation, and classical conditioning.

Pages: 284-287
Topic: Psychological/Health/Disease: Psychosocial Factors/Immune System
Skill: Conceptual   Other1:

4. Discuss the physical operation of the immune system. What systems are involved in immunological responses? How do they operate? How does Selye's general adaptation model describe the operation of the immune system?

    Answer: The immune system is a crucial component of the organism's resistance-stage resources, Selye's second stage. Systems include thymus, bone marrow, and spleen. The body transports its defenses in blood serum. The white blood cells, or leukocytes, contain much of the body's defenses and include B-cells, T-cells, and other special cell subpopulations which multiply rapidly when an antigen threat is detected. B-cells produce antibodies that circulate in serum, and protect against more common bacteria. T-cells attack specific antigens. The exhaustion stage may involve permanent immunusuppression.

Pages: 285-286
Topic: Psychological/Health/Disease: Psychosocial Factors/Immune System
Skill: Factual   Other1:

5. There appears to be a strong connection between depressed mood and suppression of immunocompetence. Describe the evidence that supports this view.

    Answer: Depressed mood has been found to be associated with HIV-1 activity among gay males. Induced negative self-evaluation was shown to have a causal relationship to diminished natural killer cell cytotoxicity, especially among subjects who were depressed and/or anxious in prior mood. The relationship between depressed mood and suppressed immunocompetence also may be partially independent of specific stressors that may evoke such feelings. A quantitative review suggested depressed mood is reliably associated with lowered white-cell count, and lowered natural killer cell activity.

Pages: 287-288
Topic: General Psychological Factors in Health and Disease: Life Style
Skill: Conceptual   Other1:

6. What are life-style factors and how do they influence physical illness? What does the research literature say about the life style-illness relationship?

    Answer: They are habits and behavior patterns under our voluntary control which are thought to play a major role in three leading causes of death: coronary heart disease, auto accidents, and alcohol-related deaths. Effects of life-style habits tend to be nonspecific. The connection between illness and these patterns is often relatively weak. However, prevention studies like the North Karelia Project, which target change in lifestyle, have been largely successful. These habits and patterns can be extremely difficult to change, as is the case with cigarette smoking and diet.

Pages: 289-292
Topic: Psychosocial Factors/Disease Processes: Heart Disease/Type A Behavior
Skill: Applied   Other1:

7. Gil is a "Type A personality." What is he like? What does this mean for his physical condition?

    Answer: He is likely to have excessive competitive drive without well-defined goals, impatience and hostility, reflected in accelerated speech and motor activity. In two major prospective studies, such individuals were found to be at higher risk for coronary heart disease. Some suggest that the underlying component of hostility/hyperaggressivity is the best predictor of the disease. Other research suggests the best predictor is general negative affect that remains unexpressed.

Pages: 292-296
Topic: Psychosocial Factors/Disease Processes: Anorexic/Bulimic Syndromes
Skill: Conceptual   Other1:

8. What are anorexia and bulimia nervosa? What are some of the factors associated with these disorders? In what ways are they similar and in what ways do they differ?

    Answer: Anorexia involves weight loss to 85 percent of expected body weight with severe dietary restriction or binge-eating with or without voluntarily purging. Bulimics have great fear of being unable to stop eating, and engage in binging episodes together with frequent and severe efforts to lose weight. Both disorders have increased dramatically in recent years, are more common in middle-class females, involve personal and family issues of power and autonomy, and can be lethal. Bulimics may be more advanced in identity level, peer relationships, sexual experience, and separation from family.

Pages: 297-298
Topic: Psychosocial Factors in Disease Processes: Essential Hypertension
Skill: Conceptual   Other1:

9. Essential hypertension is a serious disorder. What makes it so serious? What psychological factors make an individual more susceptible to essential hypertension?

    Answer: It is a primary cause of death in many cases and a major predisposing factor for other serious diseases, higher in blacks, and has no obvious warning symptoms. It has been associated with emotional stress, dietary patterns, Type A behavior pattern, and inhibition or suppression of strong urges to perform socially unacceptable acts.

Pages: 298-300
Topic: Psychosocial Factors in Disease Processes: Recurrent Headaches
Skill: Conceptual   Other1:

10. Tension and migraine headaches are two of the most common types of headaches. In what ways are the physiological and psychological factors involved in these headaches similar and different?

Answer: Migraines may begin with auras due to alterations in the brain's electrical activity, followed by localized intense pain. Tension headaches, the most common type, apparently involve emotional stress leading to contraction of muscles surrounding the skull and vascular constriction. Migraines may involve more serious vascular constriction. Both types usually appear during adolescence and recur periodically during stressful times. Tension headache sufferers may be highly reactive to stress and pain.

Pages: 300-301
Topic: Psychogenic Physical Disease: Biological Factors
Skill: Conceptual   Other1:

11. What are some of the biological factors determining the adequacy of an individual's response to stress?

Answer: Genetic liability makes some contribution, although it is difficult to separate from psychological factors based on current studies. Individuals may vary in autonomic reactivity and may be prone to show the results of stress in different organ systems. Chronically excessive autonomic activity may be associated with essential hypertension; people may vary in the regulatory function of corticovisceral control mechanisms, influencing autonomic nervous system regulation. Excessive hypothalamic activation may cause dysregulation of the endocrine system.

Pages: 301-304
Topic: Psychogenic Physical Disease: Psychosocial Factors
Skill: Conceptual   Other1:

12. Discuss the role of personality characteristics and interpersonal relationships in physiological functioning. What does the research evidence suggest about these relationships?

Answer: Particular personality factors are significantly but weakly correlated with the occurrence of certain illnesses. Some relationship exists between coronary heart disease and Type A behavior, and possibly loneliness and absence of positive social relationships. Essential hypertension has been associated with inhibition of strong urges for power or a socially unacceptable goal. Physical disease is markedly higher in those who have recently experienced marital distress, divorce, and loss of a spouse. Family problems are risk factors for eating disorders.

Topic: Psychogenic Physical Disease: Sociocultural Factors
Skill: Conceptual   Other1:

13. What are some of the sociocultural factors involved in physical illness? What does sociocultural treatment entail?

    Answer: These factors include the increased stress associated with Westernization and rapid social change, related to increases in cardiovascular disease and hypertension. Pressure on females to be thin and attractive in our society may influence eating disorders, as may expectations of high achievement and the difficult and conflicting pressures women face in contemporary society. Sociocultural measures aim at prevention in selected subgroups. Some success has been achieved, as in the North Karelia Project. Issues remain, as in difficulties encouraging preventive lifestyle changes.

Pages: 308
Topic: Treatments and Outcomes: Combined Treatment Measures
Skill: Applied   Other1:

14. Imagine that you are a psychologist. Andrea is an anorexic 17-year-old who has been assigned to you for treatment. Design an optimal treatment program for her based on what you've learned about the disorder, its causes, and treatment effectiveness.

    Answer: This disorder would best involve a combined medical and psychological treatment approach. The first step might include hospitalization to isolate her from dysfunctional family patterns and help her gain weight. Social or other rewards may be given to encourage weight gain. Cognitive-behavioral interventions in individual therapy may be effective, as they are with bulimics, for altering underlying thinking about herself and her body. Group therapy with peers may provide support for her. Family therapy also is desirable to foster clear communication, autonomy, and identity apart from family.

Pages: 308-309
Topic: Treatments and Outcomes: Sociocultural Measures
Skill: Conceptual   Other1:

15. Often we treat disorders after they have occurred. From a sociocultural perspective, what is the role of prevention in regard to psychogenic illness? Include in your answer some of the difficulties with implementing sociocultural treatments.

    Answer: Prevention has received much less attention, but has common-sense appeal and some research support. One example is the North Karelia Project, which was very effective in lowering risk for atherosclerosis and coronary heart disease. It's often very difficult to get people to change entrenched habits, like cigarette smoking and poor diets, as well as lifestyle patterns like sexual freedom without taking precautions against HIV infection. Determining and educating the right subgroups (e.g., minorities, drug abusers) can be difficult, as can be preventing "relapses" and modifying overoptimism.

CHAPTER 9   Personality Disorders

Multiple-Choice

Choose the one alternative that best completes the statement or answers the question.

Pages: 313
Topic: Personality Disorders
Skill: Factual   Other1:
1. Personality disorders in general are characterized by
   A) antisocial behavior.
   B) egocentric traits.
   C) inflexibility and maladaptive traits.
   D) eccentricity.
   Answer: C

Pages: 313
Topic: Personality Disorders
Skill: Factual   Other1:
2. Personality is usually crystallized by the end of
   A) infancy.
   B) childhood.
   C) adolescence or early adulthood.
   D) middle age.
   Answer: C

Pages: 314
Topic: Personality Disorders: Clinical Features of Personality Disorders
Skill: Applied   Other1:
3. Horace has a personality disorder, but you don't know which one. What generalization can you make about his behavior? He is most likely to
   A) repeat maladaptive behavioral patterns without learning from previous troubles.
   B) experience episodes of loss of contact with reality.
   C) experience chronic anxiety.
   D) be extremely variable in his behavior, such as being dependent in one relationship and then aloof in a different relationship.
   Answer: A

Pages: 314
Topic: Personality Disorders: Clinical Features of Personality Disorders
Skill: Conceptual   Other1:
4. The behavioral patterns of individuals with personality disorders
   A) tend to fluctuate over time.
   B) tend to normalize with experience as an individual matures.
   C) are remarkable in their tendency to shift dramatically from one kind of disorder to another.
   D) are thought to be relatively consistent over time, with little adaptation to new kinds of experiences.
   Answer: D

Pages: 314
Topic: Personality Disorders: Clinical Features of Personality Disorders
Skill: Factual   Other1:
5. Personality disorders probably originate from
   A) genetic liabilities.
   B) maladaptive cognitive styles.
   C) learning-based habit patterns.
   D) all of the above
   Answer: D

Pages: 314
Topic: Personality Disorders: Clinical Features of Personality Disorders
Skill: Factual   Other1:
6. Disturbed early attachment relationships
   A) may reflect genetic liabilities for personality disorders.
   B) may predispose a child to develop a maladaptive pattern of personality development.
   C) have little to do with later development of personality disorders.
   D) result in childhood conduct disorders but not in later personality disorders.
   Answer: B

Pages: 315
Topic: Personality Disorders: Clinical Features of Personality Disorders
Skill: Factual   Other1:
7. According to DSM-IV, personality traits
   A) cause either significant impairment in functioning or subjective distress but not necessarily both.
   B) are limited to discrete episodes of illness.
   C) are almost exclusively the result of learning from childhood experiences.
   D) are not present in the individual until late adolescence.
   Answer: A

Pages: 315
Topic: Personality Disorders: Clinical Features of Personality Disorders
Skill: Factual   Other1: In Student Study Guide
8. Personality disorders are coded on Axis _____ of DSM-IV.
   A) I
   B) II
   C) III
   D) IV
   Answer: B

Pages: 315
Topic: Personality Disorders: Clinical Features of Personality Disorders
Skill: Conceptual   Other1:
9. The reliability of personality disorder diagnoses
   A) is greater than the reliability of Axis I diagnoses.
   B) is relatively poor compared to other disorders because criteria for personality
      disorders require greater subjective inference on the part of the diagnostician.
   C) is very good, although the validity of these diagnoses is poor.
   D) is very poor, although the validity of the diagnoses is very good.
   Answer: B

Pages: 315
Topic: Personality Disorders: Clinical Features of Personality Disorders
Skill: Factual   Other1:
10. The use of semi-structured diagnostic interviews in recent research has improved the _____
    of personality disorder diagnoses.
    A) validity
    B) reliability
    C) diagnosability
    D) dimensionality
    Answer: B

Pages: 315
Topic: Personality Disorders: Clinical Features of Personality Disorders
Skill: Factual   Other1:
11. Problems with the misdiagnosis of personality disorders arise from all BUT which of the
    following?
    A) imprecise criteria requiring too much subjective clinical inference regarding whether
       the criterion is met or not
    B) categories are not mutually exclusive
    C) personality characteristics are dimensional in nature
    D) maladaptive personality traits are extremely difficult to recognize
    Answer: D

Pages: 316
Topic: Personality Disorders: Types of Personality Disorders
Skill: Factual   *Other1:*
12. Personality disorders in DSM-IV are divided into
    A) five sub-Axes.
    B) three clusters.
    C) psychotic and nonpsychotic variants.
    D) childhood and adulthood personality disorders.
    Answer: B

Pages: 316
Topic: Personality Disorders: Types of Personality Disorders
Skill: Factual   *Other1:*
13. Individuals who seem odd and eccentric to others may have personality disorders from
    A) Cluster A.
    B) Cluster B.
    C) Cluster C.
    D) proposed diagnostic categories needing further study.
    Answer: A

Pages: 316
Topic: Personality Disorders: Types of Personality Disorders
Skill: Factual   *Other1:*
14. Cluster B personality disorders are characterized by
    A) behavior that is eccentric and unusual.
    B) dramatic, emotional, and erratic behavior.
    C) anxiety and fearfulness.
    D) mistrust of others and social isolation.
    Answer: B

Pages: 316
Topic: Personality Disorders: Types of Personality Disorders
Skill: Factual   *Other1:*
15. Individuals with personality disorders who are most likely to come to the attention of
    legal authorities for their impulsive behavior are probably from
    A) Cluster A.
    B) Cluster B.
    C) Cluster C.
    D) categories in need of further study.
    Answer: B

Pages: 316
Topic: Personality Disorders: Types of Personality Disorders
Skill: Conceptual   Other1:

16. Individuals with a personality disorder who are most likely to be misdiagnosed with an anxiety disorder are probably from
    A) Cluster A.
    B) Cluster B.
    C) Cluster C.
    D) categories in need of further study.
    Answer: C

Pages: 316
Topic: Personality Disorders: Types of Personality Disorders
Skill: Factual   Other1:

17. Compared with other personality disorders, individuals with avoidant, dependent, or obsessive-compulsive personality disorders are more likely to
    A) not feel distress.
    B) seek out therapy.
    C) show episodic behaviors.
    D) have difficulties with authority figures.
    Answer: B

Pages: 316
Topic: Personality Disorders: Types of Personality Disorders
Skill: Applied   Other1:

18. Helen is suspicious and hypersensitive. She blames others for her own mistakes. She is most likely to be diagnosed with _____ personality disorder.
    A) schizoid
    B) histrionic
    C) paranoid
    D) schizotypal
    Answer: C

Pages: 316-317
Topic: Personality Disorders: Types of Personality Disorders
Skill: Conceptual   Other1:

19. The text presented the case of a forty year-old construction worker who believed that his coworkers did not like him and were laughing at him. He was typical of an individual with paranoid personality disorder because he
    A) was psychotic.
    B) was social with others in public.
    C) sought therapy.
    D) blamed others for his problems.
    Answer: D

Pages: 316
Topic: Personality Disorders: Types of Personality Disorders
Skill: Conceptual   Other1:
20. What is the relationship between paranoid personality disorder and paranoid schizophrenia?
    A) Paranoid personality disorder is a major cause of paranoid schizophrenia.
    B) They have no association.
    C) They have some symptoms in common such as suspiciousness.
    D) They are caused by the same underlying dysfunction.
    Answer: C

Pages: 318
Topic: Personality Disorders: Types of Personality Disorders
Skill: Factual   Other1:
21. An individual with schizoid personality disorder
    A) avoids others because of an extreme fear of criticism.
    B) is very likely to develop schizophrenia later on.
    C) will probably engage in criminal activity.
    D) is likely to be perceived by others as cold, distant, and aloof.
    Answer: D

Pages: 318
Topic: Personality Disorders: Types of Personality Disorders
Skill: Factual   Other1:
22. Which of these symptoms is NOT part of schizoid personality disorder?
    A) highly eccentric and idiosyncratic beliefs
    B) a lack of expressed feeling for people
    C) interpersonal detachment and aloofness
    D) a pattern of introverted "loner" behavior
    Answer: A

Pages: 318
Topic: Personality Disorders: Types of Personality Disorders
Skill: Factual   Other1:
23. Schizophrenic disorders seem to be most strongly linked genetically to _____ personality disorder.
    A) schizoid
    B) schizotypal
    C) avoidant
    D) both A and B
    Answer: B

Pages: 318-319
Topic: Personality Disorders: Types of Personality Disorders
Skill: Conceptual   Other1:
24. The text presented the case of Bill D., a 33 year-old computer analyst who was referred for a psychological evaluation. He was typical of an individual with schizoid personality disorder because he
    A) had a difficult time making friends.
    B) was suicidal.
    C) avoided others because he believed that they were trying to cause him harm.
    D) had transient auditory hallucinations.
    Answer: A

Pages: 319
Topic: Personality Disorders: Types of Personality Disorders
Skill: Factual   Other1:
25. The central problem of schizoid personality disorder is
    A) recurrent depression.
    B) a marked disregard for the feelings of others.
    C) cognitive and perceptual distortions.
    D) an inability to form attachments to other people.
    Answer: D

Pages: 319
Topic: Personality Disorders: Types of Personality Disorders
Skill: Factual   Other1:
26. In contrast to a person with schizoid personality disorder, an individual with schizotypal personality disorder is likely to
    A) show behavior that is dramatic and overstated.
    B) engage in criminal activity.
    C) have oddities of thought, perception, and speech.
    D) be socially isolated and withdrawn.
    Answer: C

Pages: 319
Topic: Personality Disorders: Types of Personality Disorders
Skill: Factual   Other1:
27. Transient psychotic symptoms when confronted with severe stress is characteristic of an individual with _____ personality disorder.
    A) histrionic
    B) schizoid
    C) schizotypal
    D) avoidant
    Answer: C

Pages: 319
Topic: Personality Disorders: Types of Personality Disorders
Skill: Applied   Other1:
28. Lawrence believes that he may have a special ability to read others' thoughts. He is waiting for a sign that will tell him whether or not he indeed possesses this special power. His beliefs are consistent with _____ personality disorder.
A) psychotic
B) schizoid
C) schizotypal
D) histrionic
Answer: C

Pages: 319
Topic: Personality Disorders: Types of Personality Disorders
Skill: Conceptual   Other1:
29. The most distinguishing characteristic of individuals with schizotypal personality disorder relative to other personality disorders is
A) extreme fear of rejection.
B) social isolation.
C) suspiciousness.
D) peculiar thought patterns.
Answer: D

Pages: 319
Topic: Personality Disorders: Types of Personality Disorders
Skill: Factual   Other1:
30. Ideas of reference, magical thinking, and digressive speech are characteristic of _____ personality disorder.
A) passive-aggressive
B) avoidant
C) schizotypal
D) paranoid
Answer: C

Pages: 320
Topic: Personality Disorders: Types of Personality Disorders
Skill: Applied   Other1:
31. Luisa is a lively and emotional graduate student. She dresses provocatively and behaves in a very seductive manner with her male professors. She has had a long string of short-lived, stormy romances. Luisa is most likely to have a diagnosis of
A) histrionic personality disorder.
B) narcissistic personality disorder.
C) dependent personality disorder.
D) passive-aggressive personality disorder.
Answer: A

Pages: 320-321
Topic: Personality Disorders: Types of Personality Disorders
Skill: Conceptual   Other1:
32. The text presented the case of Pam, a 22 year-old secretary with histrionic personality
disorder. She is typical of individuals with this diagnosis because she
A) placed excessive emphasis on her work to the exclusion of other areas of life.
B) was extremely suspicious of others.
C) was overly compliant with others.
D) was overly emotional and inappropriately seductive.
Answer: D

Pages: 320
Topic: Personality Disorders: Types of Personality Disorders
Skill: Factual   Other1:
33. Histrionic personality disorder is characterized by a pattern of
A) instability in self-image, mood, and interpersonal relationships.
B) shyness, social anxiety, and fear of criticism.
C) social withdrawal, emotional aloofness, and solitary activities.
D) excessive emotionality and attention-seeking behavior.
Answer: D

Pages: 320
Topic: Personality Disorders: Types of Personality Disorders
Skill: Conceptual   Other1:
34. The social relationships of an individual with histrionic personality disorder can be
characterized as
A) reserved and suspicious.
B) manipulative, dependent, and seductive.
C) fearful and anxious.
D) blatantly exploitative and sometimes violent.
Answer: B

Pages: 321
Topic: Personality Disorders: Types of Personality Disorders
Skill: Applied   Other1:
35. Hope believes that she is the "star" of her graduate class and that the other students
dislike her because they are jealous of her superior intelligence. She believes that she
is entitled to be exempted from an important exam because of her outstanding performance
in class. Hope probably suffers from
A) histrionic personality disorder.
B) paranoid personality disorder.
C) narcissistic personality disorder.
D) schizoid personality disorder.
Answer: C

Pages: 321
Topic: Personality Disorders: Types of Personality Disorders
Skill: Factual   Other1:
36. Which of these symptoms best characterizes narcissistic personality disorder?
    A) social indifference
    B) denial of anger and an indirect manner of expressing negative emotions toward others
    C) attitudes of superiority and self-centeredness in social relationships
    D) seductiveness and dramatic, attention-getting behavior
    Answer: C

Pages: 321
Topic: Personality Disorders: Types of Personality Disorders
Skill: Conceptual   Other1:
37. A central feature of narcissistic personality disorder is
    A) seductive and dramatic behavior.
    B) a sense of entitlement.
    C) the inability to empathize with others.
    D) both B and C
    Answer: D

Pages: 321
Topic: Personality Disorders: Types of Personality Disorders
Skill: Factual   Other1:
38. Most clinicians believe that people with narcissistic personality disorder may actually
    A) have a form of latent schizophrenia.
    B) have an underlying obsessive-compulsive disorder.
    C) be hypomanic.
    D) have a very fragile sense of self-esteem.
    Answer: D

Pages: 321
Topic: Personality Disorders: Types of Personality Disorders
Skill: Conceptual   Other1:
39. The text presented the case of a 25 year-old graduate student who complained of difficulty completing his Ph.D. in English. He was typical of an individual with narcissistic personality disorder because he
    A) withdrew from others.
    B) believed that his dissertation would revolutionize his field and was enraged at his mentor for not agreeing with him.
    C) had a long-term romantic relationship characterized by overt dependence.
    D) didn't care what anyone else thought of him.
    Answer: B

Pages: 322
Topic: Personality Disorders: Types of Personality Disorders
Skill: Conceptual   Other1:
40. As contrasted with histrionic personality disorder, narcissistic personality disorder is characterized by
    A) seeking the company of others rather than avoiding them.
    B) pleasing others rather than exploiting them.
    C) seeking admiration rather than attention.
    D) indifference to the opinions of others rather than trying to please everyone.
    Answer: C

Pages: 322
Topic: Personality Disorders: Types of Personality Disorders
Skill: Factual   Other1:
41. Individuals with narcissistic personality disorder
    A) are often seen in treatment due to interpersonal difficulties.
    B) rarely seek treatment by themselves.
    C) are very responsive to short-term cognitive therapy.
    D) can be effectively treated with tricyclic antidepressants.
    Answer: B

Pages: 322
Topic: Personality Disorders: Types of Personality Disorders
Skill: Factual   Other1:
42. An individual with antisocial personality disorder
    A) continually violates the rights of others.
    B) has low self-esteem.
    C) has social skill deficits.
    D) expresses hostility indirectly.
    Answer: A

Pages: 322
Topic: Personality Disorders: Types of Personality Disorders
Skill: Factual   Other1:
43. People with antisocial personality disorder
    A) sometimes have no prior history of conduct disorder before adolescence, although they usually do have such a history.
    B) must have had symptoms of conduct disorder before the age of fifteen.
    C) must have been in trouble with the law in order to receive this diagnosis.
    D) must have symptoms of physical violence toward others before the age of fifteen.
    Answer: B

Pages: 322
Topic: Personality Disorders: Types of Personality Disorders
Skill: Applied   Other1:
44. Henry was a charming middle-aged man who came to the attention of authorities on bigamy charges. He had a long history of courting and supposedly marrying elderly widows, then absconding with their money. His diagnosis is most likely
A) narcissistic personality disorder.
B) borderline personality disorder.
C) histrionic personality disorder.
D) antisocial personality disorder.
Answer: D

Pages: 322-323
Topic: Personality Disorders: Types of Personality Disorders
Skill: Conceptual   Other1:
45. The text presented the case of Mark, a 22 year-old individual who came to a clinic on a court order. He was typical of individuals with antisocial personality disorder because he
A) had a disproportionate sense of superiority over others.
B) had poor social skills.
C) had a long history of criminal activity.
D) was very hostile and aggressive toward the therapist.
Answer: C

Pages: 323
Topic: Personality Disorders: Types of Personality Disorders
Skill: Factual   Other1:
46. Impulsivity and extreme instability in interpersonal relationships, self-image, and mood best characterizes
A) histrionic personality disorder.
B) antisocial personality disorder.
C) avoidant personality disorder.
D) borderline personality disorder.
Answer: D

Pages: 323
Topic: Personality Disorders: Types of Personality Disorders
Skill: Factual   Other1:
47. Borderline personality disorder
A) is biologically linked to schizophrenia.
B) is no longer regarded as a disorder "bordering on" psychosis.
C) is a form of latent schizophrenia.
D) is genetically linked to schizotypal personality disorder.
Answer: B

Pages: 323
Topic: Personality Disorders: Types of Personality Disorders
Skill: Conceptual   Other1:
48. Which of the following is most typical of the interpersonal attitudes and behavior of someone with borderline personality disorder?
A) excessive trust
B) vascillation between overidealization and bitter disappointment
C) cruel and callous exploitation of others for personal gain
D) disinterest in others
Answer: B

Pages: 323
Topic: Personality Disorders: Types of Personality Disorders
Skill: Applied   Other1:
49. Loretta has a history of impulsive sexual promiscuity, chronic feelings of emptiness, and drug use. She has had several bouts of depression and impulsively attempted suicide twice. She feels that she has never had a sense of self. Loretta probably has
A) borderline personality disorder.
B) histrionic personality disorder.
C) dependent personality disorder.
D) narcissistic personality disorder.
Answer: A

Pages: 323
Topic: Personality Disorders: Types of Personality Disorders
Skill: Conceptual   Other1:
50. The text describes the case of a 26 year-old woman who was referred for hospital admission by her therapist. She was typical of individuals with borderline personality disorder because she
A) had formed an overly rigid identity at an early age.
B) was free of anxiety and depression.
C) showed excessive control of her emotions.
D) had urges to mutilate herself.
Answer: D

Pages: 324
Topic: Personality Disorders: Types of Personality Disorders
Skill: Factual   Other1:
51. Individuals with borderline personality disorder
A) may experience transient psychotic episodes.
B) are more often male than female.
C) are often indifferent to others in personal relationships.
D) are at high risk for developing schizophrenia.
Answer: A

52. About half of the individuals with borderline personality disorder also qualify for a diagnosis of _____ at some time.
   A) antisocial personality disorder
   B) schizophrenia
   C) a mood disorder
   D) histrionic personality disorder
   Answer: C

53. A key predisposing causal factor for borderline personality is
   A) exposure to extreme sibling rivalry, especially during adolescence.
   B) a lack of a coherent sense of self.
   C) being spoiled and over-indulged as a child.
   D) bouts of depression during adolescence.
   Answer: B

54. Today many clinicians believe that the relationship between borderline personality disorder and depression is
   A) not unique or special because other personality disorders are even more commonly associated with depression than is borderline personality disorder.
   B) special because it is the only personality disorder that overlaps so highly with mood disorders.
   C) one of genetic linkage.
   D) one in which depression serves as a distal necessary cause of borderline personality disorder.
   Answer: A

Topic: Personality Disorders: Types of Personality Disorders
Skill: Factual   Other1:

55. Depression in borderline individuals differs from depression in major depressives in that
    A) tricyclic antidepressants, but no other types of antidepressants, are effective in treating borderline individuals.
    B) borderline personality is characterized more by chronic feelings of loneliness, and is less amenable to antidepressant treatment.
    C) depression in borderlines usually lasts for many years.
    D) borderline individuals rarely attempt suicide.
    Answer: B

Pages: 324
Topic: Personality Disorders: Types of Personality Disorders
Skill: Factual   Other1:

56. Helena has avoidant personality disorder. She is likely to
    A) engage in a series of intense, unstable relationships.
    B) have no interest in social relationships.
    C) avoid achievement situations where she might fail.
    D) be hypersensitive to any sign of criticism or rejection.
    Answer: D

Pages: 324
Topic: Personality Disorders: Types of Personality Disorders
Skill: Conceptual   Other1:

57. In contrast to schizoid individuals, those with avoidant personality disorder
    A) are emotional and dramatic.
    B) are impulsive and self-destructive.
    C) are extremely upset by their lack of social relationships.
    D) are exploitative rather than compliant.
    Answer: C

Pages: 325
Topic: Personality Disorders: Types of Personality Disorders
Skill: Conceptual   Other1:

58. One of the key features of avoidant personality disorder is
    A) the way in which individuals with this disorder take advantage of others in subtle ways.
    B) the need to avoid situations in which one might be embarassed.
    C) the increased likelihood of engaging in risky behavior.
    D) the suspiciousness and paranoia they exhibit.
    Answer: B

Pages: 325
Topic: Personality Disorders: Types of Personality Disorders
Skill: Conceptual   Other1:
59. In contrast to dependent personality disorder, individuals with avoidant personality
disorder
A) are likely to let others make decisions for them.
B) have difficulty initiating social relationships.
C) are likely to be aloof, cold, and indifferent.
D) are indifferent to criticism.
Answer: B

Pages: 325
Topic: Personality Disorders: Types of Personality Disorders
Skill: Factual   Other1:
60. Several recent studies found substantial overlap between avoidant personality disorder and
_____, indicating that avoidant personality disorder may simply be a more extreme variant
of the same pathology.
A) generalized anxiety disorder
B) generalized social phobia
C) dysthymia
D) depressive personality disorder
Answer: B

Pages: 326
Topic: Personality Disorders: Types of Personality Disorders
Skill: Applied   Other1:
61. Hattie has a dependent personality disorder. This means that she
A) experiences little distress in her life.
B) has difficulty in initiating relationships.
C) has acute discomfort when she is alone.
D) will stand up for herself when people are taking advantage of her.
Answer: C

Pages: 326
Topic: Personality Disorders: Types of Personality Disorders
Skill: Factual   Other1:
62. Which of these features is NOT characteristic of someone with a dependent personality
disorder?
A) lack of self-confidence
B) submissiveness and compliance
C) high degree of personal initiative
D) reliance on others
Answer: C

Topic: Personality Disorders: Types of Personality Disorders
Skill: Factual   Other1:

63. Individuals with _____ personality disorder tend to build their lives around other people, subordinating their own needs in order to keep these people involved with them.
A) avoidant
B) passive-aggressive
C) histrionic
D) dependent
Answer: D

Pages: 326
Topic: Personality Disorders: Types of Personality Disorders
Skill: Conceptual   Other1:

64. The text presented the case of Sarah D., a 32 year-old mother of two and part-time tax accountant, who was typical of individuals with dependent personality disorder because she
A) finally stood up for herself once she was physically abused.
B) thought that significant others in her life were wonderful people, better than she.
C) was very dramatic and volatile emotionally.
D) was preoccupied with a fear of having to make decisions for herself.
Answer: D

Pages: 326
Topic: Personality Disorders: Types of Personality Disorders
Skill: Conceptual   Other1:

65. The fear of _____ is central for individuals with dependent personality disorder.
A) abandonment
B) humiliation
C) failing
D) intimacy
Answer: A

Pages: 327
Topic: Personality Disorders: Types of Personality Disorders
Skill: Applied   Other1:

66. Harold is perfectionistic and extremely concerned with maintaining a set routine. He probably suffers from _____ personality disorder.
A) schizoid
B) obsessive-compulsive
C) dependent
D) avoidant
Answer: B

Pages: 327
Topic: Personality Disorders: Types of Personality Disorders
Skill: Applied   Other1:
67. Jim has spent ten years writing his dissertation because he is very concerned about being absolutely correct in every detail of his work. Although he has only written twenty pages, he has spent every waking moment engaged in working on the dissertation. Harold probably suffers from _____ personality disorder.
    A) paranoid
    B) passive-aggressive
    C) obsessive-compulsive
    D) none; this is a normal case of "writer's block."
    Answer: C

Pages: 327
Topic: Personality Disorders: Types of Personality Disorders
Skill: Conceptual   Other1:
68. Most researchers today think that obsessive-compulsive personality disorder is
    A) a diathesis for obsessive-compulsive anxiety disorder.
    B) a genetic variant of obsessive-compulsive anxiety disorder.
    C) not a diathesis for obsessive-compulsive anxiety disorder.
    D) identical to obsessive-compulsive anxiety disorder.
    Answer: C

Pages: 327
Topic: Personality Disorders: Types of Personality Disorders
Skill: Conceptual   Other1:
69. The text presented the case of Alan, a dedicated train dispatcher. He was typical of individuals with obsessive-compulsive disorder in that he
    A) was close to his coworkers.
    B) got very little pleasure out of life and worried constantly about minor problems.
    C) tended to overlook details necessary for doing his job successfully.
    D) rarely displayed any irritability or anger but instead pushed such feelings away.
    Answer: B

Pages: 328
Topic: Personality Disorders: Types of Personality Disorders
Skill: Factual   Other1:
70. There is very limited empirical support for the reliability and validity of _____ personality disorder.
    A) paranoid
    B) avoidant
    C) histrionic
    D) passive-aggressive
    Answer: D

71. An individual is frequently late for work and meetings, misses appointments, forgets about assignments, refuses to follow instructions, and seems unmotivated. This is an example of _____ personality disorder.
    A) passive-aggressive
    B) avoidant
    C) narcissistic
    D) borderline
    Answer: A

72. A personality pattern characterized by dejection, self-criticism, and pessimism is
    A) avoidant personality disorder.
    B) schizotypal personality disorder.
    C) depressive personality disorder.
    D) dependent personality disorder.
    Answer: C

73. Depressive personality disorder and early-onset dysthymia
    A) are distinct disorders and respond best to very different treatments.
    B) differ in that depressive personality disorder is best characterized as a disorder in mood regulation, unlike early-onset dysthymia.
    C) are difficult to distinguish, although some evidence suggests that most patients with depressive personality disorder do not meet the criteria for early-onset dysthymia.
    D) are so similar in symptom profile that it is impossible to distinguish between them.
    Answer: C

74. Provisional categories of Axis II disorders in the DSM-IV Appendix are _____ and _____ personality disorders.
    A) dependent and depressive
    B) depressive and dysthymic
    C) passive-aggressive and depressive
    D) passive-aggressive and avoidant
    Answer: C

Pages: 328-330
Topic: Personality Disorders: Types of Personality Disorders
Skill: Factual   Other1:

75. Beck and Freeman proposed a system for integrating and differentiating personality disorders. Dimensions for characterizing individuals with different personality disorders include all BUT which of the following?
A) type of interpersonal strategies used
B) family history of psychological disorder
C) underdeveloped and overdeveloped behavioral patterns
D) characteristic core dysfunctional beliefs
Answer: B

Pages: 329
Topic: Personality Disorders: Types of Personality Disorders
Skill: Conceptual   Other1:

76. As suggested by Beck and Freeman, an example of an overdeveloped behavior pattern is control and responsibility. The corresponding underdeveloped behavior patterns are spontaneity and playfulness, respectively. This would best describe _____ personality disorder.
A) obsessive-compulsive
B) schizotypal
C) paranoid
D) dependent
Answer: A

Pages: 330
Topic: Personality Disorders: Types of Personality Disorders
Skill: Applied   Other1:

77. "If I am criticized by someone else, I will look like a complete fool." According to Beck and Freeman, this is probably a core dysfunctional belief of an individual with _____ personality disorder.
A) schizotypal
B) schizoid
C) avoidant
D) paranoid
Answer: C

Pages: 330
Topic: Personality Disorders: Causal Factors in Personality Disorders
Skill: Conceptual   Other1:
78. Little is known about causal factors in personality disorders for all BUT which of the following reasons?
    A) The level of comorbidity between different personality disorders is high.
    B) Reliability in diagnosing Axis II disorders is still problematic.
    C) Retrospective data is usually all that's available to study individuals with personality disorders.
    D) All of the above ARE reasons why little is known about it.
    Answer: D

Pages: 330
Topic: Personality Disorders: Causal Factors in Personality Disorders
Skill: Factual   Other1:
79. What is the evidence for a genetic liability for personality disorders?
    A) There is a great deal of evidence that personality disorders are almost exclusively caused by genetic factors.
    B) There is increasing evidence for a genetic contribution to some of the personality disorders.
    C) Only antisocial personality disorder has a genetic basis.
    D) Personality disorders are inherited only to the extent that they share a genetic linkage with an Axis I disorder.
    Answer: B

Pages: 330-331
Topic: Personality Disorders: Causal Factors in Personality Disorders
Skill: Factual   Other1:
80. Psychological variables often hypothesized to contribute to the development of personality disorders include all BUT which of the following?
    A) maternal stress during pregnancy
    B) childhood trauma
    C) parental devaluation of the child
    D) parental overvaluation of the child
    Answer: A

Pages: 331
Topic: Personality Disorders: Causal Factors in Personality Disorders
Skill: Factual   Other1:
81. Kohut and other psychoanalytic theorists have been influential in suggesting that _____ is involved in the origin of narcissistic personality disorder, although there is little empirical support for this hypothesis.
    A) parental overvaluation in childhood
    B) failure of the infant to experience sufficient empathic mirroring from parents in order to progress beyond primitive grandiosity
    C) the experience of repeated and severe traumas in childhood
    D) childhood sexual abuse
    Answer: B

Pages: 332-333
Topic: Personality Disorders: Treatments and Outcomes
Skill: Conceptual   Other1:
82. The text presented the case of Mrs. A., who brought her son in for treatment because of his nightmares and fear of leaving the home. This case was typical of a key problem often encountered when treating personality disorders because
    A) the person with a personality disorder was very unreliable about keeping appointments for therapy sessions.
    B) the son exhibited a personality disorder at a very early age.
    C) the son's problems were connected to the strain associated with living with another family member who had a personality disorder.
    D) psychodynamic therapy was very effective in treating the personality disorder.
    Answer: C

Pages: 333-334
Topic: Personality Disorders: Treatments and Outcomes
Skill: Conceptual   Other1:
83. Which of the following statements is NOT true of treating personality disorders?
    A) Individuals with personality disorders from Clusters A and B are more difficult to treat because of their interpersonal difficulties and reluctance to enter therapy.
    B) Treatment for individuals with dependent personality disorder ought to be altered so that excessive dependency is not fostered.
    C) Avoidant and dependent individuals are so hypersensitive to criticism that a therapist needs to be extremely careful not to hurt their feelings.
    D) Borderline personality disorder is especially amenable to cognitive treatment.
    Answer: D

Pages: 334
Topic: Personality Disorders: Treatments and Outcomes
Skill: Conceptual   Other1:
84. Cognitive therapy for personality disorders
    A) has been found to be inadequate in treating personality disorders.
    B) significantly reduces destructive acting-out behavior in individuals with severe personality disorders.
    C) is relatively new and untested in controlled studies, but appears promising.
    D) is effective only for hospitalized individuals.
    Answer: C

Pages: 334
Topic: Personality Disorders: Treatments and Outcomes
Skill: Factual   Other1:
85. The use of medication in treating borderline patients is
    A) not useful, since they do not respond to medication.
    B) controversial because of suicide risk.
    C) sometimes useful, particularly antipsychotic drugs and antidepressants like Prozac that inhibit the reuptake of serotonin.
    D) B and C
    Answer: D

Pages: 334
Topic: Personality Disorders: Treatments and Outcomes
Skill: Factual   Other1:
86. The most promising treatment for borderline personality disorder probably is
    A) a psychodynamic approach tailored to borderlines.
    B) electroconvulsive therapy.
    C) antipsychotic medication.
    D) dialectical behavior therapy.
    Answer: D

Pages: 334
Topic: Personality Disorders: Treatments and Outcomes
Skill: Factual   Other1:
87. The central disability in borderline personality disorder, according to Linehan's dialectical behavioral model, is
    A) splitting as a primary defense mechanism.
    B) self-mutilation.
    C) extreme instability in sense of self.
    D) the inability to tolerate strong states of negative affect.
    Answer: D

Pages: 334
Topic: Personality Disorders: Treatments and Outcomes
Skill: Conceptual   Other1:
88. Reducing self-destructive and self-defeating behaviors, client-centered acceptance of the patient, and learning to regulate emotions in individual and group therapy are parts of _____ therapy for borderline personality disorder.
A) psychodynamic
B) Rogerian
C) dialectical behavior
D) psychoanalytic
Answer: C

Pages: 335
Topic: Personality Disorders: Treatments and Outcomes
Skill: Conceptual   Other1:
89. Compared to many of the other personality disorders, schizotypal personality disorder is
A) one of the most amenable to treatment.
B) one of the least amenable to treatment.
C) easily treatable with medication, but not with other therapies.
D) treatable only with cognitive interventions.
Answer: B

Pages: 335
Topic: Personality Disorders: Treatments and Outcomes
Skill: Conceptual   Other1:
90. To date personality disorders from Cluster _____ have been the most amenable to treatment.
A) A
B) B
C) C
D) the provisional categories
Answer: C

Pages: 335
Topic: Antisocial Personality and Psychopathy
Skill: Factual   Other1:
91. All of the following are criteria for antisocial personality disorder in DSM-IV EXCEPT
A) at least one conviction of a felony or three convictions of a misdemeanor.
B) at least three behavioral problems after the age of fifteen.
C) at least three instances of deviant behavior before age fifteen.
D) the antisocial behavior is not a symptom of another mental disorder.
Answer: A

Pages: 335
Topic: Antisocial Personality and Psychopathy
Skill: Factual   Other1:
92. In contrast to the defining features of antisocial personality disorder in DSM-III and
    DSM-IV, the concept of psychopathy as delineated by Cleckley also includes such traits as
    A) lack of empathy.
    B) inflated and arrogant self-appraisal.
    C) glib and superficial charm.
    D) all of the above
    Answer: D

Pages: 336
Topic: Antisocial Personality and Psychopathy
Skill: Factual   Other1:
93. Research by Hare and colleagues suggests that
    A) antisocial personality disorder and psychopathy are essentially identical constructs.
    B) antisocial personality disorder, unlike psychopathy, is associated with affective and
       interpersonal traits of callousness, selfishness, and the exploitive use of others.
    C) psychopathy includes two related but separable dimensions, one involving lack of
       remorse and an exploitive use of others, and the second involving an antisocial,
       impulsive, and socially deviant life style.
    D) antisocial personality disorder has three dimensions that are entirely different than
       psychopathy.
    Answer: C

Pages: 336
Topic: Antisocial Personality and Psychopathy
Skill: Applied   Other1:
94. Imagine that you work in a prison. You would expect that the majority of inmates there
    show
    A) traits associated with psychopathy.
    B) traits associated only with the first dimension of psychopathy, such as lack of remorse
       and exploitativeness.
    C) traits associated with antisocial personality disorder, such as aggressive and deviant
       behavior.
    D) few of the traits of either psychopathy or antisocial personality disorder.
    Answer: C

Pages: 336
Topic: Antisocial Personality and Psychopathy
Skill: Conceptual   Other1:
95. One of the problems with the DSM-IV criteria for antisocial personality disorder is that
    A) these criteria lack reliability.
    B) the validity of this diagnostic category is questionable, because it fails to capture many individuals who show traits consistent with the first dimension of psychopathy, but not the second dimension.
    C) this diagnostic category is too heterogeneous because it contains individuals who may differ significantly in interpersonal and affective traits, such as the ability to feel remorse and the capacity for empathy.
    D) B and C
    Answer: D

Pages: 338
Topic: Antisocial Personality/Psychopathy: The Clinical Picture
Skill: Factual   Other1:
96. Psychopathy and antisocial personality differ in that
    A) individuals with antisocial personality, unlike psychopaths, lack the capacity to feel empathy or remorse.
    B) intelligence is negatively correlated with antisocial personality but it is generally unrelated to psychopathy.
    C) psychopaths are more often found in prison settings than are individuals with antisocial personality.
    D) psychopaths, unlike individuals with antisocial personality, tend to abuse alcohol and drugs.
    Answer: B

Pages: 339-341
Topic: Antisocial Personality/Psychopathy: The Clinical Picture
Skill: Conceptual   Other1:
97. The text presented a classic case study originally described by Hare in which Donald S. had just completed a jail sentence for bigamy. He is typical of psychopathic individuals in that he
    A) showed a repeated pattern of exploitation and illegal activity, despite periodic punishments for his behavior.
    B) was able to form a stable long-term relationship with a woman, although his other relationships were chaotic.
    C) settled down after the age of thirty-five to a position of responsibility in the community.
    D) had been involved in a series of crimes against property, but no crimes that infringed on the rights of others.
    Answer: A

Pages: 341
Topic: Antisocial Personality and Psychopathy: Causal Factors
Skill: Factual   Other1:

98. The evidence for a genetic liability for antisocial behavior and criminality shows
    A) that genetic liability clearly is the primary cause of antisocial personality.
    B) a modest heritability for criminality and antisocial personality, but only in
       interaction with certain environmental factors.
    C) that alcoholism and antisocial personality share the identical genetic liability.
    D) that there is no apparent genetic factor involved in criminality or antisocial
       behavior.
    Answer: B

Pages: 342
Topic: Antisocial Personality and Psychopathy: Causal Factors
Skill: Factual   Other1:

99. A large number of studies have found that the first dimension of psychopathy is associated
    with
    A) a very superior level of intelligence.
    B) an over-reactivity in conditioning to anxiety, which eventually causes the psychopath
       to "burn out."
    C) heightened conditioning to aversive stimuli.
    D) abnormalities in a variety of learning situations, such as avoidance learning, that may
       underlie the psychopath's impulsivity and lack of conscience.
    Answer: D

Pages: 342
Topic: Antisocial Personality and Psychopathy: Causal Factors
Skill: Factual   Other1:

100. According to Fowles's adaptation of Gray's model, psychopaths have a deficient _____ and a
    normal or overactive _____.
    A) behavioral activation system; behavioral inhibition system
    B) behavioral inhibition system; behavioral avoidance system
    C) behavioral inhibition system; behavioral activation system
    D) reward system; punishment system
    Answer: C

Pages: 342-344
Topic: Antisocial Personality and Psychopathy: Causal Factors
Skill: Factual   Other1:

101. Individuals with psychopathy
    A) are higher in sensation-seeking than normal individuals.
    B) may have difficulty delaying gratification.
    C) show reduced physiological reactivity to fearful imagery.
    D) all of the above
    Answer: D

Pages: 344
Topic: Antisocial Personality and Psychopathy: Causal Factors
Skill: Factual   *Other1: In Student Study Guide*
102. While a number of early studies linked antisocial personality formation with losing a parent at an early age, Hare suggested that the key factor was the
    A) age at which the loss occurred.
    B) emotional family disturbance before the parent left.
    C) length of the marriage before the loss.
    D) sex of the parent who left.
    Answer: B

Pages: 344
Topic: Antisocial Personality and Psychopathy: Causal Factors
Skill: Factual   *Other1:*
103. Psychopathy has been associated with
    A) sexual abuse in childhood.
    B) severe parental rejection, and lack of parental affection and supervision.
    C) lack of a father in the home during childhood and adolescence.
    D) extremely strict and restrictive parental rules with severe but consistent punishment for infractions.
    Answer: B

Pages: 345
Topic: Antisocial Personality and Psychopathy: Causal Factors
Skill: Factual   *Other1:*
104. In the longitudinal prospective studies of psychopathy and antisocial personality conducted by Robins, she found that
    A) the onset of antisocial behaviors in childhood predicted an adult diagnosis of psychopathy or antisocial personality.
    B) the onset of oppositional defiant disorder in late adolescence predicted an adult diagnosis of psychopathy or antisocial personality.
    C) the number of antisocial behaviors exhibited in childhood predicted an adult diagnosis of psychopathy or antisocial personality.
    D) A and C
    Answer: D

Pages: 345
Topic: Antisocial Personality and Psychopathy: Causal Factors
Skill: Factual   Other1:
105. Based on prospective longitudinal studies, the single best predictor of who develops an adult diagnosis of psychopathy or antisocial personality is
A) conduct disorder that begins in adolescence.
B) early oppositional defiant disorder followed by early-onset conduct disorder.
C) early disturbance in family relationships.
D) frontal-lobe abnormalities.
Answer: B

Pages: 346
Topic: Antisocial Personality and Psychopathy: Causal Factors
Skill: Factual   Other1: In Student Study Guide
106. In the Capaldi and Patterson model, the key factor that mediates the influence of the others and increases the probability of antisocial behavior in the child is
A) parental antisocial behavior.
B) divorce and other parental transitions.
C) parental stress and depression.
D) ineffective discipline and supervision.
Answer: D

Pages: 347
Topic: Antisocial Personality and Psychopathy: Treatments and Outcomes
Skill: Conceptual   Other1:
107. Based on the current empirical literature, the most promising treatment for psychopathic and antisocial personality disorder probably is
A) cognitive therapy for personality disorders.
B) behavior therapy in a controlled setting.
C) antianxiety medication and stimulants.
D) psychodynamic therapy.
Answer: B

Pages: 348
Topic: Antisocial Personality and Psychopathy: Treatments and Outcomes
Skill: Factual   Other1:
108. Beck and Freeman have developed a cognitive treatment for antisocial personality disorder that involves
    A) uncovering early repressed thoughts associated with intrapsychic anxiety.
    B) moral re-education--teaching the psychopath about ethical principles and moral points of view to fill in the gaps in the moral and spiritual education that was insufficient in childhood.
    C) aversion therapy.
    D) modifying the psychopath's self-serving dysfunctional beliefs and learning more abstract kinds of thinking using principles based on theories of moral and cognitive development.
    Answer: D

Pages: 349-351
Topic: Unresolved Issues on Axis II of DSM-IV
Skill: Conceptual   Other1:
109. Which of the following is NOT a problem that is associated with Axis II of the DSM-IV?
    A) Most people who have one personality disorder diagnosis also qualify for a diagnosis of at least one other personality disorder.
    B) Axis II diagnoses are considerably less reliable than are diagnoses made on Axis I.
    C) There is too much similarity in the symptoms exhibited by individuals who share the same Axis II diagnosis, suggesting that DSM-IV criteria for personality disorders are too narrow.
    D) Axis II is based on a categorical approach to classification rather than a dimensional approach.
    Answer: C

Pages: 351
Topic: Unresolved Issues on Axis II of DSM-IV
Skill: Conceptual   Other1:
110. With respect to the current Axis II system of DSM-IV, many researchers and clinicians (including the chair of the DSM-IV Task Force) agree that
    A) Axis II should be entirely abandoned due to the problems in reliably diagnosing personality disorders.
    B) a categorical-based system eventually should be replaced by a dimensional model of personality diagnosis.
    C) personality traits should be able to reliably fit into discrete categories; the field simply has not reached this point of development.
    D) personality traits are dimensional but also categorical in that "natural breaks" occur for most personality traits at the upper ends of severity.
    Answer: B

Short Answer

Write the word or phrase that best completes each statement or answers the question.

Pages: 313-314
Topic: Personality Disorders
Skill: Factual   Other1:
1. Briefly describe the general characteristics of a personality disorder.
   Answer: This is a disorder in which personality traits and behavior patterns are maladaptive, inflexible, and not readily adaptive to new situations. They usually significantly impair social or occupational functioning and in some cases cause a good deal of subjective emotional distress.

Pages: 315
Topic: Personality Disorders
Skill: Factual   Other1:
2. Briefly state the DSM-IV criteria for a personality disorder.
   Answer: DSM-IV requires that a personality pattern deviate markedly from the culture and be manifested in at least two areas including cognition, affectivity, interpersonal functioning, or impulse control. The pattern must be pervasive across many situations and cause impairment in social, occupational, or other areas of functioning or significant distress. The pattern is stable and of long duration.

Pages: 315
Topic: Personality Disorders
Skill: Conceptual   Other1:
3. Personality disorders are often misdiagnosed. Briefly state one reason for this problem.
   Answer: The reliability of diagnostic criteria is problematic. The criteria themselves are not very precise or easy to follow in practice. There is substantial comorbidity between personality disorders. Personality characteristics comprising criteria are dimensional in nature, ranging from normal expression of a trait to pathologically exaggerated expression, which can contribute to diagnostic unreliability.

Pages: 316
Topic: Personality Disorders: Types of Personality Disorders
Skill: Factual   Other1:
4. Briefly describe the characteristics associated with each of the personality disorder clusters in DSM-IV.
   Answer: Cluster A contains disorders characterized by odd, eccentric, and unusual behavior. Cluster B contains disorders characterized by dramatic, emotional, impulsive, and erratic behavior. Cluster C includes disorders characterized by anxiety and fearfulness.

Pages: 317
Topic: Personality Disorders: Types of Personality Disorders
Skill: Factual   Other1:
5. Identify the specific personality disorders in each of the three clusters in DSM-IV.
    Answer: Cluster A contains paranoid, schizoid, and schizotypal personality disorders.
              Cluster B includes histrionic, narcissistic, antisocial, and borderline
              personality disorders. Cluster C includes avoidant, dependent, and
              obsessive-compulsive personality disorders.

Pages: 316
Topic: Personality Disorders: Types of Personality Disorders
Skill: Applied   Other1:
6. Briefly characterize the individual with paranoid personality disorder.
    Answer: The individual is characterized by pervasive suspiciousness and mistrust of
              others, is unforgiving, hypersensitive to real or imagined criticism, and tends
              to externalize blame. The individual may experience transient psychotic
              symptoms.

Pages: 318
Topic: Personality Disorders: Types of Personality Disorders
Skill: Applied   Other1:
7. Irene has no close friends and prefers solitary activities. She has little interest in
    socializing and appears distant and aloof to others. Irene suffers from _____ personality
    disorder.
    Answer: schizoid

Pages: 318-319
Topic: Personality Disorders: Types of Personality Disorders
Skill: Conceptual   Other1:
8. What is the relationship between personality disorders and schizophrenia?
    Answer: There is genetic evidence for a relationship between schizophrenia and
              schizotypal personality disorder. It was formerly thought that schizoid and
              borderline personality patterns also were associated with schizophrenia, but
              these hypotheses have not been supported in more recent research.

Pages: 319
Topic: Personality Disorders: Types of Personality Disorders
Skill: Factual   Other1:
9. The central and distinguishing disturbance in schizotypal personality disorder is
    Answer: the presence of perceptual and cognitive problems such as magical thinking,
              ideas of reference, odd speech, and superstitious beliefs. These peculiar
              thought patterns are associated with a loosening--although not a complete
              rupture--of ties with reality.

Pages: 320
Topic: Personality Disorders: Types of Personality Disorders
Skill: Factual   Other1:
10. Briefly characterize histrionic personality disorder.
    Answer: Histrionic individuals are dramatic and emotional with an intense need to be the
             center of attention. Interpersonally they are manipulative, seductive, and
             dependent. They appear shallow and self-centered.

Pages: 321
Topic: Personality Disorders: Types of Personality Disorders
Skill: Conceptual   Other1:
11. An exaggerated need for admiration, a sense of entitlement, and lack of empathy are
    central features of _____ personality disorder.
    Answer: narcissistic

Pages: 323-324
Topic: Personality Disorders: Types of Personality Disorders
Skill: Conceptual   Other1:
12. Borderline personality disorder is notable for what symptoms?
    Answer: It is characterized by extreme instability in sense of self, mood,
             relationships, impulse control, and chronic feelings of emptiness.
             Self-mutilation and suicide attempts, which often are flagrantly manipulative,
             are common. Self-mutilation is one of the most discriminating signs for this
             condition.

Pages: 325
Topic: Personality Disorders: Types of Personality Disorders
Skill: Conceptual   Other1:
13. What is a major distinguishing feature between avoidant and dependent personality
    disorders?
    Answer: Avoidant individuals are too frightened to initiate relationships, unlike
             dependent persons.

Pages: 327
Topic: Personality Disorders: Types of Personality Disorders
Skill: Conceptual   Other1:
14. What is the relationship between obsessive-compulsive personality disorder and
    obsessive-compulsive anxiety disorder?
    Answer: It was once thought that the personality disorder is a diathesis for the anxiety
             disorder. However, recent studies found that most people meeting criteria for
             the anxiety disorder do not have traits of the personality disorder.
             Individuals with the personality disorder typically do not have the obsessions
             and ritualized compulsions of individuals with the anxiety disorder.

Pages: 328
Topic: Personality Disorders: Types of Personality Disorders
Skill: Factual   Other1:
15. The two personality disorders considered as provisional categories in DSM-IV are _____ and

_____.
Answer: passive-aggressive personality disorder; depressive personality disorder

Pages: 333
Topic: Personality Disorders: Treatments and Outcomes
Skill: Conceptual   Other1:
16. Individuals with which personality disorders are the most difficult to treat and why?
Answer: Those with disorders from Clusters A and B are the most difficult, because they
usually enter treatment at someone else's insistence or through someone else's
treatment. They have difficulties establishing a good relationship with a
therapist, act out in therapy rather than verbalizing, have high dropout rates,
and tend to be extremely angry or defensive when confronted.

Pages: 334
Topic: Personality Disorders: Treatments and Outcomes
Skill: Factual   Other1:
17. According to Linehan's dialectical behavioral therapy model for borderline personality
disorder, the central feature of this disorder that is targeted in therapy is _____.
Answer: inability to tolerate strong negative affect

Pages: 341-344
Topic: Antisocial Personality and Psychopathy: Causal Factors
Skill: Factual   Other1:
18. Identify two biological factors that have been causally implicated in psychopathy or
antisocial personality disorder.
Answer: There is a modest heritability component. In addition, there is evidence that
psychopaths tend to show deficient aversive emotional arousal, deficits in
passive avoidance learning, reduced psychic but not somatic anxiety, reduced
responsivity to aversive stimuli, sensation-seeking probably due to low levels
of arousal and deficient autonomic variability, an underactive behavioral
inhibition system, a normal or overactive behavioral activation system, and
possible frontal lobe dysfunction.

Pages: 345
Topic: Antisocial Personality and Psychopathy: Causal Factors
Skill: Factual   Other1:
19. A childhood predictor of the later development of antisocial personality disorder is the
diagnosis of _____.
Answer: oppositional defiant disorder followed by early-onset conduct disorder

Pages: 347
Topic: Antisocial Personality and Psychopathy: Treatments and Outcomes
Skill: Factual   Other1:
20. The most optimal treatment for psychopathic and antisocial personalities is
    Answer: behavioral therapy in a controlled setting as well as group therapy that
             provides an opportunity to learn to care for others and a place to be accepted
             by peers.

Essay

Write your answer in the space provided or on a separate sheet of paper.

Pages: 314-316
Topic: Personality Disorders: Clinical Features of Personality Disorders
Skill: Conceptual   Other1:
1. Discuss current difficulties with DSM-IV diagnoses of personality disorders.
   Answer: Diagnoses can be problematic because criteria do not involve objective
            behavioral standards but require too much subjective inference, so that
            reliability is poorer than for Axis I disorders. Semi-structured interviews
            improve reliability, but reliability and validity of the categories are still
            problematic. Other important difficulties arise from the fact that categories
            are not mutually exclusive and that personality traits are dimensional in
            nature, raising serious questions about the viability of a categorical approach.

Pages: 313-315
Topic: Personality Disorders: Clinical Features of Personality Disorders
Skill: Conceptual   Other1:
2. Personality disorders have a number of common characteristics regardless of the disorder.
   What are they?
   Answer: Often there is a disrupted pattern of personal relationships. The problems are
            generally longstanding, are marked by behavior that is considered troublesome to
            others, and are often associated with negative life outcomes. Traits and
            behaviors are maladaptive as well as inflexible and not readily adaptive to new
            or stressful situations. They are highly resistant to change.

Pages: 317
Topic: Personality Disorders: Types of Personality Disorders
Skill: Conceptual   Other1:
3. Differentiate between paranoid, schizoid, and schizotypal personality disorders.
   Answer: Paranoid personality disorder involves suspiciousness, hypersensitivity,
            rigidity, envy, and argumentativeness. Paranoid people constantly expect
            trickery. Schizoids show an inability to form interpersonal relationships, and
            appear cool and aloof. Schizotypals are seclusive, oversensitive, and eccentric
            with cognitive and perceptual oddities.

Pages: 317
Topic: Personality Disorders: Types of Personality Disorders
Skill: Conceptual   Other1:

4. Differentiate between histrionic, narcissistic, and borderline personality disorders.

    Answer: Histrionics are emotional and dramatic, constantly seeking attention, seductive and manipulative in relationships. Narcissists seek admiration, have a grandiose sense of self, are hypersensitive to criticism, and may have fragile self-esteem under the surface. Borderlines are characterized by extreme instability in identity and mood, are often self-destructive and impulsive, and may experience transient psychotic states.

Pages: 317
Topic: Personality Disorders: Types of Personality Disorders
Skill: Conceptual   Other1:

5. Differentiate between dependent, avoidant, and obsessive-compulsive personality disorders.

    Answer: Dependents are extremely fearful of being alone and tend to subordinate their own needs to others in order to keep them around. They allow others to make decisions and in many ways control them. Avoidants desire social relationships but avoid them out of extreme fear of criticism, derogation, and humiliation. Obsessive-compulsives are perfectionistic, rigid, overly preoccupied with work and detail to the detriment of relationships, being able to finish projects, and seeing the forest for the trees.

Pages: 328-330
Topic: Personality Disorders: Types of Personality Disorders
Skill: Conceptual   Other1:

6. Describe the cognitive model of Beck and Freeman for characterizing similarities and differences between personality disorders.

    Answer: They suggest that individuals with these disorders can be characterized on several dimensions including type of interpersonal strategy, behaviors that are over/underdeveloped, and core dysfunctional beliefs. Interpersonal strategy includes, for example, moving toward (histrionic) or away (schizoid). Overdeveloped behavior in the dependent might be compliance, with autonomy underdeveloped. "If someone dislikes me, I'm worthless," may be a core avoidant belief.

Pages: 330-332
Topic: Personality Disorders: Causal Factors in Personality Disorders
Skill: Conceptual   Other1:

7. What makes research into the causal factors of personality disorders so difficult? What is the current state of research regarding causal factors for personality disorders other than psychopathy and antisocial personality?

    Answer: Many with these disorders never seek treatment and when they do, retrospective rather than prospective studies must usually be relied on. High levels of comorbidity make it hard to disentangle causal factors. Reliability and validity of DSM-IV diagnostic categories are problematic. Moderate heritability in some disorders is evident. Early learning often is hypothesized but little research exists. Some research suggests that abuse in childhood may be related to certain personality disorders (particularly borderline). Evidence of biological and sociocultural factors is limited at present.

Pages: 333
Topic: Personality Disorders: Treatments and Outcomes
Skill: Applied   Other1:

8. Assume that you are a clinician in private practice. When are you likely to see individuals with personality disorders from Clusters A and B? If you do, what would be the most appropriate treatments?

    Answer: They usually enter as a part of someone else's treatment or when "forced." They often don't believe they have a problem or are at fault. Traditional techniques may need to be modified, such as to reassure avoidants or not foster dependency in dependents. Medication and a controlled environment may be necessary. Dialectical behavior therapy for borderlines and cognitive therapy for some other disorders are indicated. Additional treatment outcome research for personality disorders is needed, especially for personality disordered individuals who rarely seek treatment (e.g., schizoid).

Pages: 334-335
Topic: Personality Disorders: Treatments and Outcomes
Skill: Conceptual   Other1:

9. Describe Linehan's dialectical behavior therapy program. Who is it designed to be used with? What are its central assumptions? How is it implemented?

    Answer: This cognitive-behavioral model proposes that an inability to tolerate strong negative affect is central to borderlines. Treatment focuses on first reducing self-destructive and self-defeating behavior, then decreasing escapist behaviors, and increasing behavioral skills for regulating emotion and enhancing social skills. Individual and group therapy are both used in the context of an accepting, client-centered therapeutic stance.

Pages: 335-336
Topic: Antisocial Personality and Psychopathy
Skill: Applied   Other1:

10. Assume you work in a prison where you see many individuals who fit Cleckley's description of the psychopath. What are these individuals like?

    Answer: They have inadequate conscience development, lack anxiety and guilt, are irresponsible and impulsive, show a low frustration tolerance, often can impress others, reject authority, and have an inability to maintain good relationships. They are likely to exhibit features associated with the first dimension of psychopathy as described by Hare, including traits such as lack of remorse, callousness, selfishness, and an exploitative use of others. They are also likely to exhibit the deviant, aggressive, and antisocial behaviors associated with Hare's second dimension of psychopathy.

Pages: 335-341
Topic: Antisocial Personality and Psychopathy
Skill: Conceptual   Other1:

11. What is psychopathy and how is it related to DSM-IV antisocial personality disorder? What are the similarities and differences?

    Answer: Cleckley's psychopathy construct reflects two dimensions: affective and interpersonal components (lack of remorse, exploitiveness); and antisocial, deviant, and impulsive behavior (closer to the DSM-IV disorder). The DSM-IV fails to tap many individuals with characteristics of the first dimension and may have sacrificed validity for enhanced reliability. The first dimension is more stable across a lifetime and is associated with deficient aversive emotional arousal and reduced physiological responsivity to aversive stimuli.

Pages: 341-344
Topic: Antisocial Personality and Psychopathy: Causal Factors
Skill: Conceptual   Other1:

12. Discuss the literature investigating emotional arousal and fear conditioning in psychopaths. Describe these findings in terms of Gray's and Fowles's model of behavioral inhibition and activation.

    Answer: Psychopaths show deficient conditioning of anxiety to anticipation of punishment and poor passive avoidance learning. This may be associated with a deficit in the behavioral inhibition system proposed by Gray as the neural substrate of anxiety and these kinds of learning. According to Fowles, psychopaths may be normal or overactive in the behavioral activation system, prone to actively attempt to escape punishment if caught and to be overfocused on rewards. Low arousal may cause sensation-seeking behavior, and reduced reactivity to aversive stimuli suggests insensitivity to human suffering.

Pages: 345-346
Topic: Antisocial Personality and Psychopathy: Causal Factors
Skill: Conceptual   Other1:

13. What are the early warning signs of psychopathy in children? What is a typical developmental course in a case of antisocial personality?

    Answer: In Robins' prospective studies, increases in the number of antisocial behaviors in childhood correlated with the likelihood of later antisocial personality. These behaviors included theft, truancy, running away, and school problems. A typical course often begins with temperamental difficulties in infancy, argumentativeness in preschool years, hostile and defiant attitudes toward authority comprising oppositional defiant disorder by age six, and development of early-onset conduct disorder around age nine. Conduct disorder beginning in adolescence is not usually associated with psychopathy.

Pages: 346-349
Topic: Antisocial Personality and Psychopathy: Treatments and Outcomes
Skill: Conceptual   Other1:

14. Evaluate the effectiveness of the available treatments for antisocial personality disorder.

    Answer: Traditional psychodynamic therapy and medications are generally ineffective. Cognitive interventions have recently been proposed but research is needed to evaluate their effectiveness. Behavioral therapy is probably most promising, but the necessity of a controlled setting is crucial, and group rather than individual treatment also imperative. Many of these individuals improve after the age of forty without treatment. Preventive measures may be best, working with high-risk children. Early results seem promising but more time is needed for propsective study.

Pages: 349-351
Topic: Unresolved Issues on Axis II of DSM-IV
Skill: Conceptual   Other1:

15. Discuss three major limitations associated with making DSM-IV personality disorder diagnoses.

    Answer: The reliability of these diagnoses is problematic because criteria are imprecise and require far too much subjective inference. Traits are dimensional yet artificially forced into a categorical system. Different semi-structured diagnostic interviews give different diagnoses of the same individual. Many people show characteristics of more than one personality disorder, and different people with the same diagnosis may have markedly different symptoms.

CHAPTER 10 Substance-Related and Other Addictive Disorders

Multiple-Choice

Choose the one alternative that best completes the statement or answers the question.

Pages: 355
Topic: Substance-Related and Other Addictive Disorders
Skill: Factual   Other1:
1. Psychoactive drugs
    A) can lead to organic mental disorders.
    B) affect mental functioning.
    C) are illegal.
    D) A and B
    Answer: D

Pages: 355
Topic: Substance-Related and Other Addictive Disorders
Skill: Factual   Other1:
2. The two major categories of DSM-IV psychoactive substance-related addictive disorders are distinguished by whether
    A) there is organic impairment resulting from use of the substance.
    B) whether the substance is legal or illegal.
    C) whether or not the disorder involves a significant withdrawal syndrome.
    D) whether or not physiological dependence results.
    Answer: A

Pages: 355
Topic: Substance-Related and Other Addictive Disorders
Skill: Applied   Other1:
3. Alcohol abuse dementia disorder, which involves alcohol-induced physiologic changes in the brain, would be an example of
    A) psychoactive substance abuse.
    B) psychoactive substance dependence.
    C) psychoactive substance-induced organic mental disorder.
    D) toxicity.
    Answer: C

Pages: 355
Topic: Substance-Related and Other Addictive Disorders
Skill: Applied   Other1:
4. Judd has been drinking heavily for a number of years. He now has a memory defect in which he does not recognize objects he has just seen. He
   A) can correct this problem by eating properly.
   B) has alcohol abuse dementia disorder involving amnesia.
   C) is likely to die within three months as a result of his brain damage.
   D) will show a change in memory but no change in personality.
   Answer: B

Pages: 356
Topic: Substance-Related and Other Addictive Disorders
Skill: Conceptual   Other1: In Student Study Guide
5. A person who shows tolerance for a drug or withdrawal symptoms when it is unavailable illustrates
   A) psychoactive substance abuse.
   B) psychoactive substance dependence.
   C) psychoactive substance toxicity.
   D) psychoactive substance-induced organic mental disorders and syndromes.
   Answer: B

Pages: 356
Topic: Alcohol Abuse and Dependence
Skill: Factual   Other1:
6. With regard to problems faced by alcoholics,
   A) alcohol problems are related to suicide in men, but not in women.
   B) binge drinkers rarely become severely impaired, although chronic drinkers do.
   C) they tend to diminish with age.
   D) the average life span of an alcoholic is twelve years shorter than a nonalcoholic.
   Answer: D

Pages: 356
Topic: Alcohol Abuse and Dependence
Skill: Factual   Other1:
7. Which of the following statements is true about alcohol use?
   A) Alcoholism is extremely serious but rarely fatal.
   B) Alcoholism is more common in women that in men.
   C) Alcoholism increases the risk of suicide.
   D) Alcoholism is strongly associated with accidental death, but not with violent acts.
   Answer: C

Pages: 358
Topic: Alcohol Abuse and Dependence
Skill: Factual   *Other1:*

8. Which of the following statements about alcohol and alcoholism is a myth?
   A) Coffee and cold showers do nothing to sober up an individual.
   B) Withdrawal from heroin is more traumatic and potentially more lethal than withdrawal from alcohol.
   C) Alcohol is addictive, just as cocaine and heroin are.
   D) Mixing drinks is no more likely to cause intoxication than sticking to one kind of liquor.
   Answer: B

Pages: 356
Topic: Alcohol Abuse and Dependence
Skill: Factual   *Other1:*

9. Alcohol abuse
   A) is much more common among blacks than whites.
   B) usually begins in adolescence or young adulthood, and rarely begins after middle age.
   C) is the third leading cause of death in the United States.
   D) is more common among women than men.
   Answer: C

Pages: 357
Topic: Alcohol Abuse and Dependence
Skill: Factual   *Other1:*

10. Among college-aged people, the leading cause of death is
    A) suicide.
    B) alcohol-related accidents.
    C) cancer.
    D) automobile-related accidents.
    Answer: B

Pages: 359
Topic: Alcohol Abuse and Dependence: The Clinical Picture
Skill: Factual   *Other1: In Student Study Guide*

11. A person is considered intoxicated when the alcohol content of the bloodstream reaches _____ percent.
    A) 0.1
    B) 0.5
    C) 1.0
    D) 1.5
    Answer: A

Pages: 360
Topic: Alcohol Abuse and Dependence: The Clinical Picture
Skill: Factual   Other1:

12. All of the following are early warning signs of a drinking problem EXCEPT
    A) feeling guilty or embarassed the next day over behavior performed while drinking.
    B) marked increase in the amount of alcohol consumption from one month to the next.
    C) enjoying the taste of a good beer or scotch.
    D) blackouts ("pulling blanks").
    Answer: C

Pages: 361
Topic: Alcohol Abuse and Dependence: The Clinical Picture
Skill: Factual   Other1:

13. Facial and limb irregularity as well as central nervous system dysfunction are symptoms of
    A) cirrhosis.
    B) alcohol dementia disorder.
    C) fetal alcohol syndrome.
    D) alcohol-induced disorder.
    Answer: C

Pages: 360
Topic: Alcohol Abuse and Dependence: The Clinical Picture
Skill: Factual   Other1:

14. Alcohol is especially damaging to the brain and
    A) liver.
    B) spleen.
    C) kidneys.
    D) stomach.
    Answer: A

Pages: 361
Topic: Alcohol Abuse and Dependence: The Clinical Picture
Skill: Applied   Other1:

15. Bertha has been drinking to excess for many years. She is most likely to
    A) be malnourished, unless she has increased her vitamin dosage while she has been drinking.
    B) have liver damage but no brain damage.
    C) be happy-go-lucky, even though she may have experienced some interpersonal and occupational difficulties caused by her drinking.
    D) have a permanent impairment in her body's ability to utilize nutrients.
    Answer: D

Pages: 362
Topic: Alcohol Abuse and Dependence: The Clinical Picture
Skill: Applied   Other1:
16. Joey is an alcoholic. This means that he probably
    A) has organic brain damage even if no extreme organic symptoms are apparent.
    B) can recover from any deficits fairly readily, regardless of his age, as long as stops
       drinking.
    C) does not yet have any deterioration in general health.
    D) would score higher on self-esteem measures than most individuals.
    Answer: A

Pages: 362
Topic: Alcohol Abuse and Dependence: The Clinical Picture
Skill: Applied   Other1:
17. Betty was admitted to the hospital in a state of withdrawal from alcohol. She had been
    drinking excessively for years before trying to stop. She is disoriented and
    hallucinating. She suffers from
    A) alcohol amnestic disorder.
    B) alcohol withdrawal delirium, formerly known as delirium tremens.
    C) Korsakoff's psychosis.
    D) thiamine deficiency disorder.
    Answer: B

Pages: 363
Topic: Alcohol Abuse and Dependence: The Clinical Picture
Skill: Factual   Other1:
18. The central feature of alcohol amnestic disorder is
    A) the presence of hallucinations.
    B) a memory defect for recent events.
    C) acute fear and extreme suggestibility.
    D) a deep sleep, following which the individual has no memory of past events.
    Answer: B

Pages: 363
Topic: Alcohol Abuse and Dependence: The Clinical Picture
Skill: Factual   Other1:
19. Thiamine, or vitamin B, deficiency and other dietary inadequacies are thought to be the
    causes of
    A) withdrawal symptoms after a long period of alcohol abuse.
    B) alcohol withdrawal delirium, formerly known as delirium tremens.
    C) psychotic alcohol disorder.
    D) alcohol amnestic disorder.
    Answer: D

Pages: 363
Topic: Alcohol Abuse and Dependence: Causes
Skill: Conceptual   Other1:

20. Concerning the causes of alcoholism,
    A) most research evidence points to genetic liability as the primary cause of alcohol dependence in men, but not in women.
    B) there is strong evidence that individuals at risk for alcohol dependence inherit a faulty metabolism.
    C) there are probably several different patterns of causes associated with several different types of alcohol dependence.
    D) the causes of alcohol dependence are primarily psychosocial rather than biological in nature.
    Answer: C

Pages: 363
Topic: Alcohol Abuse and Dependence: Causes
Skill: Factual   Other1:

21. Having an alcoholic parent
    A) was found to be true of one-third of alcoholics.
    B) raises the risk of alcoholism in male offspring, but not in females.
    C) does not increase the risk of alcoholism in offspring unless the second parent is also an alcoholic.
    D) doesn't present any appreciable increase in risk for alcoholism in the offspring.
    Answer: A

Pages: 364
Topic: Alcohol Abuse and Dependence: Causes
Skill: Factual   Other1:

22. Men who are judged to be at high risk for developing later alcoholism
    A) tend to be passive, slightly retarded intellectually, with no apparent psychological problems.
    B) have been found to possess an excess number of pleasure centers in the brain.
    C) show different physiological patterns on a variety of measures compared with men in a control group not at risk.
    D) are physiologically identical to men who are not at risk.
    Answer: C

Pages: 366
Topic: Alcohol Abuse and Dependence: Causes
Skill: Conceptual   Other1:
23. With regard to ethnic differences in alcohol metabolism, it appears that
    A) there are no significant differences.
    B) American Indians and Asian Americans have faster metabolism than Europeans.
    C) American Indians and Asian Americans have slower metabolism than Europeans do.
    D) the research concerning alcohol metabolism is inconclusive.
    Answer: D

Pages: 366
Topic: Alcohol Abuse and Dependence: Causes
Skill: Factual   Other1:
24. Poor parenting skills and behavior among alcoholic parents have been associated with which
    of the following in their children?
    A) substance use in adolescence
    B) an increase in physical illness
    C) compulsive overachievement
    D) lowered self-esteem
    Answer: A

Pages: 366
Topic: Alcohol Abuse and Dependence: Causes
Skill: Conceptual   Other1:
25. Emotional immaturity, low frustration tolerance, impulsivity, and feelings of inadequacy
    are characteristics of
    A) siblings of alcoholics.
    B) the prealcoholic personality.
    C) the narcissistic personality.
    D) alcohol toxicity.
    Answer: B

Pages: 366
Topic: Alcohol Abuse and Dependence: Causes
Skill: Factual   Other1:
26. Addictive disorders have been linked most frequently with
    A) schizophrenia and depression.
    B) schizophrenia and antisocial personality.
    C) borderline personality disorder and antisocial personality.
    D) depression and antisocial personality.
    Answer: D

Pages: 367
Topic: Alcohol Abuse and Dependence: Causes
Skill: Applied   Other1:
27. Rosa comes to you for treatment of her alcohol abuse. You suspect that she might have some other Axis I disorder as well. Why is it important for you to evaluate her Axis I status?
    A) Treating another Axis I disorder, when present along with alcohol abuse, usually clears up the excessive drinking as well.
    B) Her genetic liability may be much stronger if the alcohol abuse is the only Axis I disorder.
    C) The co-occurrence of another mental disorder has a very significant, negative effect on likely treatment outcome.
    D) The other disorder should be treated first.
    Answer: C

Pages: 367
Topic: Alcohol Abuse and Dependence: Causes
Skill: Conceptual   Other1:
28. One of the problems with the tension-reduction model of alcoholism is that it
    A) suggests that alcoholism is a disease.
    B) suggests that alcoholism is exclusively genetically determined.
    C) does not explain why some excessive drinkers are able to maintain control over their drinking while others are not.
    D) would suggest that alcoholism is much rarer than it actually is.
    Answer: C

Pages: 367
Topic: Alcohol Abuse and Dependence: Causes
Skill: Factual   Other1:
29. The motivational model of alcohol use
    A) absolves the alcoholic of personal responsibility regarding alcohol usage.
    B) suggests that alcohol use is primarily genetically determined.
    C) suggests that alcohol is consumed because it is reinforcing to the individual.
    D) tends to overlook the effects of alcohol on mood.
    Answer: C

Pages: 367
Topic: Alcohol Abuse and Dependence: Causes
Skill: Factual   Other1:
30. The reciprocal influence model of alcohol use suggests that
    A) expectancies of social benefit can influence adolescents to begin or to continue drinking.
    B) the final common pathway of alcohol use is motivation.
    C) alcoholics are especially intolerant of stress, and thus susceptible to the tension-reducing properties of alcohol.
    D) marital partners may enable one another to continue drinking.
    Answer: A

Pages: 367
Topic: Alcohol Abuse and Dependence: Causes
Skill: Factual   Other1:
31. Excessive drinking often begins during
    A) a period of great success in an individual's life.
    B) old age.
    C) crisis periods in a marriage or other intimate personal relationship.
    D) the transition to middle age.
    Answer: C

Pages: 368
Topic: Alcohol Abuse and Dependence: Causes
Skill: Factual   Other1:
32. Many alcohol treatment programs now include
    A) biofeedback to teach individuals to reduce their alcohol cravings.
    B) financial counseling.
    C) identifying the relationship patterns that may be contributing to a drinking problem.
    D) sexual counseling.
    Answer: C

Pages: 368
Topic: Alcohol Abuse and Dependence: Causes
Skill: Factual   Other1:
33. Excessive use of alcohol is
    A) not tension-reducing, even in the short run.
    B) a major cause of divorce.
    C) usually secondary to a prior depression.
    D) the cause of depression in an alcoholic rather than the result.
    Answer: B

Pages: 368
Topic: Alcohol Abuse and Dependence: Causes
Skill: Conceptual   Other1:
34. The social context of alcohol consumption in this country
    A) is not very conducive to developing a drinking problem.
    B) is very reinforcing of alcohol consumption.
    C) causes the highest rate of alcoholism in the world.
    D) is associated with a lower rate of alcoholism than in countries that are more
       disapproving of alcohol.
    Answer: B

Pages: 368-369
Topic: Alcohol Abuse and Dependence: Causes
Skill: Factual   Other1:
35. An important factor in determining the incidence of alcoholism in a particular society is
    A) the stress level produced by the culture.
    B) whether there are clearcut changes in the seasonal patterns of the weather.
    C) cultural and religious attitudes toward drinking.
    D) A and C
    Answer: D

Pages: 368
Topic: Alcohol Abuse and Dependence: Causes
Skill: Factual   Other1:
36. The incidence of alcoholism is lowest among
    A) religious or cultural groups who prohibit the use of alcohol.
    B) religious or cultural groups who restrict the use of alcohol largely to religious
       rituals.
    C) religious or cultural groups who condone the use of alcohol as a means of reducing
       stress.
    D) A and B
    Answer: D

Pages: 369
Topic: Alcohol Abuse and Dependence: Treatments and Outcomes
Skill: Conceptual   Other1:
37. Denial is a hallmark of
    A) depression.
    B) addiction.
    C) alcoholism, but only among the most severe alcoholics.
    D) alcohol abuse, but not alcohol dependence, because those who are addicted recognize
       that they have an illness.
    Answer: B

Pages: 369
Topic: Alcohol Abuse and Dependence: Treatments and Outcomes
Skill: Factual   Other1:
38. The most effective approach to alcohol treatment appears to be
    A) cognitive-behavioral therapy on an outpatient basis.
    B) alcohol aversion therapy.
    C) a multidisciplinary approach that may also involve intensive treatment in an inpatient setting.
    D) medication with careful monitoring on an outpatient basis.
    Answer: C

Pages: 369
Topic: Alcohol Abuse and Dependence: Treatments and Outcomes
Skill: Applied   Other1:
39. The first stage in the treatment of alcoholism includes
    A) treating physical withdrawal symptoms.
    B) group psychotherapy.
    C) the use of Antabuse.
    D) the administration of antidepressants.
    Answer: A

Pages: 369
Topic: Alcohol Abuse and Dependence: Treatments and Outcomes
Skill: Applied   Other1:
40. Jim, an alcoholic, has entered an alcohol rehabilitation program. In this program, one of the strategies that will be used to help him through detoxification is
    A) Antabuse.
    B) psychodynamic therapy.
    C) an antidepressant.
    D) a tranquilizer.
    Answer: D

Pages: 370-371
Topic: Alcohol Abuse and Dependence: Treatments and Outcomes
Skill: Factual   Other1:
41. The most effective psychological treatment(s) for alcoholism in terms of long-term prognosis
    A) is individual therapy.
    B) is Antabuse.
    C) is motivational therapy.
    D) are group and behavioral therapies.
    Answer: D

Pages: 370
Topic: Alcohol Abuse and Dependence: Treatments and Outcomes
Skill: Conceptual   Other1:
42. When family therapy is used in the treatment of alcoholism, the emphasis is on
    A) the alcoholic individual as a member of a disturbed family.
    B) the psychotic thinking of the alcoholic.
    C) absolving the alcoholic of the responsibility for his or her drinking.
    D) increasing the punitiveness of the family toward the alcoholic.
    Answer: A

Pages: 371
Topic: Alcohol Abuse and Dependence: Treatments and Outcomes
Skill: Conceptual   Other1:
43. Environmental support in the treatment of alcoholism may involve
    A) the administration of minor tranquilizers on a temporary basis.
    B) exposing the alcoholic to environmental stressors that are particularly aversive,
       thereby desensitizing the alcoholic to such situations.
    C) the use of halfway houses, designed to assist them in their return to family and
       community.
    D) helping the alcoholic to learn more effective coping skills.
    Answer: C

Pages: 371
Topic: Alcohol Abuse and Dependence: Treatments and Outcomes
Skill: Factual   Other1:
44. Relapses and continued deterioration after treatment for alcohol abuse are generally
    associated with
    A) a lack of close relationships with family or friends.
    B) the individual not taking medications as prescribed.
    C) low intelligence.
    D) the individual substituting a more serious drug in place of alcohol.
    Answer: A

Pages: 371
Topic: Alcohol Abuse and Dependence: Treatments and Outcomes
Skill: Applied   Other1:
45. Janet participates in a treatment program in which she receives alcohol after an
    intramuscular injection of emetine hydrochloride, which induces nausea and vomiting. This
    is designed to
    A) induce aversive conditioning.
    B) help her gain insight into her drinking behavior.
    C) counteract the effects of Antabuse.
    D) aid in detoxification.
    Answer: A

Pages: 371
Topic: Alcohol Abuse and Dependence: Treatments and Outcomes
Skill: Factual   Other1:
46. A promising treatment for younger drinkers who are at high risk for developing later alcohol dependence is
   A) modeling-based psychotherapy.
   B) individual psychotherapy.
   C) Antabuse.
   D) skills-training, which combines social-learning theory and cognitive-behavioral strategies.
   Answer: D

Pages: 371
Topic: Alcohol Abuse and Dependence: Treatments and Outcomes
Skill: Factual   Other1:
47. Compared to a goal of total abstinence, programs which aim at self-controlled drinking for alcoholics
   A) are more successful in preventing relapse.
   B) are highly successful with individuals who have been drinking heavily from an early age, rather than with later-onset alcoholics.
   C) have been moderately successful for women, but not for men.
   D) have been consistently successful with about 15 percent of the alcoholics in any given program.
   Answer: D

Pages: 372
Topic: Alcohol Abuse and Dependence: Treatments and Outcomes
Skill: Factual   Other1:
48. Although Alcoholics Anonymous does not participate in external comparative treatment outcome studies, one study of this treatment found that
   A) its success is very limited with severe alcoholics.
   B) most people remain in the program and eventually learn to abstain from alcohol.
   C) the quasi-religious nature of the program is especially appealing to alcoholic individuals.
   D) the program is more successful in teaching controlled drinking than in getting individuals to abstain from alcohol altogether.
   Answer: A

Pages: 373
Topic: Alcohol Abuse and Dependence: Treatments and Outcomes
Skill: Factual   Other1:
49. Compared to other treatment programs, Alcoholics Anonymous
    A) is highly successful.
    B) is successful, but only with severe alcoholics who have "hit bottom."
    C) uses primarily psychodynamic interventions, although advocates of AA would disagree.
    D) has a very high drop-out rate.
    Answer: D

Pages: 373
Topic: Alcohol Abuse and Dependence: Treatments and Outcomes
Skill: Factual   Other1:
50. Under the best of circumstances, the success rate for long-term outcome following alcohol treatment is about
    A) 70 to 90 percent.
    B) 40 percent.
    C) 25 percent.
    D) 5 percent.
    Answer: A

Pages: 373
Topic: Alcohol Abuse and Dependence: Treatments and Outcomes
Skill: Factual   Other1:
51. In a long-term follow-up study of treatment for alcoholism using diverse treatment methods,
    A) 90% of the individuals remained abstinent at follow-up.
    B) many of the individuals showed drinking problems at follow-up, although the treatment did work for some individuals.
    C) virtually every individual in the study had relapsed at follow-up.
    D) about half of the individuals had begun to abuse some other substance.
    Answer: B

Pages: 373
Topic: Alcohol Abuse and Dependence: Treatments and Outcomes
Skill: Factual   Other1:
52. An important finding in alcohol treatment is that
    A) inpatient treatment is vastly superior to outpatient treatment.
    B) "check-up" follow-up sessions are very effective in the early stages of therapy.
    C) attempts to detect and treat alcohol problems through the workplace have been counterproductive.
    D) once an individual has achieved abstinence for three months, he or she is likely to remain abstinent at five-year follow-up.
    Answer: B

Pages: 374
Topic: Alcohol Abuse and Dependence: Treatments and Outcomes
Skill: Factual   Other1:
53. The text described a cognitive-behavioral treatment program aimed at relapse prevention in individuals recovering from addictions. This program includes
    A) individual therapy sessions designed to explore early experiences that led to the addiction problem.
    B) training to recognize the little decisions that put an individual into situations where relapse is more likely.
    C) immediate hospitalization upon relapse with an aversive conditioning regimen.
    D) the short-term use of Antabuse.
    Answer: B

Pages: 374
Topic: Alcohol Abuse and Dependence: Treatments and Outcomes
Skill: Applied   Other1:
54. Evan has been treated in an alcohol treatment facility where the primary treatment goal is abstinence. One of the problems he may have is
    A) that this type of treatment has been found to be much more effective for women than for men.
    B) finding any aftercare consistent with this philosophy.
    C) that he may see even a minor transgression of abstinence as having drastic significance.
    D) that this view is not consistent with the philosophy espoused by Alcoholics Anonymous.
    Answer: C

Pages: 374
Topic: Alcohol Abuse and Dependence: Treatments and Outcomes
Skill: Factual   Other1:
55. The abstinence violation effect is
    A) the relapse rate percentage used in treatment outcome studies of addicts.
    B) the effect that physiologically addicting drugs have in making continued abstinence difficult.
    C) the tendency of an abstainer to relapse completely after a minor transgression.
    D) the Alcoholics Anonymous phrase for relapsing.
    Answer: C

Pages: 375
Topic: Drug Abuse and Dependence
Skill: Factual   Other1:
56. Drug abuse and dependence typically begin during
    A) childhood.
    B) adolescence and young adulthood.
    C) middle age.
    D) old age.
    Answer: B

Pages: 375
Topic: Drug Abuse and Dependence
Skill: Factual   Other1:
57. Factors associated with drug abuse and dependence include all of the following EXCEPT
    A) gender.
    B) age.
    C) race and ethnicity.
    D) labor force status.
    Answer: A

Pages: 375
Topic: Drug Abuse and Dependence
Skill: Factual   Other1:
58. The implementation of a drug-screening program in one large setting
    A) resulted in almost half of the employees quitting.
    B) apparently served as a deterrent for drug users applying for employment.
    C) found the greatest incidence of drug use among white-collar workers.
    D) found an association between drug use and job performance.
    Answer: B

Pages: 375
Topic: Drug Abuse and Dependence: Opium and Its Derivatives (Narcotics)
Skill: Factual   Other1:
59. One of the oldest psychoactive drugs used for medicinal purposes in ancient history is
    A) heroin.
    B) morphine.
    C) opium.
    D) methadone.
    Answer: C

Pages: 376
Topic: Drug Abuse and Dependence: Opium and Its Derivatives (Narcotics)
Skill: Factual   Other1:

60. Opium derivatives include all BUT which of the following?
    A) codeine
    B) heroin
    C) cocaine
    D) morphine
    Answer: C

Pages: 376
Topic: Drug Abuse and Dependence: Opium and Its Derivatives (Narcotics)
Skill: Factual   Other1:

61. Compared with morphine, heroin
    A) is less addictive.
    B) acts more rapidly and more intensely.
    C) is more often found in current medical settings.
    D) is rarely abused.
    Answer: B

Pages: 378
Topic: Drug Abuse and Dependence: Opium and Its Derivatives (Narcotics)
Skill: Factual   Other1:

62. Opium derivatives are physiologically addicting. Thus, they are associated with
    A) withdrawal symptoms.
    B) tolerance requiring increasing doses to obtain the same effect.
    C) decreasing pleasure from the drug despite increasingly higher doses.
    D) A and B
    Answer: D

Pages: 379
Topic: Drug Abuse and Dependence: Opium and Its Derivatives (Narcotics)
Skill: Applied   Other1:

63. Tammy, a heroin addict, went through withdrawal two weeks ago. She is about to relapse.
    Which of the following statements is true about her?
    A) She is in danger of overdosing if she takes as big a dose of heroin as she had been
       taking, since her tolerance level has decreased.
    B) The heroin will have little or no effect on her the first time or two that she ingests
       it.
    C) She will be protected from overdose if she has begun an adequate diet.
    D) She is still in the middle stage of withdrawal.
    Answer: A

Pages: 378
Topic: Drug Abuse and Dependence: Opium and Its Derivatives (Narcotics)
Skill: Factual   Other1:
64. An individual who is addicted to heroin usually will experience withdrawal symptoms after about _____ without the drug.
    A) three days
    B) a week
    C) one hour
    D) eight hours
    Answer: D

Pages: 378
Topic: Drug Abuse and Dependence: Opium and Its Derivatives (Narcotics)
Skill: Factual   Other1:
65. Withdrawal from heroin
    A) is always a very painful and sometimes a dangerous process.
    B) is not always dangerous or even very painful.
    C) lasts about a month.
    D) is often fatal.
    Answer: B

Pages: 379
Topic: Drug Abuse and Dependence: Opium and Its Derivatives (Narcotics)
Skill: Factual   Other1:
66. The most frequently cited reason given by addicts for beginning to use heroin is
    A) pleasure.
    B) being forced to use it.
    C) being tricked into it.
    D) having first been treated with morphine for a prior ailment by a legitimate physician.
    Answer: A

Pages: 379
Topic: Drug Abuse and Dependence: Opium and Its Derivatives (Narcotics)
Skill: Factual   Other1:
67. The most important factors involved in the development of psychoactive drug addiction include all of the following EXCEPT
    A) genetic inheritance.
    B) learning factors such as modeling.
    C) the overproduction of natural endorphins.
    D) the mesocorticolimbic dopamine pathway (MCLP).
    Answer: C

Pages: 379
Topic: Drug Abuse and Dependence: Opium and Its Derivatives (Narcotics)
Skill: Factual   Other1:
68. There is a high incidence of _____ among heroin addicts.
   A) schizophrenia
   B) psychosis
   C) people in the health professions
   D) antisocial personality
   Answer: D

Pages: 380
Topic: Drug Abuse and Dependence: Opium and Its Derivatives (Narcotics)
Skill: Factual   Other1:
69. Addicts who were part of the narcotics subculture in several large Texas cities were found to
   A) feel inadequate in the face of the demands of adulthood.
   B) lack good sex-role identification.
   C) be under-educated, unemployed individuals from minority groups.
   D) all of the above
   Answer: D

Pages: 380
Topic: Drug Abuse and Dependence: Opium and Its Derivatives (Narcotics)
Skill: Factual   Other1:
70. Traditional treatment of heroin addiction using counseling and group therapy
   A) has been associated with about a 50% success rate.
   B) has been very unsuccessful.
   C) has been effective in helping an addict readjust to his or her community and return to financial self-sufficiency.
   D) is very successful but few addicts seek treatment.
   Answer: B

Pages: 380
Topic: Drug Abuse and Dependence: Opium and Its Derivatives (Narcotics)
Skill: Factual   Other1:
71. The effectiveness of methadone for heroin addicts is
   A) very poor.
   B) still undetermined.
   C) significantly improved when accompanied by psychosocial support.
   D) not improved with the addition of other interventions.
   Answer: C

Pages: 381
Topic: Drug Abuse and Dependence: Opium and Its Derivatives (Narcotics)
Skill: Factual   Other1:
72. Increased success of methadone treatments in recent years appears to have been due to
    A) the use of additional drugs that reduce the discomfort of withdrawal symptoms.
    B) better quality methadone.
    C) the decreased cost of methadone, which makes it more readily available to the addict.
    D) the increasing cost and unavailability of heroin.
    Answer: A

Pages: 381
Topic: Drug Abuse and Dependence: Cocaine and Amphetamines (Stimulants)
Skill: Factual   Other1:
73. The number of occasional cocaine users is _____, while the number of crack cocaine users
    is _____.
    A) increasing; decreasing
    B) increasing; stabilizing
    C) decreasing; increasing
    D) stabilizing; increasing
    Answer: C

Pages: 381
Topic: Drug Abuse and Dependence: Cocaine and Amphetamines (Stimulants)
Skill: Factual   Other1:
74. Chronic cocaine abuse is associated with
    A) acute toxic psychotic symptoms.
    B) organic amnestic disorder.
    C) permanent and severe neurological impairment.
    D) permanent impotence.
    Answer: A

Pages: 382
Topic: Drug Abuse and Dependence: Cocaine and Amphetamines (Stimulants)
Skill: Conceptual   Other1:
75. The most dangerous drug introduced to date probably is
    A) amphetamines.
    B) crack cocaine.
    C) tranquilizers.
    D) sleeping pills.
    Answer: B

Pages: 383
Topic: Drug Abuse and Dependence: Cocaine and Amphetamines (Stimulants)
Skill: Factual   Other1:
76. Factors associated with poorer outcomes in treating cocaine addiction include
    A) having financial means to continue the habit.
    B) the gender of the addict.
    C) educational level.
    D) concurrent alcoholism or antisocial personality disorder.
    Answer: D

Pages: 384
Topic: Drug Abuse and Dependence: Cocaine and Amphetamines (Stimulants)
Skill: Factual   Other1:
77. Today physicians prescribe amphetamines for all of the following EXCEPT
    A) weight loss.
    B) staying awake, such as to drive or study.
    C) treating narcolepsy.
    D) treating hyperactivity in children.
    Answer: B

Pages: 384
Topic: Drug Abuse and Dependence: Cocaine and Amphetamines (Stimulants)
Skill: Factual   Other1:
78. Chronic amphetamine abuse can lead to
    A) permanent depression.
    B) a chronic manic state.
    C) psychosis.
    D) substantial weight gain.
    Answer: C

Pages: 384
Topic: Drug Abuse and Dependence: Cocaine and Amphetamines (Stimulants)
Skill: Factual   Other1:
79. Amphetamines
    A) are psychologically addicting but minimally physiologically addicting.
    B) are psychologically and physiologically addicting.
    C) are very addicting physiologically.
    D) are not usually addicting drugs, psychologically or physiologically.
    Answer: A

Pages: 384
Topic: Drug Abuse and Dependence: Cocaine and Amphetamines (Stimulants)
Skill: Factual   Other1:
80. Withdrawal from amphetamines usually includes
    A) severe physical complications which must be closely supervised medically.
    B) no real physical pain, but depressive symptoms often occur.
    C) physical problems and severe depression that lasts for several months.
    D) psychotic symptoms.
    Answer: B

Pages: 384
Topic: Drug Abuse and Dependence: Barbituates (Sedatives)
Skill: Factual   Other1:
81. Excessive use of barbituates results in all BUT which of the following?
    A) barbituate psychosis
    B) increasing tolerance
    C) physiological dependence
    D) psychological dependence
    Answer: A

Pages: 385
Topic: Drug Abuse and Dependence: Barbituates (Sedatives)
Skill: Factual   Other1:
82. Impaired memory and concentration, sluggishness, lack of motor coordination, and brain damage are side-effects associated with excessive use of
    A) cocaine.
    B) amphetamines.
    C) barbituates.
    D) antidepressants.
    Answer: C

Pages: 385
Topic: Drug Abuse and Dependence: Barbituates (Sedatives)
Skill: Factual   Other1:
83. The most common abusers of barbituates are
    A) adolescents.
    B) college-aged people.
    C) middle-aged and older people.
    D) physicians.
    Answer: C

Pages: 385
Topic: Drug Abuse and Dependence: Barbituates (Sedatives)
Skill: Factual   Other1:
84. Barbituate withdrawal
   A) sometimes leads to an acute psychosis.
   B) is physically painless.
   C) is psychologically uncomfortable, but physical problems are very mild.
   D) involves a brief period of hyperactivity, followed by a return to normalcy.
   Answer: A

Pages: 385
Topic: Drug Abuse and Dependence: LSD and Related Drugs (Hallucinogens)
Skill: Factual   Other1: In Student Study Guide
85. The drug that was once thought to be useful for inducing "model psychoses" is
   A) cocaine.
   B) LSD.
   C) heroin.
   D) marijuana.
   Answer: B

Pages: 386
Topic: Drug Abuse and Dependence: LSD and Related Drugs (Hallucinogens)
Skill: Factual   Other1:
86. A flashback is
   A) a paranoid delusion associated with cocaine-induced toxic psychosis.
   B) a vivid recollection of childhood experiences sometimes reported by people taking cocaine.
   C) a pleasant resurgence of energy a day or two following amphetamine ingestion.
   D) an involuntary recurrence of perceptual distortions or hallucinations weeks or months after taking LSD.
   Answer: D

Pages: 386
Topic: Drug Abuse and Dependence: LSD and Related Drugs (Hallucinogens)
Skill: Factual   Other1:
87. Brief psychotherapy is an effective treatment for
   A) cocaine addiction.
   B) barbituate dependence.
   C) psychological dependence on LSD.
   D) LSD-induced psychosis.
   Answer: C

Pages: 386
Topic: Drug Abuse and Dependence: Marijuana
Skill: Factual   Other1:
88. Marijuana may be classified as a
    A) barbituate.
    B) stimulant.
    C) narcotic.
    D) mild hallucinogen.
    Answer: D

Pages: 387
Topic: Drug Abuse and Dependence: Marijuana
Skill: Factual   Other1:
89. With continued use over the long term, which of the following is associated with lethargy, passivity, and diminished self-control?
    A) amphetamines
    B) LSD
    C) marijuana
    D) caffeine
    Answer: C

Pages: 388
Topic: Drug Abuse and Dependence: Marijuana
Skill: Conceptual   Other1:
90. Marijuana
    A) is physiologically addictive.
    B) dependency responds to psychological treatment methods.
    C) does not lead to psychological dependence, unlike heroin.
    D) dependence has a potentially dangerous withdrawal syndrome.
    Answer: B

Pages: 388
Topic: Drug Abuse and Dependence: Caffeine and Nicotine
Skill: Factual   Other1:
91. Caffeine-induced organic mental disorder
    A) can be fatal.
    B) is a caffeine withdrawal syndrome.
    C) is similar in symptoms to those associated with marijuana withdrawal.
    D) is no longer recognized by the DSM.
    Answer: A

Pages: 388
Topic: Drug Abuse and Dependence: Caffeine and Nicotine
Skill: Factual   Other1:
92. Nicotine-induced organic mental disorder
    A) is a state of acute nicotine poisoning.
    B) results from ceasing or reducing the intake of nicotine-containing substances in people
       who have acquired a physical dependency on them.
    C) results in permanent impairment of brain tissue.
    D) usually lasts about a year.
    Answer: B

Pages: 388
Topic: Drug Abuse and Dependence: Caffeine and Nicotine
Skill: Factual   Other1:
93. Nicotine withdrawal symptoms usually last for
    A) several days to several weeks.
    B) about six months.
    C) about one year.
    D) several years.
    Answer: A

Pages: 389
Topic: Drug Abuse and Dependence: Caffeine and Nicotine
Skill: Factual   Other1:
94. Tobacco dependency
    A) is most effectively treated by short-term use of antianxiety medication.
    B) has a successful treatment rate of about 2 to 5 percent.
    C) has a successful treatment rate of about 20 to 25 percent.
    D) has a successful treatment rate of about 50 to 75 percent.
    Answer: C

Pages: 389
Topic: Other Addictive Disorders: Hyperobesity and Pathological Gambling
Skill: Conceptual   Other1:
95. The authors define hyperobesity as
    A) being 25 pounds or more above desirable body weight.
    B) being 50 pounds or more above desirable body weight.
    C) being 75 pounds or more above desirable weight.
    D) being 100 pounds or more above desirable weight.
    Answer: D

Pages: 389
Topic: Other Addictive Disorders: Hyperobesity and Pathological Gambling
Skill: Factual   Other1:
96. Obesity resulting from habitual overeating is considered to be more like the problems found in
    A) personality disorders.
    B) anxiety disorders.
    C) depression.
    D) dissociative disorders.
    Answer: A

Pages: 389-390
Topic: Other Addictive Disorders: Hyperobesity and Pathological Gambling
Skill: Applied   Other1:
97. Harry and Barry are identical twins who were reared apart. Harry is markedly overweight. What is likely to be true of Barry?
    A) Barry will be most like the adoptive parents who raised him with little resemblance to Harry's weight.
    B) Barry is more likely to be depressed than overweight.
    C) Barry is likely to be overweight also.
    D) It's impossible to predict.
    Answer: C

Pages: 390
Topic: Other Addictive Disorders: Hyperobesity and Pathological Gambling
Skill: Factual   Other1:
98. Adult obesity may be associated with
    A) a reduced number of adipose cells.
    B) carbohydrate withdrawal.
    C) hypersomnia.
    D) overfeeding in infancy and childhood.
    Answer: D

Pages: 390
Topic: Other Addictive Disorders: Hyperobesity and Pathological Gambling
Skill: Factual   Other1:
99. Family eating behavior patterns that place an overemphasis on food are
    A) apparently not involved in producing obesity.
    B) apparently associated with obesity in family members.
    C) only influential in producing obesity if eating is used by the family as a way of alleviating emotional distress.
    D) a risk factor in producing obesity, while genetic liability is not.
    Answer: B

Pages: 390
Topic: Other Addictive Disorders: Hyperobesity and Pathological Gambling
Skill: Factual   Other1:
100. According to the psychodynamic view, obesity is caused by
    A) fixation at the oral stage of development.
    B) a failure to resolve the Oedipal or Electra conflict.
    C) a fixation at the anal stage.
    D) sexual repression.
    Answer: A

Pages: 390
Topic: Other Addictive Disorders: Hyperobesity and Pathological Gambling
Skill: Factual   Other1:
101. Disorders that are often reported by overweight individuals entering weight loss programs
    are
    A) barbituate abuse.
    B) somatoform disorder.
    C) an affective or anxiety disorder.
    D) body dysmorphic disorder.
    Answer: C

Pages: 390
Topic: Other Addictive Disorders: Hyperobesity and Pathological Gambling
Skill: Factual   Other1:
102. Compared with individuals of normal weight, obese individuals
    A) experienced sexual abuse in childhood.
    B) are conditioned to more internal and external cues to eat.
    C) eat fewer calories but still gain weight.
    D) are actually more physically active.
    Answer: B

Pages: 390
Topic: Other Addictive Disorders: Hyperobesity and Pathological Gambling
Skill: Factual   Other1:
103. Obesity is more common among
    A) children than adults.
    B) lower-class adults and children.
    C) men than women.
    D) younger adults than older adults.
    Answer: B

Pages: 391
Topic: Other Addictive Disorders: Hyperobesity and Pathological Gambling
Skill: Factual   Other1:
104. The most effective weight-loss programs for long-term changes in eating behavior would be likely to
    A) involve the use of amphetamines.
    B) be a medically supervised fasting program.
    C) be a group support program.
    D) be a behavioral management program.
    Answer: D

Pages: 392
Topic: Other Addictive Disorders: Hyperobesity and Pathological Gambling
Skill: Conceptual   Other1:
105. Some suggest that dieting
    A) is the only cure for obesity.
    B) may not be effective in treating hyperobesity.
    C) is effective only if it is rapid and then followed by participation in support groups.
    D) will work in conjunction with medical supervision.
    Answer: B

Pages: 393-394
Topic: Other Addictive Disorders: Hyperobesity and Pathological Gambling
Skill: Applied   Other1:
106. The text presented the case of John, a compulsive gambler. He was typical of such individuals because
    A) his gambling caused harm to his family and work relationships.
    B) he also showed other significant pathology, such as major depression.
    C) he was also using stimulants.
    D) his condition was easily treated once he sought help, although it took many years before he was willing to do so.
    Answer: A

Pages: 394
Topic: Other Addictive Disorders: Hyperobesity and Pathological Gambling
Skill: Factual   Other1:
107. Pathological gambling
    A) has a very high genetic liability.
    B) is not addictive.
    C) seems to be a learned behavior pattern that is highly resistant to extinction.
    D) is primarily found among individuals in the upper class.
    Answer: C

Pages: 394
Topic: Other Addictive Disorders: Hyperobesity and Pathological Gambling
Skill: Factual   Other1:
108. Pathological gamblers tend to be
    A) violent criminals who have spent many years in prison.
    B) low in self-esteem, shy, nervous, and passive except when gambling.
    C) chronically depressed.
    D) immature, rebellious, thrill seeking, and basically psychopathic.
    Answer: D

Pages: 395
Topic: Other Addictive Disorders: Hyperobesity and Pathological Gambling
Skill: Conceptual   Other1:
109. Treatment of pathological gambling
    A) has been extremely effective using aversion therapy.
    B) is most effective when an individual has "hit bottom."
    C) is still a new research area, and there is much to learn about the most effective
       treatments.
    D) has about an 80 percent success rate for individuals in Gamblers Anonymous.
    Answer: C

Pages: 396
Topic: Unresolved Issues on the Genetics of Alcoholism
Skill: Conceptual   Other1:
110. The evidence for a genetic basis for alcoholism is
    A) inconclusive at the present time.
    B) well-established from adoption studies.
    C) clearly nonexistent.
    D) clearly established, but only for genetic transmission in males.
    Answer: A

Short Answer

Write the word or phrase that best completes each statement or answers the question.

Pages: 355-356
Topic: Substance-Related and Other Addictive Disorders
Skill: Conceptual   Other1:
1. What is the difference between psychoactive substance abuse and psychoactive substance
   dependence?
   Answer: Dependence includes more severe forms of psychoactive substance use disorders
           and usually involves a marked physiological need for increasing amounts of a
           substance to achieve the desired effects (tolerance) or withdrawal symptoms when
           the drug is unavailable.

Pages: 356-357
Topic: Alcohol Abuse and Dependence
Skill: Factual   Other1:
2. Briefly identify three problems associated with excessive alcohol consumption.
    Answer: It is the third major cause of death in the United States, and is involved in
             many accidents, violent crimes, and suicides. Organic damage results from
             long-term abuse. Damage to an individual's interpersonal and occupational life
             is often severe. An alcoholic's life span is 12 years shorter than average.

Pages: 366
Topic: Alcohol Abuse and Dependence: The Clinical Picture
Skill: Applied   Other1:
3. Briefly characterize the typical problem drinker.
    Answer: He is male, either black or white, probably unmarried, and is not highly
             educated. He is probably immature, impulsive, thrill-seeking, and doesn't
             experience hangovers.

Pages: 358
Topic: Alcohol Abuse and Dependence
Skill: Factual   Other1:
4. State three of the myths commonly associated with alcoholism.
    Answer: Mixing different types of liquor will make you more intoxicated. Alcohol is a
             stimulant, not truly addictive, less dangerous than marijuana, and helpful for
             sleeping. Coffee, exercise, and cold showers help speed the metabolism of
             alcohol. Impaired judgment does not occur before obvious signs of intoxication.
             Liver damage precedes brain damage. Heroin withdrawal is more dangerous than
             alcohol withdrawal.

Pages: 362-363
Topic: Alcohol Abuse and Dependence: The Clinical Picture
Skill: Factual   Other1:
5. Briefly identify and characterize the two alcoholic psychoses.
    Answer: Alcohol withdrawal delirium (delirium tremens) involves hallucinations,
             delusions, disorientation, acute fear, extreme suggestibility, tremors, and
             other physiological symptoms. Alcohol amnestic disorder (Korsakoff's psychosis)
             involves a memory deficit sometimes accompanied by the falsification of events
             to fill in memory gaps.

Pages: 363-366
Topic: Alcohol Abuse and Dependence: Causes
Skill: Conceptual   Other1:
6. Briefly state three possible biological causes for alcoholism.
    Answer: Genetic liability is possible; the evidence is mixed. Also possible are
             differences in conditioned physiological responses to alcohol, differences in
             other physiological measures, and possibly factors associated with ethnicity
             that involve an abnormal response to alcohol. In addition, alcohol contains
             intrinsic rewarding properties.

Pages: 367
Topic: Alcohol Abuse and Dependence: Causes
Skill: Factual   Other1:
7. What is the reciprocal influence model of alcohol use?
    Answer: This model suggests that cognitive expectations play a large role in the
             initiation and maintenance of alcohol consumption. Adolescents may begin
             drinking as a result of expectations that alcohol will increase their popularity
             and acceptance.

Pages: 368-369
Topic: Alcohol Abuse and Dependence: Causes
Skill: Conceptual   Other1:
8. How do sociocultural factors influence alcohol consumption?
    Answer: The degree of stress in a culture influences alcohol use, as do cultural and
             religious attitudes toward drinking. Also important is the degree to which a
             culture provides substitute means of satisfaction and other means of coping with
             stress.

Pages: 369-372
Topic: Alcohol Abuse and Dependence: Treatments and Outcomes
Skill: Applied   Other1:
9. Ada is an alcoholic who is brought to you for treatment. Briefly describe the treatment
    program you would prescribe for her.
    Answer: The first stage of treatment may include detoxification. Withdrawal symptoms
             may be alleviated with minor tranquilizers. Physical rehabilitation is
             important to restore proper nutrition and diet. Drugs like Antabuse may prevent
             an immediate return to drinking while psychotherapy begins. Group therapy,
             environmental intervention, and family counseling are each important. Aversive
             conditioning or behavioral self-control training might also be used. Continued
             support after treatment is important. Controlled drinking or abstinence may be
             treatment goals.

Pages: 381
Topic: Drug Abuse and Dependence: Opium and Its Derivatives (Narcotics)
Skill: Applied   Other1:

10. For those who cannot abstain from heroin, _____ treatment can enable individuals to function adequately at home and at work without giving up their addiction altogether.
    Answer: methadone or bupenorphine

Pages: 381
Topic: Drug Abuse and Dependence: Cocaine and Amphetamines (Stimulants)
Skill: Conceptual   Other1:

11. Chronic cocaine abuse may result in _____.
    Answer: acute toxic psychotic symptoms. It is also associated with depression, criminal activity, sexual dysfuntion, neurological impairment, and fatality.

Pages: 384
Topic: Drug Abuse and Dependence: Cocaine and Amphetamines (Stimulants)
Skill: Factual   Other1:

12. Briefly characterize amphetamine withdrawal.
    Answer: Amphetamines are not physiologically addicting, so abrupt withdrawal is generally painless physically. Psychological dependence, however, may result in withdrawal symptoms of depression and fatigue.

Pages: 384-385
Topic: Drug Abuse and Dependence: Barbituates (Sedatives)
Skill: Factual   Other1:

13. What are some of the problems associated with barbituate abuse?
    Answer: It can lead to increased tolerance, psychological and physiological dependence. Side effects include sluggishness, impaired memory and concentration, lack of motor coordination, depression, and mood shifts. Prolonged excessive use is associated with brain damage and personality deterioration.

Pages: 386
Topic: Drug Abuse and Dependence: LSD and Related Drugs (Hallucinogens)
Skill: Factual   Other1:

14. An involuntary recurrence of hallucinations following the use of LSD is called a _____.
    Answer: flashback

Pages: 387
Topic: Drug Abuse and Dependence: Marijuana
Skill: Applied   Other1:

15. Kay has just smoked some marijuana. Describe what she is probably experiencing.
    Answer: Her high is likely to be characterized by mild euphoria, relaxation, intensified sensory experience, a distorted sense of time, hunger, and possibly mild hallucinations and delusions. Pupils contract and eyes become bloodshot. She may be processing information more slowly than usual.

10 - Substance-Related and Other Addictive Disorders   page 398

Pages: 388
Topic: Drug Abuse and Dependence: Caffeine and Nicotine
Skill: Factual   Other1:
16. Other than alcohol, the most lethal legal substance associated with addiction probably is

_____.

Answer: nicotine

Pages: 389
Topic: Drug Abuse and Dependence: Caffeine and Nicotine
Skill: Factual   Other1:
17. The average success rate for quit-smoking programs is about _____.
Answer: 20 to 25 percent.

Pages: 389-391
Topic: Other Addictive Disorders: Hyperobesity and Pathological Gambling
Skill: Conceptual   Other1:
18. List three causal factors that have been associated with obesity.
Answer: These include genetic inheritance, overfeeding in infancy or childhood (which may be associated with a greater number of adipose cells), and early familial factors such as an overemphasis on food or using food to alleviate distress. A few cases are due to hormonal or metabolic dysfunction. Obese individuals may condition more readily to a greater variety of internal and external cues. It is also associated with lower socioeconomic class.

Pages: 392
Topic: Other Addictive Disorders: Hyperobesity and Pathological Gambling
Skill: Factual   Other1:
19. Briefly describe what is meant by establishing a "reasonable weight" as a treatment goal for an obese person.
Answer: The treatment goal involves helping a person reduce weight to a level which may be above the person's ideal, but which may be much easier to maintain.

Pages: 394
Topic: Other Addictive Disorders: Hyperobesity and Pathological Gambling
Skill: Conceptual   Other1:
20. Briefly characterize the personality of the typical compulsive gambler.
Answer: He or she is immature, rebellious, unconventional, perhaps somewhat psychopathic, unrealistic, sensation seeking, and makes extensive use of rationalizations. They are probably experiencing difficulty at home and at work. They have a strong need for adulation and recognition. Certain ethnic groups are at higher risk.

Essay

Write your answer in the space provided or on a separate sheet of paper.

Pages: 355-356
Topic: Substance-Related and Other Addictive Disorders
Skill: Factual   Other1:

1. How does the DSM-IV characterize psychoactive substance abuse and psychoactive substance-induced organic mental disorders?
   Answer: Disorders of abuse are characterized by regular and consistent use of a psychoactive substance. This category includes psychoactive substance abuse disorders, involving pathological use of a substance resulting in potentially hazardous behavior, or in continued use despite a persistent social, psychological, occupational, or health problem. Psychoactive substance dependence disorders, the other category, involves physiological dependence, which includes tolerance, withdrawal, or both. Organic mental disorders involve organic impairment from substance use.

Pages: 357-363
Topic: Alcohol Abuse and Dependence: The Clinical Picture
Skill: Factual   Other1:

2. As you have probably observed many times, alcohol is commonly used among college students. How does alcohol affect the body physiologically?
   Answer: It is a depressant that affects the higher brain centers, impairs judgment, and lowers self-control. Some loss of motor coordination is apparent. At high levels, the person may pass out or experience blackouts. It often increases sexual stimulation but lowers sexual performance. When large amounts of alcohol are ingested, the liver may be seriously overworked and eventually may suffer irreversible damage. Over time, an excessive drinker has a 1-in-10 chance of developing cirrhosis of the liver.

Pages: 360-363
Topic: Alcohol Abuse and Dependence: The Clinical Picture
Skill: Applied   Other1:

3. Jennifer is an alcoholic. She exhibits alcohol dependence. What are her likely symptoms, including psychotic reactions?
   Answer: She experiences tolerance and withdrawal. She may experience tremors, loss of control, blackouts, liver and brain damage. Her body is probably malnourished and unable to process nutrients properly. She may have alcohol withdrawal delirium upon withdrawal, or alcohol amnestic disorder, characterized by serious memory problems, falsification of events, and disorientation.

Pages: 363-368
Topic: Alcohol Abuse and Dependence: Causes
Skill: Conceptual   Other1:

4. Other than a genetic liability, what are the biological and psychosocial factors associated with alcoholism?

    Answer: Differences in brain EEG patterns and stress-response dampening with alcohol ingestion are associated with alcoholics and prealcoholics, as is a larger conditioned response to alcohol cues. Depression and antisocial personality disorder are most frequently linked to addictive disorders. Alcohol may be associated with an increased need for tension reduction. It is also associated with early family experience, including having an alcoholic parent, little supervision, greater stress, negative affect, and current marital difficulty. Expectancies of social benefit from drinking is important.

Pages: 369-372
Topic: Alcohol Abuse and Dependence: Treatments and Outcomes
Skill: Applied   Other1:

5. Jeremy has just entered a treatment program for alcohol dependence. What is he likely to encounter there?

    Answer: Biological approaches may include detoxification, adjunct use of minor tranquilizers to alleviate withdrawal symptoms, and Antabuse to encourage short-term abstinence, along with physical rehabilitation. Psychosocial interventions may include group therapy, family counseling, environmental interventions, behavioral therapy like aversive conditioning or self-control training, relapse-prevention cognitive-behavioral therapy, and participation in Alcoholics Anonymous. Continuing support after treatment is important.

Pages: 374
Topic: Alcohol Abuse and Dependence: Treatments and Outcomes
Skill: Conceptual   Other1:

6. Relapse prevention is an enormous problem in successfully treating alcoholism and other addictive disorders. Define this problem and discuss solutions to it.

    Answer: This problem involves maintaining the abstinence or self-control that was the goal of treatment. Many programs have a high success rate upon completion, but at follow-up many individuals have resumed their addictive behavior. Thus, continued support following treatment and preparation for relapse are critical for long-term success. One approach to preparing for relapse behavior is a cognitive-behavioral approach which examines the "mini-decisions" that may appear to be irrelevant to relapse, but put an individual at greater risk, and teaches preparation for the abstinence violation effect.

Pages: 378-379
Topic: Drug Abuse and Dependence: Opium and Its Derivatives (Narcotics)
Skill: Factual   Other1:

7. Describe the short-term and long-term effects of heroin.

    Answer: Opium and its derivatives, morphine, codeine and heroin, are analgesics and very
              addictive physically and psychologically. The immediate effects of heroin
              include a euphoric rush, followed by a five-hour pleasant reverie. Addicts
              begin to crave more of the drug after about eight hours, and mild to painful
              withdrawal symptoms last about a week. Long-term use is associated with marked
              deterioration in personality, health, and general functioning as well as in
              self-esteem and morality. AIDS, hepatitis, and overdose are not uncommon risks.

Pages: 364-365
Topic: Drug Abuse and Dependence: Opium and Its Derivatives (Narcotics)
Skill: Factual   Other1:

8. What do we know about the neurological factors mediating drug addiction?

    Answer: Genetic and constitutional factors may cause differences in individuals'
              physiological susceptibility and sensitivity to the effects of drugs, which may
              involve differences in the mesocorticolimbic dopamine pathway (MCLP). The MCLP
              is activated by psychoactive drugs, producing great pleasure and simultaneously
              reinforcing drug use. The MCLP is involved in emotional control, memory, and
              gratification. Repeated use of the drug causes changes in neurochemical
              structure resulting in behavioral changes, tolerance, and physical addiction.

Pages: 381-384
Topic: Drug Abuse and Dependence: Cocaine and Amphetamines (Stimulants)
Skill: Factual   Other1:

9. What are the effects and side-effects of stimulant drugs?

    Answer: Cocaine is associated with several hours of euphoria, confidence, contentment,
              general arousal, talkativeness, and sexual arousal. Chronic use may be
              associated with sexual dysfunction and acute toxic psychotic symptoms.
              Amphetamines, like cocaine, stimulate the central nervous system, causing
              appetite suppression, alertness, excitement, and a sense of well-being.
              Chronic abuse can result in brain damage and amphetamine psychosis.

Pages: 384-385
Topic: Drug Abuse and Dependence: Barbituates (Sedatives)
Skill: Conceptual   Other1:

10. What are the long-term effects of excessive barbituate use and how is withdrawal dealt with?

Answer: Long-term effects involve marked physical and psychological addiction, brain damage, personality deterioration, and impairment in memory and concentration. Withdrawal is potentially extremely dangerous and sometimes fatal. It includes anxiety, tremors, insomnia, nausea, elevated heart rate and blood pressure, weight loss, and an acute delirious psychosis. Very gradual withdrawal under medical supervision is necessary to avoid serious complications.

Pages: 385-388
Topic: Drug Abuse and Dependence: LSD and Related Drugs (Hallucinogens)
Skill: Conceptual   Other1:

11. How are marijuana and LSD similar and how do they differ?

Answer: Both are hallucinogens. Marijuana is a mild one, but LSD is potentially very powerful. Marijuana use is relatively common and is usually smoked. It results in a mild euphoria, pleasant relaxation, increased appetite, impaired short-term memory, and somewhat intensified sensory experience with occasional hallucinations. LSD differs in that it usually causes more marked perceptual distortions, mood swings, depersonalization, and flashbacks. Neither drug is physically addictive. Both can be psychologically addictive. LSD can cause acute psychosis.

Pages: 373-389
Topic: Substance-Related and Other Addictive Disorders
Skill: Conceptual   Other1:

12. Evaluate the effectiveness of psychosocial treatments for substance dependence.

Answer: Relapse is a major problem with any type of treatment of any addiction; follow-up support is critical. Prognosis is poor with greater severity of addiction and when other diagnoses co-occur. Individual psychotherapy isn't very effective with any of the addictions. Behavioral treatments have been modestly successful for alcoholism in conjunction with group and environmental interventions, but not for opiate addiction. Psychological treatment of cocaine abuse is modestly successful but dropout rates are high. Relapse prevention and support groups have been effective with marijuana dependence.

Pages: 389-391
Topic: Other Addictive Disorders: Hyperobesity and Pathological Gambling
Skill: Conceptual   Other1:

13. What are some of the causal factors associated with hyperobesity?

    Answer: Biological factors include genetic liability, advancing age and reduced physical activity, and a greater number of adipose cells, which may be due to overfeeding in infancy or childhood. Psychosocial factors include early familial overemphasis on food, use of food to alleviate emotional distress, and heightened susceptibility to acquiring conditioned responses to internal and external food cues. Obesity is also associated with lower socioeconomic status.

Pages: 393-395
Topic: Other Addictive Disorders: Hyperobesity and Pathological Gambling
Skill: Applied   Other1:

14. Geordi is a pathological gambler. If he is typical of such individuals, what is he like? What are some of the factors that encouraged him to engage in this behavior?

    Answer: He is likely to be rebellious, unconventional, immature, have a strong need for recognition and adulation, is sensation seeking and unrealistic. He probably won a substantial sum of money the first time he gambled and thereafter was susceptible to the intermittent reinforcement winning provides. He may be psychopathic. He probably has a chaotic marriage and work problems, and may have a jail record for gambling-related crime. He also may be a member of an ethnic group, such as Southeast Asian refugees from Laos, in which pathological gambling is prevalent.

Pages: 396
Topic: Unresolved Issues on the Genetics of Alcoholism
Skill: Conceptual   Other1:

15. What is the evidence for and against a genetic vulnerability factor for alcoholism? What can you conclude based on the evidence?

    Answer: Evidence comes from family history (pedigree) studies, adoption studies, twin studies, studies of individuals hypothesized to be at risk for alcoholism, and studies of ethnic differences associated with differences in the incidence of alcoholism. However, not all adoption and high-risk studies have substantiated the genetic hypothesis. Thus, the evidence remains ambiguous until further research clarifies the issue.

CHAPTER 11 Sexual Variants, Abuse, and Dysfunctions

Multiple-Choice

Choose the one alternative that best completes the statement or answers the question.

Pages: 400
Topic: Sexual Variants, Abuse, and Dysfunctions
Skill: Factual   Other1:
1. Premature ejaculation is an example of a
    A) transsexual dysfunction.
    B) paraphilia.
    C) sexual dysfunction.
    D) pedophiliac dysfunction.
    Answer: C

Pages: 400
Topic: Sexual Variants, Abuse, and Dysfunctions
Skill: Factual   Other1:
2. Research about sexuality is
    A) one of the earliest areas of research in psychology.
    B) almost non-existent.
    C) surprisingly limited due to taboos and political controversies surrounding sexual
       topics.
    D) abundant, although it is plagued by methodological problems.
    Answer: C

Pages: 401
Topic: Sociocultural/Sexual Practice/Standards: Degeneracy/Abstinence Theory
Skill: Factual   Other1:
3. The belief that masturbation and non-procreative sex are harmful because they waste semen
    is derived from
    A) onanistic insanity theory.
    B) degeneracy theory.
    C) psychoanalytic theory.
    D) neurasthenia.
    Answer: B

Pages: 401
Topic: Sociocultural/Sexual Practice/Standards: Degeneracy/Abstinence Theory
Skill: Factual   Other1:
4. Reverend Sylvester Graham was an early crusader for public health in the 1800's. He
advocated a healthy diet, physical fitness, and
A) sexual abstinence.
B) sexual moderation.
C) sexual tolerance.
D) none of the above
Answer: A

Pages: 402
Topic: Sociocultural/Sexual Practice/Standards: Degeneracy/Abstinence Theory
Skill: Conceptual   Other1:
5. The idea that masturbation and sex can cause serious physical and psychological damage has
been highly influential in _____ society.
A) New Guinean
B) Western
C) Melanesian
D) Sambian
Answer: B

Pages: 402
Topic: Sociocultural/Sexual Practices/Standards: Ritualized Homosexuality
Skill: Conceptual   Other1:
6. Societies differ markedly in their views of what is sexually normal and appropriate. This
is reflected in the very different methods that Victorian-era Americans and Sambians of
New Guinea found to handle problems stemming from the belief, common to both societies,
that _____ is necessary for physical and psychological well-being.
A) physical fitness
B) sexual abstinence
C) homosexual inhibition
D) semen conservation
Answer: D

Pages: 402
Topic: Sociocultural/Sexual Practices/Standards: Ritualized Homosexuality
Skill: Factual   Other1:

7. A striking example of cultural influences on sexual attitudes and behavior is found in the practice of _____ among Sambian individuals of Papua, New Guinea, a practice that would be considered unacceptable by many contemporary Americans.
    A) ritualized homosexuality in adolescent males
    B) ritualized homosexuality in adolescent females
    C) circumcision ceremonies for adolescent males
    D) an automatic death penalty for extramarital sex
    Answer: A

Pages: 403
Topic: Sociocultural/Sexual Practices/Standards: Homosexuality/Psychiatry
Skill: Applied   Other1:

8. Gary is gay. If he had lived in America during the first half of this century, he would most likely have been regarded as
    A) a criminal.
    B) mentally ill.
    C) mentally retarded.
    D) either A or B
    Answer: D

Pages: 403
Topic: Sociocultural/Sexual Practices/Standards: Homosexuality/Psychiatry
Skill: Factual   Other1:

9. The current position of the American Psychiatric Association and the DSM on homosexuality is that
    A) homosexual behavior is immoral but not necessarily psychologically disordered.
    B) whether or not homosexuality should be regarded as normal should be decided upon every five years by a members vote.
    C) homosexuality is not in any sense a mental disorder.
    D) homosexuality is a mental disorder, but should not be treated unless an individual is unhappy with his or her homosexuality.
    Answer: C

Pages: 405
Topic: Sociocultural/Sexual Practices/Standards: Homosexuality/Psychiatry
Skill: Factual   Other1:
10. The rate of adult homosexuality among men is
    A) between two and six percent.
    B) between fifteen and twenty percent.
    C) has decreased substantially since the onset of the AIDS epidemic.
    D) has increased substantially since American culture has become more tolerant of homosexuality.
    Answer: A

Pages: 405
Topic: Sociocultural/Sexual Practices/Standards: Homosexuality/Psychiatry
Skill: Factual   Other1:
11. Prospective and retrospective studies have found that
    A) gay men tend to have had domineering mothers and emotionally distant fathers.
    B) gay men tend to have been molested in childhood by a gay man.
    C) gay adults show more sex-atypical behavior in childhood.
    D) there are no differences in the childhoods of homosexual and heterosexual individuals.
    Answer: C

Pages: 405-406
Topic: Sociocultural/Sexual Practices/Standards: Homosexuality/Psychiatry
Skill: Factual   Other1:
12. All of the following are etiological factors that have been hypothesized to be involved in homosexuality EXCEPT
    A) early hormonal influences more typical of the opposite sex.
    B) structural features in certain areas of the brain that are more characteristic of the opposite sex.
    C) a genetic liability.
    D) genital characteristics that are more similar to the opposite sex.
    Answer: D

Pages: 406
Topic: Sociocultural/Sexual Practices/Standards: Homosexuality/Psychiatry
Skill: Factual   Other1:
13. Most research suggests that
    A) homosexuality is associated with a greater incidence of many different Axis I mental disorders than is heterosexuality.
    B) psychological adjustment is about the same in heterosexual and homosexual individuals.
    C) homosexual individuals are actually better adjusted psychologically than heterosexual individuals.
    D) homosexuals are especially likely to have Axis II mental disorders.
    Answer: B

Pages: 404-406
Topic: Sexual Variants: The Paraphilias
Skill: Factual   Other1:
14. Behavior patterns that require the use of unusual objects, rituals, or situations for full sexual satisfaction are
    A) pedophilias.
    B) paraphilias.
    C) necrophilias.
    D) fetishophilias.
    Answer: B

Pages: 406-407
Topic: Sexual Variants: The Paraphilias
Skill: Factual   Other1:
15. Paraphilias include all of the following EXCEPT
    A) gender dysphoria.
    B) voyeurism.
    C) sexual masochism.
    D) exhibitionism.
    Answer: A

Pages: 407
Topic: Sexual Variants: The Paraphilias
Skill: Applied   Other1:
16. Henry can not achieve sexual fulfillment unless he masturbates using ladies' underclothing that he has stolen from strangers' houses. According to DSM-IV, Henry has
    A) gender dysphoria.
    B) froteurrism.
    C) fetishism.
    D) coprophilia.
    Answer: C

Pages: 407
Topic: Sexual Variants: The Paraphilias
Skill: Factual   Other1:
17. Most theories of fetishism emphasize the importance of
    A) classical conditioning.
    B) operant conditioning.
    C) early sexual trauma or abuse.
    D) an exclusively homosexual orientation.
    Answer: A

Pages: 408
Topic: Sexual Variants: The Paraphilias
Skill: Factual   Other1:
18. Most transvestites
    A) are homosexual.
    B) are genetically female but physically male.
    C) are exclusively heterosexual.
    D) have very high scores on measures of neuroticism and psychoticism.
    Answer: C

Pages: 407-408
Topic: Sexual Variants: The Paraphilias
Skill: Applied   Other1:
19. Floyd dresses in women's clothes in order to achieve sexual arousal. According to the
    DSM-IV, Floyd has
    A) gender dysfunction.
    B) gender dysphoria.
    C) transsexualism.
    D) transvestic fetishism.
    Answer: D

Pages: 408
Topic: Sexual Variants: The Paraphilias
Skill: Factual   Other1:
20. When they are cross-dressed, individuals with transvestic fetishism
    A) tend to pursue homosexual encounters, even if they are predominantly heterosexual in
       orientation.
    B) show a decrease in anxiety and shyness.
    C) show a reduction in sexual arousal.
    D) believe that they have special powers, such as the ability to read others' minds and to
       foretell the future.
    Answer: B

Pages: 408-409
Topic: Sexual Variants: The Paraphilias
Skill: Applied   Other1:
21. The text presented the case of Mr. A., who enjoyed dressing up in women's clothing. He is
    typical of such individuals because
    A) he was married with children.
    B) he had a variety of other paraphilias.
    C) he was sexually abused in childhood.
    D) he was gay.
    Answer: A

Pages: 409-410
Topic: Sexual Variants: The Paraphilias
Skill: Factual   Other1:
22. A "Peeping Tom" is most likely to be
   A) an older man whose wife will no longer satisfy his sexual needs.
   B) a young man who has sadistic tendencies.
   C) a man with antisocial personality disorder.
   D) a young man who feels sexually inadequate.
   Answer: D

Pages: 410
Topic: Sexual Variants: The Paraphilias
Skill: Factual   Other1:
23. A voyeur
   A) is very rarely married.
   B) ordinarily does not engage in serious criminal activity.
   C) seeks sexual encounters with those he observes.
   D) is typically well-adjusted sexually in his other sexual activities.
   Answer: B

Pages: 410-411
Topic: Sexual Variants: The Paraphilias
Skill: Factual   Other1:
24. Most exhibitionists
   A) are not assaultive.
   B) are homosexual males.
   C) eventually proceed to commit more serious sexual crimes like rape.
   D) stalk their victims for months before exposing themselves.
   Answer: A

Pages: 411
Topic: Sexual Variants: The Paraphilias
Skill: Factual   Other1:
25. The most common sexual offense reported to police in North America and Europe, though not in most other countries, is
   A) voyeurism.
   B) exhibitionism.
   C) sadism.
   D) rape.
   Answer: B

Pages: 411
Topic: Sexual Variants: The Paraphilias
Skill: Conceptual   Other1:
26. Mild degrees of sexually sadistic behavior differ from sadism as a paraphilia in that
    A) sadistic activities are the preferred or exclusive means of sexual gratification in
       paraphilic sadism.
    B) paraphilic sadism involves bondage and "disciplinary" practices like spanking.
    C) paraphilic sadism involves the sadistic use and abuse of children for sexual
       gratification.
    D) paraphilic sadism usually involves severe mutilation of the sexual partner.
    Answer: A

Pages: 411
Topic: Sexual Variants: The Paraphilias
Skill: Factual   Other1:
27. Sadistic activities
    A) are typically carried out by individuals when they are depressed.
    B) sometimes are associated with animals or fetishistic objects.
    C) do not result in sexual gratification unless they involve sexual intercourse.
    D) always result in severe mutilation.
    Answer: B

Pages: 412
Topic: Sexual Variants: The Paraphilias
Skill: Factual   Other1:
28. Sexual masochism involves
    A) inflicting pain on others.
    B) preferring children as the sex object.
    C) receiving sexual gratification through inanimate objects.
    D) achieving sexual pleasure by having pain inflicted on the self.
    Answer: D

Pages: 412
Topic: Sexual Variants: The Paraphilias
Skill: Factual   Other1:
29. Autoerotic asphyxia is a dangerous form of
    A) sadism.
    B) masochism.
    C) fetishism.
    D) fixated pedophilia.
    Answer: B

Pages: 413
Topic: Sexual Variants: Causal Factors for Paraphilias
Skill: Factual   Other1:
30. Individuals with paraphilias
    A) are almost always female.
    B) are almost always from emotionally cold families.
    C) usually have more than one paraphilia.
    D) usually also have an antisocial personality disorder.
    Answer: C

Pages: 414
Topic: Sexual Variants: Causal Factors for Paraphilias
Skill: Factual   Other1:
31. Some research indicates that male vulnerability to sexual paraphilias may be linked to
    A) higher than average levels of testosterone.
    B) lower than average levels of testosterone.
    C) a greater dependency on visual sexual stimuli.
    D) males' reduced sensitivity to external sources of sexual stimulation.
    Answer: C

Pages: 414
Topic: Sexual Variants: Causal Factors for Paraphilias
Skill: Factual   Other1:
32. Errors in erotic target location may explain some cases of
    A) transvestism.
    B) masochism.
    C) homosexuality.
    D) gender identity disorder.
    Answer: A

Pages: 414
Topic: Sexual Variants: Gender Identity Disorders
Skill: Factual   Other1:
33. Gender _____ refers to one's sense of maleness or femaleness.
    A) identity
    B) role
    C) dysphoria
    D) preference
    Answer: A

Pages: 414
Topic: Sexual Variants: Gender Identity Disorders
Skill: Applied   Other1:
34. Wendy has always wanted to be a boy. She enjoys dressing in boys' clothing and feels uncomfortable participating in traditionally female activities. According to DSM-IV, Wendy probably has
    A) gender role disorder.
    B) gender identity disorder.
    C) transvestic fetishism.
    D) a paraphilia.
    Answer: B

Pages: 414
Topic: Sexual Variants: Gender Identity Disorders
Skill: Factual   Other1:
35. According to DSM-IV, the two components of gender identity disorder are cross-gender identification and ____.
    A) transvestic fetishism
    B) a history of childhood gender identity disorder
    C) gender role disorder
    D) gender dysphoria
    Answer: D

Pages: 414
Topic: Sexual Variants: Gender Identity Disorders
Skill: Factual   Other1:
36. Boys who express a strong desire to be a girl, show a marked preference for girls' activities, and a reluctance to engage in boys' rough play are most likely to suffer from
    A) transvestism.
    B) transsexualism.
    C) gender identity disorder of childhood.
    D) gender role dysfunction.
    Answer: C

Pages: 414
Topic: Sexual Variants: Gender Identity Disorders
Skill: Applied   Other1:
37. Andy is a boy who has been diagnosed with gender identity disorder. He is most likely to grow up to be
    A) a transsexual.
    B) a transvestic fetishist.
    C) a pedophile.
    D) a homosexual.
    Answer: D

Pages: 414
Topic: Sexual Variants: Gender Identity Disorders
Skill: Conceptual   Other1:
38. Boys outnumber girls by five to one in clinic-referred gender identity disorder. One reason for this may be that
    A) more boys than girls are sexually abused, which is a common cause of gender identity disorder.
    B) parents and peers tolerate tomboyish behavior in girls more than they do feminine behavior in boys.
    C) the traditional masculine role in society is more difficult to learn and adapt to than is the traditional feminine role.
    D) abnormal testosterone levels are associated with most cases of gender identity disorder.
    Answer: B

Pages: 415
Topic: Sexual Variants: Gender Identity Disorders
Skill: Conceptual   Other1:
39. The diagnostic status of gender identity of childhood is controversial because
    A) such children are usually unhappy primarily because society does not tolerate cross-gender behavior.
    B) some research suggests that cross-gender behavior is a very typical and normal phase of childhood.
    C) some research suggests that it is a childhood homosexuality disorder.
    D) it can not be treated except by later sex-change surgery.
    Answer: A

Pages: 415
Topic: Sexual Variants: Gender Identity Disorders
Skill: Factual   Other1:
40. Therapy for children with gender identity disorder usually includes all of the following EXCEPT
    A) training in how to reduce their cross-gender behavior.
    B) hormonal supplements to assure normal sexual development at puberty.
    C) the psychodynamic exploration of inner conflicts that may be related to gender dysphoria.
    D) easing strained relationships with parents and peers.
    Answer: B

Pages: 415
Topic: Sexual Variants: Gender Identity Disorders
Skill: Factual   Other1:
41. Adults with gender identity disorder are called
    A) transsexuals.
    B) transvestites.
    C) cross-gender disordered individuals.
    D) autogynephiliacs.
    Answer: A

Pages: 415
Topic: Sexual Variants: Gender Identity Disorders
Skill: Factual   Other1:
42. There appears to be two subtypes of _____, homosexual and nonhomosexual, which have different causes and different developmental courses.
    A) transvestism
    B) transgender disorder
    C) transsexualism
    D) paraphilia
    Answer: C

Pages: 415-416
Topic: Sexual Variants: Gender Identity Disorders
Skill: Factual   Other1:
43. Homosexual transsexuals differ from nonhomosexual transsexuals in all of the following ways EXCEPT that
    A) nonhomosexual transsexuals are almost always biological males.
    B) nonhomosexual transsexuals are not especially feminine in childhood or adulthood.
    C) nonhomosexual transsexualism is usually associated with autogynephilia, a paraphilia characterized by sexual arousal at the thought of being a woman.
    D) nonhomosexual transsexuals do not seek sex change surgery.
    Answer: D

Pages: 415
Topic: Sexual Variants: Gender Identity Disorders
Skill: Applied   Other1:
44. Alan is a homosexual transsexual. This individual is a biological male who feels like a _____ and is attracted to _____.
    A) man; women
    B) woman; men
    C) woman; women
    D) man; men
    Answer: B

Pages: 416
Topic: Sexual Variants: Gender Identity Disorders
Skill: Factual   Other1:
45. Autogynephilia is
    A) the masochistic practice involving self-strangulation during masturbation.
    B) the gender identity disorder in which a man believes that he is really a woman.
    C) a paraphilia in which a man becomes sexually aroused by the thought of being a woman.
    D) the disorder in which a homosexual man dresses like a woman, but does not feel that he
       is a woman.
    Answer: C

Pages: 416
Topic: Sexual Variants: Gender Identity Disorders
Skill: Factual   Other1:
46. The most effective treatment for gender dysphoria in transsexuals is
    A) long-term psychodynamic therapy.
    B) aversion therapy.
    C) surgical sex reassignment.
    D) There is no effective treatment at present.
    Answer: C

Pages: 416
Topic: Sexual Variants: Gender Identity Disorders
Skill: Factual   Other1:
47. An important determinant of satisfactory outcome from sex reassignment surgery appears to
    be
    A) whether the operation involves a male-to-female or a female-to-male change.
    B) whether an individual is a homosexual or nonhomosexual transsexual.
    C) the extent to which an individual was psychologically well adjusted before the surgery.
    D) the length of time that individuals live as the gender they wish to become prior to the
       surgery.
    Answer: C

Pages: 416
Topic: Sexual Abuse: Childhood Sexual Abuse
Skill: Factual   Other1:
48. Of the various forms of sexual abuse, including pedophilia, rape, and incest, only _____
    is/are included in the DSM-IV.
    A) pedophilia
    B) rape
    C) incest
    D) A and C
    Answer: A

Pages: 417
Topic: Sexual Abuse: Childhood Sexual Abuse
Skill: Factual   Other1:
49. The prevalence of childhood sexual abuse is
    A) not as common as once thought, since most accounts were based on repressed memories that turned out to be false.
    B) probably about 10 percent or higher, more common than once thought.
    C) only about 1 or 2 percent, but its long-term consequences are debilitating enough to make this a more serious problem than the low numbers would indicate.
    D) markedly lower in recent years due to media focus on the issue.
    Answer: B

Pages: 417-418
Topic: Sexual Abuse: Childhood Sexual Abuse
Skill: Factual   Other1:
50. Many children who are sexually abused
    A) show a predictable pattern of symptoms known as the "sexual abuse syndrome."
    B) exhibit fears, posttraumatic stress disorder, and poor self-esteem.
    C) show a wide variety of sexual symptoms ranging from sexual withdrawal to promiscuity.
    D) B and C
    Answer: D

Pages: 418
Topic: Sexual Abuse: Childhood Sexual Abuse
Skill: Conceptual   Other1:
51. The long-term consequences of childhood sexual abuse
    A) are almost always associated with borderline personality disorder.
    B) are rarely as serious as the short-term consequences, as individuals tend to heal with time.
    C) are thought to be associated with a wide variety of adult psychopathology, although it is difficult to establish clearcut causal links between early experiences and later behavior.
    D) are completely unknown at present.
    Answer: C

Pages: 419
Topic: Sexual Abuse: Childhood Sexual Abuse
Skill: Conceptual   Other1:

52. The text describes the example of the McMartin Preschool case. This case illustrates
    A) the difficulty that sometimes exists in establishing the truth of children's claims about sexual abuse.
    B) the difficulty of uncovering repressed memories, although such memories can be recovered accurately if enough psychotherapy is conducted.
    C) the importance of using anatomically correct dolls when questioning young children about alleged sexual abuse.
    D) the fact that children never misreport experiences of sexual abuse, especially insofar as such experiences are highly memorable events.
    Answer: A

Pages: 420-421
Topic: Sexual Abuse: Childhood Sexual Abuse
Skill: Factual   Other1:

53. In a series of studies of preschool aged children's memories of events, Ceci has found that
    A) young children tend to be highly accurate when reporting positive events, but tend to be inaccurate when reporting negative events.
    B) young children have difficulty distinguishing between real and imagined events.
    C) young children have difficulty in recalling whether repeatedly imagined events really occurred, but mental health professionals are usually able to tell whether or not the children are accurate in their memories.
    D) the use of anatomically correct dolls in interviews with young children improved the accuracy of the children's reports considerably.
    Answer: B

Pages: 420-421
Topic: Sexual Abuse: Childhood Sexual Abuse
Skill: Factual   Other1:

54. In a series of studies of preschool aged children's memories of events, Ceci has found that
    A) using anatomically correct dolls can dramatically improve the accuracy of young children's reports of what happened during a physical exam.
    B) psychologists and researchers who regularly work with children are unable to distinguish between accurate and inaccurate reports given by young preschoolers.
    C) the more often and extensively that young children are interviewed by professionals about an alleged incident of abuse, the more likely it is that the children's memory of the event will be accurate and reliable.
    D) none of the above
    Answer: B

Pages: 419-422
Topic: Sexual Abuse: Childhood Sexual Abuse
Skill: Conceptual   Other1:
55. One of the most controversial issues in psychology today concerns
    A) whether there are any serious consequences of childhood sexual abuse.
    B) whether there are any serious long-term consequences of rape and molestation in adult
       women.
    C) the validity of recovered (formerly repressed) memories of abuse.
    D) the validity of women's reports of rape.
    Answer: C

Pages: 419
Topic: Sexual Abuse: Childhood Sexual Abuse
Skill: Conceptual   Other1:
56. In the popular book "The Courage to Heal," the authors asserted: "If you are unable to
    remember any specific instances [of sexual abuse]...but still have the feeling that
    something abusive happened to you, it probably did" (p. 21). This advice
    A) is helpful in allowing victims of childhood sexual abuse to accurately recall the
       abuse.
    B) is helpful in allowing people who suspect, but who did not actually experience,
       childhood sexual abuse to accurately recall that no abuse occurred.
    C) is controversial, especially in light of research findings that even normal unrepressed
       memories can be highly inaccurate.
    D) A and B
    Answer: C

Pages: 422
Topic: Sexual Abuse: Pedophilia
Skill: Factual   Other1:
57. Pedophilia is defined by
    A) the age difference between victim and perpetrator.
    B) the bodily maturity of the victim.
    C) the bodily maturity of the perpetrator.
    D) the genders of the victim and perpetrator.
    Answer: B

Pages: 422
Topic: Sexual Abuse: Pedophilia
Skill: Factual   Other1:
58. All of the following statements are true of pedophilia EXCEPT
    A) nearly all pedophiles are male.
    B) a majority of the victims of pedophiles are female.
    C) most pedophiles are exclusively homosexual.
    D) most pedophiles are previously acquainted with the victim.
    Answer: C

Pages: 422
Topic: Sexual Abuse: Pedophilia
Skill: Factual   Other1:
59. The proportion of pedophilic encounters that are homosexual is much greater than the rate of homosexuality in the general population. This is because
    A) many more homosexuals than heterosexuals are pedophiles.
    B) most victims of pedophiles are male, probably because boys are often given greater freedom than girls are, and thus are more easily stalked.
    C) many pedophiles are relatively indifferent to the gender of their victims.
    D) most homosexuals prefer children rather than adults as sexual partners.
    Answer: C

Pages: 422
Topic: Sexual Abuse: Pedophilia
Skill: Factual   Other1:
60. Studies investigating the sexual responses of pedophiles have consistently found that
    A) pedophiles respond to erotic pictures of female children but not to erotic pictures of female adults.
    B) pedophiles respond to erotic pictures of both male and female children, but not to erotic pictures of adults.
    C) pedophiles tend to respond to erotic pictures of adults as well as to erotic pictures of children.
    D) pedophiles respond sexually to visual stimuli whether or not the stimuli are erotic in nature.
    Answer: C

Pages: 422
Topic: Sexual Abuse: Pedophilia
Skill: Factual   Other1:
61. _____ often desire mastery or dominance over their partners, and believe that their partners will benefit from sexual contact.
    A) Pedophiles
    B) Masochists
    C) Fetishists
    D) Voyeurs
    Answer: A

Pages: 422-423
Topic: Sexual Abuse: Pedophilia
Skill: Applied   Other1:

62. Patrick is a married man who molests children, but only when he is under great stress. He is known as a
    A) fixated pedophile.
    B) fixated exhibitionist.
    C) regressed pedophile.
    D) situational pedophile.
    Answer: C

Pages: 423
Topic: Sexual Abuse: Incest
Skill: Factual   Other1:

63. One reason that most people avoid sexual relations between close relatives may be that
    A) it is harder to get along with a family member than with a stranger.
    B) few people remain together long enough in a family structure to become sexually interested in one another before leaving the family.
    C) sexual interest is low toward those people to whom one is continuously exposed to from an early age.
    D) the nuclear family today fluctuates in composition so much so that there is little opportunity for attractions between relatives to develop into actual sexual activity.
    Answer: C

Pages: 423
Topic: Sexual Abuse: Incest
Skill: Factual   Other1:

64. Biologically unrelated children who were reared together in Israeli kibbutzim
    A) rarely married or had sexual relationships with one another in adulthood.
    B) tended to intermarry in adulthood.
    C) often had sexual relationships with one another in adolescence, but tended to marry individuals from outside their kibbutzim.
    D) were unable to form healthy sexual attachments with anyone outside their kibbutzim.
    Answer: A

Pages: 424
Topic: Sexual Abuse: Incest
Skill: Factual   Other1:

65. _____ incest is by far the most common kind of incest.
    A) Father-daughter
    B) Mother-son
    C) Brother-sister
    D) Brother-brother
    Answer: C

Pages: 424
Topic: Sexual Abuse: Incest
Skill: Factual   Other1:
66. Which of the following is at especially high risk for incest?
    A) a son
    B) a daughter
    C) a stepdaughter
    D) a stepson
    Answer: C

Pages: 424
Topic: Sexual Abuse: Incest
Skill: Applied   Other1:
67. Bart has had an incestuous relationship with his daughter. He is most likely to be
    A) a latent homosexual.
    B) shy, conventional, and overprotective of his daughter.
    C) happily married with a normal marital sexual relationship.
    D) a pedophile.
    Answer: B

Pages: 424
Topic: Sexual Abuse: Incest
Skill: Factual   Other1:
68. In families where incest between father and children or stepchildren occurs, the mother (assuming she knows)
    A) usually will take the children and leave her husband if she finds out about the incest.
    B) usually will protect her child from further incestuous relations, but rarely will leave her husband.
    C) often will not help or protect her child.
    D) none of the above
    Answer: C

Pages: 425
Topic: Sexual Abuse: Rape
Skill: Factual   Other1:
69. The prevalence of rape
    A) varies a great deal depending upon its definition.
    B) is lower now than in previous years.
    C) has consistently been shown to be one in every ten women.
    D) has not been studied sufficiently to make any estimates.
    Answer: A

Pages: 426
Topic: Sexual Abuse: Rape
Skill: Conceptual   Other1:
70. Rape is a crime that is probably motivated by
    A) unresolved Oedipal conflicts associated with women.
    B) aggression.
    C) either lust or aggression.
    D) lust.
    Answer: C

Pages: 426
Topic: Sexual Abuse: Rape
Skill: Factual   Other1:
71. The majority of rape victims are
    A) girls under fifteen.
    B) women in their teens and early twenties.
    C) women in their thirties and forties.
    D) elderly women, because they are the most vulnerable.
    Answer: B

Pages: 426
Topic: Sexual Abuse: Rape
Skill: Factual   Other1:
72. Rapists report that sexual motivation is
    A) not an important cause of their behavior.
    B) a very important cause of their behavior.
    C) secondary to the desire to humiliate and dominate a woman.
    D) not at all involved in causing their behavior.
    Answer: B

Pages: 426
Topic: Sexual Abuse: Rape
Skill: Conceptual   Other1:
73. All of the following facts provide evidence that rape is in part sexually motivated EXCEPT
    A) most rapes are not very aggressive in nature.
    B) at least some rapists share some of the characteristics of paraphiliacs, who are
       strongly sexually motivated.
    C) rapists cite sexual motivation as a very important cause of their behavior.
    D) unlike other violent crimes, most victims of rape are in their teens and early
       twenties.
    Answer: A

Pages: 426
Topic: Sexual Abuse: Rape
Skill: Factual   Other1:
74. Most rapes
    A) are isolated acts by an individual who never commits another rape.
    B) occur at night in a rapist's own neighborhood.
    C) are not planned, but occur impulsively.
    D) involve girls under the age of twelve.
    Answer: B

Pages: 426-427
Topic: Sexual Abuse: Rape
Skill: Conceptual   Other1:
75. "Victim-precipitated" rape is
    A) more common today than in previous decades.
    B) less common today than in previous decades.
    C) often a cause of date-rape.
    D) a myth.
    Answer: D

Pages: 427
Topic: Sexual Abuse: Rape
Skill: Applied   Other1:
76. Ted is a rapist. If he is typical of most convicted rapists, he is
    A) highly educated, handsome, and manipulative.
    B) a young man with little education who is from a lower socioeconomic class.
    C) a middle aged man who is married with children.
    D) a sexual sadist who is aroused by violence rather than by sexual stimuli.
    Answer: B

Pages: 428
Topic: Sexual Abuse: Rape
Skill: Factual   Other1:
77. Many rapists
    A) have other paraphilias such as exhibitionism and voyeurism.
    B) tend to be especially adept at interpreting women's social cues, which aids them in
       exploiting women.
    C) are obviously disturbed and therefore fairly easy to recognize.
    D) commit a rape only once and never commit an act of violence again.
    Answer: A

Pages: 428
Topic: Sexual Abuse: Rape
Skill: Factual   Other1:
78. Most men who are arrested for rape
    A) will not be convicted.
    B) are serial rapists.
    C) will only serve a brief jail sentence if convicted.
    D) all of the above
    Answer: D

Pages: 429
Topic: Sexual Abuse: Treatment and Recidivism of Sex Offenders
Skill: Applied   Other1:
79. Frederick is undergoing therapy for pedophilia. He views a series of slides of naked preschool girls and receives a shock when he becomes sexually aroused by the pictures. This treatment is called
    A) aversion therapy.
    B) distraction therapy.
    C) covert sensitization.
    D) satiation.
    Answer: A

Pages: 429
Topic: Sexual Abuse: Treatment and Recidivism of Sex Offenders
Skill: Factual   Other1:
80. The reduction of deviant sexual arousal
    A) is the most promising treatment for sex offenders.
    B) is probably insufficient without also replacing deviant sexual arousal patterns with more acceptable sexual stimuli.
    C) is only successful in treating young adult males who don't have a long history of sex offenses.
    D) in sex offenders is only possible with surgical or chemical castration.
    Answer: B

Pages: 429
Topic: Sexual Abuse: Treatment and Recidivism of Sex Offenders
Skill: Conceptual   Other1:

81. One of the problems with attempts to modify patterns of sexual arousal in sex offenders is that
    A) sex offenders always lack motivation to participate in treatment.
    B) some sex offenders can fake their phallometric arousal measurements to give the appearance that their sexual arousal patterns have changed when they really haven't.
    C) treatment occurs in laboratory settings and may not generalize to the patient's outside world.
    D) B and C
    Answer: D

Pages: 429-430
Topic: Sexual Abuse: Treatment and Recidivism of Sex Offenders
Skill: Factual   Other1:

82. Research evaluating the long-term treatment outcome of sex offenders suggests that
    A) treatment of any sort is ineffective.
    B) social skills training is the most effective method of treatment, and castration is the least effective treatment.
    C) it is not clear to what extent various treatments will reduce recidivism rates among sex offenders.
    D) aversion therapy has proven most successful in treating sex offenders provided that the degree of aversion that was conditioned was substantial.
    Answer: C

Pages: 430
Topic: Sexual Abuse: Treatment and Recidivism of Sex Offenders
Skill: Factual   Other1:

83. One of the most promising treatments for sex offenders is
    A) surgical or chemical castration, although this approach remains highly controversial.
    B) group therapy.
    C) social skills training.
    D) long-term psychodynamic therapy.
    Answer: A

Pages: 430
Topic: Sexual Abuse: Treatment and Recidivism of Sex Offenders
Skill: Factual   Other1:
84. A major problem with treatment outcome research on sex offenders is that
    A) there is little funding available for such research.
    B) there has been a lack of randomly assigned controls who are equally motivated for
       treatment in available studies.
    C) almost everyone who is treated will go on to commit another sex offense upon release.
    D) none of the above
    Answer: B

Pages: 430
Topic: Sexual Dysfunctions
Skill: Factual   Other1: In Student Study Guide
85. Impairment of either the desire for sexual gratification or of the ability to achieve it
    is termed sexual
    A) dysfunction.
    B) incompetence.
    C) perversion.
    D) variation.
    Answer: A

Pages: 430-431
Topic: Sexual Dysfunctions
Skill: Factual   Other1:
86. The four phases of human sexual response include all of the following EXCEPT
    A) excitement.
    B) resolution.
    C) orgasm.
    D) anticipation.
    Answer: D

Pages: 431-432
Topic: Sexual Dysfunctions: Dysfunctions of Sexual Desire
Skill: Applied   Other1:
87. Frank has no interest in sex, finds it extremely aversive, and avoids all genital sexual
    contact with his wife even though this causes her distress. He is suffering from
    A) male orgasmic disorder.
    B) male erectile disorder.
    C) hyperactive sexual desire disorder.
    D) sexual aversion disorder.
    Answer: D

Pages: 431
Topic: Sexual Dysfunctions: Dysfunctions of Sexual Arousal
Skill: Applied   Other1:
88. Ed would like to have sexual contact with his spouse twice a week, but she prefers to have sex twice a month. This suggests that
   A) she has hypoactive sexual desire disorder.
   B) she has sexual aversion disorder.
   C) sexual frequency preferences vary widely among otherwise normal individuals.
   D) he has hyperactive sexual desire disorder.
   Answer: C

Pages: 432
Topic: Sexual Dysfunctions: Dysfunctions of Sexual Arousal
Skill: Applied   Other1:
89. Last night Barry had difficulty achieving an erection when he was sexually intimate with his partner. It is most likely that Barry
   A) has never been able to sustain an erection during intercourse.
   B) is organically impaired.
   C) is experiencing temporary erectile difficulty.
   D) is over the age of forty.
   Answer: C

Pages: 432
Topic: Sexual Dysfunctions: Dysfunctions of Sexual Arousal
Skill: Conceptual   Other1:
90. Most cases of serious erectile problems
   A) are organic in origin.
   B) are found in men who are confused about their heterosexuality.
   C) may very well involve both organic and psychogenic causes.
   D) begin before the age of sixty.
   Answer: C

Pages: 432
Topic: Sexual Dysfunctions: Dysfunctions of Sexual Arousal
Skill: Factual   Other1:
91. Men who are over the age of seventy
   A) are able to achieve erections with the same frequency as men in their twenties.
   B) are usually unable to achieve an erection.
   C) may have some erectile difficulties, although the majority report that they are still able to have sexual intercourse.
   D) are usually unable to have sexual intercourse, although they enjoy other forms of sexual activity.
   Answer: C

Pages: 432
Topic: Sexual Dysfunctions: Dysfunctions of Sexual Arousal
Skill: Factual   Other1:

92. The proportion of erectile problems that have an organic basis
    A) is about 5 percent.
    B) is about 90 percent among men over the age of fifty.
    C) has probably been underestimated in the past, and may be close to 50 percent.
    D) is about 10 percent among men under the age of eighty.
    Answer: C

Pages: 432
Topic: Sexual Dysfunctions: Dysfunctions of Sexual Arousal
Skill: Conceptual   Other1:

93. Distinguishing between psychogenic and organic causes of erectile insufficiency
    A) is relatively easy in older males but not in younger males.
    B) is relatively easy in younger males but not in older males.
    C) is reliably determined by the nocturnal penile erection procedure.
    D) is difficult because there is no test currently available that provides reliable
       results.
    Answer: D

Pages: 432-433
Topic: Sexual Dysfunctions: Dysfunctions of Sexual Arousal
Skill: Applied   Other1:

94. Edie does not become excited when she is having sex with her partner, which causes her
    great distress. She suffers from
    A) female orgasmic disorder.
    B) female sexual arousal disorder.
    C) vaginismus.
    D) dyspareunia.
    Answer: B

Pages: 433
Topic: Sexual Dysfunctions: Orgasmic Disorders
Skill: Factual   Other1:

95. Premature ejaculation is more often associated with
    A) men over the age of fifty.
    B) younger men.
    C) men involved in adulterous or otherwise illicit sexual relationships, who may harbor
       unconscious guilt about their behavior.
    D) homosexual men.
    Answer: B

Pages: 433
Topic: Sexual Dysfunctions: Orgasmic Disorders
Skill: Factual   Other1:
96. In sexually normal men,
    A) premature ejaculation is most likely in individuals who engage in frequent intercourse.
    B) occasional masturbation makes premature ejaculation more likely.
    C) the ejaculatory reflex is to a considerable extent under voluntary control.
    D) few can tolerate as much as four minutes of stimulation without ejaculation.
    Answer: C

Pages: 433
Topic: Sexual Dysfunctions: Orgasmic Disorders
Skill: Factual   Other1:
97. Male orgasmic disorder
    A) is almost always due to organic impairment.
    B) usually involves retarded ejaculation during intercourse, but not during masturbation.
    C) is almost always associated with a particular partner.
    D) usually involves the complete inability to ejaculate.
    Answer: B

Pages: 433-434
Topic: Sexual Dysfunctions: Orgasmic Disorders
Skill: Applied   Other1:
98. Jan becomes sexually aroused during sexual intercourse with her husband, but she is
    distressed that she is unable to have an orgasm with him. Jan suffers from
    A) dyspareunia.
    B) female sexual arousal disorder.
    C) hypoactive sexual desire disorder.
    D) female orgasmic disorder.
    Answer: D

Pages: 434
Topic: Sexual Dysfunctions: Dysfunctions Involving Sexual Pain
Skill: Factual   Other1:
99. Vaginismus is
    A) painful intercourse.
    B) an involuntary vaginal muscle spasm preventing penetration.
    C) an infection of the vagina that results in painful intercourse.
    D) the psychological fear of sexual intercourse.
    Answer: B

Pages: 434
Topic: Sexual Dysfunctions: Dysfunctions Involving Sexual Pain
Skill: Factual   Other1:
100. The sexual dysfunction that is most likely to have an organic basis is
    A) male erectile disorder.
    B) premature ejaculation.
    C) vaginismus.
    D) dyspareunia.
    Answer: D

Pages: 435
Topic: Sexual Dysfunctions: Causal Factors in Sexual Dysfunctions
Skill: Conceptual   Other1:
101. A common cause of sexual dysfunction is
    A) organic impairment.
    B) aging.
    C) early sexual abuse.
    D) dysfunctional early learning.
    Answer: D

Pages: 435
Topic: Sexual Dysfunctions: Causal Factors in Sexual Dysfunctions
Skill: Factual   Other1:
102. Masters and Johnson suggested that a primary cause of orgasmic dysfunction in females may
    be
    A) early sexual trauma.
    B) early conditioning that a woman's primary sexual responsibility is to satisfy a man.
    C) early learning that sex is for procreation.
    D) early learning that premarital sex is potentially harmful.
    Answer: B

Pages: 435
Topic: Sexual Dysfunctions: Causal Factors in Sexual Dysfunctions
Skill: Conceptual   Other1:
103. For young men, masturbation and sex with prostitutes, which both involve efficient and
    impersonal achievement of orgasm, may lead to _____ in later sexual encounters.
    A) erectile disorder
    B) hypoactive sexual desire disorder
    C) male orgasmic disorder
    D) premature ejaculation
    Answer: D

Pages: 436
Topic: Sexual Dysfunctions: Causal Factors in Sexual Dysfunctions
Skill: Conceptual   Other1:
104. While many researchers have suggested that anxiety plays an important causal role in sexual dysfunctions, more recently there is evidence that _____, rather than anxiety, is responsible for inhibiting sexual arousal.
A) a genetically based organic impairment
B) a history of sexual abuse
C) cognitive distraction
D) fear of contracting AIDS
Answer: C

Pages: 437
Topic: Sexual Dysfunctions: Causal Factors in Sexual Dysfunctions
Skill: Factual   Other1:
105. Many have suggested that changes in women's roles in recent decades have resulted in an increase in the prevalence of male sexual dysfunctions. The research on this hypothesis
A) supports this idea.
B) has not yet yielded sufficient evidence to allow us to either confirm or disconfirm this hypothesis.
C) suggests that changing roles have increased the prevalence of female sexual dysfunctions rather than male sexual dysfunctions.
D) suggests that sexual dysfunctions in men and women have decreased as a result of changing female roles.
Answer: B

Pages: 437
Topic: Sexual Dysfunctions: Treatments and Outcomes
Skill: Factual   Other1:
106. The treatment of sexual dysfunctions
A) has become very successful for most female dysfunctions, but less so for male dysfunctions.
B) has become very successful for male dysfunctions, but less so for female dysfunctions.
C) has shown little progress in the past few decades.
D) has shown remarkable progress in the past few decades.
Answer: D

Pages: 438
Topic: Sexual Dysfunctions: Treatments and Outcomes
Skill: Factual   Other1:

107. In the treatment of sexual dysfunctions, one of the central issues emphasized by Masters and Johnson, as well as by those who have followed in their footsteps, is that
   A) partners of those suffering from a sexual dysfunction need to be understanding and supportive of their partners, but rarely will need any therapeutic treatment themselves.
   B) partners of those suffering from sexual dysfunction should ignore the problem so as not to reinforce it.
   C) partners of those suffering from a sexual dysfunction also are in need of help because sexual dysfunctions are not disorders of individuals but instead are disorders of relationships between individuals.
   D) partners of those suffering from a sexual dysfunction should receive individual psychotherapy from a sex therapist in order to vent their frustrations and get a better understanding of the sexual dysfunction.
   Answer: C

Pages: 439
Topic: Unresolved Issues: Long-Term Consequences of Childhood Sexual Abuse
Skill: Conceptual   Other1:

108. Most studies suggest that
   A) childhood sexual abuse is associated with avoidant personality disorder.
   B) childhood sexual abuse causes borderline personality disorder.
   C) childhood sexual abuse is not causally linked to borderline personality disorder.
   D) childhood sexual abuse is associated with borderline personality disorder, but it is not clear whether this relationship is causal.
   Answer: D

Pages: 439
Topic: Unresolved Issues: Long-Term Consequences of Childhood Sexual Abuse
Skill: Conceptual   Other1:

109. A number of studies have found that individuals who are diagnosed with borderline personality disorder more often report experiencing early sexual abuse than do individuals with other forms of psychopathology. This means that
   A) childhood sexual abuse is one cause of borderline personality disorder.
   B) borderline individuals are able to recall instances of past sexual abuse better than other individuals.
   C) borderline individuals tend to feign a history of childhood sexual abuse to gain attention and sympathy.
   D) no firm conclusion about causation can be made from this finding because a number of other plausible interpretations have not been excluded.
   Answer: D

Pages: 439-440
Topic: Unresolved Issues: Long-Term Consequences of Childhood Sexual Abuse
Skill: Conceptual   Other1:
110. Research concerning the long-term consequences of childhood sexual abuse has suffered from
    A) a lack of theory specifying more precisely the hypothesized causal mechanisms linking childhood sexual abuse to specific disorders.
    B) a reliance on research designs that require retrospective recall of past sexual abuse.
    C) a lack of prospective research which would allow one to examine sexually abused children prior to developing any specific maladaptive behavior.
    D) all of the above
    Answer: D

Short Answer

Write the word or phrase that best completes each statement or answers the question.

Pages: 400-404
Topic: Sociocultural Influences on Sexual Practices and Standards
Skill: Conceptual   Other1:
1. Perhaps nowhere are sociocultural influences more evident than in the case of sexual attitudes, standards, and practices. Briefly illustrate this point with an example from Western or other cultures.
    Answer: Nineteenth-century American beliefs about semen conservation and the origins of insanity led to strict admonitions of sexual abstinence and a masturbation taboo. Homosexuality is practiced as a socially condoned ritual in one culture, but was condemned until recently in our culture by psychologists and lawmakers. Premarital sex was taboo before the sixties, when it became acceptable and even desirable. This attitude is changing again with the growing fear of sexually transmitted diseases like AIDS.

Pages: 404
Topic: Sexual Variants: The Paraphilias
Skill: Factual   Other1:
2. What are paraphilias?
    Answer: They are a group of persistent sexual behavior patterns in which unusual objects, rituals, or situations are required for full sexual satisfaction.

Pages: 407
Topic: Sexual Variants: The Paraphilias
Skill: Applied   Other1:
3. Paul can only achieve an orgasm by masturbating while he fondles women's shoes. According to DSM-IV, he suffers from _____.
    Answer: fetishism

Pages: 408
Topic: Sexual Variants: The Paraphilias
Skill: Factual   Other1:
4. Briefly describe a typical transvestic fetishist.
   Answer: He is male, heterosexual, married, and has children. He regards himself as a male, but may feel like a woman when he dresses like one. He achieves sexual arousal and satisfaction by cross-dressing. Compared to normal individuals, he may be more controlled in impulse expression, more inhibited and uninvolved interpersonally, and more dependent. He may report a reduction in anxiety and shyness when dressed as a woman.

Pages: 409-410
Topic: Sexual Variants: The Paraphilias
Skill: Factual   Other1:
5. Briefly characterize a typical voyeur OR exhibitionist.
   Answer: The typical voyeur is a young male who feels shy and sexually inadequate around women, and thus substitutes voyeuristic behavior for normal sexual contact. If in a relationship, he is not well-adjusted sexually. The exhibitionist is a young man who usually exposes himself to a young or middle-aged female. He tends to be very consistent in the places and times in which he exposes himself. He is rarely assaultive, although there may be a subgroup of exhibitionists with antisocial personalities.

Pages: 411
Topic: Sexual Variants: The Paraphilias
Skill: Conceptual   Other1:
6. How do paraphilic sadism and paraphilic masochism differ from mild sadistic and masochistic behaviors associated with normal sexual practice?
   Answer: The critical distinction lies in whether the sadistic or masochistic activity is the preferred or exclusive means of sexual gratification.

Pages: 414
Topic: Sexual Dysfunctions: Causal Factors in Sexual Dysfunctions
Skill: Conceptual   Other1:
7. Why are men much more likely to develop paraphilias than women?
   Answer: One theory is that this is associated with men's greater dependency on visual sexual stimuli. They may be more vulnerable to conditioning to nonsexual stimulus features. The theory of erotic target location also suggests that some men may be more prone to errors in "targeting," learning which physical features are associated with a sexual target.

Pages: 414
Topic: Sexual Variants: Gender Identity Disorders
Skill: Factual   Other1:

8. What are the two components of gender identity disorder in the DSM-IV?
   Answer: They are cross-gender identification and gender dysphoria.

Pages: 414
Topic: Sexual Variants: Gender Identity Disorders
Skill: Applied   Other1:

9. Briefly describe a typical boy who has a diagnosis of gender identity disorder.
   Answer: He may prefer to dress in girls' clothing and shows a decided preference for
            girls' activities. He dislikes the rough games of other boys, and may express
            the desire to be a girl. He is often ostracized as a "sissy" by his peers.

Pages: 416
Topic: Sexual Variants: Gender Identity Disorders
Skill: Factual   Other1:

10. The most effective treatment for transsexualism is _____.
    Answer: surgical sex reassignment

Pages: 418-421
Topic: Sexual Abuse: Childhood Sexual Abuse
Skill: Factual   Other1:

11. What do we know of the reliability of children's reports of past events?
    Answer: They are not always reliable, especially with young children. Studies show that
             children who are asked to repeatedly imagine a scenario will come to believe
             that they have really experienced it. Their accounts are judged believable by
             professionals. Thus, suggestive interviews by therapists about alleged sexual
             abuse may produce inaccurate accounts of events.

Pages: 429-430
Topic: Sexual Abuse: Treatment and Recidivism of Sex Offenders
Skill: Factual   Other1:

12. Briefly describe three treatments used for sex offenders.
    Answer: Deviant arousal reduction usually involves either aversion therapy, covert
             sensitization, or satiation. These may be accompanied by an attempt to retrain
             the offender to become sexually aroused by nondeviant stimuli. Cognitive
             restructuring and social skills training are sometimes used. Surgical and
             chemical castration are often successful but controversial treatments.

Pages: 431
Topic: Sexual Dysfunctions: Dysfunctions of Sexual Desire
Skill: Factual   Other1:

13. Dysfunctions of sexual desire include _____ and _____.
    Answer: hypoactive sexual desire disorder; sexual aversion disorder

Pages: 432-433
Topic: Sexual Dysfunctions: Dysfunctions of Sexual Arousal
Skill: Applied   Other1:
14. Nancy does not become sexually aroused by her partner when they are sexually intimate, which is causing serious problems in their relationship. She suffers from _____.
    Answer: female sexual arousal disorder

Pages: 433-434
Topic: Sexual Dysfunctions: Orgasmic Disorders
Skill: Factual   Other1:
15. Identify and briefly describe an orgasmic disorder.
    Answer: Premature ejaculation involves ejaculation before, during, or soon after penetration and before a man wants to ejaculate. Male orgasmic disorder involves retarded ejaculation in one or more sexual situations. Female orgasmic disorder involves the inability to experience an orgasm or persistent delays in achieving orgasm following normal sexual excitement.

Pages: 434
Topic: Sexual Dysfunctions: Dysfunctions Involving Sexual Pain
Skill: Factual   Other1:
16. An involuntary spasm of the vaginal muscles that prevents penetration and sexual intercourse is called _____, while painful intercourse is called _____.
    Answer: vaginismus; dyspareunia

Pages: 434-435
Topic: Sexual Dysfunctions: Causal Factors in Sexual Dysfunctions
Skill: Conceptual   Other1:
17. Briefly describe how early learning experiences can play a causal role in a sexual dysfunction.
    Answer: Learning too little about sex or learning information that is incorrect can lead to false expectations and ineffective techniques. Early learning that a woman's primary sexual responsibility is to please a man may often underlie female orgasmic dysfunction. Premature ejaculation may result from early conditioning to fast and efficient masturbation or sex with prostitutes, who actively attempt to bring on quick ejaculation. Early learning that sex is dirty or sinful may impact on both women and men.

Pages: 436
Topic: Sexual Dysfunctions: Causal Factors in Sexual Dysfunctions
Skill: Conceptual   Other1:

18. What role do cognitive factors play in sexual arousal and performance?

    Answer: Some research suggests that distracting cognitions about the adequacy of one's
    performance play an important role in sexual arousal dysfunctions in both men
    and women. Dysfunctional individuals may be more easily distracted by thoughts
    about their performance. Worry about one's ability to become erect or aroused,
    or to have an orgasm in a future encounter, may perpetuate the problem.

Pages: 437-438
Topic: Sexual Dysfunctions: Treatments and Outcomes
Skill: Conceptual   Other1:

19. Following the work of Masters and Johnson, how are sexual dysfunctions construed by sex
    therapists, and what are some of the main goals of treatment?

    Answer: The sexual dysfunction is treated as a shared disorder of the relationship
    rather than as a disorder of a single individual. Treatment aims to educate, to
    remove misconceptions and fears, and to modify attitudes. Behavioral
    interventions such as sensate focus are often used to target the dysfunction
    directly.

Pages: 439-440
Topic: Unresolved Issues: Long-Term Consequences of Childhood Sexual Abuse
Skill: Conceptual   Other1:

20. What is one of the difficulties in establishing causal connections between childhood
    sexual abuse and adult psychopathology?

    Answer: Most studies of this relationship are retrospective studies, which are subject
    to a variety of methodological problems. There exists the possibility that some
    third variables may be the cause of the adult psychopathology. Therapists may
    plant ideas of repressed memories of abuse in suggestible patients.

Essay

Write your answer in the space provided or on a separate sheet of paper.

Pages: 400-404
Topic: Sociocultural Influences on Sexual Practices and Standards
Skill: Conceptual   Other1:

1. Discuss the role of sociocultural and historical influences on sexual attitudes and behavior. Provide examples to illustrate your points.
   Answer: Some aspects of sexuality are essentially universal, like the incest taboo, but most are highly variable depending upon cultural and historical context. Degeneracy theory and abstinence theory were important in shaping nineteenth and twentieth century American sexual mores. Homosexuality has been endorsed by at least one culture as desirable, but severely condemned by some people in Western culture. The psychiatric field has changed markedly over the years in its view of the normalcy of homosexuality, and social attitudes have changed somewhat as to its morality and legality.

Pages: 404-414
Topic: Sexual Variants: The Paraphilias
Skill: Factual   Other1:

2. According to DSM-IV, what are paraphilias? Identify and briefly describe each of them.
   Answer: These are persistent sexual behavior patterns in which unusual objects, rituals, or situations are required for full sexual satisfaction. They often have a compulsive quality and an individual often has more than one paraphilia. DSM-IV recognizes eight specific paraphilias: fetishism, transvestic fetishism, voyeurism, exhibitionism, sadism, masochism, pedophilia, and frotteurism. Each of these should be described.

Pages: 414-415
Topic: Sexual Variants: Gender Identity Disorders
Skill: Applied   Other1:

3. Quentin, aged ten, has a gender identity disorder. What are the features of his disorder? How would you treat him? What is his likely prognosis as an adult?
   Answer: He is probably markedly preoccupied with female interests and activities, may prefer to wear girls' clothing, and may wish that he were a girl. He avoids rough play with other boys and is not interested in stereotypical male pursuits. He has difficulty with his peers, who regard him as a sissy, and with his parents, who are alarmed at his feminine behaviors. Treatment involves easing his relationships by teaching more gender-appropriate behaviors, and helping him cope with gender dysphoria. He is more likely to be a homosexual than a transsexual as an adult.

Pages: 415-416
Topic: Sexual Variants: Gender Identity Disorders
Skill: Factual   Other1:
4. What is transsexualism? What are its subtypes and how is it treated?
    Answer: It is adult gender identity disorder, which involves cross-gender identification
             and gender dysphoria. Two subtypes exist with different causes and
             developmental courses. Homosexual transsexuals usually had childhood gender
             identity disorder and are attracted to members of their own biological sex.
             Nonhomosexual transsexuals may be bisexual, heterosexual, or asexual, were not
             especially feminine as children, and usually experience autogynephilia. They
             seek sex reassignment surgery much later than homosexual transsexuals. This is
             the only effective treatment for transsexualism.

Pages: 417-422
Topic: Sexual Abuse: Childhood Sexual Abuse
Skill: Conceptual   Other1:
5. Discuss issues surrounding attempts to determine the prevalence and actual occurrence of
    childhood sexual abuse.
    Answer: The prevalence depends on the definition of sexual abuse used. A further issue
             involves the validity of children's allegations. A variety of studies by Ceci
             and others show that young children often confuse reality and fantasy when they
             have repeatedly imagined an imaginary scenario or been asked leading questions
             about a subject. The McMartin Preschool case illustrates this danger. Another
             issue involves the validity of recovered repressed memories of childhood abuse.
             Loftus and others have shown that even nonrepressed memories can be easily
             distorted.

Pages: 422-423
Topic: Sexual Abuse: Pedophilia
Skill: Factual   Other1:
6. What is pedophilia? Describe a typical pedophile.
    Answer: Pedophilia is a paraphilia in which an adult's preferred or exclusive sexual
             partner is a prepubertal child. Most pedophiles are male and are acquainted with
             their victims, who are usually female. Pedophiles tend to be somewhat
             indifferent about their partner's gender, so that homosexual pedophilic
             interactions occur more often than in the general population. Typically the
             pedophile is interpersonally unskilled and can feel in control with children.
             Some researchers identify fixated and regressive subtypes of pedophiles.
             Pedophiles show sexual arousal to both children and adults in studies.

Pages: 423-424
Topic: Sexual Abuse: Incest
Skill: Applied   Other1:

7. Paula was sexually abused by her father for several years as an adolescent. Assuming that they are typical of an incestuous family, describe her father and mother.

   Answer: Father-daughter incest is the second most common pattern of incest. Her father is probably of lower intelligence and socioeconomic standing. He may be shy and conventional with no history of pedophilic tendencies. He is probably very devoted to his family and overprotective of Paula, which results in her feeling isolated from others. The family itself is probably isolated socially and high in conflict avoidance. Her mother was probably sexually abused as a child and, if she knows of the incest, will not help or protect Paula.

Pages: 425-426
Topic: Sexual Abuse: Rape
Skill: Conceptual   Other1:

8. Discuss the controversy over whether rape is motivated by sex or aggression.

   Answer: Some feminists and others argue that rape is motivated by the desire to dominate and humiliate a victim rather than by sexual desire for her. Some suggest a subtyping in which rapists are classified according to the relative role that aggression and lust play in their behavior. Evidence that rape is at least partially sexually motivated is that rapists themselves say that sexual desire is important, most victims are young and attractive, and rapists show sexual arousal to rape stimuli in studies.

Pages: 428-430
Topic: Sexual Abuse: Treatment and Recidivism of Sex Offenders
Skill: Conceptual   Other1:

9. Discuss the treatment of sex offenders and its efficacy.

   Answer: Treatment usually focuses on one of these goals: modifying deviant sexual arousal patterns, modifying cognitions and social skills, and reducing sexual drive. Modifying sexual arousal involves aversion therapy, covert sensitization, or satiation. It is probably ineffective unless accompanied by replacing deviant patterns with more acceptable arousal patterns. Even then offenders may fake their sexual arousal responses and positive effects may not generalize to the real world. Castration is perhaps most effective but controversial.

Pages: 430-431
Topic: Sexual Dysfunctions
Skill: Factual   Other1:

10. What are the characteristics of the four-stage sexual response cycle? Indicate how they relate to sexual dysfunctions.

    Answer: The desire stage involves desire to have sex. Excitement involves physical arousal (erection or lubrication) and subjective pleasure. Sexual tension peaks and is released during orgasm, and relaxation and happiness characterize the resolution phase. Disorders occur in any of the first three phases. Dysfunctions of the desire phase include hypoactive sexual desire disorder and sexual aversion disorder. Male erectile disorder and female sexual arousal disorder are associated with the excitement phase. Premature ejaculation and orgasmic disorders are associated with orgasm phase.

Pages: 432-433
Topic: Sexual Dysfunctions
Skill: Factual   Other1:

11. Identify and describe two of the most common sexual dysfunctions in males.

    Answer: Male erectile disorder involves the inability to achieve or sustain an erection sufficient for a satisfactory duration of penetration. Situational erectile problems are rather common. Prolonged erectile problems are rare before sixty. Premature ejaculation involves persistently ejaculating before, during, or very soon after penetration. It is more common in younger men and in those who have not had sex for a prolonged period. Male orgasmic disorder involves retarded ejaculation or the inability to ejaculate during intercourse. Such men may be able to ejaculate normally during masturbation.

Pages: 432-434
Topic: Sexual Dysfunctions
Skill: Factual   Other1:

12. Identify and describe two sexual dysfunctions that primarily affect females.

    Answer: Female sexual arousal disorder involves the absence of subjective sexual arousal feelings and associated physiological changes during most or all forms of erotic stimulation. Female orgasmic disorder involves persistent or recurrent delay in, or absence of, orgasm following normal sexual excitement. This diagnosis is somewhat more difficult to make, because of the great variability in the ways that women achieve and experience orgasms. Vaginismus involves involuntary vaginal contraction preventing penetration. Dyspareunia is painful intercourse.

Pages: 434-437
Topic: Sexual Dysfunctions: Causal Factors in Sexual Dysfunctions
Skill: Factual   Other1:

13. What do we know about the causes of sexual dysfunctions?

   Answer: Dysfunctional learning is an important factor in many of the sexual dysfunctions. Inadequate education and misinformation can contribute to faulty techniques and false expectations. Women often learn that their primary sexual responsibility is to satisfy their partner, not themselves. Men may condition early on to the fast, efficient orgasm they achieve via masturbation or sex with prostitutes, causing premature ejaculation. Anxiety and fear of inadequacy play a role in arousal disorders, as do cognitive distraction and interpersonal problems.

Pages: 437-439
Topic: Sexual Dysfunctions: Treatments and Outcomes
Skill: Factual   Other1:

14. What do we know about treating sexual dysfunctions?

   Answer: Our knowledge has increased substantially since Masters and Johnson published their work in 1970. Modern methods emphasize the shared nature of the sexual disorder, and attempt to remove misconceptions and fears about sex, so that individuals come to view sex in a natural and educated way. Behavior therapy, such as sensate focus exercises, aims directly at the dysfunction itself. Lifelong female orgasmic dysfunction is treated by educating a woman to masturbate to orgasm. Erectile problems may require physical treatment such as prostheses. Vaginismus may respond to intravaginal insertions.

Pages: 439-440
Topic: Unresolved Issues: Long-Term Consequences of Childhood Sexual Abuse
Skill: Conceptual   Other1:

15. Discuss the problems associated with studying the long-term consequences of childhood sexual abuse.

   Answer: Many studies find an association between childhood sexual abuse and borderline personality disorder or dissociative identity disorder. However, these are retrospective studies and thus are plagued by methodological problems so it is impossible to establish causality. Retrospective recall is especially problematic. There are plausible third variables (genetics) that may account for the association. Borderline individuals may be especially likely to make up reports of abuse. Dissociatives and borderlines may be more suggestible to recovering false memories of abuse.

CHAPTER 12 Schizophrenias and Delusional Disorders

Multiple-Choice

Choose the one alternative that best completes the statement or answers the question.

Pages: 443
Topic: Schizophrenias and Delusional Disorders
Skill: Factual   Other1:
1. A pervasive loss of contact with reality is called
    A) neurosis.
    B) psychosis.
    C) paranoia.
    D) dementia praecox.
    Answer: B

Pages: 443
Topic: Schizophrenias and Delusional Disorders
Skill: Conceptual   Other1:
2. The text refers to "the schizophrenias," rather than to "schizophrenia." Why?
    A) Schizophrenia also includes delusional disorders.
    B) There are three distinct factors that have been identified as causes of different types
       of schizophrenia.
    C) Schizophrenia will probably someday be recognized as consisting of several separate and
       distinct conditions.
    D) It was once thought that schizophrenia consisted of several distinct disorders,
       although we now know that is probably not true.
    Answer: C

Pages: 443
Topic: Schizophrenias and Delusional Disorders
Skill: Factual   Other1:
3. Unlike schizophrenics, individuals with delusional disorders
    A) show perceptual and cognitive symptoms in childhood.
    B) have visual as well as auditory hallucinations.
    C) may behave normally apart from their delusion.
    D) tend to have biological parents who share their disorder.
    Answer: C

Pages: 444
Topic: The Schizophrenias
Skill: Factual   Other1:
4. Kraepelin used the term "dementia praecox" to refer to
    A) a group of conditions that he believed involved progressive mental deterioration beginning early in life.
    B) a group of dementias in the elderly that bear a striking resemblance to schizophrenia.
    C) Alzheimer's dementia.
    D) syphilitic insanity, which resembles schizophrenia.
    Answer: A

Pages: 444
Topic: The Schizophrenias
Skill: Factual   Other1:
5. According to Bleuler, schizophrenia
    A) is a "split" or multiple personality.
    B) involves a split within the intellect, between the intellect and emotion, and between the intellect and external reality.
    C) is a heterogeneous disorder in terms of the multiple forms in which it is manifested.
    D) B and C
    Answer: D

Pages: 444
Topic: The Schizophrenias
Skill: Factual   Other1:
6. Schizophrenia
    A) rarely occurs outside of Western cultures.
    B) first occurs during childhood.
    C) is about three times as common in males as in females.
    D) accounts for about half of all available mental hospital beds in this country.
    Answer: D

Pages: 444
Topic: The Schizophrenias
Skill: Applied   Other1:
7. Both Leonard and Lenore are diagnosed with schizophrenia. Which of the following statements is most likely to be true?
    A) Lenore had an earlier initial onset of the disorder than Leonard.
    B) Leonard has a more severe form of the disorder.
    C) Lenore's disease is unusual, in that males are much more likely to be schizophrenic than females.
    D) Lenore has a poorer prognosis than Leonard.
    Answer: B

Pages: 444
Topic: The Schizophrenias
Skill: Conceptual   Other1:

8. Although Kraepelin used the term "praecox" to convey that the schizophrenias begin early in life, the actual age of onset of the condition
   A) typically is during the early teenage years.
   B) typically is during the mid-twenties.
   C) typically is during the mid-thirties.
   D) typically is during the mid-forties.
   Answer: B

Pages: 445-447
Topic: The Schizophrenias: A Case Study
Skill: Conceptual   Other1:

9. The text presented the case study of the Genain quadruplet girls, all four of whom became schizophrenic. These women were typical of siblings with schizophrenia because
   A) environmental factors apparently caused the differences between these women, although they shared a genetic diathesis.
   B) there was no evidence of any physiological dysfunction in any of these women.
   C) the course of the disorders were essentially similar in severity, chronicity, and eventual outcome.
   D) whenever there is a multiple birth, either all of the siblings will have schizophrenia or none of them will have it.
   Answer: A

Pages: 444-446
Topic: The Schizophrenias: A Case Study
Skill: Conceptual   Other1:

10. The Genain quadruplets, who were all concordant for schizophrenia, were typical of schizophrenics because
   A) they all showed neurological impairment of the central nervous system.
   B) their symptoms, course, and level of severity were virtually identical.
   C) they showed a progressive, irreversible deterioration once their symptoms appeared.
   D) their disorder first appeared when they were in adolescence or early adulthood.
   Answer: D

Pages: 448
Topic: The Schizophrenias: The Clinical Picture in Schizophrenia
Skill: Applied   Other1:
11. Martin has gradually become withdrawn from his friends and family and has lost his emotional responsivity. His behavior has become socially inappropriate and at times quite bizarre, although there are no obvious discrete stressors in his life. Martin is showing signs of
   A) reactive schizophrenia.
   B) process schizophrenia.
   C) positive-symptom schizophrenia.
   D) acute schizophrenia.
   Answer: B

Pages: 448
Topic: The Schizophrenias: The Clinical Picture in Schizophrenia
Skill: Applied   Other1: In Student Study Guide
12. Hester Genain was never as well off psychologically as her sisters and moved in imperceptible steps toward psychosis. She could be viewed as a(n) _____ schizophrenic.
   A) acute
   B) residual
   C) process
   D) reactive
   Answer: C

Pages: 448
Topic: The Schizophrenias: The Clinical Picture in Schizophrenia
Skill: Conceptual   Other1:
13. All of the following are differences between process and reactive forms of schizophrenia EXCEPT
   A) a gradual, insidious onset versus a sudden and dramatic onset that may occur in reaction to stress, respectively.
   B) poor prognosis versus relatively good prognosis, respectively.
   C) loss of emotional responsivity versus intense emotional turmoil, respectively.
   D) onset before puberty versus onset in early adulthood, respectively.
   Answer: D

Pages: 448
Topic: The Schizophrenias: The Clinical Picture in Schizophrenia
Skill: Conceptual   Other1:
14. Which of the following is an example of a negative symptom?
   A) hallucinations
   B) emotional turmoil
   C) emotional unresponsiveness
   D) delusions
   Answer: C

Pages: 448
Topic: The Schizophrenias: The Clinical Picture in Schizophrenia
Skill: Factual   Other1:
15. Compared to negative-symptom schizophrenia, positive-symptom schizophrenia
   A) has a better long-term prognosis.
   B) is less responsive to treatment with antipsychotic medication.
   C) has a more gradual onset.
   D) does not involve hallucinations or delusions.
   Answer: A

Pages: 448
Topic: The Schizophrenias: The Clinical Picture in Schizophrenia
Skill: Factual   Other1:
16. The majority of schizophrenic individuals
   A) have mostly negative symptoms.
   B) have mostly positive symptoms.
   C) have some mixture of positive and negative symptoms.
   D) have neither positive nor negative symptoms.
   Answer: C

Pages: 448
Topic: The Schizophrenias: The Clinical Picture in Schizophrenia
Skill: Conceptual   Other1:
17. One of the problems with research on the distinction between positive-symptom and
   negative-symptom schizophrenia is
   A) the difficulty in identifying and measuring positive and negative symptoms.
   B) lack of agreement among researchers as to what types of symptoms shoud be considered
      positive or negative.
   C) the tendency to consider the positive/negative distinction to be dichotomous rather
      than as end points of a continuum, or as two independent continua.
   D) all of the above
   Answer: D

Pages: 449
Topic: The Schizophrenias: The Clinical Picture in Schizophrenia
Skill: Factual   Other1:
18. Paranoid schizophrenics tend to be
   A) more reactive than process in type, with a more benign outcome.
   B) more disturbed in perceptual and cognitive functioning.
   C) more vulnerable genetically to schizophrenia.
   D) more process than reactive in type, with a less benign outcome.
   Answer: A

Pages: 448-449
Topic: The Schizophrenias: The Clinical Picture in Schizophrenia
Skill: Factual   Other1:
19. All of the following represent traditional attempts to characterize differences among schizophrenic subtypes EXCEPT
    A) negative-symptom/positive-symptom schizophrenia.
    B) process/reactive schizophrenia.
    C) delusional/nondelusional schizophrenia.
    D) paranoid/nonparanoid schizophrenia.
    Answer: C

Pages: 450
Topic: The Schizophrenias: The Clinical Picture in Schizophrenia
Skill: Factual   Other1:
20. The DSM-IV criteria for a diagnosis of schizophrenia requires the presence of two or more of the following symptoms EXCEPT
    A) paranoia.
    B) grossly disorganized or catatonic behavior.
    C) negative symptoms.
    D) disorganized speech.
    Answer: A

Pages: 449
Topic: The Schizophrenias: The Clinical Picture in Schizophrenia
Skill: Factual   Other1:
21. Formal thought disorder refers to
    A) disturbances in thought content, such as a belief that one's private thoughts are being broadcast to others.
    B) a withdrawal from reality.
    C) alogia, the absence of speech.
    D) disturbances in language and communication.
    Answer: D

Pages: 451
Topic: The Schizophrenias: The Clinical Picture in Schizophrenia
Skill: Factual   Other1:
22. It has been estimated that about half of all schizophrenics experience which of the following during the onset of their disorders?
    A) olfactory hallucinations
    B) the belief that their thoughts are being controlled by an outside force
    C) anhedonia, the inability to experience pleasure
    D) a breakdown in perceptual selectivity
    Answer: D

Pages: 452
Topic: The Schizophrenias: Problems in Defining Schizophrenia
Skill: Conceptual   Other1: In Student Study Guide
23. The new DSM criteria for the diagnosis of schizophrenia since 1980, according to the authors, have
    A) certainly increased diagnostic validity.
    B) increased the number of patients diagnosed as schizophrenic.
    C) probably decreased both diagnostic reliability and validity.
    D) increased diagnostic reliability.
    Answer: D

Pages: 452
Topic: The Schizophrenias: Problems in Defining Schizophrenia
Skill: Conceptual   Other1:
24. A DSM-IV diagnosis of schizophrenia
    A) is high in validity but low in reliability.
    B) is a provisional construct.
    C) refers to a single, distinctive disease entity.
    D) is based on an understanding of the causes of schizophrenia that distinguish it from other mental disorders.
    Answer: B

Pages: 452
Topic: The Schizophrenias: Subtypes of Schizophrenia
Skill: Factual   Other1:
25. The DSM delineates five subtypes of schizophrenia on the basis of
    A) the different causes of each subtype.
    B) the differing clinical pictures of each subtype.
    C) differences in underlying brain pathology associated with each subtype.
    D) the content of thought disturbance associated with each subtype.
    Answer: B

Pages: 452-453
Topic: The Schizophrenias: Subtypes of Schizophrenia
Skill: Applied   Other1:
26. A person who is in the process of breaking down and first becoming schizophrenic is most likely to fit the _____ subtype of schizophrenia.
    A) undifferentiated
    B) catatonic
    C) paranoid
    D) disorganized
    Answer: A

Pages: 452-454
Topic: The Schizophrenias: Subtypes of Schizophrenia
Skill: Applied   Other1:
27. The text presented the case of Rick Wheeler, who believed that he was Jesus and the devil
    wanted to kill him. He was NOT typical of undifferentiated schizophrenics because
    A) he would remain motionless for hours and sometimes for days at a time.
    B) his disorder had an early, gradual, and insidious onset.
    C) he was unable to keep a job and to support himself.
    D) his illness only lasted a few weeks.
    Answer: B

Pages: 453
Topic: The Schizophrenias: Subtypes of Schizophrenia
Skill: Applied   Other1:
28. Rod exhibits a rapidly changing mixture of most of the symptoms of schizophrenia. He is
    emotionally distraught, confused, excited, and experiences delusions of reference. He is
    most likely to suffer from _____ schizophrenia.
    A) paranoid
    B) catatonic
    C) undifferentiated
    D) disorganized
    Answer: C

Pages: 454
Topic: The Schizophrenias: Subtypes of Schizophrenia
Skill: Factual   Other1:
29. The central feature of catatonic schizophrenia is
    A) excited or stuperous motor symptoms.
    B) blunted or inappropriate affect.
    C) illogical or absurd delusions.
    D) an extreme stressor precipitating the symptoms.
    Answer: A

Pages: 454-455
Topic: The Schizophrenias: Subtypes of Schizophrenia
Skill: Factual   Other1:
30. During phases of catatonic excitement, an individual
    A) may be indistinguishable from a manic patient.
    B) may be impulsively violent and very dangerous to others.
    C) may attempt suicide.
    D) all of the above
    Answer: D

Pages: 455-456
Topic: The Schizophrenias: Subtypes of Schizophrenia
Skill: Applied   Other1:
31. The text presented the case study of Todd Phillips, a sixteen-year-old student in a psychiatric hospital. He was typical of catatonic schizophrenics because
    A) he was very well-adjusted prior to the onset of the disorder.
    B) he first became psychotic in childhood.
    C) he would remain frozen in strange positions for long periods of time.
    D) virtually all catatonic schizophrenics are male.
    Answer: C

Pages: 456
Topic: The Schizophrenias: Subtypes of Schizophrenia
Skill: Factual   Other1:
32. The schizophrenic subtype with the earliest onset and most severe disintegration of personality is the _____ subtype.
    A) undifferentiated
    B) paranoid
    C) disorganized
    D) catatonic
    Answer: C

Pages: 456
Topic: The Schizophrenias: Subtypes of Schizophrenia
Skill: Applied   Other1:
33. Gina is schizophrenic. She giggles a lot, acts silly, and talks "baby talk." She experiences frequent auditory hallucinations and bizarre delusions. Gina most likely belongs to the _____ subtype of schizophrenia.
    A) disorganized
    B) undifferentiated
    C) residual
    D) catatonic
    Answer: A

Pages: 457
Topic: The Schizophrenias: Subtypes of Schizophrenia
Skill: Applied   Other1:
34. Jeff has a diagnosis of schizophrenia, but he is able to maintain an unskilled job that doesn't require social contact. His cognitive functioning is relatively intact. He is most likely a(n) _____ schizophrenic.
    A) undifferentiated
    B) catatonic
    C) paranoid
    D) disorganized
    Answer: C

Pages: 457-459
Topic: The Schizophrenias: Subtypes of Schizophrenia
Skill: Applied   Other1:

35. The text presented the case study of a paranoid schizophrenic who believed that he was the reincarnation of Franklin Roosevelt, and he was the only person in the world who could thwart the Russians. He is typical of paranoid schizophrenics because
    A) he is male.
    B) he has delusions that involve themes of grandeur.
    C) he spoke in "word salad."
    D) he has prominent symptoms of a mood disorder.
    Answer: B

Pages: 459
Topic: The Schizophrenias: Subtypes of Schizophrenia
Skill: Applied   Other1:

36. Phillip had an episode of schizophrenia, but currently exhibits only a few mild signs of the disorder. He qualifies for a diagnosis of
    A) schizophreniform disorder.
    B) residual schizophrenia.
    C) schizoaffective disorder.
    D) residual schizophreniform disorder.
    Answer: B

Pages: 459
Topic: The Schizophrenias: Subtypes of Schizophrenia
Skill: Applied   Other1:

37. During the past year, John has been experiencing symptoms of both schizophrenia and major depression. John would receive a diagnosis of
    A) schizoaffective disorder.
    B) schizophreniform disorder.
    C) catatonic schizophrenia.
    D) schizobipolar disorder.
    Answer: A

Pages: 459
Topic: The Schizophrenias: Subtypes of Schizophrenia
Skill: Applied   Other1:

38. Virginia exhibits a variety of schizophrenic symptoms including delusions, auditory hallucinations, and formal thought disorder. She has been symptomatic for about a month. Virginia qualifies for a diagnosis of
    A) paranoid schizophrenia.
    B) schizoaffective disorder, manic type.
    C) undifferentiated schizophrenia.
    D) schizophreniform disorder.
    Answer: D

Topic: The Schizophrenias: Subtypes of Schizophrenia
Skill: Conceptual   Other1:
39. All cases of schizophrenia which have a recent onset will first receive a diagnosis of
A) schizoaffective disorder.
B) schizophreniform disorder.
C) undifferentiated schizophrenia.
D) general psychosis.
Answer: B

Pages: 460
Topic: The Schizophrenias: Causal Factors in Schizophrenia
Skill: Factual   Other1:
40. Studies of genetic contributions to schizophrenia
A) have identified two separate mechanisms that are involved in the genetic factor's influence on schizophrenic behavior.
B) have determined that genetic liability contributes about 50 percent of the risk of schizophrenia in any given individual.
C) have had to rely on pedigree stategies to demonstrate genetic effects.
D) have identified one of the genes that may work in concert with other genes to produce schizophrenia.
Answer: C

Pages: 460
Topic: The Schizophrenias: Causal Factors in Schizophrenia
Skill: Factual   Other1:
41. In a recent review of the most methodologically sound twin studies, Torrey and colleagues found that the overall pairwise concordance rate for schizophrenia in monozygotic twins was _____ percent compared to _____ percent in dizygotic twins.
A) 75; 25
B) 50;15
C) 28; 6
D) 10; 2
Answer: C

Pages: 460-462
Topic: The Schizophrenias: Causal Factors in Schizophrenia
Skill: Conceptual   Other1:
42. Twin studies of schizophrenia allow us to conclude that
    A) schizophrenia is a genetically caused disorder, with environmental factors playing little role in the origin of this disorder.
    B) genetic causal factors probably are involved in a predisposition to schizophrenia, although environmental factors can not be entirely disentangled from genetic factors in these twin studies.
    C) environmental factors like shared stress play as strong a role as genetic factors in the origin of schizophrenia.
    D) monozygotic twins share a higher rate of nongenetic pathogenic factors than do dizygotic twins.
    Answer: B

Pages: 461
Topic: The Schizophrenias: Causal Factors in Schizophrenia
Skill: Conceptual   Other1:
43. The results obtained from the classic twin method of investigating schizophrenia
    A) demonstrate that genetic factors make a strong contribution to developing the disorder.
    B) demonstrate that genetic factors do not play as strong a role as was previously thought.
    C) demonstrate that genetic factors make only a weak contribution to developing the disorder.
    D) are difficult to interpret because monozygotic twins may be more alike than dizygotic twins in terms of nongenetic pathogenic factors influencing their prenatal and postnatal developments.
    Answer: D

Pages: 461
Topic: The Schizophrenias: Causal Factors in Schizophrenia
Skill: Factual   Other1:
44. Compared to his nonschizophrenic identical twin, Matthew (who is schizophrenic) is more likely to
    A) have been born with physical birth defects.
    B) have been considered "different" or "odd" in childhood.
    C) have a higher intelligence level on IQ tests.
    D) be artistically or musically talented.
    Answer: B

Pages: 461-462
Topic: The Schizophrenias: Causal Factors in Schizophrenia
Skill: Factual   Other1:
45. A study of monozygotic twins who are discordant for schizophrenia found that
    A) the schizophrenic twin had genetic anomalies that the nonschizophrenic twin did not have.
    B) the schizophrenic twin suffered from birth complications that the nonschizophrenic twin did not experience.
    C) the schizophrenic twin had a variety of structural and functional abnormalities in the brain that the nonschizophrenic did not have.
    D) the schizophrenic twin suffered from viral infections in childhood that the nonschizophrenic twin did not experience.
    Answer: C

Pages: 462
Topic: The Schizophrenias: Causal Factors in Schizophrenia
Skill: Factual   Other1:
46. Studies of the offspring of nonschizophrenic co-twins from discordant twin pairs found that
    A) the offspring were no more likely to become schizophrenic than an individual drawn from the general population.
    B) the rate of schizophrenia among these offspring was higher than the rate of schizophrenia among the offspring of the schizophrenic co-twins.
    C) these offspring were at greater risk for an affective disorder than for schizophrenia.
    D) these offspring had a rate of schizophrenia that was similar to that of the offspring of the schizophrenic co-twins.
    Answer: D

Pages: 462
Topic: The Schizophrenias: Causal Factors in Schizophrenia
Skill: Conceptual   Other1:
47. Studies of the offspring of nonschizophrenic co-twins from discordant twin pairs suggest that
    A) environmental factors play a more important role than genetic factors in the origin of schizophrenia.
    B) genetic factors cause schizophrenia, while environmental factors are essentially unimportant.
    C) a genetic predisposition to schizophrenia may remain unexpressed in some individuals unless it is released by some unknown environmental factors.
    D) the heritability of schizophrenia involves the transmission of a single dominant gene.
    Answer: C

Pages: 462
Topic: The Schizophrenias: Causal Factors in Schizophrenia
Skill: Conceptual *Other1:*
48. The research strategy that allows the clearest separation of genetic and environmental factors in studying schizophrenia is
   A) the adoption strategy.
   B) twin studies.
   C) high-risk studies.
   D) family pedigree studies.
   Answer: A

Pages: 463-464
Topic: The Schizophrenias: Causal Factors in Schizophrenia
Skill: Factual *Other1:*
49. The large-scale Danish adoption study of schizophrenics found that
   A) the biological relatives of schizophrenics were more likely to also be schizophrenic than were the biological relatives of nonschizophrenic control adoptees.
   B) the adoptive relatives of schizophrenics were more likely to also be schizophrenic than were their biological relatives.
   C) the adequacy of child-rearing practices among adoptive families was highly correlated with the incidence of schizophrenia regardless of an individual's biological predisposition.
   D) there was no difference in the incidence of schizophrenia among adoptive and biological relatives of schizophrenics.
   Answer: A

Pages: 463
Topic: The Schizophrenias: Causal Factors in Schizophrenia
Skill: Factual *Other1:*
50. The "schizophrenia spectrum" refers to
   A) the subtypes of schizophrenia that are recognized by DSM-IV.
   B) the range of severity of cognitive and behavioral deterioration in individuals who have a diagnosis of schizophrenia.
   C) the psychotic mood disorders.
   D) a group of disorders that appears to share a common genetic diathesis with schizophrenia.
   Answer: D

Pages: 463
Topic: The Schizophrenias: Causal Factors in Schizophrenia
Skill: Factual   Other1:
51. Schizotypal personality disorder and schizoaffective disorder
    A) are more likely to appear in the biological relatives of schizophrenics than in the biological relatives of nonschizophrenic control adoptees.
    B) are mild forms of schizophrenia that have an environmental rather than a genetic origin.
    C) are unrelated to schizophrenia in recent analyses of the Danish adoption study data.
    D) are genetically related to the mood disorders rather than to schizophrenia.
    Answer: A

Pages: 464
Topic: The Schizophrenias: Causal Factors in Schizophrenia
Skill: Factual   Other1:
52. Schizophrenia research involving studies of high-risk children define "high risk" as
    A) having neurological impairments similar to schizophrenics.
    B) belonging to lower socioeconomic groups.
    C) being the offspring of a schizophrenic parent.
    D) being a monozygotic twin.
    Answer: C

Pages: 464
Topic: The Schizophrenias: Causal Factors in Schizophrenia
Skill: Factual   Other1:
53. In the Israeli-NIMH High-Risk Study, an index group of high-risk children reared by their biological parents was compared to a group of high-risk children raised in kibbutzim, as well as to children from matched low-risk control groups. Investigators found that
    A) high-risk and low-risk children who were raised in kibbutzim were more disturbed psychologically than were the children raised by their own parents.
    B) high-risk children tended to have a high frequency of neurological soft signs compared to low-risk children.
    C) high-risk children reared in kibbutzim were more likely to become disordered than were high-risk children raised by their schizophrenic parent.
    D) B and C
    Answer: D

Pages: 464
Topic: The Schizophrenias: Causal Factors in Schizophrenia
Skill: Conceptual   Other1:
54. Overall, high-risk studies of schizophrenia suggest that
    A) schizophrenia has an unquestionably genetic, not an environmental, origin.
    B) schizophrenia has an unquestionably environmental, not a genetic, origin.
    C) having a schizophrenic parent is a good predictor of psychological disorder, including schizophrenia.
    D) the neurological impairments found in high-risk children are caused by the defective "schizophrenic" gene that is transmitted by the schizophrenic parent.
    Answer: C

Pages: 464-465
Topic: The Schizophrenias: Causal Factors in Schizophrenia
Skill: Conceptual   Other1:
55. Taken together, the various types of genetic studies of schizophrenia suggest that
    A) schizophrenia is always accompanied by some genetic liability, although the environment also plays a role in causing the disorder.
    B) genetic liability is a sufficient, but not a necessary, cause of schizophrenia.
    C) genetic liability is probably a diathesis in some cases of schizophrenia.
    D) the evidence for a genetic predisposition to schizophrenia is weak.
    Answer: C

Pages: 465
Topic: The Schizophrenias: Causal Factors in Schizophrenia
Skill: Conceptual   Other1:
56. The general strategy in biochemical research on the etiology of schizophrenia involves
    A) using imaging devices to examine synaptic functioning in the brains of schizophrenics and their biological relatives.
    B) inducing psychotic behaviors in animals in order to study the anti-psychotic effects of various experimental drugs.
    C) measuring the relative enlargement of the third ventricle in the brains of schizophrenics.
    D) attempting to determine the site and nature of the effects of existing drugs that are successful in treating the disorder.
    Answer: D

Pages: 465
Topic: The Schizophrenias: Causal Factors in Schizophrenia
Skill: Factual   Other1:
57. According to the dopamine hypothesis, schizophrenia is caused by
   A) abnormally low levels of dopamine.
   B) an excessive level of dopaminergic activity at certain synaptic sites.
   C) the inability of dopamine to transform into norepinephrine.
   D) abnormalities in larger brain structures that are associated with dopamine pathways.
   Answer: B

Pages: 465
Topic: The Schizophrenias: Causal Factors in Schizophrenia
Skill: Factual   Other1:
58. Neuroleptic drugs
   A) increase the available amount of dopamine in neural synapses.
   B) block dopamine-mediated neural transmission.
   C) block GABA-mediated neural transmission.
   D) inhibit the reuptake of serotonin by postsynaptic neurons.
   Answer: B

Pages: 465
Topic: The Schizophrenias: Causal Factors in Schizophrenia
Skill: Conceptual   Other1:
59. Neuroleptic drugs block dopamine receptors within hours of administration, indicating that
   A) they may be useful in treating affective disorders as well as schizophrenia.
   B) their beneficial effects will not last longer than a few days.
   C) if dopamine receptors alone were involved in schizophrenia, schizophrenics wouldn't
      take weeks to show improvement after initially receiving neuroleptics.
   D) the beneficial effects of neuroleptics are immediately apparent clinically in
      schizophrenic individuals.
   Answer: C

Pages: 465-466
Topic: The Schizophrenias: Causal Factors in Schizophrenia
Skill: Conceptual   Other1:
60. Problems with the dopamine hypothesis include all of the following EXCEPT
   A) dopaminergic abnormalities have not been found to be associated with schizophrenia in
      recent studies.
   B) several types of postsynaptic dopamine receptors exist which are involved with
      different biochemical processes.
   C) second-generation antipsychotic drugs probably work through a mode of action very
      different from that of neuroleptics.
   D) schizophrenics take weeks to respond to neuroleptic drugs despite the fact that they
      act almost immediately to lower dopamine levels.
   Answer: A

Pages: 466
Topic: The Schizophrenias: Causal Factors in Schizophrenia
Skill: Conceptual   Other1:
61. The current status of biochemical theories of schizophrenic etiology indicate that
   A) the dopamine hypothesis has been replaced by the clozapine hypothesis of schizophrenia.
   B) schizophrenia does not involve abnormalities in dopaminergic activity, as had been previously thought.
   C) schizophrenia involves a more complex biochemical dysfunction than mere excessive dopaminergic activity.
   D) serotonin, and not dopamine, is the key neurotransmitter causing schizophrenic symptoms.
   Answer: C

Pages: 466
Topic: The Schizophrenias: Causal Factors in Schizophrenia
Skill: Factual   Other1:
62. One of the most reliable neurophysiological abnormalities that has been found in schizophrenics and those "at risk" for schizophrenia is
   A) a deficiency in smooth pursuit eye movement.
   B) the inability to maintain attention during information-processing tasks.
   C) anomalies in brain-wave functioning.
   D) all of the above
   Answer: D

Pages: 466-467
Topic: The Schizophrenias: Causal Factors in Schizophrenia
Skill: Factual   Other1:
63. Neurophysiological abnormalities in schizophrenics
   A) distinguish them from patients who have psychotic mood disorders.
   B) are not found in their biological relatives.
   C) probably underlie the perceptual, attentional, and cognitive symptoms of schizophrenia.
   D) are genetic in origin.
   Answer: C

Pages: 467
Topic: The Schizophrenias: Causal Factors in Schizophrenia
Skill: Factual   Other1:
64. Enlarged ventricles and sulci in the brains of some schizophrenics indicate
   A) that schizophrenia is caused by a progressive deterioration of brain tissue.
   B) the long-term use of neuroleptic drugs.
   C) that these brain abnormalities are caused by birth complications or prenatal injury.
   D) none of the above
   Answer: D

Pages: 467
Topic: The Schizophrenias: Causal Factors in Schizophrenia
Skill: Factual   Other1:
65. PET studies measuring metabolic activity in the brain have found that
    A) schizophrenics have an abnormally high level of activity in most areas of the brain.
    B) there is an abnormally high level of activation in the frontal lobes of some schizophrenics.
    C) there is an abnormally low level of activation in the frontal lobes of some schizophrenics.
    D) levels of activation increase over the years in some schizophrenics, eventually leading to a "burn-out" phenomenon.
    Answer: C

Pages: 467
Topic: The Schizophrenias: Causal Factors in Schizophrenia
Skill: Factual   Other1:
66. When some schizophrenics perform laboratory tasks involving frontal-lobe involvement,
    A) they are unable to improve their performance on the tasks even when they are given extensive and lengthy instruction, similar to brain-damaged patients.
    B) frontal lobe activation is so high that they are too distracted to maintain the attention needed to perform the tasks.
    C) they exhibit a pattern of hypofrontality.
    D) their symptoms are exacerbated.
    Answer: C

Pages: 468
Topic: The Schizophrenias: Causal Factors in Schizophrenia
Skill: Conceptual   Other1:
67. An overall review of neuroimaging studies of schizophrenia suggests that
    A) the frontal lobe, temperolimbic region, and basal ganglia are the three brain regions most strongly implicated in schizophrenia.
    B) hypofrontality is the only significant dysfunction in the brains of schizophrenics.
    C) enlarged ventricles cause reduced activity in the frontal lobes of some schizophrenics.
    D) schizophrenia involves the progressive degeneration of brain tissue.
    Answer: A

Pages: 468
Topic: The Schizophrenias: Causal Factors in Schizophrenia
Skill: Factual   Other1:
68. Few of the abnormal neuroanatomical findings in schizophrenics
    A) are found in their biological relatives.
    B) are found in schizophrenia spectrum disorders.
    C) are specific to schizophrenia compared to other disorders.
    D) are found in individuals with mood disorders.
    Answer: C

Pages: 468
Topic: The Schizophrenias: Causal Factors in Schizophrenia
Skill: Factual   Other1:
69. The seasonal effect observed by many investigators concerning schizophrenia refers to
    A) the fact that schizophrenics are rarely born during the winter months.
    B) the fact that schizophrenics' symptoms tend to worsen during the winter months.
    C) the fact that more schizophrenics than would be expected were born during the winter
       months.
    D) the increase in the hospital admissions of schizophrenics during the summer months.
    Answer: C

Pages: 468
Topic: The Schizophrenias: Causal Factors in Schizophrenia
Skill: Factual   Other1:
70. The season of birth effect
    A) has been shown to be a mere statistical artifact.
    B) appears to exist and may be associated with infectious agents, obstetrical
       complications, or both.
    C) holds true for stillbirths, but not for schizophrenics.
    D) actually has been shown to be true of bipolar disorder rather than schizophrenia.
    Answer: B

Pages: 469
Topic: The Schizophrenias: Causal Factors in Schizophrenia
Skill: Conceptual   Other1:
71. The role of biological factors in the etiology of schizophrenia
    A) has not been established.
    B) has been strongly established but only in schizophrenics who also have a genetic
       liability for schizophrenia.
    C) is clearly established but we do not know how biological factors operate to produce
       schizophrenic symptoms.
    D) is clearly established in the case of abnormal dopaminergic transmission, but not in
       neuroanatomical abnormalities.
    Answer: C

Pages: 469
Topic: The Schizophrenias: Causal Factors in Schizophrenia
Skill: Conceptual   Other1:
72. Psychosocial and biological factors are
    A) mutually exclusive in explaining the etiology of schizophrenia.
    B) now known to be mutually antagonistic.
    C) rarely investigated in interaction together, which is a major limitation in schizophrenia research.
    D) usually investigated interacting in various ways in studies of schizophrenics, but as of yet no conclusive findings have emerged.
    Answer: C

Pages: 469
Topic: The Schizophrenias: Causal Factors in Schizophrenia
Skill: Conceptual   Other1:
73. The great emphasis on studying biological determinants of schizophrenia has highlighted the importance of
    A) examining the interaction between neurophysiological and neuroanatomical factors.
    B) examining the interaction of genetic, biochemical, neurophysiological, and neuroanatomical factors.
    C) examining the interaction between genetic and biochemical factors.
    D) examining not only biological factors, but nonbiological factors as well.
    Answer: D

Pages: 469
Topic: The Schizophrenias: Causal Factors in Schizophrenia
Skill: Factual   Other1:
74. Walker and colleagues conducted a series of studies in which blind observers evaluated preschizophrenic children and their siblings in old home movies. They found that
    A) the preschizophrenic children and their siblings were indistinguishable from one another.
    B) the preschizophrenic children were more often treated harshly or ignored by their parents than were their siblings.
    C) the preschizophrenic children were more aggressive and hostile than their siblings.
    D) the preschizophrenic children showed less emotion in general, more negative than positive emotion, and had poorer motor skills than their siblings.
    Answer: D

Pages: 469
Topic: The Schizophrenias: Causal Factors in Schizophrenia
Skill: Conceptual   Other1:

75. An important point to be drawn from the studies by Walker and colleagues evaluating preschizophrenic children in old home movies is that
    A) biological impairments do not typically appear until after the onset of schizophrenia later in life.
    B) psychosocial factors preceed biological factors in the development of schizophrenia.
    C) biological factors can influence the personality and social development of children at risk for schizophrenia in very detrimental ways.
    D) biological impairment in schizophrenics and in those at risk for schizophrenia is progressive.
    Answer: C

Pages: 470
Topic: The Schizophrenias: Causal Factors in Schizophrenia
Skill: Conceptual   Other1:

76. In schizophrenia research, personality factors may be very important in
    A) mediating between biological diatheses and schizophrenic outcomes.
    B) influencing the amount of stress that an individual experiences growing up.
    C) distinguishing children at risk for schizophrenia from children at risk for other psychological disorders.
    D) all of the above
    Answer: D

Pages: 470
Topic: The Schizophrenias: Causal Factors in Schizophrenia
Skill: Factual   Other1:

77. Compared to biological research on schizophrenic etiology, psychosocial research
    A) is more plentiful and well-designed.
    B) is less important.
    C) is sparse and tends to be out-of-date.
    D) is more important.
    Answer: C

Pages: 470
Topic: The Schizophrenias: Causal Factors in Schizophrenia
Skill: Applied   Other1:
78. Linda had an initial onset of schizophrenia when she was an adolescent in 1964. When her parents conferred with doctors about Linda's illness, they were most likely told that
A) she had inherited the condition from one of them.
B) they were to blame for her illness because of faulty parenting.
C) no one knows the cause of schizophrenia, but we do know that it is not caused by faulty parenting.
D) she had been sexually abused as a child.
Answer: B

Pages: 470
Topic: The Schizophrenias: Causal Factors in Schizophrenia
Skill: Factual   Other1:
79. One of the most influential theories of schizophrenia from the 1940's through the 1960's was
A) the Oedipal/Electra Complex.
B) the schizophrenogenic mother.
C) expressed emotion.
D) interpersonal stress.
Answer: B

Pages: 471
Topic: The Schizophrenias: Causal Factors in Schizophrenia
Skill: Factual   Other1:
80. Many studies find
A) that the mothers of schizophrenics are emotionally disturbed, but the fathers are not.
B) little emotional disturbance in the parents of schizophrenics.
C) a high incidence of emotional disturbance in schizophrenics' parents.
D) that schizophrenics' mothers tend to have recurrent episodes of severe depression.
Answer: C

Pages: 471
Topic: The Schizophrenias: Causal Factors in Schizophrenia
Skill: Conceptual   Other1:
81. The emotional disturbance often found in the families of schizophrenics
A) is a major psychosocial cause of schizophrenia.
B) may be either a cause or a result of schizophrenia in a family member.
C) results from the stress of having a schizophrenic family member.
D) is a statistical artifact.
Answer: B

Pages: 471
Topic: The Schizophrenias: Causal Factors in Schizophrenia
Skill: Applied   Other1:
82. Peter and Paula are a married couple with a schizophrenic son. They are in a state of constant tension, seemingly ready to abandon the marriage at any moment. This condition is called
A) marital schism.
B) marital skew.
C) double bind.
D) expressed emotion.
Answer: A

Pages: 471
Topic: The Schizophrenias: Causal Factors in Schizophrenia
Skill: Factual   Other1:
83. Lidz and colleagues found that one characteristic pattern in the families of schizophrenics involved a collusion to regard seriously disturbed behavior in one of the parents as normal. This is called
A) marital schism.
B) marital skew.
C) double bind.
D) expressed emotion.
Answer: B

Pages: 471
Topic: The Schizophrenias: Causal Factors in Schizophrenia
Skill: Conceptual   Other1:
84. Schizophrenics often have psychologically healthy siblings who were raised together with them in the same family. This suggests that
A) family pathology is not involved in the etiology of schizophrenia.
B) parents show favoritism to some of their children over others in subtle but destructive ways.
C) no two children ever have identical childhood family experiences, even if they are twins.
D) psychosocial factors are less important than biogenetic factors in the etiology of schizophrenia.
Answer: C

Pages: 471
Topic: The Schizophrenias: Causal Factors in Schizophrenia
Skill: Factual   Other1:
85. In families where siblings were discordant for schizophrenia, the siblings who became ill
    A) were found to have been fathered by someone other than their sibling's father.
    B) had experienced a serious head trauma in adolescence.
    C) experienced family crises at critical periods of early childhood.
    D) none of the above
    Answer: C

Pages: 471
Topic: The Schizophrenias: Causal Factors in Schizophrenia
Skill: Factual   Other1:
86. A child who is constantly put into situations of paradoxical communications by his parent
    may become increasingly anxious and disorganized, eventually becoming schizophrenic. This
    theory refers to
    A) maternal skew.
    B) marital schism.
    C) double-bind communication.
    D) expressed emotion.
    Answer: C

Pages: 472
Topic: The Schizophrenias: Causal Factors in Schizophrenia
Skill: Factual   Other1:
87. Communication deviance
    A) in parents predicts the later development of schizophrenia spectrum disorders in
       offspring.
    B) in families has not been shown to be involved in the etiology of schizophrenia.
    C) in schizophrenics and their families has been shown to have the same underlying genetic
       diathesis.
    D) is found only in schizophrenics, not in their family members.
    Answer: A

Pages: 472
Topic: The Schizophrenias: Causal Factors in Schizophrenia
Skill: Factual   Other1:
88. Relapse rates in schizophrenics are highly associated with the level of _____ in their
    families.
    A) double-bind communication
    B) expressed emotion
    C) education
    D) socioeconomic class
    Answer: B

Pages: 472
Topic: The Schizophrenias: Causal Factors in Schizophrenia
Skill: Factual   Other1:
89. Expressed emotion
A) tends to increase in a family only after a family member becomes schizophrenic.
B) predicts schizophrenia before its initial onset.
C) is highly resistant to treatment.
D) involves two components, formal thought disorder and marital skew.
Answer: B

Pages: 472
Topic: The Schizophrenias: Causal Factors in Schizophrenia
Skill: Factual   Other1:
90. Schizophrenic recovery
A) is usually slow and incomplete.
B) is usually fast and often complete.
C) varies in speed and degree, with the least recovery shown by negative-symptom schizophrenics.
D) usually follows a similar course in most schizophrenics.
Answer: C

Pages: 472-473
Topic: The Schizophrenias: Causal Factors in Schizophrenia
Skill: Factual   Other1:
91. Schizophrenia
A) differs in frequency and in symptoms between different cultures.
B) does not differ between cultures in either form or frequency.
C) is more prevalent in lower socioeconomic classes in all cultures.
D) differs dramatically in frequency between different ethnic groups in America regardless of social class.
Answer: A

Pages: 474
Topic: The Schizophrenias: Treatment and Outcomes
Skill: Factual   Other1:
92. The most common method of treatment for schizophrenia today is
A) psychoanalysis.
B) cognitive therapy.
C) pharmacotherapy.
D) all of the above
Answer: C

Pages: 474
Topic: The Schizophrenias: Causal Factors in Schizophrenia
Skill: Factual   Other1:
93. Most schizophrenics today
    A) are treated in outpatient clinics.
    B) remain hospitalized for years at a time.
    C) experience only one hospitalization, and receive pharmacotherapy from family physicians.
    D) are eventually able to make a full recovery.
    Answer: A

Pages: 474
Topic: The Schizophrenias: Treatment and Outcomes
Skill: Factual   Other1:
94. The "revolving door" pattern refers to
    A) the tendency for many schizophrenics to experience intermittent hospitalizations interspersed with periods of marginal living on the outside.
    B) the fact that schizophrenics never recover completely from their illness.
    C) the rapid discharge rate of schizophrenics from mental hospitals today.
    D) the fact that most schizophrenics check themselves into and out of mental hospitals on a regular basis in order to get shelter and food.
    Answer: A

Pages: 476
Topic: The Schizophrenias: Treatment and Outcomes
Skill: Factual   Other1:
95. Hegarty and colleagues found gradual increases and decreases during circumscribed periods of time over the last century in the success of treatment outcomes for schizophrenics. These decreases in successful outcomes from 1976 to 1991 are probably due to
    A) changes in federal regulations permitting the prescription of experimental anti-psychotic drugs.
    B) political changes in which less funding was available for treatment.
    C) the adoption of stricter diagnostic criteria, which limited the diagnosis of schizophrenia to more severely disturbed patients who would be less likely to have a successful treatment outcome.
    D) chance.
    Answer: C

Pages: 474-475
Topic: The Schizophrenias: Treatment and Outcomes
Skill: Conceptual   Other1:
96. Unfortunately, there is a widespread view among many mental health professionals that schizophrenics
    A) are incurable and thus should not be helped.
    B) will probably respond to drug therapy, but psychosocial interventions are unimportant.
    C) will recover completely in most cases with drug therapy alone.
    D) should not be hospitalized so as not to encourage dependence on the system.
    Answer: B

Pages: 474-475
Topic: The Schizophrenias: Treatment and Outcomes
Skill: Factual   Other1:
97. In a recent review of studies combining biological and psychological treatments for schizophrenia, the studies suggested that
    A) pharmacotherapy was superior to psychological treatment, and equivalent to combined treatment.
    B) psychological treatment was just as effective as pharmacotherapy, and combined treatment did not produce enhanced effects.
    C) combining pharmacotherapy and psychological treatment often was superior to either treatment alone.
    D) pharmacotherapy was superior to all other treatments initially, but its effectiveness lasted for a little over a year and then declined for most schizophrenics, at which point psychological treatment became most effective.
    Answer: C

Pages: 475
Topic: Delusional (Paranoid) Disorder
Skill: Factual   Other1:
98. The DSM-IV recognizes two forms of nonschizophrenic psychotic disorders,
    A) delusional disorder and bipolar psychosis.
    B) shared psychotic disorder and bipolar psychosis.
    C) delusional disorder and paranoid disorder.
    D) shared psychotic disorder and delusional disorder.
    Answer: D

Pages: 475-476
Topic: Delusional (Paranoid) Disorder
Skill: Factual   Other1:

99. In the DSM-IV, "persecutory," "jealous," "somatic," and "grandiose" are types of
    A) schizophrenia.
    B) shared psychoses.
    C) delusional disorder.
    D) none of the above
    Answer: C

Pages: 477
Topic: Delusional (Paranoid) Disorder: The Clinical Picture
Skill: Factual   Other1:

100. Individuals with shared psychotic disorder
    A) usually also have a diagnosis of schizophrenia.
    B) are highly suggestible and tend to adopt dominant-submissive roles.
    C) tend to be biologically related, suggesting a genetic diathesis for the disorder.
    D) are almost always female.
    Answer: B

Pages: 478
Topic: Delusional (Paranoid) Disorder: The Clinical Picture
Skill: Applied   Other1:

101. An individual who is normal in most respects but who believes that he or she has a divine
    mission to preach the coming end of the world on the streetcorner is probably suffering
    from
    A) disorganized schizophrenia.
    B) delusional disorder.
    C) undifferentiated schizophrenia.
    D) grandiosity disorder.
    Answer: B

Pages: 477
Topic: Delusional (Paranoid) Disorder: The Clinical Picture
Skill: Factual   Other1:

102. The central features of a paranoid delusion include all of the following EXCEPT
    A) it is impervious to logic and reason.
    B) more and more of the individual's environment becomes incorporated into the delusional
       system.
    C) eventually an individual will act against his or her imagined enemies in what is
       usually a violent manner.
    D) it usually centers on one theme, such as an unfaithful romantic partner or a plot to be
       harmed by others.
    Answer: C

Pages: 478
Topic: Delusional (Paranoid) Disorder: The Clinical Picture
Skill: Applied   Other1:
103. Grant is diagnosed with delusional disorder. He
    A) is often incoherent and makes little sense when he speaks.
    B) appears normal apart from his delusional system.
    C) is warm and friendly at times but hostile at other times.
    D) shows relatively marked cognitive impairment, although not as severe as schizophrenic impairment.
    Answer: B

Pages: 479
Topic: Delusional (Paranoid) Disorder: The Clinical Picture
Skill: Conceptual   Other1:
104. One difficulty in diagnosing an individual with delusional disorder is
    A) that such individuals tend to be difficult to understand because of their severe cognitive impairment.
    B) that it may be difficult to determine whether a particular belief is true or false, especially if one accepts the basic premise on which it is based.
    C) this type of individual tends to become violent when evaluated and challenged by a therapist.
    D) that the individual is usually ready to back down from his or her position when challenged, although he or she will resume the belief soon after.
    Answer: B

Pages: 480
Topic: Delusional (Paranoid) Disorder: Causal Factors/Delusional Disorder
Skill: Conceptual   Other1:
105. Severe disruption in cognitive processes
    A) is typical of individuals with delusional disorder.
    B) is typical of individuals with paranoid schizophrenia.
    C) is less common in delusional disorder and paranoid schizophrenia than in other types of schizophrenia.
    D) is common to both delusional disorder and paranoid schizophrenia, which indicates that these two disorders may be genetically related.
    Answer: C

Pages: 480
Topic: Delusional (Paranoid) Disorder: Causal Factors/Delusional Disorder
Skill: Factual   Other1:
106. As children, adult individuals with delusional disorder were typically
    A) indistinguishable from their normal peers.
    B) hyperactive and aggressive.
    C) aloof and seclusive.
    D) regarded as popular by their peers but as troublemakers by adults.
    Answer: C

Pages: 480-481
Topic: Delusional (Paranoid) Disorder: Causal Factors/Delusional Disorder
Skill: Factual   Other1:
107. The typical developmental course of delusional disorder involves
    A) a sudden onset in reaction to failure or rejection, when the individual decides that he
       or she is a victim of injustice.
    B) a gradual increase in suspiciousness and scrutiny, with a moment of "paranoid
       illumination" in which the individual decides that he or she is a victim of others.
    C) an experience of extreme stress in adolescence following a chaotic childhood, which
       culminates in a mental breakdown and the appearance of delusions.
    D) a gradual deterioration in cognitive and behavioral functioning.
    Answer: B

Pages: 481
Topic: Delusional (Paranoid) Disorder: Treatments and Outcomes
Skill: Factual   Other1:
108. The treatment of individuals with delusional disorder
    A) is difficult, since few of them think they need help.
    B) usually involves neuroleptic medication, which is very successful in eliminating the
       delusional system.
    C) is usually unsuccessful unless an individual is hospitalized and given extensive
       therapy in an inpatient setting.
    D) by means of cognitive therapy is generally very successful.
    Answer: A

Pages: 482
Topic: Unresolved Issues on Schizophrenia
Skill: Conceptual   Other1:
109. One of the greatest drawbacks to progress in understanding, treating, and preventing schizophrenia is
    A) the lack of reliability in current diagnostic criteria for schizophrenia.
    B) the probable heterogeneity of schizophrenic disorders.
    C) the lack of research that exists concerning possible biological factors involved in the etiology of schizophrenia.
    D) the excessive focus on psychosocial etiological factors.
    Answer: B

Pages: 482
Topic: Unresolved Issues on Schizophrenia
Skill: Factual   Other1:
110. Based on the position taken by the authors concerning limitations of past research approaches to understanding schizophrenia, future research
    A) should become interdisciplinary in nature, incorporating biological, psychosocial, and sociocultural perspectives.
    B) should mount a concerted effort at identifying the singular underlying cause of this homogeneous disorder.
    C) should recognize that the diversity of symptoms is not due to schizophrenia being comprised of distinct disorders, but instead is one core disorder that has many possible manifestations.
    D) should focus on the interactions between various biological factors insofar as psychosocial and sociocultural factors have proven to be relatively unimportant.
    Answer: A

Short Answer

Write the word or phrase that best completes each statement or answers the question.

Pages: 448-449
Topic: The Schizophrenias: The Clinical Picture in Schizophrenia
Skill: Factual   Other1:
1. Identify and briefly describe one of the distinctions that clinicians and researchers have used to characterize different types of schizophrenia. Do not include subtypes listed in the DSM-IV.
    Answer: The process/reactive distinction characterizes schizophrenics by the suddenness and form of the onset of schizophrenia as well as by the prognosis. Paranoid and nonparanoid schizophrenics are distinguished by the well-organized character of the schizophrenic's delusions as well as their persecutory or grandiose content. Negative-symptom and positive-symptom schizophrenics are distinguished by the particular symptoms that they display.

Pages: 449-451
Topic: The Schizophrenias: The Clinical Picture in Schizophrenia
Skill: Factual   Other1:
2. Briefly describe three of the central features of schizophrenia.
    Answer: Formal thought disorder involves a failure to make sense or to think logically.
    Disturbances of thought content involve delusions and peculiar beliefs.
    Perceptual aberrations and hallucinations may be present. Individuals may have
    a disturbed sense of self, disrupted goal-directed activity, autism,
    disturbances in motor behavior, and inappropriate emotion.

Pages: 453
Topic: The Schizophrenias: Subtypes of Schizophrenia
Skill: Factual   Other1:
3. What are the five subtypes of schizophrenia recognized by DSM-IV?
    Answer: They are the undifferentiated, paranoid, catatonic, disorganized, and residual
    subtypes.

Pages: 456
Topic: The Schizophrenias: Subtypes of Schizophrenia
Skill: Applied   Other1:
4. Dick has a diagnosis of schizophrenia. He first became symptomatic at age fifteen. He is
    currently unable to care for himself and behaves in a silly and infantile manner. His
    speech is often incoherent. Dick is most likely to have a DSM-IV diagnosis of the _____
    subtype of schizophrenia.
    Answer: disorganized

Pages: 453
Topic: The Schizophrenias: Subtypes of Schizophrenia
Skill: Factual   Other1:
5. Select and describe one of the subtypes of schizophrenia that is recognized in DSM-IV.
    Answer: Undifferentiated schizophrenia involves a rapidly changing mixture of most major
    symptoms. It is most common in an initial breakdown, during stress in a person
    already schizophrenic, or in a transition to another subtype. The paranoid type
    involves delusions, usually of persecution or grandeur, and less behavioral and
    cognitive disorganization than other types. The catatonic type is notable for
    motor disturbance. The disorganized type involves emotional blunting,
    silliness, word salad, and bizarre behavior. The residual type involves mild
    symptoms in remitted individuals.

Pages: 460-462
Topic: The Schizophrenias: Causal Factors in Schizophrenia
Skill: Conceptual   Other1:
6. What do twin studies tell us about the relative contribution of genetic and environmental factors in the etiology of schizophrenia?
    Answer: They suggest that there is some genetic contribution to schizophrenia, although concordant outcomes may be associated with greater prenatal and postnatal environmental similarities for monozygotic twins compared to dizygotic twins. Thus, twin studies do not allow us to draw clearcut conclusions about the magnitude of heritability in schizophrenia.

Pages: 463-464
Topic: The Schizophrenias: Causal Factors in Schizophrenia
Skill: Factual   Other1:
7. Describe three central findings from the Danish adoption study.
    Answer: Schizophrenia was more prevalent among biological relatives of schizophrenic probands than among biological relatives of matched controls. Chronic schizophrenia was the most common schizophrenic diagnosis among those relatives. Schizotypal personality disorder and schizoaffective disorder appear to be schizophrenia spectrum disorders, also appearing with greater frequency in biological relatives of schizophrenics. There may also be an interaction between genetic diathesis and family disorganization for individuals at genetic risk for schizophrenia.

Pages: 465
Topic: The Schizophrenias: Subtypes of Schizophrenia
Skill: Factual   Other1:
8. What is the dopamine hypothesis?
    Answer: This theory states that schizophrenia is caused by excessive dopaminergic activity at certain synaptic sites in the brain. This theory guided research for many years following the discovery that neuroleptic drugs reduced dopamine levels in schizophrenics. Today it is known that the etiology of schizophrenia is much more complex.

Pages: 466
Topic: The Schizophrenias: Causal Factors in Schizophrenia
Skill: Factual   Other1:
9. Schizophrenics and their biological relatives have been shown to be deficient in their ability to track a moving target visually, which is called _____.
    Answer: smooth pursuit eye movement (SPEM)

Pages: 467-468
Topic: The Schizophrenias: Causal Factors in Schizophrenia
Skill: Factual   Other1:

10. Identify three of the structures or regions of the brain which have been implicated in schizophrenia.
    Answer: These include the presence of enlarged ventricles and sulci, undersized temporal lobe structures, lowered metabolic activation in the frontal lobes, and anomalies in the basal ganglia.

Pages: 468
Topic: The Schizophrenias: Causal Factors in Schizophrenia
Skill: Factual   Other1:

11. What is the season of birth effect? Describe one explanation for it.
    Answer: This refers to the finding that a greater number of schizophrenics are born during the winter months than would be expected. It is not known why, although some have suggested that this has to do with influenza or other infectious agents that are associated with season. Torrey and colleagues propose an infectious agent that appears to be a common factor for both schizophrenia and stillbirth risk. Obstetrical complications also have been proposed.

Pages: 469-470
Topic: The Schizophrenias: Causal Factors in Schizophrenia
Skill: Conceptual   Other1:

12. How might biological factors influence the occurrence of psychosocial stressors in individuals at risk for schizophrenia?
    Answer: They may influence the personality and social development of children in a negative way, resulting in rejection or other difficulties with peers and family members. Poorer motor skills, lack of emotion, and a relatively greater proportion of negative emotions are characteristics that have been associated with high-risk children. These may impact on the way others view and treat them.

Pages: 470-472
Topic: The Schizophrenias: Causal Factors in Schizophrenia
Skill: Factual   Other1:

13. Three of the deviant family patterns that have been suggested as causal factors in schizophrenia are _____, _____, and _____.
    Answer: the schizophrenogenic mother; marital schism; marital skew; double-bind communication; communication deviance (transactional style deviance); expressed emotion

Pages: 472
Topic: The Schizophrenias: Causal Factors in Schizophrenia
Skill: Conceptual   Other1:
14. What does research on expressed emotion tell us?
    Answer: Relapse rates for schizophrenics are significantly higher when these individuals
             return to families that are high in expressed emotion. Expressed emotion also
             predicts schizophrenia before its initial onset. Therapeutic attempts to reduce
             expressed emotion in families have had a positive effect on relapse rates.

Pages: 472-474
Topic: The Schizophrenias: Causal Factors in Schizophrenia
Skill: Factual   Other1:
15. What influence do sociocultural factors have on schizophrenia?
    Answer: They are associated with differences in prevalence among different cultures and
             socioeconomic classes, and in the content and form that the disorder takes. They
             may also influence changes in the prevalence of different subtypes of
             schizophrenia over time.

Pages: 474-475
Topic: The Schizophrenias: Treatment and Outcomes
Skill: Conceptual   Other1:
16. The major problem with the way that schizophrenia is treated today is the tendency to use
    _____ therapy almost exclusively.
    Answer: drug

Pages: 477-478
Topic: Delusional (Paranoid) Disorder: The Clinical Picture
Skill: Factual   Other1:
17. What are delusional disorder and shared psychotic disorder?
    Answer: Delusional disorder involves a usually well-elaborated delusion that often
             involves a theme of persecution or grandeur. Occasional hallucinations may
             occur, but the individual with this disorder may appear entirely normal apart
             from the delusion. There is no cognitive disorganization as is seen with
             schizophrenia. Shared psychotic disorder involves the incorporation of another
             person's delusions and psychotic patterns.

Pages: 478-481
Topic: Delusional (Paranoid) Disorder: The Clinical Picture
Skill: Factual   Other1:

18. What is the typical developmental course of delusional disorder?

   Answer: An individual may have been aloof, seclusive, and secretive in childhood.
   Usually after a series of failures, disappointments, or rejections, an
   individual will become increasingly suspicious that others are to blame for
   these events. He scrutinizes every situation for clues and becomes highly
   selective in his information-processing. He often experiences a moment of
   "paranoid illumination" when everything falls into place and he feels at last
   that he understands the nature of the conspiracy against him. More and more of
   his environment is incorporated into the delusional system.

Pages: 482
Topic: Unresolved Issues on Schizophrenia
Skill: Conceptual   Other1:

19. The text often refers to schizophrenia as a heterogeneous disorder. What does this mean?

   Answer: It means that schizophrenia is actually a group of disorders which differ in
   terms of etiology, symptoms, course, prognosis, treatment, and/or perhaps
   prevention.

Pages: 481-482
Topic: Unresolved Issues on Schizophrenia
Skill: Conceptual   Other1:

20. Describe one of the problems facing schizophrenia researchers today.

   Answer: There is a lack of communication between psychosocial and biological
   researchers. There is a view that one or the other type of research is superior
   to the other. The heterogeneity of schizophrenia itself makes it very difficult
   to study the causes of the presumably distinct disorders that comprise the group
   of schizophrenias. The likelihood of a multiplicity of factors acting in concert
   makes it very difficult to assess the relative contribution of independent
   factors. The probably polygenic inheritance involved in a genetic diathesis also
   makes such research problematic.

Essay

Write your answer in the space provided or on a separate sheet of paper.

    Pages: 445-448
    Topic: The Schizophrenias: A Case Study
    Skill: Conceptual   *Other1:*

1. The text presented the case of the Genain quadruplets, four girls who were concordant for schizophrenia. Describe these individuals in terms of similarities and differences in clinical picture (e.g., reactive vs. process type), outcome, and potential causal factors.

    Answer: The environment had a powerful impact on the women's disorder despite their being genetically identical. They differed in symptoms, course, and severity from process (Hester) to reactive (Myra), undifferentiated (Myra) to disorganized (Iris and Hester), good outcome (Myra) to poor outcome (Hester). Hester was the most biologically compromised at birth which may have influenced her family's mistreatment of her. Hester and Nora had similar neurological impairments, but Nora's outcome was much better than Hester's or Iris's, perhaps because she was treated better by her parents than they were.

    Pages: 450
    Topic: The Schizophrenias: The Clinical Picture in Schizophrenia
    Skill: Factual   *Other1:*

2. Describe the DSM-IV diagnostic criteria for schizophrenia.

    Answer: 1) Two or more of the following: delusions, hallucinations, disorganized speech, grossly disorganized or catatonic behavior, negative symptoms. 2) Markedly poor performance in work, interpersonal relations, or self-care since the onset of the disturbance. 3) Continuous signs of disturbance for at least six months. Schizoaffective disorder, mood disorder, substance abuse, medication, and medical conditions have been ruled out.

    Pages: 449-451
    Topic: The Schizophrenias: The Clinical Picture in Schizophrenia
    Skill: Factual   *Other1:*

3. Describe the central clinical features of schizophrenia.

    Answer: The central features involve disorganization of perception, cognition, and behavior. Thinking may be disordered in form and in content. Perception is often disrupted, perhaps involving a breakdown in selectivity, and may include hallucinations. Emotions may be blunted, anhedonic, inappropriate, or agitated in acute phases of illness. The sense of self or identity may be confused. Goal-directed activity is usually interrupted, behavior deteriorated, motor behavior disturbed, and the individual may withdraw from reality into an inner fantasy world.

Pages: 453
Topic: The Schizophrenias: Subtypes of Schizophrenia
Skill: Factual   Other1:

4. Describe the different types of schizophrenia that are recognized in DSM-IV, other than residual schizophrenia.

    Answer: The undifferentiated type is most common at initial onset, during stress or transition to another subtype. It involves a rapidly changing pattern of most symptoms, with emotional turmoil and fear. The disorganized type involves infantile behavior, emotional blunting, word salad, and bizarre behavior. It has an earlier onset and poorer prognosis than other types. The catatonic type involves motoric rigidity which may alternate with agitation. Paranoid schizophrenia involves delusions, usually of persecution or grandeur, vivid hallucinations, and less disorganized behavior than in other types.

Pages: 459
Topic: The Schizophrenias: The Clinical Picture in Schizophrenia
Skill: Factual   Other1:

5. What are schizophreniform and schizoaffective disorders?

    Answer: These are not considered formal subtypes of schizophrenia in DSM-IV. Schizoaffective disorder is a category for individuals who have characteristics of both schizophrenia and bipolar or major depressive disorder, such that a differential diagnosis can not be made. Schizophreniform disorder is diagnosed when schizophrenic symptoms are present but have not lasted for six months. An individual may be rediagnosed as schizophrenic after six months. Brief psychotic episodes other than early-onset schizophrenia may also be diagnosed as schizophreniform disorder.

Pages: 460-465
Topic: The Schizophrenias: Causal Factors in Schizophrenia
Skill: Conceptual   Other1:

6. Describe the various research methods used to study the role of genetic factors in the etiology of schizophrenia. What are the advantages and limitations of each method?

    Answer: Family pedigree and twin studies examine the contribution of a genetic liability by comparing changes in the prevalence of schizophrenia with increases in genetic relatedness. If schizophrenia were exclusively genetic the concordance rate for MZ twins would approach 100 percent. Environmental similarities are greater for MZ twins, however. Adoption studies attempt to do a better job of separating genetic and environmental influences by examining index cases (and controls) who were not raised by a disordered biological parent.

Pages: 460-462
Topic: The Schizophrenias: Causal Factors in Schizophrenia
Skill: Conceptual   Other1:

7. Describe the schizophrenic twin studies discussed in the text. What were the findings and how would you interpret them?

    Answer: Concordance rates among MZ twins are about 28 percent, and 6 percent among DZ twins. This argues for a partial genetic contribution to schizophrenia, although prenatal and postnatal environments of MZ twins appear to be more similar than they are for DZ twins. Genetic factors may influence psychosocial factors. An MZ twin pair may differ in genetic mutations, congenital brain abnormalities, and other potentially important etiological factors. Discordant affected co-twins also show anomalies in brain structure and function.

Pages: 462-464
Topic: The Schizophrenias: Causal Factors in Schizophrenia
Skill: Factual   Other1:

8. What have adoption studies found about the etiology of schizophrenia?

    Answer: The Danish adoption study found a greater prevalence of schizophrenia, schizotypal personality disorder, and schizoaffective disorder in the biological relatives of adopted-away schizophrenics, but no such increase in their adoptive relatives or in the biological relatives of matched controls. This suggests a moderate genetic risk. It was also found that relative family disorganization in adoptive families may interact with genetic liability to raise the risk of schizophrenia in genetically liable individuals beyond the risk they would have if placed in a healthy adoptive family.

Pages: 465-466
Topic: The Schizophrenias: Causal Factors in Schizophrenia
Skill: Factual   Other1:

9. What is the dopamine hypothesis? What is the status of this theory today?

    Answer: This theory of schizophrenic etiology was developed when scientists found that early anti-psychotic drugs acted to decrease dopaminergic activity. The theory suggests that schizophrenia is caused by excess dopamine activity at postsynaptic receptors. However, today this theory is seen as insufficient. Dopaminergic drugs act on neural sites almost immediately but it takes weeks for psychotic symptoms to subside. The dopamine system contains several types of dopamine receptors involved in different biochemical processes. Further, new drugs differ from dopamine blockers in mode of action.

Pages: 466-469
Topic: The Schizophrenias: Causal Factors in Schizophrenia
Skill: Conceptual   Other1:

10. A variety of studies have found neurophysiological and neuroanatomical anomalies associated with schizophrenia. Describe these findings and discuss how you would interpret them.

     Answer: Neurophysiological abnormalities may underlie perceptual, attentional, and information-processing dysfunctions. Schizophrenics and their relatives are often disordered in smooth pursuit eye movement, sustained attention and other information-processing tasks, and neuropsychological tests. Studies find enlarged ventricles and sulci, hypofrontality, and abnormalities of temporal lobes and basal ganglia in schizophrenics, and related anomalies in schizotypals and in children at genetic risk. This suggests an inherited biological vulnerability, though not necessarily specific to schizophrenia.

Pages: 459-474
Topic: The Schizophrenias: Causal Factors in Schizophrenia
Skill: Conceptual   Other1:

11. What is the current status of research on the role of genetic and psychosocial factors in the etiology of schizophrenia?

     Answer: Most research today is biogenetic, with an enormous lack of attention to psychosocial factors and to interdisciplinary research and communication. Evidence suggests a moderate genetic liability for some cases of schizophrenia, although the magnitude of heritability, the mechanism of transmission, and the specific gene loci are unknown. Many biological anomalies have been found in schizophrenics' relatives, again suggesting a genetic liability, but how these anomalies cause psychotic symptoms is unknown and most findings are not specific to schizophrenia. Deviant communication may be causal.

Pages: 469-472
Topic: The Schizophrenias: Causal Factors in Schizophrenia
Skill: Factual   Other1:

12. Much psychosocial schizophrenia research has focused on the family life of schizophrenics. Describe three of the more influential theories, and what the research evaluating these theories has found.

     Answer: Starting in the 1940's, the theory of the schizophrenogenic mother appeared. She was seen as cold and rejecting, yet also eliciting dependence from her child for her own emotional satisfaction. This theory was not born out empirically. Other theories include double-bind theory (also unsupported by research), Lidz's studies of marital skew and schism, and family communication deviance. Studies usually find emotional disturbance in parents. Communication deviance and EE have been found to predict the onset of schizophrenia. Bidirectionality of effects is common.

Pages: 474-475
Topic: The Schizophrenias: Treatment and Outcomes
Skill: Applied   Other1:

13. Imagine that you are a psychologist who is asked to design a treatment program for a schizophrenic individual. What would you include and why?

Answer: Pharmacotherapy is important in treating such an individual to reduce psychotic symptoms. However, other interventions should be included to help the individual cope with everyday responsibilities, social skills, and the impact that the illness has on various areas of the individual's life. Family therapy to educate family members and to reduce EE (and subsequent probablility of relapse) are important.

Pages: 475-481
Topic: Delusional (Paranoid) Disorder: The Clinical Picture
Skill: Factual   Other1:

14. Describe the characteristic clinical picture and developmental course of delusional disorder.

Answer: A child who later develops this disorder is often secretive, aloof, and seclusive, which may cause further interpersonal difficulties. As an adult, the onset of the disorder usually follows several disappointments or failures, initially increasing one's hostility and defenses by blaming others and enhancing selective perceptions. A moment of paranoid illumination may occur, in which the delusion crystallizes. The person builds a pseudo-community around his or her delusional system which is impervious to logic or reason. Themes usually involve persecution or grandeur. Violence may result.

Pages: 481-482
Topic: Unresolved Issues on Schizophrenia
Skill: Conceptual   Other1:

15. What are some of the problems involved in schizophrenia research today?

Answer: One difficulty is in defining the construct of schizophrenia. DSM-IV relies on symptoms, with very reliable diagnostic criteria but somewhat questionable validity. Schizophrenia is probably heterogeneous, but it is not known how to carve it into distinct disorders each with its own set of causal factors. It is extremely difficult to disentangle environmental from genetic effects in research, especially without knowledge of specific gene loci involved in the vulnerability. The deep schism between biological and psychosocial researchers prevents studying interactions between these variables.

CHAPTER 13 Brain Disorders and Other Cognitive Impairments

Multiple-Choice

Choose the one alternative that best completes the statement or answers the question.

Pages: 486
Topic: Brain Impairment and Adult Disorder
Skill: Factual   Other1:
1. The difference between neurological problems and psychopathological problems
    A) is that psychopathological symptoms do not have a physiological basis.
    B) is nonexistent.
    C) is that neurological problems always cause psychopathology.
    D) is that psychopathology can result from neurological damage, or can exist in the
       absence of demonstrable brain anomalies.
    Answer: D

Pages: 486
Topic: Brain Impairment/Adult Disorder: Adult Brain Damage/Mental Function
Skill: Applied   Other1:
2. Mary ingested small amounts of lead, which resulted in mild, diffuse brain damage. She is
    most likely to show
    A) severe disorientation.
    B) emotional overreactivity.
    C) hallucinations.
    D) attentional impairments.
    Answer: D

Pages: 486
Topic: Brain Impairment/Adult Disorder: Adult Brain Damage/Mental Function
Skill: Factual   Other1:
3. A circumscribed area of abnormal change in brain structure is a
    A) pseudodementia.
    B) focal lesion.
    C) diffuse lesion.
    D) neuropsychopathological lesion.
    Answer: B

Pages: 486-487
Topic: Brain Impairment/Adult Disorder: Adult Brain Damage/Mental Function
Skill: Factual   Other1:

4. Focal brain lesions
    A) occur only in adults and only following a direct injury to the brain.
    B) often occur with progressive brain disease that spreads over numerous focal sites.
    C) involve diffuse damage following oxygen deprivation or the ingestion of toxins.
    D) result in psychopathological symptoms, but not in neuropsychological deficits.
    Answer: B

Pages: 487
Topic: Brain Impairment/Adult Disorder: Adult Brain Damage/Mental Function
Skill: Applied   Other1:

5. Maria has a focal brain lesion. She may exhibit
    A) great trouble remembering past events, but little trouble remembering recent events.
    B) a heightened preoccupation with personal standards of hygiene and appearance.
    C) difficulty in initiating behavior.
    D) good abstract reasoning but poor understanding of concrete concepts.
    Answer: C

Pages: 487
Topic: Brain Impairment/Adult Disorder: Adult Brain Damage/Mental Function
Skill: Applied   Other1:

6. Impairment in orientation is one consequence of a focal brain lesion. An example of this would be
    A) an individual who has difficulty initiating behaviors.
    B) an individual who has difficulty coordinating motor activity with visual stimuli.
    C) an individual who is unable to locate himself or herself in time or space.
    D) an individual who manifests inappropriate emotions with a lack of emotional control.
    Answer: C

Pages: 487
Topic: Brain Impairment/Adult Disorder: Adult Brain Damage/Mental Function
Skill: Factual   Other1:

7. Which of the following types of impairments are associated with focal brain lesions?
    A) memory deficits
    B) difficulties with learning and comprehension
    C) poor control over hygiene and sexuality
    D) all of the above
    Answer: D

Pages: 487
Topic: Brain Impairment/Adult Disorder: Adult Brain Damage/Mental Function
Skill: Conceptual   Other1:
8. An individual with neuropsychological damage
    A) will not usually show manifest psychopathology.
    B) will almost always evidence moderate to severe psychopathology.
    C) usually manifests psychopathology that is very consistent and predictable.
    D) may have psychopathological symptoms, but these occur as a consequence of the
       individual reacting to being neurologically impaired rather than as the direct effects
       of the damage itself.
    Answer: A

Pages: 487
Topic: Brain Impairment/Adult Disorder: Adult Brain Damage/Mental Function
Skill: Factual   Other1:
9. Brain damage
    A) varies in its effects on different individuals depending on their previous level of
       personality integration and life situation.
    B) varies between individuals only insofar as the location or severity of the damage
       varies.
    C) does not vary in its neurological effects on different individuals, but does vary in
       terms of its psychopathological effects.
    D) none of the above
    Answer: A

Pages: 488
Topic: Brain Impairment/Adult Disorder: Adult Brain Damage/Mental Function
Skill: Factual   Other1:
10. The text uses the example of "hardware" and "software" as analogies for
    A) memory and attention.
    B) recall and recognition.
    C) brain and psychological experience.
    D) subcortex and cortex.
    Answer: C

Pages: 488
Topic: Brain Impairment/Adult Disorder: Adult Brain Damage/Mental Function
Skill: Conceptual   Other1:
11. Using a computer analogy,
    A) neurological disorders are the result of a software "glitch."
    B) neurological disorders are the result of a breakdown in hardware.
    C) neurological disorders are faulty software that may cause a breakdown in some of the
       hardware components.
    D) Computer analogies are misleading in this case.
    Answer: B

Pages: 488
Topic: Brain Impairment/Adult Disorder: Adult Brain Damage/Mental Function
Skill: Conceptual   Other1:
12. Using a computer analogy, the extensive breakdown of hardware preventing new information from being encoded and old information from being retrieved is
    A) focal damage.
    B) dementia.
    C) the amnestic syndrome.
    D) mental retardation.
    Answer: B

Pages: 488
Topic: Brain Impairment/Adult Disorder: Adult Brain Damage/Mental Function
Skill: Factual   Other1:
13. Once cells and neural pathways in the brain have been destroyed,
    A) the functions that they controlled are irretrievably lost.
    B) they make partial improvement in function impossible.
    C) psychological abilities are more likely to be lost than physical abilities.
    D) they rarely regenerate.
    Answer: D

Pages: 489
Topic: Brain Impairment/Adult Disorder: Adult Brain Damage/Mental Function
Skill: Applied   Other1:
14. Micah has suffered brain damage in the left hemisphere. He is most likely to suffer a loss of functioning in
    A) language.
    B) gestalt processing.
    C) the left side of his body.
    D) reasoning on a nonverbal level.
    Answer: A

Pages: 489
Topic: Brain Impairment/Adult Disorder: Adult Brain Damage/Mental Function
Skill: Factual   Other1:
15. Deficits in intuitive reasoning, and configural and spatial processing are associated with damage to the
    A) temporal lobes.
    B) left hemisphere.
    C) right hemisphere.
    D) frontal lobes.
    Answer: C

Pages: 489
Topic: Brain Impairment/Adult Disorder: Adult Brain Damage/Mental Function
Skill: Conceptual   Other1:
16. Brain-behavior relationships
   A) are straightforward due to the specialization of different brain regions for different functions.
   B) are straightforward for sensory and motor skills, but not for higher mental processes.
   C) are difficult to predict, since almost any given behavior is produced by activity in many parts of the brain.
   D) none of the above
   Answer: C

Pages: 490
Topic: Brain Impairment/Adult Disorder: Adult Brain Damage/Mental Function
Skill: Applied   Other1:
17. Monty has suffered damage to the frontal lobes. He is most likely to show
   A) passivity, apathy, and perseverative thought.
   B) a loss of functioning to the right side of the body.
   C) a deficit in receptive language.
   D) distortions in his body image.
   Answer: A

Pages: 490
Topic: Brain Impairment/Adult Disorder: Adult Brain Damage/Mental Function
Skill: Factual   Other1:
18. Damage to temporal lobe structures causes
   A) impulsivity and attentional problems.
   B) visual impairments.
   C) difficulty with fine motor movements.
   D) memory problems.
   Answer: D

Pages: 490
Topic: Brain Impairment/Adult Disorder: Adult Brain Damage/Mental Function
Skill: Factual   Other1:
19. An important limitation with the DSM-IV is that neuropsychological disorders are sometimes coded on Axis _____, but at other times neurological disease processes are coded on Axes
   _____ .
   A) III; I and IV
   B) I; II and IV
   C) I; I and V
   D) I; I and III
   Answer: D

Pages: 490
Topic: Brain Impairment/Adult Disorder: Neuropsychological Disorder/HIV-1
Skill: Factual   Other1:
20. Neuropsychological symptom syndromes differ from mood and personality disorders in that the former
    A) include hallucinations and delusions.
    B) exclude manic symptoms.
    C) include obvious motor skill deficits.
    D) are presumed to reflect underlying brain pathology.
    Answer: D

Pages: 491
Topic: Brain Impairment/Adult Disorder: Neuropsychological Disorder/HIV-1
Skill: Factual   Other1:
21. Widespread disorganization of mental processes that develops rapidly and that may result in coma is
    A) dementia.
    B) delirium.
    C) Alzheimer's disease.
    D) reterograde amnesia.
    Answer: B

Pages: 491
Topic: Brain Impairment/Adult Disorder: Neuropsychological Disorder/HIV-1
Skill: Factual   Other1:
22. Delirious states
    A) tend to be acute conditions that rarely last longer than a week.
    B) are usually caused by the progressive deterioration of brain tissue.
    C) are rarely serious.
    D) tend to interfere somewhat with an individual's daily activity, although the individual should be able to continue with ordinary tasks.
    Answer: A

Pages: 491
Topic: Brain Impairment/Adult Disorder: Neuropsychological Disorder/HIV-1
Skill: Factual   Other1:
23. Dementia involves
    A) a rapid onset.
    B) generalized disturbance in brain metabolism.
    C) progressive deterioration of brain functioning.
    D) a diffuse reaction to toxic substances.
    Answer: C

Pages: 491
Topic: Brain Impairment/Adult Disorder: Neuropsychological Disorder/HIV-1
Skill: Applied   Other1:
24. Irv is in the earliest phase of dementia. His symptoms most likely include
    A) personality deterioration and loss of moral sensibility.
    B) memory deficits for recent events.
    C) loss of emotional control.
    D) inability to care for his hygiene and appearance.
    Answer: B

Pages: 492
Topic: Brain Impairment/Adult Disorder: Neuropsychological Disorder/HIV-1
Skill: Factual   Other1:
25. The most common cause of dementia is
    A) intracranial tumors.
    B) severe or repeated head injury.
    C) drug toxicity.
    D) degenerative brain disease.
    Answer: D

Pages: 492
Topic: Brain Impairment/Adult Disorder: Neuropsychological Disorder/HIV-1
Skill: Factual   Other1:
26. The amnestic syndrome involves deficits in
    A) long-term memory.
    B) memory for words and concepts.
    C) abstract reasoning.
    D) short-term memory.
    Answer: D

Pages: 492
Topic: Brain Impairment/Adult Disorder: Neuropsychological Disorder/HIV-1
Skill: Conceptual   Other1:
27. Dementia and the amnestic syndrome differ in that
    A) dementia does not involve memory deficits.
    B) dementia is not reversible, whereas the amnestic syndrome rarely lasts longer than a
       few months.
    C) memory loss is progressive in amnestic syndrome.
    D) in amnestic syndrome, overall cognitive functioning remains relatively intact.
    Answer: D

Pages: 493
Topic: Brain Impairment/Adult Disorder: Neuropsychological Disorder/HIV-1
Skill: Factual   Other1:
28. Neuropsychological delusional syndrome
    A) often is caused by retarded cerebrovascular development.
    B) often is caused by pseudodementia.
    C) often is caused by drug abuse.
    D) all of the above
    Answer: C

Pages: 493
Topic: Brain Impairment/Adult Disorder: Neuropsychological Disorder/HIV-1
Skill: Factual   Other1:
29. Neuropsychological mood syndrome most closely resembles
    A) anxiety disorders.
    B) depressive disorders.
    C) schizophrenia.
    D) all of the above
    Answer: B

Pages: 493
Topic: Brain Impairment/Adult Disorder: Neuropsychological Disorder/HIV-1
Skill: Factual   Other1:
30. A severely depressed syndrome that appears like dementia is called
    A) major depression, melancholic type.
    B) major depression, neuropsychological type.
    C) secondary depression.
    D) pseudodementia.
    Answer: D

Pages: 493
Topic: Brain Impairment/Adult Disorder: Neuropsychological Disorder/HIV-1
Skill: Factual   Other1:
31. The essential feature of neuropsychological personality syndromes is
    A) manic or depressive states caused by impaired cerebral functioning.
    B) false beliefs arising out of known or suspected brain damage.
    C) neuroses arising out of known or suspected brain damage.
    D) a change in general personality style or traits following brain impairment.
    Answer: D

Pages: 493
Topic: Brain Impairment/Adult Disorder: Neuropsychological Disorder/HIV-1
Skill: Factual   Other1:
32. In neuropsychological personality syndrome,
    A) the cause is always associated with ingestion of toxins or substance abuse.
    B) there are many etiologies associated with the syndrome.
    C) the personality change is positive in some cases but distinctly negative in other
       cases.
    D) symptoms usually appear during the final stage of a progressive brain disorder.
    Answer: B

Pages: 494
Topic: Brain Impairment/Adult Disorder: Neuropsychological Disorder/HIV-1
Skill: Factual   Other1:
33. The HIV-1 virus
    A) causes opportunistic infections in the body which sometimes spread to the brain.
    B) can directly cause disruptions in bodily functioning, but does not directly affect the
       central nervous system.
    C) can itself cause disruptive brain changes.
    D) causes general paresis.
    Answer: C

Pages: 494
Topic: Brain Impairment/Adult Disorder: Neuropsychological Disorder/HIV-1
Skill: Applied   Other1:
34. Melanie has AIDS dementia complex. This is most likely
    A) caused by a secondary infection associated with AIDS.
    B) localized to the occipital lobe of her brain.
    C) to involve a generalized loss of cognitive functioning.
    D) to affect female AIDS patients far more often than male patients for reasons as yet
       unknown.
    Answer: C

Pages: 494
Topic: Brain Impairment/Adult Disorder: Neuropsychological Disorder/HIV-1
Skill: Factual   Other1:
35. AIDS dementia complex
    A) usually appears soon after HIV infection.
    B) appears after the development of full-blown AIDS.
    C) is primarily associated with males and not females.
    D) usually begins with psychomotor slowing, diminished concentration, and mild memory
       difficulties.
    Answer: D

Pages: 494
Topic: Brain Impairment/Adult Disorder: Neuropsychological Disorder/HIV-1
Skill: Factual   Other1:

36. Neurological problems
    A) diagnosable as AIDS dementia complex appear in as many as 38 percent of AIDS patients.
    B) are apparent in subtler form in many individuals with AIDS-related complex and HIV infection.
    C) are rare in AIDS patients, except in a minority who have been infected with HIV for a long period of time.
    D) A and B
    Answer: D

Pages: 494
Topic: Brain Impairment/Adult Disorder: Neuropsychological Disorder/HIV-1
Skill: Factual   Other1:

37. Treatment for AIDS dementia complex
    A) is nonexistent at present.
    B) involves anti-psychotic medication and dietary monitoring.
    C) is sometimes successful with antiviral medication, although this success may be temporary.
    D) is successful but only when individuals do not yet exhibit full-blown AIDS.
    Answer: C

Pages: 495
Topic: Brain Impairment/Adult Disorder: Dementia of the Alzheimer's Type
Skill: Factual   Other1:

38. Mental disorders accompanying the brain degeneration of old age are called
    A) presenile dementias.
    B) senile dementias.
    C) Huntington's dementias.
    D) Pick's disorders.
    Answer: B

Pages: 495
Topic: Brain Impairment/Adult Disorder: Dementia of the Alzheimer's Type
Skill: Factual   Other1:

39. Presenile Alzheimer's dementia is
    A) associated with an especially slow and gradual progression.
    B) a milder version of senile Alzheimer's dementia.
    C) probably associated with a substantial genetic contribution.
    D) exclusively associated with frontal lobe impairment.
    Answer: C

Pages: 495-496
Topic: Brain Impairment/Adult Disorder: Dementia of the Alzheimer's Type
Skill: Conceptual   Other1:
40. The real nature of Alzheimer's disease is
A) merely the product of the aging process as manifested in the brain.
B) a specific disease process.
C) an organ system failure associated with the cumulative exposure to an array of risk factors.
D) unknown; any of the above answers coud be correct.
Answer: D

Pages: 496
Topic: Brain Impairment/Adult Disorder: Dementia of the Alzheimer's Type
Skill: Factual   Other1:
41. The rate of Dementia of the Alzheimer's Type (DAT) is
A) about one in ten people over age sixty-five in the United States.
B) declining in Western countries with improvements in living conditions.
C) about 50 percent in individuals over the age of sixty-five.
D) artificially inflated by inaccurate statistical analyses of epidemiological data.
Answer: A

Pages: 496
Topic: Brain Impairment/Adult Disorder: Dementia of the Alzheimer's Type
Skill: Factual   Other1:
42. Pick's disease
A) is a subtype of Alzheimer's dementia.
B) is genetically related to Huntington's disease.
C) is a presenile dementia more common in women than in men.
D) has a rapid onset but is rarely fatal.
Answer: C

Pages: 496
Topic: Brain Impairment/Adult Disorder: Dementia of the Alzheimer's Type
Skill: Factual   Other1:
43. Huntington's disease
A) often begins with florid psychotic symptoms.
B) is a genetically determined form of presenile dementia.
C) can be cured once it has begun but can not be prevented.
D) is often caused by environmental toxins.
Answer: B

Pages: 497
Topic: Brain Impairment/Adult Disorder: Dementia of the Alzheimer's Type
Skill: Factual   Other1:
44. In Dementia of the Alzheimer's Type (DAT),
    A) symptoms often begin with a person's gradual withdrawal from social life and other interests.
    B) the disease is debilitating but rarely fatal.
    C) individuals are reduced to a vegetative state within about three years of first showing symptoms.
    D) most individuals become markedly paranoid and assaultive.
    Answer: A

Pages: 497
Topic: Brain Impairment/Adult Disorder: Dementia of the Alzheimer's Type
Skill: Factual   Other1:
45. Individuals who have Dementia of the Alzheimer's Type (DAT)
    A) may vary in symptoms from day to day.
    B) may recover permanently if the disease has not progressed too far.
    C) rarely degenerate to the point that they can not care for themselves at all.
    D) will remain physically healthy despite their cognitive deterioration.
    Answer: A

Pages: 497
Topic: Brain Impairment/Adult Disorder: Dementia of the Alzheimer's Type
Skill: Factual   Other1:
46. About half of all individuals with Dementia of the Alzheimer's Type (DAT)
    A) die within three to five years.
    B) end up in a vegetative state.
    C) display a course of simple deterioration.
    D) develop paranoid delusions, hallucinations, and become violently assaultive.
    Answer: C

Pages: 497-498
Topic: Brain Impairment/Adult Disorder: Dementia of the Alzheimer's Type
Skill: Applied   Other1:
47. The text presented a case study of a retired engineer who was hospitalized by his wife and son. He was typical of many patients with Dementia of the Alzheimer's Type (DAT) in that
    A) he had become violent toward family members.
    B) his recall of recent events was intact, but his long-term memory was severely impaired.
    C) he showed a course of simple deterioration.
    D) he became hypochondriacal and performed repetitive, meaningless rituals.
    Answer: C

Pages: 499
Topic: Brain Impairment/Adult Disorder: Dementia of the Alzheimer's Type
Skill: Factual   Other1:
48. Treatment of Dementia of the Alzheimer's Type (DAT) usually includes
    A) neuroleptic medication.
    B) surgery to repair damaged neural circuits.
    C) medication and a calm, reassuring social environment.
    D) neurological imaging.
    Answer: C

Pages: 498-499
Topic: Brain Impairment/Adult Disorder: Dementia of the Alzheimer's Type
Skill: Factual   Other1:
49. The end stage of Alzheimer's disease is characterized by all of the following EXCEPT
    A) a vegetative state.
    B) continuous delirium.
    C) depression.
    D) death.
    Answer: C

Pages: 499
Topic: Brain Impairment/Adult Disorder: Dementia of the Alzheimer's Type
Skill: Factual   Other1:
50. The fundamental neuropathology of Dementia of the Alzheimer's Type (DAT) involves
    A) an excessive number of dopaminergic postsynaptic receptor sites.
    B) the accumulation of environmental toxins within brain cell nuclei.
    C) malformations of cells in the parietal lobes.
    D) granulovacuoles, tangled neurofibrils, and senile plaques.
    Answer: D

Pages: 499
Topic: Brain Impairment/Adult Disorder: Dementia of the Alzheimer's Type
Skill: Factual   Other1:
51. The depletion of _____ is strongly implicated in Dementia of the Alzheimer's Type (DAT).
    A) dopamine
    B) serotonin
    C) beta amyloid
    D) acetylcholine
    Answer: D

Pages: 499
Topic: Brain Impairment/Adult Disorder: Dementia of the Alzheimer's Type
Skill: Factual   Other1:
52. Evidence for the involvement of acetylcholine (ACh) in Alzheimer's disease comes from all of the following EXCEPT
    A) the earliest and most severely affected neurons in Alzheimer's disease are involved in the release of ACh.
    B) a promising new diagnostic test for Alzheimer's disease appears to depend on the effects of ACh.
    C) senile plaques and granulovacuoles appear only in cells associated with ACh pathways.
    D) a drug that increases the availability of ACh has proven temporarily helpful in improving cognitive function in some Alzheimer's patients.
    Answer: C

Pages: 500
Topic: Brain Impairment/Adult Disorder: Dementia of the Alzheimer's Type
Skill: Factual   Other1: In Student Study Guide
53. Dementia of the Alzheimer's Type (DAT) has been linked to _____, which is due to a trisomy involving chromosome 21.
    A) Huntington's chorea
    B) Down syndrome
    C) MID
    D) Tay-Sach's disease
    Answer: B

Pages: 500
Topic: Brain Impairment/Adult Disorder: Dementia of the Alzheimer's Type
Skill: Factual   Other1:
54. According to recent discoveries made by researchers at Duke University, _____ may play a key role in the etiology of Dementia of the Alzheimer's Type (DAT).
    A) amyloid
    B) acetylcholine
    C) apoliproprotein-E
    D) all of the above
    Answer: C

Pages: 500
Topic: Brain Impairment/Adult Disorder: Dementia of the Alzheimer's Type
Skill: Factual   Other1:
55. In the etiology of Alzheimer's disease, environmental factors
    A) play a minimal role, since there is a genetic basis for the disorder.
    B) are involved in late-onset Alzheimer's, but not in early-onset Alzheimer's.
    C) probably play an important role, since many monozygotic twins are discordant for
       Alzheimer's.
    D) cause most instances of the disorder.
    Answer: C

Pages: 500-501
Topic: Brain Impairment/Adult Disorder: Dementia of the Alzheimer's Type
Skill: Factual   Other1:
56. The treatment of Alzheimer's dementia
    A) at best allows only a temporary interruption of the course of the disease.
    B) is successful in reversing the course of the disease in about half of the cases using
       acetylcholine-enhancing drugs.
    C) focuses on the alteration of faulty genes on chromosome 21.
    D) involves the use of neuroleptic drugs.
    Answer: A

Pages: 501
Topic: Brain Impairment/Adult Disorder: Dementia of the Alzheimer's Type
Skill: Applied   Other1:
57. Eli is an Alzheimer's patient who has begun to wander off at night and make inappropriate
    sexual advances. A therapeutic intervention that might work best to control these
    behaviors is
    A) cognitive therapy.
    B) neuroleptic medication.
    C) antidepressant medication.
    D) behavioral therapy.
    Answer: D

Pages: 501
Topic: Brain Impairment/Adult Disorder: Dementia of the Alzheimer's Type
Skill: Applied   Other1:
58. Melinda cares for her mother who has Dementia of the Alzheimer's Type (DAT). Melinda
    A) is likely to find taking care of her mother somewhat stressful but rewarding.
    B) is at high risk for depression and psychotropic drug abuse.
    C) is probably in denial about the course and outcome of her mother's disorder.
    D) will probably also develop Alzheimer's disease.
    Answer: B

Pages: 501
Topic: Brain Impairment/Adult Disorder: Dementia of the Alzheimer's Type
Skill: Factual   Other1:
59. Nursing home care for Alzheimer's patients
   A) almost always results in more rapid deterioration.
   B) may result in rapid deterioration if the institution lacks social support and
      stimulation.
   C) is about half as expensive as home care.
   D) is not commonly used because of the great costs involved.
   Answer: B

Pages: 502
Topic: Brain Impairment/Adult Disorder: Dementia of the Alzheimer's Type
Skill: Factual   Other1:
60. Vascular dementia (VAD)
   A) is a variant of late-onset Dementia of the Alzheimer's Type (DAT).
   B) is a pseudodementia.
   C) is caused by strokes.
   D) is the most common form of dementia.
   Answer: C

Pages: 502
Topic: Brain Impairment/Adult Disorder: Dementia of the Alzheimer's Type
Skill: Factual   Other1:
61. Compared to Dementia of the Alzheimer's Type (DAT), vascular dementia (VAD)
   A) does not involve general brain atrophy and behavioral impairment.
   B) usually begins before the age of fifty.
   C) sometimes can be medically managed to reduce the likelihood of further strokes and
      deterioration.
   D) has a very different clinical picture, especially late in the course of the disorder.
   Answer: C

Pages: 502
Topic: Brain Impairment and Adult Disorder: Disorders Involving Head Injury
Skill: Factual   Other1:
62. All of the following are general types of traumatic head injury distinguished by
   clinicians EXCEPT
   A) brain stem injury.
   B) closed head injury.
   C) skull fracture.
   D) penetrating head injury.
   Answer: A

Pages: 502
Topic: Brain Impairment and Adult Disorder: Disorders Involving Head Injury
Skill: Applied   Other1:
63. Reba has recently regained clear consciousness after sustaining a serious head injury in an automobile accident. She probably is experiencing which of the following?
A) retrograde amnesia
B) postgrade amnesia
C) convulsions
D) coma
Answer: A

Pages: 502
Topic: Brain Impairment and Adult Disorder: Disorders Involving Head Injury
Skill: Factual   Other1:
64. Anterograde amnesia is
A) an amnesia that follows a trauma-induced coma.
B) an inability to remember events leading up to a head injury.
C) an inability to remember events during variable periods of time after a head injury.
D) a delirium associated with severe head injuries.
Answer: C

Pages: 503
Topic: Brain Impairment and Adult Disorder: Disorders Involving Head Injury
Skill: Factual   Other1:
65. A person who is rendered unconscious by a head trauma
A) will usually lapse into a coma before regaining consciousness.
B) will usually pass through stages of stupor and confusion as the person returns to consciousness.
C) will usually experience serious cerebral edema.
D) will usually suffer from permanently reduced general intelligence and difficulty resuming prior occupational tasks.
Answer: B

Pages: 503
Topic: Brain Impairment and Adult Disorder: Disorders Involving Head Injury
Skill: Factual   Other1:
66. The severity and duration of residual symptoms following brain injury depend on
A) the nature and extent of the damage.
B) a person's premorbid personality.
C) the immediacy of treatment.
D) all of the above
Answer: D

Pages: 503
Topic: Brain Impairment and Adult Disorder: Disorders Involving Head Injury
Skill: Factual   Other1:
67. Most of the recovery from severe brain injury
    A) does not occur until after months, and sometimes years, of therapy.
    B) is in cognitive functioning rather than in behavioral problems.
    C) occurs in the earliest posttrauma phase.
    D) emerges spontaneously long after the injury occurred.
    Answer: C

Pages: 503
Topic: Brain Impairment and Adult Disorder: Disorders Involving Head Injury
Skill: Factual   Other1:
68. Pressure on regions of the brain caused by the accumulation of blood is called
    A) subdural hematoma.
    B) petechial hemorrhage.
    C) intracranial hemorrhage.
    D) brain contusion.
    Answer: A

Pages: 503-504
Topic: Brain Impairment and Adult Disorder: Disorders Involving Head Injury
Skill: Applied   Other1:
69. Stone suffers from slurred speech, impaired memory and concentration, and involuntary movements. He probably has
    A) AIDS dementia complex.
    B) Alzheimer's disease.
    C) encephalopathy from petechial hemorrhaging ("punch drunk").
    D) organic personality syndrome.
    Answer: C

Pages: 504
Topic: Brain Impairment and Adult Disorder: Disorders Involving Head Injury
Skill: Conceptual   Other1:
70. Mild brain concussions and contusions
    A) usually go unnoticed by the individual who experiences them.
    B) may result in postimpact confusion and subtle residual impairment.
    C) do not result in permanent neurological impairment.
    D) result in subdural hematoma.
    Answer: B

Pages: 504-505
Topic: Brain Impairment and Adult Disorder: Disorders Involving Head Injury
Skill: Applied   Other1:
71. Phineas Gage, the nineteenth century man whose brain was pierced by a crowbar, would today be considered to have
    A) amnestic syndrome.
    B) vascular dementia.
    C) neurological personality syndrome.
    D) pseudodementia.
    Answer: C

Pages: 506
Topic: Brain Impairment and Adult Disorder: Disorders Involving Head Injury
Skill: Factual   Other1:
72. All of the following predict a favorable prognosis in cases of head injury EXCEPT
    A) a short period of unconsciousness or posttraumatic amnesia.
    B) appropriate rehabilitation and retraining interventions.
    C) motivation to recover.
    D) a brief period of anterograde amnesia following injury.
    Answer: D

Pages: 506
Topic: Brain Impairment and Adult Disorder: Disorders Involving Head Injury
Skill: Factual   Other1:
73. An alcoholic
    A) will show less decline in cognitive functioning following head injury.
    B) is more likely to experience a head injury.
    C) has a poor prognosis for recovery from head injury.
    D) B and C
    Answer: D

Pages: 506
Topic: Mental Retardation
Skill: Factual   Other1:
74. A disorder that is functionally equivalent to mental retardation but that has its onset after age seventeen must be considered
    A) a late-onset type of mental retardation.
    B) a dementia.
    C) to have a relatively favorable prognosis.
    D) to be of relatively brief duration.
    Answer: B

Pages: 506
Topic: Mental Retardation
Skill: Factual   Other1:
75. In contrast to other developmental disorders, mental retardation is diagnosed in DSM-IV on
    A) Axis I.
    B) Axis II.
    C) Axis III.
    D) Axes I and III.
    Answer: B

Pages: 507
Topic: Mental Retardation
Skill: Factual   Other1:
76. Initial diagnoses of mental retardation
    A) are usually made shortly after birth.
    B) are usually apparent in the first few years of life.
    C) peak at age fifteen.
    D) are rarely made after the age of eight or nine.
    Answer: C

Pages: 507
Topic: Mental Retardation
Skill: Factual   Other1:
77. DSM-IV considers an individual to be retarded if that person's IQ score is below _____ and
    is accompanied by significant limitations in adaptive functioning, both of which must
    begin before the age of _____.
    A) 100; ten
    B) 85; fifteen
    C) 70; eighteen
    D) 50; twenty
    Answer: C

Pages: 508
Topic: Mental Retardation: Levels of Mental Retardation
Skill: Applied   Other1:
78. Nedra has a "borderline" IQ. This means that
    A) her IQ is between 50 and 70.
    B) her IQ is between 71 and 84.
    C) her IQ is between 85 and 99.
    D) her IQ is on the border of profound mental retardation and can't be precisely
       determined.
    Answer: B

Pages: 508
Topic: Mental Retardation: Levels of Mental Retardation
Skill: Applied   Other1:
79. Mona is moderately retarded. This means that
    A) she is considered "educable."
    B) she is unable to speak and remains dependent on others for all physical care.
    C) she is able to support herself and live independently.
    D) she can be trained to master certain routine skills with specialized instruction.
    Answer: D

Pages: 508
Topic: Mental Retardation: Levels of Mental Retardation
Skill: Factual   Other1:
80. Severely retarded people
    A) have an IQ between 20 and 40.
    B) are usually diagnosed in infancy because of obvious physical malformations.
    C) have very poor motor and speech development.
    D) all of the above
    Answer: D

Pages: 509
Topic: Mental Retardation: Levels of Mental Retardation
Skill: Applied   Other1:
81. Noreen is profoundly retarded. She is most likely to
    A) develop limited levels of personal hygiene.
    B) achieve a fair command of speaking but not be able to read or write.
    C) have poor health and a short life expectancy.
    D) have a mental age of an average four-to-seven-year-old child.
    Answer: C

Pages: 509
Topic: Mental Retardation: Brain Defects in Mental Retardation
Skill: Factual   Other1:
82. Mental retardation that is organically caused
    A) comprises only about 5 percent of all cases of mental retardation.
    B) is usually at least moderate and often is severe.
    C) is always profound.
    D) is usually mild or borderline.
    Answer: B

Pages: 509
Topic: Mental Retardation: Brain Defects in Mental Retardation
Skill: Factual   Other1:
83. Genetic factors
    A) are very common in most levels of retardation.
    B) are clearly involved in the more severe forms of retardation.
    C) are involved only in cases of profound retardation.
    D) are involved only in Down syndrome.
    Answer: B

Pages: 509
Topic: Mental Retardation: Brain Defects in Mental Retardation
Skill: Factual   Other1:
84. A baby is more likely to have brain damage if the mother
    A) drank alcohol before conception.
    B) contracted German measles or certain other infections during pregnancy.
    C) had a blood transfusion during the first three months of pregnancy.
    D) chose to have a home delivery rather than giving birth in a hospital.
    Answer: B

Pages: 510
Topic: Mental Retardation: Brain Defects in Mental Retardation
Skill: Factual   Other1:
85. Compared with normal birth weight babies, babies who are born weighing less than about five to six pounds
    A) have no greater risk of mental retardation.
    B) have a high rate of neurological disorders and often mental retardation.
    C) tend to have physical defects but no significant mental impairment.
    D) are likely to experience later psychopathology but rarely exhibit mental retardation.
    Answer: B

Pages: 510
Topic: Mental Retardation: Brain Defects in Mental Retardation
Skill: Factual   Other1:
86. Current thinking about the role of malnutrition during early development
    A) suggests that it is causally involved in many mild to moderate cases of mental retardation.
    B) suggests that malnutrition has no association with mental retardation, as was once thought.
    C) suggests that malnutrition has only an indirect relationship to mental retardation.
    D) suggests that brain damage due to prenatal deficiencies in essential nutrients can be reversed in infancy with proper diet.
    Answer: C

Pages: 510
Topic: Mental Retardation: Organic Retardation Syndromes
Skill: Applied   Other1:
87. Noah is mentally retarded. He has a flat and broad face and nose, almond-shaped eyes, and thick eyelids. He has
    A) Klinefelter's syndrome.
    B) Down syndrome.
    C) Turner's syndrome.
    D) Number 18 trisomy syndrome.
    Answer: B

Pages: 512
Topic: Mental Retardation: Organic Retardation Syndromes
Skill: Factual   Other1:
88. Individuals with Down syndrome
    A) rarely live beyond the age of fifteen.
    B) are more affectionate and placid than normal youngsters.
    C) show their greatest deficits in verbal and language-related skills.
    D) show an increase in severity of retardation with an increase in their physical anomalies.
    Answer: C

Pages: 511
Topic: Mental Retardation: Organic Retardation Syndromes
Skill: Factual   Other1:
89. An example of mental retardation caused by a sex chromosome abnormality is
    A) Neimann-Pick's disease.
    B) Tay-Sachs disease.
    C) Klinefelter's syndrome.
    D) Number 18 trisomy syndrome.
    Answer: C

Pages: 512
Topic: Mental Retardation: Organic Retardation Syndromes
Skill: Factual   Other1:
90. A trisomy 21 syndrome refers to
    A) phenylketonuria.
    B) microcephaly.
    C) any form of genetically caused mental retardation.
    D) Down syndrome.
    Answer: D

Pages: 512-513
Topic: Mental Retardation: Organic Retardation Syndromes
Skill: Factual   Other1:
91. The incidence of Down syndrome
    A) increases in mothers over forty.
    B) increases in mothers under fifteen.
    C) increases in fathers over fifty-five.
    D) all of the above
    Answer: D

Pages: 513
Topic: Mental Retardation: Organic Retardation Syndromes
Skill: Applied   Other1:
92. Nat has just been born with phenylketonuria. This means that
    A) he appears normal.
    B) he is destined to develop severe or profound retardation as he gets older.
    C) he has distinctive facial features at birth.
    D) he has inherited a faulty dominant gene from his father.
    Answer: A

Pages: 513
Topic: Mental Retardation: Organic Retardation Syndromes
Skill: Factual   Other1:
93. Early detection and treatment of phenylketonuria
    A) is not possible with current technology.
    B) may allow the deterioration process to be arrested so that an individual achieves
       normal or borderline intelligence.
    C) prevents physical illness but not mental deterioration.
    D) should begin by age ten in order for there to be no ill effects from the disorder.
    Answer: B

Pages: 513-514
Topic: Mental Retardation: Organic Retardation Syndromes
Skill: Factual   Other1:
94. Abnormal differences in head shape and size
    A) are caused by the lack of a particular liver enzyme.
    B) always have a genetic basis.
    C) include microcephaly and macrocephaly.
    D) are not associated with mental retardation.
    Answer: C

Pages: 514
Topic: Mental Retardation: Organic Retardation Syndromes
Skill: Factual   Other1:
95. Individuals with microcephaly
A) are notable for the large size of their heads.
B) usually stop brain development at the fourth or fifth month of fetal life.
C) are not usually diagnosed until they are around six months of age.
D) are always profoundly retarded and usually die within two years of birth.
Answer: B

Pages: 514
Topic: Mental Retardation: Organic Retardation Syndromes
Skill: Applied   Other1:
96. Mary is an infant whose upper part of the head is slowly enlarging relative to her face
and the rest of her body. She has
A) hydrocephalus.
B) microcephaly.
C) macrocephaly.
D) Turner's syndrome.
Answer: A

Pages: 514-515
Topic: Mental Retardation: Cultural-Familial Mental Retardation
Skill: Factual   Other1:
97. Adverse sociocultural conditions
A) play a greater role than was previously thought in the development of mental
retardation.
B) may exacerbate genetically determined cases of mental retardation, but do not
themselves cause retardation.
C) always involve extreme sensory and social deprivation during early life, which results
in occasional cases of mild mental retardation.
D) do not play a causal or exacerbating role in mental retardation.
Answer: A

Pages: 515
Topic: Mental Retardation: Cultural-Familial Mental Retardation
Skill: Factual   Other1:
98. In a study of children born to slum-dwelling Milwaukee mothers,
    A) environmental impoverishment was associated with a general deficit in the children's IQ by aged two.
    B) children were normal in IQ initially, but the children's IQ declined over the next ten years regardless of their mothers' IQ.
    C) while the children had similar IQs initially, the children born to mothers with IQs below 80 showed a progressive decline in their own IQs relative to the children born to mothers with IQs over 80.
    D) environmental impoverishment played little role in the IQs of the children assessed regardless of the children's age.
    Answer: C

Pages: 515-516
Topic: Mental Retardation: Cultural-Familial Mental Retardation
Skill: Factual   Other1:
99. Research suggests that
    A) mothers with low IQs do not stimulate adequate intellectual growth in their children.
    B) cultural-familial mental retardation is usually associated with brain pathology as well as social impoverishment.
    C) children born to mothers with low IQs improve dramatically in intellectual functioning once they begin school.
    D) cultural-familial mental retardation is usually moderate to severe.
    Answer: A

Pages: 516
Topic: Mental Retardation: The Problem of Assessment
Skill: Factual   Other1:
100. The assessment of _____ and intellectual functioning are required to diagnose mental retardation.
    A) etiology
    B) parental IQs
    C) social competence
    D) sensory-motor deficits
    Answer: C

Pages: 516
Topic: Mental Retardation: The Problem of Assessment
Skill: Factual   Other1:
101. The assessment of mental retardation
    A) requires the competent administration of an IQ test, which is a reliable indicator of retardation.
    B) is difficult both in terms of the IQ testing and in determining levels of social competence.
    C) is one of the most straightforward diagnostic tasks, relative to diagnosing psychopathology.
    D) is impossible unless the etiology of the mental retardation is known.
    Answer: B

Pages: 516-517
Topic: Mental Retardation: Treatments, Outcomes, and Prevention
Skill: Factual   Other1:
102. Mentally retarded children who are institutionalized
    A) often are severely retarded and were institutionalized at an early age.
    B) are almost always from the highest socioeconomic class.
    C) often are adolescents who are mildly retarded and who became problematic in social areas.
    D) A and C
    Answer: D

Pages: 517
Topic: Mental Retardation: Treatments, Outcomes, and Prevention
Skill: Factual   Other1:
103. Training and education for the mentally retarded
    A) is extensive and promising.
    B) is extensive for the severely retarded, but not for mildly retarded individuals.
    C) is inadequate given that it can be very beneficial when properly done.
    D) is limited to Head Start programs and "mainstreaming."
    Answer: C

Pages: 519
Topic: Specific Learning Disorders
Skill: Factual   Other1:
104. Specific learning disorders
    A) often begin in adolescence or adulthood.
    B) are generalized developmental disorders of childhood.
    C) are circumscribed and may occur in very bright children.
    D) are usually genetic in origin.
    Answer: C

Pages: 520
Topic: Specific Learning Disorders: The Clinical Picture
Skill: Conceptual   Other1:
105. Learning disabled children are usually identified when
    A) they are infants and early developmental milestones are not met.
    B) they are in preschool and not able to keep up with other children.
    C) their academic performance fails to live up to expected achievement level.
    D) they attempt to do college work and have unexpected difficulties.
    Answer: C

Pages: 521
Topic: Specific Learning Disorders: Causal Factors in Learning Disorders
Skill: Factual   Other1:
106. Dyslexic learning disabilities are most likely to be caused by
    A) anoxia at birth.
    B) subtle impairments of the central nervous system.
    C) a defect in the brain's laterality of function.
    D) a genetic vulnerability.
    Answer: D

Pages: 522
Topic: Specific Learning Disorders: Treatments and Outcomes
Skill: Factual   Other1:
107. It is difficult to treat learning disabled children because
    A) it's not yet known what is "wrong" with them.
    B) most of them are so discouraged by the time they are identified as learning disabled
        that they do not want to be helped.
    C) their neuropsychological defects can't be corrected.
    D) there is little funding available in most school districts.
    Answer: A

Pages: 522
Topic: Specific Learning Disorders: Treatments and Outcomes
Skill: Factual   Other1:
108. The long-term outcome for learning disabled adults is
    A) positive, as their disabilities tend to diminish with age.
    B) entirely dependent on the support they received from family and school staff.
    C) variable, with many adults continuing to have difficulties while others manage very
        well.
    D) very poor, as few learning disabled children are able to finish high school and find
        suitable jobs.
    Answer: C

Pages: 523
Topic: Unresolved Issues on Cultural-Familial Retardation
Skill: Conceptual   Other1:
109. African Americans are disproportionately represented among those labeled "retarded." This is in part due to
   A) ethnic differences in IQ caused by differences in brain size.
   B) the fact that African Americans as a group have been seriously disadvantaged in the standard educational system and it is successful engagements in this system, not intelligence, that IQ tests have been designed to measure.
   C) the fact that exposure to extracurricular cultural enrichment is associated with IQ and school performance, and may be lacking in the lives of many impoverished minorities.
   D) B and C
   Answer: D

Pages: 523
Topic: Unresolved Issues on Cultural-Familial Retardation
Skill: Factual   Other1:
110. Head Start programs
   A) are very successful in equipping preschool children from disadvantaged backgrounds for academic success.
   B) may produce short-term gains, but these are likely to disappear without general environmental enrichment.
   C) made no difference in the performance of children from disadvantaged backgrounds.
   D) none of the above
   Answer: B

Short Answer

Write the word or phrase that best completes each statement or answers the question.

Pages: 487
Topic: Brain Impairment/Adult Disorder: Adult Brain Damage/Mental Function
Skill: Factual   Other1:
1. Briefly identify three of the consequences of focal brain lesions.
   Answer: These include impairment of memory, orientation, learning, comprehension, judgment, emotional control, initiation of behavior, controls over proprietary and ethical conduct, language, visuospatial ability, and apathy.

Pages: 490
Topic: Brain Impairment/Adult Disorder: Neuropsychological Disorder/HIV-1
Skill: Factual   Other1:
2. What are the four categories of neurological symptom syndromes?
   Answer: They are delirium and dementia, amnestic syndrome, neuropsychological delusional and mood syndromes, and neuropsychological personality syndrome.

Pages: 492
Topic: Brain Impairment/Adult Disorder: Neuropsychological Disorder/HIV-1
Skill: Factual   Other1:

3. What is the amnestic syndrome?
    Answer: This involves an inability to recall ongoing events more than a few minutes
    after they've occurred, although long-term memory and memory for words and
    concepts remain largely intact. The primary memory deficit may be in the
    retrieval of information. This syndrome is most often caused by alcohol and
    barbituate addiction, and may be reversed in some cases.

Pages: 494
Topic: Brain Impairment/Adult Disorder: Neuropsychological Disorder/HIV-1
Skill: Factual   Other1:

4. What are the clinical features and course in individuals with AIDS dementia complex (ADC)?
    Answer: The onset of the disorder usually begins in the late phase of HIV infection.
    Initial features include psychomotor slowing and clumsiness, and mild
    difficulties with memory and concentration. Dementia usually appears quickly
    after the onset of these symptoms. The later phase of this dementia includes
    psychotic thinking, apathy, confusion, regression, and withdrawal. Individuals
    become bedridden and incontinent before death.

Pages: 496-499
Topic: Brain Impairment/Adult Disorder: Dementia of the Alzheimer's Type
Skill: Factual   Other1:

5. Briefly describe the clinical features and course of Dementia of the Alzheimer's Type
    (DAT).
    Answer: Symptoms usually begin with a gradual withdrawal, a decrease in mental
    alertness, and intolerance of change in routine. Thoughts and activities may
    become childish; impaired memory, confusion, agitation, and empty speech may
    emerge. The course is one of simple deterioration in about half the cases, with
    a paranoid orientation occurring in some cases. Eventually a patient is reduced
    to a vegetative state and dies of a disease that overwhelms the person's limited
    defenses.

Pages: 499-500
Topic: Brain Impairment/Adult Disorder: Dementia of the Alzheimer's Type
Skill: Factual   Other1:

6. Name three of the biological causal factors thought to be implicated in Dementia of the
    Alzheimer's Type (DAT).
    Answer: These factors include reduced levels of acetylcholine; neuropathy involving the
    accumulation of senile plaques, neurofibrillary tangles, and granulovacuoles;
    and a genetic vulnerability which may be associated with a gene mutation on
    chromosome 21. Genetic vulnerability may involve a blood protein,
    apoliproprotein-E (Apo-E), which may enhance the buildup of beta amyloid in
    senile plaques or neurofibrillary tangling.

Pages: 502
Topic: Brain Impairment/Adult Disorder: Dementia of the Alzheimer's Type
Skill: Factual   Other1:

7. A series of strokes, or cerebral infarcts, may be associated with a neuropsychological disorder that is called _____ .
   Answer: vascular dementia (VAD; formerly multi-infarct dementia)

Pages: 502-504
Topic: Brain Impairment and Adult Disorder: Disorders Involving Head Injury
Skill: Applied   Other1:

8. Zeke just suffered a serious head injury that rendered him unconscious for about ten minutes. What symptoms is he likely to experience?
   Answer: He probably has retrograde amnesia, and feels dizzy and confused as he regains consciousness. An intracranial hemorrhage may occur. If it involves pinpoint spots of bleeding, this is called petechial hemorrhages. The accumulation of blood may cause subdural hematoma, which is potentially serious. Excessive swelling, called cerebral edema, may also occur. Subtle to severe neurological impairments may persist, or he may recover completely.

Pages: 507
Topic: Mental Retardation: Levels of Mental Retardation
Skill: Factual   Other1:

9. The DSM-IV recognizes four levels of severity of mental retardation: _____, _____, _____, and _____ .
   Answer: mild; moderate; severe; profound

Pages: 508
Topic: Mental Retardation: Levels of Mental Retardation
Skill: Conceptual   Other1:

10. Briefly distinguish mild from moderate mental retardation.
    Answer: Mild retardation involves an IQ of about 50 to 70. The mildly retarded individual is considered "educable," and attains the adult intellectual level of an average eight-to-eleven-year-old. These individuals attain an adolescent level of social adjustment but require supervision because of poor judgment. They don't often show obvious physical signs of retardation, and may become self-supporting and independent. Moderately retarded individuals have an IQ from about 35 to 55, are considered "trainable," with an eventual intellectual level comparable to a normal four-to-seven-year-old.

Pages: 512
Topic: Mental Retardation: Organic Retardation Syndromes
Skill: Factual   Other1:

11. Mental retardation caused by a trisomy of chromosome 21 is called _____ .
    Answer: Down syndrome

Pages: 511-514
Topic: Mental Retardation: Organic Retardation Syndromes
Skill: Factual   Other1:

12. Other than Down syndrome, identify three other forms of mental retardation that have a strong biological etiology.
    Answer: These include PKU, microcephaly, macrocephaly, hydrocephalus, Tay-Sachs disease, Turner's syndrome, Klinefelter's syndrome, Niemann-Pick's disease, Bilirubin encephalopathy, congenital rubella, and Number 18 trisomy syndrome.

Pages: 514-515
Topic: Mental Retardation: Cultural-Familial Mental Retardation
Skill: Conceptual   Other1:

13. What is cultural-familial mental retardation?
    Answer: This type of mental retardation involves causal factors associated with adverse sociocultural conditions, especially involving a deprivation of social, cultural, and intellectual stimulation. Other factors such as a genetic liability may be involved in some of these cases as well. This retardation is mild, and may be due to low IQ mothers' inability to provide adequate stimulation for intellectual growth.

Pages: 518
Topic: Mental Retardation: Treatments, Outcomes, and Prevention
Skill: Factual   Other1:

14. Placing retarded children in classrooms with normal children, which is referred to as _____, may result in self-esteem deficits for the less able children.
    Answer: mainstreaming

Pages: 520
Topic: Specific Learning Disorders: The Clinical Picture
Skill: Conceptual   Other1:

15. How are learning disabled children identified?
    Answer: Their academic achievement in one or more school subjects fails to meet the level of expected performance. Their IQs, family backgrounds, and exposure to cultural norms are consistent with at least average achievement in school.

Pages: 520
Topic: Specific Learning Disorders: The Clinical Picture
Skill: Factual   Other1:

16. Learning disorders involving reading are called _____.
    Answer: dyslexia

Pages: 520-521
Topic: Specific Learning Disorders: Causal Factors in Learning Disorders
Skill: Conceptual   Other1:

17. What do we know about causal factors in learning disorders?
    Answer: Research has not supported the hypotheses that learning disorders are caused by
             specific central nervous system dysfunction or disruption of normal brain
             laterality. A twin study found that monozygotic twins were 100 percent
             concordant for dyslexia, strongly suggesting a genetic basis for at least some
             learning disorders. Nevertheless, biological hypotheses tend to be vague on
             mechanisms and, with the exception of dyslexia, do not have a strong record
             supporting them. Psychosocial hypotheses also have done poorly.

Pages: 522
Topic: Specific Learning Disorders: Treatments and Outcomes
Skill: Conceptual   Other1:

18. What is the major difficulty associated with treating children with learning disorders?
    Answer: Because we do not have a confident grasp on what is "wrong" with the average LD
             child, we have had limited success in treating these children.

Pages: 523
Topic: Unresolved Issues on Cultural-Familial Retardation
Skill: Conceptual   Other1:

19. In essence, what do IQ tests measure?
    Answer: They were designed to predict academic achievement. They do not exhaustively
             measure the concept of intelligence and IQ test scores should not be viewed as
             being equivalent to intelligence.

Pages: 523
Topic: Unresolved Issues on Cultural-Familial Retardation
Skill: Conceptual   Other1:

20. Why might African-Americans be disproportionately represented among those labeled as
    mildly retarded?
    Answer: This ethnic group tends to score below Caucasians on IQ tests. IQ tests measure
             ability to perform academically, which is associated with exposure to
             extracurricular cultural products. African-Americans do not have the same
             advantages in this regard as Caucasians, and thus may not score as well on IQ
             tests.

Essay

Write your answer in the space provided or on a separate sheet of paper.

Pages: 486-490
Topic: Brain Impairment/Adult Disorder: Adult Brain Damage/Mental Function
Skill: Factual   Other1:

1. What is the difference between diffuse brain damage and focal brain lesions? What are the general effects of these different types of brain damage?
    Answer: Diffuse brain damage refers to the type of widespread damage that might occur with moderate oxygen deprivation or the ingestion of toxic substances. Attentional and self-monitoring impairments are quite common. Severe diffuse damage results in dementia. Focal brain lesions are circumscribed areas of abnormal change in brain structure, such as might be due to traumatic injury or progressive brain disease. Common symptoms include impairment of memory, orientation, learning, judgment, emotional control, and language. These symptoms also appear in progressively diffuse damage.

Pages: 487-488
Topic: Brain Impairment/Adult Disorder: Adult Brain Damage/Mental Function
Skill: Conceptual   Other1:

2. Use a computer analogy involving hardware and software to describe brain dysfunction.
    Answer: The human brain is like a highly programmable system of hardware with pschosocial experience as the functional equivalent of software. Organic mental disorders have hardware defects as their primary cause. The direct symptoms of such a breakdown are limited and to a certain extent predictable, but have pervasive effects on the software. These effects are known clinically as dementia. Less extensive hardware damage results in more variation in the mental symptoms manifested.

Pages: 488-490
Topic: Brain Impairment/Adult Disorder: Adult Brain Damage/Mental Function
Skill: Conceptual   Other1:

3. How do the extent and location of a neuropsychological disorder impact on the behavioral manifestations of the disorder? Include in your response the specific indicators of damage to the different lobes of the brain.
    Answer: In general, the greater the amount of tissue damage, the greater the impairment of function. Location may play a significant role because of specialization. Damage to frontal areas can produce passivity and apathy, or impulsiveness and distractibility. Damaged parietal lobes may produce distortions of body image or language function. Damage to temporal lobes disrupts an early stage of memory storage, eating, sexuality, and the emotions. Damage to the occipital lobe produces visual impairments and visual association deficits.

Pages: 490-493
Topic: Brain Impairment/Adult Disorder: Neuropsychological Disorder/HIV-1
Skill: Factual   Other1:

4. What characterizes a neurological symptom syndrome? Describe these various specific syndromes.

   Answer: They involve symptom clusters that may behaviorally resemble schizophrenia, or mood or personality disorders, but presumably have an underlying organic basis. More than one syndrome may be present and syndrome patterns may change over time. Delirium involves rapid widespread disorganization of higher mental processes. Dementia is a progressive deterioration of brain functioning. The amnestic syndrome involves a deficit in recalling ongoing events probably due to problems with retrieval. Delusional, mood, and personality syndromes resemble psychopathological disorders.

Pages: 493-495
Topic: Brain Impairment/Adult Disorder: Neuropsychological Disorder/HIV-1
Skill: Applied   Other1:

5. Martin has contracted the HIV-1 virus. What are the possible neurological and neuropsychological problems that he may face as the disease progresses?

   Answer: AIDS-related complex may result in subtle neurological impairments. AIDS dementia complex (ADC) involves more generalized degeneration of brain tissue with atrophy, edema, inflammation, and demyelination. Clinical features begin with psychomotor slowing and mild cognitive difficulties, with dementia then occurring rapidly. Brain damage is concentrated in central white matter and subcortical gray matter. The end stage ADC involves being bedridden and incontinent, and eventually culminates in death.

Pages: 495-499
Topic: Brain Impairment/Adult Disorder: Dementia of the Alzheimer's Type
Skill: Factual   Other1:

6. Describe the diagnosis, clinical features, course, and prognosis of Dementia of the Alzheimer's Type (DAT). How is it associated with aging?

   Answer: Diagnosis usually is made after all other possibilities are ruled out, but a recent test involving an abnormal reaction to a drug causing pupil dilation appears promising. Onset usually involves gradual withdrawal. Behavior becomes increasingly childish, cognitive difficulties appear and worsen, and personality changes occur. The outcome is a vegetative state followed by death. Half of the cases involve simple deterioration. Some suggest that Alzheimer's is an early normal aging of the brain. Some suggest advancing age is associated with increased exposure to multiple risk factors for DAT.

Pages: 499-500
Topic: Brain Impairment/Adult Disorder: Dementia of the Alzheimer's Type
Skill: Conceptual   Other1:

7. What do we know about the causes of Dementia of the Alzheimer's Type (DAT)?

   Answer: The fundamental neuropathy involves the accumulation of senile plaques with beta amyloid cores, neurofibrillary tangling, and granulovacuoles. Recently a gene mutation on chromosome 21 (hence the association with Down syndrome) was found that may increase beta amyloids or neurofibrillary tangling. Environmental factors are also important since many monozygotic twins are discordant for DAT. Acetylcholine (ACh), a neurotransmitter involved in memory mediation, is deficient in DAT brains. The earliest cells to be destroyed in DAT are involved in ACh release.

Pages: 500-502
Topic: Brain Impairment/Adult Disorder: Dementia of the Alzheimer's Type
Skill: Applied   Other1:

8. Ernst is a sixty-five-year-old man who has Alzheimer's disease. How would you go about treating him?

   Answer: Tacrine may provide temporary improvement in cognitive functioning, but no treatment exists currently that can halt or reverse the disease. Other medications may help in controlling symptoms like agitation and depression. Behavioral approaches may be useful in controlling problematic behaviors like poor self-care, wandering off, and inappropriate sexual behavior. A calm, reassuring, and predictable environment helps the patient. The caregiver probably also needs support and relief. Institutionalization should involve sufficient levels of stimulation.

Pages: 502-506
Topic: Brain Impairment and Adult Disorder: Disorders Involving Head Injury
Skill: Factual   Other1:

9. Describe the clinical features associated with mild, moderate, and severe brain injury.

   Answer: Even mild injury may result in residual subtle neurological impairment. Chronic headaches, irritability, anxiety, and dizziness are common after moderate injury. An injury serious enough to cause unconsciousness usually involves retrograde amnesia, subsequent stupor and confusion, and intracranial hemorrhage such as petechial hemorrhages. If sufficient blood accumulates, serious subdural hematoma may occur. Cerebral edema is also dangerous. Lowered intelligence and loss of adult roles may follow severe injury. Personality changes and epilepsy are less common aftereffects.

Pages: 502-506
Topic: Brain Impairment and Adult Disorder: Disorders Involving Head Injury
Skill: Factual   Other1:

10. Describe the favorable and unfavorable prognostic indicators that are associated with head injury.

    Answer: Favorable prognostic indicators include brief (or no) unconsciousness and amnesia, minimal or no cognitive impairment, well-integrated personality, higher education, motivation, a favorable life situation to return to, early intervention, and appropriate rehabilitation. Poor indicators include anterograde amnesia, especially severe injuries or those involving highly specialized regions that mediate important functions that can't be retrained, history of alcoholism or emotional or organic conditions, and lack of immediate treatment.

Pages: 506-507
Topic: Mental Retardation: Levels of Mental Retardation
Skill: Factual   Other1:

11. How does DSM-IV characterize and classify mental retardation? Describe the different levels of retardation recognized by DSM-IV.

    Answer: DSM-IV defines mental retardation as subaverage general intellectual functioning with significant limitations of adaptive functioning. It recognizes four levels of retardation based on IQ. Mildly retarded (IQ 50-70) are "educable," can achieve an 8-to-11-year-old's intellectual level, an adolescent social level, and self-sufficiency in adulthood. Moderately retarded (IQ 35-55) are "trainable," achieve a 4-to-7-year-old's intellectual level, and semi-independence. Severely retarded (IQ 20-40) can learn some self-care and simple tasks. Profoundly retarded are in lifelong custodial care.

Pages: 509-510
Topic: Mental Retardation: Brain Defects in Mental Retardation
Skill: Factual   Other1:

12. What do we know about the causes of mental retardation?

    Answer: About 25 percent of all cases involve known brain pathology, most being moderate or severe. All profound cases involve obvious organic impairment. Other causes include genetic factors (Down syndrome, PKU), infections (HIV-1, rubella), toxic agents (carbon monoxide, alcohol), prematurity and physical injury at birth, malnutrition (although perhaps indirectly), and ionizing radiation.

Pages: 510-514
Topic: Mental Retardation: Organic Retardation Syndromes
Skill: Factual   Other1:

13. Identify and describe three organic mental retardation syndromes.

Answer: Down symdrome is caused by trisomy of chromosome 21, which increases with parental age. It involves characteristic physical anomalies and defects, and moderate to severe retardation. PKU is a genetic disease involving two recessive genes in which the liver lacks an enzyme needed to metabolize phenylalanine, which in untreated individuals builds up and causes retardation. Other genetic disorders include Tay-Sachs, Turner's, and Klinefelter's syndromes. Cranial abnormalities also cause certain types of retardation like microcephaly and macrocephaly.

Pages: 514-516
Topic: Mental Retardation: Cultural-Familial Mental Retardation
Skill: Conceptual   Other1:

14. What is cultural-familial mental retardation and what are its causes? Include in your discussion the study of slum-dwelling Milwaukee children born to mothers with IQs above and below 80.

Answer: This type of mild retardation is associated with adverse sociocultural factors involving lack of normal environmental stimulation. It may be associated with severe deprivation by disturbed parents, but more often is associated with impoverished families and mothers who have low IQs. The Milwaukee study found that these children began with average IQs but the children born to low-IQ mothers declined in IQ over the years while the other children did not, presumably due to lack of intellectual stimulation.

Pages: 519-522
Topic: Specific Learning Disorders
Skill: Factual   Other1:

15. What are learning disorders, their causes, outcomes, and treatment?

Answer: They involve inadequate development in a circumscribed area, and are determined when a child's academic achievement does not meet expectations. The exact nature and causes of these disorders are unknown, but a gene region on chromosome 6 has recently been associated with dyslexia. Previous hypotheses of specific central nervous system dysfunction and imbalanced brain laterality were not supported by research. Treatment is limited due to lack of understanding of the disorder. Some but not all adults continue to have difficulties with deficits in specific areas and with self-esteem.

CHAPTER 14 Disorders of Childhood and Adolescence

Multiple-Choice

Choose the one alternative that best completes the statement or answers the question.

Pages: 527
Topic: Disorders of Childhood and Adolescence
Skill: Factual   Other1:
1. Today the field of study that attempts to understand childhood disorders emphasizes the importance of developmental changes that normally take place in a child or adolescent. This field often is referred to as
    A) childhood psychopathology, which subsumes disorders of adolescence as well as childhood.
    B) developmental psychopathology.
    C) childhood and adolescent psychopathology.
    D) developmental psychology.
    Answer: B

Pages: 527
Topic: Disorders of Childhood and Adolescence
Skill: Factual   Other1:
2. Which of the following is TRUE concerning disorders in children?
    A) Early conceptions suggested that children were very different than adults.
    B) Progress in understanding the maladaptive patterns of youth has exceeded the efforts to deal with adult patterns.
    C) The majority of problem children today receive psychological treatment, although this was not always true in the past.
    D) About 15 percent of American children have psychological disorders.
    Answer: D

Pages: 527
Topic: Disorders of Childhood and Adolescence
Skill: Factual   Other1:
3. Among children,
    A) maladjustment is diagnosed more often in boys than in girls.
    B) the most common diagnosis is conduct disorder.
    C) maladjustment is found more commonly in Great Britain than in the United States.
    D) the majority who have psychological disorders receive treatment.
    Answer: A

Pages: 528
Topic: Maladaptive Behavior/Different Life Periods: Clinical Pictures
Skill: Conceptual   Other1:

4. The clinical picture in childhood disorders
    A) is essentially the same as in adult disorders.
    B) is the same for anxiety disorders, but different for such psychotic disorders as
       schizophrenia.
    C) is the same only for those disorders that are also found in adulthood.
    D) is different even for those disorders that are also found in adulthood.
    Answer: D

Pages: 528
Topic: Maladaptive Behavior/Different Life Periods: Clinical Pictures
Skill: Conceptual   Other1:

5. Compared with the emotional disturbances of adulthood, the disorders of childhood tend to
    be
    A) persistent and longer lasting.
    B) short-lived, undifferentiated, and changeable.
    C) specific and clearly defined.
    D) more serious.
    Answer: B

Pages: 528
Topic: Maladaptive Behavior/Different Life Periods: Young Children
Skill: Conceptual   Other1:

6. Compared with adults, young children
    A) are less vulnerable to traumatic events that would bother most adults.
    B) have a more stable sense of identity.
    C) perceive immediate threats as disproportionately important.
    D) are ironically better able to cope with stressful events.
    Answer: C

Pages: 529
Topic: Maladaptive Behavior/Different Life Periods: Young Children
Skill: Factual   Other1:

7. The most distress for children following natural or other disasters is associated with
    each of the following EXCEPT
    A) being female.
    B) being a younger child.
    C) being given crisis intervention counseling close in time to when the disaster occurred.
    D) being male.
    Answer: D

Pages: 529
Topic: Maladaptive Behavior/Different Life Periods: Young Children
Skill: Factual   Other1:
8. Interventions in the four-stage model of managing children's adjustment in a disaster include
   A) short-term use of sedatives during the days immediately following a disaster.
   B) identifying children at high risk for problems and removing them from their usual environment to minimize exposure to disaster-related stimuli.
   C) programs that promote transition back into routine activities.
   D) cognitive interventions to teach children how to distract themselves from thoughts about the disaster.
   Answer: C

Pages: 528
Topic: Maladaptive Behavior/Different Life Periods: Young Children
Skill: Conceptual   Other1:
9. When considering whether a child's behavior is abnormal, it is imperative to consider whether the behavior is
   A) age-appropriate.
   B) condoned by the child's parents.
   C) condoned by the child's peer group.
   D) B and C
   Answer: A

Pages: 528-529
Topic: The Classification of Childhood and Adolescent Disorders
Skill: Factual   Other1:
10. The first diagnostic system that included childhood disorders became available
   A) prior to the diagnostic system for adults.
   B) with Kraepelin's classic textbook on the classification of mental disorders.
   C) when the DSM-I was published.
   D) when the DSM-II was published.
   Answer: C

Pages: 529-530
Topic: The Classification of Childhood and Adolescent Disorders
Skill: Factual   Other1:
11. Early classification systems for childhood disorders were limited in all of the following ways EXCEPT
   A) they ignored the important role that the environment plays in the way children's symptoms are expressed.
   B) a child's developmental level was not taken into consideration.
   C) they ignored disorders that had no adult counterpart.
   D) they used a dimensional system of classification rather than a categorical system.
   Answer: D

14 - Disorders of Childhood and Adolescence   page 527

Pages: 530
Topic: The Classification of Childhood and Adolescent Disorders
Skill: Factual   Other1:
12. A researcher gathers symptomatic information about a child's presenting symptoms from a variety of sources. The researcher then submits these data to statistical analysis to determine the child's characteristics. This is the
    A) dimensional strategy of classification.
    B) deficit strategy of classification.
    C) structural strategy of classification.
    D) categorical strategy of classification.
    Answer: A

Pages: 530
Topic: The Classification of Childhood and Adolescent Disorders
Skill: Factual   Other1:
13. The most widely researched and used dimensional strategy for assessing childhood behavior problems is
    A) the Structured Clinical Interview for Childhood Disorders.
    B) the Child Behavior Checklist.
    C) Thematic Apperception Test.
    D) the Rorschach Inkblot Test.
    Answer: B

Pages: 530
Topic: The Classification of Childhood and Adolescent Disorders
Skill: Factual   Other1: In Student Study Guide
14. Which of these would NOT fit under Aschenbach's internalizing dimension?
    A) anxiety
    B) social withdrawal
    C) depression
    D) aggression
    Answer: D

Pages: 530
Topic: The Classification of Childhood and Adolescent Disorders
Skill: Factual   Other1:
15. Compared with a categorical approach to classification, a dimensional approach
    A) is not concerned about the relative frequency of aberrant behaviors among different groups.
    B) assumes that behaviors are continuous and thus aberrant behaviors are found even among "normals."
    C) assumes that aberrant behaviors are discrete and noncontinuous.
    D) contains many classes defined by few, often rare, behaviors.
    Answer: B

Pages: 531
Topic: Disorders of Childhood: Attention-Deficit Hyperactivity Disorder
Skill: Factual   Other1:
16. Attention-deficit hyperactivity disorder is characterized by
    A) an increasing frequency from age six to age sixteen.
    B) a greater frequency in girls than in boys.
    C) mild to moderate mental retardation.
    D) difficulties that interfere with effective task-oriented behavior.
    Answer: D

Pages: 531
Topic: Disorders of Childhood: Attention-Deficit Hyperactivity Disorder
Skill: Factual   Other1:
17. The childhood disorder most frequently referred to mental health centers is
    A) attention-deficit hyperactivity disorder.
    B) conduct disorder.
    C) separation anxiety disorder.
    D) childhood depression.
    Answer: A

Pages: 531
Topic: Disorders of Childhood: Attention-Deficit Hyperactivity Disorder
Skill: Factual   Other1:
18. Attention-deficit hyperactivity disorder is associated with
    A) exaggerated or excessive muscle activity.
    B) distractibility.
    C) impulsivity and low frustration tolerance.
    D) all of the above.
    Answer: D

Pages: 531
Topic: Disorders of Childhood: Attention-Deficit Hyperactivity Disorder
Skill: Factual   Other1: In Student Study Guide
19. Which of the following is NOT a usual characteristic of children with ADHD?
    A) low frustration tolerance
    B) lower in intelligence
    C) great difficulties in getting along with their parents
    D) higher in anxiety
    Answer: D

Pages: 531
Topic: Disorders of Childhood: Attention-Deficit Hyperactivity Disorder
Skill: Applied   Other1:
20. Oswald has attention-deficit hyperactivity disorder. If he is typical of most such individuals, then he
A) has above average intelligence.
B) gets along well with his peers but has difficulty at home.
C) is immature.
D) is socially inhibited.
Answer: C

Pages: 531
Topic: Disorders of Childhood: Attention-Deficit Hyperactivity Disorder
Skill: Factual   Other1:
21. As a rule, hyperactive children
A) are anxious.
B) are above average in intelligence.
C) do poorly in school.
D) are viewed positively by their peers.
Answer: C

Pages: 531
Topic: Disorders of Childhood: Attention-Deficit Hyperactivity Disorder
Skill: Conceptual   Other1:
22. The text described the case of an eight-year-old girl who was typical of children with attention-deficit hyperactivity disorder because she
A) got along well with peers, but not with adults.
B) was very disruptive and demanding with peers and adults.
C) was of average to above average intelligence.
D) had a significant organic brain disorder.
Answer: B

Pages: 531
Topic: Disorders of Childhood: Attention-Deficit Hyperactivity Disorder
Skill: Conceptual   Other1:
23. One of the major difficulties confronting researchers who study the etiology of attention-deficit hyperactivity disorder is
A) the lack of reliable assessment instruments for diagnosing hyperactivity.
B) the overwhelming accumulation of genetic studies that identify a genetic contribution but do not examine possible environmental influences.
C) the difficulty in isolating food additives from children's diets in order to study their effects.
D) none of the above
Answer: A

Pages: 532
Topic: Disorders of Childhood: Attention-Deficit Hyperactivity Disorder
Skill: Conceptual   Other1:
24. The current evidence regarding food additives and hyperactivity suggests that
    A) food additives are a major source of hyperactivity.
    B) food additives are a minor but important source of hyperactivity.
    C) food additives affect boys differently than girls, resulting in hyperactivity in boys but not in girls.
    D) food additives do not cause hyperactivity in children.
    Answer: D

Pages: 532
Topic: Disorders of Childhood: Attention-Deficit Hyperactivity Disorder
Skill: Factual   Other1:
25. Which of the following is TRUE concerning hyperactivity?
    A) Parental personality problems are related to hyperactivity in children.
    B) Food additives are one primary causal factor.
    C) Siblings of hyperactive children do not show any greater incidence of academic difficulties than would be expected in siblings of normal children.
    D) Parents of hyperactive children are no more likely to have clinical diagnoses than are parents of other children.
    Answer: A

Pages: 532
Topic: Disorders of Childhood: Attention-Deficit Hyperactivity Disorder
Skill: Applied   Other1:
26. Oliver has attention-deficit hyperactivity disorder. The pharmacological treatment of choice for his disorder is
    A) antianxiety drugs.
    B) stimulant medication.
    C) sedating medication.
    D) antidepressant medication.
    Answer: B

Pages: 532
Topic: Disorders of Childhood: Attention-Deficit Hyperactivity Disorder
Skill: Conceptual   Other1:
27. Otis has hyperactivity and is taking Ritalin. This drug is likely to
    A) increase his attention and concentration.
    B) decrease his attention and concentration.
    C) increase his intelligence.
    D) decrease his intelligence.
    Answer: A

Pages: 533
Topic: Disorders of Childhood: Attention-Deficit Hyperactivity Disorder
Skill: Conceptual   Other1:
28. One of the problems with using drugs to treat hyperactivity is that
    A) children whose restlessness is the result of environmental conditions are not eligible
        to receive the drugs.
    B) the long-term effects of these drugs are not known.
    C) such drugs appear to accelerate the growth process.
    D) these drugs cause short-term benefits in academic performance but the long-term effects
        on school performance are negative.
    Answer: B

Pages: 533
Topic: Disorders of Childhood: Attention-Deficit Hyperactivity Disorder
Skill: Conceptual   Other1:
29. The most effective treatment for hyperactivity is
    A) behavioral therapy.
    B) medication.
    C) behavioral therapy plus medication.
    D) unclear insofar as research evidence exists to support each of the above approaches.
    Answer: D

Pages: 533
Topic: Disorders of Childhood: Attention-Deficit Hyperactivity Disorder
Skill: Factual   Other1:
30. Many studies have found that young adults who were hyperactive as children
    A) had fewer psychiatric problems as adults than control subjects.
    B) had the same number of psychiatric problems as adults as did control subjects.
    C) had a greater number of problems as adults than did control subjects.
    D) had a greater number of psychotic behaviors as adults than did control subjects.
    Answer: C

Pages: 533
Topic: Disorders of Childhood: Attention-Deficit Hyperactivity Disorder
Skill: Factual   Other1:
31. Compared with boys whose hyperactivity did not persist into later adolescence or early
    adulthood, boys with persistent hyperactivity were more likely to
    A) develop conduct disorders.
    B) develop schizophrenia or another psychotic disorder.
    C) have a lower rate of substance abuse.
    D) develop a serious mood disorder.
    Answer: A

Pages: 534
Topic: Disorders of Childhood: Conduct Disorders
Skill: Factual   Other1:
32. Pat has a conduct disorder. The focus of this diagnosis would be on Pat's
    A) anxiety or mood disturbance.
    B) legal record.
    C) bizarre behavior, such as hallucinations or delusions.
    D) aggressive or antisocial behavior.
    Answer: D

Pages: 535
Topic: Disorders of Childhood: Conduct Disorders
Skill: Factual   Other1:
33. It is difficult, if not impossible, to distinguish the early stages in the development of
    an antisocial personality from
    A) an attention-deficit hyperactivity disorder.
    B) separation anxiety disorder.
    C) the personality pattern expressed by an abused child.
    D) a conduct disorder.
    Answer: D

Pages: 535
Topic: Disorders of Childhood: Conduct Disorders
Skill: Factual   Other1:
34. The essential symptomatic behavior in the conduct disorders is
    A) a persistent violation of rules and a disregard for the rights of others.
    B) withdrawal, crying, and the avoidance of contact with others.
    C) unrealistic fears, oversensitivity, and chronic anxiety.
    D) problems in conduct that lead to deficits in problem solving.
    Answer: A

Pages: 535
Topic: Disorders of Childhood: Conduct Disorders
Skill: Factual   Other1:
35. Oppositional defiant disorder
    A) is a diagnosis that often follows conduct disorder when a child continues his or her
        problem behavior in adolescence.
    B) almost always precedes the development of conduct disorder.
    C) will almost always turn into conduct disorder within a year.
    D) is unlike conduct disorder in that its risk factors differ significantly.
    Answer: B

Pages: 535
Topic: Disorders of Childhood: Conduct Disorders
Skill: Factual   Other1:
36. Oppositional defiant disorder
   A) usually begins by the age of six.
   B) has as risk factors family discord and socioeconomic disadvantage.
   C) is more common in the upper classes, whereas conduct disorder is more common in the
      lower classes.
   D) A and B
   Answer: D

Pages: 535-537
Topic: Disorders of Childhood: Conduct Disorders
Skill: Factual   Other1:
37. The major causal factors in conduct disorders appear to involve all of the following
   EXCEPT
   A) mild neuropsychological problems.
   B) difficult temperament.
   C) excessive viewing of violence on television.
   D) low verbal intelligence.
   Answer: C

Pages: 536
Topic: Disorders of Childhood: Conduct Disorders
Skill: Conceptual   Other1:
38. Early neurological vulnerabilities may interact with _____ to produce a self-perpetuating
   cycle resulting in conduct disorder.
   A) serious childhood disease
   B) the early loss of the mother
   C) home and school environments
   D) overprotective parents
   Answer: C

Pages: 536
Topic: Disorders of Childhood: Conduct Disorders
Skill: Factual   Other1:
39. An adult diagnosis of psychopathy or antisocial personality disorder is
   A) most often associated with conduct disorder that begins in adolescence.
   B) most often associated with mild mental retardation.
   C) most often associated with oppositional defiant disorder and early-onset conduct
      disorder.
   D) not significantly associated with any particular childhood disorder.
   Answer: C

Pages: 536
Topic: Disorders of Childhood: Conduct Disorders
Skill: Conceptual   Other1:
40. Early-onset and later-onset conduct disorder are distinguished by
    A) the fact that few individuals with later-onset conduct disorder go on to develop antisocial personality in adulthood.
    B) the fact that later-onset, but not early-onset, conduct disorder is associated with neurological impairment.
    C) risk factors associated with later-onset conduct disorder, including lower verbal intelligence and impulsivity.
    D) all of the above
    Answer: A

Pages: 536-537
Topic: Disorders of Childhood: Conduct Disorders
Skill: Factual   Other1:
41. The families of children with conduct disorders typically
    A) accept the child's behavior as "normal."
    B) provide the child with harsh but consistent discipline.
    C) involve rejection and neglect.
    D) are overprotective.
    Answer: C

Pages: 537
Topic: Disorders of Childhood: Conduct Disorders
Skill: Applied   Other1:
42. Paddy, fifteen years old, has a conduct disorder. He is aggressive and has been admitted to an inpatient unit. If he is typical of most such individuals in this setting, then this treatment
    A) will only make his behavior worse.
    B) will have only a temporary effect without modifying the environment that he will return to.
    C) will have a permanent effect as long as it is tough and challenging.
    D) will have a permanent effect as long as it is caring, empathic, and supportive.
    Answer: B

Pages: 537
Topic: Disorders of Childhood: Conduct Disorders
Skill: Factual   Other1:

43. In the cohesive family model,
    A) children at risk for conduct disorder are removed from their families and placed into a cohesive foster family structure for a period of time.
    B) the parent-child interaction is regarded as the origin of the child's problems and is thus the focus of treatment.
    C) the parents and not the child are treated, as the child's problems are seen as resulting from ineffective parenting skills.
    D) parents are trained to attend more frequently to the child's negative behaviors.
    Answer: B

Pages: 537
Topic: Disorders of Childhood: Conduct Disorders
Skill: Factual   Other1:

44. Treatment of conduct disordered children
    A) is difficult because parents are usually not willing to participate.
    B) has been successful with the cohesive family model.
    C) that involves placing a child with a foster family often does not work or has only a temporary effect.
    D) all of the above
    Answer: D

Pages: 537
Topic: Disorders of Childhood: Conduct Disorders
Skill: Factual   Other1:

45. The relationship between aggressiveness in children and the later commission of violent crimes and damage to public property in adulthood is
    A) low for both males and females.
    B) high for males, but low for females.
    C) low for males, but high for females.
    D) high for both males and females.
    Answer: B

Pages: 537-538
Topic: Disorders of Childhood: Conduct Disorders
Skill: Applied   Other1:

46. Quentin has been placed in a treatment program for children with conduct disorders. This program will be most successful if it
    A) emphasizes punishment in an effort to "teach him a lesson."
    B) emphasizes personal insight into his behavior.
    C) uses medication within the treatment program.
    D) teaches behavioral management techniques to his parents.
    Answer: D

Pages: 538
Topic: Disorders of Childhood: Delinquent Behavior
Skill: Factual   Other1:
47. The term juvenile delinquency
    A) refers to behavior in which a single individual rather than a group performs some aggressive action.
    B) is a diagnostic term used in DSM-IV to refer to adolescents with conduct disorder.
    C) includes only acts that involve either destruction of property or aggressiveness towards a victim.
    D) includes unlawful destructive or violent acts committed by an individual who is younger than a state determined age.
    Answer: D

Pages: 539
Topic: Disorders of Childhood: Delinquent Behavior
Skill: Conceptual   Other1:
48. Children who run away from home
    A) often run away in an effort to escape from an intolerable home situation.
    B) are much more likely to be male than female.
    C) are most likely to repeat the running away if they are running away from situations such as fights with parents.
    D) all of the above
    Answer: A

Pages: 538
Topic: Disorders of Childhood: Delinquent Behavior
Skill: Factual   Other1:
49. Which of the following is true regarding delinquent behavior?
    A) Juveniles are disproportionately represented among those who commit violent crimes.
    B) Most juveniles who are arrested do not have a prior police record.
    C) The incidence of delinquent acts for females is declining, while it is rising for males.
    D) Male delinquents are most commonly arrested for murder.
    Answer: A

Pages: 538
Topic: Disorders of Childhood: Delinquent Behavior
Skill: Factual   Other1:
50. Delinquent acts are committed
    A) equally by individuals in all social classes.
    B) disproportionately often by middle- and upper-class youths.
    C) primarily by lower-class minority youths.
    D) about equally by socially disadvantaged white and nonwhite youths.
    Answer: D

Pages: 538
Topic: Disorders of Childhood: Delinquent Behavior
Skill: Conceptual   Other1:
51. Moffitt recently suggested that researchers investigating the etiology of delinquency modify their view of delinquency to include
   A) children as well as adolescents.
   B) recognition of the heterogeneity of delinquency and its origins.
   C) the nature of the delinquent acts committed.
   D) children under the age of eight.
   Answer: B

Pages: 538
Topic: Disorders of Childhood: Delinquent Behavior
Skill: Factual   Other1:
52. Some research suggests that two subgroups of delinquents exist, with a "continuous" delinquent group
   A) characterized by a significant genetic liability to criminality.
   B) characterized by significant brain pathology and the presence of multiple learning disabilities.
   C) evolving sequentially from oppositional defiant disorder to conduct disorder and adult antisocial personality.
   D) exhibiting delinquent acts throughout adolescence, including increasingly aggressive behavior from about age eight to eighteen, and a relatively rapid deescalation during young adulthood.
   Answer: C

Pages: 539-540
Topic: Disorders of Childhood: Delinquent Behavior
Skill: Factual   Other1:
53. Among the causal factors of delinquency, it appears that
   A) learning disabilities are linked to delinquency.
   B) a relatively large number of delinquency cases involve brain pathology.
   C) there is a genetic transmission of a predisposition to antisocial behavior.
   D) individuals with brain pathology whose inner controls are impaired become more impulsive and delinquent as they enter adulthood.
   Answer: C

Pages: 540
Topic: Disorders of Childhood: Delinquent Behavior
Skill: Factual   Other1:
54. Delinquent acts that are directly associated with behavior disorders, such as hyperactivity, typically involve
A) about half of all cases of delinquency.
B) impulsivity and emotional instability.
C) sexual violence.
D) several learning disabilities but an average level of intelligence.
Answer: B

Pages: 540
Topic: Disorders of Childhood: Delinquent Behavior
Skill: Factual   Other1:
55. Delinquent acts commonly occur as by-products of
A) drug abuse.
B) psychological disorders.
C) low intelligence.
D) sexual abuse.
Answer: A

Pages: 540
Topic: Disorders of Childhood: Delinquent Behavior
Skill: Factual   Other1:
56. Delinquency appears to occur among a disproportionate number of youths coming from
A) homes with large, extended families involving grandparents.
B) homes characterized by parental conflict.
C) homes broken by the death of a parent.
D) two-parent families.
Answer: B

Pages: 541
Topic: Disorders of Childhood: Delinquent Behavior
Skill: Applied   Other1:
57. Quinn, who has been involved in delinquent acts, comes from a family in which his father was the rejecting parent. His father most likely
A) was passive and uninvolved.
B) was dependent on the mother to enforce the rules of the household.
C) used physically punitive methods of discipline.
D) was overprotective and smothering.
Answer: C

Pages: 541
Topic: Disorders of Childhood: Delinquent Behavior
Skill: Factual   Other1:
58. In general, studies have found that higher rates of delinquency occur in families that
    A) provide less parental supervision for the child.
    B) are overly strict in limit-setting.
    C) utilize material rewards as the primary method of influencing the children's behavior.
    D) allow children too little freedom.
    Answer: A

Pages: 541
Topic: Disorders of Childhood: Delinquent Behavior
Skill: Factual   Other1:
59. Children who are delinquent
    A) have usually been involved in incest.
    B) typically come from homes in which one of the parents has died.
    C) are rarely encouraged by their parents to engage in such behavior.
    D) often have a parent, particularly a father, with antisocial traits.
    Answer: D

Pages: 541
Topic: Disorders of Childhood: Delinquent Behavior
Skill: Factual   Other1:
60. Girls who engage in serious promiscuity
    A) are often covertly encouraged to be promiscuous by their fathers.
    B) often have experienced incest and other types of early sexual activity.
    C) often have experienced a high incidence of parental absence and harsh, inconsistent
       discipline.
    D) all of the above
    Answer: D

Pages: 542
Topic: Disorders of Childhood: Delinquent Behavior
Skill: Factual   Other1:
61. Delinquent gangs
    A) have been decreasing in membership since the Los Angeles riots following the Rodney
       King trial.
    B) are the choice for most delinquents.
    C) are comprised of delinquents from lower socioeconomic classes.
    D) are a means of gaining status and approval among youths who feel rejected by society.
    Answer: D

Pages: 542
Topic: Disorders of Childhood: Delinquent Behavior
Skill: Factual   Other1:
62. Key components of successful treatment for delinquents who are institutionalized include all of the following EXCEPT
A) medication.
B) removal from an aversive environment.
C) redirection of peer pressure in the direction of resocialization rather than delinquency.
D) parental counseling and modifying related environmental circumstances.
Answer: A

Pages: 543
Topic: Disorders/Childhood: Anxiety Disorders of Childhood and Adolescence
Skill: Factual   Other1: In Student Study Guide
63. Children diagnosed as suffering from anxiety disorders usually attempt to cope with their fears by
A) becoming overly dependent on others.
B) denying the existence of fearful things.
C) developing compulsive behaviors.
D) indulging in "guardian angel" fantasies.
Answer: A

Pages: 543
Topic: Disorders/Childhood: Anxiety Disorders of Childhood and Adolescence
Skill: Factual   Other1:
64. Separation anxiety disorders
A) are more common in girls than in boys.
B) involve children who have fears that are not specific to a particular situation.
C) involve unrealistic fears, oversensitivity, self-consciousness, and chronic anxiety.
D) involve children who tend to reject parental support as a means of coping with their anxiety.
Answer: C

Pages: 544
Topic: Disorders/Childhood: Anxiety Disorders of Childhood and Adolescence
Skill: Applied   Other1:
65. The text presented the case of Cindy, an overweight eleven-year-old girl who had overanxious disorder. She was typical of most such individuals because she
A) had few somatic problems.
B) was conscientious and preoccupied with safety.
C) was anxious about her own well-being but confident in her dealings with others.
D) showed excessive anxiety primarily when she was separated from her parents.
Answer: B

Pages: 544
Topic: Disorders/Childhood: Anxiety Disorders of Childhood and Adolescence
Skill: Factual   Other1:

66. Children with anxiety disorders
    A) are insensitive to ordinary anxiety cues, especially physiological cues.
    B) have parents who use harsh and inconsistent punishment.
    C) have parents who are cold and rejecting.
    D) have feelings of insecurity that have been undermined by early losses or other traumatic experiences.
    Answer: D

Pages: 544
Topic: Disorders/Childhood: Anxiety Disorders of Childhood and Adolescence
Skill: Factual   Other1:

67. Childhood anxiety disorders are associated with each of the following factors EXCEPT
    A) an unusual constitutional sensitivity.
    B) maladaptive learning from an overprotective parent.
    C) moving to a new school.
    D) a deficit in conditionability to aversive stimuli.
    Answer: D

Pages: 545
Topic: Disorders/Childhood: Anxiety Disorders of Childhood and Adolescence
Skill: Factual   Other1: In Student Study Guide

68. Typically, children with anxiety disorders
    A) become adolescents with maladaptive avoidance behavior.
    B) become adults with idiosyncratic thinking and behavior.
    C) become suicidal when they reach thirty.
    D) have experiences that reduce their fears and insecurity.
    Answer: D

Pages: 545
Topic: Disorders/Childhood: Anxiety Disorders of Childhood and Adolescence
Skill: Conceptual   Other1:

69. Pharmacological treatment of childhood anxiety disorders
    A) has become more common but remains controversial.
    B) is now thought to be dangerous because of the long-term side-effects that have been documented.
    C) has been very successful, especially in the treatment of overanxious disorder.
    D) is the most frequent treatment used today.
    Answer: A

Pages: 545
Topic: Disorders/Childhood: Anxiety Disorders of Childhood and Adolescence
Skill: Factual   Other1:
70. Behavioral interventions with anxiety-disordered children
    A) are substantially less successful than other forms of therapy.
    B) are often helpful, especially if they involve in vivo desensitization approaches.
    C) are helpful in clinical settings but not in school settings.
    D) only work in conjunction with medication and family therapy.
    Answer: B

Pages: 546
Topic: Disorders/Childhood: Anxiety Disorders of Childhood and Adolescence
Skill: Conceptual   Other1:
71. Compared to adults, children
    A) are more easily treated because they are able to recover more quickly from negative
       events.
    B) are usually more motivated for therapy and better able to talk openly and honestly
       about their problems.
    C) are usually easier to diagnose.
    D) are more difficult to diagnose and treat.
    Answer: D

Pages: 546
Topic: Disorders/Childhood: Anxiety Disorders of Childhood and Adolescence
Skill: Conceptual   Other1:
72. In the treatment of childhood disorders, family therapy
    A) sees the family as functional.
    B) is easier to conduct with children than it is with adults.
    C) sometimes outperforms alternative treatment methods, such as some forms of individual
       therapy.
    D) assumes that deviant family patterns are the result of the individual child's
       pathology, rather than the other way around.
    Answer: C

Pages: 546
Topic: Disorders/Childhood: Anxiety Disorders of Childhood and Adolescence
Skill: Conceptual   Other1:
73. Play therapy
    A) evolved out of efforts to apply behavioral therapy to children.
    B) involves a structure provided by the therapist so that feelings and emotions can be
       expressed.
    C) assumes that children are potentially as insightful and as motivated for self-change as
       are adults.
    D) is less effective than other treatment methods with children.
    Answer: B

74. Which of the following statements about childhood depression is NOT true?
    A) The phenomemon of childhood depression has only recently been recognized as a clinical syndrome since the inception of DSM-IV.
    B) Depression is twice as common in girls as in boys.
    C) Depressive symptoms occur relatively frequently in children and adolescents, with an estimate ranging from 13 to 23 percent of children manifesting these symptoms.
    D) A marked rise in depressive symptoms occurs during the teenage years.
    Answer: A

75. Depressive disorders during childhood and adolescence
    A) are not persistent and are usually overcome within a few days.
    B) are very rare, although they can be very serious when they occur.
    C) involve behaviors that are fundamentally different from the behaviors associated with depression in adults.
    D) show a lifetime prevalence rate of about 20 percent among high school students.
    Answer: D

76. An important causal factor in childhood depressive disorders appears to be
    A) maladaptive learning.
    B) unconscious conflicts associated with the oral stage.
    C) adoption at birth.
    D) a hereditary hormonal imbalance.
    Answer: A

Pages: 547
Topic: Disorders of Childhood: Childhood Depression
Skill: Applied   Other1:
77. Phoebe, who is depressed, has a six-month-old daughter. Phoebe's interactions with her daughter are likely to lead to
A) avoidant behavior by the child that will end once Phoebe is no longer depressed.
B) avoidant behavior by the child that will continue even when Phoebe is no longer depressed.
C) clingy and dependent behavior by the child that will end once Phoebe is no longer depressed.
D) clingy and dependent behavior by the child that will continue even when Phoebe is no longer depressed.
Answer: B

Pages: 547-548
Topic: Disorders of Childhood: Childhood Depression
Skill: Factual   Other1:
78. In the treatment of childhood depression,
A) young children are just as likely to benefit from verbal, insight oriented therapy as are older children.
B) a supportive emotional environment does not seem to be as important with children as it does with adults.
C) antidepressant medication is as successful as it is with adults.
D) psychological interventions appear to be more effective than antidepressant pharmacotherapy.
Answer: D

Pages: 548
Topic: Disorders of Childhood: Other Symptom Disorders
Skill: Applied   Other1:
79. Quincy, age seven, has been wetting the bed twice a week since his parent's divorce four months ago. He had no problem wetting the bed for the year previous to this. Quincy would be diagnosed as having
A) primary functional enuresis.
B) secondary functional enuresis.
C) primary functional encopresis.
D) secondary functional encopresis.
Answer: B

Pages: 548
Topic: Disorders of Childhood: Other Symptom Disorders
Skill: Factual   *Other1:*

80. Enuresis
   A) occurs more often in girls than in boys.
   B) diminishes with age more quickly for boys than for girls.
   C) may be caused by organic or by psychological factors.
   D) always involves psychological regression to an earlier phase of toilet-training.
   Answer: C

Pages: 549
Topic: Disorders of Childhood: Other Symptom Disorders
Skill: Factual   *Other1:*

81. The most effective treatment for enuresis is
   A) imipramine.
   B) a hormone replacement medication.
   C) conditioning procedures.
   D) psychotherapy.
   Answer: C

Pages: 549
Topic: Disorders of Childhood: Other Symptom Disorders
Skill: Factual   *Other1:*

82. The typical encopretic child
   A) is female.
   B) is over the age of thirteen.
   C) is likely to soil his or her clothing under stress.
   D) soils his or her clothing in order to "get back at" parents.
   Answer: C

Pages: 549
Topic: Disorders of Childhood: Other Symptom Disorders
Skill: Factual   *Other1:*

83. Most children with encopresis
   A) report that they do not know when they need to have a bowel movement.
   B) soil themselves in school, resulting in rejection by peers.
   C) do not have a medical condition associated with this disorder.
   D) do not respond to medical or psychological treatment.
   Answer: A

Pages: 549-550
Topic: Disorders of Childhood: Other Symptom Disorders
Skill: Factual   Other1:

84. Which of the following is TRUE concerning sleepwalking disorder?
    A) About 5 percent of children experience regular or periodic sleepwalking episodes.
    B) Sleepwalking episodes usually last from fifteen to thirty minutes.
    C) Awakening an individual who is sleepwalking will result in severe physiological stress for the person.
    D) People who walk in their sleep do not hurt themselves.
    Answer: B

Pages: 550
Topic: Disorders of Childhood: Other Symptom Disorders
Skill: Applied   Other1:

85. The text described the case of seven-year-old Bobby who walked in his sleep. This case illustrated
    A) the successful short-term use of tranquilizing medicines.
    B) a successful behavioral treatment of sleepwalking.
    C) how psychotherapy can be used to resolve underlying unconscious conflicts associated with sleepwalking.
    D) the causal connection between enuresis and sleepwalking.
    Answer: B

Pages: 551
Topic: Disorders of Childhood: Other Symptom Disorders
Skill: Factual   Other1:

86. Tics
    A) are usually not noticed by the individual performing the act.
    B) are often related to enuresis.
    C) occur most frequently in adults, but occasionally they also occur in children.
    D) almost always have an organic basis.
    Answer: A

Pages: 551
Topic: Disorders of Childhood: Other Symptom Disorders
Skill: Factual   Other1:

87. Tourette's syndrome
    A) usually begins between the ages of seven and fourteen.
    B) probably has an organic basis.
    C) is an extreme tic disorder involving multiple motor and vocal patterns.
    D) all of the above
    Answer: D

Pages: 552
Topic: Pervasive Developmental Disorder: Autism
Skill: Factual   Other1:
88. Autism
    A) includes deficits in language development but not reality testing.
    B) includes deficits in reality testing but not motor development.
    C) includes deficits in language and motor development as well as reality testing.
    D) includes deficits in social functioning but not motor development or reality testing.
    Answer: C

Pages: 552
Topic: Autism: The Clinical Picture in Autistic Disorder
Skill: Applied   Other1:
89. William is an autistic child. He is probably
    A) severely lacking in emotional expression.
    B) unable to utter any meaningful sounding words.
    C) relatively withdrawn and uncommunicative.
    D) aggressive and frequently attacks others.
    Answer: C

Pages: 552
Topic: Autism: The Clinical Picture in Autistic Disorder
Skill: Factual   Other1:
90. Persistent repetition of a few words at a time is characteristic of many autistic
    children. This is called
    A) speech delay.
    B) imitative speech.
    C) echolalia.
    D) word salad.
    Answer: C

Pages: 552-553
Topic: Autism: The Clinical Picture in Autistic Disorder
Skill: Factual   Other1:
91. Autistic children
    A) vary a great deal in their impairments and capabilities.
    B) are homogeneous with respect to their lack of emotional expression.
    C) are homogeneous with respect to language dysfunction.
    D) are usually of average or above-average intelligence despite their cognitive deficits.
    Answer: A

Pages: 552-553
Topic: Autism: The Clinical Picture in Autistic Disorder
Skill: Factual   Other1:
92. Which of the following statements about autism is FALSE?
    A) Autistic children are often preoccupied with maintaining a routine in their environments.
    B) Autistic children are often partially or completely deaf, which contributes to their social isolation.
    C) Autistic children often engage in self-stimulating and repetitive activities.
    D) Autistic children often become obsessed with unusual objects like rocks or trees.
    Answer: B

Pages: 554
Topic: Autism: Causal Factors in Autism
Skill: Factual   Other1:
93. Autism
    A) is caused primarily by prenatal exposure to infectious agents.
    B) is caused primarily by exposure to mothers who have been described as "emotional refrigerators."
    C) is probably the most heritable of the various forms of psychopathology discussed in the text.
    D) all of the above
    Answer: C

Pages: 554
Topic: Autism: Causal Factors in Autism
Skill: Conceptual   Other1:
94. Autism, while probably heterogeneous in etiology,
    A) is apparently sometimes genetically linked to fragile X syndrome in males.
    B) rarely involves genetic causal factors.
    C) usually involves adverse environmental factors during pregnancy.
    D) usually is associated with the experience of anoxia during birth.
    Answer: A

Pages: 554
Topic: Autism: Treatments and Outcomes
Skill: Conceptual   Other1:
95. In the treatment of autism,
    A) anti-psychotic drugs are most successful in reducing symptoms.
    B) a new anti-hypertensive drug has proved to be markedly successful in treating symptoms.
    C) medication is generally not useful unless a child's behavior is unmanageable by other means.
    D) medications exacerbate symptoms rather than ameliorating them, and thus should be avoided.
    Answer: C

Pages: 555
Topic: Autism: Treatments and Outcomes
Skill: Conceptual   Other1:
96. Which of the following treatments for autism has been LEAST effective?
    A) structured inpatient treatment focusing on formal schooling
    B) a two-year behavioral program of intensive one-on-one interactions with therapists
    C) treating symptoms with antihypertensive medications
    D) home-based behavioral treatment programs using parents as agents of behavior change
    Answer: C

Pages: 556-557
Topic: Planning Better Programs/Help Children and Youth: Special Factors
Skill: Factual   Other1:
97. All of the following statements about the psychological treatment of children and adolescents are true EXCEPT
    A) Treatment usually must involve the parents as well as the child, since many disorders of childhood are associated with parental and familial problems.
    B) Treatment is as effective as treatment for adults, but fraught with special problems and considerations.
    C) Treatment always requires the consent of the parents if the individual is under the age of eighteen, and many parents do not have the time, money, or interest to see that their children receive treatment.
    D) Home-based treatment using the parents as change agents can be very successful if the parents are motivated to participate.
    Answer: C

Pages: 556
Topic: Planning Better Programs/Help Children and Youth: Special Factors
Skill: Conceptual   Other1:
98. Treatment without parental consent is NOT permitted
    A) in the case of a mature minor.
    B) in the case of an emancipated minor.
    C) in emergency situations.
    D) in cases where a child asks for treatment.
    Answer: D

Pages: 557
Topic: Planning Better Programs/Help Children and Youth: Special Factors
Skill: Conceptual   Other1:
99. Most of the behavior disorders specific to childhood appear to
    A) be organic in nature.
    B) grow out of pathogenic family interactions.
    C) be persistent through adulthood.
    D) respond to insight oriented therapy.
    Answer: B

Pages: 557
Topic: Planning Better Programs/Help Children and Youth: Special Factors
Skill: Applied   Other1:
100. Paula, parent of a disruptive nine-year-old, is in a treatment program that emphasizes using parents as change agents. This type of program
    A) has not been found to be successful.
    B) focuses on helping parents understand the child's behavior disorder and administer appropriate reinforcement techniques.
    C) is helpful, but is usually not important since children's problems are not related to family interactions.
    D) is used primarily with parents who have had their children removed from them.
    Answer: B

Pages: 558
Topic: Planning Better Programs/Help Children and Youth: Special Factors
Skill: Factual   Other1:
101. In placing children outside the family,
    A) most facilities are only available to provide protective care during the day.
    B) there have been few reports of unsuitable placement facilities, and therefore most children do well when placed outside the home.
    C) they will do better than they did at home even if they are put into a series of foster homes.
    D) it is important to work toward permanent placement after every effort has been made to hold a family together.
    Answer: D

Pages: 558
Topic: Planning Better Programs/Help Children and Youth: Special Factors
Skill: Factual   Other1:
102. The identification of children who are at special risk and early intervention
    A) have become a primary focus for clinicians during the past twenty years.
    B) do not seem to have had any significant positive effects.
    C) are effective only if the child is removed from the family situation.
    D) should only be used when treatment for acute problems is not possible.
    Answer: A

Pages: 559
Topic: Planning Better Programs to Help Children and Youth: Child Abuse
Skill: Applied   Other1:

103. Patty has been physically abused by her parents. If she is typical of many such children, then she
  A) will show impaired cognitive ability and memory.
  B) will have difficulties with family members, but not with peers.
  C) is likely to exhibit the "compensation effect" by not abusing her own children when she becomes a parent.
  D) may develop an anxiety disorder but is not likely to show depressive symptoms.
  Answer: A

Pages: 560
Topic: Planning Better Programs to Help Children and Youth: Child Abuse
Skill: Applied   Other1:

104. Opal, age ten, was sexually abused by her stepfather. She experiences intense psychological symptoms. If she is typical of most such children, then within eighteen months she will
  A) show a significant worsening of symptoms.
  B) begin to act out, probably to the point of making suicidal gestures.
  C) show no change in her symptoms.
  D) show substantial improvement in her psychological symptoms.
  Answer: D

Pages: 560
Topic: Planning Better Programs to Help Children and Youth: Child Abuse
Skill: Conceptual   Other1:

105. The problem with conceptualizing the residual symptoms of sexual abuse as a type of posttraumatic stress disorder is that
  A) the symptoms of sexual abuse are not as long-lasting as are the symptoms of PTSD.
  B) this conceptualization may miss some of the serious effects, such as prolonged depression and anxiety.
  C) the symptoms of PTSD and sexual abuse are not similar.
  D) the concept of PTSD does not apply to children and adolescents.
  Answer: B

Pages: 561
Topic: *Planning Better Programs to Help Children and Youth: Child Abuse*
Skill: Factual   Other1:
106. In studies of the treatment and prevention of child abuse, it has been found that
    A) most prevention efforts are not effective because high-risk parents cannot be identified.
    B) adults who were abused are at no greater risk for abusing their children than adults who were not abused.
    C) peer-initiated efforts at increasing social interactions between abused children and their abusers is effective in reducing the risk of further abuse, although the negative consequences of the original abuse remains unchanged.
    D) training high-risk parents in behaviorally oriented child management skills is effective in reducing the risk for abuse.
    Answer: D

Pages: 562
Topic: *Planning Better Programs/Help Children/Youth: Child Advocacy Programs*
Skill: Factual   Other1:
107. One of the major problems with child advocacy efforts has been that
    A) legal and political groups have not been involved in such efforts.
    B) government efforts are fragmented, with little coordination of various services.
    C) there has never been an effort to coordinate government services.
    D) mental health professionals have been overinvolved and governmental agents have been underinvolved in the planning to help children.
    Answer: B

Pages: 562
Topic: *Unresolved Issues on Parental Pathology and Childhood Disorders*
Skill: Conceptual   Other1:
108. The research on the transmission of emotional problems from parents to children indicates that
    A) the stress and symptoms that parents experience influence children's behavior, rather than specific parental diagnoses resulting in specific childhood disorders.
    B) children tend to inherit specific disorders from parents who have adult variants of those same disorders.
    C) children of emotionally disturbed parents are often high achievers as a way of escaping family problems.
    D) parental symptomatology does not seem to have much of an effect on children.
    Answer: A

Pages: 563
Topic: Unresolved Issues on Parental Pathology and Childhood Disorders
Skill: Factual   Other1:
109. Recent research on childhood psychopathology and divorce suggests that
   A) parental pathology rather than divorce is what produces disorder in a child, at least for conduct disordered boys.
   B) divorce causes short-term problems for children, but they seem to grow out of these problems by the end of adolescence.
   C) divorce causes few short-term problems for children, but they tend to have long-term difficulties in social and romantic relationships.
   D) parental divorce alone accounts for most childhood problems.
   Answer: A

Pages: 563
Topic: Unresolved Issues on Parental Pathology and Childhood Disorders
Skill: Factual   Other1:
110. In an investigation of the relationship between parental pathology and childhood problems, the Rochester longitudinal study found that
   A) the specific diagnosis of the mother had the greatest impact on the development of behavior problems in children.
   B) socioeconomic status and severity of mother's illness were the biggest risk factors for childhood problems.
   C) multiple risk factors were no more likely to increase risk of childhood problems than was the presence of a single risk factor, contrary to what had been predicted.
   D) there was no association between parental pathology and childhood disorders, raising serious questions about the presumed transmission of psychopathology from parent to child.
   Answer: B

Short Answer

Write the word or phrase that best completes each statement or answers the question.

Pages: 527-530
Topic: Maladaptive Behavior/Different Life Periods: Young Children
Skill: Conceptual   Other1:
1. Briefly describe three of the special considerations one must take into account when diagnosing children as opposed to adults.
   Answer: They are less able to describe and reflect on their problems. They depend on parents for identifying problems, coping with them, and seeking help. Families have an important influence on symptoms expressed. Their coping resources are more limited because of their cognitive limitations. Developmental level is an important factor to consider in terms of the age-appropriateness of behaviors.

Pages: 530
Topic: The Classification of Childhood and Adolescent Disorders
Skill: Factual   Other1:
2. The DSM-IV uses a _____ system of classification, whereas many researchers in developmental psychopathology prefer a _____ strategy.
    Answer: categorical; dimensional

Pages: 531
Topic: Disorders of Childhood: Attention-Deficit Hyperactivity Disorder
Skill: Factual   Other1:
3. Briefly describe three of the clinical features of Attention-deficit Hyperactivity Disorder (ADHD).
    Answer: These features include excessive motor activity, impulsivity, distractibility, poor attention, difficulty following instructions, and poor relationships with peers, teachers, and family members.

Pages: 532-533
Topic: Disorders of Childhood: Attention-Deficit Hyperactivity Disorder
Skill: Conceptual   Other1:
4. The two most effective types of treatment for Attention-deficit Hyperactivity Disorder are _____ and _____.
    Answer: medication; behavioral therapy

Pages: 535-536
Topic: Disorders of Childhood: Conduct Disorders
Skill: Factual   Other1:
5. In its most serious manifestation, early-onset conduct disorder is likely to be preceded by _____ disorder, and followed by adult _____ disorder.
    Answer: oppositional defiant; antisocial personality (psychopathy, sociopathy)

Pages: 535-537
Topic: Disorders of Childhood: Conduct Disorders
Skill: Factual   Other1:
6. What are some of the causal factors that have been identified in the etiology of conduct disorder?
    Answer: Research suggests a genetic liability leading to low verbal intelligence, neuropsychological impairment, and difficult temperament. These may interact with familial and other environmental factors to establish a vicious downward cycle. Social rejection is another important factor, as is family dysfunction, especially when it involves harsh and inconsistent discipline, inadequate supervision, and parental pathology.

Pages: 538
Topic: Disorders of Childhood: Conduct Disorders
Skill: Conceptual   Other1:

7. What is the difference between conduct disorder and juvenile delinquency?

    Answer: Juvenile delinquency is a legal term referring to legal violations committed by minors. Conduct disorder is a psychiatric diagnosis for children who persistently and repetitively violate rules and social norms and show disregard for others' rights. Thus, a juvenile delinquent may not have a diagnosis of conduct disorder, and not all conduct disordered children or adolescents commit delinquent acts.

Pages: 539
Topic: Disorders of Childhood: Delinquent Behavior
Skill: Factual   Other1:

8. What kind of children typically run away from home and why do they do so?

    Answer: They are usually between ages eleven and fourteen, at least half are girls and many are from the suburbs. Three general categories exist in explaining why children run away: to get out of destructive family situations, to better the family situation, or because of a secret problem like an unwanted pregnancy. Many in the first category experience physical or sexual abuse at home. Another subset called "run-to's" typically seek pleasure like drugs or escape from school, and are likely to run away over and over. Some children are encouraged to leave by parents.

Pages: 538-542
Topic: Disorders of Childhood: Delinquent Behavior
Skill: Factual   Other1:

9. Briefly identify three of the causal factors that have been implicated in the etiology of delinquency.

    Answer: These factors include genetic determinants, brain damage, low intelligence, psychological disorders like hyperactivity or psychosis, antisocial traits, drug use, parental absence, family conflict, parental rejection, faulty discipline, antisocial parental models, isolated family, undesirable peer influence, feelings of alienation and rebellion, and being rejected by society.

Pages: 543-545
Topic: Disorders/Childhood: Anxiety Disorders of Childhood and Adolescence
Skill: Applied   Other1:

10. Johnny is a seven-year-old boy who is typical of a child with separation anxiety disorder. What is he like clinically and how might his anxiety disorder have developed?

    Answer: He is anxious and upset when separated from a major attachment figure or familiar surroundings. He is probably overly dependent on his parents, shy, self-conscious, chronically anxious, and has many unrealistic fears. He may have been born with a heightened constitutional sensitivity and conditionability to aversive stimuli. Parental overprotectiveness may have undermined feelings of adequacy and conveyed that the world is a dangerous place. Overanxious parents model excessive anxiety. He may be hypercritical of himself or have experienced failures that no one helped him deal with.

Pages: 545-548
Topic: Disorders of Childhood: Childhood Depression
Skill: Conceptual   Other1:

11. How does childhood depression compare with adult depression in clinical picture and treatment?

    Answer: The adult diagnostic criteria in DSM-IV are used reliably with children, and thus the symptom picture is similar almost by definition. In terms of treatment, children do not respond to tricyclic antidepressants nearly as well as do adults. Children may also be more likely than adults to accidently overdose on medication. An important facet of psychological therapy is providing a supportive environment as well as for them to learn more adaptive coping strategies and effective emotional expression. Play therapy is generally successful with younger children.

Pages: 548-549
Topic: Disorders of Childhood: Other Symptom Disorders
Skill: Factual   Other1:

12. The two childhood disorders involving inappropriate elimination are _____ and _____.

    Answer: enuresis (functional enuresis); encopresis (functional encopresis)

Pages: 550-551
Topic: Disorders of Childhood: Other Symptom Disorders
Skill: Applied   Other1:

13. Give an example of a treatment procedure used for sleepwalking disorder or tics.

    Answer: A behavioral intervention for sleepwalking was described in the text in which a boy was conditioned to wake up as signs of a somnambulism-causing nightmare began, rather than sleepwalking, while he acted out in play mastery over the monster of his nightmare. Other behavioral interventions for tics and sleepwalking may be coupled with medications.

Pages: 551
Topic: Disorders of Childhood: Other Symptom Disorders
Skill: Factual   Other1:
14. Describe Tourette's syndrome.
     Answer: This disorder involves multiple motor and vocal patterns including
              uncontrollable head movements accompanied by grunts, barks, and other sounds.
              Coprolalia sometimes occurs. It is more common in males and probably has an
              organic basis.

Pages: 552-554
Topic: Autism: The Clinical Picture in Autistic Disorder
Skill: Factual   Other1:
15. What are the central features of autism?
     Answer: They include perceptual-cognitive deficits, impaired language development with
              frequent echolalia, social withdrawal, repetitious and bizarre behavior,
              self-stimulation, obsessive preoccupation with unusual objects and with
              maintaining regularity and consistency in the environment.

Pages: 554
Topic: Autism: Causal Factors in Autism
Skill: Factual   Other1:
16. What is the role of genetic factors in autism?
     Answer: Autism is probably the most heritable mental disorder, as twin studies showed
              nearly a 100 percent concordance rate for autism in monozygotic twins. It is
              linked genetically to fragile X syndrome in males. However, the genetic and
              nongenetic factors involved in the etiology of autism are probably
              heterogeneous.

Pages: 558-562
Topic: Planning Better Programs/Help Children and Youth: Special Factors
Skill: Conceptual   Other1:
17. What is the importance of early intervention strategies for children?
     Answer: These strategies attempt to identify children at risk for later problems in
              order to intervene to prevent the child from becoming disturbed and to enhance a
              child's coping resources. This has been shown to be effective in
              natural-disaster situations, in school-based groups for children whose parents
              are divorcing, for children experiencing other traumatic events, and in reducing
              the risk of child abuse.

Pages: 559-560
Topic: Planning Better Programs to Help Children and Youth: Child Abuse
Skill: Applied   Other1:

18. Nancy has been physically and sexually abused by her father. What problems is she likely to have compared to normal children?
    Answer: She may have impaired cognitive and memory abilities. Socially she is likely to be more insensitive and maladjusted. She probably exhibits depressive symptoms and has an external locus of control. She is at risk for substance abuse, poor sexual adjustment, difficulty in romantic relationships, a tendency to use dissociative defense mechanisms, and low self-esteem.

Pages: 560
Topic: Planning Better Programs to Help Children and Youth: Child Abuse
Skill: Factual   Other1:

19. What factors are associated with parents who abuse their children?
    Answer: They are likely to be under thirty, in a lower socioeconomic class, and to show some psychological disturbance. Their personality traits include aggression, being nonconforming, selfish, and lacking in impulse control. They tend to be experiencing a higher-than-average degree of frustration, and many stressors are present in their lives at the time of the abuse. They are likely to abuse in response to a child's misbehavior, which serves as a trigger.

Pages: 561-562
Topic: Planning Better Programs/Help Children/Youth: Child Advocacy Programs
Skill: Factual   Other1:

20. Groups that try to obtain better conditions for mentally disturbed children are called _____ groups.
    Answer: child advocacy

Essay

Write your answer in the space provided or on a separate sheet of paper.

> Pages: 528-530
> Topic: *Maladaptive Behavior in Different Life Periods*
> Skill: *Conceptual*   Other1:

1. One of the major issues in child psychopathology is whether child disorders should be considered as separate and distinct from adult disorders. Take a position on either side of this debate. Provide reasons for your position. In your answer, include examples of disorders from DSM-IV that support your position.

   Answer: Some disorders such as autism have no adult equivalent. Others, such as depression, are reliably diagnosed using adult criteria. Even disorders that are primarily problems of childhood, however, reflect developmental level. In childhood disorders, environmental factors play a more important role in symptom expression. Children have less self-understanding and perspective than adults, and thus fewer coping resources. They are also more dependent on other people. Age-appropriateness is central to determining whether a given behavior is abnormal in children.

> Pages: 530
> Topic: *The Classification of Childhood and Adolescent Disorders*
> Skill: *Conceptual*   Other1:

2. Differentiate between categorical and dimensional strategies in the classification of childhood mental disorders. Describe which applies to DSM-IV and indicate how the other approach could be incorporated into the diagnostic system.

   Answer: The categorical strategy (e.g., DSM-IV) is based on the disease model and involves describing a class or category in terms of the behaviors characteristic of that class of children. Categorical systems often have many classes defined by relatively few symptoms. The dimensional strategy (e.g., the Child Behavior Checklist) involves applying statistical methods to provide dimensions for the widely observed symptoms manifested by children. It conceptualizes behaviors as continuous and may be found in normal children. These systems usually have few classes covering numerous related behaviors.

Pages: 531
Topic: Disorders of Childhood: Attention-Deficit Hyperactivity Disorder
Skill: Applied   Other1:

3. Orlando has attention-deficit hyperactivity disorder (ADHD) and has been referred to a psychologist. What is likely to be his clinical presentation in terms of intellectual, social, and motor abilities?

    Answer: Orlando may be slightly below average in intelligence and does poorly in school. He is rather immature with a low frustration tolerance. He is likely to be impulsive, disruptive, and highly distractible. He will have great difficulty following instructions and obeying rules, resulting in problems with parents and teachers. Peers will also view him negatively. He will show excessive or exaggerated muscular activity, constantly fidgeting and running around haphazardly.

Pages: 532-533
Topic: Disorders of Childhood: Attention-Deficit Hyperactivity Disorder
Skill: Applied   Other1:

4. Orlando has attention-deficit hyperactivity disorder (ADHD). He has been referred to a clinic for treatment. What treatment program will most likely be successful?

    Answer: Some controversy regarding the most effective treatment for ADHD exists. Research suggests that the combination of psychotherapy and medication is more effective than either one alone. With this approach, Orlando may receive a stimulant, such as Ritalin, to reduce overactivity and distractibility. Also included would be behavioral therapy techniques that use positive reinforcement and the structuring of learning materials and tasks to minimize error and maximize immediate feedback. He may outgrow some of his hyperactive behavior as he reaches his middle teens.

Pages: 532-534
Topic: Disorders of Childhood: Attention-Deficit Hyperactivity Disorder
Skill: Conceptual   Other1:

5. What are some of the concerns that have been raised concerning the use of stimulant medication in the treatment of children with attention-deficit hyperactivity disorder (ADHD)? How do these concerns weigh in against the benefits of medication?

    Answer: Benefits include reducing distractibility and overactivity, so that severely disturbed children may be able to function in a regular classroom for the first time when they begin medication. Relationships with family and peers are apt to be markedly improved. Concerns include unknown and possibly serious long-term side effects, especially in still developing children; the importance of an accurate diagnosis before prescribing these drugs; and whether the drugs are sometimes used for adults' convenience rather than the child's best interests. Parental monitoring is crucial.

Pages: 534-537
Topic: Disorders of Childhood: Conduct Disorders
Skill: Conceptual   Other1:

6. What are conduct disorders? What evidence exists for the heterogeneity of this construct?

   Answer: Conduct disorders involve repetitive violation of rules or social norms and disregard for others' rights. Research suggests differences in etiology, course, and prognosis between early-onset and later-onset conduct disorder. The former usually evolves by age nine from oppositional defiant disorder. This subgroup may have a genetic predisposition to low verbal intelligence, mild neuropsychological problems of attention and impulse control, difficult temperament, and adult antisocial personality. Late-onset usually begins and ends in adolescence and doesn't share these risk factors.

Pages: 538-542
Topic: Disorders of Childhood: Delinquent Behavior
Skill: Conceptual   Other1:

7. Delinquent behavior is a major social and cultural problem. Describe the causal factors involved in such behavior, including personal, family, peer, and sociocultural issues.

   Answer: Personal pathology involves genetic determinants, brain damage and low intelligence, psychological disorders, antisocial traits, and drug abuse. Pathogenic family patterns involve broken homes, parental rejection and faulty discipline, antisocial parental models, and an isolated family. Undesirable peer relationships, alienation and rebellion, social rejection, and delinquent gangs are also factors. A subgroup of "continuous" delinquents evolves from early-onset conduct disorder and oppositional defiant disorder. Social mimicry of delinquent peers is important in adolescent-only delinquency.

Pages: 543-545
Topic: Disorders/Childhood: Anxiety Disorders of Childhood and Adolescence
Skill: Factual   Other1:

8. Describe the clinical features and causal factors associated with the major childhood anxiety disorders.

   Answer: Separation anxiety disorder involves excessive anxiety at separation from parent or home, oversensitivity, self-consciousness, and chronic anxiety. Overanxious disorder involves excessive generalized worry, often expressed somatically, with possible perfectionism and obsessional self-doubt. Causal factors involve (a) unusual constitutional sensitivity, (b) an undermining of feelings of adequacy and security, (c) the "modeling" effect of an overanxious and protective parent, and (d) the failure of an indifferent or detached parent to provide adequate guidance for a child's development.

Pages: 545-547
Topic: Disorders of Childhood: Childhood Depression
Skill: Applied   Other1:
9. Nancy is experiencing childhood depression. What is her likely clinical presentation and what are the probable causes of her disorder?
    Answer: Childhood depression includes symptoms of withdrawal, crying, avoiding eye contact, physical complaints, poor appetite, and even aggressive behavior. She may be suicidal, so this must be carefully assessed. Causal factors may involve a genetic liability. Also important is the role of maladaptive learning associated with parental models who are depressed with constricted mood. Research shows persistent avoidance reactions in the infants of such mothers. Also possible is the transmission of a depressogenic attributional style as a risk factor for childhood depression.

Pages: 545-548
Topic: Disorders/Childhood: Anxiety Disorders of Childhood and Adolescence
Skill: Factual   Other1:
10. Discuss the treatment of childhood anxiety disorders and childhood depression.
    Answer: Antianxiety and antidepressant drugs are more common today for treating anxiety, although their effectiveness has not been established and there is often diagnostic uncertainty due to comorbidity. Tricyclics for depression aren't very effective and may have dangerous side effects. Behavioral interventions such as highly specific in vivo desensitization are helpful for anxiety, but family or play therapy may be more effective. Therapy for depression usually follows the anxiety model. Short-term residential treatment and psychotherapy are effective. Emotional support is a crucial component.

Pages: 548-551
Topic: Disorders of Childhood: Other Symptom Disorders
Skill: Factual   Other1:
11. Describe one of the behavior disorders of childhood that involves a single outstanding symptom. Also discuss its causes and treatment.
    Answer: Functional enuresis is the habitual involuntary discharge of urine after the age of expected continence and is not organically caused. Functional encopresis refers to inappropriate bowel movements after age four. Tics involve a persistent, intermittent, usually localized muscle twitch or spasm. Tourette's syndrome, an extreme tic disorder involving multiple motor and vocal patterns, is probably organic. Sleepwalking disorder involves repeated episodes of somnambulism without later recall. Medical causes must be ruled out in these disorders. Behavioral treatment is generally most effective.

Pages: 551-554
Topic: Autism: The Clinical Picture in Autistic Disorder
Skill: Applied   Other1:

12. Donald is a typical six-year-old boy with a diagnosis of autism. What is he like?

Answer: Autism is a heterogeneous disorder with some variability among individuals in severity of impairment. Donald's symptoms may have been apparent in his first few weeks of life, but were probably obvious before thirty months of age. He shows deficits in perceptual-cognitive functioning, social connectedness, language development, and sense of identity. He probably engages in repetitive and bizarre behaviors and self-stimulation. He may be preoccupied with unusual objects, hypersensitive to auditory stimuli, and strongly in need of maintaining regularity and familiarity in his environment.

Pages: 554-555
Topic: Autism: Treatments and Outcomes
Skill: Conceptual   Other1:

13. Discuss research on the etiology of autism and its treatment.

Answer: Family and twin studies suggest a genetic liability, and in fact autism may be the most heritable form of psychopathology in the text. Recently a genetic defect related to the fragile X syndrome in males was linked to autism. Other genetic defects may be caused by radiation or other prenatal damage. Evidence suggests a subtle inborn constitutional defect involving perceptual-cognitive processing and ability to relate to the world. Prognosis is generally poor regardless of treatment, although most success has been shown by home-based and intensive long-term residential behavioral programs.

Pages: 556-561
Topic: Planning Better Programs/Help Children and Youth: Special Factors
Skill: Conceptual   Other1:

14. Discuss the special factors associated with diagnosing and treating children and adolescents. Include child abuse in your discussion.

Answer: A child depends on others to get help in identifying and assisting with problems. Many children are at the mercy of families that are dysfunctional, benignly neglectful, abusive, uneducated, or unconcerned about their well-being. They are unable to describe their problems with the same insight and complexity an adult might have. Their symptoms are often determined by familial context. Parents usually require treatment as well, and little change is possible in the long run without changing the family. Early intervention before problems like child abuse become acute is important.

Pages: 562-563
Topic: Unresolved Issues on Parental Pathology and Childhood Disorders
Skill: Conceptual   Other1:

15. What do we know about the relationship between parental psychopathology and childhood disorders?

     Answer: Research has strongly established a correlation, but the exact nature of the mechanisms of transmission and the direction of causality are complicated factors to identify and disentangle. Specific disorders in parents do not simply result in specific children's disorders. Instead, the types of symptoms exhibited by parents (e.g., constricted affect, inattention) influence a child's behavior. Genetic relationships often exist but are difficult to disentangle from environmental factors. Although the mechanisms haven't been established, parental psychopathology is probably associated at times.

CHAPTER 15 Clinical Assessment

Multiple-Choice

Choose the one alternative that best completes the statement or answers the question.

Pages: 567
Topic: Clinical Assessment
Skill: Conceptual   Other1:
1. Compared with diagnosing medical conditions, diagnosing psychological disorders
   A) rarely allows confirmation of the diagnosis with physical tests.
   B) does not involve identification of the causes of the disorders.
   C) tends to be an ongoing process that continues during treatment.
   D) all of the above
   Answer: D

Pages: 568
Topic: Clinical Assessment
Skill: Conceptual   Other1:
2. One of the problems associated with an initial (pretreatment) clinical assessment is that
   A) the clinician has so much critical information that a decision is difficult to make.
   B) decisions must often be made within a constrained time frame.
   C) treatment must be delayed until the assessment is completed, which often can take
      several monthss.
   D) few psychological assessment tools are available that are appropriate for this early
      stage.
   Answer: B

Pages: 568
Topic: Clinical Assessment
Skill: Factual   Other1:
3. Screening is the use of psychological assessment
   A) to identify individuals who are either unfit or highly unsuited for a particular
      assignment or job.
   B) to determine who should be discharged from a hospital.
   C) to indicate when therapy should be terminated.
   D) to establish a baseline against which to evaluate the effects of treatment.
   Answer: A

Pages: 568
Topic: Clinical Assessment
Skill: Conceptual   Other1:
4. Pretreatment clinical assessment is often done for all of the following reasons EXCEPT
    A) to determine the need for hospitalization.
    B) to determine a treatment plan.
    C) to establish a baseline of various psychological functions in order to evaluate the
       effect of treatment.
    D) to diagnose the underlying physical illness that is producing a given disorder.
    Answer: D

Pages: 568
Topic: The Information Sought in Assessment
Skill: Conceptual   Other1:
5. When conducting an initial clinical assessment, the clinician must first
    A) identify the problem.
    B) establish a treatment plan.
    C) determine whether medication is needed.
    D) determine whether the patient's family should be involved in the treatment.
    Answer: A

Pages: 568
Topic: The Information Sought in Assessment
Skill: Conceptual   Other1:
6. Formal diagnosis of psychological disorders
    A) is unimportant provided the clinician has a good basic understanding of the client's
       environmental pressures and resources.
    B) can help in planning and managing appropriate treatment.
    C) is usually not necessary for health insurance reimbursement, provided the clinician
       writes out his or her clinical impressions.
    D) is more important for treatment than for research.
    Answer: B

Pages: 569
Topic: The Information Sought in Assessment
Skill: Conceptual   Other1:
7. For most clinicians the primary purpose of assessment is to
    A) obtain a formal diagnosis.
    B) gain a basic understanding of the individual.
    C) determine whether the individual should be placed on medication.
    D) establish a baseline of the patient's personality characteristics.
    Answer: B

Pages: 569
Topic: The Information Sought in Assessment
Skill: Conceptual   Other1:

8. In conducting psychological assessment, a clinician focuses on whether the client
    A) has behavioral excesses.
    B) has behavioral deficits.
    C) has maladaptive personality characteristics.
    D) all of the above.
    Answer: D

Pages: 569
Topic: The Information Sought in Assessment
Skill: Conceptual   Other1:

9. When conducting a psychological assessment, it is essential to include a description of
    A) long-term personality characteristics.
    B) the quality of prenatal care.
    C) teacher and peer evaluations.
    D) medical problems experienced by biological parents.
    Answer: A

Pages: 569
Topic: The Information Sought in Assessment
Skill: Factual   Other1:

10. Integrating diverse bits of information about an individual into a meaningful picture,
    which includes hypotheses about why a person is behaving in maladaptive ways, is known as
    A) a social context analysis.
    B) a dynamic formulation.
    C) clinical integration.
    D) diversification analysis.
    Answer: B

Pages: 569-570
Topic: Varying Types of Assessment Data
Skill: Conceptual   Other1:

11. When conducting a clinical assessment, a mental health professional will tend to use
    procedures and assessment techniques
    A) that are comprehensive, covering a wide range of theoretical orientations.
    B) that elicit information about symptomatic behavior or possible causal factors that are
       emphasized by a given theoretical framework.
    C) that match the clinical features of a patient, such as using an assessment tool
       designed to identify intrapsychic conflicts when seeing a patient who appears to have
       such conflicts.
    D) that will determine whether or not a patient's problems are due to underlying organic
       malfunctioning.
    Answer: B

Pages: 569
Topic: Varying Types of Assessment Data
Skill: Factual   Other1:

12. A mental health professional who focuses primarily on the biological causes of behavior would most likely be a
    A) cognitively oriented behaviorist.
    B) behavioral psychologist.
    C) psychiatrist.
    D) psychoanalytically oriented clinician.
    Answer: C

Pages: 570
Topic: Varying Types of Assessment Data
Skill: Conceptual   Other1:

13. In conducting a psychological assessment, a behaviorally oriented clinician would focus on
    A) the functional relationships between environmental events and behavior.
    B) unstructured personality assessment techniques, such as the Rorschach inkblot test.
    C) interview techniques that uncover the processes blocking personal growth.
    D) personal confrontations to pinpoint difficulties in interpersonal relationships.
    Answer: A

Pages: 570
Topic: Importance of Rapport Between the Clinician and the Client
Skill: Applied   Other1:

14. Nell was ordered by the court to undergo psychological assessment following two reports that she was physically abusing her children. The assessment will be used to help determine whether she will be able to regain custody of her children. Nell is likely to
    A) establish a good rapport with the clinician who's assessing her in order to "win over" the clinician.
    B) establish a poor rapport with the clinician because she is being forced to undergo the testing.
    C) have a different quality of rapport and motivational set than she would if she were voluntarily seeking help, which the clinician must take into account.
    D) show test-taking behavior that is virtually the same as what she would show if she were voluntarily seeking help.
    Answer: C

15. A general physical examination would be absolutely necessary as part of the assessment procedure for
    A) any psychological disorder.
    B) a somatoform disorder.
    C) a separation anxiety disorder.
    D) a snake phobia.
    Answer: B

16. An electroencephalogram (EEG)
    A) is an invasive procedure to the brain.
    B) involves a series of X-ray pictures of the brain taken from different angles.
    C) provides a description of the brain's metabolic functioning.
    D) measures brain-wave patterns in waking and sleeping states.
    Answer: D

17. Divergences from normal EEG patterns of brain electrical activity are known as
    A) dysfunctional arhythmias.
    B) dysregulatory alpha waves.
    C) circadian disregulation.
    D) dysrhythmias.
    Answer: D

18. One procedure that provides information about the brain's structural characteristics is
    A) the electroencephalogram.
    B) an angiogram.
    C) computerized axial tomography.
    D) positron emission tomography.
    Answer: C

Pages: 571
Topic: Assessment of the Physical Organism: The Neurological Examination
Skill: Applied   Other1:
19. Rowena's physician is suggesting that she have a PET scan. The physician wants to obtain a more specific understanding of her brain pathology by measuring her brain's
    A) electrical activity.
    B) structural characteristics.
    C) intellectual capacity.
    D) metabolic processes.
    Answer: D

Pages: 572
Topic: Assessment of the Physical Organism: The Neurological Examination
Skill: Conceptual   Other1:
20. The primary advantage of nuclear magnetic resonance imaging (MRI) over the CAT scan is that the MRI
    A) is not an invasive procedure.
    B) provides better differentiation and clarity.
    C) measures the metabolic processes of the brain.
    D) allows one to examine brain functioning as opposed to simple brain structure.
    Answer: B

Pages: 572
Topic: Assessment of the Physical Organism: The Neurological Examination
Skill: Applied   Other1:
21. Enlarged cerebrospinal fluid spaces are present within the brains of some schizophrenic individuals. These enlarged spaces and other types of abnormalities of brain structure are measured most accurately with
    A) positron emission tomography.
    B) nuclear magnetic resonance imaging.
    C) computerized axial tomography.
    D) the electroencephalogram.
    Answer: B

Pages: 572
Topic: Assessment of the Physical Organism: The Neuropsychological Exam
Skill: Factual   Other1:
22. Measuring any alteration in behavioral or psychological functioning as a result of organic brain pathology is done through
    A) neuropsychological assessment.
    B) nuclear magnetic resonance imaging.
    C) computerized axial tomography.
    D) positron emission tomography.
    Answer: A

Pages: 572-573
Topic: Assessment of the Physical Organism
Skill: Factual   Other1:
23. Neuropsychological tests
    A) are especially useful in measuring an individual's performance on perceptual-motor tasks.
    B) can be given only through means of a highly individualized array of tests.
    C) can be given only through means of a highly standardized battery of tests.
    D) are unable to provide information as to the possible location of brain damage.
    Answer: A

Pages: 573
Topic: Assessment of the Physical Organism: The Neuropsychological Exam
Skill: Factual   Other1:
24. The Halstead-Reitan battery is
    A) a personality inventory.
    B) the newest form of positron emission tomography.
    C) a neuropsychological examination.
    D) a form of computerized axial tomography.
    Answer: C

Pages: 573
Topic: Assessment of the Physical Organism: The Neuropsychological Exam
Skill: Factual   Other1:
25. The Tactual Performance Test, Speech Sounds Perception Test, and Finger Oscillation Test are all parts of the
    A) Thematic Apperception Test.
    B) Brief Psychiatric Rating Scale.
    C) Halstead-Reitan battery.
    D) mental status exam.
    Answer: C

Pages: 573
Topic: Assessment of the Physical Organism: The Neuropsychological Exam
Skill: Conceptual   Other1:
26. The major advantage of the Halstead-Reitan battery over the Luria-Nebraska in assessing neuropsychological functioning is that the Halstead-Reitan
    A) is more manageable for a patient who is seriously ill.
    B) takes much less time to administer.
    C) yields more information.
    D) does not require a professional to administer it.
    Answer: C

Pages: 574
Topic: Psychosocial Assessment: Assessment Interviews
Skill: Factual   Other1:
27. Which of the following is often considered the central element of the assessment process?
    A) the MMPI
    B) the TAT
    C) the Rorschach Inkblot Test
    D) the assessment interview
    Answer: D

Pages: 574
Topic: Psychosocial Assessment: Assessment Interviews
Skill: Factual   Other1:
28. Two interviewers assessing the same client arrive at the same conclusion about the client. This is known as
    A) validity.
    B) reliability.
    C) convergence.
    D) clinical integrity.
    Answer: B

Pages: 574
Topic: Psychosocial Assessment: Assessment Interviews
Skill: Applied   Other1:
29. Dr. White is doing research in which she must diagnose clients at a mental health clinic. Because diagnostic reliability is of great concern in research, she will most likely establish diagnoses by using
    A) open-ended interviews.
    B) standardized structured interviews.
    C) the mental status exam.
    D) time-limited interviews that last the same length of time for each client, although the questions may differ.
    Answer: B

Pages: 574
Topic: Psychosocial Assessment: Assessment Interviews
Skill: Conceptual   Other1:
30. Compared with a controlled and structured type of assessment interview, a flexible interview
    A) is more reliable.
    B) is more valid.
    C) is often used because clinicians are overconfident in the accuracy of their own methods and judgments.
    D) shows higher correlations with other clinical tools, such as the MMPI.
    Answer: C

Pages: 574
Topic: Psychosocial Assessment: Assessment Interviews
Skill: Factual   Other1:
31. The reliability of the assessment interview may be enhanced by the use of
    A) a flexible, open-ended interview rather than a structured interview.
    B) the TAT.
    C) the Rorschach test.
    D) rating scales.
    Answer: D

Pages: 574
Topic: Psychosocial Assessment: Assessment Interviews
Skill: Factual   Other1:
32. Rating scales can be useful adjuncts to the assessment interview for all of the following
    reasons EXCEPT
    A) they provide a clinician with quantitative data.
    B) they provide an overall comprehensive profile of a client.
    C) they provide useful screening information about possible neuropsychological problems
       underlying clinical symptoms.
    D) they provide information about specific problems that may need immediate intervention.
    Answer: C

Pages: 574
Topic: Psychosocial Assessment: Assessment Interviews
Skill: Factual   Other1: In Student Study Guide
33. Clinical interviews have been criticized as unreliable and evidence of this unreliability
    includes the finding that different clinicians often arrive at different formal diagnoses.
     For this reason, recent versions of the DSM have emphasized an approach that
    A) employs a hierarchical structure.
    B) employs multidimensional assessments.
    C) requires confirmation by convergent information.
    D) employs "operational" assessment.
    Answer: D

Pages: 575
Topic: Psychosocial Assessment: Assessment Interviews
Skill: Factual   Other1:
34. Compared with the clinical interview, computerized programs
    A) are unable to obtain important information such as social history.
    B) can provide the clinician with a wealth of reliable data.
    C) are too simplistic to be used clinically.
    D) are more likely than open-ended clinical interviews to yield erroneous conclusions.
    Answer: B

Pages: 575
Topic: Psychosocial Assessment: Assessment Interviews
Skill: Factual   Other1:
35. Excessive reliance on computerized assessment can introduce error because
    A) research indicates that people are less likely to respond honestly to a computer than
       to a clinician.
    B) computer programs do not have the capacity to ask all of the questions needed in order
       to make a clinical diagnosis.
    C) the complexity of human behavior leads to many exceptions to any rule, leaving no
       adequate substitute for expert clinical judgment.
    D) none of the above; computerized assessment does not lead to assessment errors.
    Answer: C

Pages: 576
Topic: Psychosocial Assessment: Assessment Interviews
Skill: Factual   Other1:
36. The "D-Tree" is a computer software program designed to guide practitioners through the
    diagnostic process by presenting appropriate questions to the clinicians. When the
    clinician obtains all relevant information from an interviewee, the D-Tree will generate a
    DSM-IV diagnosis. The D-Tree is an example of
    A) a decision tree approach to assessment.
    B) an open-ended approach to assessment.
    C) an unstructured but systematic and highly controlled approach to assessment.
    D) an exciting new approach to assessment, although research has not yet demonstrated
       whether it yields reliable clinical diagnoses.
    Answer: A

Pages: 574-575
Topic: Psychosocial Assessment: Assessment Interviews
Skill: Conceptual   Other1:
37. Which of the following would NOT be appropriate for a clinician to use in order to enhance
    diagnostic reliability?
    A) a standardized interview format
    B) a flexible, unstructured interview format
    C) a computerized diagnostic interview
    D) a rating scale
    Answer: B

Pages: 575
Topic: Psychosocial Assessment: The Clinical Observation of Behavior
Skill: Applied   Other1:
38. Rita is in therapy with a behaviorally oriented clinician. The clinician provides instructions in how to observe and report her own behavior in various natural settings. This procedure is known as
    A) self-monitoring.
    B) self-talk.
    C) self-analysis.
    D) self-growth.
    Answer: A

Pages: 575
Topic: Psychosocial Assessment: The Clinical Observation of Behavior
Skill: Conceptual   Other1:
39. Rating scales are important in clinical observation because they
    A) are more unstructured than are interviews.
    B) gather more extensive information than do interviews.
    C) are likely to be used equally by clinicians of different perspectives.
    D) encourage reliability.
    Answer: D

Pages: 577
Topic: Psychosocial Assessment: The Clinical Observation of Behavior
Skill: Factual   Other1:
40. One of the rating scales most widely used for recording observations in clinical practice and psychiatric research is the
    A) Brief Psychiatric Rating Scale.
    B) Thematic Apperception Test.
    C) Computerized Diagnostic Interview for Children.
    D) Rorschach Inkblot Test.
    Answer: A

Pages: 578
Topic: Psychosocial Assessment: The Clinical Observation of Behavior
Skill: Conceptual   Other1:
41. A clinician is using the Brief Psychiatric Rating Scale with a client. The advantage of this approach is that it
    A) replaces the interview.
    B) is a flexible, unstructured, self-report instrument.
    C) allows the clinician to compare the client's symptoms with the symptoms of other psychiatric patients.
    D) allows the client to rate his or her own behavior using a standardized format.
    Answer: C

Pages: 578
Topic: Psychosocial Assessment: The Clinical Observation of Behavior
Skill: Factual   Other1:
42. The Brief Psychiatric Rating Scale and the Hamilton Rating Scale for Depression are especially useful in
    A) inpatient hospital settings.
    B) outpatient mental health clinics.
    C) clinical research.
    D) clinical settings that specialize in treating children and adolescents.
    Answer: C

Pages: 578
Topic: Psychosocial Assessment: The Clinical Observation of Behavior
Skill: Applied   Other1:
43. Rona carries a beeper that produces a small tone at unexpected intervals. She then writes down whatever thoughts the signal interrupted. This is a form of
    A) self-analysis.
    B) self-growth.
    C) self-monitoring.
    D) self-actualization.
    Answer: C

Pages: 578
Topic: Psychosocial Assessment: The Clinical Observation of Behavior
Skill: Factual   Other1:
44. When it is important to observe the client's behavior and not feasible to do so in a natural setting, the psychologist may ask
    A) the client to complete an MMPI.
    B) the client's entire family to meet together so that interactions may be studied.
    C) the individual to engage in self-monitoring.
    D) the client to participate in a flexible interview.
    Answer: B

Pages: 579
Topic: Psychosocial Assessment: The Clinical Observation of Behavior
Skill: Factual   Other1:
45. An often-used procedure that enables a clinician to observe a client's behavior directly is
    A) a beeper system to produce "thought reports."
    B) role-playing.
    C) self-monitoring.
    D) the computerized interview.
    Answer: B

46. Psychological tests are
    A) indirect means of assessing psychological characteristics.
    B) unstructured means of assessing behavior.
    C) direct means of assessing behavior.
    D) observational means of assessing behavior.
    Answer: A

47. Psychological tests
    A) do not involve subjectivity in scoring and interpretation.
    B) tend to be limited in reliability to more specific personality traits.
    C) usually do not involve comparisons of different people.
    D) are standardized sets of procedures for obtaining samples of behavior.
    Answer: D

48. Which of the following is a more reliable and precise method of assessment?
    A) role-playing
    B) the unstructured clinical interview
    C) unstandardized observation
    D) psychological testing
    Answer: D

49. The most widely used test for measuring adult intelligence is the
    A) Peabody Picture Vocabulary Test.
    B) MMPI.
    C) Wechsler Adult Intelligence Scale-Revised.
    D) Halstead-Reitan battery.
    Answer: C

Pages: 579
Topic: Psychosocial Assessment: Psychological Tests
Skill: Applied   Other1:

50. John, a six-year-old boy, is being assessed for possible intellectual deficits. Of the following tests, which is most likely to be used?
    A) Stanford-Binet
    B) Brief Psychiatric Rating Scale
    C) Rorschach Inkblot Test
    D) Hamilton Rating Scale
    Answer: A

Pages: 579
Topic: Psychosocial Assessment: Psychological Tests
Skill: Applied   Other1:

51. Roger, a young adult, is being assessed to evaluate the presence of organic brain damage. Of the following tests, which is most likely to be used?
    A) Stanford-Binet
    B) Rorschach Inkblot Test
    C) WAIS-R
    D) Brief Psychiatric Rating Scale
    Answer: C

Pages: 580
Topic: Psychosocial Assessment: Personality Tests
Skill: Factual   Other1: In Student Study Guide

52. Personality tests are often grouped into two categories,
    A) behavioral and psychodynamic.
    B) conscious and unconscious.
    C) projective and objective.
    D) verbal and performance.
    Answer: C

Pages: 580
Topic: Psychosocial Assessment: Personality Tests
Skill: Factual   Other1: In Student Study Guide

53. The aim of a projective test is to
    A) predict a person's future behavior.
    B) compare a patient's responses to those of persons who are known to have mental disorders.
    C) assess the way a patient perceives ambiguous stimuli.
    D) assess the role of organic factors in a patient's thinking.
    Answer: C

Pages: 580
Topic: Psychosocial Assessment: Personality Tests
Skill: Conceptual   Other1:

54. The projective test technique assumes that
    A) reliability and validity are important concepts for tests of intellectual abilities but
       not for tests of personality.
    B) the direct observation of behavior is meaningless in the clinical setting.
    C) clinicians should make as little inference as possible in evaluating responses to
       psychological tests.
    D) individuals will reveal their own inner problems and conflicts in responses that they
       make to unstructured stimuli.
    Answer: D

Pages: 580
Topic: Psychosocial Assessment: Personality Tests
Skill: Factual   Other1:

55. Which of the following is NOT a projective test?
    A) Rorschach Test
    B) Thematic Apperception Test
    C) Sentence-Completion Test
    D) MMPI
    Answer: D

Pages: 580-581
Topic: Psychosocial Assessment: Personality Tests
Skill: Factual   Other1:

56. The Rorschach Test
    A) is the most useful projective test because it takes just a few minutes to administer.
    B) can be unreliable because of the subjective nature of test interpretation.
    C) yields specific behavioral descriptions.
    D) is more reliable than other projective tests because it requires little inference on
       the part of the clinician.
    Answer: B

Pages: 581
Topic: Psychosocial Assessment: Personality Tests
Skill: Conceptual   Other1:
57. Some people criticize the Rorschach Test for having negligible validity. Which of the following statements may be made in defense of the Rorschach?
    A) The administration of the Rorschach is very complicated and requires extensive training.
    B) Research by Exner and others has started to empirically evaluate possible links between Rorschach scores and external criteria like diagnoses.
    C) It isn't possible to quantify and evaluate the kinds of statements about psychodynamic issues that are yielded by the Rorschach.
    D) The Rorschach Test has been used by clinicians for over eighty years.
    Answer: B

Pages: 581
Topic: Psychosocial Assessment: Personality Tests
Skill: Factual   Other1:
58. In an effort to increase reliability of the Rorschach Test,
    A) the number of inkblots has been increased.
    B) the test has been altered to incorporate more true-false statements.
    C) a computer-based interpretation system has been developed.
    D) the test has been merged with the MMPI.
    Answer: C

Pages: 581
Topic: Psychosocial Assessment: Personality Tests
Skill: Applied   Other1:
59. Russell is taking a test that involves making up stories based on a series of simple pictures. Russell is taking the
    A) Thematic Apperception Test.
    B) Rorschach Inkblot Test.
    C) Picture Completion Test.
    D) Sentence Completion Test.
    Answer: A

Pages: 581
Topic: Psychosocial Assessment: Personality Tests
Skill: Conceptual   Other1:
60. The assumption underlying the Thematic Apperception Test is that people
    A) can monitor their own behavior.
    B) are aware of their own impulses.
    C) are highly resistant to questioning in interviews.
    D) will project their own inner conflicts on to ambiguous pictures.
    Answer: D

Pages: 581
Topic: Psychosocial Assessment: Personality Tests
Skill: Factual   Other1:
61. Scoring and interpretation systems used with the TAT
   A) have increased the reliability and validity of the TAT by providing a standardized objective system that clinicians can use.
   B) have not been utilized extensively by clinicians because there is little evidence of their making a clinically significant contribution.
   C) are rather straightforward and easy to use.
   D) turn the test from being a projective test into an objective test.
   Answer: B

Pages: 582
Topic: Psychosocial Assessment: Personality Tests
Skill: Conceptual   Other1:
62. The TAT is a good example of how
   A) revising a psychological test can improve the test.
   B) clinicians sometimes will continue to use instruments that have failed to demonstrate reliability even after decades of use.
   C) standardized scoring systems can enhance the reliability and clinical utility of projective tests.
   D) scientists continually update and modernize psychological tests.
   Answer: B

Pages: 582
Topic: Psychosocial Assessment: Personality Tests
Skill: Applied   Other1:
63. John is taking a test in which he is provided with the beginnings of sentences and he is asked to fill in the parts that are missing. John is most likely taking the
   A) Rorschach Inkblot Test.
   B) Thematic Apperception Test.
   C) MMPI.
   D) Sentence Completion Test.
   Answer: D

Pages: 582
Topic: Psychosocial Assessment: Personality Tests
Skill: Factual   Other1:
64. Compared with other projective tests, the Sentence Completion test
   A) uses norms.
   B) is more structured.
   C) is more reliable.
   D) is more valid.
   Answer: B

Pages: 582
Topic: Psychosocial Assessment: Personality Tests
Skill: Conceptual   Other1:
65. In spite of numerous limitations, projective tests have a place in clinical settings that
    A) have well-trained staff who are sufficiently experienced in the use of such tests to
       make clinically useful judgments about a person's psychodynamic functioning.
    B) needs to conduct extensive individual psychological evaluations.
    C) do not value the importance of reliability and validity of psychological tests, which
       is true of most well-trained clinical psychologists.
    D) focus on treatment of disorders that are responsive to structural short-term
       interventions.
    Answer: A

Pages: 583
Topic: Psychosocial Assessment: Personality Tests
Skill: Factual   Other1:
66. Compared to projective tests, a major advantage of objective tests is that they are
    A) developed within a psychodynamic framework.
    B) more amenable to objectively based quantification, thereby enhancing reliability.
    C) less structured.
    D) more engaging for the test taker, thereby increasing the test taker's motivational set.
    Answer: B

Pages: 583
Topic: Psychosocial Assessment: Personality Tests
Skill: Factual   Other1:
67. The most widely used personality test for both clinical assessment and psychopathology
    research in the United States is the
    A) MMPI/MMPI-2.
    B) Rorschach Test.
    C) WAIS-R.
    D) TAT.
    Answer: A

Pages: 583
Topic: Psychosocial Assessment: Personality Tests
Skill: Applied   Other1:
68. Robert is taking a test on which he is to answer true or false to a large number of items
    such as, "I often feel as if things were not real." Robert is taking
    A) the Rorschach Test.
    B) the Sentence Completion Blank.
    C) the MMPI-2.
    D) the TAT.
    Answer: C

Pages: 583
Topic: Psychosocial Assessment: Personality Tests
Skill: Factual   Other1:

69. The authors of the MMPI developed the item selection method known as
    A) content validity.
    B) test-retest reliability.
    C) rational analysis.
    D) empirical keying.
    Answer: D

Pages: 583
Topic: Psychosocial Assessment: Personality Tests
Skill: Applied   Other1:

70. A psychologist is utilizing the item selection method known as empirical keying to
    construct a personality test. This psychologist will
    A) select items that appear related to the construct in question, such as depression.
    B) utilize his or her clinical judgment in deciding which items are ultimately to be
       included in the test.
    C) utilize his or her theoretical perspective in deciding which items are ultimately to be
       included in the test.
    D) select a given item solely on the basis of the item's ability to discriminate between a
       given diagnostic group and normals, regardless of the content of the items.
    Answer: D

Pages: 583
Topic: Psychosocial Assessment: Personality Tests
Skill: Conceptual   Other1:

71. In general, interpreting an individual's responses on the MMPI-2 involves the assumption
    that
    A) the individual does not have a psychotic disturbance.
    B) the individual has either a documented IQ in the average range (90-110) or higher, or
       has completed high school or its equivalent.
    C) if the testee's responses closely approximate that of a particular pathological group,
       then the testee probably shares other psychologically significant characteristics with
       that group.
    D) everyone has at least some psychopathology, no matter how mild.
    Answer: C

Pages: 583
Topic: Psychosocial Assessment: Personality Tests
Skill: Factual   Other1:
72. Each of the clinical scales on the MMPI-2 is designed to measure
    A) tendencies to respond in psychologically deviant ways.
    B) the individual's behavioral responses in certain predetermined situations.
    C) a distinct DSM diagnosis.
    D) whether an individual is lying or faking on the test.
    Answer: A

Pages: 583
Topic: Psychosocial Assessment: Personality Tests
Skill: Factual   Other1:
73. The MMPI contains all of the following EXCEPT
    A) behavioral rating scales.
    B) clinical scales.
    C) validity scales.
    D) "special" scales, which were developed after the original MMPI was completed, four of
       which became so widely used that they were added to the MMPI profile form.
    Answer: A

Pages: 583
Topic: Psychosocial Assessment: Personality Tests
Skill: Factual   Other1:
74. The validity scales on the MMPI-2 are designed to detect whether an individual
    A) is experiencing a psychotic disorder.
    B) has answered the questions in a straightforward, honest manner.
    C) is experiencing test-anxiety.
    D) has the reading level necessary to understand the items adequately.
    Answer: B

Pages: 583
Topic: Psychosocial Assessment: Personality Tests
Skill: Applied   Other1: In Student Study Guide
75. A clinical researcher devises a new psychological test that assesses neuroticism. She is
    concerned with the possibility that some individuals might not answer the questions in a
    straightforward, accurate way. To determine whether an individual is honest, she should
    A) factor analyze the responses.
    B) make use of actuarial interpretation.
    C) construct a validity scale.
    D) test the instrument on a group of college students.
    Answer: C

Pages: 583
Topic: Psychosocial Assessment: Personality Tests
Skill: Factual   Other1:
76. An example of a clinical scale on the MMPI-2 is the
    A) defensiveness scale.
    B) ego strength scale.
    C) lie scale.
    D) schizophrenia scale.
    Answer: D

Pages: 583
Topic: Psychosocial Assessment: Personality Tests
Skill: Applied   Other1:
77. Deanna obtained a high score on the Schizophrenia scale of the MMPI-2. This means that she
    A) qualifies for a DSM-IV diagnosis of schizophrenia.
    B) has delusions and/or hallucinations.
    C) shows some propensities typical of the schizophrenic population.
    D) all of the above
    Answer: C

Pages: 584
Topic: Psychosocial Assessment: Personality Tests
Skill: Factual   Other1:
78. One of the most common uses of the MMPI is as a diagnostic standard. This means that
    A) individual items are analyzed for bizarre responses.
    B) the clinician uses the MMPI as the standard against which other tests in a battery are compared.
    C) the individual's profile pattern is compared with profiles of known patient groups to suggest a broad descriptive diagnosis for the individual under study.
    D) the clinician focuses on objective content themes that may exist in an individual's responses.
    Answer: C

Pages: 584
Topic: Psychosocial Assessment: Personality Tests
Skill: Factual   Other1:
79. In interpreting an MMPI-2, a psychologist finds that an individual has endorsed an unusually large number of items about fears, and concludes that the individual may very well be preoccupied with fear. This is an example of an approach to MMPI interpretation known as
   A) profile interpretation.
   B) content interpretation.
   C) descriptive interpretation.
   D) reference interpretation.
   Answer: B

Pages: 584
Topic: Psychosocial Assessment: Personality Tests
Skill: Applied   Other1:
80. "The MMPI is superficial and does not adequately reflect the complexities of an individual taking the test." This criticism is most likely to be said by a _____ oriented clinician.
   A) psychodynamically
   B) behaviorally
   C) cognitively
   D) biologically
   Answer: A

Pages: 584
Topic: Psychosocial Assessment: Personality Tests
Skill: Applied   Other1:
81. "The MMPI and the entire genre of personality tests are too oriented toward measuring unobservable mentalistic constructs." This criticism is most likely to be said by a _____ oriented clinician.
   A) psychodynamically
   B) behaviorally
   C) cognitively
   D) humanistically
   Answer: B

Pages: 584
Topic: Psychosocial Assessment: Personality Tests
Skill: Factual   *Other1:*
82. In revising the MMPI, the MMPI-2 has
    A) been based on a new and more representative standardization sample than was used in the
       original scale.
    B) a modernized item pool.
    C) retained the clinical scales in their original form, although some items were deleted
       or reworded.
    D) all of the above
    Answer: D

Pages: 584
Topic: Psychosocial Assessment: Personality Tests
Skill: Factual   *Other1:*
83. A key feature of the MMPI-2 is that
    A) the clinical scales measure the same properties of personality organization as they
       always have.
    B) the validity scales have been discarded.
    C) it can now be used with children under age twelve.
    D) it now incorporates more items from behavioral and cognitive theoretical perspectives.
    Answer: A

Pages: 588
Topic: Psychosocial Assessment: Personality Tests
Skill: Applied   *Other1:*
84. Dr. Doe is developing a psychological test by means of factor analysis. Assuming that Dr.
    Doe's test is reliable and valid, the test will
    A) provide a DSM-IV diagnosis of an Axis I disorder for an individual.
    B) measure several basic traits in a precise and selective manner.
    C) provide DSM-IV diagnoses of both Axis I and Axis II disorders for an individual.
    D) measure multiple traits that are highly interrelated.
    Answer: B

Pages: 588
Topic: Psychosocial Assessment: Personality Tests
Skill: Conceptual   *Other1:*
85. One limitation of the MMPI-2 is that it
    A) cannot detect whether an individual is attempting to distort his or her responses.
    B) requires a clinical interview as a supplement to the test itself.
    C) is based on factor analysis, which often leads to measures that sacrifice validity for
       the sake of reliability without intending to do so.
    D) requires an individual to be literate.
    Answer: D

Pages: 589
Topic: Psychosocial Assessment: Personality Tests
Skill: Factual   Other1:
86. Computer-based MMPI interpretation systems typically employ
    A) actuarial procedures.
    B) schematic interpretation.
    C) rational analysis.
    D) factor analysis.
    Answer: A

Pages: 589
Topic: Psychosocial Assessment: Personality Tests
Skill: Conceptual   Other1:
87. One of the problems with actuarial data for an instrument like the MMPI is that
    A) the collection of such data is relatively inexpensive, which has led to the
       accumulation of so many actuarial-based profiles that many subjects "fit" two or more
       profile types.
    B) the potential number of significantly different profiles is limited.
    C) the profiles of many subjects do not "fit" the profile types for which actuarial data
       are available.
    D) the generated profiles are relatively useless for predicting behavior.
    Answer: C

Pages: 589
Topic: Psychosocial Assessment: Personality Tests
Skill: Applied   Other1:
88. A psychologist utilizes a computer interpretation of the MMPI. This interpretation will
    A) yield a profile pattern that probably is not accurate with regard to the psychologist's
       client.
    B) replace the clinician's subjective diagnostic judgment with an objective, accurate
       diagnosis.
    C) probably rely on general clinical lore and the wisdom of expert clinicians rather than
       on actuarial data when reporting rare conditions such as suicide.
    D) have been written by a statistical analyst, resulting in an analysis that must be
       translated by the psychologist into clinically useful terms.
    Answer: C

Pages: 589
Topic: Psychosocial Assess: Psychological Assessment/Forensic/Legal Cases
Skill: Applied   Other1:
89. Attorneys in a civil court case would like to establish that an individual is cognitively impaired. To evaluate the question of cognitive impairment, forensic psychologists would be most likely to use
A) the WAIS-R.
B) the MMPI.
C) the Halstead-Reitan Battery.
D) A and C
Answer: D

Pages: 590
Topic: Psychosocial Assess: Psychological Assessment/Forensic/Legal Cases
Skill: Applied   Other1:
90. Jose was ordered to undergo psychological testing by a court. He is uncooperative but agreed reluctantly to take the tests. A forensic psychologist might best deal with this situation by
A) relying more on projective tests than on personality tests insofar as the former are not as prone to be contaminated by a testee's test-taking attitude.
B) adopting a stern and even threatening attitude in order to intimidate Jose into participating appropriately in the test taking.
C) using a test like the MMPI-2 which contains scales that can covertly assess his cooperativeness and truthfulness.
D) offering an incentive like financial compensation for participating appropriately.
Answer: C

Pages: 590
Topic: Psychosocial Assessment: Psychological Tests in Personnel Screening
Skill: Factual   Other1:
91. The use of personality tests in personnel screening is most likely to be used with
A) job applicants who have histories of previous psychiatric hospitalizations.
B) individuals applying for positions that require a high level of emotional stability.
C) individuals applying for positions that require having certain personality characteristics.
D) individuals in large corporations, due to the expense involved.
Answer: B

Pages: 591
Topic: Psychosocial Assessment: Psychological Tests in Personnel Screening
Skill: Factual   Other1:
92. In contrast to personnel screening, the object of personnel selection is to
   A) screen in appropriate job applicants.
   B) screen out inappropriate applicants.
   C) evaluate whether the personality characteristics of a job applicant provide a good
      match to the requirements of the job.
   D) A and C
   Answer: D

Pages: 591
Topic: Psychosocial Assessment: Psychological Tests in Personnel Screening
Skill: Conceptual   Other1:
93. Psychological testing may be done in personnel screening and in personnel selection. The
   difference between these two uses influence the types of tests used. Unlike personnel
   screening, testing in personnel selection is likely to involve
   A) measures of normal personality characteristics.
   B) a self-report inventory.
   C) measures of emotional instability and maladjustment.
   D) measures especially designed to identify personality disorders.
   Answer: A

Pages: 591
Topic: Psychosocial Assessment: Psychological Tests in Personnel Screening
Skill: Applied   Other1:
94. A psychologist who is employed in personnel screening, as opposed to personnel selection,
   would most likely use
   A) the MMPI-2.
   B) an employment interview.
   C) an evaluation of previous work record.
   D) all of the above
   Answer: D

Pages: 591
Topic: Psychosocial Assessment: Psychological Tests in Personnel Screening
Skill: Conceptual   Other1:
95. According to psychologists who use psychological tests for preemployment testing,
   A) such tests do not need good reliability to be useful in this setting.
   B) psychological tests do not invade an individual's privacy.
   C) psychological tests should not be used as the sole means of determining whether a
      person should be hired.
   D) employment interviews are rarely useful as a source of information prior to a person
      being hired.
   Answer: C

Pages: 591-592
Topic: Psychosocial Assessment: Psychological Tests in Personnel Screening
Skill: Factual   Other1:
96. In order for a psychological test to be used in personnel screening, it must be shown that
    A) the test does not discriminate against ethnic minorities.
    B) the test is valid for the particular application for which it is to be used.
    C) the test is the single best source of information about an individual.
    D) A and B
    Answer: D

Pages: 592
Topic: Psychosocial Assessment: Psychological Tests in Personnel Screening
Skill: Conceptual   Other1:
97. One of the advantages of using the MMPI-2 in personnel screening is that the MMPI-2
    A) can be read by individuals with second grade reading ability.
    B) does not discriminate against ethnic minority subjects.
    C) measures normal personality instead of psychopathology.
    D) was originally validated in personnel screening situations.
    Answer: B

Pages: 593
Topic: Psychosocial Assessment: A Psychological Case Study
Skill: Conceptual   Other1:
98. The text presented the case of Esteban, a twenty-one-year-old student from Colombia.
    Although a number of assessment specialists participated in the assessment, which is
    unusual, in other respects the psychological assessment used in this case was typical
    because
    A) an interview was used exclusively for obtaining information.
    B) the various tests used yielded very contradictory information.
    C) the assessment included a general physical exam conducted by the psychologist.
    D) the family history was important in understanding Esteban.
    Answer: D

Pages: 593
Topic: Psychosocial Assessment: A Psychological Case Study
Skill: Factual   Other1:
99. The text presented the case of Esteban, a twenty-one-year-old student from Colombia. Some
    psychologists believe that the Rorschach Inkblot Test is particularly appropriate for
    cases like Esteban's because the Rorschach
    A) is not culture bound.
    B) is more appropriate for college students than the MMPI.
    C) is not as biased toward members of ethnic minorities as is the MMPI.
    D) provides a more structured situation than other projective tests.
    Answer: A

Pages: 586-594
Topic: Psychosocial Assessment: A Psychological Case Study
Skill: Applied   Other1:
100. The text presented the case study of Esteban, a twenty-one-year-old student from Colombia. The MMPI-2 computer-based report was typical of such reports because
    A) there was a large discrepancy between the report based on the MMPI and that based on the MMPI-2.
    B) the report was invalid because Esteban is a member of an ethnic minority.
    C) the report provided diagnostic and treatment considerations.
    D) the report was not used appropriately in Esteban's treatment.
    Answer: C

Pages: 586-594
Topic: Psychosocial Assessment: A Psychological Case Study
Skill: Conceptual   Other1:
101. The text presented the case study of Esteban, a twenty-one-year-old student from Columbia. The MMPI-2 computer-based report suggested several possible diagnoses, such as schizophrenia and a severe personality disorder, and further indicated that an Organic Brain Syndrome or Substance-Induced Organic Mental Disorder are possible conditions that need to be evaluated. These aspects of the MMPI-2 computer-based report illustrate how diagnostically
    A) inaccurate the MMPI-2 can be in some cases since Esteban's DSM-IV diagnosis did not match any of the computer-generated diagnoses.
    B) accurate the MMPI-2 can be in some cases since Esteban's DSM-IV diagnosis was schizophrenia.
    C) accurate the MMPI-2 can be in some cases since Esteban's DSM-IV diagnosis was Schizotypal Personality Disorder.
    D) accurate the MMPI-2 can be in some cases since Esteban's DSM-IV diagnosis was Organic Personality Syndrome on Axis I and Borderline Personality Disorder on Axis II.
    Answer: D

Pages: 586-594
Topic: Psychosocial Assessment: A Psychological Case Study
Skill: Conceptual   Other1:
102. The text presented the case study of Esteban, a twenty-one-year-old student from Columbia.
 Comparison of the MMPI-2 computer-based report to the Rorschach computer-based report
 illustrates that
     A) the MMPI-2 report was superior to the Rorschach report in terms of the portrayal of
        Esteban's functioning.
     B) the Rorschach report was superior to the MMPI-2 report in terms of the portrayal of
        Esteban's functioning.
     C) both reports provided some useful information but overall were highly inaccurate in
        their portrayals of Esteban's functioning.
     D) it is important not to rely solely on one test in that the reports provided useful and
        complementary information about Esteban's functioning.
     Answer: D

Pages: 594
Topic: The Integration of Assessment Data
Skill: Factual   Other1:
103. The integration of various assessment data into a coherent working model for use in
 planning or changing treatment for a given patient usually is done by
     A) computer.
     B) clinicians in individual private practices.
     C) a social worker or clinical technician.
     D) a psychiatrist or general physician.
     Answer: B

Pages: 594
Topic: The Integration of Assessment Data
Skill: Factual   Other1:
104. Within a clinic or hospital setting, integration of assessment data is usually done
     A) by the staff social worker.
     B) by a psychologist.
     C) by an interdisciplinary team.
     D) by no one, as results do not get integrated.
     Answer: C

Pages: 595
Topic: The Integration of Assessment Data
Skill: Factual   Other1:
105. Clinical assessment data are commonly used
   A) in the initial stages of treatment, but not during the course of therapy.
   B) during the course of therapy, but not during the initial stages of treatment.
   C) both in the initial stages of treatment and during the course of therapy.
   D) in the period before treatment has begun, but not after the treatment has begun.
   Answer: C

Pages: 595
Topic: The Integration of Assessment Data
Skill: Conceptual   Other1:
106. The accuracy of assessment is
   A) not very important because assessment rarely affects treatment decisions.
   B) very important because the decisions using assessment results have far-reaching
      implications.
   C) much more important at the beginning of treatment than at discharge or termination.
   D) much more important at the end than at the beginning of treatment.
   Answer: B

Pages: 595
Topic: The Integration of Assessment Data
Skill: Factual   Other1:
107. Which of the following is most accurate regarding the limitations of the assessment
   process?
   A) The theoretical orientation of the clinician is an important factor in the
      interpretation of test data.
   B) Even the worst psychological test data usually leads to adequate treatment planning.
   C) Most objective personality scales do not have a sufficient base of validation studies
      to make them clinically useful.
   D) Most clinicians overemphasize stressors and other life circumstances as the causes of a
      patient's problems and therefore underutilize personality tests.
   Answer: A

Pages: 596
Topic: Unresolved Issues on the Use of Computerized Assessment
Skill: Conceptual   Other1:
108. The use of computers in psychological testing
    A) has been decreasing in recent years as studies suggest that computerized tests lack validity.
    B) results in the elimination of the clinician from the interpretation of assessment.
    C) is important for the administration of tests, but rarely in the interpretation of tests.
    D) increases efficiency and reliability.
    Answer: D

Pages: 596
Topic: Unresolved Issues on the Use of Computerized Assessment
Skill: Factual   Other1: In Student Study Guide
109. The American Psychological Association's (APA's) guidelines on computer-based assessment assume that computerized test results will be used as
    A) a last resort only.
    B) final recommendations.
    C) the sole basis for diagnosis.
    D) working hypotheses.
    Answer: D

Pages: 597
Topic: Unresolved Issues on the Use of Computerized Assessment
Skill: Factual   Other1:
110. One of the major advantages of using computerized assessment is that
    A) it frees up time for doing those things that can only be accomplished by a highly skilled clinician.
    B) even untrained individuals can use such assessment in a competent fashion.
    C) the assessment booklets and answer sheets support the warm, personal style that clinicians hope to convey to their clients.
    D) the clinician can be replaced by the computer in the interpretation process.
    Answer: A

Short Answer

Write the word or phrase that best completes each statement or answers the question.

Pages: 567-568
Topic: Clinical Assessment
Skill: Conceptual   Other1:
1. Briefly describe one way in which medical and psychological diagnoses differ.
    Answer: A medical diagnosis generally involves objective testing with external criteria
         for confirmation and validation. The cause of the disease or its mechanism are
         generally known as a part of the diagnosis. A psychological diagnosis does not
         usually allow for such objective confirmatory testing. It also tends to be
         symptom-based and to involve an ongoing process.

Pages: 571
Topic: Assessment of the Physical Organism: The Neurological Examination
Skill: Factual   Other1:
2. A preliminary neurological screening device involving the measure of brain electrical
    activity involves use of the ____.
    Answer: electroencephalogram (EEG)

Pages: 571-572
Topic: Assessment of the Physical Organism: The Neurological Examination
Skill: Factual   Other1:
3. What method might a neurologist use if she or he wished to look for structural anomalies
    in the brain?
    Answer: She or he might use either a CAT scan or an MRI.

Pages: 571
Topic: Assessment of the Physical Organism: The Neurological Examination
Skill: Applied   Other1:
4. Dr. Black hypothesizes that his patient has a dysfunction in metabolic functioning of the
    frontal lobes. What method would be best for him to use to test his hypothesis?
    Answer: a PET scan

Pages: 572-573
Topic: Assessment of the Physical Organism: The Neuropsychological Exam
Skill: Factual   Other1:
5. What information does neuropsychological assessment provide?
    Answer: It can establish the presence of cognitive, perceptual, and motor impairment.
         It also provides information about the nature of the impairment and possibly
         about the area of the brain involved.

Pages: 573
Topic: Assessment of the Physical Organism: The Neuropsychological Exam
Skill: Factual   Other1:
6. A widely used neuropsychological test is the _____.
    Answer: Halstead-Reitan Battery; Luria-Nebraska; Halstead-Wepman Aphasia Screening Test

Pages: 574-575
Topic: Psychosocial Assessment: Assessment Interviews
Skill: Conceptual   Other1:
7. Name one way in which the reliability of the clinical interview may be enhanced.
    Answer: A clinician may use a standardized interview format, a computerized diagnostic
             interview, or rating scales in conjunction with the interview.

Pages: 575-579
Topic: Psychosocial Assessment: The Clinical Observation of Behavior
Skill: Factual   Other1:
8. What are two methods of behavioral observation that a clinician might use?
    Answer: These include the clinician's own direct observation, which may take place in
             natural settings; self-monitoring of behavior and cognitions; and self-report
             and clinical rating scales. Observation in contrived situations and role-playing
             can also be very informative.

Pages: 579
Topic: Psychosocial Assessment: Psychological Tests
Skill: Factual   Other1:
9. The most commonly used intelligence test for adults is the _____.
    Answer: WAIS-R

Pages: 580-583
Topic: Psychosocial Assessment: Personality Tests
Skill: Conceptual   Other1:
10. What is the major difference between projective and objective personality tests?
     Answer: Projective tests are unstructured, using ambiguous stimuli like inkblots and
              pictures, and eliciting unstructured responses. They are based on the
              assumption that an individual projects conflicts, motives, and wishes onto the
              stimuli. Objective tests use highly structured stimuli and elicit highly
              structured responses like "true/false" responses. Objective tests lend
              themselves to greater quantification and therefore greater reliability in
              scoring and interpretation.

Pages: 580-581
Topic: Psychosocial Assessment: Personality Tests
Skill: Factual   Other1:
11. Briefly describe the Rorschach Test and the main assumption that forms the basis for using this test.
    Answer: This is a projective test in which a person is shown a series of ten inkblots
             and asked to describe what he or she sees in them. The assumption on which the
             test is based is that people will project their inner conflicts, motives, and
             wishes onto the inkblots.

Pages: 581
Topic: Psychosocial Assessment: Personality Tests
Skill: Applied   Other1:
12. Dinah was asked to look at a series of pictures and to tell a story about each one. She
    was taking the _____.
    Answer: Thematic Apperception Test (TAT)

Pages: 583
Topic: Psychosocial Assessment: Personality Tests
Skill: Factual   Other1:
13. The most frequently used and well-researched psychosocial assessment device is the _____.
    Answer: MMPI

Pages: 583
Topic: Psychosocial Assessment: Personality Tests
Skill: Factual   Other1:
14. How was the MMPI developed?
    Answer: It was developed through a process of empirical keying. A large battery of
             true/false items were administered to a sample of normal individuals and to a
             variety of other homogeneous diagnostic groups. Items for the MMPI were then
             selected on the basis of their discriminative ability.

Pages: 583-585
Topic: Psychosocial Assessment: Personality Tests
Skill: Factual   Other1:
15. Describe the different types of scales that are included in the MMPI.
    Answer: This test consists of over 500 true/false items which can be grouped into 10
             clinical scales, a number of validity scales, and hundreds of special scales.
             Four of the special scales have been used so routinely that they were
             incorporated into the MMPI profile.

Pages: 584
Topic: Psychosocial Assessment: Personality Tests
Skill: Factual   Other1:
16. What are diagnostic standard and content interpretation?

　Answer: These are two uses of the MMPI. The MMPI can be used as a diagnostic standard, in which an individual's profile is compared against profiles of known patient groups to generate a general descriptive diagnosis. In content interpretation, a clinician evaluates the content themes of an individual's MMPI.

Pages: 588
Topic: Psychosocial Assessment: Personality Tests
Skill: Factual   Other1:
17. What is factor analysis and how is it used in the development of personality tests?

　Answer: This is a statistical procedure whereby a large array of intercorrelated measures can be reduced to a minimum number of factors that purportedly represent basic and relatively independent traits. It can be used in the development of objective psychological tests, the goal being to measure one trait at a given time with maximum precision and selectivity. A personality profile can then be drawn showing the degree to which such traits are characteristic of an individual.

Pages: 589
Topic: Psychosocial Assessment: Personality Tests
Skill: Factual   Other1:
18. What procedure is typically used in developing a computer-based MMPI interpretation system? Identify and briefly describe this process.

　Answer: Such interpretation systems typically rely on actuarial procedures in which behavioral descriptions and other characteristics of many subjects with distinct profiles are stored in the computer and compared with an individual's profile that is submitted to the computer for interpretation.

Pages: 589-592
Topic: Psychosocial Assessment: Psychological Tests in Personnel Screening
Skill: Factual   Other1:
19. Other than a clinical setting, identify two settings in which psychological assessment is used.

　Answer: These include assessment for personnel selection, personnel screening, forensic contexts, and school settings.

Pages: 596-597
Topic: Unresolved Issues on the Use of Computerized Assessment
Skill: Factual   Other1:
20. Why do some clinicians object to the use of computerized assessment?
    Answer: They object for a variety of reasons: fear of dehumanizing the clinical
             process, lack of familiarity with research on reliability of this approach, fear
             of loss of professional standards in the use and interpretation of psychological
             tests, fear of being replaced by computers, and fear that it will lead to
             unnecessary overtesting.

Essay

Write your answer in the space provided or on a separate sheet of paper.

Pages: 568-570
Topic: The Information Sought in Assessment
Skill: Applied   Other1:
1. A psychologist plans to use assessment in working with a client. What does this
   psychologist hope to gain from the assessment? What of the person will be assessed?
   Answer: The psychologist hopes to gain a basic understanding of the individual's
            history, intellectual functioning, personality characteristics, and
            environmental pressures and resources. This is more important than a formal
            diagnosis taken in isolation. The assessment might include an objective
            description of the individual's behavior, a description of any relevant
            long-term personality characteristics, the social context in which the
            individual operates, and a formulation of the individual that would allow the
            clinician to develop hypotheses about the client's future behavior.

Pages: 570
Topic: Importance of Rapport Between the Clinician and the Client
Skill: Conceptual   Other1:
2. Why is good rapport between clinician and client important to assessment? What factors
   comprise good rapport?
   Answer: It is important because a client may be anxious and defensive in being asked to
            provide deeply personal information to a stranger. Good rapport can help to set
            the client at ease, increasing the likelihood that the information given is
            complete and accurate. Elements of good rapport include educating the client as
            to how the testing can help him or her as well as to the laws regarding
            confidentiality. Warmth and empathy are obviously of central importance.

Pages: 571-572
Topic: Assessment of the Physical Organism: The Neurological Examination
Skill: Factual   Other1:

3. Describe the differences between an electroencephalogram (EEG), a CAT scan, a PET scan, and an MRI.

    Answer: An EEG measures the brain's electrical activity. Where dysrythmias occur, further specialized techniques can be used to arrive at precise diagnoses. A CAT scan uses X-rays to examine anomalies in the brain's structural characteristics. The PET scan allows for appraisal of brain functioning by measuring its metabolic activity. The MRI measures variations in magnetic fields of various organs and structural parts of the body. The MRI thus allows visualization of the brain's anatomic features and provides greater precision and quality than the CAT scan.

Pages: 572-574
Topic: Assessment of the Physical Organism
Skill: Factual   Other1:

4. Describe some of the tasks that might be included in an assessment of a client based on a neuropsychological examination. What might the neuropsychologist learn from these tests?

    Answer: The tasks on the commonly used Halstead-Reitan Battery include the Category Test, the Tactual Performance Test, the Rhythm Test, the Speech Sounds Performance Test, and the Finger Oscillation Task. The clinician can evaluate the nature and severity of an individual's cognitive, behavioral, psychological, and intellectual impairment, as well as its possible brain location, even before it becomes apparent in scans. Tests may be individualized for a given patient.

Pages: 574-575
Topic: Psychosocial Assessment: Assessment Interviews
Skill: Conceptual   Other1:

5. Describe the different types of interviews that can be used by a clinician. What are the advantages and disadvantages of these specific types of interviews, and of the interview process generally?

    Answer: The interview may vary from a simple set of questions, such as the mental status exam, to a more extended format. Highly structured interviews like the computerized diagnostic interview for DSM-IV result in higher reliability. The flexible format interview is subject to error and has been criticized as an unreliable source of information. Nevertheless, excessive reliance on structured interviews can introduce error due to the complexity of human behavior.

Pages: 575-579
Topic: Psychosocial Assessment: The Clinical Observation of Behavior
Skill: Applied   Other1:

6. Richard is seriously depressed. What are the different observational methods that the behaviorally oriented clinician can use in assessing Richard? What are the advantages and disadvantages of each?

Answer: Direct observation is important, although this will probably not occur in a natural setting. Self-monitoring and self-reports can be used, providing insight into the individual's perceptions accompanied by the limitations of self-report measures. Rating scales, such as the Hamilton Rating Scale for Depression, organize information and encourage reliability and objectivity. Family assessment, contrived situations, and role-playing are other important observational methods.

Pages: 579-583
Topic: Psychosocial Assessment: Personality Tests
Skill: Conceptual   Other1:

7. What are the major differences between projective and objective tests? What are the advantages and disadvantages of each method?

Answer: Projective tests are unstructured, relying on ambiguous stimuli. Subjects' responses are not constrained by a preselected format. Underlying these tests is the assumption that individuals project their own conflicts, motives, and wishes into the situation. Interpretation involves subjective judgment. Objective tests are structured, resulting in quantification that enhances reliability. They are cost-effective, highly reliable, and objective; they also can be scored and administered by computer. They may be too mechanistic and require adequate reading ability.

Pages: 580-582
Topic: Psychosocial Assessment: Personality Tests
Skill: Applied   Other1:

8. Rodney sought treatment for anxiety. He is being assessed by a clinician with projective techniques. Describe three techniques that might be used. What are the advantages and disadvantages of these approaches?

Answer: The Rorschach Test, the Thematic Apperception Test, and the Sentence Completion Test are three such tests. These tests allow the individual to describe vague, unstructured stimuli. Projective tests are aimed at discovering the ways in which an individual's past learning and self-structure result in the organization and perception of ambiguous information. Projective tests have been criticized because of poor reliability and validity.

Pages: 583-589
Topic: Psychosocial Assessment: Personality Tests
Skill: Factual   Other1:
9. The MMPI is the most widely used personality assessment measure. How was it developed and what kind of information can be obtained from it?

Answer: The MMPI was developed using empirical keying, administering a pool of items to a control group of normal individuals and groups of patients having particular psychiatric diagnoses. Items were selected on the basis of their discriminative ability. The MMPI can be used as a diagnostic standard to generate general descriptive diagnoses as well as for content interpretation. Three validity scales, ten clinical scales, and numerous special scales can be interpreted.

Pages: 571-589
Topic: Psychosocial Assessment: Personality Tests
Skill: Applied   Other1:
10. Rochelle has sought help from a psychologist. She complains of headaches following a minor auto accident a year ago. She also appears to be depressed, as she is not sleeping well and often cries. Describe how Rochelle might be assessed by the psychologist. In your description include some type of interview, projective test, objective test, and two other assessment methods.

Answer: The interview could be flexible, semi-structured, or standardized. Some structure would enhance reliability and allow specific diagnostic probes concerning depressive symptoms. Perhaps the most reliable projective test would be the Rorschach, provided that a standardized scoring and interpretive system was used. The most reliable and informative objective test would be the MMPI-2. Other measures could include rating scales, observation, and tests like the WAIS-R and Halstead-Reitan Battery to determine the possiblity of neuropsychological impairment associated with the auto accident.

Pages: 574-589
Topic: Psychosocial Assessment: Personality Tests
Skill: Conceptual   Other1:
11. Discuss issues of reliability, validity, and clinical utility as they pertain to psychosocial assessment.

Answer: The general type (e.g., projective, objective, interview) of assessment tool and the specific test chosen within that general class vary tremendously in reliability in both scoring and interpretation. They also vary in the type of information elicited, so that a psychodynamic clinician may find projectives more useful than an MMPI-2, despite their lower reliability, and a behaviorist may have little use for a projective over an objective rating scale. Research to validate tests varies in quantity, quality, and findings. The MMPI is the most well-validated personality test.

Pages: 589-590
Topic: Psychosocial Assess: Psychological Assessment/Forensic/Legal Cases
Skill: Factual   Other1:

12. How is psychological assessment used in forensic cases?

    Answer: Intellectual and neuropsychological tests are most often used to establish legal incompetence and cognitive impairments in damage suits. Psychosocial assessment is most often used to assess psychological adjustment in cases of custody, claims of psychological damages, and to establish legal insanity. The MMPI-2 is useful to assess a person's honesty and other characteristics of his or her test-taking attitude in court-ordered testing. The WAIS-R, Halstead-Reitan, and MMPI-2 are the most frequently used tests in forensic settings.

Pages: 590-592
Topic: Psychosocial Assessment: Psychological Tests in Personnel Screening
Skill: Conceptual   Other1:

13. How is psychological testing used in personnel screening and personnel selection? Are these uses of psychological testing justified?

    Answer: It is used in screening to assess psychopathology and emotional instability for jobs requiring high levels of psychological stability. The MMPI is often used. Selection of personnel involves "screening in" individuals with certain desirable personality characteristics. In this case, a measure of normal personality like the 16 Personality Factor Inventory would be used. In some cases (e.g., airline pilots and police officers) the safety of many people is at stake. Some tests involve invasion of privacy but are considered warranted if the placement decisions are for the "public good."

Pages: 594-596
Topic: The Integration of Assessment Data
Skill: Conceptual   Other1:

14. Psychosocial assessment can be an invaluable tool. At the same time, assessment has numerous limitations. Describe four of these limitations.

    Answer: The instrument or the clinician may be culturally biased. The theoretical orientation of the clinician inevitably influences assessment. Many clinicians overemphasize internal traits without due attention to the possible role of stressors or other external circumstances in a person's life. Many psychological assessment procedures have not been sufficiently validated. There is always a possibility that some assessment data--and any diagnostic label or treatment based on them--may be inaccurate.

Pages: 596-597
Topic: Unresolved Issues on the Use of Computerized Assessment
Skill: Conceptual   Other1:

15. In what ways are computers used in psychological assessment? What are the advantages of computerized assessment? What arguments against its use have been suggested?

Answer: They can be used in test administration, scoring, and interpretation. They can enhance reliability, efficiency, and can be cost-effective. Some clinicians dislike this approach due to lack of familiarity with these programs or the fear that they will lead to a dehumanized or unprofessional approach to clinical work. Some believe that insufficient validity research exists. Software programs do exist that have no sound research support.

CHAPTER 16 Biologically Based Therapies

Multiple-Choice

Choose the one alternative that best completes the statement or answers the question.

Pages: 601
Topic: Early Attempts at Biological Intervention
Skill: Factual   Other1:
1. The idea that a disordered mind might be healed by treatment directed at the body
    A) goes back to ancient times.
    B) became prominent during the Middle Ages.
    C) was developed shortly after the Industrial Revolution.
    D) became prominent during the early twentieth century.
    Answer: A

Pages: 601
Topic: Early Attempts at Biological Intervention
Skill: Conceptual   Other1:
2. In the search for biological treatments for disordered behavior,
    A) little progress has been made in the use of drugs for disordered behaviors.
    B) most such behavior has been shown to be due to genetic defects.
    C) hormonal factors have been discarded as explanations for all but the most severely
       disordered behavior.
    D) we still have no reliable knowledge of point-to-point correspondence between certain
       behaviors and particular events in the brain at cellular or subcellular levels.
    Answer: D

Pages: 602
Topic: Early Attempts at Biological Intervention
Skill: Factual   Other1:
3. The treatment of disordered behavior through purging the body of unwanted substances was a
    typical treatment in all of the following EXCEPT
    A) ancient Rome.
    B) the Middle Ages.
    C) the eighteenth century.
    D) the twentieth century.
    Answer: D

Pages: 602
Topic: Early Attempts at Biological Intervention
Skill: Applied   Other1:
4. Sirus shows disordered behavior. His physician recommends that Sirus be treated with laxatives and emetics in an effort to purge his body. Sirus probably lived
   A) in the eighteenth century.
   B) in the nineteenth century.
   C) in the early part of the twentieth century.
   D) in the middle part of the twentieth century.
   Answer: A

Pages: 602
Topic: Early Attempts at Biological Intervention
Skill: Factual   Other1:
5. Medical treatments of the mentally disordered, such as bleeding,
   A) have been shown to be somewhat effective but only for severely disordered behavior.
   B) were not generally used for physical diseases.
   C) often have been influenced by advances in other sciences.
   D) died out in the fourth century, only to be revived in the nineteenth century.
   Answer: C

Pages: 602
Topic: Early Attempts at Biological Intervention
Skill: Factual   Other1:
6. After the discovery of electricity, many efforts were made to use electrical stimulation to alter mental states. This is an example of
   A) the barbaric procedures of earlier times.
   B) how the physical treatment of mental illness began.
   C) medical procedures deriving from developments in other sciences.
   D) one of the rare cases in which an early psychological treatment was developed from a sound scientific theory.
   Answer: C

Pages: 602
Topic: Early Attempts at Biological Intervention
Skill: Factual   Other1:
7. In general, as more has been learned in various subfields of medicine, treatment measures have become
   A) more benign but also more risky.
   B) more invasive and also more risky.
   C) more benign and also less risky.
   D) more invasive but also less risky.
   Answer: C

Pages: 602
Topic: Early Attempts at Biological Intervention
Skill: Conceptual   Other1:

8. Relative to other branches of medicine, psychiatry
   A) has developed more quickly in its treatment methods.
   B) has developed quickly in treatment options even though it has been slow to uncover the causes of mental disorders.
   C) has developed slowly both in understanding and in treating mental disorders.
   D) has been fairly quick to uncover the causes of most mental disorders, but slow to discover treatments for them.
   Answer: C

Pages: 603
Topic: Early Attempts at Biological Intervention: Coma/Convulsive Therapies
Skill: Factual   Other1:

9. Insulin coma therapy
   A) is remarkably effective though risky.
   B) decreases the glucose (sugar) in the patient's blood until the patient goes into shock, which is terminated after an hour or more by administering glucose.
   C) was introduced in the early twentieth century as a physiological treatment for schizophrenia.
   D) B and C
   Answer: D

Pages: 603
Topic: Early Attempts at Biological Intervention: Coma/Convulsive Therapies
Skill: Factual   Other1:

10. The use of convulsion therapy to treat schizophrenia was originally based on the mistaken idea that
    A) convulsions would drive out demons from a psychotic individual.
    B) schizophrenia and epilepsy rarely co-occur.
    C) convulsions cause a radical reorganization of brain cells that results in the subsiding of schizophrenic symptoms.
    D) individuals with diabetes are unusually well-adjusted psychologically.
    Answer: B

Pages: 603
Topic: Early Attempts at Biological Intervention: Coma/Convulsive Therapies
Skill: Factual   Other1:

11. Insulin coma therapy
    A) is a rather benign and ineffective form of treatment.
    B) causes an acute deficiency of glucose in the blood.
    C) was introduced as a treatment for anxiety disorders.
    D) is most effective with individuals who are manic.
    Answer: B

Pages: 603
Topic: Early Attempts at Biological Intervention: Coma/Convulsive Therapies
Skill: Factual   Other1:
12. Where insulin coma therapy was effective, it appears that
    A) the effect may have been due to some other factor.
    B) the effect was obtained primarily with chronic schizophrenic patients.
    C) the relapse rate was high.
    D) A and C
    Answer: D

Pages: 603
Topic: Early Attempts at Biological Intervention: Coma/Convulsive Therapies
Skill: Factual   Other1:
13. Insulin coma therapy has largely disappeared because
    A) it was ineffective and carried great medical risks.
    B) it was effective but carried great medical risks.
    C) even though it had few medical risks, it was ineffective.
    D) more effective treatments were developed even though these newer treatments carried
       greater medical risks.
    Answer: A

Pages: 603
Topic: Early Attempts at Biological Intervention: Coma/Convulsive Therapies
Skill: Factual   Other1:
14. Electrostimulation was developed when it was discovered that
    A) anxiety could be reduced by electrical stimulation to the skin.
    B) melancholic depression could be treated effectively with mild electrical stimulation.
    C) symptoms of general paresis could be reduced, although only temporarily, through
       electrical stimulation.
    D) anxiety was caused by an abnormally high amount of electrical activity in the brain.
    Answer: B

Pages: 603
Topic: Early Attempts at Biological Intervention: Coma/Convulsive Therapies
Skill: Factual   Other1:
15. Electroconvulsive therapy (ECT) is more widely used today than insulin therapy because ECT
    A) is more effective with schizophrenia and carries fewer medical risks.
    B) is more effective with schizophrenia even though it carries greater medical risks.
    C) is more effective with depression and carries fewer medical risks.
    D) is more effective with depression even though it carries greater medical risks.
    Answer: C

Pages: 603
Topic: Early Attempts at Biological Intervention: Coma/Convulsive Therapies
Skill: Factual   Other1:
16. The mechanism through which electroconvulsive therapy (ECT) works is
    A) through changes in brain serotonin levels.
    B) through changes in both brain serotonin and norepinephrine levels.
    C) through changes in the sensitivity of neurotransmitter receptors.
    D) unknown.
    Answer: D

Pages: 604
Topic: Early Attempts at Biological Intervention: Coma/Convulsive Therapies
Skill: Factual   Other1:
17. Bilateral electroconvulsive therapy
    A) is more effective with individuals who have bipolar disorder than it is with major
       depression.
    B) involves passing an electrical current across one hemisphere of the brain.
    C) is no longer used because of serious side effects such as permanent memory loss.
    D) has been shown to be more effective than unilateral ECT in some studies, although other
       studies have found equivalent effectiveness.
    Answer: D

Pages: 603-604
Topic: Early Attempts at Biological Intervention: Coma/Convulsive Therapies
Skill: Applied   Other1:
18. Sarah is receiving electroconvulsive therapy. She will
    A) lose consciousness for about three hours following the procedure.
    B) experience violent muscle contractions and possibly bone fractures if she is not given
       muscle relaxants.
    C) receive an electrical current of five volts for about one hour.
    D) experience a severe increase in her blood sugar level, resulting in a coma.
    Answer: B

Pages: 604
Topic: Early Attempts at Biological Intervention: Coma/Convulsive Therapies
Skill: Applied   Other1:
19. Sarah has just received her first treatment of electroconvulsive therapy. She is most
    likely to
    A) experience auditory hallucinations for a brief time afterward.
    B) suffer tonic and clonic seizures over the next week.
    C) feel more clearheaded and less depressed following the first two to three sessions.
    D) have amnesia for the period immediately preceding the therapy.
    Answer: D

Pages: 604-605
Topic: Early Attempts at Biological Intervention: Coma/Convulsive Therapies
Skill: Factual   Other1:
20. Which of the following statements about electroconvulsive therapy (ECT) is NOT true?
    A) Unilateral ECT is more effective than bilateral ECT but has more serious side effects.
    B) Unilateral ECT has fewer side effects but may be less effective than bilateral ECT.
    C) A recent review of the last fifty years of research suggests that ECT is effective for patients with manic disorders who have not responded to medication.
    D) A low-energy pulsating electrical stimulus may be safer than the standard treatment.
    Answer: A

Pages: 605
Topic: Early Attempts at Biological Intervention: Coma/Convulsive Therapies
Skill: Factual   Other1:
21. Compared to the 1940s, the use of electroconvulsive therapy is now more difficult to defend because
    A) it has been shown to cause severe and permanent memory impairment.
    B) there are effective alternative approaches available.
    C) individuals continue to break vertebrae during the seizures caused by ECT.
    D) it is ineffective with individuals suffering from schizophrenia, the population for whom it was developed.
    Answer: B

Pages: 605
Topic: Early Attempts at Biological Intervention: Coma/Convulsive Therapies
Skill: Factual   Other1:
22. Supporters of electroconvulsive therapy believe that it is the only effective way of dealing with some individuals who have
    A) severe depression and who are suicidal.
    B) severe panic disorder.
    C) schizophrenia.
    D) antisocial personality disorder.
    Answer: A

Pages: 605
Topic: Early Attempts at Biological Intervention: Coma/Convulsive Therapies
Skill: Factual   Other1:
23. With regard to electroconvulsive therapy, there is
    A) considerable doubt as to whether this procedure helps anyone.
    B) little doubt that this procedure is effective in the treatment of schizophrenia.
    C) little doubt that it causes extreme brain damage.
    D) little doubt that this procedure is effective in the treatment of endogenous depression.
    Answer: D

Pages: 605
Topic: Early Attempts at Biological Intervention: Coma/Convulsive Therapies
Skill: Factual   Other1:
24. According to extensive investigation of electroconvulsive therapy (ECT) conducted by NIMH, the most likely medical problems that are often associated with ECT today are
    A) vertebrae fractures.
    B) mortality.
    C) brain damage.
    D) none, as all of the risks have been virtually eliminated.
    Answer: D

Pages: 605
Topic: Early Attempts at Biological Intervention: Coma/Convulsive Therapies
Skill: Factual   Other1:
25. Compared with other somatic treatments, such as barbituate anesthetics, ECT procedures result in
    A) significantly higher injury rates, but about the same mortality rates.
    B) significantly higher injury and mortality rates.
    C) about the same injury rates, but significantly higher mortality rates.
    D) about the same injury and mortality rates.
    Answer: D

Pages: 605
Topic: Early Attempts at Biological Intervention: Coma/Convulsive Therapies
Skill: Factual   Other1:
26. According to the NIMH Consensus Development Conference on electroconvulsive therapy, the effect of ECT has been well established for
    A) obsessive-compulsive disorder.
    B) delusional and endogenous depression, as well as acute mania.
    C) schizophrenia.
    D) dysthymic disorder.
    Answer: B

Pages: 605
Topic: Early Attempts at Biological Intervention: Coma/Convulsive Therapies
Skill: Factual   Other1:
27. According to the NIMH Consensus Development Conference, electroconvulsive therapy can be effectively used with all of the following disorders EXCEPT
    A) delusional depression.
    B) endogenous depression.
    C) dysthymia.
    D) acute mania.
    Answer: C

Pages: 605
Topic: Early Attempts at Biological Intervention: Coma/Convulsive Therapies
Skill: Applied   Other1:
28. Steven is a psychiatrist who suffers from a dysthymic disorder that appears to have begun as a result of his wife's death two years ago. His own psychiatrist has recommended ECT. Steven should
    A) refuse the treatment because ECT is not an effective treatment for dysthymia.
    B) refuse the treatment unless he has already received antidepressant medication with no success.
    C) accept the treatment and make sure that it is followed by the use of lithium.
    D) accept the treatment and make sure that it is followed by the use of antidepressant medication.
    Answer: A

Pages: 605
Topic: Early Attempts at Biological Intervention: Coma/Convulsive Therapies
Skill: Applied   Other1:
29. Stephanie is suffering from a delusional depression and is suicidal. She recently received eight sessions of electroconvulsive therapy and her depression appears to have been alleviated. The next step would be to
    A) give her twelve more sessions of ECT to make sure that the depression is cured.
    B) put her under observation for one month in the hospital to see if the depression returns.
    C) place her on a maintenance dose of antidepressant medication.
    D) release her from the hospital with no follow-up unless she becomes depressed again.
    Answer: C

Pages: 605
Topic: Early Attempts at Biological Intervention: Coma/Convulsive Therapies
Skill: Factual   Other1:
30. The relapse rates associated with electroconvulsive therapy are
    A) low.
    B) high for delusional patients, but low for individuals with other diagnoses.
    C) high unless the treatment is followed by maintenance doses of antidepressant medication.
    D) high unless the treatment is followed by maintenance doses of antidelusional medication.
    Answer: C

Pages: 605
Topic: Early Attempts at Biological Intervention: Coma/Convulsive Therapies
Skill: Factual   Other1:
31. Some researchers believe that the effect of electroconvulsive therapy is due to
    A) induced changes in the levels of certain neurotransmitters.
    B) a severing of the connections between the limbic system and the frontal lobes.
    C) the alteration of the occipital cortex.
    D) a reduction of arousal in the brain stem.
    Answer: A

Pages: 604
Topic: Early Attempts at Biological Intervention: Coma/Convulsive Therapies
Skill: Applied   Other1:
32. The text presented the case of Ms. McCall, a well-educated woman who received ECT
    treatments. Ms. McCall was an appropriate patient for these treatments because
    A) her depression was mild but chronic.
    B) she showed symptoms of depression together with problematic behavior associated with
       aggressive impulses.
    C) her depression was secondary to a primary diagnosis of recurrent schizophrenia.
    D) she was severely depressed.
    Answer: D

Pages: 604
Topic: Early Attempts at Biological Intervention: Coma/Convulsive Therapies
Skill: Applied   Other1:
33. The text presented the case of Ms. McCall, a well-educated woman who received ECT
    treatments. Ms. McCall was typical of individuals who receive ECT because she
    A) was schizophrenic and needed one session of ECT to respond.
    B) was schizophrenic and needed a series of ECT sessions to respond.
    C) was depressed and needed one session of ECT to respond.
    D) was depressed and needed a series of ECT sessions to respond.
    Answer: D

Pages: 604
Topic: Early Attempts at Biological Intervention: Coma/Convulsive Therapies
Skill: Factual   Other1:
34. The type of ECT that produces the fewest side effects is
    A) unilateral ECT with a higher-energy, constant electrical stimulus.
    B) unilateral ECT with a lower-energy, pulsating electrical stimulus.
    C) bilateral ECT with a higher-energy, constant electrical stimulus.
    D) bilateral ECT with a lower-energy, pulsating electrical stimulus.
    Answer: B

Pages: 606
Topic: Early Attempts at Biological Intervention: Psychosurgery
Skill: Factual   Other1:
35. A prefrontal lobotomy involves separating the deeper centers of the brain from
    A) the frontal lobes.
    B) the occipital lobes.
    C) the temporal lobes.
    D) the parietal lobes.
    Answer: A

Pages: 606
Topic: Early Attempts at Biological Intervention: Psychosurgery
Skill: Factual   Other1:
36. The initial reports concerning psychosurgery were
    A) highly negative, but were ignored.
    B) neutral, and suggested that the procedure be used since there was no more effective
       treatment at that time.
    C) cautiously optimistic.
    D) enthusiastic and downplayed complications.
    Answer: D

Pages: 606
Topic: Early Attempts at Biological Intervention: Psychosurgery
Skill: Factual   Other1:
37. The side effects of prefrontal lobotomy include
    A) mental retardation.
    B) an inability to inhibit impulses.
    C) an undesirable shallowness or absence of feelings.
    D) B and C
    Answer: D

Pages: 607
Topic: Early Attempts at Biological Intervention: Psychosurgery
Skill: Applied   Other1:
38. The text presented the case of Rosemary Kennedy, who received a prefrontal lobotomy. Her
    case is a good example of
    A) the positive effects that were often achieved with this procedure.
    B) how the procedure usually had little impact.
    C) the negative and tragic effects often caused by this procedure.
    D) how this kind of procedure could be effective if used concurrently with antipsychotic
       drugs.
    Answer: C

Pages: 606
Topic: Early Attempts at Biological Intervention: Psychosurgery
Skill: Factual   Other1:
39. Psychosurgical procedures began to decline with the advent of
    A) psychotherapy.
    B) antianxiety drugs.
    C) antidepressant drugs.
    D) antipsychotic drugs.
    Answer: D

Pages: 606-607
Topic: Early Attempts at Biological Intervention: Psychosurgery
Skill: Factual   Other1:
40. Compared with the past, psychosurgery today is
    A) used more often but involves more circumspect procedures.
    B) sometimes used as a last resort for individuals with intractable psychoses.
    C) sometimes used to prepare individuals for a later administration of antipsychotic
       drugs.
    D) prohibited by law in the United States.
    Answer: B

Pages: 606
Topic: Early Attempts at Biological Intervention: Psychosurgery
Skill: Factual   Other1:
41. In the mid-1970s, Congress called a national commission to evaluate the effects of
    psychosurgery. This commission suggested that modern psychosurgery
    A) results in some surprisingly beneficial effects, although often achieved at the expense
       of losing certain cognitive capacities.
    B) is not as dangerous as was previously believed.
    C) results in death in about 20 percent of the cases.
    D) is ineffective with all disorders for which it has been used.
    Answer: A

Pages: 606-607
Topic: Early Attempts at Biological Intervention: Psychosurgery
Skill: Factual   Other1:
42. Psychosurgery today
    A) involves very precise and localized destruction of brain tissue.
    B) is only permitted by law in the case of a severe suicidal depression that has continued
       for at least five years.
    C) is only used in the case of brain tumors.
    D) none of the above
    Answer: A

Pages: 606
Topic: Early Attempts at Biological Intervention: Psychosurgery
Skill: Factual   Other1: In Student Study Guide
43. A modern psychosurgical technique known as "cingulotomy" is used to remove the subjective experience of
    A) depression.
    B) guilt.
    C) mania.
    D) pain.
    Answer: D

Pages: 607
Topic: Early Attempts at Biological Intervention: Psychosurgery
Skill: Factual   Other1:
44. The current recommendations for psychosurgery include all of the following EXCEPT
    A) a severely disturbed patient has not responded to any other form of treatment considered standard for that disorder.
    B) a patient is rationally able to give informed consent for the procedure.
    C) a patient is so severely disturbed that he or she is unable to give informed consent for medical procedures, in which case a family member (preferably a biological parent) must provide consent.
    D) attempts have been made to treat the patient by other means for a period of at least five years and the patient is experiencing extreme disability symptoms.
    Answer: C

Pages: 608
Topic: Early Attempts at Biological Intervention: Psychosurgery
Skill: Factual   Other1:
45. Research on the new psychosurgical procedures
    A) is in its early stages, thereby preventing any firm conclusions.
    B) suggests that few individuals experience negative side effects, including suicide.
    C) indicates that about two-thirds of severe obsessive-compulsive patients responded well to these procedures.
    D) all of the above
    Answer: D

Pages: 608
Topic: The Emergence of Pharmacological Methods of Treatment
Skill: Factual   Other1:
46. In the treatment of mental disorders, the early goal of pharmacology was to
    A) bring the course of the disorder under control.
    B) change psychotic disorders into neurotic disorders.
    C) soothe and calm patients so that they would be more manageable.
    D) stimulate patients in an effort to excite the intellectual functioning of the
       individual.
    Answer: C

Pages: 608
Topic: The Emergence of Pharmacological Methods of Treatment
Skill: Factual   Other1:
47. One of the problems with the early medical compounds used to treat mental disorders was
    that these medications
    A) caused death in significant numbers.
    B) often caused more serious disorders.
    C) excited individuals to the point that many experienced manic states.
    D) produced severe drowsiness.
    Answer: D

Pages: 608
Topic: The Emergence of Pharmacological Methods of Treatment
Skill: Factual   Other1:
48. Little real progress was made in the treatment of mental disorders with drugs until the
    A) 1940s.
    B) 1950s.
    C) 1960s.
    D) 1970s.
    Answer: B

Pages: 608-609
Topic: Pharmacological Methods of Treatment: Types of Drugs Used in Therapy
Skill: Factual   Other1: In Student Study Guide
49. Antipsychotic, antidepressant, antianxiety, and lithium compounds are all referred to as
    _____ drugs.
    A) hallucinogenic
    B) mind-expanding
    C) narcotic
    D) psychotropic
    Answer: D

Pages: 609
Topic: Pharmacological Methods of Treatment: Types of Drugs Used in Therapy
Skill: Factual   Other1:
50. A critical factor to consider in psychotropic drug administration is the fact that
    A) individuals can differ in critical ways in the dosage that they require for a
       therapeutic effect.
    B) most psychotropic drugs are dangerous and thus should be used only under the
       supervision of a friend or family member.
    C) most individuals are unable to metabolize these kinds of drugs.
    D) most of these drugs cause serious side effects and should only be used as a last
       resort.
    Answer: A

Pages: 609
Topic: Pharmacological Methods of Treatment: Types of Drugs Used in Therapy
Skill: Applied   Other1:
51. Scott has schizophrenic symptoms and is taking an antipsychotic drug. This drug will
    A) sedate him sufficiently so that he will be easier to manage despite his psychotic
       symptoms.
    B) decrease his cognitive functioning but stabilize his mood.
    C) serve as a major tranquilizer, making a tranquil patient even more tranquil.
    D) reduce the intensity of his psychotic symptoms.
    Answer: D

Pages: 609
Topic: Pharmacological Methods of Treatment: Types of Drugs Used in Therapy
Skill: Factual   Other1:
52. Antianxiety drugs and antipsychotic drugs are similar in that they both
    A) elevate mood.
    B) decrease psychotic symptoms.
    C) reduce depressive symptoms.
    D) reduce tension.
    Answer: D

Pages: 609
Topic: Pharmacological Methods of Treatment: Types of Drugs Used in Therapy
Skill: Factual   Other1:
53. Prior to the introduction of antipsychotic drugs in mental hospitals, most patients
    A) were too disturbed to be treated effectively by the staff, who focused primarily on
       controlling patients' behavior.
    B) were treated by behavioral interventions.
    C) were given alcohol and reserpine to sedate them.
    D) received antianxiety drugs.
    Answer: A

Pages: 609
Topic: Pharmacological Methods of Treatment: Types of Drugs Used in Therapy
Skill: Factual   Other1:
54. Prior to the introduction of antipsychotic drugs in mental hospitals, the staff of such hospitals was most concerned with
    A) utilizing the newest treatment methods of psychoanalysis and other psychological therapies.
    B) maintaining control over patients.
    C) providing a supportive environment.
    D) milieu therapy.
    Answer: B

Pages: 609
Topic: Pharmacological Methods of Treatment: Types of Drugs Used in Therapy
Skill: Factual   Other1:
55. The form of psychosocial therapy in which the entire facility is regarded as a therapeutic community is known as
    A) milieu therapy.
    B) community therapy.
    C) rational therapy.
    D) Gestalt therapy.
    Answer: A

Pages: 609
Topic: Pharmacological Methods of Treatment: Types of Drugs Used in Therapy
Skill: Applied   Other1:
56. Sterling is a patient in a mental ward in which patients participate in the regulation of their own activities. This would be considered
    A) rational therapy.
    B) milieu therapy.
    C) cognitive therapy.
    D) Gestalt therapy.
    Answer: B

Pages: 609
Topic: Pharmacological Methods of Treatment: Types of Drugs Used in Therapy
Skill: Factual   Other1:
57. The first major psychotropic drug that showed encouraging effects with manic, schizophrenic, and other patients in the early 1950s was
    A) Haldol.
    B) Thoridazine.
    C) Stelazine.
    D) Reserpine.
    Answer: D

Pages: 609
Topic: Pharmacological Methods of Treatment: Types of Drugs Used in Therapy
Skill: Factual   Other1:
58. Reserpine was associated with which of the following side effects?
    A) low blood pressure
    B) severe depression in patients with a prior history of depression
    C) tardive dyskinesia
    D) A and B
    Answer: D

Pages: 609
Topic: Pharmacological Methods of Treatment: Types of Drugs Used in Therapy
Skill: Factual   Other1:
59. Reserpine is
    A) still a major drug used in the treatment of schizophrenia.
    B) no longer used because it induces manic symptoms in too many patients.
    C) now used mainly for control of hypertension.
    D) the subject of major lawsuits because of a large number of fatalities.
    Answer: C

Pages: 609-610
Topic: Pharmacological Methods of Treatment: Types of Drugs Used in Therapy
Skill: Applied   Other1:
60. Steffie, a patient in a mental hospital in the late 1950s, was diagnosed with
    schizophrenia. She was most likely treated with
    A) Thorazine.
    B) Haldol.
    C) Reserpine.
    D) Imipramine.
    Answer: A

Pages: 609-610
Topic: Pharmacological Methods of Treatment: Types of Drugs Used in Therapy
Skill: Factual   Other1:
61. The drug that became the treatment of choice for schizophrenia in the 1950s was
    A) Reserpine.
    B) Thorazine.
    C) Imipramine.
    D) Haldol.
    Answer: B

Pages: 610
Topic: Pharmacological Methods of Treatment: Types of Drugs Used in Therapy
Skill: Conceptual   Other1:
62. Thorazine became the treatment of choice for schizophrenia instead of Reserpine because
    Thorazine
    A) had a greater sedative effect.
    B) had a greater activating effect.
    C) was less expensive.
    D) produced virtually the same benefits but with fewer undesirable side effects.
    Answer: D

Pages: 610
Topic: Pharmacological Methods of Treatment: Types of Drugs Used in Therapy
Skill: Factual   Other1: In Student Study Guide
63. Virtually all of the antipsychotic drugs accomplish the same biochemical effect, which is
    A) blocking dopamine receptors.
    B) blocking the production of noradrenalin.
    C) stimulating the production of endorphins.
    D) stimulating the production of glutamic acid.
    Answer: A

Pages: 610
Topic: Pharmacological Methods of Treatment: Types of Drugs Used in Therapy
Skill: Applied   Other1:
64. Sheryl takes a high dose of Prolixin to treat her schizophrenia. She may complain of any
    of the following side effects EXCEPT
    A) tremors of the extremities.
    B) muscular stiffness.
    C) mania.
    D) dry mouth.
    Answer: C

Pages: 610
Topic: Pharmacological Methods of Treatment: Types of Drugs Used in Therapy
Skill: Factual   Other1:
65. The side effects associated with antipsychotic drugs
    A) tend to be similar among different individuals.
    B) are common primarily when an antidepressant drug is also administered.
    C) are rare but tend to be permanent when they occur.
    D) are often relieved by substituting another drug of the same class.
    Answer: D

Pages: 610
Topic: Pharmacological Methods of Treatment: Types of Drugs Used in Therapy
Skill: Factual   Other1:
66. The schizophrenic individuals most likely to respond to antipsychotic drug therapy are those with
    A) acute schizophrenia.
    B) chronic schizophrenia.
    C) negative-symptom schizophrenia.
    D) none of the above
    Answer: A

Pages: 610
Topic: Pharmacological Methods of Treatment: Types of Drugs Used in Therapy
Skill: Factual   Other1:
67. Tardive dyskinesia is a side effect of prolonged use of
    A) antianxiety agents.
    B) antidepressant drugs.
    C) antipsychotic drugs.
    D) all psychotropic drugs.
    Answer: C

Pages: 610
Topic: Pharmacological Methods of Treatment: Types of Drugs Used in Therapy
Skill: Factual   Other1:
68. Tardive dyskinesia
    A) is a short-term side effect of antipsychotic drugs.
    B) involves involuntary movements of the tongue, lips, and extremities.
    C) is associated primarily with the presence of positive symptoms, such as hallucinations, delusions, and thought disturbances.
    D) involves dry mouth and Parkinson-like immobility of the facial muscles.
    Answer: B

Pages: 610
Topic: Pharmacological Methods of Treatment: Types of Drugs Used in Therapy
Skill: Factual   Other1:
69. Tardive dyskinesia symptoms
    A) decrease quickly once the dosage of an antipsychotic drug is reduced.
    B) are more likely in young schizophrenics who use antipsychotics than in older schizophrenics.
    C) are due to an imbalance between norepinephrine and serotonin activity in the brain.
    D) can occur months or years after antipsychotic drug treatment is initiated and even after use of the drug has been stopped.
    Answer: D

Pages: 610-611
Topic: Pharmacological Methods of Treatment: Types of Drugs Used in Therapy
Skill: Factual   Other1:
70. Which of the following statements about tardive dyskinesia is FALSE?
    A) It is associated with aging.
    B) It is associated with negative symptoms.
    C) It can now be easily controlled with drug therapy, which has become a universal adjunct to antipsychotic drug therapy.
    D) Its manifestation may fluctuate over time in a given patient.
    Answer: C

Pages: 611
Topic: Pharmacological Methods of Treatment: Types of Drugs Used in Therapy
Skill: Applied   Other1:
71. Sheena suffers from tardive dyskinesia. The best course of treatment is to
    A) administer continuous dosages of antipsychotic drugs.
    B) increase the dosage of antipsychotic drugs.
    C) discontinue her use of antipsychotic drugs.
    D) switch to a different antipsychotic drug.
    Answer: C

Pages: 611
Topic: Pharmacological Methods of Treatment: Types of Drugs Used in Therapy
Skill: Factual   Other1:
72. "Target dosing" is
    A) administering antipsychotic medication when symptoms appear, rather than continuously.
    B) administering antipsychotic medication only to a subset of schizophrenic individuals (such as those with negative symptoms) who are specifically "targeted" for treatment.
    C) targeting some schizophrenics for treatment with antipsychotic drugs, and some schizophrenics for treatment with antidepressants or lithium.
    D) prescribing different types of antipsychotic drugs for different types of psychotic symptoms.
    Answer: A

Pages: 611
Topic: Pharmacological Methods of Treatment: Types of Drugs Used in Therapy
Skill: Factual   Other1:
73. Recent research suggests that schizophrenic individuals who receive lower doses, rather than normal doses, of antipsychotic drugs are more likely to
    A) show greater improvement.
    B) develop tardive dyskinesia.
    C) relapse.
    D) suffer from chronic schizophrenia.
    Answer: A

Pages: 611
Topic: Pharmacological Methods of Treatment: Types of Drugs Used in Therapy
Skill: Factual   Other1:
74. To reduce negative side effects of antipsychotic drugs, psychiatrists
    A) use continuous administration of antipsychotic drugs.
    B) combine antidepressants with the antipsychotic drugs.
    C) combine antianxiety agents with the antipsychotic drugs.
    D) administer lower doses of antipsychotic drugs.
    Answer: D

Pages: 611-612
Topic: Pharmacological Methods of Treatment: Types of Drugs Used in Therapy
Skill: Applied   Other1:
75. The text presented the case of Ms. W., a nineteen-year-old who suffered from
    hallucinations over a three-month period. She was typical of individuals who respond to
    antipsychotic drugs because she
    A) evidenced tardive dyskinesia immediately after taking the first few doses of the drugs.
    B) showed positive symptoms.
    C) was on the drugs for four years before evidencing a full recovery.
    D) needed other drugs to control the effects of tardive dyskinesia.
    Answer: B

Pages: 612
Topic: Pharmacological Methods of Treatment: Types of Drugs Used in Therapy
Skill: Factual   Other1:
76. A recent and encouraging antipsychotic medication, especially for phenothiazine-resistant
    schizophrenics, is
    A) clozapine.
    B) stelazine.
    C) thorazine.
    D) Buspar.
    Answer: A

Pages: 612
Topic: Pharmacological Methods of Treatment: Types of Drugs Used in Therapy
Skill: Factual   Other1:
77. In groups of treatment-resistant individuals with schizophrenia,
    A) Haldol has been found effective in 30-60 percent of cases.
    B) Haldol has been found effective in 60-90 percent of cases.
    C) Clozapine has been found effective in 30-60 percent of cases.
    D) Clozapine has been found effective in 60-90 percent of cases.
    Answer: C

Pages: 612
Topic: Pharmacological Methods of Treatment: Types of Drugs Used in Therapy
Skill: Factual   Other1:
78. Compared with other antipsychotic drugs, clozapine has the advantage of
    A) being considerably less expensive.
    B) effectively treating 30-60 percent of individuals who have been treatment-resistant to phenothiazines.
    C) having fewer and less serious side effects.
    D) reducing depressive symptoms as well as schizophrenic symptoms.
    Answer: B

Pages: 612
Topic: Pharmacological Methods of Treatment: Types of Drugs Used in Therapy
Skill: Factual   Other1:
79. Disadvantages associated with clozapine include all of the following EXCEPT
    A) its side effects can be fatal.
    B) it is very expensive.
    C) it tends to diminish in effectiveness after a few months.
    D) it requires careful monitoring due to the possibility of serious side effects.
    Answer: C

Pages: 612
Topic: Pharmacological Methods of Treatment: Types of Drugs Used in Therapy
Skill: Factual   Other1:
80. Two of the basic classes of antidepressant drugs include
    A) phenothiazines and benzodiazepines.
    B) MAO inhibitors and benzodiazepines.
    C) phenothiazines and tricyclics.
    D) MAO inhibitors and tricyclics.
    Answer: D

Pages: 612
Topic: Pharmacological Methods of Treatment: Types of Drugs Used in Therapy
Skill: Factual   Other1:
81. MAO inhibitors
    A) selectively inhibit the reuptake mechanism involved in serotonergic transmission.
    B) inhibit the enzyme that helps break down the monoaminic neurotransmitters, such as serotonin and norepinephrine.
    C) inhibit the over-production of norepinephrine.
    D) all of the above
    Answer: B

Pages: 612
Topic: Pharmacological Methods of Treatment: Types of Drugs Used in Therapy
Skill: Factual   Other1:
82. The exact mechanism by which MAO inhibitors reduce depressive symptoms is by
    A) decreasing levels of serotonin.
    B) decreasing levels of serotonin and norepinephrine.
    C) increasing levels of norepinephrine.
    D) none of the above, as we do not know exactly how these drugs operate to reduce
       depression.
    Answer: D

Pages: 613
Topic: Pharmacological Methods of Treatment: Types of Drugs Used in Therapy
Skill: Applied   Other1:
83. Seth suffers from depression and has never before received treatment. Prior to the
    introduction of the "second-generation" antidepressants, he most likely would have been
    treated with
    A) a tricyclic, because tricyclics are widely believed to be more effective than MAO
       inhibitors, although the tricyclics also have more dangerous side effects than the MAO
       inhibitors.
    B) a tricyclic because tricyclics are widely believed to be more effective and to have
       less dangerous side effects than the MAO inhibitors.
    C) an MAO inhibitor because MAO inhibitors are widely believed to be more effective than
       tricyclics, although the MAO inhibitors also have more dangerous side effects than the
       tricyclics.
    D) an MAO inhibitor because MAO inhibitors are widely believed to be more effective and to
       have less dangerous side effects than tricyclics.
    Answer: B

Pages: 613
Topic: Pharmacological Methods of Treatment: Types of Drugs Used in Therapy
Skill: Factual   Other1:
84. Prozac differs from the MAO inhibitors and tricyclics because Prozac
    A) is more addictive.
    B) is chemically unrelated to these other classes of drugs.
    C) does not affect the levels of norepinephrine and serotonin activity.
    D) has no serious side effects.
    Answer: B

Pages: 613
Topic: Pharmacological Methods of Treatment: Types of Drugs Used in Therapy
Skill: Factual   Other1:
85. The difference between tricyclic antidepressants and the more recent second-generation antidepressants, the SSRIs, is that
    A) tricyclics increase the availability of norepinephrine and serotonin, while SSRIs decrease this availability.
    B) tricyclics decrease the availability of norepinephrine and serotonin, while SSRIs increase this availability.
    C) SSRIs inhibit the activity of the enzyme responsible for the breakdown of serotonin in the synaptic cleft.
    D) SSRIs selectively target serotonin re-uptake.
    Answer: D

Pages: 613
Topic: Pharmacological Methods of Treatment: Types of Drugs Used in Therapy
Skill: Factual   Other1:
86. The most popular antidepressant drug of the 1990s is
    A) Imipramine.
    B) Xanax.
    C) Valium.
    D) Prozac.
    Answer: D

Pages: 613
Topic: Pharmacological Methods of Treatment: Types of Drugs Used in Therapy
Skill: Conceptual   Other1:
87. Soon after Prozac was put on the market, a controversy erupted in the media over whether Prozac is associated with an enhanced risk of suicide. Recent studies have examined this issue and have found that
    A) Prozac is indeed associated with enhanced suicidal risk but only in adolescents.
    B) Prozac actually is associated with enhanced risk of manic episodes, not suicide.
    C) Prozac is no more associated with suicide than other antidepressants.
    D) tricyclics rather than Prozac are associated with enhanced risk of suicide.
    Answer: C

Pages: 613
Topic: Pharmacological Methods of Treatment: Types of Drugs Used in Therapy
Skill: Factual   Other1:
88. Tetracyclics like Desyrel and Trazodone
    A) are sometimes used to treat non-schizophrenic psychoses.
    B) are sometimes used to treat erectile dysfunctions.
    C) are antibiotics.
    D) are sometimes used to treat depression.
    Answer: D

Pages: 613
Topic: Pharmacological Methods of Treatment: Types of Drugs Used in Therapy
Skill: Factual   Other1:
89. Pharmacological treatment of depression differs from drug therapy for schizophrenia in that
    A) antidepressants often produce dramatic results and with long-term use are effective in prevention for patients subject to recurrent depressive episodes.
    B) antidepressants only suppress depressive symptoms whereas antipsychotics eliminate psychotic symptoms altogether.
    C) once medication is terminated, depressed people rarely relapse whereas schizophrenics typically relapse.
    D) schizophrenics are highly suggestible and respond readily to placebos, whereas nonpsychotic depressed individuals do not.
    Answer: A

Pages: 613
Topic: Pharmacological Methods of Treatment: Types of Drugs Used in Therapy
Skill: Factual   Other1:
90. Long-term administration of antidepressants
    A) is associated with tardive dyskinesia and other serious side effects.
    B) is often needed due to the high probability of relapse when the drugs are discontinued.
    C) is not recommended due to their addictive potential.
    D) is not recommended due to the severe, potentially life-threatening syndrome induced by withdrawal from antidepressants.
    Answer: B

Pages: 613-614
Topic: Pharmacological Methods of Treatment: Types of Drugs Used in Therapy
Skill: Factual   Other1:
91. In the treatment of depression with antidepressant drugs, it has been found that
    A) no consistent patient characteristic has emerged as a marker of whether a patient would respond better to medication as opposed to other forms of treatment such as cognitive therapy.
    B) tardive dyskinesia is a more common side effect than was previously believed.
    C) the newer drugs, such as Prozac, have a greater risk of suicide than other antidepressants.
    D) pharmacological treatment for depression often produces only mild results.
    Answer: A

Pages: 614
Topic: Pharmacological Methods of Treatment: Types of Drugs Used in Therapy
Skill: Factual   Other1:
92. Antidepressants are used successfully with all of the following disorders EXCEPT
    A) bulimia.
    B) obsessive-compulsive disorder.
    C) panic disorder.
    D) delusional disorder.
    Answer: D

Pages: 614
Topic: Pharmacological Methods of Treatment: Types of Drugs Used in Therapy
Skill: Factual   Other1:
93. The two major classes of drugs used in the treatment of anxiety are
    A) barbituates and propanediols.
    B) barbituates and phenothiazines.
    C) benzodiazepines and propanediols.
    D) benzodiazepines and phenothiazines.
    Answer: C

Pages: 614
Topic: Pharmacological Methods of Treatment: Types of Drugs Used in Therapy
Skill: Factual   Other1:
94. Compared with other types of anxiety-reducing drugs, benzodiazepines
    A) diminish generalized anxiety and leave adaptive behaviors largely intact.
    B) have a low addictive potential and a high margin of dosage safety.
    C) are rarely used in the treatment of insomnia.
    D) operate mainly through the reduction of muscle tension.
    Answer: A

Pages: 614-615
Topic: Pharmacological Methods of Treatment: Types of Drugs Used in Therapy
Skill: Applied   Other1:
95. Suzanne is taking a benzodiazepine to treat her anxiety. She should be concerned that
    A) mania is a relatively common side effect.
    B) she may become addicted to the drug.
    C) while her anxiety is likely to be diminished, her adaptive behaviors also are likely to
       become impaired.
    D) when taken in high dosages, the drugs have potentially serious effects on a woman's
       reproductive ability.
    Answer: B

Pages: 615
Topic: Pharmacological Methods of Treatment: Types of Drugs Used in Therapy
Skill: Factual   Other1:

96. Benzodiazepines appear to produce their effects by
    A) increasing the amount of norepinephrine in the synapses.
    B) stimulating the production of serotonin.
    C) decreasing the amount of dopamine at the synapses.
    D) increasing the activity of gamma aminobutyric acid (GABA) in certain parts of the brain, such as the limbic system.
    Answer: D

Pages: 615
Topic: Pharmacological Methods of Treatment: Types of Drugs Used in Therapy
Skill: Factual   Other1:

97. Flurazepam (Dalmane) is a benzodiazepine, which is the most common class of drug prescribed as sleep medications. In their evaluation of the use of benzodiazepines and other drugs as sleep medications, the Institute of Medicine (IOM) of the National Academy of Sciences concluded that
    A) regular ingestion of Dalmane can result in a buildup of toxic substances in the body that may reach critical levels within a week.
    B) Dalmane overdose is usually not lethal in itself but may interact with other drugs, such as alcohol, to produce lethal effects.
    C) in spite of its problems, Dalmane diminishes the number of deaths attributable to sleeping pill medication compared to earlier types of "hypnotic" drugs, such as barbituates.
    D) A and B
    Answer: D

Pages: 616-617
Topic: Pharmacological Methods of Treatment: Types of Drugs Used in Therapy
Skill: Factual   Other1:

98. One of the problems with lithium is that it
    A) is effective for depression, but has little effect on manic symptoms.
    B) must be administered in a hospital setting.
    C) is associated with a number of side effects, including possible toxicity and long-term kidney damage.
    D) can only be taken for a few months or at best a year before tolerance develops.
    Answer: C

Pages: 616
Topic: Pharmacological Methods of Treatment: Types of Drugs Used in Therapy
Skill: Factual   Other1:

99. Lithium
   A) was developed initially to treat schizophrenia.
   B) has few side effects even at high levels.
   C) can be toxic if not very carefully monitored.
   D) can be used with a variety of patients because it is one of the safest drugs.
   Answer: C

Pages: 617
Topic: Pharmacological Methods of Treatment: Types of Drugs Used in Therapy
Skill: Factual   Other1:

100. Lithium is effective in all of the following groups EXCEPT
   A) some cases of bipolar depression.
   B) manic states.
   C) a subset of unipolar depressives.
   D) all of the above
   Answer: D

Pages: 616
Topic: Pharmacological Methods of Treatment: Types of Drugs Used in Therapy
Skill: Factual   Other1:

101. In the treatment of manic states, lithium
   A) must be administered within a narrow dosage range in order to be effective.
   B) results in tardive dyskinesia if taken over long periods of time.
   C) is ineffective for individuals who also experience depressive states.
   D) has been found to be only modestly effective.
   Answer: A

Pages: 617
Topic: Pharmacological Methods of Treatment: Types of Drugs Used in Therapy
Skill: Factual   Other1:

102. Lithium works by
   A) reducing the amount of dopamine at the synapses.
   B) increasing the amount of norepinephrine at the synapses.
   C) increasing the amount of serotonin at the synapses.
   D) a process that is unknown.
   Answer: D

103. Recently the tricyclic drug carbamazepine (Tegretol) has been found to be
    A) effective for rapidly cycling mood changes in bipolar disorder.
    B) highly toxic for bipolar patients, although it is not toxic for unipolar patients.
    C) most effective in the treatment of acute manic states.
    D) ineffective in the treatment of bipolar disorder.
    Answer: A

104. In the treatment of children,
    A) antianxiety drugs have been found to be effective.
    B) antipsychotic drugs have been found to be effective.
    C) antidepressant drugs have been found to be effective.
    D) all of the above
    Answer: D

105. One of the problems with using psychotropic drugs with children is that
    A) they are effective, but for only a small minority of those children treated.
    B) these drugs work but for different disorders than is the case with adults.
    C) such high dosages are needed to be effective that the children are placed in serious
       danger.
    D) such drugs may be physically dangerous and in some cases a child's problem may become
       even more serious.
    Answer: D

106. One of the most successful drug treatments for a childhood disorder is
    A) tricyclics for autism.
    B) benzodiazepines for childhood depression.
    C) stimulants for hyperactivity.
    D) MAO inhibitors for separation anxiety disorder.
    Answer: C

Pages: 618
Topic: Pharmacological Methods of Treatment: A Biopsychosocial Perspective
Skill: Conceptual   Other1:
107. Pharmacological therapy
   A) will often result in relapse when drugs are discontinued unless psychotherapy is
      included in an individual's treatment program.
   B) is usually sufficient by itself to effect a cure in some disorders, though drugs must
      be continued indefinitely.
   C) is usually sufficient by itself as a treatment for the most severe disorders like
      schizophrenia.
   D) is most effective when individuals are not very disturbed.
   Answer: A

Pages: 618
Topic: Pharmacological Methods of Treatment: A Biopsychosocial Perspective
Skill: Applied   Other1:
108. The text discussed the case of Osherhoff v. Chestnut Lodge. This case concerned a
   physician who was treated at an exclusively psychoanalytic facility. This case is
   important because it suggested that
   A) patients must be given a thorough physical examination before being offered
      medications.
   B) patients are not responsible for their actions if they are taking their medications.
   C) therapists in the future could conceivably be found negligent by a court for not
      providing medication to patients.
   D) patients cannot receive medication unless psychotherapy has been offered to them.
   Answer: C

Pages: 618
Topic: Pharmacological Methods of Treatment: A Biopsychosocial Perspective
Skill: Factual   Other1:
109. The combination of psychotropic medication and psychosocial approaches appears to be most
   useful in the treatment of
   A) mild disorders.
   B) treatment-resistant disorders in which major mental disorders and persistent
      personality disorders are involved.
   C) organic brain disorders such as dementia.
   D) few disorders as the combination does not appear to be more effective than either type
      of treatment alone.
   Answer: B

Pages: 621
Topic: Unresolved Issues: Pharmacology Opened the Door/Personality Change?
Skill: Factual   Other1:
110. In his book "Listening to Prozac," Kramer suggests that
   A) Prozac is in danger of being used not only to ameliorate disorders but of being misused for its pleasing personality-transforming characteristics, suggesting we may be entering an era of "cosmetic psychopharmacology."
   B) Prozac should be more widely available due to its ability to enhance feeling and functioning in normal individuals.
   C) Prozac is ineffective as an antidepressant.
   D) Prozac be withdrawn from the market because of widespread abuse of the drug.
   Answer: A

Short Answer

Write the word or phrase that best completes each statement or answers the question.

Pages: 601-609
Topic: Early Attempts at Biological Intervention
Skill: Factual   Other1:
1. Identify three of the methods used to treat mental disorders prior to the nineteenth century.
   Answer: These treatments included purging, bleeding, inducing convulsions, and the use of herbs like snakeroot (rauwolfia).

Pages: 603
Topic: Early Attempts at Biological Intervention: Coma/Convulsive Therapies
Skill: Conceptual   Other1:
2. The idea that epilepsy and schizophrenia rarely co-occur led to the development of _____ to treat mental disorders.
   Answer: inducing convulsions

Pages: 604
Topic: Early Attempts at Biological Intervention: Coma/Convulsive Therapies
Skill: Applied   Other1:
3. How should electroconvulsive therapy (ECT) be administered in order to minimize side effects?
   Answer: It should be administered unilaterally using a lower-energy pulsating electrical stimulus.

Pages: 605
Topic: Early Attempts at Biological Intervention: Coma/Convulsive Therapies
Skill: Factual   Other1:
4. Briefly describe two of the findings of the Consensus Development Conference conducted by NIMH to investigate ECT?
    Answer: They found that the risks traditionally associated with ECT had been mostly eliminated. ECT was associated with the most success in treating delusional and endogenous depression as well as some cases of acute mania. It was least successful in treating schizophrenia and some depressions like dysthymia. Relapse rates were found to be high without follow-up treatment with antidepressants.

Pages: 606
Topic: Early Attempts at Biological Intervention: Psychosurgery
Skill: Factual   Other1:
5. What is a prefrontal lobotomy?
    Answer: It involves the surgical severing of connections between frontal lobes and deeper brain centers underlying the frontal lobes.

Pages: 606
Topic: Early Attempts at Biological Intervention: Psychosurgery
Skill: Factual   Other1:
6. What are the two principal side-effects of prefrontal lobotomy?
    Answer: This procedure may either produce an unnatural tranquillity in an individual involving emotional shallowness or absence of feeling, or it may have the opposite effect in which an individual is permanently unable to control impulses.

Pages: 606-607
Topic: Early Attempts at Biological Intervention: Psychosurgery
Skill: Factual   Other1:
7. Under what conditions would psychosurgery be performed today?
    Answer: It would only be performed for intractable psychoses, severe and chronically debilitating obsessive-compulsive disorder, and for control of severe pain in terminal illness. It is recommended today that an individual only be considered for psychosurgery if he or she has not responded to standard methods of treatment for a period of at least five years and is rationally capable of understanding the procedure and providing informed consent.

Pages: 610
Topic: Pharmacological Methods of Treatment: Types of Drugs Used in Therapy
Skill: Factual   Other1:
8. The most common class of antipsychotic drugs is the _____.
    Answer: phenothiazines

Pages: 610
Topic: Pharmacological Methods of Treatment: Types of Drugs Used in Therapy
Skill: Factual   Other1:

9. What is tardive dyskinesia?

    Answer: It is a potentially debilitating side effect of antipsychotic drugs when used over a long period of time or at high dosages. It involves a disturbance of motor control, particularly of facial muscles and limbs. It may be due to imbalances in dopamine and acetylcholine.

Pages: 611
Topic: Pharmacological Methods of Treatment: Types of Drugs Used in Therapy
Skill: Conceptual   Other1:

10. Describe one way in which clinicians attempt to circumvent the problem of tardive dyskinesia.

    Answer: They may withdraw a patient immediately when symptoms of tardive dyskinesia appear. They may administer drugs to control tardive dyskinesia symptoms, though this is not recommended. They may use target dosing, administering antipsychotics when psychotic symptoms appear rather than continuously. They may also use lower dosages than standard dosages of antipsychotics.

Pages: 612-613
Topic: Pharmacological Methods of Treatment: Types of Drugs Used in Therapy
Skill: Factual   Other1:

11. How do MAO inhibitors, tricyclics, and SSRIs operate on the brain?

    Answer: MAOIs inhibit the activity of the enzyme that breaks down norepinephrine and serotonin in the synaptic cleft. Tricyclics inhibit the reuptake of serotonin and norepinephrine once they have been released into the synapse. SSRIs selectively inhibit the reuptake of serotonin.

Pages: 614
Topic: Pharmacological Methods of Treatment: Types of Drugs Used in Therapy
Skill: Factual   Other1:

12. Besides barbituates, the two major classes of antianxiety drugs are _____ and _____.
    Answer: propanediols; benzodiazepines

Pages: 615
Topic: Pharmacological Methods of Treatment: Types of Drugs Used in Therapy
Skill: Factual   Other1:

13. What effect do the benzodiazepines have on the brain?

    Answer: They stimulate the activity of the neurotransmitter GABA, especially in certain parts of the brain known to be implicated in anxiety, such as the limbic system. GABA is thought to be functionally deficient in individuals with generalized anxiety.

Pages: 616-617
Topic: Pharmacological Methods of Treatment: Types of Drugs Used in Therapy
Skill: Factual   Other1:
14. The drug of choice for treating bipolar disorder is _____.
    Answer: lithium

Pages: 616
Topic: Pharmacological Methods of Treatment: Types of Drugs Used in Therapy
Skill: Conceptual   Other1:
15. What is the most notable difficulty in treating bipolar patients with lithium?
    Answer: Lithium has a very narrow dosage in which it is therapeutically effective, and
             this dosage level is very near the level at which lithium can become toxic.

Pages: 617
Topic: Pharmacological Methods of Treatment: Drug Therapy For Children
Skill: Conceptual   Other1:
16. What are two of the special considerations that a clinician should have when prescribing
    psychotropic drugs for children?
    Answer: It must be clear that drugs are not simply being used to minimize annoying
             behavior in children. Dosage levels may be very difficult to establish, since
             excessive blood levels of certain drugs can be physically dangerous and can even
             produce worsening of symptoms. Further, long-term side effects of these drugs
             are not known, a special consideration for still developing children.

Pages: 617
Topic: Pharmacological Methods of Treatment: Drug Therapy For Children
Skill: Factual   Other1:
17. One of the most successful uses of drug therapy in children is the use of stimulants for

    _____.
    Answer: hyperactivity (ADHD)

Pages: 618-621
Topic: Pharmacological Methods of Treatment: A Biopsychosocial Perspective
Skill: Conceptual   Other1:
18. What are two of the major general limitations associated with pharmacological therapy?
    Answer: These include undesirable and dangerous side effects, determining accurate
             dosages, using drugs without any other forms of associated treatment, and
             overusing and misusing drugs like the benzodiazepines and Prozac.

Pages: 618
Topic: Pharmacological Methods of Treatment: A Biopsychosocial Perspective
Skill: Conceptual   Other1:

19. The case described in the text of Osherhoff versus Chestnut Lodge, in which a physician sued the treatment facility that had treated him for depression, was notable in its preliminary court arbitration. Although the case was settled out of court before a final judgment was rendered, what did the preliminary court arbitration indicate and what is the major implication of this case?

    Answer: The preliminary court arbitration indicated an initial award of damages to Dr. Osherhoff. In spite of being settled out of court, the possibility that therapists may be liable for failing to provide medication to patients is an important and potentially disruptive new development in the field.

Pages: 621
Topic: Unresolved Issues: Pharmacology Opened the Door/Personality Change?
Skill: Conceptual   Other1:

20. Why is the popularity of Prozac controversial?

    Answer: It seems to have beneficial effects beyond reducing the depressive symptoms it was developed to target. It sometimes seems to transform personalities and make relatively normal people feel better than normal. This may be dehumanizing and dangerous if widespread. Kramer suggests that Prozac operates to reduce an individual's sensitivity to criticism and rejection. Many nondepressed individuals could become overly insensitive and even potentially dangerous if their sensitivity to others were markedly reduced. Kramer cautions readers about the dawning of an era of "cosmetic psychopharmacology."

Essay

Write your answer in the space provided or on a separate sheet of paper.

Pages: 601-610
Topic: Early Attempts at Biological Intervention
Skill: Factual   Other1:

1. Discuss the main historical attempts to treat psychological problems with biological methods from ancient times up to the introduction of psychotropic medication.

    Answer: Ancient Greeks like Hippocrates believed that mental disorders were organically caused and thus could be treated by using physical methods. Purging the body of undesirable substances with emetics and laxatives was done in ancient Rome, medieval times, and into the eighteenth century. The medieval Paracelsus induced convulsions to cure "lunacy." Bleeding was common in the eighteenth century. Often new psychiatric methods arose as discoveries were made in other sciences, like electrical stimulation and drug-induced convulsive therapies. Debilitating psychosurgery was common from 1935 to 1955.

Pages: 601-609
Topic: Early Attempts at Biological Intervention
Skill: Factual   Other1:

2. Describe two biological treatments used in the past but rarely, if ever, used today. Why were these treatments discarded?

    Answer: Purging and bleeding were two common primitive treatments. Insulin coma therapy was used as a treatment for schizophrenia. Insulin is administered until the patient goes into a hypoglycemic coma. Results have been disappointing. Prefrontal lobotomies were used for numerous disorders. Serious side effects, including death, and the advent of the major antipsychotic drugs resulted in a decrease in the use of psychosurgical procedures. Certain drugs, such as barbituates for anxiety and reserpine for schizophrenia, have now been replaced by more effective pharmacological treatments.

Pages: 603-605
Topic: Early Attempts at Biological Intervention: Coma/Convulsive Therapies
Skill: Applied   Other1:

3. Sondra is a patient in an inpatient facility. Her psychiatrist is recommending electroconvulsive therapy. How will this therapy be administered and what are the potential side effects?

    Answer: Her psychiatrist may use bilateral ECT or unilateral ECT on Sondra's nondominant hemisphere with either continuous or lower-energy, pulsating stimulation. Unilateral ECT causes fewer side effects with little or no loss in therapeutic effectiveness. In bilateral ECT, electrical stimulation is passed from one side of the head to the other. Sedatives and muscle relaxants are used to prevent violent contractions. Side effects include amnesia for the period immediately preceding the therapy and possibly long-term memory impairment.

Pages: 603-605
Topic: Early Attempts at Biological Intervention: Coma/Convulsive Therapies
Skill: Applied   Other1:

4. Seth is an inpatient in a psychiatric hospital. His psychiatrist recommends electroconvulsive therapy. In order to make an informed decision about receiving this treatment, what should Seth know about the effectiveness and risks of this procedure?

    Answer: ECT appears to be effective for delusional depression, "endogenous" depression, and acute mania. It is not effective for dysthymia or schizophrenia. Maintenance doses of antidepressant medication probably must follow ECT to prevent relapse. He should know that unilateral ECT may reduce the chance of memory impairment over bilateral ECT, and that lower-energy, pulsating electrical stimulation may lessen the risk of cognitive impairment compared to continuous stimulation. He should also know that bilateral ECT has been found to be more effective than or equally effective to unilateral ECT.

Pages: 606-608
Topic: Early Attempts at Biological Intervention: Psychosurgery
Skill: Factual   Other1:

5. Describe prefrontal lobotomies as they were traditionally performed in the United States. Include in your answer when the procedure was most commonly performed, what the procedure entailed in general terms, and a description of the main side effects and complications resulting from the procedure.

   Answer: Prefrontal lobotomies were popular in America between 1935 and 1955, when antipsychotic drugs were introduced. This procedure involves severing the frontal lobes from deeper brain centers. Initial deleterious side effects were dismissed for a variety of reasons, such as maintaining control over mental patients and gaining professional respectability. The operation produced an unnatural tranquility with an absence of feeling, or a permanent loss in the ability to control one's impulses. In addition, a complication of this procedure was death in about 1 to 4 percent of patients.

Pages: 609
Topic: Pharmacological Methods of Treatment: Types of Drugs Used in Therapy
Skill: Conceptual   Other1:

6. Describe the effect that antipsychotic drugs had on changing the typical mental hospital.

   Answer: Antipsychotic drugs were introduced in the mid-1950s. Prior to this, the staffs of mental hospitals were primarily concerned with the maintenance of control because of the patients' bizarre and potentially violent behavior. The ward patients often fulfilled the common stereotypes of people "gone mad." Nudity, screaming, and the threat of violence were pervasive. Antipsychotic drugs brought a dramatic change. One could now get to know one's patients on a personal level and could initiate milieu therapy, developing a constructive environment where patients could regulate their own activities.

Pages: 610-611
Topic: Pharmacological Methods of Treatment: Types of Drugs Used in Therapy
Skill: Applied   Other1:

7. Pete suffers from schizophrenia. He has been placed on antipsychotic drugs. Under what conditions may he experience side effects and what are the potential side effects?

   Answer: With persistent use or at high dosage, he may experience dryness of the mouth and throat, muscular stiffness, jaundice, and a Parkinson-like syndrome involving tremors of the extremities and immobility of the facial muscles. A particularly troublesome side effect of long-term antipsychotic drug use is tardive dyskinesia, a motor disturbance involving involuntary movements of facial muscles and limbs. It is more common in negative symptom schizophrenics, alcohol-abusing schizophrenics, and in people over age fifty-five.

Pages: 610-611
Topic: Pharmacological Methods of Treatment: Types of Drugs Used in Therapy
Skill: Applied   Other1:
8. Ginny, who suffers from schizophrenia, has been told that she has tardive dyskinesia. What is this disorder and what is the cause? Is there any way to treat this problem? Could it have been prevented?

   Answer: Tardive dyskinesia involves involuntary movements of the tongue, lips, jaw, and extremities. The individual may show involuntary limb movements and usually shows characteristic chewing movements. This is a result of persistent use or high dosages of antipsychotic medication. Discontinuing the antipsychotic medication is the favored treatment. Using lower doses of standard drugs is a good preventive measure with no loss in therapeutic effectiveness. Target dosing is another option, administering antipsychotics intermittently as needed. Drugs to control tardive symptoms aren't recommended.

Pages: 612-614
Topic: Pharmacological Methods of Treatment: Types of Drugs Used in Therapy
Skill: Conceptual   Other1:
9. What are the advantages and disadvantages of the different types of antidepressant medications?

   Answer: Tricyclics were most commonly used prior to the 1990s because of limited side effects compared to MAOIs. MAOIs are more toxic, require troublesome dietary restrictions, and may have less potent therapeutic effects. "Second generation" antidepressants or SSRIs like Prozac are not fatal in overdose like the tricyclics can be, but may cause nervousness, nausea, insomnia, agitation, or high blood pressure. Prozac has become the preferred antidepressant. Antidepressants are effective, useful in preventing recurrence of depression, but relapse rates often are high upon discontinuing medication.

Pages: 614-616
Topic: Pharmacological Methods of Treatment: Types of Drugs Used in Therapy
Skill: Conceptual   Other1:
10. What are the different types of antianxiety drugs? What are their advantages and disadvantages?

    Answer: Barbituates are seldom used in treatment today because they have high addictive potential and a low margin of dosage safety. Propanediols operate mainly through the reduction of muscular tension, but may reduce adaptive functioning. Benzodiazepines are the most widely prescribed class of antianxiety drugs because they diminish generalized fear yet leave adaptive behaviors largely intact. They are highly addictive and sudden withdrawal is dangerous. Benzodiazepines are overprescribed for sleeping and can have lethal effects in interaction with other drugs such as alcohol.

Pages: 612-616
Topic: Pharmacological Methods of Treatment: Types of Drugs Used in Therapy
Skill: Factual   Other1:

11. What do we know about how the various classes of antidepressant and antianxiety drugs operate in the brain?

Answer: MAOIs inhibit the activity of the enzyme that breaks down serotonin and norepinephrine in the synaptic cleft. Tricyclics inhibit the reuptake of serotonin and norepinephrine once they've been released into the synapse. They decrease the number and sensitivity of certain types of receptors while increasing the responsiveness of others. SSRIs selectively inhibit serotonin re-uptake. Benzodiazepines stimulate GABA activity in anxiety-related brain regions like the limbic system. GABA is thought to be functionally deficient in people with generalized anxiety.

Pages: 616-617
Topic: Pharmacological Methods of Treatment: Types of Drugs Used in Therapy
Skill: Applied   Other1:

12. William has just been placed on lithium to treat his bipolar disorder. What can you tell him about this treatment, including the biochemical basis of lithium, its effectiveness, and potential side effects?

Answer: The biochemical basis of lithium's therapeutic effect is unknown. Hypotheses center around altering electrolyte balances, which may affect neurotransmitters. It is effective in promptly resolving about 75 percent of clearly defined manic states, but relapse may be as high as 40 percent. It must be monitored closely because there is a narrow range for effectiveness of the drug, and it can be toxic. It can have serious long-term complications, including kidney damage and memory problems. Short-term effects include lethargy, uncoordination, and loss of hypomanic "highs."

Pages: 617
Topic: Pharmacological Methods of Treatment: Drug Therapy For Children
Skill: Conceptual   Other1:

13. How are psychotropic drugs used with children? Do you think that these drugs should be used with individuals in this age group?

Answer: Antianxiety, antipsychotic, and antidepressant drugs have all been proven effective with children. Stimulants are very successful in attenuating attentional impairment associated with ADHD. Special considerations, however, must be taken because dosages are more difficult to determine. These drugs may be dangerous and even worsen symptoms if dosage level is not properly prescribed. Long-term side effects are unknown and may be of greater concern in patients who are still growing. This must be weighed carefully against the potential benefits.

Pages: 618-620
Topic: Pharmacological Methods of Treatment: A Biopsychosocial Perspective
Skill: Conceptual   Other1:
14. Modern psychopharmacology has brought some dramatic changes in the treatment of mental disorders. What are the problems in the use of psychotropic medications?

Answer: Undesirable side effects may arise with any of the drugs. Matching drug and dosage to the needs of a given individual can be difficult. The use of medications in isolation from other treatment methods is usually inappropriate and ineffective because drugs themselves do not cure disorders. Relapse rates are high upon discontinuation. Psychosocial therapy may help to maintain and increase the gains made with drugs. The combination of psychotropic medication and psychosocial approaches can be especially useful for severely disturbed patients.

Pages: 621
Topic: Unresolved Issues: Pharmacology Opened the Door/Personality Change?
Skill: Conceptual   Other1:
15. What is the controversy concerning the widespread popularity of Prozac? What do you think about this issue?

Answer: This drug has personality-altering properties in individuals, possibly involving reduced sensitivity to criticism and rejection, that make it popular beyond its intended use. People seek prescriptions just to feel happier than normal. This raises disturbing questions in that the goal of treating a disorder may become superceded by quite different goals, such as "cosmetic pharmacology." Social groups may someday be composed of pharmacologically synthetic personalities. The authors believe that human behavior is far too complex to be altered so radically by medications at hand.

CHAPTER 17 Psychologically Based Therapies

Multiple-Choice

Choose the one alternative that best completes the statement or answers the question.

Pages: 625
Topic: Psychologically Based Therapies
Skill: Conceptual   Other1:
1. Professional psychotherapy is distinguished from informal helping relationships by the fact that therapeutic interventions
    A) are guided by theoretical preconceptions.
    B) do not involve active or directive actions on the part of therapists.
    C) do not involve the same degree of warmth and empathy.
    D) involve few of the characteristics found in informal relationships.
    Answer: A

Pages: 625
Topic: Psychologically Based Therapies
Skill: Conceptual   Other1:
2. The conviction underlying all psychotherapy is that
    A) psychopathology is caused by psychosocial factors.
    B) unconscious conflicts underlie psychopathology, even if therapy doesn't need to identify them in order to be effective.
    C) cognitions are the primary source of individuals' problems.
    D) therapy can help an individual develop more adaptive ways of perceiving, evaluating, and behaving.
    Answer: D

Pages: 626
Topic: An Overview of Psychological Treatment: Who Receives Psychotherapy?
Skill: Factual   Other1:
3. Individuals vary tremendously in their degree of motivation for psychological treatment. One of the most highly motivated patient groups is comprised of individuals who
    A) have experienced a recent crisis or trauma and feel that they can not manage on their own.
    B) have somatic symptoms and were referred to a therapist by a physician who could find nothing physically wrong with them.
    C) are referred by a court to undergo therapy.
    D) have entered therapy because a spouse has threatened divorce if they don't seek therapy.
    Answer: A

Pages: 626-627
Topic: An Overview of Psychological Treatment: Who Receives Psychotherapy?
Skill: Factual   Other1:

4. The client who is most likely to become resistant to therapy as the therapy progresses is the one who entered therapy because of
   A) a sudden, highly stressful situation.
   B) feeling that his or her potential has not been realized.
   C) a lengthy history of maladjustment and interpersonal problems.
   D) relatively minor problems.
   Answer: C

Pages: 626-627
Topic: An Overview of Psychological Treatment: Who Receives Psychotherapy?
Skill: Factual   Other1:

5. Individuals who seem to have the best prognosis for personality change are those who
   A) have endured long-term problems and are highly motivated to change.
   B) have narcissistic disorders with healthy levels of self-esteem.
   C) are the most severely disturbed, such as schizophrenics.
   D) exhibit the YAVIS pattern--are young, attractive, verbal, intelligent, and successful.
   Answer: D

Pages: 626-627
Topic: An Overview of Psychological Treatment: Who Receives Psychotherapy?
Skill: Conceptual   Other1:

6. Psychological treatment, such as psychotherapy,
   A) is applicable to a relatively limited range of problems.
   B) can be very helpful for individuals with major psychoses.
   C) has relatively greater success when a therapist takes the characteristics of a
      particular client into account in determining the treatment of choice.
   D) B and C
   Answer: D

Pages: 627
Topic: Psychological Treatment: Who Provides Psychotherapeutic Services?
Skill: Factual   Other1: In Student Study Guide

7. The member of the mental health team who has specialization in personality theory, psychological assessment, and psychotherapy is a
   A) psychiatrist.
   B) clinical psychologist.
   C) psychiatric social worker.
   D) pastoral counselor.
   Answer: B

Pages: 628
Topic: Psychological Treatment: Who Provides Psychotherapeutic Services?
Skill: Factual   Other1:

8. Unlike professional personnel, paraprofessionals in psychotherapy
A) have limited training and work under the direction of a mental health professional.
B) must have undergraduate degrees but not graduate degrees.
C) are usually employed in hospital settings.
D) primarily conduct psychodynamic kinds of therapy.
Answer: A

Pages: 628
Topic: Psychological Treatment: Who Provides Psychotherapeutic Services?
Skill: Factual   Other1:

9. In contrast to a clinical psychologist, a counseling psychologist
A) has a master's degree instead of a Ph.D.
B) usually works with individuals who have problems not involving serious mental
   disorders, although at present this difference is not as evident as it once was.
C) usually oversees the work of paraprofessionals instead of seeing clients.
D) usually works as an advisor to businesses.
Answer: B

Pages: 628
Topic: An Overview of Psychological Treatment: The Therapeutic Relationship
Skill: Conceptual   Other1:

10. The most crucial element in determining the success or failure of psychotherapy with a
given client probably is the client's
A) emotional depth.
B) cognitive processing.
C) motivation to change.
D) intellectual capacity.
Answer: C

Pages: 629
Topic: An Overview of Psychological Treatment: The Therapeutic Relationship
Skill: Conceptual   Other1:

11. Flexibility in using a variety of interactive styles is an important aspect of the
therapist's role in the therapeutic process because
A) it is important that a client view the therapist as a friend.
B) effective therapy depends to some extent on a good match between client and therapist.
C) the therapist must foster dependency in the earlier phases of therapy, and independence
   in later phases.
D) none of the above
Answer: B

Pages: 629
Topic: An Overview of Psychological Treatment: The Therapeutic Relationship
Skill: Applied   Other1:
12. Andrea begins therapy and expects that the therapy will help her. This expectancy
    A) may be enough by itself to produce positive change.
    B) is necessary to produce positive change.
    C) is helpful in psychodynamic therapy, but irrelevant to cognitive and behavioral
       interventions.
    D) is irrelevant to the change process.
    Answer: A

Pages: 630-631
Topic: Psychological Treatment: A Perspective on Therapeutic Pluralism
Skill: Conceptual   Other1:
13. According to the authors' CAPER framework of therapeutic strategies, therapy is
    essentially
    A) targeted at an individual's cognitions and affects.
    B) a matter of creating a feedback loop between the client and the client's environment.
    C) a matter of interrupting the psychopathology-sustaining loop.
    D) focused on changing behavior by processing the physiological components of a client's
       reactions.
    Answer: C

Pages: 631
Topic: Psychological Treatment: A Perspective on Therapeutic Pluralism
Skill: Factual   Other1:
14. According to the authors' CAPER framework of therapeutic strategies, behavioral approaches
    are an example of _____ therapies.
    A) Type A
    B) Type P
    C) Type C
    D) Type R
    Answer: D

Pages: 630-631
Topic: Psychological Treatment: A Perspective on Therapeutic Pluralism
Skill: Conceptual   Other1:
15. According to the authors' CAPER framework of therapeutic strategies, psychopathology involves a self-sustaining loop. One implication of this is that
    A) it is imperative to discover the cause or causes of the maladaptive behavior in order to interrupt the loop.
    B) it is important to delineate the specific characteristics of this loop for each client because it must be interrupted at its point of origin.
    C) the question of how a given client's abnormal behavior began is not especially relevant to the current therapy.
    D) the therapist need not be concerned with how a client's behavior affects the environment insofar as the client is conceived of as a conglomerate of mutually influencing cognitions, affects, and physiological states.
    Answer: C

Pages: 630-631
Topic: Psychological Treatment: A Perspective on Therapeutic Pluralism
Skill: Conceptual   Other1:
16. The authors' CAPER framework of therapeutic strategies suggests that
    A) whether or not a particular therapeutic strategy will be successful with any given client depends on the kind of feedback loop that supports that client's abnormal behavior.
    B) the effectiveness of therapeutic strategies follows this order, from most to least effective: cognitive, affective, physiological, environmental, response.
    C) positive change in the client can be effected by intervening at any one of a number of points in the continuous feedback loop.
    D) the environment will eventually provide corrective feedback to a client so that he or she can self-correct abnormal behavior.
    Answer: C

Pages: 631
Topic: Psychodynamic Therapy
Skill: Applied   Other1:
17. Dr. Michael's therapeutic approach involves freeing a client from the tremendously energy-draining process of repression so that the client can turn his or her energies to better personality integration and more effective living. Dr. Michael most likely practices _____ therapy.
    A) psychodynamic
    B) gestalt
    C) cognitive
    D) systemic
    Answer: A

Pages: 632-634
Topic: Psychodynamic Therapy: Freudian Psychoanalysis
Skill: Factual   Other1:
18. All of the following are fundamental techniques of classical psychoanalysis EXCEPT
    A) analysis of free association.
    B) analysis of counter-resistance.
    C) analysis of transference.
    D) analysis of dreams.
    Answer: B

Pages: 633
Topic: Psychodynamic Therapy: Freudian Psychoanalysis
Skill: Factual   Other1:
19. An altered state of consciousness involving extreme suggestibility is known as
    A) transference.
    B) hypnosis.
    C) free association.
    D) dreamwork.
    Answer: B

Pages: 633
Topic: Psychodynamic Therapy: Freudian Psychoanalysis
Skill: Applied   Other1:
20. Andrea is in therapy and has regressed to being a five-year-old child. The therapist is most likely
    A) employing an interpersonal therapy.
    B) attempting to flood the client with images through an in vivo behavioral procedure.
    C) using hypnosis within a psychoanalytic framework.
    D) using rational-emotive therapy.
    Answer: C

Pages: 632
Topic: Psychodynamic Therapy: Freudian Psychoanalysis
Skill: Factual   Other1:
21. The basic rule of free association is that
    A) the client must say whatever comes into his or her mind without censoring.
    B) the client must relate to the therapist as if he or she were a significant person from the client's past.
    C) the client must respond with one word in response to each of the psychoanalyst's stimulus words.
    D) the client must be willing to regress to childhood under hypnosis within the therapy session.
    Answer: A

Pages: 632
Topic: Psychodynamic Therapy: Freudian Psychoanalysis
Skill: Factual   Other1:
22. Freud believed that free association
    A) revealed the contents of the preconscious.
    B) involved associations that are not random, but are determined like other events.
    C) yielded information about the unconscious if properly interpreted.
    D) all of the above
    Answer: D

Pages: 632
Topic: Psychodynamic Therapy: Freudian Psychoanalysis
Skill: Factual   Other1:
23. According to psychoanalytic theory, the "royal road to the unconscious" is through
    A) free association.
    B) dream analysis.
    C) analysis of resistance.
    D) hypnosis.
    Answer: B

Pages: 632
Topic: Psychodynamic Therapy: Freudian Psychoanalysis
Skill: Factual   Other1:
24. In dream analysis within a psychoanalytic framework, the analyst
    A) uses the Dictionary of Dream Symbolism that was developed by Sigmund Freud and his
       followers.
    B) assumes that dreams may sometimes be important to understand unconscious conflicts, but
       only if the conflicts are obvious in the manifest content of the dream.
    C) will attempt to interpret the manifest content of the dream by having a client free
       associate to the latent content of the dream.
    D) will attempt to understand the latent content of the dream by studying the manifest
       content of the dream and the client's preconscious associations to the manifest
       content.
    Answer: D

Pages: 632
Topic: Psychodynamic Therapy: Freudian Psychoanalysis
Skill: Applied   Other1:
25. Ian is in psychoanalytic therapy. He is talking about an important childhood experience and keeps switching topics. His analyst will
A) think that he is regressing to an earlier cognitive level of development.
B) help Ian push this experience deeper into the preconscious until Ian is ready to talk about it.
C) interpret this as resistance.
D) assume that the childhood experience is not as important as Ian believes it to be.
Answer: C

Pages: 632
Topic: Psychodynamic Therapy: Freudian Psychoanalysis
Skill: Applied   Other1: In Student Study Guide
26. A son of a critical father comes to therapy one day and with no provocation is extremely hostile in his remarks to the therapist. The therapist might consider that _____ is occurring.
A) free association
B) countertransference
C) transference
D) positive transference
Answer: C

Pages: 632-634
Topic: Psychodynamic Therapy: Freudian Psychoanalysis
Skill: Factual   Other1:
27. Within a transference relationship, the analyst
A) confronts the client directly, challenging the client to recognize his or her inadequacies.
B) interprets the client's responses as examples of resistance.
C) strengthens the client's ego defenses by providing emotional support and extra caring.
D) acts in a detached and impersonal manner in order to let the client project his or her own neurotic conflicts onto the analyst.
Answer: D

Pages: 634
Topic: Psychodynamic Therapy: Freudian Psychoanalysis
Skill: Applied   Other1:
28. One reason that all psychoanalysts must undergo analysis themselves is that
A) they must learn about themselves so as to better manage counter-transference.
B) they must learn how to resolve their own analyst's counter-transference neurosis.
C) this will allow them to be free of any of their own unconscious conflicts.
D) this will free them of all counter-transference in their future dealings with patients.
Answer: A

Pages: 634
Topic: Psychodynamic Therapy: Freudian Psychoanalysis
Skill: Applied   Other1:

29. Adam is in psychoanalytic treatment. He is reliving a pathogenic past relationship in the context of his relationship with his analyst, thereby recreating the neurosis in real life. This experience is often referred to as
    A) secondary transference.
    B) transference neurosis.
    C) secondary neurosis.
    D) repetitive neurosis.
    Answer: B

Pages: 634
Topic: Psychodynamic Therapy: Freudian Psychoanalysis
Skill: Factual   Other1:

30. According to psychoanalytic principles, the key element in effecting a psychoanalytic "cure" is considered to be
    A) the resolution of the Oedipal conflict.
    B) the development of a warm and close therapy relationship.
    C) the resolution of the transference neurosis.
    D) the elimination of resistance.
    Answer: C

Pages: 634
Topic: Psychodynamic Therapy: Freudian Psychoanalysis
Skill: Conceptual   Other1:

31. According to the authors' CAPER framework of therapeutic strategies, psychoanalysis is an example of _____ therapy.
    A) Type C
    B) Type A
    C) Type E
    D) Type P
    Answer: C

Pages: 635
Topic: Psychodynamic Therapy: Psychodynamic Therapy Since Freud
Skill: Factual   Other1:

32. Object-relations therapy and other interpersonally oriented psychodynamic therapies
    A) suggest that the id is the most important component of the individual's personality in determining the quality of a person's relationships.
    B) focus on the disruptive effects that the superego has on social relationships.
    C) emphasize that unconscious attitudes toward early significant figures impact on a person's current interpersonal relationships, not just on the relationship with a therapist.
    D) assume that early relationships with significant others are relatively unimportant, and instead therapy should focus on the here and now.
    Answer: C

Pages: 635
Topic: Psychodynamic Therapy: Psychodynamic Therapy Since Freud
Skill: Conceptual   Other1:

33. Object-relations therapists tend to focus on correcting their clients' distorted views of the interpersonal environment. In this respect, the approach is most like
    A) cognitive therapy.
    B) behavioral therapy.
    C) assertiveness training.
    D) Gestalt therapy.
    Answer: A

Pages: 635
Topic: Psychodynamic Therapy: Psychodynamic Therapy Since Freud
Skill: Factual   Other1:

34. Compared with traditional Freudian analysis, psychodynamic therapists currently place greater emphasis on
    A) current life situations.
    B) interpersonal relationships.
    C) current ego functioning.
    D) all of the above
    Answer: D

Pages: 635
Topic: Psychodynamic Therapy: Evaluation of Psychodynamic Therapy
Skill: Factual   Other1:

35. Psychoanalytically oriented psychotherapy
    A) remains the treatment of choice for individuals who are primarily seeking extensive self-insight, although it is very expensive and there is little research data concerning its efficacy.
    B) has clearly been shown to be ineffective.
    C) has been subjected to more rigorous research scrutiny than have other therapy approaches.
    D) is best suited for individuals who suffer from severe psychopathology because of its intensive and long-term nature.
    Answer: A

Pages: 636
Topic: Behavior Therapy
Skill: Conceptual   Other1:

36. The ultimate goal of behavior therapy is to
    A) create an atmosphere conducive to regaining control over one's thoughts and feelings.
    B) help the client gain greater insight into the causes of his or her behavior.
    C) bring desired responses under the control of the individual.
    D) change distorted cognitions.
    Answer: C

Pages: 636
Topic: Behavior Therapy: Extinction
Skill: Applied   Other1:

37. Five-year-old Alex has learned some "naughty" words and delights in trying to shock grown-ups with them. His parents have decided to ignore him when he uses these words in the hope that he will eventually stop using them if he gets no reaction out of them. This is an example of
    A) implosion.
    B) desensitization.
    C) extinction.
    D) modeling.
    Answer: C

Pages: 637
Topic: Behavior Therapy: Extinction
Skill: Applied   Other1:

38. Taryne is undergoing flooding in therapy to treat her fear of flying. This means that she
    A) imagines flying while her therapist describes a variety of gruesome scenes.
    B) initially imagines nonanxiety-arousing scenes, followed by scenes of increasing anxiety.
    C) places herself in real-life situations that are frightening, such as sitting in an airplane.
    D) focuses on understanding the irrationality of her fear by such techniques as examining safety statistics.
    Answer: C

Pages: 637-638
Topic: Behavior Therapy: Extinction
Skill: Factual   Other1:

39. Which of the following is true regarding extinction procedures for the treatment of anxiety disorders?
    A) Reports on the effectiveness of implosive therapy and flooding have been generally unfavorable.
    B) Many clients respond favorably to implosion or flooding, although some clients do not respond and a few suffer an exacerbation of symptoms.
    C) Extensive research suggests that implosion therapy is vastly superior to flooding in treating most anxiety disorders.
    D) Most individuals with anxiety disorders are unwilling to confront their fears directly in flooding procedures.
    Answer: B

Pages: 638
Topic: Behavior Therapy: Extinction
Skill: Factual   Other1:

40. Repeatedly self-inducing "false alarm" somatic cues in order to extinguish panic is a modified form of which behavioral technique?
    A) flooding
    B) implosion
    C) systematic desensitization.
    D) aversion therapy.
    Answer: A

Pages: 638
Topic: Behavior Therapy: Systematic Desensitization
Skill: Conceptual   Other1:

41. Jake becomes anxious at the thought of bridges. On his way to work he drives many miles out of his way to avoid bridges. Each time he avoids this situation he is being
    A) positively reinforced, which makes treatment especially difficult.
    B) negatively reinforced, which makes treatment especially difficult.
    C) positively reinforced, which makes treatment easier.
    D) negatively reinforced, which makes treatment easier.
    Answer: B

Pages: 638
Topic: Behavior Therapy: Systematic Desensitization
Skill: Conceptual   Other1:

42. A therapeutic technique that is based on the principle of eliciting a competing or antagonistic response to a fearful stimulus is
    A) systematic desensitization.
    B) implosive therapy.
    C) exposure therapy.
    D) response shaping.
    Answer: A

Pages: 638
Topic: Behavior Therapy: Systematic Desensitization
Skill: Factual   Other1: In Student Study Guide

43. All of the following are steps in Wolpe's approach to systematic desensitization EXCEPT
    A) asking the client to imagine anxiety-producing situations while relaxing.
    B) constructing a hierarchy of anxiety-producing situations.
    C) placing the client in anxiety-producing life situations.
    D) training the client to relax.
    Answer: C

Pages: 638-639
Topic: Behavior Therapy: Systematic Desensitization
Skill: Applied   Other1:

44. Scott is undergoing systematic desensitization to alleviate anxiety. In this treatment, he will
    A) enter a state of relaxation, which serves as an antagonistic response to the anxiety elicited by imagining a fearful situation.
    B) be exposed initially to the fearful stimulus in vivo followed by in vitro exposure.
    C) go through the entire hierarchy in one session, which usually takes about four hours.
    D) be exposed initially to the most fearful stimulus in his hierarchy and work through to the least fearful stimulus.
    Answer: A

Pages: 639
Topic: Behavior Therapy: Systematic Desensitization
Skill: Conceptual   Other1:
45. The essential element in the behavioral treatment of anxiety is
    A) positive reinforcement.
    B) confidence.
    C) relaxation.
    D) exposure.
    Answer: D

Pages: 639
Topic: Behavior Therapy: Systematic Desensitization
Skill: Conceptual   Other1:
46. In general, unless circumstances do not permit it, a therapist would select which of the
    following techniques as the most effective method for treating anxiety?
    A) systematic desensitization
    B) implosive therapy
    C) flooding
    D) hypnosis
    Answer: C

Pages: 639
Topic: Behavior Therapy: Aversion Therapy
Skill: Factual   Other1:
47. Aversion therapy is based primarily on the principle of
    A) extinction.
    B) negative desensitization.
    C) "false alarms."
    D) punishment.
    Answer: D

Pages: 640
Topic: Behavior Therapy: Aversion Therapy
Skill: Factual   Other1:
48. The method of choice today for aversion therapy is
    A) differential reinforcement of other responses.
    B) emetic therapy.
    C) electric shock.
    D) Antabuse.
    Answer: A

Pages: 640
Topic: Behavior Therapy: Aversion Therapy
Skill: Factual   Other1:
49. One of the problems with aversion therapy is that
   A) new behaviors induced by aversion therapy do not automatically and easily generalize to other situations.
   B) an alternative form of gratification must be substituted for the maladaptive behavior.
   C) the aversive stimulus must be so severe to be effective that current thinking regards this approach as unethical.
   D) A and B
   Answer: D

Pages: 640-641
Topic: Behavior Therapy: Modeling
Skill: Factual   Other1:
50. Modeling
   A) is fundamentally based on learning through trial and error.
   B) is no longer used as a therapeutic strategy.
   C) can promote the learning of complex skills, such as social skills in a shy, withdrawn client.
   D) is only useful in therapy as an adjunct to other therapeutic strategies.
   Answer: C

Pages: 641
Topic: Behavior Therapy: Systematic Use of Reinforcement
Skill: Factual   Other1:
51. Contingency management programs
   A) use reinforcement to elicit and maintain effective behavior.
   B) are an example of Type R therapy, according to the authors' CAPER model.
   C) have been very successful, especially in institutional settings.
   D) all of the above
   Answer: D

Pages: 641
Topic: Behavior Therapy: Systematic Use of Reinforcement
Skill: Applied   Other1:
52. The text reported the case of a three-year-old autistic boy who was reinforced initially for picking up eyeglass frames, then for holding them, then for carrying them around, and then for putting the frames on his head. This is an example of
   A) response shaping.
   B) modeling.
   C) aversion therapy.
   D) extinction.
   Answer: A

Pages: 642
Topic: Behavior Therapy: Systematic Use of Reinforcement
Skill: Factual   Other1:
53. The ultimate goal of extrinsic reinforcement programs like token economies is
    A) to eliminate undesirable behaviors.
    B) to increase adaptive behaviors to a level where they become reinforcing in their own right.
    C) to teach chronic mental patients how to manage their money when they will leave the hospital.
    D) none of the above
    Answer: B

Pages: 642
Topic: Behavior Therapy: Systematic Use of Reinforcement
Skill: Factual   Other1:
54. Which of the following is true regarding token economies?
    A) The use of token economies has declined in recent years, which is unfortunate in view of their effectiveness.
    B) Their effectiveness has yet to be demonstrated with chronic schizophrenic clients.
    C) Their effectiveness has been demonstrated with adults but not generally with children.
    D) Token economies have traditionally relied excessively on physical punishment.
    Answer: A

Pages: 642
Topic: Behavior Therapy: Systematic Use of Reinforcement
Skill: Factual   Other1:
55. Behavioral contracting
    A) must cover many behaviors of a given client for the contract to be successful.
    B) typically utilizes tokens as the major external incentive, and is most commonly used in institutional settings.
    C) often is used to identify specific behaviors that are to be changed and to maximize the chances that these changes will occur.
    D) has been shown to be highly successful in the long-term modification of interpersonal behavior.
    Answer: C

Pages: 642-643
Topic: Behavior Therapy: Assertiveness Therapy
Skill: Applied   Other1:
56. Samantha has difficulty standing up for herself when others try to take advantage of her. Her therapist is working with her to practice expressing her feelings in a more open way in the therapy office. Later Samantha will try these new behaviors in real-life situations. This method of therapy is called
A) systematic desensitization.
B) assertiveness training.
C) behavioral contracting.
D) response shaping.
Answer: B

Pages: 643
Topic: Behavior Therapy: Biofeedback Treatment
Skill: Factual   Other1:
57. The treatment approach in which a person is taught to influence his or her own physiological processes is known as
A) differential reinforcement.
B) differential sensitization.
C) response shaping.
D) biofeedback.
Answer: D

Pages: 644
Topic: Behavior Therapy: Biofeedback Treatment
Skill: Applied   Other1:
58. Daniel is participating in a biofeedback program for decreasing anxiety. This treatment
A) will not help him.
B) may help him, although he probably would have been helped just as much by a less costly relaxation training procedure.
C) has a high chance of generalizing successfully to situations outside of therapy.
D) will help him more than other treatments if his anxiety is accompanied by, and is perhaps due to, migraine headaches.
Answer: B

Pages: 644
Topic: Behavior Therapy: Evaluation of Behavior Therapy
Skill: Conceptual   Other1:
59. All of the following are advantages of using behavior therapy compared with psychoanalysis EXCEPT
    A) the treatment approach is precise.
    B) the learning principles used in behavior therapy have been shown to have scientific validity.
    C) behavior therapy is effective for psychological disorders involving problems with self-identity, such as personality disorders.
    D) behavior therapy is more cost-effective and efficient.
    Answer: C

Pages: 644
Topic: Behavior Therapy: Evaluation of Behavior Therapy
Skill: Factual   Other1:
60. Research suggests that behavior therapy is particularly effective in treating
    A) sexual dysfunctions.
    B) anxiety disorders.
    C) psychoses.
    D) all of the above
    Answer: D

Pages: 645
Topic: Cognitive-Behavior Therapy
Skill: Conceptual   Other1:
61. Cognitive-behavioral therapy
    A) denies the importance of reinforcement and punishment.
    B) assumes that cognitive processes influence affect, motivation, and behavior.
    C) assumes that behavior must change prior to the change of cognitions.
    D) suggests that the therapist should take a less active role than is typically the case in behavior therapies.
    Answer: B

Pages: 645
Topic: Cognitive-Behavior Therapy
Skill: Applied   Other1:
62. Abby is participating in cognitive-behavioral therapy to treat her depression. Her therapist
    A) will focus on changing behaviors to change the cognitions.
    B) will ignore past experiences as determinants of her behavior.
    C) will be nondirective in helping her change.
    D) will help her conduct "experiments" to test a variety of hypotheses about the accuracy of her cognitions.
    Answer: D

Pages: 645
Topic: Cognitive-Behavior Therapy: Rational-Emotive Therapy
Skill: Factual   Other1:
63. Rational-emotive therapy assumes that
    A) emotions rather than cognitions are primary causal factors in abnormal behavior.
    B) thoughts are important, but are less important than the objective situation in
       determining behavior.
    C) thoughts and emotions are relatively independent.
    D) irrationality is a central feature of psychological problems.
    Answer: D

Pages: 645
Topic: Cognitive-Behavior Therapy: Rational-Emotive Therapy
Skill: Applied   Other1:
64. According to rational-emotive therapy, which of the following is one of the irrational
    beliefs at the core of psychological maladjustment?
    A) One should be loved by everyone for everything one does.
    B) Happiness is achieved by action.
    C) It is undesirable when things are not the way we would like them to be.
    D) One should do everything possible, within one's means, to live a fulfilling life.
    Answer: A

Pages: 646
Topic: Cognitive-Behavior Therapy: Rational-Emotive Therapy
Skill: Factual   Other1:
65. Rational-emotive therapy
    A) focuses on altering cognitions rather than on targeting behavior change.
    B) concentrates on the relationship between therapist and client.
    C) is essentially antagonistic to humanistic therapy.
    D) includes disputing a person's false beliefs through rational confrontation.
    Answer: D

Pages: 646
Topic: Cognitive-Behavior Therapy: Stress-Inoculation Therapy
Skill: Applied   Other1:
66. Samuel's therapist is teaching him to change the self-statements he makes in
    stress-producing situations. Samuel's therapist has explained that the first phase of
    treatment, cognitive preparation, involves exploration of how Samuel's self-statements can
    influence later performance and behavior. Samuel is undergoing what kind of therapy?
    A) assertiveness therapy
    B) Meichenbaum's stress-inoculation therapy
    C) Ellis's rational-emotive therapy
    D) Beck's cognitive-behavioral therapy
    Answer: B

Pages: 646
Topic: Cognitive-Behavior Therapy: Stress-Inoculation Therapy
Skill: Factual   Other1:

67. Stress-inoculation therapy usually involves three phases. These include all of the following EXCEPT
    A) venting the feelings associated with the experience of stress.
    B) exploring attitudes about the problem situation and the self-statements associated with them.
    C) applying new self-statements to real-life situations.
    D) learning and rehearsing new self-statements.
    Answer: A

Pages: 647
Topic: Cognitive-Behavior Therapy: Beck's Cognitive-Behavior Therapies
Skill: Factual   Other1:

68. Beck's cognitive-behavioral therapy
    A) assumes that problems like depression result from illogical thinking.
    B) concentrates on the identification of unconscious impulses.
    C) focuses on first producing behavioral changes, in order to subsequently change cognitions.
    D) attempts to change cognitions by debate and persuasion.
    Answer: A

Pages: 647
Topic: Cognitive-Behavior Therapy: Beck's Cognitive-Behavior Therapies
Skill: Applied   Other1:

69. Selective perception, overgeneralization, and absolutistic thinking are examples of
    A) core irrational beliefs.
    B) self-statements.
    C) contingent thoughts about oneself, the future, and the world.
    D) logical errors found in a maladjusted individual's automatic thoughts.
    Answer: D

Pages: 647
Topic: Cognitive-Behavior Therapy: Beck's Cognitive-Behavior Therapies
Skill: Applied   Other1:

70. Kelly is depressed. Her therapist does not try to directly persuade her to change her view. Instead, her therapist has her conduct a series of "experiments" designed to test the validity of her beliefs. The therapist is using
    A) stress-inoculation therapy.
    B) Beck's cognitive-behavioral therapy.
    C) Rogers's client-centered therapy.
    D) Ellis's rational-emotive therapy.
    Answer: B

Pages: 647
Topic: Cognitive-Behavior Therapy: Beck's Cognitive-Behavior Therapies
Skill: Factual   Other1:
71. Each of the following would be typical of Beck's cognitive-behavior therapy EXCEPT
    A) scheduling pleasurable activities into a client's daily schedule.
    B) identifying and changing depressogenic schemas.
    C) encouraging the client to accomplish a series of tasks, arranged from least to most difficult, that will disconfirm false beliefs and provide successful experiences.
    D) having the therapist take a nondirective approach while the client takes a directive approach, thereby encouraging autonomy and independence in the client.
    Answer: D

Pages: 648
Topic: Cognitive-Behavior Therapy: Beck's Cognitive-Behavior Therapies
Skill: Applied   Other1:
72. The text presented the case of a fifty-three-year-old depressed engineer who had received numerous treatments for his depression, including ECT, but they were only modestly successful. The client is typical of individuals who undergo Beck's cognitive-behavior therapy for depression because
    A) the focus of therapy was to identify, evaluate, and modify his cognitive distortions.
    B) the therapist used a debate format in order to persuade him that his depression was caused by his core irrational beliefs.
    C) he relapsed following his first sessions of cognitive-behavior therapy because he wasn't concurrently on antidepressants.
    D) initial sessions of therapy focused on the client's dysfunctional childhood as the primary origin of his current maladaptive cognitions.
    Answer: A

Pages: 649
Topic: Cognitive-Behavior Therapy: Evaluation
Skill: Factual   Other1:
73. Research on the efficacy of rational-emotive therapy
    A) suggests that it is superior to exposure therapies in treating more severe anxiety disorders, such as agoraphobia.
    B) suggests that it is inferior to exposure therapies in treating more severe anxiety disorders, such as agoraphobia.
    C) is surprisingly limited in that little research has been conducted to evaluate its efficacy.
    D) B and C
    Answer: D

Pages: 649
Topic: Cognitive-Behavior Therapy: Stress-Inoculation Therapy
Skill: Factual   Other1:
74. Research suggests that stress-inoculation therapy is particularly suited to
    A) the treatment of severe anxiety disorders.
    B) the treatment of problems that appear to occur in the absence of stressful life circumstances.
    C) increasing the adaptive capabilities of individuals who are vulnerable to developing problems in stressful situations.
    D) the treatment of endogenous depression.
    Answer: C

Pages: 649
Topic: Cognitive-Behavior Therapy: Evaluation
Skill: Factual   Other1:
75. In the treatment of depression, Beck's cognitive-behavioral therapy appears to be
    A) generally successful, but significantly less effective than drug treatment.
    B) comparable to drug treatment in all but perhaps the most severe cases.
    C) superior to drug treatment in reducing relapse.
    D) B and C
    Answer: D

Pages: 649
Topic: Cognitive-Behavior Therapy: Evaluation
Skill: Factual   Other1:
76. Research suggests that cognitive-behavioral therapy is effective in treating all of the following EXCEPT
    A) bulimia.
    B) panic disorder.
    C) conduct disorder in children.
    D) alcoholism.
    Answer: D

Pages: 650
Topic: Humanistic-Experiential Therapies
Skill: Conceptual   Other1:
77. Humanistic-experiential therapies are based on the assumption that
    A) unconscious impulses are a primary determinant of behavior.
    B) people have the freedom and the responsibility to control and modify their own behavior.
    C) the therapist should act like a caring parent, taking responsibility for the direction and success of therapy.
    D) group therapy is more effective than individual therapy.
    Answer: B

Pages: 650-651
Topic: Humanistic-Experiential Therapies
Skill: Factual   Other1:

78. In psychodrama, a client acts out problem situations in a theater-like setting in order to
    A) clarify for the therapist the nature of the problem.
    B) demonstrate the problem to his or her spouse and other family members.
    C) achieve emotional catharsis and enhanced understanding.
    D) overcome social anxiety.
    Answer: C

Pages: 650
Topic: Humanistic-Experiential Therapies: Client-Centered Therapy
Skill: Factual   Other1:

79. Client-centered therapy is most closely associated with
    A) Albert Ellis.
    B) Asron Beck.
    C) Albert Bandura.
    D) Carl Rogers.
    Answer: D

Pages: 650
Topic: Humanistic-Experiential Therapies: Client-Centered Therapy
Skill: Factual   Other1:

80. Client-centered therapy was developed in the 1940s as an innovative alternative to
    A) drug treatment.
    B) psychoanalysis.
    C) behavior therapy.
    D) all of the above
    Answer: B

Pages: 650
Topic: Humanistic-Experiential Therapies: Client-Centered Therapy
Skill: Conceptual   Other1:

81. The primary objective of client-centered therapy is to help clients
    A) free themselves from the constraints that prevent them from healing themselves, thereby
       allowing them to accept and be themselves.
    B) explore their true feelings, thereby allowing them to rid themselves of "ugly
       feelings," such as hate and anger.
    C) search for the feelings that they wish to have and to then take "positive action" in
       acquiring these desired feelings while minimizing undesired feelings.
    D) B and C
    Answer: A

Pages: 650
Topic: Humanistic-Experiential Therapies: Client-Centered Therapy
Skill: Applied   Other1:
82. Allan's therapist emphasizes unconditional acceptance. This therapist believes that Allan must become more self-aware and self-accepting. Allan is working with a
    A) client-centered therapist.
    B) behavior therapist.
    C) psychoanalyst.
    D) rational-emotive therapist.
    Answer: A

Pages: 650
Topic: Humanistic-Experiential Therapies: Client-Centered Therapy
Skill: Factual   Other1:
83. In client-centered therapy, the therapist
    A) places a great emphasis on interpretation.
    B) has the client do homework in which the client carries out a series of experiments.
    C) restates in other words what the client is saying without any judgment or interpretation, assuming that the client is the primary actor in the curative process.
    D) provides advice in a warm, caring manner in an attempt to restructure the client's feelings and cognitions.
    Answer: C

Pages: 652
Topic: Humanistic-Experiential Therapies: Client-Centered Therapy
Skill: Factual   Other1:
84. Carl Rogers was notable in
    A) developing rational-emotive therapy.
    B) adding a cognitive emphasis to existential therapy.
    C) expanding the use of interpretation within therapy.
    D) being one of the first to conduct empirical research on psychotherapy.
    Answer: D

Pages: 652
Topic: Humanistic-Experiential Therapies: Client-Centered Therapy
Skill: Factual   Other1:
85. Compared with pure client-centered therapy as originally practiced by Rogers, current client-centered therapists are more likely to
    A) emphasize unconditional positive regard as a curative factor in therapy.
    B) suggest that the client is the primary actor in the curative process.
    C) see the self as active and capable of sound value choices.
    D) go beyond simple reflection and clarification in an attempt to focus the client and speed up the curative process.
    Answer: D

Pages: 652
Topic: Humanistic-Experiential Therapies: Existential Therapy
Skill: Factual   Other1:
86. Existential therapists
    A) believe that a key focus of therapy involves confronting clients in a way that allows them to establish their own values and meaning in their lives.
    B) challenge the client to confront the "shoulds" and "oughts" present in the client's irrational thinking.
    C) assume that behavior must change before the client can adequately alter his or her feelings.
    D) believe that all behavior is determined.
    Answer: A

Pages: 652
Topic: Humanistic-Experiential Therapies: Existential Therapy
Skill: Factual   Other1:
87. Existential therapists
    A) emphasize the unique responsibility of people to reflect on and question their own existence.
    B) encourage clients to make authentic choices about their own values and being.
    C) emphasize the importance of authenticity in the interaction between therapist and client.
    D) all of the above
    Answer: D

Pages: 653
Topic: Humanistic-Experiential Therapies: Gestalt Therapy
Skill: Factual   Other1:
88. Integrating thought, feeling, and action is most strongly emphasized in
    A) Gestalt therapy.
    B) existential therapy.
    C) Beck's cognitive therapy.
    D) stress-inoculation therapy.
    Answer: A

Pages: 653
Topic: Humanistic-Experiential Therapies: Gestalt Therapy
Skill: Factual   Other1:
89. The main goal of Gestalt therapy is
    A) to help clients become aware of how their own personalities affect the way in which other people treat them.
    B) to help clients become more attuned to the feelings of others.
    C) to increase clients' self-awareness and self-acceptance.
    D) to increase clients' ability to interact with others in an effective manner, especially in a group setting.
    Answer: C

Pages: 653
Topic: Humanistic-Experiential Therapies: Gestalt Therapy
Skill: Factual   Other1:
90. Gestalt therapy
    A) is used almost exclusively in an individual setting.
    B) asks clients to act out fantasies concerning feelings and conflicts.
    C) is more cognitive than even the cognitive therapies.
    D) holds that dreams have no useful significance in therapy.
    Answer: B

Pages: 653
Topic: Humanistic-Experiential Therapies: Gestalt Therapy
Skill: Applied   Other1:
91. In her therapy, Amy was asked to pretend to be one of the objects in a recent dream she had, and to report on the experience. Her therapist used a _____ approach to therapy.
    A) client-centered
    B) gestalt
    C) existential
    D) cognitive-behavioral
    Answer: B

Pages: 653
Topic: Humanistic-Experiential Therapies: Gestalt Therapy
Skill: Conceptual   Other1:
92. "Taking care of unfinished business" by resolving old traumas and conflicts in order to become more realistically self-aware and more self-accepting is a central goal of
    A) rational-emotive therapy.
    B) behavior therapy.
    C) gestalt therapy.
    D) existential therapy.
    Answer: C

Pages: 654
Topic: Humanistic-Experiential Therapies: Evaluation
Skill: Factual   Other1:
93. Humanistic-existential therapies have been criticized for
A) their lack of systematized models of human behavior and abnormal behavior.
B) being too mechanistic and impersonal.
C) challenging clients excessively, resulting in an excessively high deterioration rate.
D) their excessively strict adherence to agreed-upon therapeutic procedures.
Answer: A

Pages: 654
Topic: Therapy For Interpersonal Relationships
Skill: Factual   Other1:
94. A "systemic" approach to therapy is most appropriately associated with
A) humanistic therapy.
B) existential therapy.
C) cognitive therapy.
D) therapy for interpersonal relationships.
Answer: D

Pages: 655
Topic: Therapy/Interpersonal Relationships: Couples Counseling/(Marital)
Skill: Factual   Other1:
95. One of the greatest impediments to marital happiness is
A) the assumption by one or both partners that marriage involves friendship.
B) faulty role expectations.
C) believing that keeping channels of communication open will help solve problems.
D) the use of nonverbal communication.
Answer: B

Pages: 656
Topic: Therapy/Interpersonal Relationships: Couples Counseling/(Marital)
Skill: Conceptual   Other1:
96. In couples counseling that uses Rogerian techniques, the partners would be taught to
A) reinforce instances of desired behavior.
B) focus on cognitive distortions.
C) employ more effective listening techniques.
D) resolve a transference within the marital relationship.
Answer: C

Pages: 656
Topic: Therapy/Interpersonal Relationships: Couples Counseling/(Marital)
Skill: Factual   Other1:

97. In a study comparing behavioral marital therapy with psychodynamic marital therapy and a waiting-list control group, it was found that
   A) both therapy groups were superior to the waiting-list control group, and neither therapy group was more effective than the other.
   B) the behavior therapy group was superior to the other two groups.
   C) the psychodynamic therapy group was superior to the other two groups.
   D) there were no differences among the three groups.
   Answer: A

Pages: 656
Topic: Therapy/Interpersonal Relationships: Couples Counseling/(Marital)
Skill: Factual   Other1:

98. A long-term follow-up study of the efficacy of marital therapy with both partners undergoing therapy together, compared with other types of therapy in which the partners were not in therapy together, found that
   A) marital therapy was no more effective than individual therapy with one of the partners.
   B) marital therapy was significantly more effective than other therapies.
   C) other therapies were more effective than marital therapy.
   D) neither marital therapy nor other therapies were effective in helping intimate relationships in the long run.
   Answer: B

Pages: 656
Topic: Interpersonal Relationships: Family Therapy
Skill: Factual   Other1:

99. Family therapy
   A) involves treating every member of a family individually in therapy.
   B) has yet to be used in any large-scale manner because it is so new.
   C) assumes that the disorder shown by the "identified client" is often only a symptom of a larger family problem.
   D) developed in response to the large number of families who sought assistance for family problems.
   Answer: C

Pages: 656-657
Topic: Interpersonal Relationships: Family Therapy
Skill: Conceptual   Other1:
100. The Partridge family is participating in structural family therapy as a result of their 15-year-old daughter's problems with bulimia. In this type of therapy,
   A) it is assumed that if the family context changes, then the daughter's behavior will change.
   B) each member of the family will be treated individually, with family sessions about once a month.
   C) it is assumed that the "identified patient" is probably the only "normal" member of the family.
   D) the therapist will focus on uncovering past problems and latent resentments within the family.
   Answer: A

Pages: 656-657
Topic: Interpersonal Relationships: Family Therapy
Skill: Factual   Other1:
101. The emphasis of Satir's widely used conjoint family therapy is
   A) on enhancing the independence and self-sufficiency of each family member.
   B) on decoding the family's "structural map."
   C) on improving faulty communication and interactions so that family members can better meet each other's needs.
   D) on treating all of the individual family members in individual therapy before treating them conjointly.
   Answer: C

Pages: 657
Topic: Interpersonal Relationships: Family Therapy
Skill: Factual   Other1:
102. In structural family therapy,
   A) the therapist is very directive in order to break up the existing power structure in the family.
   B) the focus is on past interactions as they have given rise to present problems.
   C) the therapist initially acts like one of the family and participates in family interactions.
   D) the therapist adopts a Rogerian approach, focusing on good listening skills and clarification.
   Answer: C

Pages: 658
Topic: Interpersonal Relationships: Family Therapy
Skill: Factual   Other1:
103. The most recent reviews of research into the efficacy of various family therapy approaches suggest that
    A) all types of family therapy are equally effective.
    B) family therapy is no more effective than being in a waiting-list control group.
    C) experientially and analytically oriented approaches are more successful than other therapeutic approaches.
    D) behavioral family therapy is more successful than other approaches to family therapy, such as structural family therapy.
    Answer: D

Pages: 658-659
Topic: The Integration of Therapy Approaches
Skill: Conceptual   Other1:
104. One of the problems with integrating different therapy approaches is that
    A) no common language or set of basic assumptions unites the various therapy schools.
    B) few advocates of these different approaches believe that it is necessary or desirable to do so.
    C) some therapies, such as behavior therapy, cannot be used in conjunction with current biological therapies.
    D) so little research has been done on therapy that we do not yet know whether most forms of therapy are effective.
    Answer: A

Pages: 659-660
Topic: The Evaluation of Success in Psychotherapy: Problems of Evaluation
Skill: Conceptual   Other1:
105. One of the major problems in evaluating the efficacy of psychotherapy is that
    A) outcome data in the form of change scores from tests given before and after treatment may reflect a statistical artifact, like regression to the mean, rather than true therapeutic change.
    B) outcome data can come from a variety of sources, such as the client, therapist, and family members, but each source has limitations.
    C) the psychological tests administered to clients are not necessarily valid indicators of how clients will behave in real life.
    D) all of the above
    Answer: D

Pages: 660-661
Topic: The Evaluation of Success in Psychotherapy: Problems of Evaluation
Skill: Factual   Other1:
106. The authors suggest that when the design of an outcome study adheres to established modes of evaluating the efficacy of drugs, then it may not be possible to conduct a completely valid outcome study comparing the efficacy of psychosocial treatments with drug treatments. Why?
A) Therapist attributes may be critical in determining outcome from psychosocial therapies, whereas attributes associated with the therapist prescribing medication are largely irrelevant.
B) The "active ingredient" of psychosocial treatments are much more clearly defined than in drug treatments, making it extremely difficult to draw firm conclusions about differences in effectiveness.
C) If a drug treatment shows superior efficacy in comparison to psychosocial treatment, this superiority may not be due to the drug treatment but to some other "active ingredient" that is associated with the drug treatment.
D) B and C
Answer: A

Pages: 661
Topic: The Evaluation of Success in Psychotherapy: Problems of Evaluation
Skill: Conceptual   Other1:
107. The NIMH-sponsored multisite study of the treatment of depression found a statistically significant interaction between treatment site and type of treatment. This
A) was most apparent in the least severely disturbed patients.
B) was due to the differences in the characteristics of the patients treated at the different sites.
C) suggests that the relative outcomes of the various therapies was substantially affected by the characteristics of the therapists administering them.
D) indicated that drug therapy is the treatment of choice for severe depression.
Answer: C

Pages: 662
Topic: Evaluation of Success in Psychotherapy: Social Values/Psychotherapy
Skill: Conceptual   Other1:
108. One of the problems with psychotherapy is that
A) it is a science and thus should not be involved in issues associated with values and ethics.
B) it is usually done in a "social vacuum" that is not involved with the society at large.
C) some individuals are referred for treatment so that the therapist can help them to adjust to situations that the therapist may consider maladaptive.
D) it is value-free.
Answer: C

Pages: 663
Topic: Unresolved Issues on Psychotherapy
Skill: Factual   Other1:
109. Deterioration effects from psychotherapy occur for many reasons, including all of the following EXCEPT
    A) certain types of disorders, like borderline personality disorder, are extremely difficult to treat and are more prone than other disorders to deterioration effects.
    B) external events that occur in a client's life during therapy may impact negatively on the client's adjustment.
    C) a detached, impersonal style on the part of the therapist.
    D) an overly aggressive and abruptly defense-challenging therapeutic style.
    Answer: C

Pages: 663-664
Topic: Unresolved Issues on Psychotherapy
Skill: Factual   Other1:
110. Sexual intimacies between therapist and client
    A) are almost nonexistent.
    B) have yet to be addressed by the professional community.
    C) are most likely to occur with clients who are children.
    D) are nearly always destructive of client functioning in the long run.
    Answer: D

Short Answer

Write the word or phrase that best completes each statement or answers the question.

Pages: 627-628
Topic: Psychological Treatment: Who Provides Psychotherapeutic Services?
Skill: Factual   Other1:
1. Based on the text, what are the differences between a clinical psychologist and a counseling psychologist?
    Answer: A clinical psychologist has both research and clinical skill specialization with a one-year internship in a psychiatric hospital or mental health center. A clinical psychologist may have a PhD or a PsyD in psychology. A counseling psychologist also has a PhD in psychology but the internship is usually in a marital- or student-counseling setting. Normally, a counseling psychologist deals with problems not involving serious mental disorders, although this difference at present is not as evident as it once was.

Pages: 628-629
Topic: An Overview of Psychological Treatment: The Therapeutic Relationship
Skill: Conceptual   Other1:
2. What are two of the more important factors that a client brings to the therapeutic relationship?
    Answer: These include the motivation to change, the expectation of being helped, and other personal resources like intelligence, previous experience of success in life, ability to verbalize, and severity of psychopathology.

Pages: 630-631
Topic: Psychological Treatment: A Perspective on Therapeutic Pluralism
Skill: Factual   Other1:
3. In the authors' CAPER framework of therapeutic strategies, what do the letters stand for?
    Answer: They reflect five areas that might be targeted for therapeutic intervention: cognitive, affective, physiologic, environmental, and behavioral response areas. Therapies are classified according to their primary emphasis with regard to these five areas.

Pages: 632
Topic: Psychodynamic Therapy: Freudian Psychoanalysis
Skill: Factual   Other1:
4. In psychoanalytic therapy, a patient will project attitudes and feelings left over from previous relationships onto the analyst. This phenomenon is called _____.
    Answer: transference

Pages: 636-639
Topic: Behavior Therapy: Extinction
Skill: Conceptual   Other1:
5. What are two behavior therapy interventions that are based on the principle of extinction?
    Answer: These include implosive therapy, flooding, and systematic desensitization.

Pages: 640-641
Topic: Behavior Therapy: Modeling
Skill: Applied   Other1:
6. Dr. Smith is treating a woman who is spider phobic. During their sessions, Dr. Smith handles spiders without fear while she watches him. This is an example of the intervention called _____.
    Answer: modeling

Pages: 642-643
Topic: Behavior Therapy: Assertiveness Therapy
Skill: Applied   Other1:

7. Ted has difficulty standing up for himself when others try to take advantage of him. He can not ask for things that he wants and needs in his relationships with others. Ted's therapist is helping him to express his thoughts and feelings openly, with due regard for the rights of others. Ted is typical of a client undergoing what kind of therapy?
    Answer: assertiveness therapy

Pages: 643-644
Topic: Behavior Therapy: Biofeedback Treatment
Skill: Factual   Other1:

8. What does treatment outcome research suggest about the efficacy of biofeedback?
    Answer: It suggests that it is probably no more than an elaborate means of inducing relaxation. The effects of these procedures rarely generalize beyond the laboratory and, when compared with relaxation training, do not prove superior.

Pages: 646-647
Topic: Cognitive-Behavior Therapy: Stress-Inoculation Therapy
Skill: Factual   Other1:

9. What is stress-inoculation therapy?
    Answer: This is a kind of self-instructional training focused on altering self-statements that an individual makes in stressful situations, in order to alter stress-induced emotional and physiological responses. Like other cognitive-behavioral therapies, stress-inoculation therapy assumes that a person's problems result from maladaptive beliefs that are leading to negative emotional states and maladaptive behavior. The three stages typically included in this approach are cognitive preparation, skill acquisition and rehearsal, and application and practice.

Pages: 647
Topic: Cognitive-Behavior Therapy: Beck's Cognitive-Behavior Therapies
Skill: Conceptual   Other1:

10. Automatic thoughts, overgeneralization, absolutistic thinking, and dysfunctional schemas are concepts associated with _____ therapy.
    Answer: Beck's cognitive-behavior

Pages: 649
Topic: Cognitive-Behavior Therapy: Evaluation
Skill: Factual   Other1:

11. Research has shown that cognitive-behavior therapy is most effective with which disorders?
    Answer: It is effective in treating depression, panic disorder, generalized anxiety disorder, bulimia, childhood conduct disorder, substance abuse, and certain personality disorders.

Pages: 650-652
Topic: Humanistic-Experiential Therapies: Client-Centered Therapy
Skill: Factual   Other1:
12. What are two of Carl Rogers's major contributions to the field of clinical psychology?
    Answer: He developed client-centered therapy, emphasized a nondirective approach,
            stressed the importance of the therapist-client relationship and of a
            therapeutic context involving warm, unconditional positive regard. He was among
            the first to conduct empirical research on psychotherapy.

Pages: 651-653
Topic: Humanistic-Experiential Therapies
Skill: Applied   Other1:
13. Briefly describe one example of group therapy.
    Answer: One example is psychodrama, in which an individual acts out problem situations
            in a theatre-like setting while other patients form the audience. Gestalt
            therapy also makes frequent use of group settings. Each of the types of
            therapies has been applied to group treatment.

Pages: 652-653
Topic: Humanistic-Experiential Therapies: Existential Therapy
Skill: Applied   Other1:
14. Maryann feels that her life has lost its meaning. Although she has been quite successful,
    her various accomplishments no longer hold meaning for her. As she grows older, she is
    overwhelmed with a sense of dread that this is all that life has left for her. She is a
    good candidate for _____ therapy.
    Answer: existential

Pages: 653
Topic: Humanistic-Experiential Therapies: Gestalt Therapy
Skill: Applied   Other1:
15. "I am a tree. I am firmly rooted, but I sway in the wind. I am afraid that I will fall
    down if the winds become too strong." This statement is by a client who is undergoing
    _____ therapy.
    Answer: gestalt

Pages: 656
Topic: Therapy/Interpersonal Relationships: Couples Counseling/(Marital)
Skill: Factual   Other1:

16. What does outcome research suggest about the efficacy of marital therapy?

    Answer: It is more effective in five-year follow-up when couples undergo treatment together than when other types of therapies are used. All forms of therapy are better than no therapy at all for marital problems. Behavioral and insight-oriented psychodynamic marital therapies were found to be equally effective in one study. Marital therapy may also be effective as an adjunct in the treatment of individual problems, such as depression, alcohol abuse, and phobias.

Pages: 657
Topic: Interpersonal Relationships: Family Therapy
Skill: Factual   Other1:

17. Briefly describe structural family therapy.

    Answer: This is based on systems theory and involves focus on present interactions between family members. A "structural map" is first delineated by the therapist, which contains information about boundaries, dominance, power, and blame. The therapist initially acts like one of the family, participating in family interactions as an insider. The therapist then uses himself or herself as a change agent by altering customary interactions among family members.

Pages: 659-661
Topic: The Evaluation of Success in Psychotherapy: Problems of Evaluation
Skill: Conceptual   Other1:

18. What are two of the problems encountered by researchers conducting treatment outcome studies?

    Answer: These problems include how to measure outcome and statistical artifacts, how to handle drop-outs, and how to compare psychosocial with biological treatments.

Pages: 661
Topic: The Evaluation of Success in Psychotherapy: Problems of Evaluation
Skill: Conceptual   Other1:

19. NIMH sponsored an extensive and expensive multisite treatment outcome study in which cognitive-behavior, interpersonal, imipramine with clinical management, and placebo with clinical management were compared in treating depression. An important finding was a statistically significant treatment-by-sites interaction. What does this mean and why is it important?

    Answer: This means that the relative effectiveness of the treatment varied depending on the site, which essentially means that the relative effectiveness varied depending on characteristics of the therapists administering them. This illustrates the importance, as well as the problem, of therapist variables in outcome research. It is very difficult to isolate the "active ingredient" of psychosocial treatments given the abundance of therapist variables.

Pages: 663-664
Topic: Unresolved Issues on Psychotherapy
Skill: Conceptual   Other1:
20. What do studies suggest about sexual relationships between psychotherapists and clients?
    Answer: They are not uncommon and constitute a large proportion of the complaints filed
             with state boards. Most victims are female and some are children. These
             relationships can be very destructive to clients' functioning. They can also be
             difficult to prove and often do not result in license-revocation.

Essay

Write your answer in the space provided or on a separate sheet of paper.

Pages: 626-630
Topic: An Overview of Psychological Treatment: The Therapeutic Relationship
Skill: Applied   Other1:
1. Michael is entering therapy. What factors will influence the therapeutic relationship he
   develops with the therapist?
   Answer: Motivation to change is probably the most crucial element. The expectation of
            receiving help can bring about some improvement regardless of the methods used
            by the therapist. The flexibility of the therapist and the match between
            therapist and client will also be important. Other personal resources can also
            be important, including YAVIS factors. Treatment history can also be very
            important.

Pages: 630-631
Topic: Psychological Treatment: A Perspective on Therapeutic Pluralism
Skill: Factual   Other1:
2. Describe the authors' CAPER framework of psychotherapeutic strategies. How does it
   conceptualize the typical therapy client? Give examples of each of the five types of
   therapeutic interventions.
   Answer: This model conceptualizes the client in terms of interdependent cognitive,
            affective, and physiologic states, which result in behavioral responses that
            impact on the environment. The environment, in turn, provides feedback to the
            individual which confirms the person's cognitive-affective-physiologic system.
            Therapeutic interventions can target any one of these five areas to effect
            change. Type C therapy includes RET and cognitive-behavior therapy. Type A
            includes flooding and implosion. Type P includes biofeedback. Type E includes
            couples. Type R includes aversion therapy and modeling.

Pages: 632-634
Topic: Psychodynamic Therapy: Freudian Psychoanalysis
Skill: Applied   Other1:
3. Tabitha has entered therapy with a Freudian psychoanalyst. In general terms, describe the approach this analyst is most likely to follow.
    Answer: The analyst will assume a passive, detached stance. Analysis is intensive and long-term, focused on resolving unconscious conflicts by uncovering repressed memories and wishes. The basic techniques include free association, analysis of dreams, analysis of resistance, and analysis of transference.

Pages: 636-639
Topic: Behavior Therapy
Skill: Applied   Other1:
4. David has a fear of flying. Describe three behavior therapy procedures that might be used to treat his problem, and the advantages and disadvantages of each.
    Answer: Implosion is an extinction procedure in which the client is asked to imagine aversive scenes associated with anxiety. Repeated exposure in a safe setting causes the stimulus to lose its anxiety-eliciting power. Flooding involves in vivo confrontation of feared situations. Both procedures are very effective, but can exacerbate problems. Systematic desensitization involves eliciting a competing response, relaxation, while imagining or experiencing anxiety-producing stimuli arranged in a graduated hierarchy. It is also effective. In vivo procedures are usually more effective than in vitro.

Pages: 641-642
Topic: Behavior Therapy: Systematic Use of Reinforcement
Skill: Applied   Other1:
5. Thea is an aggressive eleven-year-old who has been sent to a residential treatment facility. Describe how two of the following three procedures could be used to alter her aggressiveness: response shaping, token economies, and behavioral contracting.
    Answer: Response shaping involves reinforcing gradual approximations of a response that is not initially in an individual's behavior repertoire. Token economies reinforce appropriate behaviors with tangible reinforcers that can later be exchanged for desired objects or privileges. Behavioral contracting involves an agreement between two parties, stipulating the reward to be given if certain behavioral conditions are satisfied.

Pages: 645-649
Topic: Cognitive-Behavior Therapy
Skill: Conceptual   Other1:

6. Ellis's rational-emotive therapy (RET) and Beck's cognitive-behavior therapy for depression are two of the major approaches to cognitive-behavior therapy. In what ways are they similar and different?

    Answer: RET suggests that core irrational beliefs are at the center of most maladjustment, and thoughts cause maladaptive emotions and behavior. RET attempts to restructure an individual's belief system and self-evaluation through actively disputing beliefs, rational confrontation, and homework. Beck's cognitive-behavioral therapy also focuses on changing cognitions, but does so through gathering information and conducting experiments designed to provide the client with empirical tests of beliefs and success experiences. Later, underlying depressogenic schemas (vulnerability factors) are targeted.

Pages: 650-653
Topic: Humanistic-Experiential Therapies
Skill: Conceptual   Other1:

7. What are the basic tenets of client-centered therapy? How does it differ from existential therapy?

    Answer: The goal of client-centered therapy is to help clients gain self-acceptance by removing obstacles to natural growth. Clients learn this by the therapist providing a psychological climate in which clients can feel unconditionally accepted and valued. Therapists are nondirective and reflective. The goal of existential psychotherapy is to encourage an individual to accept freedom and responsibility for creating meaning and value in his or her own life in an authentic manner. This therapy focuses on creating the self rather than on defining the self.

Pages: 651-653
Topic: Humanistic-Experiential Therapies: Gestalt Therapy
Skill: Conceptual   Other1:

8. What is gestalt therapy? How is it related to psychodrama?

    Answer: Gestalt therapy seeks the integration of thought, feeling, and action by teaching clients to recognize emotions and bodily processes they have been blocking from awareness. This allows working through "unfinished business" from the past that has been carried into the present. It is often conducted in a group setting, where the individual is encouraged to act out parts of a conflict or dream. Psychodrama can be used in a gestalt approach. It involves acting out problem situations in order to increase understanding and achieve emotional catharsis.

Pages: 635-654
Topic: The Evaluation of Success in Psychotherapy
Skill: Factual   Other1:

9. What does the treatment outcome research suggest regarding the efficacy of psychodynamic, behavioral, cognitive-behavioral, and humanistic-experiential approaches to treatment?

    Answer: From what little research exists, psychoanalysis is not very effective given its long-term and costly nature. It is limited in applicability, and best suited to the YAVIS patient with no serious psychopathology. Exposure therapies are very effective, in vivo more than in vitro, for many adult and child anxiety disorders and for OCD. Contingency management procedures are very effective, especially in institutional settings. Beck's therapy is highly successful with depression, anxiety, bulimia, and conduct disorder. Little research exists about humanistic therapies. Gestalt can be helpful.

Pages: 654-656
Topic: Therapy/Interpersonal Relationships: Couples Counseling/(Marital)
Skill: Applied   Other1:

10. Antoinette and Terry have sought assistance for their relationship from a couples therapist. As a typically distressed married couple, what kinds of problems are they probably experiencing? How would you address these problems in therapy?

    Answer: Their distress probably includes faulty role expectations, poor communication, blaming each other for problems, using little nonverbal communication, insensitivity to each other's feelings and needs, and little problem-solving behavior. Therapy might emphasize improving communication patterns, acknowledging one's own contribution to marital problems, identifying and renegotiating role expectations. The couple might be taught Rogerian listening techniques and helped to design a behavioral reinforcement program.

Pages: 656-658
Topic: Interpersonal Relationships: Family Therapy
Skill: Factual   Other1:

11. How did family therapy develop? What are the principles and goals behind it?

    Answer: It developed when many therapists noticed high relapse after patients returned to the familial environment following successful individual treatment. It regards the identified patient as reflecting larger family problems, so the entire family is treated in order to achieve more enduring change. Conjoint family and structural family therapies are the most widely used. These involve improving faulty communication and family interaction patterns so that individual's needs are better met. Structured family therapy is based on systems theory.

Pages: 658-659
Topic: The Integration of Therapy Approaches
Skill: Conceptual   Other1:

12. There is a movement toward integrating the various psychosocial therapeutic approaches instead of emphasizing their differences. What factors encourage this integration and what factors inhibit it?

    Answer: Behavioral and psychoanalytic proponents have acknowledged important features of one another's approaches. Research shows that behavioral methods are effective in the treatment of many disorders, but the simple application of technique alone does not bring about change. "Relationship" factors are exceedingly important. Neither of these treatment methods is invariably more effective than the other. Inhibiting factors include the lack of a common language, difficulty in training students in many different therapeutic approaches, and basic conceptual differences about etiology and goals.

Pages: 659-662
Topic: The Evaluation of Success in Psychotherapy
Skill: Conceptual   Other1:

13. What are some of the problems researchers face when conducting treatment outcome research?

    Answer: Difficulties arise in determining what sources of information to use as criteria of effectiveness, how to define success, and the procedures used to compare biological treatments with psychosocial treatments. There are limitations with each of the possible measures of therapeutic change, difficulties deciding how to treat dropouts, statistical artifacts associated with change scores, and how to deal with therapist characteristics when comparing biological and psychosocial treatments.

Pages: 662-663
Topic: Evaluation of Success in Psychotherapy: Social Values/Psychotherapy
Skill: Applied   Other1:

14. In what ways do social values affect psychotherapy? In your answer, include an example that illustrates the dilemma faced by a therapist who is asked to change a behavior that may or may not be viewed by the therapist as being personally objectionable.

    Answer: Science is not value-free and does not take place in a social vacuum. Social context may define or otherwise influence an individual's problems, as well as a therapist's approach to the problem. The decision to produce one behavior and to eliminate another is a choice that includes an implicit value judgment on the part of the therapist, either in the direction of upholding social convention or producing social change.

Pages: 663-664
Topic: Unresolved Issues on Psychotherapy
Skill: Factual   Other1:

15. Some studies suggest that about 10 percent of therapist-client interactions result in negative outcomes. What are some of the factors associated with deterioration in therapy?

Answer: The nature of the presenting disorder is a factor, with some disorders like borderline personality disorder being notable for deterioration in therapy. External, uncontrollable factors such as divorce may occur while a client is in therapy that may impact negatively on functioning. The "match" between therapist and client is important. Particular therapeutic techniques are better suited to some problems than others. Sexual exploitation by therapists is especially destructive.

CHAPTER 18 Contemporary Issues in Abnormal Psychology

Multiple-Choice

Choose the one alternative that best completes the statement or answers the question.

Pages: 667
Topic: Contemporary Issues in Abnormal Psychology
Skill: Factual   Other1:
1. Efforts toward prevention in the mental health field
    A) have been the focus of mental health professionals since the 1930s.
    B) are the most common form of treatment in the mental health field.
    C) are based on little empirical research.
    D) are much more expensive in the long run than other treatment efforts.
    Answer: C

Pages: 667
Topic: Contemporary Issues in Abnormal Psychology
Skill: Factual   Other1:
2. Compared with treatment methods, prevention programs
    A) are less difficult to justify to the public.
    B) are more cost-effective in the short-run.
    C) are attractive to the public, but not to politicians.
    D) can be far less costly in the long-run.
    Answer: D

Pages: 667
Topic: Contemporary Issues in Abnormal Psychology
Skill: Factual   Other1:
3. If hospitalization of a patient is necessary, current treatment efforts focus on
    A) returning the individual to the community as quickly as possible with whatever
       aftercare may be needed.
    B) long-term hospitalization.
    C) treating an individual in retreats far away from the stresses of everyday life.
    D) discharging the patient within seventy-two hours unless a court orders the hospital to
       continue inpatient treatment.
    Answer: A

Pages: 668
Topic: Perspectives on Prevention
Skill: Factual   Other1:
4. Primary prevention
   A) involves efforts to reduce the spread of a problem that has already developed.
   B) is aimed at reducing the possibility of disease or disorder and fostering positive health.
   C) typically includes emergency or crisis intervention.
   D) seeks to reduce the long-term consequences of disorders or serious problems.
   Answer: B

Pages: 668
Topic: Perspectives on Prevention
Skill: Applied   Other1:
5. Emergency psychotherapy and crisis intervention programs are examples of
   A) primary prevention.
   B) absolute prevention.
   C) tertiary prevention.
   D) secondary prevention.
   Answer: D

Pages: 668
Topic: Perspectives on Prevention: Primary Prevention
Skill: Factual   Other1:
6. Recent recommendations by an NIMH-sponsored panel at a conference on prevention suggested that
   A) the influence of some risk factors depends on developmental factors.
   B) most risk factors are highly idiosyncratic and difficult to identify.
   C) protective factors do little in the long run to lower the risk of psychological problems.
   D) risk factors are highly specific to a given disorder.
   Answer: A

Pages: 668
Topic: Perspectives on Prevention: Primary Prevention
Skill: Factual   Other1:
7. The NIMH-sponsored panel on prevention reported each of the following findings EXCEPT that
   A) generic risk factors exist for many diverse disorders.
   B) multiple risk factors have additive effects on vulnerability.
   C) many protective factors can prevent development of disorder even in high-risk individuals.
   D) risk factors have a highly specific relationship to specific disorders.
   Answer: D

Pages: 669
Topic: Perspectives on Prevention: Primary Prevention
Skill: Factual   Other1:

8. The NIMH-sponsored panel on prevention found that generic risk factors for mental health problems include all of the following EXCEPT
   A) school problems.
   B) family circumstances.
   C) physical unattractiveness.
   D) interpersonal problems.
   Answer: C

Pages: 669
Topic: Perspectives on Prevention: Primary Prevention
Skill: Factual   Other1:

9. Epidemiological studies are particularly important in efforts directed at
   A) primary prevention.
   B) secondary prevention.
   C) tertiary prevention.
   D) psychotherapy rather than prevention.
   Answer: A

Pages: 669
Topic: Perspectives on Prevention: Primary Prevention
Skill: Conceptual   Other1:

10. Epidemiological studies are particularly important in primary prevention efforts because they
    A) identify those individuals in need of hospitalization.
    B) show where resources are needed to help people with severe disorders.
    C) suggest which groups of individuals are at high risk for mental disorders.
    D) identify the causes of various mental disorders.
    Answer: C

Pages: 669-674
Topic: Perspectives on Prevention: Primary Prevention
Skill: Applied   Other1:

11. Primary prevention efforts include all of the following EXCEPT
    A) genetic counseling.
    B) establishing a routine of healthy diet and physical exercise.
    C) establishing a drug education program for elementary school children.
    D) a crisis line in a suicide prevention center.
    Answer: D

Pages: 670
Topic: Perspectives on Prevention: Primary Prevention
Skill: Conceptual   Other1:
12. Primary prevention aimed at developing optimal functioning would
    A) focus on halfway houses rather than hospitalization for individuals with schizophrenia.
    B) help individuals develop the needed skills for establishing satisfying interpersonal relationships.
    C) provide outpatient therapy services for individuals with psychological problems.
    D) develop crisis intervention services in communities throughout the country.
    Answer: B

Pages: 670
Topic: Perspectives on Prevention: Primary Prevention
Skill: Applied   Other1:
13. "Family life" classes in high school are designed to help teenagers understand marital and pregnancy issues before these events occur. These classes are examples of
    A) tertiary prevention.
    B) absolute prevention.
    C) secondary prevention.
    D) primary prevention.
    Answer: D

Pages: 671
Topic: Perspectives on Prevention: Primary Prevention
Skill: Conceptual   Other1: In Student Study Guide
14. All of the following are sociocultural efforts toward primary prevention of mental disorders EXCEPT
    A) economic planning.
    B) penal systems.
    C) public education.
    D) social security.
    Answer: B

Pages: 671
Topic: Perspectives on Prevention: Primary Prevention
Skill: Conceptual   Other1:
15. One of the problems with sociocultural measures of primary prevention is that
    A) there have as yet been no such efforts.
    B) the benefits of these efforts are generally far in the future.
    C) such prevention is so easily achieved that such efforts are often overlooked.
    D) the payoff for these efforts tends to be short-term and evaporates quickly.
    Answer: B

Pages: 671
Topic: Perspectives on Prevention: Primary Prevention
Skill: Factual   Other1:
16. In the "Say It Straight" program, youngsters were educated about the dangers of drug and alcohol abuse, and received assertiveness training in how to refuse using them. Compared with other youngsters, youngsters who received the program showed
    A) no differences in drug and alcohol-related behavior.
    B) a lower rate of drug and alcohol-related suspensions from school immediately after the program, but not at follow-up.
    C) a lower rate of drug-related behavior but no difference in alcohol-related behavior.
    D) a lower rate of drug and alcohol-related suspensions from school at follow-up.
    Answer: D

Pages: 672
Topic: Perspectives on Prevention: Primary Prevention
Skill: Factual   Other1:
17. Some intervention programs identify high-risk teenagers and provide special approaches to circumvent their further use of alcohol or other potentially dangerous drugs. Such programs
    A) are ineffective in deterring alcohol and drug abuse.
    B) depend on a consistently enforced alcohol and drug policy in the schools.
    C) are tertiary prevention programs.
    D) are typically family-based efforts.
    Answer: B

Pages: 672
Topic: Perspectives on Prevention: Primary Prevention
Skill: Factual   Other1:
18. Parents typically
    A) overestimate their own children's drug and alcohol use.
    B) have an accurate view of their own children's drug and alcohol use.
    C) underestimate their own children's drug and alcohol use.
    D) have considerable knowledge about their children's drug and alcohol use, much to the surprise of their children.
    Answer: C

Pages: 672
Topic: Perspectives on Prevention: Primary Prevention
Skill: Factual   Other1:
19. One of the major problems in family-based intervention programs for adolescent drug abuse is that
A) many programs report low rates of cooperation and participation by families.
B) parents do not seem capable of learning the skills necessary to deal with drug-related issues.
C) such programs are not likely to work because each member of the family needs individual, not family, therapy.
D) parents typically overestimate their own children's drug and alcohol use, which leads to difficulties in their relationships with their children.
Answer: A

Pages: 673
Topic: Perspectives on Prevention: Primary Prevention
Skill: Factual   Other1:
20. Programs designed to help youngsters overcome negative pressures from peers
A) emphasize using teachers and parents to reinforce the importance of self-control.
B) are typically utilized as soon as possible after a youngster has developed a problem.
C) focus on teaching social skills and assertiveness.
D) are ineffective.
Answer: C

Pages: 673
Topic: Perspectives on Prevention: Primary Prevention
Skill: Applied   Other1:
21. Wayne, age fourteen, is in a program designed to enhance his competency in basic life skills as well as his overall sense of self-worth. Such a program
A) can be useful only if his parents are involved.
B) is effective in reducing the impact of tobacco, alcohol, and marijuana use.
C) has been shown to be effective, but only if it is implemented prior to age nine.
D) will be most effective if it utilizes his teachers rather than his peer group.
Answer: B

Pages: 673
Topic: Perspectives on Prevention: Primary Prevention
Skill: Factual   Other1:
22. Most primary prevention strategies concerned with adolescents rely on
A) educating parents.
B) family-based interventions.
C) increasing adolescents' self-esteem.
D) a combination of different intervention strategies.
Answer: D

Pages: 673
Topic: Perspectives on Prevention: Primary Prevention
Skill: Conceptual   Other1:
23. The major problem in evaluating primary prevention programs is that
    A) they are used with children, but not adults.
    B) the programs are usually so powerful in changing behavior that they are difficult to measure.
    C) the intervention may be only remotely connected to the behavior being targeted for change.
    D) the costs are prohibitive.
    Answer: C

Pages: 673
Topic: Perspectives on Prevention: Primary Prevention
Skill: Factual   Other1:
24. Some critics of drug and alcohol-prevention programs for adolescents suggest that these problems are not amenable to such programs because
    A) drug and alcohol problems are genetically determined.
    B) drug and alcohol problems are the result of early socialization processes and thus must be addressed early in life.
    C) these programs are more effective for minority individuals than middle-class individuals.
    D) these programs ignore the role of peer pressure in drug abuse.
    Answer: B

Pages: 673
Topic: Perspectives on Prevention: Primary Prevention
Skill: Factual   Other1:
25. A well-controlled longitudinal study of children ages five to eighteen found that the greatest predictor of alcohol and drug abuse in adolescence was
    A) peer pressure.
    B) negative environmental influence.
    C) the lack of alcohol and drug education programs during middle school.
    D) clear psychological maladjustment in early childhood.
    Answer: D

Pages: 674
Topic: Perspectives on Prevention: Primary Prevention
Skill: Factual   Other1:
26. Substantial, well-designed, and long-range prevention programs for alcohol and drug abuse
    A) are being developed and funded at record rates.
    B) have become the primary tool in the "war on drugs."
    C) may not be funded because many recent programs have shown poor results.
    D) are not likely to be funded even though most recent programs have shown excellent results.
    Answer: C

Pages: 674
Topic: Perspectives on Prevention: Secondary Prevention
Skill: Factual   Other1:
27. Secondary prevention emphasizes
    A) reducing the long-term consequences of maladaptive behavior through early intervention.
    B) the early detection and prompt treatment of maladaptive behavior in a person's community setting.
    C) the prevention of maladaptive behavior before it occurs.
    D) A and B
    Answer: D

Pages: 674
Topic: Perspectives on Prevention: Secondary Prevention
Skill: Factual   Other1:
28. Long-term consultation and educational services designed to reduce the consequences of some identified maladaptive behavior is
    A) absolute prevention.
    B) secondary prevention.
    C) tertiary prevention.
    D) primary prevention.
    Answer: B

Pages: 674
Topic: Perspectives on Prevention: Secondary Prevention
Skill: Factual   Other1:
29. Crisis intervention
    A) is an example of primary prevention.
    B) is an example of tertiary prevention.
    C) is an idea with good intentions, but has been shown to be ineffective.
    D) developed in response to a need for immediate help for individuals faced with extremely stressful situations.
    Answer: D

Pages: 674
Topic: Perspectives on Prevention: Secondary Prevention
Skill: Factual   Other1:
30. Short-term crisis therapy and telephone hot lines are
    A) forms of tertiary prevention.
    B) ineffective.
    C) forms of secondary prevention.
    D) forms of primary prevention.
    Answer: C

Pages: 674-675
Topic: Perspectives on Prevention: Secondary Prevention
Skill: Applied   Other1:
31. A family has sought short-term crisis therapy to deal with a suicide attempt by the father. In this therapy,
    A) the therapist will attempt to return the disrupted family to a previous level of functioning.
    B) the therapist will attempt to change the basic family structure.
    C) the focus will be on short-term use of medication.
    D) the therapist probably will see the father alone rather than the entire family.
    Answer: A

Pages: 674
Topic: Perspectives on Prevention: Secondary Prevention
Skill: Conceptual   Other1:
32. If a problem involves psychological disturbance in a family member, then short-term crisis therapy will
    A) help the family come to terms with institutionalizing the disturbed individual so that they can move on with their own lives.
    B) typically evolve into long-term family therpy.
    C) mobilize the support of other family members to help the disturbed person and ease disruption of family life.
    D) emphasize medicating the individual.
    Answer: C

Pages: 675
Topic: Perspectives on Prevention: Secondary Prevention
Skill: Applied   Other1:
33. The text described the case of Leah, a seventeen-year-old girl who was brought into a hospital by her family after she attempted suicide. This case illustrates
    A) the deep changes in family structure that are typically brought about through family crisis intervention.
    B) the limited scope that family crisis intervention often has.
    C) the helpfulness and resources that family members usually bring to bear on assisting the disturbed family member.
    D) the long-term positive effects that short-term family crisis intervention usually has.
    Answer: B

Pages: 675
Topic: Perspectives on Prevention: Secondary Prevention
Skill: Applied   Other1:
34. The text presented the case of Leah, a seventeen-year-old girl who was brought into a hospital by her family after she attempted suicide. This case is typical of crisis intervention services because
    A) Leah was hospitalized.
    B) the family was highly motivated to change.
    C) an immediate solution for the emergency was needed.
    D) follow-up was initiated every six months for aftercare.
    Answer: C

Pages: 675
Topic: Perspectives on Prevention: Secondary Prevention
Skill: Conceptual   Other1:
35. Compared with standard family therapy, family crisis intervention
    A) takes more time.
    B) uses follow-up.
    C) does not involve changing the basic family functioning.
    D) is aimed at resolving the underlying dynamics of the family.
    Answer: C

Pages: 676
Topic: Perspectives on Prevention: Secondary Prevention
Skill: Factual   Other1:
36. In crisis intervention, the major initial focus is to
    A) isolate the individual from other family members.
    B) rapidly assess what is wrong and how serious it is.
    C) remove the individual from his or her surroundings.
    D) find appropriate medication for the individual.
    Answer: B

Pages: 676
Topic: Perspectives on Prevention: Secondary Prevention
Skill: Factual   Other1:
37. Of all the treatment approaches discussed in the text, the approach that is probably the most discouraging to therapists is
   A) crisis intervention.
   B) having to institutionalize individuals.
   C) treating families.
   D) caring for the chronically mentally ill.
   Answer: A

Pages: 676
Topic: Perspectives on Prevention: Secondary Prevention
Skill: Factual   Other1:
38. The group of individuals who are most likely to directly provide secondary prevention efforts are
   A) community mental health professionals, such as psychologists.
   B) secondary care professionals, such as teachers.
   C) primary care professionals, such as police personnel.
   D) secondary prevention professionals, such as pastoral counselors.
   Answer: A

Pages: 676
Topic: Perspectives on Prevention: Secondary Prevention
Skill: Factual   Other1:
39. Community mental health centers were designed to provide consultation and education services to primary care personnel who have frequent contact with members of the community. These services typically
   A) are not provided because of the extent to which these centers must provide direct services themselves.
   B) are usually provided to police and correctional personnel.
   C) are usually provided to social workers.
   D) are usually provided to teachers.
   Answer: A

Pages: 676-677
Topic: Perspectives on Prevention: Secondary Prevention
Skill: Factual   Other1:
40. Compared with natural disasters, such as hurricanes and floods, air disasters
   A) are less prone to affect rescue personnel.
   B) do not involve the same sense of blame and anger that occurs with natural disasters.
   C) occur far away from home and thus do not involve the sense of community that is present in response to natural disasters.
   D) lack secondary victims.
   Answer: C

Pages: 677
Topic: Perspectives on Prevention: Secondary Prevention
Skill: Factual   Other1:
41. Assume that your community experiences a flood. To decrease the impact of this disaster and reduce emotional distress, psychological intervention should occur
A) immediately after the disaster.
B) within one week of the disaster.
C) in a setting that keeps the victim isolated from news about the disaster.
D) only for those who are exhibiting symptoms of posttraumatic stress disorder.
Answer: A

Pages: 677
Topic: Perspectives on Prevention: Secondary Prevention
Skill: Applied   Other1:
42. Warren has just been involved in an airplane crash. He experienced only minor injuries, but there were some deaths. His crisis counselor should
A) wait to counsel him until he has had a few days to process the event emotionally.
B) provide a long-term perspective and remain objective.
C) isolate Warren from other family members temporarily.
D) first administer a battery of psychological tests in order to determine whether the accident had any negative impact on him.
Answer: B

Pages: 677-678
Topic: Perspectives on Prevention: Secondary Prevention
Skill: Factual   Other1:
43. Which of the following is TRUE when people experience a disaster?
A) Immediate crisis intervention is relatively unimportant, provided that aftercare services are provided.
B) Those who function well at the disaster site may experience later difficulties.
C) The most experienced rescue workers do not experience significant difficulties either at the disaster site or later on.
D) They usually do not want to talk about their experiences.
Answer: B

Pages: 678
Topic: Perspectives on Prevention: Secondary Prevention
Skill: Factual   Other1:
44. All of the following are standard procedures in most communities following major disasters EXCEPT for
A) telephone hot-line counseling.
B) debriefing sessions.
C) short-term milieu therapy sessions.
D) immediate crisis intervention.
Answer: C

Pages: 678
Topic: Perspectives on Prevention: Secondary Prevention
Skill: Conceptual   Other1:
45. The text illustrates secondary prevention efforts by describing the procedures and interventions that are provided to victims and emergency workers in the wake of an air-crash disaster. The overriding goal of these efforts is to
    A) provide aftercare psychological services to passenger-victims, surviving family members, and rescue personnel.
    B) instill the hope of surviving psychologically.
    C) prevent the development of more severe psychological disorders.
    D) instill protective factors that will help victims to cope should they ever be faced with another major disaster.
    Answer: C

Pages: 678
Topic: Perspectives on Prevention: Tertiary Prevention
Skill: Factual   Other1:
46. Efforts aimed at reducing the impact of a disorder and restoring an individual to functioning once a mental health problem has been identified is known as
    A) secondary prevention.
    B) tertiary prevention.
    C) post-trauma prevention.
    D) primary prevention.
    Answer: B

Pages: 678
Topic: Perspectives on Prevention: Tertiary Prevention
Skill: Factual   Other1:
47. In milieu therapy, the
    A) staff provides positive, but not negative, feedback to patients.
    B) hospital environment becomes a crucial aspect of treatment.
    C) patients are expected to conduct their own group therapy sessions while a staff member observes.
    D) patients are encouraged to willingly accept all treatment decisions made for them by the staff.
    Answer: B

Pages: 678
Topic: Perspectives on Prevention: Tertiary Prevention
Skill: Applied   Other1:
48. Andrew, an individual with depression, is participating in milieu therapy in his inpatient ward. This means that Andrew will
    A) be more heavily medicated in order to allow him the greater freedom associated with this type of therapy.
    B) receive a multimodal therapy package including individual, group, and family therapy.
    C) be responsible for a group of more dysfunctional patients.
    D) be encouraged to become involved in all decisions made concerning him.
    Answer: D

Pages: 679
Topic: Perspectives on Prevention: Tertiary Prevention
Skill: Applied   Other1:
49. Alexandra, who suffers from schizophrenia, is in an inpatient ward that emphasizes social-learning programs. This means that
    A) her primary source of therapy will still be her medication.
    B) she will participate in learning based programs that help shape socially acceptable behavior.
    C) the social groups to which she belongs on the ward are seen as the primary sources of treatment.
    D) she will participate in social programs, such as group therapy.
    Answer: B

Pages: 679
Topic: Perspectives on Prevention: Tertiary Prevention
Skill: Factual   Other1:
50. Among patients labeled as psychotic and admitted to mental hospitals, about _____ percent can be discharged within a few weeks or at most a few months.
    A) 10-30
    B) 30-50
    C) 50-70
    D) 70-90
    Answer: D

Pages: 679
Topic: Perspectives on Prevention: Tertiary Prevention
Skill: Factual   Other1:
51. One long-term study compared outcomes for chronic schizophrenic inpatients receiving either milieu therapy, a social-learning treatment program, or traditional mental hospital treatment. This study found that
    A) milieu therapy was the most effective, followed by traditional treatment, with social-learning treatment being the least effective.
    B) milieu therapy and social-learning treatment were the most effective, and equally so, with traditional treatment being the least effective.
    C) social-learning treatment was the most effective, followed by milieu therapy, with traditional treatment being the least effective.
    D) social-learning and traditional treatments were the most effective, and equally so, with milieu therapy being the least effective.
    Answer: C

Pages: 680-681
Topic: Perspectives on Prevention: Tertiary Prevention
Skill: Factual   Other1:
52. For individuals with chronic schizophrenia, adequate aftercare following a hospitalization
    A) reduces rehospitalization rates.
    B) helps such individuals with self-image and self-esteem, but has little effect on rehospitalization rates.
    C) should be abrupt rather than gradual and drawn-out.
    D) increases the long-term expense of the individual's care.
    Answer: A

Pages: 680
Topic: Perspectives on Prevention: Tertiary Prevention
Skill: Applied   Other1:
53. Caitlin, who suffers from schizophrenia, participates in an aftercare program. This means that she
    A) holds a day job outside the hospital but returns there at night.
    B) has no better chance of staying out of the hospital than if she were not participating in such a program.
    C) has a significantly reduced chance of staying out of the hospital than if she were not participating in such a program.
    D) is probably no longer mentally disturbed, especially if she has participated in the program for several years.
    Answer: C

Pages: 680
Topic: Perspectives on Prevention: Tertiary Prevention
Skill: Conceptual   Other1:

54. In a study with seriously disturbed mental patients, the patients lived in a "Lodge" and were given full responsibility for operating the Lodge, for regulating each other's behavior, for earning money, and for purchasing and preparing food. The results of this study suggest that
    A) community-based living is not a realistic goal for most seriously disturbed patients.
    B) most seriously disturbed patients are able to adjust to living in the outside world under the right circumstances.
    C) most seriously disturbed patients are not able to function adequately in the community even under the best of circumstances.
    D) A and C
    Answer: B

Pages: 681
Topic: Perspectives on Prevention: Tertiary Prevention
Skill: Factual   Other1:

55. Compared with full inpatient psychiatric treatment, partial hospitalization in a day treatment setting is
    A) less effective, but much cheaper.
    B) less effective and at a higher cost.
    C) as effective and much cheaper.
    D) as effective but at a higher cost.
    Answer: C

Pages: 681
Topic: Perspectives on Prevention: Tertiary Prevention
Skill: Factual   Other1:

56. The major problem of community-based treatment facilities for individuals with chronic disorders is that
    A) of gaining the acceptance and support of community residents.
    B) these programs are very expensive, especially when compared with traditional treatment programs.
    C) many professionals are needed to run these facilities.
    D) they lack empirical evidence concerning their effectiveness.
    Answer: A

Pages: 681
Topic: Controversial Issues and the Mentally Disordered
Skill: Factual   Other1:
57. Forensic psychology deals with
    A) the legal status of felons and other criminals.
    B) the legal status of the mentally ill.
    C) investigating the causes of criminal behavior in the mentally ill.
    D) the treatment of individuals who have been judged to be legally insane.
    Answer: B

Pages: 682
Topic: Controversial Issues and the Mentally Disordered
Skill: Factual   Other1:
58. Which of the following is a basic legal right for individuals suffering from mental disorders?
    A) Mentally ill, but not mentally retarded, individuals have a right to receive treatment.
    B) Mentally retarded, but not mentally ill, individuals have a right to receive treatment.
    C) Patients have a right to freedom from custodial confinement if they are not dangerous to themselves or others and if they can safely survive outside custody.
    D) Patients have a right to demand particular treatments, such as electroconvulsive therapy.
    Answer: C

Pages: 682
Topic: Controversial Issues and the Mentally Disordered
Skill: Factual   Other1:
59. Which of the following is TRUE concerning the legal rights of individuals suffering from mental disorders?
    A) Released state mental hospital patients have the right to live in the community, but they must notify their neighbors that they are mental patients.
    B) Patients have a right to refuse certain treatments.
    C) A patient need not be paid for work performed in a state or private hospital.
    D) An individual has a right to the best treatment available.
    Answer: B

Pages: 682
Topic: Controversial Issues and the Mentally Disordered
Skill: Factual   Other1:

60. Which of the following is TRUE concerning the basic legal rights of individuals suffering from mental disorders?
    A) A person can be confined without demonstrable evidence of the need for institutionalization for no more than thirty days.
    B) The judge protects individuals during the commitment process, since lawyers are not permitted to be retained until evidence of the need for commitment has been produced.
    C) Individuals are not permitted to receive financial compensation for work performed in state or private mental hospitals.
    D) Individuals have the right to receive treatment in less restrictive facilities than mental institutions.
    Answer: D

Pages: 681-682
Topic: Controversial Issues/Mentally Disordered: The Commitment Process
Skill: Factual   Other1:

61. To place an individual in a mental institution against his or her will, it must be shown that the individual is
    A) mentally ill.
    B) dangerous to self or to others, or unable to provide for his or her basic physical needs.
    C) refusing to receive a treatment, such as electroconvulsive therapy, which is being recommended by a psychiatrist or psychologist.
    D) A and B
    Answer: D

Pages: 681
Topic: Controversial Issues/Mentally Disordered: The Commitment Process
Skill: Factual   Other1:

62. In most cases of psychiatric hospitalization, individuals
    A) enter the hospital voluntarily.
    B) are involuntarily hospitalized because they are unable to make responsible decisions about hospitalization.
    C) are involuntarily hospitalized because they are in need of treatment or care in a hospital.
    D) are involuntarily hospitalized because they are dangerous to themselves.
    Answer: A

Pages: 682
Topic: Controversial Issues/Mentally Disordered: The Commitment Process
Skill: Factual   Other1:
63. Which of the following is TRUE concerning involuntary commitment?
    A) Any concerned person, such as a relative, can file the petition for a commitment hearing.
    B) A commitment hearing must be held as soon as possible once the individual is brought to the psychiatric hospital.
    C) A psychiatrist is the only person who can file the petition or do the examination for commitment.
    D) A psychologist must be part of the examining team that decides whether the individual should be committed.
    Answer: A

Pages: 683
Topic: Controversial Issues/Mentally Disordered: The Commitment Process
Skill: Factual   Other1:
64. If an individual is involuntarily committed, then
    A) the patient loses all of his or her civil rights.
    B) the commitment period becomes indefinite with no further evaluations.
    C) the hospital must report to the court within sixty days as to whether the person needs to be confined even longer.
    D) the court turns the case over to a psychiatrist or psychologist, who is then responsible for determining when the individual can be released from the hospital.
    Answer: C

Pages: 683
Topic: Controversial Issues/Mentally Disordered: The Commitment Process
Skill: Factual   Other1:
65. In an emergency hospitalization,
    A) a petition for commitment must be filed with the court before the individual can be detained.
    B) an individual can be detained without a commitment hearing under a "hold order," usually not to exceed seventy-two hours.
    C) a physician must sign a statement saying that imminent danger exists.
    D) B and C
    Answer: D

Pages: 683
Topic: Controversial Issues/Mentally Disordered: Assessment/"Dangerousness"
Skill: Factual   Other1:
66. The majority of psychiatric patients
    A) were assaultive prior to their admission to psychiatric facilities.
    B) are assaultive at the time of admission to psychiatric facilities.
    C) need special safety precautions and close supervision at the time of their admissions.
    D) are not considered dangerous.
    Answer: D

Pages: 683
Topic: Controversial Issues/Mentally Disordered: Assessment/"Dangerousness"
Skill: Factual   Other1:
67. A recent review of the relationship between violence and mental disorder suggests that
    A) there is no relationship between violence and mental illness.
    B) increased risk of violence in the mentally ill is apparently limited to currently
       psychotic individuals.
    C) mental illness is fairly often associated with violence, although most mentally ill
       individuals commit but a single violent act in their lifetime.
    D) when mental illness and violence co-occur, the violence almost always precedes and is
       causally implicated in the mental disorder.
    Answer: B

Pages: 683
Topic: Controversial Issues/Mentally Disordered: Assessment/"Dangerousness"
Skill: Conceptual   Other1:
68. Determining that a given patient is potentially dangerous
    A) is a relatively easy judgment for mental health professionals to make.
    B) is a crucial but difficult judgment from both therapeutic and legal standpoints.
    C) is not important in most involuntary commitments.
    D) has become less important as the number of psychiatric hospitalizations has decreased.
    Answer: B

Pages: 684
Topic: Controversial Issues/Mentally Disordered: Assessment/"Dangerousness"
Skill: Applied   Other1:
69. The text presented the case of Ms. Eva B., who was brutally stabbed to death by her former husband, who had been judged by two staff psychiatrists not to be dangerous. This case illustrated
    A) how rarely mental health professionals make mistakes when assessing dangerousness.
    B) that patients with mental disorders are more dangerous under high doses of medication.
    C) that professionals have considerable difficulty accurately appraising "dangerousness" in some individuals.
    D) that mental health professionals rarely disagree in their judgments concerning "dangerousness."
    Answer: C

Pages: 684-685
Topic: Controversial Issues/Mentally Disordered: Assessment/"Dangerousness"
Skill: Factual   Other1:
70. All of the following are associated with difficulty in predicting the future occurrence of violence EXCEPT
    A) how dangerousness is defined.
    B) the influence of unforseeable situational circumstances.
    C) the presence of "masked" schizophrenic or manic delusions.
    D) lack of information about an individual's prior history of violence.
    Answer: C

Pages: 684-685
Topic: Contemporary Issues in Abnormal Psychology
Skill: Factual   Other1:
71. Violent acts are particularly difficult to predict because they are
    A) determined almost exclusively by the individual's personality traits.
    B) determined almost exclusively by situational circumstances.
    C) determined by an interaction of unpredictable situational circumstances and the individual's personality traits.
    D) completely unpredictable in principle.
    Answer: C

Pages: 685
Topic: Controversial Issues/Mentally Disordered: Assessment/"Dangerousness"
Skill: Factual   Other1:
72. Mental health professionals
    A) underestimate the percentage of patients who are dangerous.
    B) overestimate the percentage of patients who are dangerous.
    C) underestimate the percentage of outpatients who are dangerous, but overestimate the percentage of inpatients who are dangerous.
    D) overestimate the percentage of outpatients who are dangerous, but underestimate the percentage of inpatients who are dangerous.
    Answer: B

Pages: 685
Topic: Controversial Issues/Mentally Disordered: Assessment/"Dangerousness"
Skill: Factual   Other1:
73. The use of personality tests to determine the likelihood of an individual committing an aggressive act
    A) is the most accurate means of predicting violence.
    B) can not take into account the important role of environmental circumstances.
    C) results in an underestimation of such acts.
    D) is no longer used by forensic psychologists due to lack of predictive validity.
    Answer: B

Pages: 685
Topic: Controversial Issues/Mentally Disordered: Assessment/"Dangerousness"
Skill: Factual   Other1:
74. The single best predictor of future violent behavior is
    A) a prior history of violence.
    B) personality traits of aggressiveness and impulsivity.
    C) extreme over-control of emotions.
    D) none of the above, as there is no single best predictor of violent behavior.
    Answer: D

Pages: 685
Topic: Controversial Issues/Mentally Disordered: Assessment/"Dangerousness"
Skill: Applied   Other1:
75. The most difficult type of aggressive behavior to predict is the
    A) sudden impulsive act of a seemingly well-controlled and "normal" individual.
    B) carefully planned act of a psychopath.
    C) act of an individual with an intermittent history of committing violence.
    D) act of an individual who reveals hostility and impulsive aggression on psychological tests.
    Answer: A

Pages: 685-686
Topic: Controversial Issues/Mentally Disordered: Assessment/"Dangerousness"
Skill: Factual   Other1:
76. Studies in violence prediction suggest that prediction can be vastly improved by taking into account
    A) demographic data on family background, history of violence, friendships, and substance abuse.
    B) the content of a psychotic individual's delusion.
    C) homelessness.
    D) intelligence level.
    Answer: A

Pages: 686
Topic: Controversial Issues/Mentally Disordered: Assessment/"Dangerousness"
Skill: Factual   Other1:
77. Based on the ruling in the case of <u>Tarasoff</u> v. <u>The Regents of the University of California et al</u>.
    A) therapists are legally obligated to warn potential victims of threats to their safety.
    B) individuals cannot be hospitalized until after they have committed a dangerous act.
    C) the violation of patient confidentiality is illegal.
    D) therapists should not confine a client unless the determination of "dangerousness" can be made with reasonable certainty.
    Answer: A

Pages: 686
Topic: Controversial Issues/Mentally Disordered: Assessment/"Dangerousness"
Skill: Factual   Other1:
78. "The protective privilege [of confidentiality in the psychotherapeutic relationship] ends where the public peril begins." This determination was made in the
    A) M'Naughton decision.
    B) Tarasoff decision.
    C) Hinckley decision.
    D) O'Donaldson decision.
    Answer: B

Pages: 686
Topic: Controversial Issues/Mentally Disordered: Assessment/"Dangerousness"
Skill: Factual   Other1:
79. The Tarasoff decision
    A) was later amended in Tarasoff II from a legal obligation to warn a potential victim, to a legal obligation to protect the potential victim.
    B) leaves many areas of application confusing and unclear.
    C) has been rejected in favor of the inviolability of confidentiality in some states.
    D) all of the above
    Answer: D

Pages: 687-688
Topic: Controversial Issues/Mentally Disordered: The Insanity Defense
Skill: Factual   Other1:
80. Which of the following is TRUE regarding the insanity defense?
    A) The insanity defense is used in about 15 percent of cases.
    B) Legal insanity no longer requires establishing the absence of guilty intent.
    C) The use of the insanity defense is very successful.
    D) Individuals acquitted of crimes by reason of insanity spend less time confined than
       individuals convicted of crimes.
    Answer: D

Pages: 688
Topic: Controversial Issues/Mentally Disordered: The Insanity Defense
Skill: Factual   Other1:
81. The insanity defense applies to a perpetrator's state of mind
    A) prior to committing the crime.
    B) at the time of the crime.
    C) at the time of arraignment by the police.
    D) at the time of the trial.
    Answer: B

Pages: 688
Topic: Controversial Issues/Mentally Disordered: The Insanity Defense
Skill: Applied   Other1:
82. "When I committed the crime, I was laboring under a defect of reason and did not know that
    what I was doing was wrong." This individual is using the
    A) M'Naughten Rule.
    B) Durham Rule.
    C) irresistible impulse rule.
    D) American Law Institute standard.
    Answer: A

Pages: 688
Topic: Controversial Issues/Mentally Disordered: The Insanity Defense
Skill: Factual   Other1:
83. The broadest of the insanity rules is the
    A) M'Naghten Rule.
    B) irresistible impulse rule.
    C) Durham Rule.
    D) Diminished Capacity Rule.
    Answer: C

Pages: 688
Topic: Controversial Issues/Mentally Disordered: The Insanity Defense
Skill: Factual   Other1:

84. The federal Insanity Defense Reform Act shifted the burden of proof for the insanity defense from the persecution to the defense. This has been
    A) very successful in discouraging the use of the insanity defense.
    B) very successful in expanding the insanity defense so that it is applicable to many more individuals.
    C) disastrous in that it has slowed down legal proceedings so much that criminal courts are backlogged.
    D) very unpopular with the general public.
    Answer: A

Pages: 689
Topic: Controversial Issues/Mentally Disordered: The Insanity Defense
Skill: Factual   Other1:

85. A defendant has been found "guilty but mentally ill." This means that the individual will
    A) be hospitalized instead of placed under the custody of the correctional system.
    B) remain in the custody of the correctional department until a full sentence is served even if he or she is considered in no further need of treatment.
    C) serve the sentence in a community halfway house rather than in prison.
    D) be hospitalized until well, and then be placed in the custody of the correctional department until the full sentence is served.
    Answer: B

Pages: 690
Topic: Controversial Issues/Mentally Disordered: Deinstitutionalization
Skill: Factual   Other1:

86. The deinstitutionalization of patients in large, state mental hospitals was seen as a way to
    A) lower the hospital population to manageable numbers.
    B) reduce state spending.
    C) rid society of inhumane custodial hospitals.
    D) all of the above
    Answer: D

Pages: 690
Topic: Controversial Issues/Mentally Disordered: Deinstitutionalization
Skill: Conceptual   Other1:
87. The reduction in the number of patients in public mental institutions was based on the assumption that
    A) community-based care would be provided.
    B) psychotherapy had reached the point where it could solve the patients' problems.
    C) medication was sufficient to keep patients stabilized without further treatment.
    D) hospitalization would shift from the large institutions to small community mental health hospitals.
    Answer: A

Pages: 690-691
Topic: Controversial Issues/Mentally Disordered: Deinstitutionalization
Skill: Factual   Other1:
88. One of the problems with the deinstitutionalization movement is that
    A) medication is not useful in the management of patients.
    B) community mental health centers were set up to provide inpatient, but not outpatient, services.
    C) no one thought of alternative forms of care before patients were released from the mental institutions.
    D) countless patients were discharged to fates that were even more dehumanizing than the conditions in the hospitals.
    Answer: D

Pages: 690
Topic: Controversial Issues/Mentally Disordered: Deinstitutionalization
Skill: Factual   Other1:
89. Over the past twenty years, the number of patients in state and county mental institutions has
    A) increased significantly.
    B) remained stable.
    C) decreased slightly.
    D) decreased significantly.
    Answer: D

Pages: 692
Topic: Controversial Issues/Mentally Disordered: Deinstitutionalization
Skill: Factual   Other1:
90. The increase in homeless people in major cities has been attributed in large part to
    A) crowded conditions in mental hospitals which has resulted in a lack of beds, and thus to deinstitutionalization.
    B) the overmedication of deinstitutionalized patients by psychiatrists.
    C) the premature or inappropriate discharge of patients from psychiatric hospitals.
    D) the presence of deinstitutionalized schizophrenics who are not responsive to medication.
    Answer: C

Pages: 691
Topic: Controversial Issues/Mentally Disordered: Deinstitutionalization
Skill: Factual   Other1:
91. Former mental patients typically have a problem functioning in society because
    A) they need a reintroduction to society with regular and adequate follow-up.
    B) they are not given sufficient medication to control their symptoms.
    C) they avoid the help available at community mental health centers.
    D) they are typically mildly to moderately retarded.
    Answer: A

Pages: 691-692
Topic: Controversial Issues/Mentally Disordered: Deinstitutionalization
Skill: Factual   Other1:
92. The discharge planning and aftercare services provided former mental patients are
    A) seriously deficient.
    B) slightly below adequate.
    C) adequate, but not superior.
    D) excellent.
    Answer: A

Pages: 692
Topic: Controversial Issues/Mentally Disordered: Deinstitutionalization
Skill: Factual   Other1:
93. Among the homeless population,
    A) 33 percent have chronic mental illnesses.
    B) 33 percent have severe addiction problems.
    C) 33 percent are likely to commit violent acts.
    D) A and B
    Answer: D

Pages: 692
Topic: Controversial Issues/Mentally Disordered: Deinstitutionalization
Skill: Factual   Other1:
94. Programs designed to reintegrate former mental patients into the community
    A) focus on acute patients instead of chronic patients.
    B) have not been very successful at preventing hospital readmissions.
    C) employ staff members who formerly were employed at large, state mental institutions.
    D) maintain the individual in the community and out of the hospital at all costs.
    Answer: B

Pages: 692
Topic: Controversial Issues/Mentally Disordered: Deinstitutionalization
Skill: Factual   Other1:
95. Of the money spent on mental health care,
    A) 70 percent is spent on hospitalization.
    B) 30 percent is spent on hospitalization.
    C) 70 percent is spent on posthospitalization programs.
    D) 70 percent is spent caring for chronic patients who are permanently hospitalized.
    Answer: A

Pages: 692
Topic: Controversial Issues/Mentally Disordered: Deinstitutionalization
Skill: Factual   Other1:
96. The "privatization" of the mental health system refers to
    A) the increasing emphasis in mental hospitals on inpatients' legal right to privacy.
    B) a shift in funding for mental health care from the public sector to the private sector.
    C) the trend for private health insurance companies to refuse to cover inpatient
       hospitalizations.
    D) deinstitutionalization.
    Answer: B

Pages: 692
Topic: Controversial Issues/Mentally Disordered: Deinstitutionalization
Skill: Factual   Other1:
97. As the number of patients in state mental hospitals has decreased,
    A) case-management approaches involving paraprofessionals have been terminated.
    B) community mental health centers have become the largest single setting to care for the
       mentally ill.
    C) the number of emotionally disturbed individuals being admitted to large private
       institutions has increased.
    D) private nursing home facilities have decreased.
    Answer: C

Pages: 692
Topic: Controversial Issues/Mentally Disordered: Deinstitutionalization
Skill: Conceptual   Other1:
98. Privatization has resulted in
    A) more homeless people being admitted to private institutions.
    B) more socioeconomically advantaged people being represented among psychiatric inpatients.
    C) more elderly people being admitted to psychiatric hospitals.
    D) better care for patients in both private and public institutions.
    Answer: B

Pages: 693
Topic: Controversial Issues/Mentally Disordered: Deinstitutionalization
Skill: Factual   Other1:
99. Currently the largest single setting to care for the chronic mentally ill is
    A) inpatient units at community mental health centers.
    B) large, state mental hospitals.
    C) large private hospitals.
    D) nursing homes.
    Answer: D

Pages: 693
Topic: Organized Efforts for Mental Health: U.S. Efforts for Mental Health
Skill: Factual   Other1:
100. In the U.S., the first comprehensive mental health bill was passed by the Congress in the
    A) 1920s.
    B) 1940s.
    C) 1960s.
    D) 1980s.
    Answer: B

Pages: 693
Topic: Organized Efforts for Mental Health: U.S. Efforts for Mental Health
Skill: Factual   Other1:
101. The National Mental Health Act provided for the establishment of a center for research and training in mental health, which would also serve as headquarters for the administration of a federal grant-in-aid program. This center is called
    A) NIOSH.
    B) NAMH.
    C) NIMH.
    D) NIAAA.
    Answer: C

Pages: 694
Topic: Organized Efforts for Mental Health: U.S. Efforts for Mental Health
Skill: Factual   Other1:
102. In the 1980s,
    A) federal aid for mental health programs increased considerably.
    B) the number of patients in state mental hospitals increased dramatically.
    C) state and local governments were no longer able to fund mental health programs
        adequately due to severe cuts in federal support for mental health programs.
    D) the number of professional organizations in the mental health field decreased
        considerably.
    Answer: C

Pages: 694
Topic: Organized Efforts for Mental Health: U.S. Efforts for Mental Health
Skill: Applied   Other1:
103. Establishing and maintaining high professional and ethical standards, promoting exchange
    of information, and setting standards and procedures for the accreditation of
    undergraduate and graduate training programs represent just a few of the functions of the
    A) NIMH.
    B) APA.
    C) NAMH.
    D) WHO.
    Answer: B

Pages: 694
Topic: Organized Efforts for Mental Health: U.S. Efforts for Mental Health
Skill: Factual   Other1:
104. The role of voluntary mental health agencies
    A) has not been especially great since the mental hospital reforms of the nineteenth
        century.
    B) is dependent on government funding, which was slashed in the 1960s.
    C) is crucial in planning and implementing mental health programs.
    D) is chaotic at present due to uncertainty about the future of national health care
        legislation.
    Answer: C

Pages: 695
Topic: Organized Efforts for Mental Health: U.S. Efforts for Mental Health
Skill: Factual   Other1:
105. Which of the following is TRUE regarding the use of mental health resources in private industry?
A) Private industry typically does not acknowledge the importance of mental health-promoting factors in the work place and therefore dramatically underutilizes mental health resources.
B) Primary prevention programs have been routinely used in private industry for many decades.
C) Many companies have recently begun providing psychological services through employee assistance programs.
D) Psychological services are provided on an extremely limited basis, even at the most elite private corporations.
Answer: C

Pages: 696
Topic: Organized Efforts for Mental Health: International Efforts
Skill: Factual   Other1:
106. In understanding and treating mental disorders, the World Health Organization at the present time has
A) almost completely ignored the impact of physical disease on mental health.
B) almost completely ignored ethnic and cultural differences.
C) focused exclusively on physcial diseases, not on mental health.
D) been very much aware of the interrelationship between physical, psychosocial, and sociocultural factors.
Answer: D

Pages: 697
Topic: Challenges for the Future: The Individual's Contributions
Skill: Conceptual   Other1:
107. The history of abnormal psychology makes it clear that
A) the field can be profoundly changed and improved through individual effort.
B) international efforts in dealing with mental disorders are doomed to failure until the biological causes of serious mental disorders are found.
C) more domestic and fewer international efforts are needed.
D) we are no further today in understanding mental disorders than we were in the time of Pinel, Dix, and Beers.
Answer: A

Pages: 697
Topic: Challenges for the Future: The Individual's Contributions
Skill: Conceptual   Other1:
108. Preventive measures are the most effective long-range approach to the solution of
    A) individual, but not group, mental health problems.
    B) group, but not individual, mental health problems.
    C) both individual and group mental health problems.
    D) neither individual nor group mental health problems.
    Answer: C

Pages: 698-699
Topic: Unresolved Issues on The Law-Mental Health Interface
Skill: Conceptual   Other1:
109. One of the difficulties at the interface of mental health and the legal system is
    A) a psychologist is called upon to make professional judgments about such matters as
       malingering and individual responsibility when definitive judgments about such matters
       are unattainable from a scientific persprective.
    B) the law's refusal to recognize the existence of dissociative identity disorder.
    C) the refusal of courts to use a psychologist's testimony unless it is corroborated by
       five other mental health professionals.
    D) the DSM-IV uses different standards to determine legal insanity than the courts do.
    Answer: A

Pages: 699-700
Topic: Unresolved Issues on The Law-Mental Health Interface
Skill: Conceptual   Other1:
110. All of the following are issues or difficulties at the interface of mental health and the
    legal system EXCEPT
    A) there is a need for mutual inquiry by legal scholars and mental health professionals in
       order to arrive at a balanced and equitable approach to problems associated with the
       insanity defense, yet collaborative efforts have been historically rare.
    B) the use of dissociative identity disorder (multiple personality) as a basis for
       pleading "not guilty by reason of insanity."
    C) the use of psychological experts by both prosecutors and defense attorneys, often
       resulting in disagreements between experts on either side of the case, which can be a
       source of embarassment to the mental health profession.
    D) the use of the "insanity defense" when a defendant in actuality was not psychotic at
       the time of committing the crime.
    Answer: D

Short Answer

Write the word or phrase that best completes each statement or answers the question.

Pages: 667
Topic: Contemporary Issues in Abnormal Psychology
Skill: Conceptual   Other1:
1. What is one of the major problems associated with implementing broad prevention programs?
   Answer: It can be difficult to convince legislators and the public that funding for such costly programs may be fiscally wise in the long run. Without knowing causes of mental disorders, it is hard to tailor programs to prevent them. Research demonstrating the efficacy and cost-effectiveness of such programs is difficult.

Pages: 668
Topic: Perspectives on Prevention: Primary Prevention
Skill: Factual   Other1:
2. What is primary prevention?
   Answer: It is aimed at reducing the possibility of disease or disorder prior to their occurrence, and promoting mental health.

Pages: 668-669
Topic: Perspectives on Prevention: Primary Prevention
Skill: Factual   Other1:
3. Identify five of the generic risk factors for mental disorders that were identified by the recent NIMH-sponsored panel on prevention.
   Answer: These include low social class, communication deviance, child abuse, low self-esteem, stressful life events, academic failure, racial injustice, extreme poverty, peer rejection, subnormal intelligence, and several others that are summarized in Table 18.1.

Pages: 669-671
Topic: Perspectives on Prevention: Primary Prevention
Skill: Applied   Other1:
4. Give an example of a biological, a psychosocial, and a sociocultural primary prevention strategy.
   Answer: Biological strategies include genetic counseling, prenatal care, postnatal care, and physical health strategies like improving diet and exercise in order to achieve greater physical and psychological well-being. Psychosocial strategies include skill development and preparatory education for coping with life problems like parenting. Sociocultural strategies include producing positive social change in living conditions that will foster healthy development and functioning, such as economic planning and social legislation directed at ensuring adequate health care for all.

Pages: 674
Topic: Perspectives on Prevention: Secondary Prevention
Skill: Factual   Other1:
5. What is secondary prevention?
    Answer: It emphasizes the early detection and prompt treatment of maladaptive behavior, with the goal of preventing or minimizing potential long-term consequences.

Pages: 675
Topic: Perspectives on Prevention: Secondary Prevention
Skill: Conceptual   Other1:
6. How does family crisis intervention differ from family therapy?
    Answer: Family crisis intervention is short-term, and its goal is usually limited to returning a disrupted family to the level of precrisis functioning, rather than changing basic family functioning as in family therapy.

Pages: 674-676
Topic: Perspectives on Prevention: Secondary Prevention
Skill: Factual   Other1:
7. Identify two modes of therapeutic intervention that are used when people are confronted with a crisis or major disaster.
    Answer: short-term crisis intervention therapy; telephone hot-line counseling and information dissemination; postcrisis debriefing of secondary victims.

Pages: 678
Topic: Perspectives on Prevention: Tertiary Prevention
Skill: Factual   Other1:
8. _____ prevention involves efforts aimed at reducing the impact of a disorder and restoring a person to functioning once a mental health problem has been identified.
    Answer: Tertiary

Pages: 678
Topic: Perspectives on Prevention: Tertiary Prevention
Skill: Factual   Other1:
9. What is milieu therapy?
    Answer: It is the use of a hospital environment as a therapeutic community in which patients are encouraged to take responsibility for their own behavior and treatment. Staff expectations are clearly communicated to patients. Patients are encouraged to become involved in all decisions made and all actions taken concerning them. Patients belong to social groups on the ward, which provides group cohesiveness, support, and encouragement.

Pages: 679
Topic: Perspectives on Prevention: Tertiary Prevention
Skill: Applied   Other1:

10. One example of a social-learning program is _____.
    Answer: a token economy

Pages: 679
Topic: Perspectives on Prevention: Tertiary Prevention
Skill: Factual   Other1:

11. In an extensive, long-term study of chronically hospitalized schizophrenics, traditional
    hospital care was compared with milieu therapy and social-learning programs. What did
    this study find?
    Answer: It found that both therapies were more effective in measures of improved overall
            functioning and hospital releases than traditional hospital care, and
            social-learning treatment was more effective than milieu therapy. At follow-up,
            90 percent of the released patients from the social-learning program remained
            continuously in the community, compared with 70 percent of the released patients
            who had milieu therapy and less than 50 percent who had traditional treatment.

Pages: 680-681
Topic: Perspectives on Prevention: Tertiary Prevention
Skill: Applied   Other1:

12. Identify two types of psychiatric hospital aftercare programs.
    Answer: These include halfway houses and other community-based group living facilities,
            the Fairweather Lodge program, and day hospital facilities.

Pages: 681
Topic: Controversial Issues and the Mentally Disordered
Skill: Factual   Other1:

13. The legal status of the mentally ill is the province of _____ psychology.
    Answer: forensic

Pages: 683
Topic: Controversial Issues/Mentally Disordered: The Commitment Process
Skill: Factual   Other1:

14. The major reason for committing a mentally ill person to a psychiatric facility
    involuntarily is
    Answer: the individual is a danger to self or others.

Pages: 683-685
Topic: Controversial Issues/Mentally Disordered: Assessment/"Dangerousness"
Skill: Factual   Other1:

15. What two factors are highly associated with risk for committing a violent act? Include in your answer two characteristics about the person, as opposed to environmental circumstances, that may trigger a violent act.
    Answer: Two key predictors include being actively psychotic and having a past history of violence. Personality traits of hostility, aggressiveness, impulsivity, poor judgment, and so on may also be useful, though many people showing these traits never do act on them.

Pages: 685
Topic: Controversial Issues/Mentally Disordered: Assessment/"Dangerousness"
Skill: Factual   Other1:

16. What are two of the sources of information used by psychologists in assessing whether an individual is dangerous?
    Answer: They may use psychological testing, knowledge about an individual's history with regard to violence, and knowledge of any current environmental factors that may put an individual "over the edge." Studies have also shown that prediction can be improved with demographic data on family background, friendships, and substance abuse.

Pages: 686
Topic: Controversial Issues/Mentally Disordered: Assessment/"Dangerousness"
Skill: Conceptual   Other1:

17. What is the importance of the Tarasoff case?
    Answer: This ruling established the legal obligation for a mental health professional to violate confidentiality in order to warn someone that a client has threatened to harm them. In Tarasoff II, the duty to warn was changed to the duty to protect a prospective victim. The duty to protect may be discharged if the therapist makes "reasonable efforts" to inform potential victims and an appropriate law enforcement agency of the pending threat.

Pages: 688
Topic: Controversial Issues/Mentally Disordered: The Insanity Defense
Skill: Applied   Other1:

18. Attorney Brown claims that his client was unaware of the nature and quality of the crime that he's accused of committing. This attorney is invoking the _____ Rule.
    Answer: M'Naughten

Pages: 690
Topic: Controversial Issues/Mentally Disordered: Deinstitutionalization
Skill: Factual   Other1:
19. The movement to reduce the number of inpatients in public hospitals and to integrate them into the community is called _____.
    Answer: deinstitutionalization

Pages: 695
Topic: Organized Efforts for Mental Health: U.S. Efforts for Mental Health
Skill: Factual   Other1:
20. Recent research concerning mental health risk factors has suggested that serious unrecognized problems exist in the workplace in the areas of job design and work conditions. What are two of these problems?
    Answer: These problems include work load, work pace, work schedule, role stressors, career security factors, interpersonal relations, and job content.

Essay

Write your answer in the space provided or on a separate sheet of paper.

Pages: 668
Topic: Perspectives on Prevention
Skill: Factual   Other1:
1. Describe the three types of prevention. Provide an example of each type.
   Answer: Primary prevention focuses on altering conditions that can cause or contribute to mental disorders and establishing conditions that foster positive mental health. Prenatal care is an example. Secondary prevention emphasizes the early detection and prompt treatment of maladaptive behavior. Crisis intervention is an example. Tertiary prevention involves efforts aimed at reducing the impact of a disorder, such as mental health rehabilitation efforts.

Pages: 668-669
Topic: Perspectives on Prevention: Primary Prevention
Skill: Factual   Other1:

2. Recently an NIMH-sponsored panel on prevention provided suggestions for national prevention programs that included a list of risk factors and protective factors for mental illness. What were their findings?

    Answer: They found that risk factors have a complex relationship to clinical disorders, in that disorders appear to have a host of differing risk factors rather than just a single risk factor. Risk factors may fluctuate developmentally, where some risk factors operate only in a limited span of developmental years while others operate over a much longer developmental span. Also, multiple risk factors can have culmulative effects, generic risk factors are shared by many disorders, and protective factors exist which can reduce risk of later mental disorder.

Pages: 668-671
Topic: Perspectives on Prevention: Primary Prevention
Skill: Applied   Other1:

3. What are some primary prevention efforts that could be instituted to minimize schizophrenia?

    Answer: Primary prevention focuses on altering conditions that can cause or contribute to mental disorders and establishing conditions that foster positive mental health. Family planning, including both prenatal and postnatal care, would be useful primary prevention efforts. Genetic counseling would also be useful. Psychosocial measures would assist individuals with developing physical, intellectual, emotional, and social competencies before the problems developed. Sociocultural measures would focus on providing a supportive community and creating social conditions that foster healthy development.

Pages: 671-674
Topic: Perspectives on Prevention: Primary Prevention
Skill: Factual   Other1:

4. Describe existing prevention programs aimed at alcohol and drug abuse. How effective are they?

    Answer: Many of these programs are school-based and attempt to educate children and adolescents about the dangers of abuse before they begin to use these substances. Research suggests that these programs are more effective when they include assertiveness training in how to resist peer pressure to use. Fair and consistent school policies regarding alcohol and drug use are crucial in school-based programs for high-risk teens. Programs to increase self-esteem are helpful. Some research suggests that these programs are limited because of underlying psychological difficulties and poverty.

Pages: 674-678
Topic: Perspectives on Prevention: Secondary Prevention
Skill: Applied   Other1:

5. You have been asked to develop secondary prevention strategies in your community for individuals with psychological problems. Describe programs you would develop.

    Answer: Crisis intervention with face-to-face short-term crisis therapy and telephone hot lines should be implemented immediately upon the occurrence of a crisis. Hot lines are important for disseminating accurate information as well as providing an additional counseling resource. Consultation and education of intermediaries, such as teachers and police personnel, would expand the range of victims who could be helped. Postdisaster intervention for rescue workers is also important.

Pages: 674-678
Topic: Perspectives on Prevention: Secondary Prevention
Skill: Applied   Other1:

6. Assume that an airplane disaster has just occurred in your community. What types of secondary prevention strategies are needed to deal with this disaster? What is the role of counselors, and how should they act in dealing with this disaster?

    Answer: Secondary prevention strategies include crisis therapy, telephone hot-line counseling services, and postdisaster debriefing sessions. Counselors need to respond immediately. They provide objective emotional support, serve as a source of information and a buffer against misinformation, and provide direct, effective suggestions to promote adaptation. They allow the victim to vent intense emotions, which may include anger and blame in the case of airline disasters, while providing hope and a long-term perspective.

Pages: 678-679
Topic: Perspectives on Prevention: Tertiary Prevention
Skill: Factual   Other1:

7. The mental hospital can be a therapeutic community, but is sometimes merely a custodial institution. What are some of the programs that have been designed to make hospitals into therapeutic communities?

    Answer: Milieu therapy focuses on clearly communicating staff expectations to patients. Both positive and negative feedback are used to encourage appropriate verbalizations and actions by patients. A self-care, do-it-yourself attitude prevails, in which patients are encouraged to become involved in all decisions made and all actions taken concerning them. Group cohesiveness among patients is encouraged, providing patients with support as well as group pressure to maintain control over behavior. One of the most beneficial aspects of this approach seems to be the interaction among patients themselves.

Pages: 680-681
Topic: Perspectives on Prevention: Tertiary Prevention
Skill: Applied   Other1:

8. How can tertiary prevention help formerly hospitalized mental patients to readjust to life outside the hospital?

    Answer: Aftercare programs generally can reduce relapse rates significantly. These are usually live-in community-based facilities run by the former patients residing there. The "Fairweather Lodge" has been very successful with actively psychotic former inpatients. Day hospital facilities are less costly but as effective as inpatient treatment provided patients are carefully selected. Similar community-based homes are effective for individuals who share a common problem like alcoholism or drug addiction.

Pages: 682
Topic: Controversial Issues/Mentally Disordered: The Commitment Process
Skill: Factual   Other1:

9. Describe three basic legal rights of individuals suffering from mental disorders that have been established through court actions.

    Answer: Individuals suffering from mental disorders have the right to treatment, have a right to freedom from custodial confinement if they are not dangerous to themselves or others and if they can safely survive outside of custody, have the right to be paid for work they perform in private facilities, have the right to legal counsel at commitment hearings, have the right to live in a community, have the right to refuse certain treatments, have the right to less restrictive treatment, and have the right not to be confined unless there is clear and convincing evidence that confinement is necessary.

Pages: 681-683
Topic: Controversial Issues/Mentally Disordered: The Commitment Process
Skill: Applied   Other1:

10. Assume that your friend is threatened with an involuntary commitment. What needs to be shown for your friend to be committed? What are the steps involved in this commitment? What rights, if any, does your friend have?

    Answer: Several conditions beyond mental illness usually must be met. The person must be judged to be dangerous to self or others, incapable of providing for his or her basic needs, and unable to make responsible decisions about hospitalization and/or in need of treatment or care in a hospital. A petition for a commitment hearing is filed, and a judge appoints two examiners. If the individual is committed, then the hospital must report to the court at intervals as to whether the person still needs to be confined. The person has the right to legal counsel throughout the commitment process.

Pages: 683-687
Topic: Controversial Issues/Mentally Disordered: Assessment/"Dangerousness"
Skill: Applied   Other1:

11. A psychologist sees a client in therapy. This client is making threats, suggesting that she may hurt or kill others and then kill herself. What issues must the psychologist address concerning the need to predict "dangerousness"? What are the pertinent issues concerning the "duty to warn?"

    Answer: The psychologist must determine whether the client is dangerous. This is difficult given that the definition of "dangerous" is unclear. The psychologist must also rely on personality tests and previous history regarding violence (if available) in making this determination, which minimizes the important causal role of unforeseen environmental factors. In most states, the psychologist has a duty to make "reasonable efforts" to warn a potential victim and law enforcement agencies if the client makes an explicit threat. However, some states uphold absolute confidentiality, repudiating Tarasoff.

Pages: 688
Topic: Controversial Issues/Mentally Disordered: The Insanity Defense
Skill: Factual   Other1:

12. Describe three of the five legal precedents that have been established for defining the insanity defense.

    Answer: M'Naughten: Defect of reason at the time of committing the act, so they did not know the nature and quality of the act or that the act was wrong. Irresistible Impulse: Individual was compelled beyond his or her will to commit the act. Durham: Individual is not responsible if the unlawful act was the product of mental disease or defect. ALI: Individual by reason of mental disease/defect lacks capacity to recognize the criminal nature of the act or to conform to law. IDRA: Defense must prove that individual had severe mental disorder; was unable to appreciate the criminal character of the act.

Pages: 690-693
Topic: Controversial Issues/Mentally Disordered: Deinstitutionalization
Skill: Factual   Other1:

13. The deinstitutionalization movement has produced great changes in the mental health field. What are these changes? What are the problems that have occurred as a result of this movement? Is there any way to correct these problems?

    Answer: Deinstitutionalization has resulted in a significant reduction in public hospital populations, but programs to help patients adjust gradually were woefully inadequate, due mostly to funding cuts. Some of these individuals have joined the ranks of the homeless. Others were not ready for community living and could not successfully adapt to the outside world, and thus relapsed. Privatization of mental health care has resulted in more advantaged people comprising inpatients in private institutions, and private nursing home facilities now contain the largest group of chronically mentally ill.

Pages: 693-695
Topic: Organized Efforts for Mental Health: U.S. Efforts for Mental Health
Skill: Factual   Other1:
14. Discuss some of the organized efforts to improve mental health in the United States.
    Answer: Congress established NIMH in 1946 as a center to promote more training and
             research, and as headquarters for administering a grant-in-aid program. Over
             the years its powers have expanded. Other federal institutions have been formed
             to deal with alcohol and drug abuse. Volunteer groups have performed invaluable
             services in planning and implementing community programs. Private industry is
             beginning to provide psychological services to some employees. Professional
             groups like APA promote professional communication, lobby, and set ethical,
             educational, and training standards.

Pages: 698-699
Topic: Unresolved Issues on The Law-Mental Health Interface
Skill: Conceptual   Other1:
15. Discuss one of the unresolved issues facing mental health professionals who work in the
    legal system.
    Answer: Therapists are asked to make professional judgments about legal issues that they
             have no scientific way of ascertaining. Making definitive judgments about a
             person's state of mind at the time of committing a crime is fraught with
             problems. Making definitive judgments about malingering is critical but also
             exceedingly difficult. The use of dissociative identity disorder as a basis for
             an insanity defense is full of interesting but potentially dangerous
             ramifications, such as a person feigning DID and being acquitted of murder by
             reason of insanity.